UNIX®
Network
Programming

W. Richard Stevens

Health Systems International

PRENTICE HALL
Englewood Cliffs, New Jersey 07632

Library of Congress Cataloging-in-Publication Data

Stevens, W. Richard.
    UNIX network programming / W. Richard Stevens.
        p.   cm.
    Includes bibliographical references.
    ISBN 0-13-949876-1
    1. UNIX (Computer operating system) 2. Computer networks.
    I. Title.
    QA76.76.063S755 1990
    005.7'1--dc20   89-25576
                                                              CIP

To Sally, Bill, and Ellen.

Editorial/production supervision: **Brendan M. Stewart**
Cover design: **Lundgren Graphics Ltd.**
Manufacturing buyer: **Ray Sintel**

Prentice Hall Software Series
Brian W. Kernighan, Advisor

 © 1990 by Prentice-Hall, Inc.
A Division of Simon & Schuster
Englewood Cliffs, NJ 07632

UNIX® is a registered trademark of AT&T.

Printed in the United States of America
10 9 8 7 6 5 4 3

ISBN 0-13-949876-1

Prentice-Hall International (UK) Limited, *London*
Prentice-Hall of Australia Pty. Limited, *Sydney*
Prentice-Hall Canada Inc., *Toronto*
Prentice-Hall Hispanoamericana, S.A., *Mexico*
Prentice-Hall of India Private Limited, *New Delhi*
Prentice-Hall of Japan, Inc., *Tokyo*
Simon & Schuster Asia Pte. Ltd., *Singapore*
Editora Prentice-Hall do Brasil, Ltda., *Rio de Janeiro*

Contents

Preface

Introduction

There has been an explosive growth in computer networks during the 1980s. The development of software to be used in these networks is still considered a mysterious art by some. This is not true. But little exists in writing about networking software—its design, development and coding.

Many excellent books and papers have been written in the last 20 years on the engineering design and analysis of computer networks and the protocols used by these networks. The intent of this book, however, is to concentrate on the development of *software* to use a computer network.

This book provides both the required basics that are needed to develop networking software along with numerous case studies of existing network applications. We can understand how to develop networking software and see where improvements can be made by critically examining some existing applications

A requisite for understanding how to develop software for a network is an understanding of interprocess communication (IPC). Sometimes there is a tendency when writing a new application to develop a monolithic solution. This is one large program that does everything. This approach has been fostered in recent years with the move towards 32-bit address spaces and larger amounts of memory on computer systems. An alternative approach is to distribute an application among multiple processes. These processes communicate with each other using IPC. Once we have divided an application among multiple processes, we can consider running the processes on different systems.

Organization of the Book

This text is divided into four parts.

1. The framework of a Unix process (Chapter 2), and IPC between processes on a single system (Chapter 3).

2. An overview of networking (Chapter 4), and a description of some networking protocols currently in use (Chapter 5): TCP/IP, Xerox NS (XNS), IBM's SNA, NetBIOS, the OSI protocols, and UUCP. These two chapters provide the networking background required for the remainder of the text.

3. Transport layer interfaces: Berkeley sockets and System V TLI (Chapters 6 and 7). These are the interfaces that an application uses to communicate across a network.

4. Networking examples (Chapters 8 through 18). The specific examples covered are: security, time and date servers, file transfer, line printer spoolers, remote command execution, remote login, remote tape drive access, and remote procedure calls.

This book can be used as a text for undergraduates or graduate students in computer science and related disciplines. This book is also intended for computer professionals who are interested in understanding or developing networking software. Chapters 2 and 3 can be used in an intermediate level programming course, to provide an overview of Unix process control and a detailed description of Unix IPC. Chapters 6 through 18 can be used in a networking course to provide actual examples of networking applications.

A reading familiarity with Unix and C would be beneficial, as all the programming examples are presented in this environment. A knowledge of networking is not assumed—the necessary building blocks are presented in Chapters 4 and 5.

The Examples in the Text

This is a practical book that contains many pictures (diagrams) and about 15,000 lines of C source code (including comments). Many pictures are used throughout the text, since when multiple processes are involved in an application, we have to keep track of which process is doing what. The starting point for any multiple-process network application is to draw a picture of which processes are executing on the different systems, and what each process is responsible for (network communication, file access, user interface, etc.).

The source code is included to provide actual code for the reader to follow and understand. Some of the source code has been written from scratch by the author (the TFTP implementation and the Berkeley Unix line printer client, for example), and some has been taken from the first release of the "BSD Networking Software." This Berkeley software contains most of the networking code from the 4.3BSD distribution. It is available to anyone, for a nominal fee, from the University of California at Berkeley. It is significant because it provides a readily available implementation of the TCP/IP and Xerox NS protocol suites. Numerous changes have been made by the author to this Berkeley software that is included in the text, mainly in the areas of readability.

All the programs in this book have been tested by the author and have been included in the text directly from their source files. The software was tested on the following systems: a VAX 8650 running 4.3BSD and a Compaq 386 running AT&T System V Release 3.2. Additional testing of the IPC examples in Chapter 3 was done on a DEC MicroVAX running Ultrix-32, an AT&T Unix PC running a variant of System V Release 2, and an IBM PC AT running SCO Xenix.

Acknowledgments

First and foremost, I am grateful to my wife, Sally, and our children, Bill and Ellen, for enduring throughout the course of this longer-than-planned project. Their love, support, and encouragement helped make this book possible.

Next, I would like to thank Gary Wright of HSI. He was the first one to read each chapter as it was finished, and was my sounding board for new ideas. He also helped with the exercises. His insistence on good programming techniques helped many of the examples.

Many thanks to the technical reviewers used by Prentice Hall: Brian Kernighan (AT&T Bell Laboratories), Craig Partridge (Editor, ACM SIGCOMM *Computer Communication Review*), Alix Vasilatos (Open Software Foundation), and Peter Honeyman (University of Michigan). Their insight, comments, criticisms, and suggestions added greatly to the final result. Thanks especially to Brian Kernighan for his initial support of the manuscript and for his *many* readings of it, at different stages. Thanks to John Wait, my editor at Prentice Hall, for his support and help while writing the book.

Doug McCallum (Interactive Systems Corp.) explained the use of stream pipes under System V, and David W. Dougherty (AT&T Bell Laboratories) explained the undocumented features of System V pseudo-terminals. Dave Crocker (Digital Equipment Corp., Western Research Laboratory) helped in obtaining the WIN/TCP software used in Chapter 7.

I would also like to thank Health Systems International, especially Ron Bernier and Rich Averill, for their support while writing this book. Thanks to all the others at HSI who helped in various ways during the course of the project. Thanks also to Judith Bender for her copy editing help.

Much of the what I have learned over the years has come from the Usenet community. Some of the ideas in this book and some of the exercises have come directly from Usenet discussions. To all the members of this community I give a sincere thanks.

This book was produced by the author using AT&T's Documenter's Workbench, Release 2.0 (`grap`, `pic`, `tbl`, `eqn`, and `ditroff`) on a VAX 8650 running 4.3BSD. The source code was included in the text using the `loom` program provided by David R. Hanson (Princeton University). The index was generated using software written by Jon Bentley and Brian Kernighan. PostScript output was produced by the TranScript package from Adobe Systems. Final camera-ready copy was produced on a Linotronic 300 typesetter.

The author would like to hear from any readers with comments, suggestions, or bug reports: `netbook@hsi.com` or `uunet!hsi!netbook`.

W. Richard Stevens

1

Introduction

1.1   History

Computer networks have revolutionized our use of computers. They pervade our every-day life, from automated teller machines, to airline reservation systems, to electronic mail services, to electronic bulletin boards. There are many reasons for the explosive growth in computer networks.

- The proliferation of personal computers and workstations during the 1980s helped fuel the interest and need for networks.

- Computer networks used to be expensive and were restricted to large universities, government research sites, and large corporations. Technology has greatly reduced the cost of establishing computer networks, and networks are now found in organizations of every size.

- Many computer manufacturers now package networking software as part of the basic operating system. Networking software is no longer regarded as an add-on that only a few customers will want. It is now considered as essential as a text editor.

- We are in an information age and computer networks are becoming an integral part in the dissemination of information.

Computer systems used to be stand-alone entities. Each computer was self-contained and had all the peripherals and software required to do a particular job. If a particular feature was needed, such as line printer output, a line printer was attached to

1

the system. If large amounts of disk storage were needed, disks were added to the system. What helped change this is the realization that computers and their users need to *share* information and resources.

Information sharing can be electronic mail or file transfer. Resource sharing can involve accessing a peripheral on another system. Twenty years ago this type of sharing took place by exchanging magnetic tapes, decks of punched cards, and line printer listings. Today computers can be connected together using various electronic techniques called *networks*. A network can be as simple as two personal computers connected together using a 1200 baud modem, or as complex as the TCP/IP Internet, which connects over 150,000 systems together. The number of ways to connect a computer to a network are many, as are the various things we can do once connected to a network. Some typical network applications are

- Exchange electronic mail with users on other computers. It is commonplace these days for people to communicate regularly using electronic mail.

- Exchange files between systems. For many applications it is just as easy to distribute the application electronically, instead of mailing diskettes or magnetic tapes. File transfer across a network also provides faster delivery.

- Share peripheral devices. Examples range from the sharing of line printers to the sharing of magnetic tape drives. A large push towards the sharing of peripheral devices has come from the personal computer and workstation market, since often the cost of a peripheral can exceed the cost of the computer. In an organization with many personal computers or workstations, sharing peripherals makes sense.

- Execute a program on another computer. There are cases where some other computer is better suited to run a particular program. For example, a time-sharing system or a workstation with good program development tools might be the best system on which to edit and debug a program. Another system, however, might be better equipped to run the program. This is often the case with programs that require special features, such as parallel processing or vast amounts of storage. The National Science Foundation (NSF) has connected the six NSF supercomputer centers using a network, allowing scientists to access these computers electronically. Years ago, access to facilities such as this would have required mailing decks of punched cards or tapes.

- Remote login. If two computers are connected using a network, we should be able to login to one from the other (assuming we have an account on both systems). It is usually easier to connect computers together using a network, and provide a remote login application, than to connect every terminal in an organization to every computer.

We'll consider each of these applications in more detail in the later chapters of this text.

1.2   Layering

Given a particular task that we want to solve, such as providing a way to exchange files
between two computers that are connected with a network, we divide the task into pieces
and solve each piece. In the end we connect the pieces back together to form the final
solution. We could write a single monolithic system to solve the problem, but experience
has shown that solving the problem in pieces leads to a better, and more extensible, solution.

It is possible that part of the solution developed for a file transfer program can also
be used for a remote printing program. Also, if we're writing the file transfer program
assuming the computers are connected with an Ethernet, it could turn out that part of this
program is usable for computers connected with a leased telephone line.

In the context of networking, this is called *layering*. We divide the communication
problem into pieces (layers) and let each layer concentrate on providing a particular function. Well-defined interfaces are provided between layers.

1.3   OSI Model

The starting point for describing the layers in a network is the International Standards
Organization (ISO) *open systems interconnection* model (OSI) for computer communications. This is a 7-layer model shown in Figure 1.1.

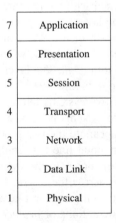

Figure 1.1 OSI 7-layer model.

The OSI model provides a detailed standard for describing a network. Most computer
networks today are described using the OSI model. In Chapter 5, each of the networks
we describe is shown against the OSI model.

The transport layer is important because it is the lowest of the seven layers that provides reliable data transfer between two systems. The layers above the transport layer can assume they have an error-free communications path. Details such as sequence control, error detection, retransmission and flow control are handled by the transport layer and the layers below it.

1.4   Processes

A fundamental entity in a computer network is a *process*. A process is a program that is being executed by the computer's operating system. When we say that two computers are communicating with each other, we mean that two processes, one running on each computer, are in communication with each other.

We describe processes in the Unix operating system in detail in Chapter 2. In Chapter 3 we describe the various forms of interprocess communication (IPC) provided by Unix to allow processes on a single computer to exchange information. In Chapters 6 and 7 we expand the interprocess communication to include processes on different systems that are connected by a network.

1.5   A Simplified Model

This book is mainly concerned with the top three layers of the OSI model—the session, presentation, and application layers—along with the interface between these three layers and the transport layer beneath them. We'll often combine these three layers into one and call it the *process* layer. Additionally, we'll usually combine the bottom two layers into a single layer and call it the *data-link* layer. We'll use a simplified, 4-layer version of the OSI model, illustrated in Figure 1.2.

In Figure 1.2 we show two systems that are connected with a network. The actual connection between the two systems is between the two data-link layers, the solid horizontal line. Although it appears to the two processes that they are communicating with each other (the dashed horizontal line between the two process layers), the actual data flows from the process layer, down to the transport layer, down to the network layer, down to the data-link layer, across the physical network to the other data-link layer, up through the network layer, then the transport layer to the other process.

Layering leads to the definitions of *protocols* at each layer. Even though physical communication takes place at the lowest layer (the physical layer in the OSI model), protocols exist at every layer. The protocols that are used at a given layer, the four horizontal lines in Figure 1.2, are also called *peer-to-peer protocols* to reiterate that they are used between two entities at the same layer. We'll discuss various protocols at the data-link, network, and transport layers, in Chapter 5. The later chapters, which describe specific applications, present various application-specific protocols at the process layer.

Since the data always flows between a given layer and the layer immediately above it or immediately below it, the *interfaces* between the layers are also important for

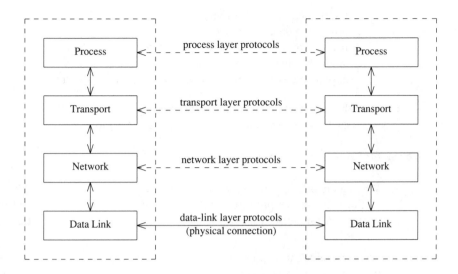

Figure 1.2 Simplified 4-layer model.

network programming. Chapters 6 and 7 provide detailed descriptions of two interfaces between the transport layer and the layer above it: Berkeley sockets and the AT&T Transport Layer Interface (TLI). The Berkeley socket interface is then used in the remaining chapters for most of the examples.

Another feature of the model shown in Figure 1.2 is that often the layers up through and including the transport layer (layers 1 through 4 of the OSI model) are included in the host operating system. This is the case for 4.3BSD and System V, the two examples used in this text.

1.6 Client–Server Model

The standard model for network applications is the *client–server* model. A *server* is a process that is waiting to be contacted by a *client* process so that the server can do something for the client. A typical (but not mandatory) scenario is as follows:

- The server process is started on some computer system. It initializes itself, then goes to sleep waiting for a client process to contact it requesting some service.

- A client process is started, either on the same system or on another system that is connected to the server's system with a network. Client processes are often initiated by an interactive user entering a command to a time-sharing system. The client process sends a request across the network to the server requesting service of some form. Some examples of the type of service that a server can provide are

    ○ return the time-of-day to the client,

    ○ print a file on a printer for the client,

    ○ read or write a file on the server's system for the client,

    ○ allow the client to login to the server's system,

    ○ execute a command for the client on the server's system.

- When the server process has finished providing its service to the client, the server goes back to sleep, waiting for the next client request to arrive.

We can further divide the server processes into two types.

1. When a client's request can be handled by the server in a known, short amount of time, the server process handles the request itself. We call these *iterative servers*. A time-of-day service is typically handled in an iterative fashion by the server.

2. When the amount of time to service a request depends on the request itself (so that the server doesn't know ahead of time how much effort it takes to handle each request), the server typically handles it in a concurrent fashion. These are called *concurrent servers*. A concurrent server invokes another process to handle each client request, so that the original server process can go back to sleep, waiting for the next client request. Naturally, this type of server requires an operating system that allows multiple processes to run at the same time. (More on this in the next chapter.) Most client requests that deal with a file of information (print a file, read or write a file, for example) are handled in a concurrent fashion by the server, as the amount of processing required to handle each request depends on the size of the file.

We'll see examples of both types of servers in later chapters.

1.7 Plan of the Book

The goal of the book is to develop and present examples of processes that are used for communication between different computer systems. In Figure 1.3, the chapters in this book are compared to the OSI model.

    To develop applications at the process layer, a thorough understanding of a process is required. Chapter 2 develops the process terminology for the Unix system. The emphasis is on process control and signals. Chapter 3 describes methods by which multiple processes on a single computer can communicate with each other—interprocess communication, or IPC. Understanding how independent processes communicate on a single computer system is a requisite to understanding IPC between processes on different systems. Chapter 3 also describes file locking and record locking under Unix, as these are often required when multiple processes are used for a task.

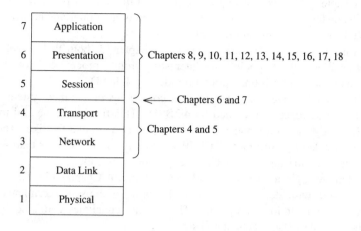

Figure 1.3 Outline of book compared to 7-layer OSI model.

Chapter 4 provides an overview of networking and the terminology used to describe the services provided by a network. Various communication protocol suites are described in Chapter 5. The emphasis is on the services provided to an application process by the protocol suite. We concentrate on the TCP/IP and Xerox NS (XNS) protocol suites, since they are used in the examples in the later chapters. We also cover the following protocol suites: IBM's SNA, NetBIOS, the OSI protocols, and UUCP. SNA is important since most Unix vendors today provide support for SNA. NetBIOS is used in many personal computer networks, which Unix systems need to communicate with. The OSI protocols, while still in their infancy, will be more important in the coming decade. An overview of UUCP is provided since it is the oldest of the Unix networking solutions, and is still widely used. An understanding of where these different protocol suites fit with regard to each other is important.

Chapters 6 and 7 describe the two predominant interfaces provided by Unix today, between the transport layer and an application process: Berkeley sockets and System V TLI. The Berkeley socket interface is then used for most of the examples in the later chapters.

The final eleven chapters contain detailed examples of actual process-level application programs. Chapter 8 describes various utility functions that are used in the remaining chapters. This includes converting network names into addresses, and timeout and retransmission algorithms for unreliable protocols.

Security is an issue we'll encounter in almost every application, and we cover it in Chapter 9. We describe the security techniques currently used by the 4.3BSD system along with the newer Kerberos system.

Chapter 10 is the first chapter describing a specific network application: obtaining the time and date from another computer on the network. Chapter 11 describes the ubiquitous Internet ''ping'' program, which has become an everyday tool on most TCP/IP networks. We also present a similar application using the Xerox NS protocols.

Chapter 12 is a complete presentation of a file transfer program—the TCP/IP Trivial File Transfer Protocol (TFTP). File transfer is an important network application and TFTP is one of the simpler protocols.

Line printer spoolers are covered in Chapter 13, both the Berkeley and System V print spoolers. Print spoolers are interesting from a process control viewpoint, in addition to the network printing option provided by 4.3BSD.

Chapter 14 covers the execution of commands on another system. We concentrate on the rcmd function provided by 4.3BSD. This function is central to what are called the Berkeley "r" commands: rcp, rdump, rlogin, and the like. These programs are often provided by third-party TCP/IP vendors for systems other than 4.3BSD, and have become de facto standards for Unix networking applications.

Remote login across a network is the topic of Chapter 15. This chapter also concerns itself with details of terminal handling and pseudo-terminals, both important features in remote login programs. This chapter concludes with a complete presentation of the 4.3BSD rlogin client and server.

In Chapter 16 we describe the use of a tape drive across a network, specifically the 4.3BSD rmt protocol. This has become an important topic with workstations and personal computers that have disks but not tape drives.

Chapter 17 is concerned with performance. This includes the performance of the various IPC techniques from Chapter 3, along with the performance of a network. Since a network is often used for file transfer and tape drive access, typical performance figures for disk drives and tape drives are also covered.

Chapter 18 covers remote procedure calls (RPC), a technique used to simplify the programming of network applications. We cover three RPC implementations: Sun RPC, Xerox Courier, and Apollo NCA.

1.8   A History of Unix Networking

The first Unix network application was UUCP, the Unix-to-Unix copy program, and all its associated commands. UUCP was developed around 1976 [Redman 1989] and its first major release outside AT&T was with Version 7 Unix in 1978. UUCP is a batch-oriented system that is typically used between systems with dial-up telephone lines or systems that are directly connected. Its major uses are for distributing software (file transfer) and electronic mail. We'll say more about the programs that comprise UUCP in Section 5.7. It is interesting that the first Unix networking application is still in wide use today.

The program cu was also distributed with Version 7 Unix in 1978, and has been available with almost every Unix system since then. Although not strictly part of a specific networking package, it provides a remote login capability to another computer system. The cu program was typically used to connect to another system using a dial-up telephone line. A rewritten version of cu was distributed with 4.2BSD where it was called tip.

In 1978 Eric Schmidt developed a network application for Unix as part of his Masters degree at Berkeley. This network was called "Berknet" and was first distributed with the Berkeley release of Version 7 Unix for the PDP-11—the 2.xBSD systems. It provided file transfer, electronic mail, and remote printing. It was widely used on the Berkeley campus. Typically the systems were directly connected with 9600 baud RS-232 lines. This software moved to the VAX with the 4.xBSD releases, then it was slowly replaced with the faster Ethernet-based local area networks that started with the 4.2BSD system.

In September 1980 Bolt, Beranek, and Newman (BBN) was contracted by the Defense Advanced Research Projects Agency (DARPA) of the Department of Defense (DoD) to develop an implementation of the TCP/IP protocols for Berkeley Unix on the VAX [Walsh and Gurwitz 1984]. A version for the 4.1BSD system was turned over to Berkeley in the Fall of 1981. This was then integrated by Berkeley into the 4.2BSD system that was being developed. The 4.2BSD system was released in August 1983 and with it the growth of local area networks, based mainly on Ethernet technology, grew rapidly. These 4.2BSD systems also allowed the computers to connect to the ARPANET, which also saw enormous growth in the early 1980s. With the 4.2BSD system the socket interface was provided, which we describe in Chapter 6 and use for most of the examples in the remainder of the text.

Networking development during this period was also underway at AT&T, however, other than UUCP, the results usually did not propagate outside AT&T. This is in contrast to the networking developments at Berkeley, which were widely disseminated. Fritz, Hefner, and Raleigh [1984] describe a network based on a HYPERchannel high-speed local network. Its development started around 1980 and it connected various types of systems running different versions of Unix: VAX 780, PDP-11/70, IBM 370, and AT&T 3B20S. The versions of Unix were the AT&T versions of System III and System V. The network was batch-oriented and supported file transfer, remote command execution, remote printing, and electronic mail.

Various third-party networking packages appeared for System V in the mid-1980s. These typically supported the TCP/IP protocol suite and were often developed by the vendor who developed the interface hardware.

The streams I/O facility was first described in Ritchie [1984b]. It did not get widely distributed outside the Bell Labs research environment, however, until System V Release 3.0 in 1986. The Transport Layer Interface (TLI), which we describe in Chapter 7, was provided with this release of System V [Olander, McGrath, and Israel 1986]. Various third-party networking packages (mainly for the TCP/IP protocol suite) based on TLI started to appear around 1988.

2

The Unix Model

2.1   Introduction

The examples in this text are from the Unix operating system—both the Berkeley 4.3BSD system and AT&T's Unix System V. All examples are based on one or more processes executing under the Unix operating system. This chapter provides an overview of the services provided by Unix for a process.

First some fundamental definitions are developed, followed by an overview of input and output under Unix. We next consider signals and process control, both important concepts when multiple processes are being used to perform an application. This leads to the development of a skeleton daemon process in Section 2.6. This skeleton daemon, and many of the concepts required to develop it, will be used in later chapters.

You might want to go through this chapter quickly, returning to it as needed when going through later chapters.

2.2   Basic Definitions

We need to define some basic terms that are used in describing a Unix process. This section is a glossary for the remainder of the text. (An attempt has been made to keep all definitions "in order." That is, if the definition of B references A, then the definition of A should precede B. Unfortunately a few forward references must be made.)

The C Programming Language

C is the programming language used for the examples throughout this text. In 1989 the work leading to the ANSI standard for the C language was completed. This version of the language is described in Kernighan and Ritchie [1988]. C compilers conforming to the ANSI standard started to appear in 1988. The earlier version of the language, which is still the predominant version, is documented in Kernighan and Ritchie [1978].

The example code in this text is written using the C language as it exists before its ANSI standard. The only exception is to show isolated function definitions with their associated argument lists, in which case the more compact ANSI version, using function prototypes, is used.

Standard C Library

Every C compiler provides a library of frequently used functions. Unix systems typically store this library in the file /lib/libc.a. Unix programmers are often unaware of this library, as it is automatically included by the Unix cc command (which invokes the C compiler and optionally the link editor also).

Until the ANSI C standard, there was never a standard definition of what functions are in this library. Appendix B of Kernighan and Ritchie [1988] provides a summary of the library defined by the ANSI standard.

When we use the term ''standard C library'' in this text, we are referring to the Unix version, which includes some functions not defined by the ANSI standard. This is because the standard Unix C library contains two sets of functions: those that should be provided with any C compiler (the standard I/O library, malloc, etc.) and those that correspond to Unix system calls (read, write, ioctl, pipe, etc.). Many C compilers for operating systems other than Unix try to emulate as many of the Unix-specific functions as possible.

Unix Versions

There are various versions and flavors of Unix in use today. Three versions are predominant. (For a more detailed history of the development of Unix, see Bach [1986] and Ritchie [1984a].)

1. AT&T Unix System V.

    The first release of System V was in 1983. Numerous interprocess communication facilities were provided with System V: message queues, semaphores, and shared memory. There have been various releases of System V. Its evolution has been

    *   Unix System V Release 2.0 (April 1984). This release was a general upgrade from its predecessor.

- Unix System V Release 2.0, enhancement release (November 1984). This enhancement release contained some important features: advisory file and record locking, and demand paging.

- Unix System V Release 3.0 (1986). This release was a major enhancement to Release 2.0. It provided: RFS (Remote File System), streams, TLI (Transport Layer Interface) and TPI (Transport Provider Interface), shared libraries, and mandatory file and record locking.

- Unix System V Release 3.1 (1987). This was a general upgrade.

- Unix System V Release 3.2 (mid-1988). This release supported the Intel 80386 processor. This release also provided binary compatibility with programs written for the Xenix system (described below).

- Unix System V Release 4.0 (late 1989). This release was a merging of AT&T System V with Sun Microsystems SunOS (a 4.xBSD derivative). It also has features of Microsoft's Xenix System V, and provides a C compiler that conforms to the ANSI X3J11 international standard.

From a networking perspective, the introduction of streams, TLI, and TPI with Release 3.0 made the development of network applications easier for the programmer. The provision for file and record locking in the enhancement release of 2.0 also simplified the coding of network applications.

2. Berkeley Software Distributions.

The Virtual VAX-11 Version of the 4.3 Berkeley Software Distribution (4.3BSD) was released in April 1986 by the Computer Systems Research Group (CSRG) at the University of California at Berkeley. Its predecessors, 4.1cBSD and 4.2BSD, circa 1982–1983, were the first widespread Unix systems with substantial network support. Indeed, the integral support for the DARPA Internet protocols (TCP/IP) and various vendors' Ethernet hardware in the BSD system led to the establishment of many local area networks. Many computer system vendors have taken the Berkeley system and ported it to hardware platforms other than the VAX. Additionally, many vendors have started with 4.3BSD and added many features and commands from System V.

In June 1988 a revision to the 4.3BSD system was released by Berkeley, referred to as the "4.3BSD Tahoe" distribution. This release was an interim release intended for testing and evaluation by experienced users. The name "Tahoe" refers to a particular CPU manufactured by Computer Consoles, Inc. that is supported by this release. Of particular interest, is the networking support provided by this release. The release notes contain the following: "Note that the Berkeley network source code is *not* public domain. However, as it contains no code licensed by AT&T or others, it is owned by the Regents of the University of California, Berkeley. It is provided as is, without any warranty, for any purpose. It may be used, modified or redistributed in source or binary forms, as long as due credit is given to the University and the University copyright notices are retained." This provides a readily available source code implementation of the DARPA Internet protocols (TCP/IP) and the Xerox NS protocols, along with the Berkeley socket interface.

3. Microsoft Xenix, System V.

    Microsoft Xenix System V is similar to AT&T Unix System V Release 2.0. The Xenix system has been ported to many different hardware environments, usually running on the Intel 8086, 80286, and 80386 processors. This includes the IBM Personal Computer family and its many look alikes.

This text is mainly concerned with the interprocess communication facilities and the networking features of System V Release 3 and 4.3BSD. When necessary we specify the release of System V. When describing the features that are specific to the Berkeley Software Distribution, we'll refer to it as 4.3BSD.

Unix Standardization

There are activities underway to provide additional standardization of the various versions of Unix.

The Institute of Electrical and Electronics Engineers (IEEE) Standard 1003.1−1988 defines a standard operating system interface and environment based on Unix. It is the first of a group of proposed standards known as *POSIX*. Its goal is to aid the portability of applications software at the source code level. This standard [IEEE 1988] focuses at the C language interface to the operating system.

X/Open is an international group of computer vendors that was started in 1984. They have produced a seven-volume portability guide [X/Open 1989] that addresses both the kernel interface and many of the utility programs that are usually provided by a Unix system. Volume 7 of this reference describes XTI, the X/Open Transport Interface. XTI is similar to the System V Release 3 Transport Layer Interface (TLI), which we describe in Chapter 7.

Unix Manuals

Occasional references are made to the Unix manual pages for additional details on a certain feature. We assume the 8-section format used by both 4.3BSD [Berkeley 1986a, 1986b, 1986c] and System V [AT&T 1989b]. References of the form "see the *tty*(4) manual page" refer to the entry for *tty* in Section 4 of the Unix manual.

Kernel

The *kernel* is the operating system. The kernel provides services such as a filesystem, memory management, CPU scheduling, and device I/O for programs. Typically the kernel interacts directly with the underlying hardware, but there are some implementations of Unix where the Unix kernel interacts with another operating system that in turn controls the hardware.

Program

A *program* is an executable file. It is usually created by a link editor and resides on a disk file. The only way a program can be executed by the Unix system is by issuing the exec system call (described later in this chapter). We sometimes refer to a program as a *program file*.

Process

A *process* is an instance of a program that is being executed by the operating system. The only way a new process can be created by the Unix system is by issuing the fork system call (described later in this chapter).

Some operating systems use the term *task* instead of process. A multitasking operating system can execute more than one task (process) at a time. Also, it is possible for a single program to be executing as many different processes at the same time. For example, there might be ten users running the same text editor program.

System Calls

A Unix kernel provides a limited number (typically between 60 and 200) of direct entry points through which an active process can obtain services from the kernel. These are named *system calls*. The actual machine instructions required to invoke a system call, along with the method used to pass arguments and results between the process and the kernel, vary from machine to machine. For example, on the VAX a process executes a chmk instruction (change mode to kernel) to invoke a system call. The low-order 16 bits of this instruction are interpreted by the kernel to specify which system call is being invoked. Arguments and results are passed between the process and the kernel using the general registers on the VAX and its condition code. The C programmer, however, does not need to worry about the actual steps required to invoke each system call. The standard Unix C library provides a C interface to each system call. This makes the actual system calls appear as normal C functions to the programmer. We use the terms *system call* and *function* interchangeably in this text, when the difference is not significant.

The distinction between a system call and a function is also confounded because some System V system calls are implemented by 4.3BSD as functions. For example, the time system call which we describe at the end of Section 2.2 is a system call under System V, but a function that calls the gettimeofday system call under 4.3BSD.

Most system calls return −1 if an errors occurs, or a value greater than or equal to zero if all is OK. A global integer variable errno is provided by the C interface to the Unix system calls. If an error occurred during a system call, errno contains the system error number. The header file <errno.h> contains the names and values of these error numbers. The errno value should be examined only after an error has occurred, since successful system calls do not reset its value to zero.

Some system calls and functions provided by the standard C library return a structure of information in addition to an integer value indicating success or error. For example, the stat and fstat system calls, described later in this section, return a pointer to the structure, not the structure itself. This is partly historical, since earlier versions of C did not support the passing of structures as either arguments or return values. It is also faster to pass a pointer to a structure than to pass an entire structure.

C Start-up Function

A C program normally starts execution with a function called main. For example, a complete C program is

```
main()
{
        printf("hello world\n");
}
```

But, most C compilers arrange for a special start-up function to be called when a C program is executed. This start-up function handles any initialization that is required, and then calls the function main. When the main function either returns or exits (by calling the exit function), a special exit function provided by the C start-up function is also invoked. A function can return either implicitly by "falling off the end" (i.e., by reaching the terminating right brace that ends a function, as in the example above), or explicitly by executing a return statement. The exit function typically flushes the standard I/O buffers and then terminates the process by calling the operating system's _exit system call (described later in this chapter). Figure 2.1 shows a picture of this.

The program shown above that prints "hello world" should have either the statement return(0) or the statement exit(0) immediately after the call to printf. Otherwise the exit status of the program in unpredictable.

Argument List

Whenever a program is executed, a variable-length argument list is passed to the process. (We show how this is done when we discuss the exec system call, later in this chapter.) The argument list is an array of pointers to character strings. There is an upper bound on the size of the argument list, often 5120 bytes or 10240 bytes.

Typically a program is executed when a command line is entered on a terminal. For example, if we enter the line

```
echo hello world
```

to a Unix shell, the program echo is executed and is passed three argument strings: echo, hello, and world. The process is then free to do whatever it wants with these arguments once it starts execution.

A C program is passed its argument list by the C start-up function as arguments to

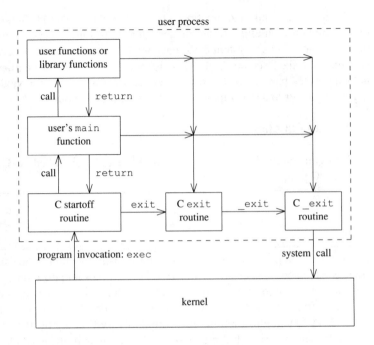

Figure 2.1 C start-up and termination functions.

the `main` function. The `main` function is declared as

```
main(argc, argv)
int     argc;
char    *argv[];
{
}
```

The first argument is an integer specifying the number of argument strings. This value is always greater than or equal to one, since a program is always passed at least one argument: the name by which it is invoked. The second argument is an array of pointers to character strings. In C an equivalent declaration for the second argument is

```
char **argv;
```

Each pointer in the `argv` array points to the character representation of that argument. The number of entries in the array is specified by the first argument. Most Unix systems add an extra element to the array (`argv[argc]`) containing a NULL pointer, but this is not guaranteed. (ANSI standard C and POSIX both require this NULL pointer.)

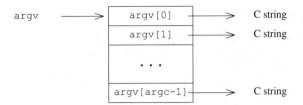

For the `echo` example shown above the picture is

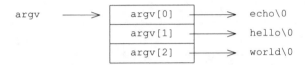

We explicitly show the null byte at the end of each argument, indicating that these are C strings.

The argument list, both the `argv` array of pointers and the character strings pointed to, are in the data space of the process. The process is free to do anything it likes with this data. Unix typically places this data on the initial stack when a program is invoked. A `main` function is also free to ignore its arguments, if desired. The program shown earlier that prints ''hello world'' does this.

Environment List

Whenever a program is executed, it is also passed a variable-length list of environment variables. The environment variables are passed to the C `main` function as an array of pointers to C strings, like the argument list is passed. But, since a count of the number of elements in this array of pointers is not provided, it must be terminated by a NULL pointer. These are accessible to the program as an optional third argument

```
main(argc, argv, envp)
int     argc;
char    *argv[];
char    *envp[];
{
}
```

The environment strings are usually of the form

variable=string

The following C program prints the values of all environment strings

```
main(argc, argv, envp)
int     argc;
char    *argv[];
char    *envp[];
{
        int     i;

        for (i = 0; envp[i] != (char *) 0; i++)
                printf("%s\n", envp[i]);
        exit(0);
}
```

Its output looks like

```
HOME=/usr1/stevens
SHELL=/bin/csh
TERM=att630
USER=stevens
PATH=/usr1/stevens/bin:/usr/local/bin:/usr/ucb:/bin:/usr/bin
EXINIT=set optimize redraw shell=/bin/csh
```

The C start-up function provides an external variable named environ that can also be used to access the environment list. This variable is declared in a C program as

```
extern char **environ;
```

An equivalent program to the one above is

```
main(argc, argv)
int     argc;
char    *argv[];
{
        int             i;
        extern char     **environ;

        for (i = 0; environ[i] != (char *) 0; i++)
                printf("%s\n", environ[i]);
        exit(0);
}
```

The reason for providing this additional copy of the pointer to the environment list is to provide user functions other than main easy access to the environment list, without having to pass its value from one function to the next. Indeed, the typical use of the environment list is for a program to obtain the value of a specific variable from the list, using the function getenv provided by the C library. For example, the following program prints the value of the environment variable HOME, if it is defined.

```
main()
{
        char    *ptr, *getenv();

        if ( (ptr = getenv("HOME")) == (char *) 0)
                printf("HOME is not defined\n");
        else
                printf("HOME=%s\n", ptr);
        exit(0);

}
```

The getenv function returns either a pointer to a specified environment variable, or a NULL pointer if that variable is not defined in the environment.

Like the argument list, both the array of environment pointers and the character strings pointed to, are in the data space of the process. The process can modify these if desired, but be aware that modifying environment strings has no effect on the parent process. When the process that modifies its environment strings terminates, the memory contents of the process are discarded. The only value passed by the terminating process to its parent process by the operating system is the 8-bit argument to the exit function. (The parent and child could, of course, mutually agree to exchange anything they like, using a disk file or some form or interprocess communication.) A process can, however, modify its environment to affect any child processes that it creates, as we will see in the exec system call in the next section.

We'll return to the argument list and the environment list when we discuss the exec system call later in this chapter. Additionally, we'll need to establish an initial environment list for a process in the remote shell server in Section 14.3. In Chapter 15 we'll need to access both the SHELL variable, to invoke the correct shell process for a user, and the TERM variable for our remote login example.

Process (continued)

A process typically has the arrangement shown in Figure 2.2. The *user context* of a process consists of the portions of the address space that are accessible to the process while it is running in user mode.

- The *text* portion of a process contains the actual machine instructions that are executed by the hardware. On many operating systems this portion of a process is set read-only so that the process cannot modify its instructions. This allows multiple instances of a single program to share a single copy of the text (shared text). When a program is executed by the operating system, the text portion is read into memory from its disk file, unless the operating system supports shared text and a copy of the program is already being executed.

- The *data* portion contains the program's data. It is possible for this to be divided into three pieces:

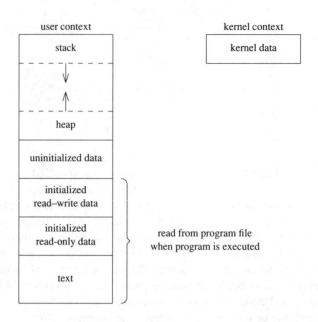

Figure 2.2   Typical arrangement of a user process.

○ *Initialized read-only data* contains data elements that are initialized by the program and are read-only while the process is executing. This area can be used for items such as literal strings that the programmer can initialize, but not change. Not many operating systems, however, currently support a read-only data area.

○ *Initialized read–write data* contains data elements that are initialized by the program and may have their values modified during execution of the process.

○ *Uninitialized data* contains data elements that are not initialized by the program but are set to zero before the process starts execution. These may be modified during the execution of the process. The Unix system calls the uninitialized data *bss*. The advantage of providing uninitialized data is that the system does not need to allocate space in the program file (on disk) for this area, since it is initialized to zero by the operating system before the process begins. In addition to saving disk space, this feature also reduces the amount of time required to read a program from disk into memory.

● The *heap* is used while a process is running to allocate more data space dynamically to the process.

● The *stack* is used dynamically while the process is running to contain the stack frames that are used by many programming languages. These stack frames contain the return address linkage for each function call and also the data elements required by a function.

A gap is shown between the heap and the stack to indicate that many operating systems leave some room between these two portions, so that both can grow dynamically during the execution of a process. This area between the heap and stack is also where the shared memory segments are usually allocated, as we'll describe in Section 3.11.

In the following C program

```
int      debug = 1;
char     *progname;

main(argc, argv)
int      argc;
char     *argv[];
{
        int      i;
        char     *ptr, *malloc();

        progname = argv[0];
        printf("argc = %d\n", argc);
        for (i = 1; i < argc; i++) {
                ptr = malloc(strlen(argv[i]) + 1);
                strcpy(ptr, argv[i]);
                if (debug)
                        printf("%s\n", ptr);
        }
}
```

the strings "argc = %d\n" and "%s\n" can be stored as read-only data. The integer variable debug is an initialized, read–write variable, and the character pointer progname is an uninitialized read–write variable. The variables i and ptr are called automatic variables. They are stored on the stack while the main function is executing. Finally, the storage space allocated by the malloc function is on the heap. (The function malloc from the standard C library allocates dynamic storage. Its argument specifies the number of bytes required, and it returns a pointer to the allocated area.) The machine instructions comprising the functions main, printf, strlen, strcpy, and malloc are all in the text segment.

The *kernel context* of a process is maintained and accessible only to the kernel. This area contains information that the kernel needs to keep track of the process and to stop and restart the process while other processes are allowed to execute. Typical elements in this area are the machine registers corresponding to the process, the physical locations and sizes of each portion of the process, and so on. This area is not accessible to the process while it is running. A portion of the kernel context of a process is stored in the *process table*. This table is a data structure within the kernel that contains one entry per process. Many of the process parameters that we describe in this section (process ID, effective user ID of a process, and so on) are stored in the process table.

For much of this text we can use a simplified picture of a typical process. We combine all the data segments (the initialized read-only data, the initialized read–write data, the uninitialized data, the heap, and the stack) into a single area labeled *data*.

```
+-------------------+
|       data        |
+-------------------+
|       text        |
+-------------------+
```

Process ID (PID)

Every process has a unique *process ID* or *PID*. The PID is an integer, typically in the range 0 through 30000. The kernel assigns the PID when a new process is created and a process can obtain its PID using the `getpid` system call.

```
int getpid();
```

The process with process ID 1 is a special process called the `init` process, which we describe later. Process ID 0 is also a special kernel process termed either the "swapper" or the "scheduler." On virtual memory implementations of Unix the process with process ID 2 is typically a kernel process termed the "pagedaemon." Other than these special processes, there are no special meanings associated with other process ID values.

Parent Process ID

Every process has a parent process, and a corresponding *parent process ID*. The kernel assigns the parent process ID when a new process is created and a process can obtain its value using the `getppid` system call.

```
int getppid();
```

The following C program prints the PID and parent process ID of a process.

```
main()
{
        printf("pid = %d, ppid = %d\n", getpid(), getppid());
        exit(0);
}
```

The output of the program could be

```
pid = 6731, ppid = 110
```

Real User ID

Each user is assigned a positive integer *user ID*. A process can obtain the real user ID of the user executing the process by calling the `getuid` system call.

```
unsigned short getuid();
```

The file `/etc/passwd` (described below) maintains the mapping between login names and numeric user IDs.

The numeric user ID is used, for example, in the filesystem to record the owner of a file. For most login names on a Unix system, there is a unique user ID assigned to each user.

Real Group ID

Along with a numeric user ID (see above), each user is also assigned a positive integer *group ID*. A process can obtain its real group ID by calling the `getgid` system call.

```
unsigned short getgid();
```

The group ID is typically used to aggregate the users of a Unix system into project groups or administrative departments.

Unlike user IDs, there are typically many users with the same group ID. The file `/etc/group` (described below) maintains the mapping between group names and numeric group IDs.

Each file on a system also has recorded for it the group ID of the owner of the file. The user ID and group ID of a file are used by the Unix filesystem to grant access to the file (described later in this section).

Effective User ID

Each process also has an *effective user ID*. A process can obtain its effective user ID by calling the `geteuid` system call.

```
unsigned short geteuid();
```

Normally this value is the same as the real user ID. It is possible, however, for a program to have a special flag set that says "when this program is executed, change the effective user ID of the process to be the user ID of the owner of this file." A program with this special flag is said to be a *set-user-ID* program. This feature provides additional permissions to users while the set-user-ID program is being executed.

When a program file has its set-user-ID bit set, and the file's owner ID is zero (the superuser), we call this a "set-user-ID root" program.

We'll use this feature in Chapter 7 to assign a name to a System V named stream pipe using the `mknod` system call. We'll also use this feature in Chapter 15 to change the file access permissions for a pseudo-terminal device.

Effective Group ID

Each process also has an *effective group ID*. A process can obtain its effective group ID by calling the `getegid` system call.

```
unsigned short getegid();
```

Normally this value is the same as the real group ID. A program can, however, have a special flag set that says "when this program is executed, change the effective group ID of the process to be the group ID of the owner of this file.'' A program with this special flag is said to be a *set-group-ID* program. Like the set-user-ID feature, this provides additional permissions to users while the set-group-ID program is being executed.

We'll encounter all four of these IDs when we discuss the security aspects of network programming.

Superuser

User ID zero is special—it identifies the *superuser*. The login name for the superuser is usually *root*. The superuser is allowed unrestricted access to files and additional permissions over other processes. For example, the superuser can terminate any other process on the system, a privilege not available to other user IDs.

A process with an effective user ID of zero is termed a superuser process. When a system function is said to be ''restricted to the superuser'' this means that the process must have an effective user ID of zero to do the specified operation.

Password File

Each line in the `/etc/passwd` file has the following format:

login-name : *encrypted-password* : *user-ID* : *group-ID* : *miscellany* : *login-directory* : *shell*

There are seven fields, separated from each other by colons. The *login-name* is the name you enter in response to the `login:` prompt when logging on to the system. This field is sometimes called the *user name*. The *encrypted-password* field can be empty, in which case you are not prompted for a password. Since the passwords in this file are encrypted, this file is always readable by anyone. The *user-ID* and *group-ID* fields are the numeric values described above. The *login-directory* specifies your initial current working directory. The *shell* field specifies the pathname of a program that is invoked when you login. All these fields are described in more detail later in this chapter. Two typical entries are

```
root:x7flmVqMxGl4g:0:10:The Superuser:/:/bin/ksh
stevens:u0ud5eOq2MpaZ:224:5:Richard Stevens:/usr1/stevens:/bin/ksh
```

The standard C library provides two functions to search the `/etc/passwd` file, looking for a matching user ID or login name.

```
#include <pwd.h>

struct passwd *getpwuid(int uid);

struct passwd *getpwnam(char *name);
```

The include file `<pwd.h>` defines a structure with the following elements:

```
struct passwd {
    char    *pw_name;        /* login-name */
    char    *pw_passwd;      /* encrypted-password */
```

```
int       pw_uid;              /* user-ID */
int       pw_gid;              /* group-ID */
int       pw_quota;            /* BSD-only; not used */
char      *pw_age;             /* System V-only; password age */
char      *pw_comment;         /* not used */
char      *pw_gecos;           /* miscellany */
char      *pw_dir;             /* login-directory */
char      *pw_shell;           /* shell */
};
```

(The order of the elements in this structure might be different on your Unix system, but their names are as shown above.) Both the functions shown above return either a pointer to a `passwd` structure that has been filled in with the values from the appropriate entry in the /etc/passwd file, or NULL if a matching entry is not found. The getpwuid function searches for a matching user ID while the getpwnam function searches for a matching login name.

We'll encounter these two functions in the later chapters that cover line printer access, remote command execution, and remote login. The getpwnam function is used, for example, when a login name is passed between a client and server. The reason for using the name, instead of the user ID, is that your user ID might be different on the different systems on which you have a valid account. Therefore, the client has to obtain your login name by

```
struct passwd    *pwd;

pwd = getpwuid( getuid() );
```

The server then uses getpwnam to turn the name into your user ID.

Shadow Passwords

System V Release 3.2 introduced *shadow passwords*. This feature stores the encrypted passwords in a separate file, /etc/shadow and the *encrypted-password* field of the /etc/passwd file is set to an asterisk. The new shadow file, /etc/shadow, is set so that only the superuser can read the file and the original file, /etc/passwd, remains readable by anyone.

The problem with the original password file scheme is that even with a one-way encryption algorithm for the password field, intruders were taking copies of the /etc/passwd file and using common words as guesses. Since many users set their passwords to common words (their family names, common computer terms, common words backwards, and the like) a brute force search would often yield numerous valid passwords.

Another feature that was introduced with shadow passwords is *password aging*. This allows the system administrator to specify both the minimum and maximum number of days between password changes for a user.

Group File

Each line in the /etc/group file has the following format:

group-name : *encrypted-password* : *group-ID* : *user-list*

There are four fields, separated from each other by colons. The *group-name* is the name of the group. The *encrypted-password* is used by the System V newgrp command, described below. This field is ignored by 4.3BSD. Since the passwords in this file are encrypted, this file is always readable by anyone. The *group-ID* field is the numeric value described earlier. The *user-list* is a comma separated list of the *login-names* allowed in this group.

The handling of groups is different between System V and 4.3BSD. With 4.3BSD, you can be a member of up to 16 groups, in addition to the group specified in your password file entry (the *real group ID*). When you login, the /etc/group file is scanned, and you become a member of each group which contains your *login-name* in the *user-list*. We call this list of group IDs that you belong to the *group access list*. This list is used only for determining resource accessibility, as described below under ''File Access Permissions.'' 4.3BSD provides the following function to initialize the group access list.

```
int initgroups(char *name, int basegid);
```

This function scans the /etc/group file and adds all the groups which list the *name* to the group access list. The *basegid* is also included in the group access list. It is usually the group ID value found in the /etc/passwd file entry for the user. We'll use this function in the rshd daemon in Section 14.3.

System V restricts you to belong to a single group at a time. The command

```
newgrp group-name
```

is provided to allow you to change your *real group ID* to the value associated with the *group-name* in the /etc/group file. If the *encrypted-password* field is not blank, and if your login name is not in the *user-list*, you are prompted for the password. If the newgrp command is executed without any arguments, your group identification returns to the group specified in the password file. The System V manual discourages the use of passwords in the /etc/group file. Instead, any users who should have the privileges of the group should be named in the *user-list*.

The standard C library provides two functions to search the /etc/group file, looking for a matching group ID or group name.

```
#include <grp.h>

struct group *getgrgid(int gid);

struct group *getgrnam(char *name);
```

The include file `<grp.h>` defines a structure with the following elements:

```
struct group {
        char     *gr_name;          /* group-name */
        char     *gr_passwd;        /* encrypted-password */
        int       gr_gid;           /* group-ID */
        char     **gr_mem;          /* array of ptrs to user-list */
};
```

Both the functions shown above return either a pointer to a `group` structure that has been filled in with the values from the appropriate entry in the `/etc/group` file, or `NULL` if a matching entry is not found. The `getgrgid` function searches for a matching group ID while the `getgrname` function searches for a matching group name.

Shells

A Unix *shell* is a program that sits between an interactive user and the kernel. Typical shells are command line interpreters that read commands from a user at a terminal (or from a file) and execute the commands. The Unix shells are more than command line interpreters—they are programming languages.

One or more of the three following shell programs are typically found on a Unix system:

- the Bourne shell: `/bin/sh`
- the KornShell: `/bin/ksh`
- the C shell: `/bin/csh`

The Bourne shell is from Version 7 Unix and is found on almost every Unix system. The KornShell is a newer replacement for the Bourne shell and contains features not in the Bourne shell, such as command line editing. The C shell is found on 4.3BSD systems.

When you login to a Unix system, the *shell* program from your password file entry is executed as your *login shell*. If this field in your password file entry is empty, the Bourne shell is invoked by default.

Filename

Every Unix file, directory, or special file has a *filename*. Some Unix systems limit the filename to 14 characters, but 4.3BSD allows filenames up to 255 characters. The only ASCII characters that are *not* allowed in a filename are the ASCII NUL character ('\0') and the slash character ('/'). 4.3BSD has the additional restriction that the high-order bit of each byte (the parity bit) must be zero. The '/' separates the filenames in a pathname (see below) and the '\0' terminates a pathname. But, it is not recommended to use characters that might be interpreted specially by the shells (such as an asterisk), or to use unprintable ASCII characters.

Pathname

A *pathname* is a null terminated character string that is built from one or more *filename*s. The filenames in a pathname are separated from one another with the slash ('/'). A pathname can optionally begin with a slash, indicating that the path begins at the root directory (described below). A pathname that does not begin with a slash is called a *relative pathname* and the path begins at the current working directory (also described below). A pathname that begins with a slash is sometimes called an *absolute pathname* or a *full pathname*. The pathname consisting of a / by itself refers to the root directory. The strings `junk.1` and `doc/book/chapter1` are relative pathnames, and the string `/usr/lib` is an absolute pathname.

There is a difference between a *filename* and a *pathname*. Filenames appear only in directories and as elements of pathnames. Pathnames are the null terminated C strings that are passed from a process to the kernel when a specific file is referenced. Nevertheless, most users and many books refer to strings such as `/usr/lib/crontab` as a filename, when it is really a pathname.

File Descriptor

A *file descriptor* is a small integer used to identify a file that has been opened for I/O. The allowable values are from zero up to some maximum, depending on the system. Older Unix systems such as Version 7 had a limit of 20 open files per process, which allowed file descriptors between 0 and 19. Most systems now provide for more than 20 open files per process. Many Unix programs, including the shells, associate file descriptors 0, 1, and 2 with the standard input, standard output, and standard error, respectively, of a process. File descriptors are assigned by the kernel when the following system calls are successful: `open`, `creat`, `dup`, `pipe`, and `fcntl`.

4.3BSD also uses small integers to refer to sockets, as we'll describe in Chapter 6. These are referred to as *socket descriptors*. 4.3BSD refers to both file descriptors and socket descriptors as just *descriptors*, differentiating between them only when necessary. For some system calls, a socket descriptor is identical to a file descriptor—the `dup` system call, for example. But some 4.3BSD system calls only work with socket descriptors (e.g., `connect`). Socket descriptors are assigned by the kernel when the following system calls are successful: `accept`, `pipe`, `socket`, and `socketpair`.

Files

Every file has many attributes. The `stat` and `fstat` system calls return the attributes of a specified file to the caller.

```
#include <sys/types.h>
#include <sys/stat.h>

int stat(char *pathname, struct stat *buf);

int fstat(int fildes, struct stat *buf);
```

If the system call was successful, zero is returned, otherwise −1 is returned.

The file `<sys/types.h>` is provided by 4.3BSD and System V. It defines numerous data types using the C language *typedef* construct. We'll encounter some of the data types defined in this file in the example that follows, and in later chapters.

The `stat` structure that is filled in by these system calls is defined in the `<sys/stat.h>` header file as:

```
struct stat {
    ushort   st_mode;     /* file type and file access permissions */
    ino_t    st_ino;      /* i-node number */
    dev_t    st_dev;      /* ID of device containing a directory
                             entry for this file */
    short    st_nlink;    /* number of links */
    ushort   st_uid;      /* user ID */
    ushort   st_gid;      /* group ID */
    dev_t    st_rdev;     /* ID of device, for character special or
                             block special files */
    off_t    st_size;     /* file size in bytes */
    time_t   st_atime;    /* time of last file access */
    time_t   st_mtime;    /* time of last file modification */
    time_t   st_ctime;    /* time of last file status change */
    long     st_blksize;  /* optimal block size for filesystem
                             operations; 4.3BSD only */
    long     st_blocks;   /* actual number of blocks allocated;
                             4.3BSD only */
};
```

The `st_mode` field of the `stat` structure contains the file type, the file access permissions (9 bits), the set-user-ID bit, the set-group-ID bit and the sticky bit. (We describe all these terms below.) The following bit masks are defined in the `<sys/stat.h>` header file, to determine the file type.

```
#define S_IFMT   0170000   /* type of file */
#define         S_IFREG   0100000   /* regular */
#define         S_IFDIR   0040000   /* directory */
#define         S_IFCHR   0020000   /* character special */
#define         S_IFBLK   0060000   /* block special */
#define         S_IFLNK   0120000   /* symbolic link - BSD only */
#define         S_IFSOCK  0140000   /* socket - BSD only */
#define         S_IFIFO   0010000   /* fifo - System V only */
```

The file types, coded in the `st_mode` variable are

- A *regular file*, also called an *ordinary file* contains zero or more data bytes.
- A *directory* contains the names and i-node numbers of other files. (An i-node is a data structure on the disk that contains information about a file, such as where on the disk the file is located.)
- A *character special file* and a *block special file* are I/O devices that appear as regular files in the Unix filesystem. The handling of special files depends on the actual device being referenced.
- A *fifo* is a first-in first-out queue, also known as a *named pipe*. These are in System V, but not 4.3BSD, and are covered in the next chapter.
- A *symbolic link* is a file that contains the pathname of another file. These are only provided by 4.3BSD.
- A *socket* is a special type of file provided by 4.3BSD that we cover in Chapter 6.

The following program prints the type of a file:

```
/*
 * Print the type of file for each of the command line arguments.
 */

#include         <sys/types.h>
#include         <sys/stat.h>

main(argc, argv)
int      argc;
char     *argv[];
{
        int              i;
        struct stat      statbuff;
        char             *ptr;

        for (i = 1; i < argc; i++) {
                printf("%s: ", argv[i]);
                if (stat(argv[i], &statbuff) < 0)
                        err_sys("fstat error");

                switch (statbuff.st_mode & S_IFMT) {
                case S_IFDIR:   ptr = "directory";              break;
                case S_IFCHR:   ptr = "character special";      break;
                case S_IFBLK:   ptr = "block special";          break;
                case S_IFREG:   ptr = "regular";                break;
#ifdef S_IFLNK
                case S_IFLNK:   ptr = "symbolic link";          break;
#endif
#ifdef S_IFSOCK
                case S_IFSOCK:  ptr = "socket";                 break;
#endif
#ifdef S_IFIFO
```

```
                       case S_IFIFO:   ptr = "fifo";                      break;
#endif
                       default:        ptr = "** unknown mode **";  break;
                       }
                       printf("%s\n", ptr);
               }
         exit(0);
}
```

This program processes its command line arguments, printing the file type of each argument. If the program is compiled and link edited into the file a.out and executed as

```
    a.out /dev/tty /dev/ra0a /usr/lib /etc/passwd
```

the output is

```
    /dev/tty: character special
    /dev/ra0a: block special
    /usr/lib: directory
    /etc/passwd: regular
```

Note that this program works under both 4.3BSD and System V, since the conditional compilation feature of the C language determines which file types are supported. The function err_sys is called when an error is returned by the stat system call. This function, and other error handling functions that are used throughout this text, are listed in the "Standard Error Routines" section of Appendix A.

We'll use these two system calls for a variety of purposes. In Section 7.9 we'll need to obtain the major and minor device numbers, st_rdev, (described later in this section) for a stream pipe. In Section 9.2 we'll use fstat to verify the owner of a file and to obtain the file's access permissions. In our implementation of the Trivial File Transfer Protocol in Chapter 12 we'll use stat to obtain the file access permissions for files and directories that are being accessed from a remote system. In our 4.3BSD line printer spooler in Section 13.3 we'll use stat to obtain the size of the file being printed. In Chapter 15 we'll use stat to check the existence of a pseudo-terminal device entry.

File Access Permissions

As described earlier, every process has four IDs associated with it.

- real user ID
- real group ID
- effective user ID
- effective group ID

Additionally, every file has the following attributes (in addition to others that we won't consider here):

- owner's user ID (a 16-bit integer)
- owner's group ID (a 16-bit integer)

- user-read permission (a 1-bit flag)
- user-write permission (a 1-bit flag)
- user-execute permission (a 1-bit flag)

- group-read permission (a 1-bit flag)
- group-write permission (a 1-bit flag)
- group-execute permission (a 1-bit flag)

- other-read permission (a 1-bit flag)
- other-write permission (a 1-bit flag)
- other-execute permission (a 1-bit flag)

- set-user-ID (a 1-bit flag)
- set-group-ID (a 1-bit flag)

The Unix kernel goes through the following tests to determine if a process can access a file. If any of the following are true, access is allowed.

1. If the effective user ID of the process is zero (the superuser), access is allowed.

2. If the effective user ID of the process matches the user ID of the owner of the file, *and* if the appropriate owner access permission bit for the file is set, access is allowed. The test after the *and* means that the file's user-read permission bit must be set if the process wants to read the file, or the file's user-write permission bit must be set if the process wants to write to the file, or that the file's user-execute permission bit must be set if the process wants to execute the file.

3. If the effective user ID of the process does *not* match the user ID of the owner of the file, *and* if the effective group ID of the process matches the group ID of the owner of the file, *and* if the appropriate group access permission bit (group-read, group-write, group-execute) for the file is set, access is allowed. Under 4.3BSD the group ID test includes both the effective group ID of the process and the list of group IDs in the group access list for the process.

4. If the effective user ID of the process does *not* match the user ID of the owner of the file, *and* if the effective group ID of the process does not match the group ID of the owner of the file, *and* if the appropriate "other" access permission bit (other-read, other-write, other-execute) for the file is set, access is allowed.

Note that the group test is done only if the user IDs are not the same. Similarly, the "other" test is done only if the user IDs are not the same and if the group IDs don't match.

File Access Mode Word

The bit flags described above have a fixed position in what is termed the file access *mode* word. This encoding of the bits in the mode word is used by the access, chmod, creat, mknod, msgctl, open, semctl, shmctl, stat, fstat, and umask system calls. Figure 2.3 shows the octal value for these bits. (Octal values tend to be used for the mode specification, because the user, group, and "other" access bits are each 3 bits wide.)

octal value	Meaning
04000	Set user ID on execution
02000	Set group ID on execution
01000	Save text image after execution ("sticky bit")
00400	Read by user
00200	Write by user
00100	Execute by user
00040	Read by group
00020	Write by group
00010	Execute by group
00004	Read by other
00002	Write by other
00001	Execute by other

Figure 2.3   Allocation of bits in the file access mode word.

Note that the user access bits are isolated from the access mode using a mask of 0700. The group access bits are isolated using a mask of 070, and the other access bits are isolated using a mask of 07.

If the "sticky bit" is set, and if the file is an executable program with read-only text, a copy of the text is left in the swap area after the program has finished executing, so that the next time it is executed it will start faster.

File permissions and the file access mode are important in any network application that does file transfer. We'll use these, for example, in our implementation of the Trivial File Transfer Protocol client and server in Chapter 12. Additionally, in Chapter 13 we'll see how the 4.3BSD line printer daemon uses the file access mode to maintain certain status information for a printer.

File Mode Creation Mask

Each process has a *file mode creation mask*. It is set with the umask system call

```
int umask(int cmask);
```

The low-order 9 bits of *cmask* specify the file mode creation mask for the process. These 9 bits specify the user access bits, group access bits and other access bits, as described above. This system call returns the previous value of the file mode creation mask for the process. (This is one of the few system calls, along with exit, getpid, getpgrp, getppid, getuid, geteuid, getgid, getegid that cannot fail and does not have an error return.)

The file mode creation mask is used when a new file or directory is created. The mask specifies which bits in the new file are to be *cleared*. For example, if we create a new file with a mode of octal 0664 (read–write by user, read–write by group, and read by other) and if the file mode creation mask is octal 022, the group-write bit is turned off, giving the file an actual mode of octal 0644.

We'll use this system call in our skeleton daemon process, which we develop in Section 2.6.

Major and Minor Device Numbers

Every I/O device has a *major device number* and a *minor device number*. The combination of these two device numbers is held in a datatype whose name is `dev_t`, which is defined in the header file `<sys/types.h>`. Typically the major and minor numbers are each stored in an 8-bit byte, and the `dev_t` datatype is a short integer (16 bits).

For disk drives, the major device number usually specifies the disk controller and the minor device number specifies both the drive and the partition on the drive. For example, a controller that supports up to 8 drives can use minor device numbers 0–7 for up to 8 partitions on the first drive, 8–15 for the partitions on the second drive, and so on. Terminal multiplexors typically use the major device number to specify the actual terminal multiplexor device and the minor device number for each terminal line on the multiplexor.

We'll return to these device numbers in Chapter 7 when we describe the streams clone mechanism.

Directories

A *directory* is a special type of file that the kernel maintains. It is special since only the kernel modifies directories, but processes can read directories. A directory has a pathname, just like a regular file, but the contents of a directory is a list of filename and i-node number pairs. On System V each filename occupies up to 14 bytes and an i-node number occupies 2 bytes, for 16 bytes per directory entry. 4.3BSD uses a different structure that allows variable-length directory entries, since each filename can occupy up to 255 characters.

When a new directory is created, the kernel automatically makes entries named '.' and '..' (called dot and dot-dot, respectively). The first one refers to the directory itself, and the second refers to the parent directory.

4.3BSD and System V Release 3 allow a process to create a new directory with the `mkdir` system call.

```
int mkdir(char *pathname, int mode);
```

The *mode* specifies the low-order 12 bits of the directory's file mode, which might be modified by the file mode creation mask for the process.

Earlier Unix systems, Version 7 through System V Release 2, didn't provide this system call, requiring the process to use the `mknod` system call to create a directory. The problem is that the `mknod` system call is restricted to the superuser (except for FIFOs, which are described in the next chapter). The program that exists to create directories, `mkdir`, has to invoke the `mknod` system call, so it must have its set-user-ID bit on with an owner of root. A program invokes a Unix command using the `system` function, supplied by the standard C library.

```
int system(char *string);
```

This function invokes the Bourne shell to execute the specified command `string`. A typical sequence to create a directory is:

```
char  buff[1024], dirname[1024];

sprintf(buff, "mkdir %s", dirname);
if (system(buff) != 0) {
        /* error handling */
}
```

The `sprintf` function is from the standard I/O library and it formats an output string into a character array (`buff`). The value returned by `system` is the value passed to the `exit` system call (described in a later section) by the specified command.

Current Working Directory

Each process has associated with it a *current working directory*. The current working directory specifies the starting point for pathnames that do not begin with a '/'. The value for the current working directory is initialized from the *login-directory* field of the `/etc/passwd` file when you login. A process can change its current working directory with the `chdir` system call.

```
int chdir(char *pathname);
```

A zero is returned by this system call if all is OK, otherwise −1 is returned.

We'll return to this system call in Section 2.6 when we develop our skeleton daemon process. We'll also use it in our remote command server in Section 14.3, to change to a user's login directory.

Process Group ID

Every process is a member of a process group that is identified by a positive integer *process group ID*. Unlike the process ID, which is always unique for a process, the process group ID is usually not unique. Typically multiple processes have the same process group ID and these processes are called *members* of the process group.

If the process group ID equals the process ID for a process, that process is called a *process group leader*. If the two IDs are not equal, then the process group ID for any process is the process ID of the process group leader.

Process groups are used by the `kill` system call, which is described later in this chapter. It is possible to send a signal (also described later in this chapter) using the `kill` system call to all processes belonging to a specified process group.

The value of the process group ID is obtained by calling the `getpgrp` system call. The System V version is

```
int getpgrp();
```

which returns the process group of the current process. The 4.3BSD version is

```
int getpgrp(int pid);
```

If the *pid* argument is zero, this returns the process group of the current process, otherwise it returns the process group of the process whose process ID is *pid*.

Unlike the process ID and the parent process ID, a process can change its process group ID using the `setpgrp` system call. Under System V a process is only able to change its process group ID to be equal to its process ID, effectively becoming a process group leader.

```
int setpgrp();
```

This system call returns the new process group ID, which is the process ID of the calling process. 4.3BSD allows a process to set the process group ID of a process to any integer value.

```
int setpgrp(int pid, int pgrp);
```

If the *pid* is zero, the call applies to the current process. If the *pid* is nonzero, then the affected process must have the same effective user ID as the current process, or the current process must have superuser privileges.

Terminal Group ID and Control Terminal

Each process can be a member of a terminal group that is identified by a positive integer *terminal group ID*. The terminal group ID is the process ID of the process group leader that opened the terminal—typically the login shell that is invoked when you login to a Unix system. This process is called the *control process* for a terminal. A terminal has only a single control process.

The terminal group ID identifies the *control terminal* for a process group. The control terminal is used for dispatching signals (described later) when certain terminal keys are pressed and when a login shell terminates. When a process that is both a process group leader and the control process for a terminal (typically the login shell) calls the `exit` function to terminate, the "hangup" signal is sent to each process in the process group (i.e., all remaining processes that are descendants of the login shell). The control terminal is referenced automatically by the device whose name is `/dev/tty`. If a program wants to be certain that it is reading or writing to the control terminal, regardless of how the standard input or standard output are redirected, it can open and use this device.

Under Unix System V, a process is not able to examine or set its terminal group ID. But the `setpgrp` system call disassociates the calling process from its control terminal, if the calling process is not already a process group leader. Under 4.3BSD, the `ioctl` system call can be used by a process to set (`TIOCSPGRP`) or examine (`TIOCGPGRP`) the terminal group ID for its control terminal.

We return to the control terminal and the interaction between it and the terminal group ID Section 2.6 when we discuss daemon processes.

Socket Group ID

4.3BSD supports the notion of a process group for sockets, similar to what we just described for terminals. (Sockets are used in the Berkeley networking system. We describe them in detail in Chapter 6.) Every socket that is open has an associated *socket group ID*. A process sets or examines this value using the `fcntl` system call, as we'll describe in Section 6.11. If this value is less than zero, its absolute value specifies a process group ID. If this value is greater than zero, it specifies a process ID. Unlike the terminal group ID, the socket group ID can refer to either a group of processes or a single process. The socket group ID specifies the process or process group to be notified when certain conditions exist on a socket.

Time-of-Day

In Chapters 8 and 11 we'll need to measure the amount of time it takes a network message to go from a client to a server, and have a response returned by the server.

4.3BSD provides the `gettimeofday` system call, which returns the number of seconds since 00:00:00 GMT, January 1, 1970. It also returns some timezone information, which we won't need for our examples.

```
#include <sys/time.h>

int gettimeofday(struct timeval *tvalptr, struct timezone *tzoneptr);

struct timeval {
  long  tv_sec;     /* seconds since 00:00:00 GMT, Jan. 1, 1970 */
  long  tv_usec;    /* and microseconds */
};
```

It returns zero if all is OK, with the structure pointed to by the *tvalptr* filled in. All our calls to this system call specify a *tzoneptr* of NULL, which means we're not interested in this information. Refer to the *gettimeofday*(2) manual page for all the details.

System V provides the `times` system call. This returns the amount of processor time used by the calling process, in addition to the current clock time.

```
#include <sys/types.h>
#include <sys/times.h>

long times(struct tms *ptr);

struct tms {
  time_t  tms_utime;    /* user time */
  time_t  tms_stime;    /* system time */
  time_t  tms_cutime;   /* user time, children */
  time_t  tms_cstime;   /* system time, children */
};
```

The current clock time is returned as the long integer value of the system call.† Unfortunately, this value is measured in the number of clock ticks since some arbitrary point in time, usually the time the system was booted. The number of clock ticks per second is specified by the constant `HZ` in the system header file `<sys/param.h>`. It is usually 60 or 100. We are only interested in measuring the difference between two of these values, so it won't matter that they are not from a known reference point in the past.

In our remote procedure call examples in Chapter 18 we'll need to obtain the current time-of-day. The `time` system call returns the number of seconds since 00:00:00 GMT, January 1, 1970. The 4.3BSD version of this is just an interface to the `gettimeofday` system call, which we described above, and is provided for compatibility with other versions of Unix.

```
long time(long *ptr);
```

The number of seconds is always returned as the value of the system call. Additionally, if the *ptr* argument is not NULL, the value is also returned through this pointer.

2.3   Input and Output

There are two methods available under Unix for doing input and output:

- the Unix system calls for I/O,
- the standard I/O library.

The Unix system calls for I/O (`open`, `read`, `write`, etc.) are direct entry points into the kernel. The standard I/O library, on the other hand, is a set of functions that provides a higher level interface between a process and the kernel, providing features such as buffering, line-by-line input, formatted output, and the like. The ANSI standard defines the

---

† 4.3BSD provides a `times` function, however it is not compatible with the System V system call. The 4.3BSD function returns zero or one, not the current clock time.

standard I/O library precisely, providing portability among many different operating systems. With network programming, however, there are times when the Unix system calls must be used.

Appendix B of Kernighan and Ritchie [1988] provides a summary of the library defined by the ANSI standard. We'll briefly review the Unix system calls for input and output that we'll be using throughout the text.

open **System Call**

A file is opened by

```
#include <fcntl.h>

int open(char *pathname, int oflag, [ , int mode ] );
```

In early versions of Unix there was not an optional third argument and the *oflag* value was specified as a binary constant: 0 (open for reading), 1 (open for writing), or 2 (open for reading and writing). Newer versions (System V and 4.3BSD) allow symbolic specification of the *oflag* argument (which can be combined by or'ing them together):

O_RDONLY	Open for reading only
O_WRONLY	Open for writing only
O_RDWR	Open for reading and writing
O_NDELAY	Do not block on open or read or write
O_APPEND	Append to end of file on each write
O_CREAT	Create the file if it doesn't exist
O_TRUNC	If the file exists, truncate its length to zero
O_EXCL	Error if O_CREAT and the file already exists

Most implementations define O_RDONLY as 0, O_WRONLY as 1, and O_RDWR as 2, for compatibility with older programs. The third argument, *mode*, is optional and is required only if O_CREAT is specified (see the creat system call below). open returns a file descriptor if successful, otherwise −1 is returned.

In Section 3.2 we'll use the O_EXCL flag in our file locking example. Also, we'll discuss the effect of the O_NDELAY flag on pipes and FIFOs in Section 3.5.

creat **System Call**

A new file is created by

```
int creat(char *pathname, int mode);
```

If successful, creat returns a file descriptor and the file is opened for writing, otherwise −1 is returned. The *mode* specifies the low-order 12 bits of the file access mode word. This value is modified by the low-order 9 bits of the file mode creation mask, as described earlier with the umask system call. The file's owner ID is set to the effective user ID of the process and the file's group ID is set to the effective group ID of the process. If the file already exists, its length is truncated to zero, and the file's mode and owners are not changed.

`close` System Call

An open file is closed by

```
int close(int fildes);
```

When a process terminates, all open files are automatically closed by the kernel.

`read` System Call

Data is read from an open file using

```
int read(int fildes, char *buff, unsigned int nbytes);
```

If the `read` is successful, the number of bytes read is returned—this can be less than the *nbytes* that was requested. If the end of file is encountered, zero is returned. If an error is encountered, −1 is returned.

`write` System Call

Data is written to an open file using

```
int write(int fildes, char *buff, unsigned int nbytes);
```

The actual number of bytes written is returned by the system call. This is usually equal to the *nbytes* argument. If an error occurs, −1 is returned. Both `read` and `write` specify their *nbytes* argument as an unsigned integer, so that more than 32767 bytes can be read or written in one operation on a system that has 16-bit integers. An unsigned 16-bit integer still places a limit of 65534 bytes per `read` or `write`, since zero indicates an end-of-file and −1 indicates an error.

With network programming we must be prepared for a `read` or `write` to return a positive value that is less than the *nbytes* argument. This is not an error, but happens because of the buffering that can take place within the network. In Section 6.6 we'll develop some functions that handle this condition.

`lseek` System Call

Every open file has a "current byte position" associated with it. This is measured as the number of bytes from the start of the file. The `creat` system call sets the file's position to the beginning of the file, as does the `open` system call, unless the O_APPEND flag is specified. The `read` and `write` system calls update the file's position by the number of bytes read or written. Before a `read` or `write`, an open file can be positioned using

```
long lseek(int fildes, long offset, int whence);
```

The *offset* and *whence* arguments are interpreted as follows:

- If *whence* is 0, the file's position is set to *offset* bytes from the beginning of the file.

- If *whence* is 1, the file's position is set to its current position plus the *offset*. The *offset* can be positive or negative.

- If *whence* is 2, the file's position is set to the size of the file plus the *offset*. The *offset* can be positive or negative.

The file's offset can be greater than the file's current size, in which case the next `write` to the file will extend the file. A file's position can never be less than zero. `lseek` returns the new long integer byte offset of the file, or −1 if an error occurred.

`dup` **and** `dup2` **System Calls**

An existing file descriptor is duplicated by

```
int dup(int fildes);
```

This returns a new file descriptor that shares the following with the original *filedes*:

- both refer to the same file or pipe (pipes are discussed in the next chapter),

- the access mode of the new file descriptor is the same as that of the original: read, write, or read/write,

- both file descriptors share the same file position.

It is guaranteed that the new file descriptor returned by `dup` is the lowest numbered available file descriptor. We will see many examples of this system call in later chapters.
4.3BSD provides another variant of this system call

```
int dup2(int oldfildes, int newfiledes);
```

Here the *newfiledes* argument specifies the new descriptor value that is desired. If this new descriptor value is already in use, it is first released, as if a `close` had been done.
We'll examine the duplication of descriptors later in this chapter when we describe file sharing. We'll encounter both of these system calls in our remote login example in Chapter 15.
Another way to duplicate a descriptor is with the `fcntl` system call, which we now describe.

`fcntl` **System Call**

The `fcntl` system call is used to change the properties of a file that is already open.

```
#include <fcntl.h>

int fcntl(int filedes, int cmd, int arg);
```

The *cmd* argument must be one of the following. (Unless noted otherwise, these commands are valid for both System V and 4.3BSD.)

F_DUPFD   Duplicate the file descriptor, similar to the dup system call. Unlike dup, however, this system call allows us to specify the lowest number that the new file descriptor is to assume—the value of *arg*. The new descriptor is returned as the value of the system call.

F_SETFD   Set the close-on-exec flag for the file to the low-order bit of *arg*. If the low-order bit of *arg* is set, the file is closed on an exec system call (described later in this chapter). Otherwise the file remains open across an exec.

F_GETFD   Return the close-on-exec flag for the file as the value of the system call.

F_SETFL   Set the status flags for this file to the value of *arg*. The allowable status flags are formed by or'ing together the following constants:

     O_NDELAY   (System V only) Set the file for nonblocking I/O.

     O_APPEND   (System V only) Have all writes append to the end of this file.

     O_SYNC   (System V only) Enable the synchronous write option.

     FNDELAY   (BSD only) Set the file for nonblocking I/O. This option is only available for terminals and sockets.

     FAPPEND   (BSD only) Have all writes append to the end of this file.

     FASYNC   (BSD only) Enable the SIGIO signal to be sent to the process group when I/O is possible. This option is only available for terminals and sockets.

F_GETFL   Return the status flags for this file as the value of the system call.

F_GETOWN   (BSD only) Return the value of the process ID or the process group ID that is set to receive the SIGIO and SIGURG signals. A positive return value indicates a process ID and a negative value (other than −1) is the negative of the process group ID.

F_SETOWN   (BSD only) Set the process ID or the process group ID to receive the SIGIO and SIGURG signals to the value of *arg*. A positive value specifies a process ID and a negative values specifies a process group ID.

F_GETLK, F_SETLK, and F_SETLKW
     (System V only) These three commands are for record locking, which we describe in Section 3.2.

Many of these features (asynchronous I/O, record locking, signals) are described in more detail in later chapters.

`ioctl` **System Call**

The `ioctl` system call is also used to change the behavior of an open file.

```
#include <sys/ioctl.h>          /* BSD only */

int ioctl(int filedes, unsigned long request, char *arg);
```

This system call performs a variety of control functions on terminals, devices, sockets (BSD), and streams (System V). The BSD include file `<sys/ioctl.h>` contains the definitions for *request* for all possible operations. Under System V different header files are used depending on the type of operation being performed. For example, `<termio.h>` contains the *request* values for terminal operations. Historically, the greatest use for `ioctl` has been to change terminal characteristics: the baud rate, parity, number of bits per character, and so on. It is also used for a plethora of other device-specific operations.

We'll return to this system call when we cover Berkeley sockets and System V streams in Chapters 6 and 7. We also use it in Chapter 15 to change the characteristics of a terminal device.

The main difference between `fcntl` and `ioctl` is that the former is intended for any open file, while the latter is intended for device-specific operations. This separation of function, however, is less than perfect.

2.4   Signals

A signal is a notification to a process that an event has occurred. Signals are sometimes called "software interrupts." Signals usually occur asynchronously. By this we mean that the process doesn't know ahead of time exactly when a signal will occur. Signals can be sent

- by one process to another process (or to itself),
- by the kernel to a process.

Before describing the conditions under which signals are sent, let's first give the names for all the signals. Every signal has a name, specified in the header file `<signal.h>`. Figure 2.4 summarizes the names of all the signals along with their description and default action. The column labeled "Note" specifies if the signal is specific to either 4.3BSD or System V. Rows without either of these two notes are common to both systems.

Name	Note	Description	Default action
SIGALRM		Alarm clock	Terminate
SIGBUS		Bus error	Terminate with core image
SIGCLD		Death of a child process	Discarded
SIGCONT	4.3BSD	Continue after SIGSTP	Discarded
SIGEMT		EMT instruction	Terminate with core image
SIGFPE		FPE instruction	Terminate with core image
SIGHUP		Hangup	Terminate
SIGILL		Illegal instruction	Terminate with core image
SIGINT		Interrupt character	Terminate
SIGIO	4.3BSD	I/O is possible on a file descriptor	Discarded
SIGIOT		IOT instruction	Terminate with core image
SIGKILL		Kill	Terminate
SIGPIPE		Write on a pipe with no one to read it	Terminate
SIGPOLL	System V	Selectable event on a streams device	Terminate
SIGPROF	4.3BSD	Profiling timer alarm	Terminate
SIGPWR	System V	Power fail	Terminate
SIGQUIT		Quit character	Terminate with core image
SIGSEGV		Segmentation violation	Terminate with core image
SIGSTOP	4.3BSD	Stop	Stop (suspend) process
SIGSYS		Bad argument to system call	Terminate with core image
SIGTERM		Software termination signal	Terminate
SIGTRAP		Trace trap	Terminate with core image
SIGTSTP	4.3BSD	Stop signal generated from keyboard	Stop (suspend) process
SIGTTIN	4.3BSD	Background read from control terminal	Stop (suspend) process
SIGTTOU	4.3BSD	Background write to control terminal	Stop (suspend) process
SIGURG	4.3BSD	Urgent condition present on socket	Discarded
SIGUSR1		User defined signal 1	Terminate
SIGUSR2		User defined signal 2	Terminate
SIGVTALRM	4.3BSD	Virtual time alarm	Terminate
SIGWINCH	4.3BSD	Window size change	Discarded
SIGXCPU	4.3BSD	CPU time limit exceeded	Terminate
SIGXFSZ	4.3BSD	File size limit exceeded	Terminate

Figure 2.4 Unix signals.

How and when are signals sent? There are five conditions that generate signals.

1. The `kill` system call allows a process to send a signal to another process or to itself. The name *kill* is somewhat a misnomer, since a signal does not always terminate a process. Some signals do indeed kill the receiving process, while others are used to inform the process of some condition that the receiving process then handles.

   ```
   int kill(int pid, int sig);
   ```

   As expected, a process is not able to send a signal to any other arbitrary process. To send a signal, the sending process and the receiving process must both have the same effective user ID, or the sending process must be the superuser.

The `kill` system call does many different things, depending on the values of its arguments.

- If the *pid* argument is zero, the signal is sent to all processes in the sender's process group.

- If the *pid* argument is −1, and the sender is not the superuser, the signal is sent to all processes whose real user ID equals the effective user ID of the sending process.

- If the *pid* argument is −1, and the sender is the superuser, the signal is sent to all processes, other than the system processes (normally the processes with PIDs of 0 and 1).

- If the *pid* argument is negative, but not −1, the signal is sent to all processes whose process group ID equals the absolute value of *pid*. (We'll use this feature in our remote command server in Section 14.3.)

- If the *sig* argument is zero, error checking is done but no signal is sent. This can be used to test the validity of the *pid*. Note that in order for this to work, all the signals listed in Figure 2.4 must have a value of one or more, which is indeed the case.

2. The `kill` command is also used to send signals. This command is a program that takes its command line arguments and issues a `kill` system call, so all the restrictions and options listed above apply here also.

3. Certain terminal characters generate signals. For example, every interactive terminal has associated with it an interrupt character and a quit character. The interrupt character (typically Control-C or Delete) terminates a process that is running—it generates a `SIGINT` signal. The quit character (typically Control-backslash) terminate a process that is running and generates a core image of the process—it generates a `SIGQUIT` signal. The core image can then be used with a debugger for post mortem analysis of the process. One is able to set the interrupt character and the quit character to be almost any terminal character desired.

In addition to these two terminal control characters, 4.3BSD provides a terminal suspend character (typically Control-Z) to generate a `SIGTSTP` signal immediately, and a delayed terminal suspend character (typically Control-Y). The latter generates a `SIGTSTP` signal when the process attempts to read the character, instead of when it is typed. (We'll return to both of these terminal suspend signals in Chapter 15 when we describe the remote login client program.)

These terminal-generated signals are sent not only to the process that is running, but to all processes in the control group of the terminal. These terminal-generated signals are normally sent from the kernel to a process.

4. Certain hardware conditions generate signals. For example, floating point arithmetic errors generate a `SIGFPE` error. Referencing an address outside a process' address

space generates a SIGSEGV signal. The specific hardware conditions and the signals that they generate, can differ from one Unix implementation to another. These types of signals are normally sent from the kernel to a process.

5. Certain software conditions that are noticed by the kernel cause signals to be generated. For example, the SIGURG signal is generated when out-of-band data arrives on a socket. (More on this in Chapter 6.)

Having described what signals are and how they are generated, what can a process do with a signal?

1. A process can provide a function that is called whenever a specific type of signal occurs. This function, called a signal handler, can do whatever the process wants to handle the condition. This is called *catching* the signal.

2. A process can choose to ignore a signal. All signals, other than SIGKILL, can be ignored. The SIGKILL signal is special, since the system administrator must have a guaranteed way of terminating any process.

3. A process can allow the default to happen, as indicated in the column labeled ''Default'' in Figure 2.4. Normally a process is terminated on receipt of a signal, with certain signals generating a core image of the process in its current working directory. But, under 4.3BSD, the default action for the SIGURG, SIGCONT, SIGIO, and SIGWINCH signals is to be ignored. Further, the default action under 4.3BSD for the SIGSTOP, SIGTSTP, SIGTTIN, and SIGTTOU signals is to stop the process.

A process specifies how it wants a signal handled by calling the signal system call.†

```
#include <signal.h>

int (*signal (int sig, void (*func)(int)))(int);
```

What this declaration says is that signal is a function that returns a pointer to a function that returns an integer. The *func* argument specifies the address of a function that doesn't return anything (void). There are two special values for the *func* argument: SIG_DFL to specify that the signal is to be handled in the default way, and SIG_IGN to specify that the signal is to be ignored. The signal system call always returns the previous value of *func* for the specified signal.

To specify, for example, that the SIGUSR1 signal is to be ignored

```
signal(SIGUSR1, SIG_IGN);
```

---

† There are some exceptions to this. The SIGIO, SIGPOLL, and SIGURG signals all require the process to execute additional system calls if it wants to catch the signal. We'll discuss these signals in Chapters 6 and 7.

To have the function `myintr` called when the `SIGINT` signal is generated, only if this signal is not currently being ignored, we write:

```
#include <signal.h>

extern void    myintr();

  . . .

if (signal(SIGINT, SIG_IGN) != SIG_IGN)
        signal(SIGINT, myintr);
```

When a function is called to handle a signal, the integer signal number is passed as the first argument to the function. This allows a single function to handle multiple signals, determining at run time which signal occurred. Some of the hardware generated signals pass additional arguments to the signal handling function, which we don't consider here. If the signal handling function returns, the process that received the signal continues from where it was interrupted.

We now consider each signal and some of its specifics. Several of the signals are used for implementation dependent hardware exceptions. These signals show their lineage back to the original PDP-11 version of Unix. On the PDP-11, the low-core interrupt vectors correspond to the following conditions: bus error, illegal instruction, trace trap, IOT trap, power fail, and EMT trap. IOT and EMT, for example, are the mnemonics for two actual PDP-11 instructions that transferred control from a user process into the kernel. Signals corresponding to these PDP-11 mnemonics still exist, although their meanings are different on systems other than a PDP-11.

SIGALRM   A process can set an alarm clock by calling the `alarm` system call.

```
unsigned int alarm(unsigned int sec);
```

The *sec* argument specifies the number of seconds to elapse before the kernel is to send the process a `SIGALRM` signal. The argument specifies the "real time" (also called the "wall clock time"), not the CPU time. If the argument is zero, any previous alarm clock for the process is cancelled. This system call is used for setting software timeouts. We'll use it in Chapter 11, for example, with the Internet ping program to send a network message to another system every second. The value returned by the function is the time remaining, if any, from the previous call to the function.

We'll also use the `sleep` function in later chapters, to pause for a specified number of seconds.

```
unsigned int sleep(unsigned int sec);
```

The `sleep` function usually sets a `SIGALRM` signal, which it catches. There are numerous details on how this function can interact with a

SIGALRM signal that the process has already established, which we won't consider. Also, the 4.3BSD version doesn't return a value, while the System V version returns the amount of unslept time if the sleep is terminated early by the process catching some other signal.

SIGBUS This signal is generated by an implementation dependent hardware fault.

SIGCLD This signal is sent to the parent process when a child process terminates. Unlike most signals that we listed in Figure 2.4, this one is discarded if the process does not catch it. Under 4.3BSD, this signal also indicates that the status of a child process has changed. This is more general than just indicating the death of a child process. The change in status can be the death of a child process, or it can be that a child process is stopped by a SIGSTOP, SIGTTIN, SIGTTOU, or SIGTSTP signal. (This signal is officially called SIGCHLD in 4.3BSD. We'll use the name SIGCLD, as this name is acceptable to both 4.3BSD and System V.) We discuss this signal in more detail when we cover the exit and wait system calls later in this chapter. We also discuss it in Section 6.16 when we describe the 4.3BSD inetd daemon.

SIGCONT (4.3BSD) When a 4.3BSD process that has been stopped (see the SIGSTOP and SIGTSTP descriptions below) is continued, this signal is sent. A full screen editor that has been stopped, for example, can repaint the screen when it is continued.

SIGEMT This signal is generated by an implementation dependent hardware fault.

SIGFPE This signal is generated by an implementation dependent hardware condition. 4.3BSD on the VAX, for example, uses this signal to indicate floating point conditions (e.g., floating point underflow) and integer arithmetic conditions (e.g., divide by zero).

SIGHUP When a terminal is closed, the *hangup* signal is sent to every process for which it is the control terminal. This signal is also sent to all processes in a process group when the process group leader terminates.

SIGILL This signal is generated by an implementation dependent hardware condition.

SIGINT This *interrupt* signal is usually generated when you enter the interrupt key on the terminal.

SIGIO (4.3BSD) This signal indicates that I/O is possible on a file descriptor. 4.3BSD uses this signal to provide a form of asynchronous I/O for a process. We discuss this signal in Section 6.12.

SIGIOT This signal is generated by an implementation dependent hardware fault. Additionally, the System V version of abort sends this signal to the current process. (This is a case of a process sending a signal to itself.) The abort function is called by a process to generate a core image and terminate, when an abnormal error condition exists. The 4.3BSD version of `abort` sends a `SIGILL` signal to itself to terminate with a core image.

SIGKILL   This signal is the only guaranteed way to terminate a process, since the receiving process cannot ignore or catch this signal.

SIGPIPE   When a process writes to a pipe or FIFO and there are no processes reading from the pipe or FIFO, this signal is sent to the writer. Pipes and FIFOs are covered in the next chapter. Additionally, this signal is generated by 4.3BSD when a process writes to a socket that has become disconnected. Berkeley sockets are discussed in Chapter 6.

SIGPOLL   (System V) A selectable event has occurred on a streams device. System V provides this signal to allow a process to do asynchronous I/O on one or more streams devices. We'll cover this signal in Section 7.12.

SIGPROF   (4.3BSD) 4.3BSD provides three alarm clock mechanisms: the `SIGALRM` feature, which measures the "real time" of a process, a virtual timer (`SIGVTALRM`), which measures the "virtual time" of a process (the time while a process is running), and a profile timer (`SIGPROF`), which measures both the virtual time and the time spent by the kernel executing on behalf of the process. The `SIGPROF` signal is used by interpreters to profile the execution of a program being interpreted.

SIGPWR   (System V) This signal indicates a power fail, but its operation is implementation dependent. The System V manual discourages one from using this signal, so we will ignore it.

SIGQUIT   This signal is usually generated when you enter the quit key on the terminal. This is similar to the `SIGINT` signal, but the `SIGQUIT` signal also generates a core image.

SIGSEGV   This signal is generated by an implementation dependent hardware fault. A segmentation violation is typically generated when a process references a memory address that it is not allowed to access.

SIGSTOP   (4.3BSD) This signal stops a process. Like the `SIGKILL` signal, the `SIGSTOP` signal cannot be ignored or caught. This provides a way for the system administrator to stop a process. A process that has been stopped is continued with the `SIGCONT` signal.

SIGSYS   This signal indicates that an invalid system call was invoked. Also, for historical reasons, this signal is also generated when the *whence* argument to the `lseek` system call is not 0, 1, or 2.

SIGTERM   Software termination signal. This is the default signal sent to a process when the `kill` command is used. (Do not confuse the `kill` command with the system call of the same name.)

SIGTRAP   This signal is used along with the `ptrace` system call to allow a process to be run with tracing enabled. This feature is used by debuggers, and is not discussed further in this text.

SIGTSTP   (4.3BSD) This signal is sent to a process when the suspend key (typically Control-Z) or the delayed suspend key (typically Control-Y) is entered on the keyboard. A process that has been suspended (stopped) is continued with the `SIGCONT` signal. We'll discuss these signals later in this chapter when we describe the job-control facilities provided by 4.3BSD.

SIGTTIN   (4.3BSD) This signal is generated when a process in the background attempts to read from its control terminal. Since confusion results when more than one process reads from a terminal device, 4.3BSD generates this signal. If the process ignores this signal, the process is stopped by default.

SIGTTOU   (4.3BSD) This signal is similar to the `SIGTTIN` signal above, but is generated when a background process attempts to write to its control terminal. By default a background process is allowed to write to its control terminal, but you can specify that a background write is to generate this signal instead.

SIGURG   (4.3BSD) An urgent condition (such as out-of-band data) is present. This signal and the concept of out-of-band data are discussed in Section 6.14. This signal is also used by the pseudo-terminal device driver, which we discuss in Section 15.10.

SIGUSR1   There are two user defined signals that can be used to communicate between processes. Note that if a signal is used for communication between two or more processes, the only information provided the receiving process is the signal type—it cannot obtain the process ID of the sending process. The signal carries no information other than it occurred. For this reason, signals are not frequently used for communication between processes.

SIGUSR2   See the `SIGUSR1` signal above.

SIGVTALRM (4.3BSD) See the `SIGPROF` signal description.

SIGWINCH   (4.3BSD) The size of the terminal window has changed. We describe this signal in Section 15.8.

SIGXCPU   (4.3BSD) 4.3BSD allows resource limits to be set by a process that affect the process and any new processes it creates. These limits are

- the amount of CPU time to be used by each process,
- the largest size of any single file that can be created,
- the maximum size of the data segment for a process,
- the maximum size of the stack segment for a process,

- the maximum size of a core image that can be generated,
- the maximum size of a process' resident set size.

The `SIGXCPU` signal indicates that the process has exceeded its CPU time.

`SIGXFSZ`   (4.3BSD) This signal indicates that the process has exceeded its file size limit. See the list of process resources above.

Reliable Signals

The signal facilities provided by Unix were unreliable in earlier versions. What we mean by this is that race conditions existed such that signals could get lost—an event could occur to generate a signal but the process would never get notified. Changes were made in both 4.3BSD and in System V Release 3 to provide reliable signals. (Unfortunately, the enhancements made by Berkeley and AT&T are not compatible.) The following features were added to provide more reliable signals:

- Signals handlers remain installed after a signal occurs. Earlier versions of Unix reset the action associated with a signal to `SIG_DFL` right before the user's signal handler was called. This meant that any occurrence of the same signal, before the user's signal handler could call the `signal` system call again, would be lost.

- A process must be able to prevent selected signals from occurring when desired. But we don't want to signal discarded (we could do that with the `SIG_IGN` action). Instead, we want the signal to be remembered, so that when we're ready the signal is delivered. 4.3BSD terms this *blocking* a signal and System V calls it *holding* a signal.

- While a signal is being delivered to a process, that signal is blocked (held). By this we mean that if a signal is generated a second time, while the process is handling its first occurrence, the signal handler is not called again. Instead, the second occurrence of the signal is remembered. If the signal handler that is processing the first occurrence of the signal returns normally, only then it is called again to handle the remembered signal.

4.3BSD supports the concept of a signal mask. It is an integer that specifies one or more signal values. The `sigmask` macro, defined in the `<signal.h>` header file, generates signal masks. For example, to generate a mask containing the values for the `SIGQUIT` and `SIGINT` signals, we write

```
int   mask;

mask = sigmask(SIGQUIT) | sigmask(SIGINT);
```

The 4.3BSD implementation uses one bit in a 32-bit integer for each signal value. (This limits the total number of signals to 32.) To block one or more signals, we call the `sigblock` system call.

```
int sigblock(int mask);
```

The set of signals specified by the *mask* are added to the set of signals currently blocked. This system call returns the signal mask that was in effect before the call. A signal is unblocked by calling

```
int sigsetmask(int mask);
```

with a *mask* that doesn't contain the signal that we want to unblock.

Typically we have a critical region of code within which we don't want certain signals to occur. Assume we want to block the SIGQUIT and SIGINT signals. The code to do this is

```
int      oldmask;

oldmask = sigblock( sigmask(SIGQUIT) | sigmask(SIGINT) );

/* critical region */

sigsetmask(oldmask);       /* reset the mask to what it was */
```

We'll see an actual example of this in Section 15.11 when we discuss the remote login client.

System V doesn't support the concept of a signal mask. Instead, the signal functions take one signal value as an argument. To hold (block) a signal

```
int sighold(int sig);
```

is called, with the signal value as the argument. The system call

```
int sigrelse(int sig);
```

is called to release a signal that has been held. Both of these system calls return −1 on an error, or zero if all is OK. Under System V our example above is

```
sighold(SIGQUIT);
sighold(SIGINT);

/* critical region */

sigrelse(SIGQUIT);
sigrelse(SIGINT);
```

Another feature that both 4.3BSD and System V provide with their reliable signals is the ability to release one or more signals that are blocked, while waiting for a signal to occur. For example, if we use a signal handler to set a global variable to indicate when a signal occurs, we want to examine this variable with that signal blocked. Without using reliable signals, we would code

```
int     flag = 0; /* global variable set when SIGINT occurs */

...
for ( ; ; ) {
        while (flag == 0)
                pause();   /* wait for a signal to occur */
        /* the signal has occurred, process it */
        ...
}
```

But this contains an error. If the signal occurs after the test of the `flag` variable, but before the call to `pause`, the signal can be lost. What we want to do is block the `SIGINT` signal while we're testing the global variable. Under 4.3BSD we write

```
int     flag = 0; /* global variable set when SIGINT occurs */

for ( ; ; ) {
        sigblock(sigmask(SIGINT));
        while (flag == 0)
                sigpause(0); /* wait for a signal to occur */
        /* the signal has occurred, process it */
        ...
}
```

The `sigpause` system call sets a new signal mask (the argument of 0) and waits for a signal to occur. Since we block the `SIGINT` signal before testing the `flag` variable, the race condition is avoided. Note that the unblocking of the signal and the pause have to be combined into a single system call. If we called `sigblock` first, to unblock the signal, followed by a call to `pause`, there is still a chance that the signal could occur between the two system calls. We'll see some other race conditions that can occur between independent system calls in the next chapter when we discuss record locking. Also, we'll show an actual example of the `sigpause` system call in Section 6.12 when we discuss asynchronous I/O.

Under System V we can also atomically release a signal and wait for a signal to occur, using the `sigpause` system call.

```
int     flag = 0; /* global variable set when SIGINT occurs */

for ( ; ; ) {
        sighold(SIGINT);
        while (flag == 0)
                sigpause(SIGINT); /* wait for a signal to occur */
        /* the signal has occurred, process it */
        ...
}
```

This System V version is slightly different from the 4.3BSD version. The System V `sigpause` can only be used with one signal value. It checks to see if that specific signal, `SIGINT` in the example above, has been received and held, and if so, the action for that signal is taken. If that specific signal has not been received and held, then the process waits for any signal to occur. Here is a case where the 4.3BSD signal mask concept is preferable, since the signal mask allows multiple signal values to be handled at once.

4.3BSD provides another new feature with its reliable signals. Normally when a signal occurs during a ''slow'' system call, that system call is interrupted and it returns with an error of `EINTR`. The process is supposed to test for this error return and reissue the system call, if desired. Slow system calls are usually those that can block. For example, a read from a terminal device or a network device is considered a slow system call, since either can cause the process to wait until some data is available to be read. A read from a disk file, however, never blocks, so it would never be interrupted. System V defines the slow system calls as: `ioctl`, `open`, `pause`, `read`, `sigpause`, `wait`, and `write`. In addition, 4.3BSD can interrupt the following system calls: `accept`, `connect`, `flock`, `readv`, `recv`, `recvfrom`, `recvmsg`, `send`, `sendto`, `sendmsg`, and `writev`. When the revised signal mechanisms were introduced with 4.2BSD, they included the automatic restart of interrupted system calls. With 4.3BSD, however, it became an option that can be overridden. We'll show an example in Chapter 15 when we want a `read` system call to be interrupted when a signal occurs (i.e., we don't want the kernel to restart it automatically).

One problem with the automatic restarting of certain system calls by 4.3BSD is that not all the interrupted system calls are automatically restarted. The only ones that are automatically restarted are `flock`, `ioctl`, `read`, `readv`, `wait`, `write`, and `writev`. For example, `accept` and `recvfrom` are never automatically restarted. This means we still have to be aware of the possibility of encountering an interrupted system call when doing network programming.

2.5   Process Control

Network programming involves the interaction of two or more processes. We now examine the ways in which programs are executed and how processes are created and terminated. This is an important topic that we'll encounter in almost every chapter of this text.

`fork` **System Call**

The only way in which a new process is created by Unix is for an existing process to execute the `fork` system call.†

```
int fork();
```

The `fork` system call creates a copy of the process that was executing. The process that executed the `fork` is called the *parent process* and the new process is called the *child process*. The `fork` system call is called once (by the parent process) but it returns twice (once in the parent and once in the child). The only difference in the returns from the `fork` system call is that the return value in the parent process is the process ID of the newly created child process, while the return value in the child process is zero. If the `fork` system call is not successful, −1 is returned. Should the child wish to obtain the process ID of its parent process, it can call the `getppid` system call. An example of the `fork` system call is

```
main()
{
        int     childpid;

        if ( (childpid = fork()) == -1) {
                perror("can't fork");
                exit(1);
        } else if (childpid == 0) {
                /* child process */
                printf("child: child pid = %d, parent pid = %d\n",
                                        getpid(), getppid());
                exit(0);
        } else {
                /* parent process */
                printf("parent: child pid = %d, parent pid = %d\n",
                                        childpid, getpid());
                exit(0);
        }
}
```

We show the `fork` operation as

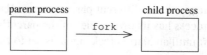

Realize that if the text segment can be shared, then both the parent and child can share the text segment after the `fork`.

---

† This does not apply to the `init` process, which has a process ID of 1, and is started specially by the kernel when the Unix system is initialized. Readers interested in these details should consult Bach [1986] or Leffler et al. [1989].

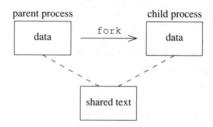

Also, realize that the child's copy of the data segment is a copy of the parent's data segment when the `fork` operation takes place. It is *not* a copy from the corresponding program's disk file.

One important feature of the `fork` operation is that the files that were open in the parent process before the `fork` are shared by the child process after the `fork`. This feature provides an easy way for the parent process to open specific files or devices and pass these open files to the child process. After the `fork` the parent closes the files that it opened for the child, so that both processes are not sharing the same file. We will see many examples of this later in the text.

Regarding the process variables that were defined in the previous sections, the values of the following in the child process are copied from the parent process.

- real user ID
- real group ID
- effective user ID
- effective group ID
- process group ID
- terminal group ID
- root directory
- current working directory
- signal handling settings
- file mode creation mask

The child process differs from the parent process in the following ways:

- the child process has a new, unique process ID,
- the child process has a different parent process ID,
- the child process has its own copies of the parent's file descriptors,
- the time left until an alarm clock signal is set to zero in the child.

There are two uses for the `fork` operation.

1. A process wants to make a copy of itself so that one copy can handle an operation while the other copy does another task. This is typical for network servers. We will see many examples of this later in the text.

2. A process wants to execute another program. Since the only way to create a new process is with the `fork` operation, the process must first `fork` to make a copy of itself, then one of the copies (typically the child process) issues an `exec` (described below) to execute the new program. This is typical for programs such as shells.

We'll encounter both of these uses in the examples later in this text.

`exit` **System Call**

A process terminates by calling the `exit` system call. This system call never returns to the caller. When `exit` is called, an integer exit status is passed by the process to the kernel. This exit status is then available to the parent process of the exiting process through the `wait` system call (described below). Only the low-order 8 bits of the exit status should be used, allowing a process to terminate with an exit status in the range 0 through 255. By convention, a process that terminates normally returns an exit status of zero, while the nonzero values are used to indicate an error condition.

One must be careful to differentiate between the `exit` system call and the `exit` function provided by the standard C library—see Figure 2.3. The version provided by the C library is a function that first allows the standard I/O library to flush any partially filled buffers, and then invokes the `exit` system call. Another function is provided by the standard C library, `_exit`, and this function invokes the system call immediately. The `_exit` function should be called by a process that wants to avoid any standard I/O cleanup from taking place.

Some additional ramifications of the `exit` system call are discussed below with the `wait` system call.

`exec` **System Call**

The only way in which a program is executed by Unix is for an existing process to issue the `exec` system call.† The `exec` system call replaces the current process with the new program. The process ID does not change. We refer to the process that issues the `exec` system call as the *calling process*, and the program that is `exec`ed as the *new program*. Many Unix manuals incorrectly refer to the new program as the *new process*, but realize that it is really a new program executing in the context of the calling process. A new process is *not* created by Unix.

There are six different versions of the `exec` function.

---

† Again, we are not considering the initial bootstrap sequence of the operating system, or how the `init` program is executed by the operating system.

```
int execlp(char *filename, char *arg0, char *arg1, ..., char *argn,
           (char *) 0);

int execl(char *pathname, char *arg0, char *arg1, ..., char *argn,
          (char *) 0);

int execle(char *pathname, char *arg0, char *arg1, ..., char *argn,
           (char *) 0, char **envp);

int execvp(char *filename, char **argv);

int execv(char *pathname, char **argv);

int execve(char *pathname, char **argv, char **envp);
```

The exec functions return to the caller only if an error occurs. Otherwise control passes
to the start of the new program. The relationship between these six functions is shown in
Figure 2.5.

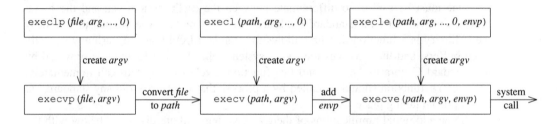

Figure 2.5 exec functions.

There are many ways to look at these six functions.

1. The three functions in the top row specify each argument string as a separate argu-
    ment to the exec function, with a NULL pointer terminating the variable number of
    arguments.† The three functions in the second row have built an *argv* array, contain-
    ing the pointers to the argument strings. This argv array must contain a NULL
    pointer to specify its end, since a count is not specified.

---

† A common error that became evident when Unix was moved to the Intel 80286-based systems,
using "large memory model" programming, was to code this NULL pointer as '0' instead of
'(char *) 0'. With the large memory model, a pointer is 32 bits while an integer is typically
16 bits, so this coding error passes a 16-bit value to a function expecting a 32-bit argument.

2. The two functions in the left column specify a *filename* argument. This is converted into a *pathname* using the current `PATH` environment variable. If there does not exist a variable in the current environment named `PATH` then a default search path of "`:/bin:/usr/bin`" is used. If the *pathname* argument to `execlp` or `execvp` contains a slash (/) anywhere in the string, the `PATH` variable is not used. The four functions in the right two columns specify a fully qualified *pathname* argument.

3. The four functions in the left two columns do not specify an explicit environment pointer. Instead the current value of the external variable `environ` is used for building an environment list that is passed to the new program. The two functions in the right column specify an explicit environment list. The *envp* array of pointers must be terminated by a NULL pointer.

The program invoked by the `exec` system call inherits the following attributes from the process that calls `exec`.

- process ID
- parent process ID
- process group ID
- terminal group ID
- time left until an alarm clock signal
- root directory
- current working directory
- file mode creation mask
- real user ID
- real group ID
- file locks

Two attributes that can change when a new program is `exec`ed are

- effective user ID,
- effective group ID.

If the set-user-ID bit is set for the program being `exec`ed, the effective user ID is changed to the user ID of the owner of the program file. Similarly, if the set-group-ID bit is set for the program, the effective group ID is set to the group ID of the owner of the program file.

The status of signals is handled specially when the new program is `exec`ed. Any signals that were set to terminate the calling process will terminate the new program, and any signals that were set to be ignored by the calling process will still be ignored. The difference is that signals that were set to be caught by the calling process can no longer be caught, since the function address that was passed to the `signal` system call is now meaningless in the new program. To handle this, any signals that were set to be caught in the calling process are changed to terminate the program.

`wait` **System Call**

A process can wait for one of its child processes to finish by executing the `wait` system call.

        int wait(int *status);

The value returned by `wait` is the process ID of the child process that terminated. If the process that calls `wait` does not have any child processes, `wait` returns a value of −1 immediately. If the process that calls `wait` has one or more child processes that has not yet terminated, then the calling process is suspended by the kernel until one of its child processes terminates. When a child process terminates and `wait` returns, if the *status* argument is not `NULL`, the value passed to `exit` by the terminating child process is stored in the *status* variable. Some additional information is also returned by `wait`. There are three conditions for which `wait` returns a process ID as its return value.

1. A child process called `exit`.

2. A child process was terminated by a signal.

3. A child process was being traced and the process stopped. This occurs when one process is tracing the execution of another process, such as when a debugger is being used to step through a process. We will not discuss this option—refer to Bach [1986] for additional details.

Each of these three cases returns different information in the *status* variable, as shown in Figure 2.6.

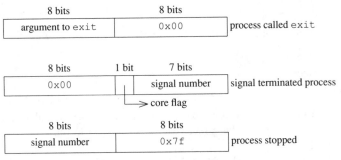

Figure 2.6   Values returned by the `wait` system call.

Signal numbers are greater than zero, otherwise it would be impossible to distinguish between the three cases. The *core flag* bit is one if the terminated process generated a core file, otherwise it is zero.

As mentioned previously, a process has a single parent process, but it can have many child processes. The following steps are done by the kernel when a process `exits`.

- If the parent process of the `exit`ing process has called the `wait` system call, the parent process is notified that a child process has terminated (i.e., the `wait` system call returns to the parent). The parent process is passed the child's exit status (the child's argument to the `exit` function), if the parent's *status* argument was nonzero.

- If the parent process of the `exit`ing process is not executing a `wait`, the terminating process is marked as a *zombie process*. A zombie process is one that has terminated, but its parent has not `wait`ed for it yet. The kernel releases all the resources being used by a zombie process (its memory, for example) but has to at least maintain its exit status, until its parent `wait`s for it.

- The parent process ID of all the terminating process' child processes is set to 1 (the `init` process). This is described in more detail below.

- If the process ID, process group ID, and terminal group ID fields of the terminating process are all equal, the hangup signal, `SIGHUP`, is sent to each process that has a process group ID equal to that of the terminating process.

What happens to the parent process ID of a child process when the parent process terminates before the child process? There are three possible scenarios to consider.

1. The child process terminates before the parent process. This is the "normal" condition when we are entering commands to an interactive shell (assuming we don't logout before waiting for a command to complete).

   (a) If the parent process has already executed a `wait`, then the `wait` returns to the parent process with the process ID of the child that terminated.

   (b) If the parent process has not executed a `wait`, then the child process becomes a *zombie* process, as mentioned above.

2. The parent process terminates before its child processes. This presents a problem, since the parent process IDs of any child processes are no longer valid, once the parent terminates. The way Unix handles this is to find all processes (active or zombie) whose parent process ID equals the process ID of the terminating process. For these child processes that are about to be orphaned, Unix sets their parent process ID to 1, the process ID of the `init` process. The `init` process, therefore, becomes the parent process of any orphaned processes. The `init` process never terminates.† Other than having its parent process ID changed, an executing child process is not aware that its parent process has terminated.

---

† If the `init` process were to terminate while the system were in multiuser mode, no new users would be able to login to the system. The 4.3BSD kernel checks for this condition in the `exit` system call and automatically reboots the kernel if the `exit`ing process has a process ID of 1.

When a process `exits`, a `SIGCLD` signal is generated in the parent process. But by default, this signal is ignored, as shown in Figure 2.3. Many programs are unaware of this signal. The purpose of this signal is to allow the parent process to call `wait` to obtain the `exit` status of its child process. If a process knows that it will spawn child processes, this is one technique to prevent its children from becoming zombies. As mentioned earlier, if the parent does not `wait` for a child process that has terminated, that child becomes a zombie, until the parent also terminates. System V allows a process to prevent any of its child processes from becoming zombies. To do this, the parent has to execute

```
signal(SIGCLD, SIG_IGN);
```

to ignore this signal. This tells the kernel that the process is not interested in the `exit` status of its children. From this point on, the kernel will not generate zombie processes from the children of this process. Instead, their `exit` status is discarded. 4.3BSD does not provide this feature. We'll return to this signal in Section 2.6 when we discuss a general daemon process.

`wait3` **System Call**

4.3BSD provides a variant of the `wait` system call.

```
#include <sys/wait.h>
#include <sys/time.h>
#include <sys/resource.h>

int wait3(union wait *status, int options, struct rusage *rusage);
```

The main use is to set the *options* argument to `WNOHANG` to prevent the system call from blocking if there aren't any children wishing to report status. In this case the return value is zero. Otherwise the return value is either a positive process ID or −1 if an error occurred. The *rusage* argument allows the caller to obtain CPU usage information of its children. If a child process has terminated, the value returned in *status* is the same as we described for the `exit` system call.

We'll use this system call with our skeleton daemon at the end of this chapter, when we want to assure that we don't block.

Process Relationships

We mentioned a special process above, the `init` process. This process always has a process ID of 1. When a Unix system is started for normal multiuser operation, the kernel invokes the program `/etc/init` to start things up. The `init` process runs with a user ID of zero, so that it has superuser privileges. The operation of `init` depends on the Unix system.

   1. Under 4.3BSD, `init` executes the shell script `/etc/rc`. This file does some

normal housekeeping chores and then starts the normal daemon processes (more on these in the next section). `init` then reads the file `/etc/ttys` to determine which terminals are to be activated for multiuser operation.

2. Under Unix System V, `init` reads the file `/etc/inittab`, which specifies the actions to be taken under different circumstances. For normal multiuser operation the file `/etc/rc` is executed, and this program starts most daemon processes. When this program finishes, the `/etc/inittab` file specifies which terminals are to be activated for multiuser operation. (The System V `init` program and its `/etc/inittab` file provide for additional capabilities, based on a user-specified "run level" of the system. Refer to the System V Administrator Reference Manual for all the details.)

Regardless of the Unix system, for each of the terminals to be activated, the `init` process `forks` a copy of itself, and then each child process `execs` the `/etc/getty` program. This gives the picture shown in Figure 2.7.

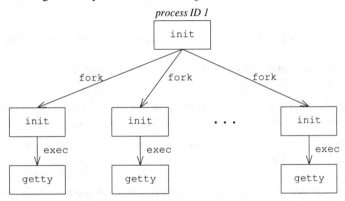

Figure 2.7   `getty` processes waiting for users to login.

`getty` sets the terminal's speed, outputs a greeting message, and waits for you to enter your login name. After your login name is entered, `getty` `execs` the program `/bin/login`, passing it your login name as an argument. The `login` program then looks up the login name in the `/etc/passwd` file and prompts you for a password, if required. If you enter a login name to the second `getty` shown in Figure 2.7, the picture becomes as shown in Figure 2.8. The other `getty` processes in Figure 2.8 are waiting for someone to enter a login name.

The programs that have been run so far, `init`, `getty`, and `login`, have all been running with a user ID and an effective user ID of zero (the superuser). Also note that the process ID does not change when an `exec` occurs, so all the processes starting from the `forked` copy of `init` have the same process ID. Now that the `login` program knows who is logging in, it does the following:

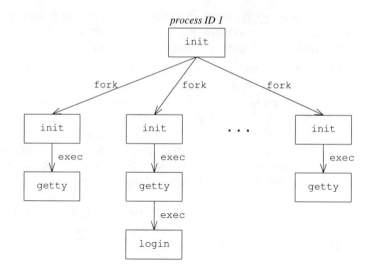

Figure 2.8 `getty` processes after one user has entered a login name.

- Sets the current working directory to the *login-directory* field from the password file entry. This is done by calling the `chdir` system call.

- Sets the group ID and the user ID, in that order, to the values specified in the password file entry. This is done by calling the `setgid` and `setuid` system calls.

- `exec`s the shell program specified by the password file entry, or `/bin/sh` if one is not specified.

Unless the person logging in is the superuser (whose *login-name* is usually `root`), the effect of the `setgid` and `setuid` calls is to lower the privilege of the process. These two system calls are restricted to the superuser, since it is not possible for any user to change their user ID or group ID to become some other user. Since the `login` program is running with a user ID of zero, it is allowed to change its user ID. Note also that `login` must change its group ID first, so that its user ID is still zero when it calls the `setuid` system call. If it were to try these two in the opposite order, it would not have superuser privileges when it tried to execute the `setgid` call, and it would fail. If your shell is the Bourne shell, Figure 2.9 shows the `exec` of the login shell.

The shell that is invoked by `login` is known as the *login shell*. The parent process ID of all processes shown in Figure 2.9, other than the original `init` process (whose process ID is 1), is 1. This is because when `init` `forks` its child processes, the parent process ID of the child process is 1, and the parent process ID does not change when an `exec` occurs.

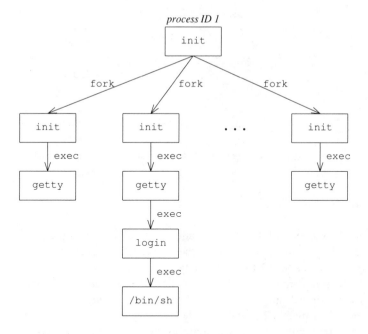

Figure 2.9 `getty` processes after one login shell is started.

Looking only at a shell process, its normal action is to wait for the interactive user to enter a command line, which it then executes. For example, if you enter

    date

the actions taken are

1. The shell `fork`s a copy of itself and `wait`s for the child process to terminate.

2. The child process uses the `PATH` environment variable, to look for an executable file with the name `date`. If the environment variable were

    `PATH=/usr1/stevens/bin:/usr/local/bin:/usr/ucb:/bin:/usr/bin`

   the shell looks in the directory `/usr1/stevens/bin`, then the directory `/usr/local/bin`, and so on. Assuming the executable program is located in `/bin/date` the child process `exec`s that program.

3. When the `date` program finishes, it calls `exit` with its return status, which terminates the child process and allows the `wait` to return to the parent process.

Figure 2.10 summarizes these actions of the shell.

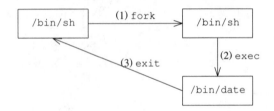

Figure 2.10   Normal shell invocation of an interactive command.

Job Control

Job control is a feature of 4.3BSD that allows you to start multiple processes from a terminal and have some control over their execution. Each process, or pipeline of
processes, is called a *job*. More accurately, a *job* is a collection of one or more processes
that share the same process group ID. One important feature of job control is your ability
to share the terminal among the jobs. Job control requires support from the terminal
driver, the signal mechanism, and the shell. Being aware of job control is important to
network programming. Our remote login example in Chapter 15 has to be aware of job
control.

It used to be easy to distinguish between the C shell, which supports job control and
the Bourne shell, which doesn't. But we need to better qualify the terms. In this text
we'll distinguish between a *job-control shell* and a shell that doesn't support job control.
When we use these terms we're also describing the underlying Unix system. For example, although the C shell supports job control under 4.3BSD, it has been ported to
System V where it doesn't support job control. Similarly the KornShell supports job control if the underlying system provides it. When we refer to a job-control shell we mean
either the C shell or the KornShell, running on a version of Unix that supports job control.

As an example, consider the processes when you enter the following command to a
Bourne shell:†

```
make > make.out 2>&1 &
```

This executes the program `make` in the background (i.e., the shell doesn't wait for it to
finish before allowing you to enter another command). Its standard output is redirected
to the file `make.out`. The notation `2>&1` instructs the shell to create file descriptor 2
(standard error) as a duplicate of file descriptor 1 (standard output). This redirects both

---

† The `make` program is a standard Unix utility that assists in the construction and maintenance of
other programs. It typically invokes the C compiler and the link editor to build an executable
program. For our purposes, we're using it as an example because it is a program that is often run in
the background and it `exec`s other programs.

the standard output and the standard error from `make` to the file `make.out`. This `make` process probably invokes other processes, such as the C compiler, `cc`. Assume while this process is running in the background, you enter

```
vi main.c
```

to edit a file. At this point, since the Bourne shell is not a job-control shell, the processes are shown in Figure 2.11.

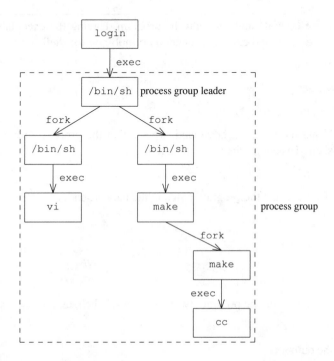

Figure 2.11   Process group.

The original interactive shell that `login` invokes (termed the login shell) is called the *process group leader*. Its process group ID equals its process ID. All of its child processes (those beneath it in the process tree shown in Figure 2.11) have a process group ID equal to the login shell's process ID. A child process can remove itself from the process group that it inherits by calling the `setpgrp` system call. This makes the calling process a process group leader in its own process group, and any processes created by this child process will, by default, belong to this new process group. We will see in the next section how a daemon process wants to remove itself from its inherited process group and create its own process group.

Let's look at the creation of process groups by both a job-control shell and a non-job-control shell. The following program prints its process ID and its process group ID.

```
main()
{
        printf("pid = %d, pgrp = %d\n", getpid(), getpgrp(0));
        exit(0);
}
```

If we compile and link edit the program, leaving the executable program in the default file a.out and execute it under a non-job-control shell as

```
a.out
```

we get

```
pid = 1173, pgrp = 1117
```

Using the Unix ps command, we see that the process with a PID of 1117 is our login shell. Executing the program again yields

```
pid = 1174, prgrp = 1117
```

If we execute the program twice in the background, as

```
a.out & a.out &
```

the output is

```
pid = 1175, pgrp = 1117
pid = 1176, pgrp = 1117
```

If we execute the program twice, from a subshell, as

```
( a.out & a.out & )
```

the output is

```
pid = 1178, pgrp = 1117
pid = 1179, pgrp = 1117
```

Placing the commands within parentheses tells the shell to execute a subshell that will in turn execute the command list. (The command list is everything between the parentheses.) The missing process ID, 1177, belongs to the subshell.

This description of process groups applies to shells that don't support job control. But a job-control shell does things differently. A job-control shell that is a login shell makes each child process the leader of its own process group. Executing the same program as above, from the C shell, as

```
a.out
```

generates

```
pid = 2524, pgrp = 2524
```

Since the process ID equals the process group ID, this process is a process group leader. Executing the program again gives

```
pid = 2525, pgrp = 2525
```

If the program is executed twice in the background, as

```
a.out & a.out &
```

the output is

```
pid = 2527, pgrp = 2527
pid = 2526, pgrp = 2526
```

Each child process is put into its own process group. But if we execute the program twice from a subshell, as

```
( a.out & a.out & )
```

with the C shell we get

```
pid = 2530, pgrp = 2528
pid = 2529, pgrp = 2528
```

Here the login C shell places the subshell (whose process ID is 2528) into its own process group. This subshell, however, is not a login shell, so its child processes (process IDs 2529 and 2530) remain in its process group. The KornShell output for this example would be

```
pid = 2530, pgrp = 2530
pid = 2529, pgrp = 2529
```

Here we see that a job-control KornShell does execute the parenthesized command list in a subshell (whose process ID is 2528) but this subshell places each of the background commands in its own process group.

This difference in the handling of process groups for child processes also affects the sending of signals. Recall that the `kill` system call with a *pid* argument of zero, sends the signal to all processes in the sender's process group. Also, since a non-job-control shell places child processes of a login shell in the same process group as the login shell, when the login shell terminates, the SIGHUP signal is sent to any child processes that still belong to the process group of the login shell. With a job-control shell, however, a child process of a login shell is not affected when the login shell terminates.

File Sharing

The sharing of files across a `fork` system call merits further review, as it nicely describes the sharing of files between Unix processes. There are three kernel tables used to access a file, which we show in Figure 2.12.

- Every process has a *process table* entry. One portion of the process table is an array of file pointers. The file descriptors described earlier are just indexes into this array.

- The file pointers in the process table point to entries in the *file table*. The file table is where the current file position for all open files in the system is maintained. This position is modified and returned by the `lseek` system call, and updated by every `read` and `write` system call.

- At the right side of the picture is the *i-node* table. Every open file has an entry in the i-node table. An i-node table entry contains all the information read from the i-node on disk, along with some other fields that the kernel needs to maintain while the file is open (such as a count of how many processes have the file open).

From the early versions of Unix the arrangement of these three tables has been to allow file sharing and avoid duplicate data storage by keeping different information in each table. Since the i-node table does not keep the file's current position, an i-node entry for a file can be shared by any number of processes. A common operation that must be handled is if two or more processes are reading the same file at some point in time—the file position of one process must be independent of the other. If the file's position were kept in the i-node table, processes could not share an i-node table entry.

Another case that must be handled is a process that `forks` a child process and then `execs` some other process. Consider the example

```
cc test.c > cc.out 2>&1
```

This redirects both the standard output and the standard error to the same file, `cc.out`. (The Unix program `cc` is the C compiler. It typically invokes all the passes of the compiler, which are each separate executable programs, then the assembler, and then the link editor.) When the `cc` process `forks` and `execs` all these programs, it is essential that all these processes share the file positions for file descriptors 1 and 2 with the parent. This way an error message from the first pass is written to the file `cc.out` and the file position updated accordingly. If the next pass outputs a message to this file, it must write its output after the output from the first pass. Similarly if the third pass writes another message, its write must start from the ending file position from the previous pass. The only way to have the file position shared like this, is to have the parent and child processes reference the same file table entry for every open file. In Figure 2.12, the entry labeled ''fd i'' is shared between the parent and child.

This example also shows a case where two file descriptors in a single process must be shared—the redirection of the standard output and the standard error output must point to the same file table entry. This is so that output to either one updates a single file position accordingly. Since the file descriptor for the standard error on the `cc` command line above is created using the `dup` system call, this system call must have the new file descriptor that it returns, point to the same file table entry as the existing file descriptor (the argument to `dup`).

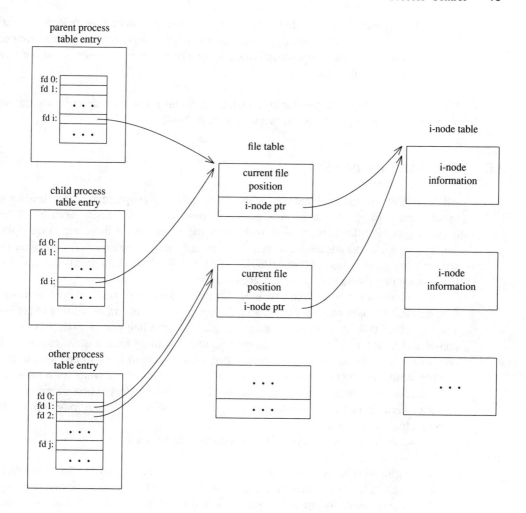

Figure 2.12 The sharing of files between processes.

We can state a few rules about the sharing of file pointers.

1. The only time a single process table entry contains pointers to the same file table entry is from a dup system call.

2. If a single process opens the same file more than once, each open returns a file descriptor that points to a unique file table entry, but all these file table entries point to the same i-node table entry.

3. A file table entry can only have more than one process table entry pointing to it from a fork operation. Normally there is no way for two unrelated processes to share a single file table entry.

4. If the parent and child do not coordinate the use of a shared file from a `fork` (if the parent, for example, does not wait for the child to terminate before referencing the file), then any changes made by one of the two processes to the file position affects the other.

We return to this topic of file sharing in Chapters 6 and 7 when we describe the passing of an open file descriptor between two unrelated processes.

2.6   Daemon Processes

All the definitions and explanations up to this point in this chapter have been leading up to the actual writing of a skeleton of a daemon process, which we now describe. While daemon processes have been used with Unix for many years, there are some subtle details that must be considered, to provide a robust daemon process. The ideas in this section come from Lennert [1986, 1987]. Williams [1989] provides details on how these features are implemented in System V Release 4.0.

A daemon is a process that executes "in the background" (i.e., without an associated terminal or login shell) either waiting for some event to occur, or waiting to perform some specified task on a periodic basis. For example, the line printer examples that we consider in Chapter 13 have a daemon process that is waiting for a request to print a file on a line printer. A remote login program that allows users to login to one system from another system on the network, would have a daemon process that waits for a request to come across the network for someone to login. A standard Unix process named `cron` performs periodic tasks at given times during the day, taking its instructions from the file `/usr/lib/crontab`.

Consider the different ways a daemon process can be started.

1. During system start-up. Most system daemons are started by the initialization script `/etc/rc`, which is executed by `/etc/init` when the system is brought up multiuser. When a daemon is started by `/etc/rc` it will have superuser privileges.

2. From the system's `/usr/lib/crontab` file on a periodic basis. Daemons invoked this way can have superuser privileges, since the `cron` program itself runs as superuser.

3. From a user's `crontab` file on a periodic basis. This ability of ordinary users to create their own `crontab` files is provided by System V, not 4.3BSD.

4. By executing the `at` command, which schedules a job for execution at some later time.

5. From a user terminal, as a foreground job or as a background job. This is usually done when testing a daemon.

Other than the case where you start a daemon from a terminal, the other examples all generate a daemon that is not connected to a terminal. Indeed, it is the normal interaction of a login terminal, the process group associated with that terminal, and all the associated interactions of signals, that generate the problem areas that must be handled correctly when writing a daemon.

Typical *system* daemons (such as the line printer daemon) have by the following characteristics:

- They are started once, when the system is initialized.

- Their "lifetime" is the entire time that the system is operating; usually they do not die and get restarted later.

- They spend most of their time waiting for some event to occur at which time they perform their service.

- They frequently spawn other processes to handle service requests.

We now look at the details of initiating and executing daemon processes, and develop a set of rules for coding a daemon. These rules are intended to provide a robust daemon that is capable of being invoked by any of the ways listed above. In addition, we handle cases that might not occur in all daemons—writing error messages on start-up to a terminal, for example. If your daemon does not do this, then you need not worry about reacquiring a control terminal.

Part of the problem with coding a daemon is that a Unix process has little control or knowledge about who invoked it (i.e., who its parent process is) and under what conditions it was invoked (i.e., was it invoked as a background process from a login shell or by the system initialization). There is some information that is obtainable, for example if the parent process ID is 1, then the daemon was probably invoked by the `init` process. We must say "probably" because there is a chance that the process that invoked the daemon did an `exit` before the daemon got started, orphaning the daemon so that the daemon's parent process ID gets set to 1 by the kernel. It is also hard to determine other characteristics of the daemon's process environment, such as its current working directory, and whether it currently has a control terminal or not. Our approach is to assume the worst and provide a daemon capable of being invoked by any other process.

Close All Open File Descriptors

All unnecessary file descriptors should be closed. This especially applies to standard input, standard output, and the standard error, since they were probably inherited from the process that `exec`ed the daemon. The code fragment

```
#include <sys/param.h>

for (i = 0; i < NOFILE; i++)
        close(i);
```

will close all open files. The constant NOFILE defines the maximum number of open files per process. Some daemons specify the constant 20 in the limit of the loop, and others use the <stdio.h> constant _NFILE as the upper limit. This constant is available under System V. 4.3BSD provides the getdtablesize system call, which returns the number of entries in the file descriptor table for a process.

Change Current Working Directory

The current working directory for a process is held open by the kernel for the life of the process. The mounted filesystem to which this directory belongs cannot be unmounted while an active process has its current working directory in that filesystem. To allow the system administrator to unmount a filesystem, a daemon should execute

```
chdir("/");
```

to change its current working directory to the root directory.

An exception to this rule are the daemons which execute a chdir to the directory where they do all their work. For example, the System V line printer spooler changes to the /usr/spool/lp directory, since that is its home directory for all its operations. Indeed, this spooler cannot operate unless this directory is available.

Be aware that if the daemon terminates with a core image, the kernel tries to create the file core in the current working directory of the process. If you are testing a new daemon and don't have superuser privilege, you may not have permission to write this file in the root directory. In this case you might want to change the working directory to /tmp, for example.

Reset the File Access Creation Mask

A process inherits its file access creation mask from its parent. A daemon should execute

```
umask(0);
```

to reset this mask. This prevents any files created by the daemon from having their access bits modified. For example, if a daemon specifically created a file with a mode of 0660, so that only the user and group could read and write the file, but the umask value was 060, the group read and write permissions would be turned off. If the daemon required the group permissions to be on, so that some other process in that group could access the file, this umask value prevents it.

Run in the Background

If a daemon is started from a login session without being placed in the background (with the shell's & operator), the daemon will tie up the terminal while it is executing. If the daemon is started from a shell script (such as /etc/rc) without being placed in the background, the daemon will cause the processing of the shell script to stop until the daemon finishes. To avoid either of these, the daemon should do a fork and have the parent `exit`, allowing the actual daemon to continue in the child process.

Disassociate from Process Group

Any process inherits its process group ID from the process that `exec`ed it. By belonging to some process group, the daemon is susceptible to signals sent to the entire process group. To prevent this from affecting a daemon, the daemon should disassociate from its inherited process group and form its own process group.

The daemon calls the `setpgrp` system call to set its process group ID equal to its process ID, making the calling process a process group leader, in a new process group. Under System V, the call is

```
setpgrp();
```

while under 4.3BSD we have

```
setpgrp(0, getpid());
```

Ignore Terminal I/O Signals

On systems that support job control, you control the ability of a background job to produce output on the control terminal with an `stty` option. (`stty` is a Unix program that allows you to enable or disable certain terminal characteristics.) If background writes are not allowed, the process is sent the `SIGTTOU` signal when it attempts to write to the control terminal. The best solution is to disassociate the daemon process from its controlling terminal, as we do below. But if the daemon does want to write some error messages on the control terminal when started, it should ignore this signal.

```
#ifdef SIGTTOU
        signal(SIGTTOU, SIG_IGN);
#endif
```

The use of the `#ifdef` allows this code to be compiled only on a system that supports this signal, since it is 4.3BSD-specific and not in System V. It is also a good idea to ignore the other terminal-related job-control signals: `SIGTTIN` and `SIGTSTP`.

Signals, Process Groups, and Control Terminals (Revisited)

The handling of signals, process groups, and control terminals is so important in a multiple-process environment that we revisit them now. Figure 2.13 shows the relevant kernel data structures. Figure 2.13 shows a process structure that contains all the information for a single process.†

---

† Technically, the control terminal pointer is not contained in the process structure, but in another per-process structure, the user area. Also, the socket structure is really pointed to by a file table entry, which is pointed to by a file descriptor entry. These details are not important for our discussion.

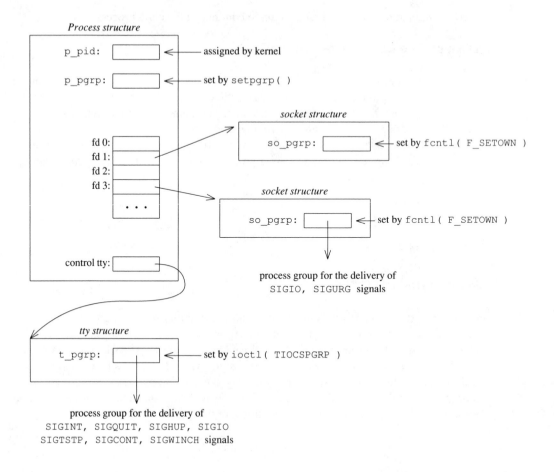

Figure 2.13 Kernel data structures for the various process groups.

We also show the tty structure, of which there is one for every terminal or pseudo-terminal, and two socket structures. (We cover pseudo-terminals in Chapter 15.) To recapitulate what we've already described in previous sections of this chapter, every process has

- a unique process ID, `p_pid`. This value is assigned by the kernel when the process is created.

- a process group ID, `p_pgrp`. This value can be changed by a process with the `setpgrp` system call (whose arguments and semantics differ slightly between System V and 4.3BSD). When this value equals the process ID for a process, that process is termed a process group leader.

- a pointer to a socket structure for every socket that the process has open (4.3BSD only).

- a pointer to the tty structure for the control terminal of the process. This pointer can be NULL if the process does not have a control terminal. Under 4.3BSD this pointer can be set to NULL with an `ioctl` of `TIOCNOTTY`. As we discussed earlier in this chapter, under System V a process can't specifically change this pointer, but the `setpgrp` system call has the side effect of setting this pointer to NULL, if the calling process is not already a process group leader. The kernel uses this pointer from the process table to the corresponding tty structure, when a process opens its control terminal, `/dev/tty`.

Every terminal and pseudo-terminal has a tty structure that contains

- the current terminal group ID, `t_pgrp`. This field identifies the process group to receive the signals associated with the terminal: `SIGINT`, `SIGQUIT`, `SIGHUP`, `SIGIO`, `SIGTSTP`, `SIGCONT`, and `SIGWINCH`. The first three signals are common to both 4.3BSD and System V, while the latter four are 4.3BSD-specific. This terminal group ID can be changed under 4.3BSD with an `ioctl` of `TIOCSPGRP`.

Every socket on a 4.3BSD system has a socket structure that contains

- a socket group ID, `so_pgrp`. The value in this field for each socket can be either a process ID or a process group ID. This field identifies the process or process group to receive the `SIGIO` and `SIGURG` signals for the socket. In Section 6.11 we discuss the exact form of the `fcntl` system call that changes this value for a socket.

The terminal group ID in the tty structure is changed by a job-control shell to refer to the current foreground job each time a new foreground job is started. This is why we carefully labelled the `t_pgrp` field as the ''current'' terminal group ID. A non-job-control shell never changes the terminal group ID field, in which case it always contains the process ID of the login shell.

Note that we have at least two different process groups: `p_pgrp`, which is the process group of the process, `t_pgrp` which is the process group of the terminal, and possibly one or more `so_pgrp`s, which are the process groups for each open socket. The process group ID fields in the socket structure and in the tty structure are used for delivering signals that arise from a socket or a terminal. These are the two types of I/O that can generate signals.

The kernel assigns a control terminal to a process when a terminal device that is not already a control terminal is opened for the first time. The conditions under which the kernel assigns a control terminal to a process differ between System V and 4.3BSD.

- 4.3BSD assigns a control terminal to a process only if the process group ID is zero.

- System V assigns a control terminal to a process only if the process is a process group leader (i.e., process group ID equals process ID).

The assignment of a control terminal is typically done by the `getty` process, and the control terminal is inherited by a child process over a `fork` system call. Under normal conditions, the control terminal is the terminal on which you login to the system.

Disassociate from Control Terminal

Like the process group ID, the terminal group ID of a process is inherited from the process that `execs` it. If a daemon is invoked from a login session, it inherits the control terminal of the session.

Under System V, a process disassociates itself from its control terminal (if it has one) by calling the `setpgrp` system call. In addition to making the calling process a process group leader, as described above, if the process is *not* already a process group leader when it calls `setpgrp`, this call disassociates the process from its control terminal. Therefore we can use this system call to do two things—remove ourself from the inherited process group and disassociate from the inherited control terminal. But the only way a process can guarantee that it is not already a process group leader when it calls `setpgrp` is to do a `fork` and then call `setpgrp` from the child process. Since the process group ID is copied from the parent to the child across the `fork`, and since the child will have a different process ID from the parent, we are certain the child is not a process group leader. By doing the `fork` described previously (to run in the "background") we handle this condition. The System V code is

```
if (fork() != 0)
        exit(0);  /* parent process */

/* first child process */

setpgrp();      /* change process group and lose control tty */
```

Under 4.3BSD a process removes its association with its controlling terminal by opening the file `/dev/tty` and issuing a `TIOCNOTTY` ioctl for the device. The 4.3BSD code is

```
if (fork() != 0)
        exit(0);                             /* parent process */

/* first child process */

setpgrp(0, getpid());                        /* change process group */

if ( (fd = open("/dev/tty", O_RDWR)) >= 0) {
        ioctl(fd, TIOCNOTTY, (char *) 0); /* lose control tty */
        close(fd);
}
```

Don't Reacquire a Control Terminal

If the daemon were to open a terminal device after disassociating itself from its control terminal as above, it could reacquire a control terminal. The reasons a daemon could open a terminal device are to log error messages to /dev/tty or /dev/console, for example. Even if the daemon closes the terminal device when its finished with it, the device can still be considered the control terminal for the daemon process.

4.3BSD only allows a process to acquire a control terminal if the process has a process group ID of zero. Since our daemon does a setpgrp above, to become a process group leader, it is not possible for it to reacquire a control terminal.

The status of our 4.3BSD daemon is as follows:

- it does not have a control terminal,

- it is a process group leader in its own group,

- it cannot acquire a control terminal, since it has a nonzero process group ID.

We mentioned above that System V assigns a control terminal to a process only if the process is a process group leader. With the call to setpgrp we have made the daemon a process group leader. If the daemon stops being a process group leader, it can never reacquire a control terminal. To do this we have the daemon fork again and have the parent (which is the child process from the first fork) terminate, with the child continuing. But when the first child calls exit it causes the hangup signal, SIGHUP, to be sent to all processes belonging to the process group of the exiting process. This means the second child will receive this signal. To avoid this, the daemon calls signal to ignore the hangup signal, before calling fork. (Recall from earlier that the signal settings are copied from the parent to the child across a fork.) The code for System V, including the steps already shown above, is

```
if (fork() != 0)
        exit(0);                /* parent process */

/* first child process */

setpgrp();         /* change process group and lose control tty */

signal(SIGHUP, SIG_IGN);

if (fork() != 0)
        exit(0);                /* first child process */

/* second child process continues as daemon */
```

The call to `exit` by the first child process has another effect on the second child process. The `exit` system call must set the process group ID of all members of a process group to zero when the process group leader (i.e., the first child) terminates. This is because there is a chance that some other process will be created in the future with the same process ID as the terminating process. If this were not done by the kernel, and if the other processes in this group (such as the second child process) were still in existence when the process ID is reused, they would contain an invalid process group ID.

The status of our System V daemon, the second child process, is as follows:

- it does not have a control terminal,

- its process group ID is zero, therefore as long as it never calls `setpgrp` again, it can never become a process group leader,

- it cannot acquire a control terminal since it is not a process group leader.

System V `inittab` File

System V provides a file `/etc/inittab` that is read by the `init` process and used to control its actions as the system changes state. The "states" are called *run levels* and specify single-user mode or multiuser mode, with various levels of multiuser mode available. Without spending pages describing all the features of the System V `init` process, we must note how it affects the operation of daemons. Each line in the `inittab` file is of the form

> *id* : *run-level* : *action* : *command-line*

Historically (i.e., before System V) most daemons were invoked from the `/etc/rc` file when the system went into multiuser mode. System V provides a feature where an entry in the `inittab` file can specify an *action* of `respawn`. This tells `init` to start the process, do not wait for it to complete, but if it does terminate, restart the process. This type of entry is typically used to restart the `getty` processes on the terminal lines used in multiuser operation. The *action* can also be `once`, which causes the process to be started only once when the run level of the system matches the *run level* of the entry in the inittab file, and not wait for its completion and not restart the process if it does terminate. If the rules developed above for coding a System V daemon were followed, and if the daemon were started from the inittab file with an *action* of respawn, once the parent process terminates, init will respawn the process again, and again, and again. To avoid this condition, our daemon should detect whether it was invoked by the init process, and if so, avoid the forks and exits shown above. The real solution is *not* to invoke a daemon like this, with the init process trying to respawn it every time it terminates. Usually the daemon process should not terminate unless

- it is through with its tasks, in which case it should not immediately be respawned.
- the system is going from multiuser to single-user. In this case the daemon should catch some signal that tells it to terminate gracefully. For example, a line printer daemon should shut down the line printers in an orderly fashion.

Unfortunately there is no guaranteed method for the daemon to determine how it was invoked. As mentioned earlier, a process can determine if its parent process ID is 1, but an ambiguity exists—if the daemon is started by hand from a login shell, and if the shell terminates before the daemon gets started, the exit from the shell will set the daemon's parent to be the init process. Alternately, a command line flag can be specified to indicate whether the daemon is started from the inittab file or by hand. This, however, depends on the option being entered correctly every time the daemon is started, either from the inittab file, or by hand for testing. A common error is to examine the *command-line* from the inittab file used to invoke the daemon, and enter this verbatim when starting the daemon by hand.

Daemon Termination

Both System V and 4.3BSD use the SIGTERM signal to notify all running processes that the system is going from multiuser to single-user. This signal is sent by the init process, which then waits for the processes to terminate. If a process doesn't terminate after some amount of time (5 seconds for 4.3BSD, 20 seconds for System V) the SIGKILL signal is sent to the process, which it can't ignore. A daemon should catch the SIGTERM signal and use it to stop its operation gracefully.

Handle SIGCLD Signals

Sometimes a daemon is interested in the exit status of its child processes, and other times it isn't. But if it doesn't care, and if it doesn't handle the SIGCLD signals that its children generate, the child processes become zombies and just waste system resources. We'll provide an option in our skeleton daemon for the caller to signify that its not interested in its children. For this case, under System V we can set the action for the SIGCLD signal to SIG_IGN. As we discussed earlier with the wait system call, this is a special feature of System V that tells the kernel not to generate zombies from children

of the calling process. With 4.3BSD we'll set the signal catcher for the SIGCLD signal
to the following function.

```
/*
 * This is a 4.3BSD SIGCLD signal handler that can be used by a
 * server that's not interested in its child's exit status, but needs to
 * wait for them, to avoid clogging up the system with zombies.
 *
 * Beware that the calling process may get an interrupted system call
 * when we return, so they had better handle that.
 */

#include        "systype.h"

#include        <sys/wait.h>
#include        <signal.h>

sig_child()
{
#ifdef  BSD
        /*
         * Use the wait3() system call with the WNOHANG option.
         */

        int             pid;
        union wait      status;

        while ( (pid = wait3(&status, WNOHANG, (struct rusage *) 0)) > 0)
                ;
#endif
}
```

Skeleton Daemon

We can now use all the techniques and code fragments developed in this section to write
a skeleton function that a daemon should call when it is started.

```
/*
 * Initialize a daemon process.
 */

#include        <stdio.h>
#include        <signal.h>
#include        <sys/param.h>
#include        <errno.h>
extern int      errno;

#ifdef  SIGTSTP          /* true if BSD system */
#include        <sys/file.h>
#include        <sys/ioctl.h>
#endif

/*
```

```
 * Detach a daemon process from login session context.
 */

daemon_start(ignsigcld)
int     ignsigcld;       /* nonzero -> handle SIGCLDs so zombies don't clog */
{
        register int    childpid, fd;

        /*
         * If we were started by init (process 1) from the /etc/inittab file
         * there's no need to detach.
         * This test is unreliable due to an unavoidable ambiguity
         * if the process is started by some other process and orphaned
         * (i.e., if the parent process terminates before we are started).
         */

        if (getppid() == 1)
                goto out;

        /*
         * Ignore the terminal stop signals (BSD).
         */

#ifdef SIGTTOU
        signal(SIGTTOU, SIG_IGN);
#endif
#ifdef SIGTTIN
        signal(SIGTTIN, SIG_IGN);
#endif
#ifdef SIGTSTP
        signal(SIGTSTP, SIG_IGN);
#endif

        /*
         * If we were not started in the background, fork and
         * let the parent exit.  This also guarantees the first child
         * is not a process group leader.
         */

        if ( (childpid = fork()) < 0)
                err_sys("can't fork first child");
        else if (childpid > 0)
                exit(0);        /* parent */

        /*
         * First child process.
         *
         * Disassociate from controlling terminal and process group.
         * Ensure the process can't reacquire a new controlling terminal.
         */

#ifdef  SIGTSTP         /* BSD */

        if (setpgrp(0, getpid()) == -1)
```

```
                    err_sys("can't change process group");

            if ( (fd = open("/dev/tty", O_RDWR)) >= 0) {
                    ioctl(fd, TIOCNOTTY, (char *)NULL); /* lose controlling tty */
                    close(fd);
            }

#else   /* System V */

            if (setpgrp() == -1)
                    err_sys("can't change process group");

            signal(SIGHUP, SIG_IGN);            /* immune from pgrp leader death */

            if ( (childpid = fork()) < 0)
                    err_sys("can't fork second child");
            else if (childpid > 0)
                    exit(0);          /* first child */

            /* second child */
#endif

out:
            /*
             * Close any open files descriptors.
             */

            for (fd = 0; fd < NOFILE; fd++)
                    close(fd);

            errno = 0;                /* probably got set to EBADF from a close */

            /*
             * Move the current directory to root, to make sure we
             * aren't on a mounted filesystem.
             */

            chdir("/");

            /*
             * Clear any inherited file mode creation mask.
             */

            umask(0);

            /*
             * See if the caller isn't interested in the exit status of its
             * children, and doesn't want to have them become zombies and
             * clog up the system.
             * With System V all we need do is ignore the signal.
             * With BSD, however, we have to catch each signal
             * and execute the wait3() system call.
             */
```

```
            if (ignsigcld) {
#ifdef   SIGTSTP
                int     sig_child();

                signal(SIGCLD, sig_child);        /* BSD */
#else
                signal(SIGCLD, SIG_IGN);          /* System V */
#endif
            }
}
```

2.7   Summary

This chapter is a summary of the important features of the Unix operating system that are used in network programming. We'll encounter signals and process control in most of the examples that we develop and examine later in the text. The final section of this chapter, the development of the `daemon_start` function, brings together most of the topics discussed in the chapter.

Exercises

2.1   If a process modifies an environment variable, by changing one of the strings pointed to by the `environ` pointer, what effect does this have on its parent process? What effect does this have on any child processes it invokes?

2.2   What effect does the following have:

```
setuid(getuid());
```

(Hint: refer to the BSD line printer client in Section 13.3)

2.3   Both the functions `getpwuid` and `getpwnam` return a pointer to a structure that the function fills in. Where do you think this structure is stored? (Check the appropriate manual pages for your system.)

2.4   Some network servers compare a user's encrypted password with the `pw_passwd` field in the `passwd` structure. What happens when the server is running on a system that has a shadow password file?

2.5   Investigate the `access` system call (which we have not described here) on your Unix system. We'll use this system call in the remote shell server in Section 14.3. Write a similar function that uses the effective user ID and the effective group ID.

2.6   If multiple processes are appending records to a file, is there any difference between having each process `open` the file with the `O_APPEND` flag, versus having each process issue an `lseek` to the end of the file before each `write`?

2.7   Implement the `sleep` function using the `alarm` system call. Be sure to handle the case of an alarm that is already set. Do you need reliable signals to do this correctly?

2.8   Why doesn't `fork` return the process ID of the parent to the child and return zero to the parent?

2.9   Implement the `system` function. (Hint: see Kernighan and Pike [1984].)

2.10 If a process that is run by a shell sets its file access creation mask to zero, does this affect other processes that are run after it by the shell?

3

Interprocess Communication

3.1 Introduction

Since network programming involves the interaction of two or more processes, we must look carefully at the different methods that are available for different processes to communicate with each other. In traditional single process programming, different modules within the single process can communicate with each other using global variables, function calls, and the arguments and results passed back and forth between functions and their callers. But, when dealing with separate processes, each executing within its own address space, there are more details to consider. When time-shared, multiprogramming operating systems were developed over 20 years ago, one design goal was to assure certain that separate processes wouldn't interfere with each other. For two processes to communicate with each other, they must both agree to it, and the operating system must provide some facilities for the *Interprocess Communication* (IPC).

While some form of IPC is required for network programming, the use of IPC is by no means restricted to processes executing on different systems, communicating through a network of some form. Indeed, there are many instances where IPC can and should be used between processes on a single computer system. We can diagram two processes using IPC on a single computer system as shown in Figure 3.1.

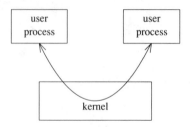

Figure 3.1   IPC between two processes on a single system.

This figure shows the information between the two processes going through the kernel; although this is typical, it is not a requirement for IPC.

To expand this to processes on different systems, using some form of networking between the two systems, we have the picture shown in Figure 3.2.

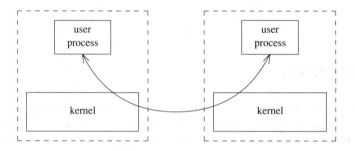

Figure 3.2   IPC between two processes on different systems.

In this chapter we consider several different methods of IPC.

- pipes
- FIFOs (named pipes)
- message queues
- semaphores
- shared memory

Before going into the IPC sections, we first describe file and record locking, an integral and necessary part of many multiple process systems.

3.2   File and Record Locking

There are occasions when multiple processes want to share some resource. It is essential that some form of mutual exclusion be provided so that only one process at a time can access the resource.

Consider the following scenario, which comes from the line printer daemon examples that we consider in more detail in Chapter 13. The process that places a job on the print queue (to be printed at a later time by another process) has to assign a unique sequence number to each print job. We cannot use the process ID as the sequence number, as it is possible for a print job to exist long enough for a given process ID to be reused. The technique used by the Unix print spoolers is to have a file for each printer that contains the next sequence number to be used. The file is just a single line containing the sequence number in ASCII. Each process that needs to assign a sequence number goes through three steps:

- it reads the sequence number file,
- it uses the number,
- it increments the number and writes it back.

The problem is that in the time it takes a single process to execute these three steps, another process can perform the same three steps. Chaos can result. What is needed is for a process to be able to set a *lock* to say that no other process can access the file until the first process is done. Here is a simple program that does these three steps. The functions my_lock and my_unlock are called to lock the file at the beginning, and unlock the file when the process is done with the sequence number.

```
#define SEQFILE "seqno"          /* filename */
#define MAXBUFF    100

main()
{
        int     fd, i, n, pid, seqno;
        char    buff[MAXBUFF + 1];

        pid = getpid();
        if ( (fd = open(SEQFILE, 2)) < 0)
                err_sys("can't open %s", SEQFILE);

        for (i = 0; i < 20; i++) {
                my_lock(fd);                        /* lock the file */

                lseek(fd, 0L, 0);                   /* rewind before read */
                if ( (n = read(fd, buff, MAXBUFF)) <= 0)
                        err_sys("read error");
                buff[n] = '\0';         /* null terminate for sscanf */

                if ( (n = sscanf(buff, "%d\n", &seqno)) != 1)
                        err_sys("sscanf error");
                printf("pid = %d, seq# = %d\n", pid, seqno);

                seqno++;                /* increment the sequence number */

                sprintf(buff, "%03d\n", seqno);
                n = strlen(buff);
                lseek(fd, 0L, 0);                   /* rewind before write */
                if (write(fd, buff, n) != n)
```

```
                              err_sys("write error");

                my_unlock(fd);                       /* unlock the file */
        }
}
```

To show the results when locking is not used, the following functions provide no locking at all.

```
/*
 * Locking routines that do nothing.
 */

my_lock(fd)
int     fd;
{
        return;
}

my_unlock(fd)
int     fd;
{
        return;
}
```

If the sequence number is initialized to one, and a single copy of the program is run, we get the following output:

```
        pid = 118,  seq# = 1
        pid = 118,  seq# = 2
        pid = 118,  seq# = 3
        pid = 118,  seq# = 4
        pid = 118,  seq# = 5
        pid = 118,  seq# = 6
        pid = 118,  seq# = 7
        pid = 118,  seq# = 8
        pid = 118,  seq# = 9
        pid = 118,  seq# = 10
        pid = 118,  seq# = 11
        pid = 118,  seq# = 12
        pid = 118,  seq# = 13
        pid = 118,  seq# = 14
        pid = 118,  seq# = 15
        pid = 118,  seq# = 16
        pid = 118,  seq# = 17
        pid = 118,  seq# = 18
        pid = 118,  seq# = 19
        pid = 118,  seq# = 20
```

When the sequence number is again initialized to one, and the program (whose name is
a.out) is run twice, using the shell command

```
a.out & a.out &
```

we get the following output:

```
pid = 186, seq# = 1              pid = 186, seq# = 10
                                 pid = 186, seq# = 11
pid = 187, seq# = 1
pid = 187, seq# = 2              pid = 187, seq# = 6
pid = 187, seq# = 3              pid = 187, seq# = 7
pid = 187, seq# = 4              pid = 187, seq# = 8
pid = 187, seq# = 5              pid = 187, seq# = 9
pid = 187, seq# = 6              pid = 187, seq# = 10
pid = 187, seq# = 7
pid = 187, seq# = 8              pid = 186, seq# = 12
pid = 187, seq# = 9              pid = 186, seq# = 13
pid = 187, seq# = 10             pid = 186, seq# = 14
                                 pid = 186, seq# = 15
pid = 186, seq# = 2              pid = 186, seq# = 16
pid = 186, seq# = 3              pid = 186, seq# = 17
pid = 186, seq# = 4              pid = 186, seq# = 18
pid = 186, seq# = 5              pid = 186, seq# = 19
                                 pid = 186, seq# = 20
pid = 187, seq# = 5
                                 pid = 187, seq# = 11
pid = 186, seq# = 6              pid = 187, seq# = 12
pid = 186, seq# = 7              pid = 187, seq# = 13
pid = 186, seq# = 8              pid = 187, seq# = 14
pid = 186, seq# = 9
```

(The output has been put into two columns and spaces inserted between the consecutive
lines of output for a single process to make the output more readable.) This is not what
we want. The first process (PID 186) reads the file and prints its value (1). Before this
value gets incremented and written back to the file, the second process (PID 187) reads
the file and uses the CPU while it updates the sequence number all the way to 10. Only
then does the first process run again, and it resets the sequence number back to two.
What has happened is that the operating system has switched between the two processes
somewhere in the middle of the three steps outlined earlier. Note that each process reads,
increments, and writes the sequence number file exactly 20 times (there are exactly 40
lines of output), but the sequence number keeps getting incremented then reset to some
earlier value by the other process.

     What we need is some way to allow a process to ''lock out'' other processes from
accessing the sequence number file while the three steps are being performed.

Advisory Locking versus Mandatory Locking

Advisory locking means that the operating system maintains a correct knowledge of which files have been locked by which processes, but it does not prevent some process from writing to a file that is locked by another process. A process can ignore an advisory lock and write to a file that is locked, if the process has adequate permissions. Advisory locks are fine for what are called *cooperating processes*. The programming of daemons used by network programming is an example of cooperative processes—the programs that access a shared resource, such as the sequence number file, are all under control of the system administrator. In our example, as long as the actual file containing the sequence number is not writable by any process, some random process cannot write to the file while it is locked. The other type of file locking, *mandatory locking*, is provided by some systems. Mandatory locks mean that the operating system checks every `read` and `write` request to verify that the operation does not interfere with a lock held by a process.

System V Release 2 provides advisory locking, as does 4.3BSD, while System V Release 3 provides both advisory and mandatory locking. By default, System V Release 3 provides advisory locking. To enable mandatory locking for a particular file, we must turn the group-execute bit *off* and turn the set-group-ID bit *on* for the file. Note that it makes no sense to have the set-user-ID bit on for a file without having the user-execute bit on also, and similarly for the set-group-ID bit and the group-execute bit. Therefore the mandatory locking option was added to System V Release 3 in this way, without affecting any existing user software. New system calls were not required. The `ls` command on System V Release 3 was enhanced to look for this special combination of bits and note that the file is marked for mandatory locking.

File Locking versus Record Locking

File locking locks an entire file, while *record locking* allows a process to lock a specified portion of a file. The definition of a record for Unix record locking is given by specifying a starting byte offset in the file and the number of bytes from that position. The term *record locking* is derived from other operating systems that enforce a record structure on disk files. A better term for the Unix feature is *range locking* since the Unix kernel does not support the concept of "records." It is a range of the file that is locked. Whether this range has any resemblance to a record is up to the application.

The System V `lockf` function has the calling sequence

```
#include <unistd.h>

int lockf(int fd, int function, long size);
```

where *function* has one of the following values:

> F_ULOCK   Unlock a previously locked region
> F_LOCK   Lock a region (blocking)
> F_TLOCK   Test and lock a region (nonblocking)
> F_TEST   Test a region to see if it is locked

The `lockf` function uses the current file offset (which the process can set using the `lseek` system call) and the *size* argument to define the "record." The record starts at the current offset and extends forward for a positive *size*, or extends backwards for a negative *size*. If the *size* is zero, the record affected extends from the current offset through the largest file offset (the end of file). Doing an `lseek` to the beginning of the file followed by a `lockf` with a *size* of zero locks the entire file.

   The `lockf` function provides both the ability to set a lock and to test if a lock is set. When the *function* is F_TLOCK and the region is already locked by another process, the calling process is put to sleep until the region is available. This is termed *blocking*. The F_TLOCK operation, however, is termed a *nonblocking* call—if the region is not available, `lockf` returns immediately with a value of −1 and `errno` set to either EAGAIN or EACCES.† Also, the F_TEST operation allows a process to test if a lock is set, without setting a lock. Note that to do a *nonblocking* lock, we must use the F_TLOCK operation. If we write

```
    ...
    if (lockf(fd, F_TEST, size) == 0) {
            rc = lockf(fd, F_LOCK, size);
            ...
    }
```

there is a chance that some other process can issue a `lockf` call between the F_TEST and the F_LOCK, which causes the F_LOCK to block. The F_TLOCK provides the ability to do the test and set in a single operation, which is needed.

   An example of a nonblocking lock is if a daemon is started and it wants to assure that only a single copy of it is running. When the daemon starts, it executes a nonblocking lock on a specified file. If the lock succeeds, then the daemon is the only copy running, but if it fails the daemon can exit, since it knows that a copy is already running. We will see an example of this exact scenario in the 4.3BSD line printer spooler in Section 13.2.

System V Release 2 Advisory Locking

The original System V Release 2 did not provide any type of file or record locking. But the enhanced version of System V Release 2 provided advisory file and record locking.

---

† System V Release 2 and System V Release 3 both return EACCES. The System V Release 3 manual warns that "portable application programs should expect and test for either value."

With System V Release 3, mandatory file and record locking are provided. Our locking functions are

```
/*
 * Locking routines for System V.
 */

#include        <unistd.h>

my_lock(fd)
int     fd;
{
        lseek(fd, 0L, 0);                       /* rewind before lockf */
        if (lockf(fd, F_LOCK, 0L) == -1)        /* 0L -> lock entire file */
                err_sys("can't F_LOCK");
}

my_unlock(fd)
int     fd;
{
        lseek(fd, 0L, 0);
        if (lockf(fd, F_ULOCK, 0L) == -1)
                err_sys("can't F_ULOCK");
}
```

System V record locking is really provided by the fcntl system call. The lockf function is provided by the standard C library as an interface to the fcntl system call.

4.3BSD Advisory Locking

We continue our sequence number example using the advisory file locking provided by 4.3BSD. The flock system call is provided to lock and unlock a file.

```
#include <sys/file.h>

int flock(int fd, int operation);
```

fd is a file descriptor of an open file, and *operation* is built from the following constants:

LOCK_SH	Shared lock
LOCK_EX	Exclusive lock
LOCK_UN	Unlock
LOCK_NB	Don't block when locking

More than one shared lock can be applied to a file at any time, but a file cannot have both a shared lock and an exclusive lock, or multiple exclusive locks at any time. The permissible locking operations are

`LOCK_SH`	Shared lock (blocking)
`LOCK_EX`	Exclusive lock (blocking)
`LOCK_SH	LOCK_NB`	Shared lock (nonblocking)
`LOCK_EX	LOCK_NB`	Exclusive lock (nonblocking)
`LOCK_UN`	Unlock

If the lock was successful, zero is returned by `flock`, otherwise −1 is returned. If the lock fails because the file is already locked and a nonblocking lock was requested (`LOCK_NB`), the global `errno` is set to EWOULDBLOCK. This lets us code our locking functions as follows:

```
/*
 * Locking routines for 4.3BSD.
 */

#include        <sys/file.h>

my_lock(fd)
int     fd;
{
        if (flock(fd, LOCK_EX) == -1)
                err_sys("can't LOCK_EX");
}

my_unlock(fd)
int     fd;
{
        if (flock(fd, LOCK_UN) == -1)
                err_sys("can't LOCK_UN");
}
```

We can now use these locking functions and run our program under System V or 4.3BSD. Executing the shell command

```
a.out & a.out &
```

yields the output

```
pid = 308, seq# = 1              pid = 308, seq# = 22
                                 pid = 308, seq# = 23
pid = 307, seq# = 2              pid = 308, seq# = 24
pid = 307, seq# = 3              pid = 308, seq# = 25
pid = 307, seq# = 4              pid = 308, seq# = 26
pid = 307, seq# = 5              pid = 308, seq# = 27
pid = 307, seq# = 6
pid = 307, seq# = 7              pid = 307, seq# = 28
pid = 307, seq# = 8              pid = 307, seq# = 29
pid = 307, seq# = 9              pid = 307, seq# = 30
pid = 307, seq# = 10
pid = 307, seq# = 11             pid = 308, seq# = 31
pid = 307, seq# = 12             pid = 308, seq# = 32
pid = 307, seq# = 13             pid = 308, seq# = 33
pid = 307, seq# = 14             pid = 308, seq# = 34
pid = 307, seq# = 15
                                 pid = 307, seq# = 35
pid = 308, seq# = 16             pid = 307, seq# = 36
pid = 308, seq# = 17             pid = 307, seq# = 37
pid = 308, seq# = 18
pid = 308, seq# = 19             pid = 308, seq# = 38
pid = 308, seq# = 20             pid = 308, seq# = 39
pid = 308, seq# = 21             pid = 308, seq# = 40
```

(Again we have inserted blank lines at the points when the process ID changes and made the output multicolumn.) This is the way this example should work—the sequence number increments up to 40 in order.

Other Unix Locking Techniques

There are three features of the Unix filesystem implementation that can be exploited to provide a type of locking. These techniques create and use an ancillary file as an indicator that the process has the shared resource locked. If the ancillary file exists, the resource is locked by some other process, otherwise the calling process must create the ancillary file to lock the resource. The three techniques that we show in this section use the following features:

1. The link system call fails if the name of the new link to the file already exists.

2. The creat system call fails if the file already exists *and* if the caller does not have write permission for the file.

3. Newer versions of Unix, including both 4.3BSD and System V, support options to the open system call that cause it to fail if the file already exists.

The first two techniques are applicable to all versions of Unix, and have been used since Version 7 (or earlier).

A first idea is to create the ancillary file and use it as an indicator that a process has a lock on some other file. This won't work, however, since the `creat` system call does not fail if the file already exists. If the file does exist, `creat` truncates the file to zero length.

Another idea is to test if the ancillary file exists, and if not, create the file.

```
if ( (fd = open(file, 0)) < 0)
        fd = creat(file, 0644);
    . . .
```

This won't work either, as it takes two separate system calls to test if a file exists (`open`), and then create the file if it does not exist (`creat`). In the time between the two system calls some other process can do the same test and then `creat` the same file. When the process that was interrupted runs again, it issues the `creat` system call, but no error occurs even though the file already exists.

Our first correct implementation uses the fact that the `link` system call fails if the name of the new link to the file already exists.

```
int link(char *existingpath, char *newpath);
```

This system call takes an existing file and creates another directory link to that file. (Recall that a Unix file can have any number of links (i.e., names) that refer to the same file.) Unlike the `creat` system call, if the new pathname specified by the `link` already exists, an error is returned and the global `errno` is set to `EEXIST`. Our technique is to create a unique temporary file, whose name is based on the process ID of the process. Once this file is created, we try to form another `link` to it, under the "well-known" name of the ancillary lock file. If the `link` succeeds, then the process has the lock, and the lock file is pointed to by two directory entries—the temporary filename based on the process ID and the well-known name of the lock file. The temporary filename can now be removed, leaving only a single link to the file. Using this technique for our lock functions, we have

```
/*
 * Locking routines using the link() system call.
 */

#define LOCKFILE        "seqno.lock"

#include         <sys/errno.h>
extern int       errno;

my_lock(fd)
int      fd;
{
        int      tempfd;
        char     tempfile[30];

        sprintf(tempfile, "LCK%d", getpid());

        /*
```

```
        * Create a temporary file, then close it.
        * If the temporary file already exists, the creat() will
        * just truncate it to 0-length.
        */

       if ( (tempfd = creat(tempfile, 0444)) < 0)
             err_sys("can't creat temp file");
       close(tempfd);

       /*
        * Now try to rename the temporary file to the lock file.
        * This will fail if the lock file already exists (i.e., if
        * some other process already has a lock).
        */

       while (link(tempfile, LOCKFILE) < 0) {
             if (errno != EEXIST)
                    err_sys("link error");
             sleep(1);
       }
       if (unlink(tempfile) < 0)
             err_sys("unlink error for tempfile");
}

my_unlock(fd)
int     fd;
{
       if (unlink(LOCKFILE) < 0)
             err_sys("unlink error for LOCKFILE");
}
```

The second technique uses the fact that the `creat` system call returns an error if the file exists *and* write permission is denied. In describing this system call in Section 2.3, we stated that it truncates an existing file to zero-length if it already exists. This is normally true, but if the file access permissions don't allow writing to the file for the process calling `creat`, it fails and `errno` is set to `EACCES`. There is one caveat to this technique—this error is not returned if the process has superuser permissions, since the superuser can write to any file. Our technique is to create a temporary lock file with all write permissions disabled, and if the `creat` succeeds, the calling process knows it has the lock, and the sequence number file can be safely modified. The unlock operation removes the temporary lock file, since the `unlink` system call succeeds if the caller has write permission in the directory. The caller does not need either read or write permission for the file being unlinked. Our code for this technique is

```
/*
 * Locking routines using a creat() system call with all
 * permissions turned off.
 */

#include         <sys/errno.h>
extern int       errno;
```

```
#define LOCKFILE        "seqno.lock"
#define TEMPLOCK        "temp.lock"

my_lock(fd)
int     fd;
{
        int     tempfd;

        /*
         * Try to create a temporary file, with all write
         * permissions turned off.  If the temporary file already
         * exists, the creat() will fail.
         */

        while ( (tempfd = creat(TEMPLOCK, 0)) < 0) {
                if (errno != EACCES)
                        err_sys("creat error");
                sleep(1);
        }
        close(tempfd);
}

my_unlock(fd)
int     fd;
{
        if (unlink(TEMPLOCK) < 0)
                err_sys("unlink error for tempfile");
}
```

The third technique uses the option flags for the `open` system call that are provided by most recent versions of Unix—both 4.3BSD and System V, for example, provide it. The `<fcntl.h>` header file defines the option flags for the `open` system call. If both O_CREAT and O_EXCL are specified, the `open` fails if the file already exists, otherwise the file is created. The POSIX standard [IEEE 1988] specifically states that the test for the existence of the file and the creation of the file if it doesn't exist, must be atomic with regard to other processes trying to do the same thing.

Our code for this technique is

```
/*
 * Locking routines using a open() system call with both
 * O_CREAT and O_EXCL specified.
 */

#include         <fcntl.h>
#include         <sys/errno.h>
extern int       errno;

#define LOCKFILE         "seqno.lock"
#define PERMS            0666

my_lock(fd)
int      fd;
{
```

```
        int     tempfd;

        /*
         * Try to create the lock file, using open() with both
         * O_CREAT (create file if it doesn't exist) and O_EXCL
         * (error if create and file already exists).
         * If this fails, some other process has the lock.
         */

        while ( (tempfd = open(LOCKFILE, O_RDWR|O_CREAT|O_EXCL, PERMS)) < 0) {
                if (errno != EEXIST)
                        err_sys("open error for lock file");
                sleep(1);
        }
        close(tempfd);
}

my_unlock(fd)
int     fd;
{
        if (unlink(LOCKFILE) < 0)
                err_sys("unlink error for lock file");
}
```

There are a few points to consider about these three techniques.

1. The first two techniques work under any version of Unix.

2. These techniques take longer to execute than actual file locking system calls, as multiple system calls (such as `creat`, `close`, `link`, and `unlink`) are required, and several filesystem operations are required.

3. An ancillary lock file is required, in addition to the file containing the resource that is shared. In our example, we need both the sequence number file and the ancillary lock file. Since the lock file must be created each time it is needed, a single file cannot be used.

4. Ancillary files such as a lock file might be left around after a system crash and some technique must be devised to handle this (i.e., remove old lock files).

5. The `link` system call in the first technique cannot create a link between files on different logical filesystems, so the temporary file cannot normally be placed in the `/tmp` filesystem. (Many larger Unix systems place the `/tmp` directory in its own filesystem.)

6. The second technique does not work if the processes competing for the resource run with superuser privileges.

7. When the ancillary lock is owned by another process, the process wanting the lock doesn't know when to check again. In our examples we wait for one second. The ideal condition is for the process wanting the lock to be notified when the lock is available.

8. The process that obtains the lock can terminate, intentionally or unintentionally, without releasing the lock.

Cases 4 and 8 require some technique for another process to determine when an existing lock is not in use. A common solution is to assume a timeout period based on the application (a few minutes, perhaps) and remove locks that are older than this. The last-access time or last-modify time in the `stat` structure for the lock file can be used to determine how long a lock has been around. Since this technique fails if the resource is really in use for longer than the timeout period, an enhancement to this is to store the process ID of the process that has the lock in the lock file. This way, the `kill` system call, with a signal argument of zero can be used to determine if the process is still in existence. (We'll see a similar example in Section 13.2—the 4.3BSDline printer spooler stores the process ID of the current server in a file so that it can `kill` it at a later time, if necessary.)

Given the potential problems with these older techniques, true record locking or file locking should be used when available.

We'll return to this file locking example in Section 3.10 when we present another solution using semaphores.

3.3   A Simple Client–Server Example

The client–server example shown in Figure 3.3 is used throughout this chapter for illustration of the various methods of IPC.

The client reads a filename from the standard input and writes it to the IPC channel. The server reads this filename from the IPC channel and tries to open the file for reading. If the server can open the file, it responds by reading the file and writing it to the IPC channel, otherwise the server responds with an ASCII error message stating that it can't open the file. The client then reads from the IPC channel, writing what it receives to the standard output. If the file can't be read by the server, the client reads an error message from the IPC channel. Otherwise the client reads the contents of the file.

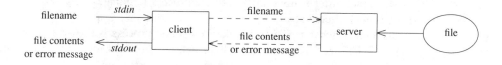

Figure 3.3 Client–server example.

The two dashed lines in Figure 3.3, between the client and server, correspond to some form of IPC.

3.4   Pipes

Pipes are provided with all flavors of Unix. A pipe provides a one-way flow of data. A pipe is created by the `pipe` system call.

```
int pipe(int *filedes);
```

Two file descriptors are returned—*filedes[0]* which is open for reading, and *filedes[1]* which is open for writing. Pipes are of little use within a single process, but here is a simple example that shows how they are created and used.

```
main()
{
        int     pipefd[2], n;
        char    buff[100];

        if (pipe(pipefd) < 0)
                err_sys("pipe error");

        printf("read fd = %d, write fd = %d\n", pipefd[0], pipefd[1]);
        if (write(pipefd[1], "hello world\n", 12) != 12)
                err_sys("write error");

        if ( (n = read(pipefd[0], buff, sizeof(buff))) <= 0)
                err_sys("read error");

        write(1, buff, n);       /* fd 1 = stdout */

        exit(0);
}
```

The output of this program is

```
hello world
read fd = 3, write fd = 4
```

Note that the "hello world" string is printed on the standard output *before* the output of the `printf`. The reason for this is because the `printf` output is buffered by the standard I/O library, and since its output does not fill a standard I/O buffer (typically 512 or 1024 bytes), the buffer is not output until the process terminates. The `write` function, however, is not buffered at all.

A diagram of what a pipe looks like in a single process is shown in Figure 3.4. A pipe has a finite size, always at least 4096 bytes. The rules for reading and writing a pipe—when there is either no data in the pipe, or when the pipe is full—are provided in the next section on FIFOs.

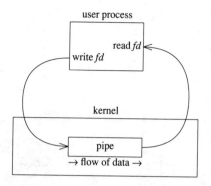

Figure 3.4   Pipe in a single process.

Pipes are typically used to communicate between two different processes in the following way. First, a process creates a pipe and then `forks` to create a copy of itself, as shown in Figure 3.5.

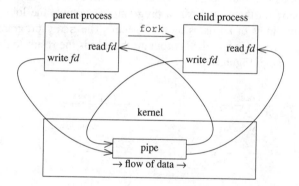

Figure 3.5   Pipe in a single process, immediately after `fork`.

Next the parent process closes the read end of the pipe and the child process closes the write end of the pipe. This provides a one-way flow of data between the two processes as shown in Figure 3.6.

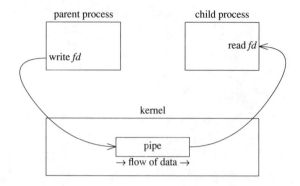

Figure 3.6 Pipe between two processes.

When a user enters a command such as

```
who | sort | lpr
```

to a Unix shell, the shell does the steps shown above to create three processes with two pipes between them. (who is a program that outputs the login names, terminal names, and login times of all users on the system. The sort program orders this list by login names, and lpr is a 4.3BSD program that sends the result to the line printer.) We show this pipeline in Figure 3.7.

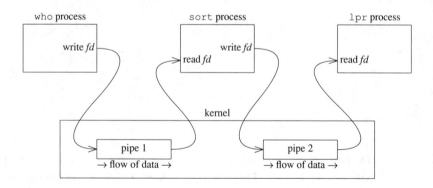

Figure 3.7 Pipes between three processes in a shell pipeline.

Note that all the pipes shown so far have all been unidirectional, providing a one-way flow of data only. When a two-way flow of data is desired, we must create two pipes and use one for each direction. The actual steps are

- create pipe 1, create pipe 2,
- fork,
- parent closes read end of pipe 1,

- parent closes write end of pipe 2,
- child closes write end of pipe 1,
- child closes read end of pipe 2.

This generates the picture shown in Figure 3.8.

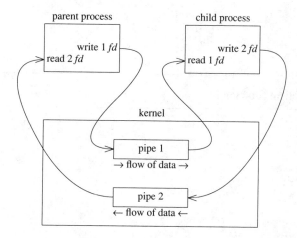

Figure 3.8 Two pipes to provide a bidirectional flow of data.

Let's now implement the client–server example described in the previous section using pipes. The `main` function creates the pipe and `forks`. The client then runs in the parent process and the server runs in the child process.

```
main()
{
        int     childpid, pipe1[2], pipe2[2];

        if (pipe(pipe1) < 0 || pipe(pipe2) < 0)
                err_sys("can't create pipes");

        if ( (childpid = fork()) < 0) {
                err_sys("can't fork");

        } else if (childpid > 0) {                      /* parent */
                close(pipe1[0]);
                close(pipe2[1]);

                client(pipe2[0], pipe1[1]);

                while (wait((int *) 0) != childpid)     /* wait for child */
                        ;

                close(pipe1[1]);
                close(pipe2[0]);
                exit(0);
```

```
        } else {                                        /* child */
                close(pipe1[1]);
                close(pipe2[0]);

                server(pipe1[0], pipe2[1]);

                close(pipe1[0]);
                close(pipe2[1]);
                exit(0);
        }
}
```

The client function is

```
#include         <stdio.h>

#define MAXBUFF        1024

client(readfd, writefd)
int     readfd;
int     writefd;
{
        char    buff[MAXBUFF];
        int     n;

        /*
         * Read the filename from standard input,
         * write it to the IPC descriptor.
         */

        if (fgets(buff, MAXBUFF, stdin) == NULL)
                err_sys("client: filename read error");

        n = strlen(buff);
        if (buff[n-1] == '\n')
                n--;                            /* ignore newline from fgets() */
        if (write(writefd, buff, n) != n)
                err_sys("client: filename write error");;

        /*
         * Read the data from the IPC descriptor and write
         * to standard output.
         */

        while ( (n = read(readfd, buff, MAXBUFF)) > 0)
                if (write(1, buff, n) != n)        /* fd 1 = stdout */
                        err_sys("client: data write error");
        if (n < 0)
                err_sys("client: data read error");
}
```

The server function is

```
#include          <stdio.h>

#define MAXBUFF          1024

server(readfd, writefd)
int     readfd;
int     writefd;
{
        char            buff[MAXBUFF];
        char            errmesg[256], *sys_err_str();
        int             n, fd;
        extern int      errno;

        /*
         * Read the filename from the IPC descriptor.
         */

        if ( (n = read(readfd, buff, MAXBUFF)) <= 0)
                err_sys("server: filename read error");
        buff[n] = '\0';          /* null terminate filename */

        if ( (fd = open(buff, 0)) < 0) {
                /*
                 * Error.  Format an error message and send it back
                 * to the client.
                 */

                sprintf(errmesg, ": can't open, %s\n", sys_err_str());
                strcat(buff, errmesg);
                n = strlen(buff);
                if (write(writefd, buff, n) != n)
                        err_sys("server: errmesg write error");
        } else {
                /*
                 * Read the data from the file and write to
                 * the IPC descriptor.
                 */

                while ( (n = read(fd, buff, MAXBUFF)) > 0)
                        if (write(writefd, buff, n) != n)
                                err_sys("server: data write error");
                if (n < 0)
                        err_sys("server: read error");
        }
}
```

The function sys_err_str returns a pointer to an error message string that it builds, based on the system's errno value. This function, and other error handling functions that are used throughout the book, are listed in the ''Standard Error Routines'' section of Appendix A.

The standard I/O library provides a function that creates a pipe and initiates another process that either reads from the pipe or writes to the pipe.

```
#include <stdio.h>

FILE *popen(char *command, char *type);
```

command is a shell command line. It is invoked by the Bourne shell, so the PATH environment variable is used to locate the *command*. A pipe is created between the calling process and the specified command. The value returned by popen is a standard I/O FILE pointer that is used for either input or output, depending on the character string *type*. If the value of *type* is r the calling process reads the standard output of the *command*. If the *type* is w the calling process writes to the standard input of the command. If the popen call fails, a value of NULL is returned. The function

```
#include <stdio.h>

int pclose(FILE *stream);
```

closes an I/O *stream* that was created by popen, returning the exit status of the *command*, or −1 if the *stream* was not created by popen.

We can provide another solution to our client–server example using the popen function and the Unix cat program.

```
#include        <stdio.h>

#define MAXLINE        1024

main()
{
        int     n;
        char    line[MAXLINE], command[MAXLINE + 10];
        FILE    *fp;

        /*
         * Read the filename from standard input.
         */

        if (fgets(line, MAXLINE, stdin) == NULL)
                err_sys("filename read error");

        /*
         * Use popen to create a pipe and execute the command.
         */

        sprintf(command, "cat %s", line);
        if ( (fp = popen(command, "r")) == NULL)
                err_sys("popen error");

        /*
         * Read the data from the FILE pointer and write
         * to standard output.
```

```
*/
        while ((fgets(line, MAXLINE, fp)) != NULL) {
                n = strlen(line);
                if (write(1, line, n) != n)
                        err_sys("data write error");
        }

        if (ferror(fp))
                err_sys("fgets error");

        pclose(fp);
        exit(0);
}
```

Another use of popen is to determine the current working directory of a process. Recall that the chdir system call changes the current working directory for a process, but there is not an equivalent system call to obtain its current value. System V provides a getcwd function to do this. 4.3BSD provides a similar, but not identical function, getwd.

The following program obtains the current working directory and prints it, using the Unix pwd command.

```
#include         <stdio.h>

#define MAXLINE           255

main()
{
        FILE    *fp;
        char    line[MAXLINE];

        if ( (fp = popen("/bin/pwd", "r")) == NULL)
                err_sys("popen error");

        if (fgets(line, MAXLINE, fp) == NULL)
                err_sys("fgets error");

        printf("%s", line);      /* pwd inserts the newline */

        pclose(fp);
        exit(0);
}
```

The biggest disadvantage with pipes is that they can only be used between processes that have a parent process in common. This is because a pipe is passed from one process to another by the fork system call, and the fact that all open files are shared between the parent and child after a fork. There is no way for two totally unrelated processes to create a pipe between them and use it for IPC.

3.5   FIFOs

FIFO stands for *First In, First Out*. A Unix FIFO is similar to a pipe. It is a one-way
flow of data, with the first byte written to it being the first byte read from it. Unlike
pipes, however, a FIFO has a name associated with it, allowing unrelated processes to
access a single FIFO. Indeed, FIFOs are also called *named pipes*. FIFOs are in
System V but not 4.3BSD. FIFOs came with System III Unix, but have never been well
documented, and are therefore ignored by most programmers. FIFOs are used by the
System V line printer system, as we see in Section 13.4.

A FIFO is created by the `mknod` system call. This call is normally reserved to the
superuser to create new device entries, but any user can create a FIFO.

```
int mknod(char *pathname, int mode, int dev);
```

The *pathname* is a normal Unix pathname, and this is the name of the FIFO. The *mode*
argument specifies the file mode access mode (read and write permissions for owner,
group, and world) and is logically or'ed with the `S_IFIFO` flag from `<sys/stat.h>`
to specify that a FIFO is being created. The *dev* value is ignored for a FIFO. A FIFO
can also be created by the `mknod` command, as in

```
/etc/mknod name p
```

Once a FIFO is created, it must be opened for reading or writing, using either the `open`
system call, or one of the standard I/O open functions—`fopen`, or `freopen`. Note that
it takes three system calls to create a FIFO and open it for reading and writing (`mknod`,
`open`, and `open`) while the single `pipe` system call does the same thing.

The `O_NDELAY` flag for a file, which is set either on the call to `open` or by calling
`fcntl` after the file has been opened, sets the "no delay" flag for either a pipe or a
FIFO. (Since a pipe is opened as part of the `pipe` system call, the only way to set this
flag for a pipe is with the `fcntl` system call.) The effect of this flag is shown in Figure 3.9.

The reason the first two rows in Figure 3.9 have the restriction for read-only or
write-only is that if a FIFO is opened by a process for *both* reading and writing, there
can't be any waiting for a reader or writer.

A pipe or FIFO follows these rules for reading and writing:

- A `read` requesting less data than is in the pipe or FIFO returns only the requested
  amount of data. The remainder is left for subsequent `read`s.

- If a process asks to read more data than is currently available in the pipe FIFO,
  only the data available is returned. The process must be prepared to handle a
  return value from `read` that is less than the requested amount.

- If there is no data in the pipe or FIFO, and if no processes have it open for writing, a `read` returns zero, signifying the end of file. If the reader has specified
  `O_NDELAY`, it cannot tell if a return value of zero means there is no data currently
  available or if there are no writers left.

Condition	Normal	O_NDELAY set
open FIFO, read-only with no process having the FIFO open for writing	wait until a process opens the FIFO for writing	return immediately, no error
open FIFO, write-only with no process having the FIFO open for reading	wait until a process opens the FIFO for reading	return an error immediately, errno set to ENXIO
read pipe or FIFO, no data	wait until there is data in the pipe or FIFO, or until no processes have it open for writing; return a value of zero if no processes have it open for writing, otherwise return the count of data	return immediately, return value of zero
write, pipe or FIFO is full	wait until space is available, then write data	return immediately, return value of zero

Figure 3.9 Effect of O_NDELAY flag on pipes and FIFOs.

- If a process `writes` less than the capacity of a pipe (which is at least 4096 bytes) the `write` is guaranteed to be *atomic*. This means that if two processes each write to a pipe or FIFO at about the same time, either all the data from the first process is written, followed by all the data from the second process, or vice versa. The system does not mix the data from the two processes—i.e., part of the data from one process, followed by part of the data from the other process. If, however, the `write` specifies more data than the pipe can hold, there is no guarantee that the `write` operation is atomic.

- If a process `writes` to a pipe or FIFO, but there are no processes in existence that have it open for reading, the `SIGPIPE` signal is generated, and the `write` returns zero with `errno` set to `EPIPE`. If the process has not called `signal` to handle the `SIGPIPE` notification, the default action is to terminate the process. The only way the `write` returns is if the process either ignores the `SIGPIPE` signal, or if it handles the signal and returns from its signal handler.†

Consider a daemon that uses a FIFO to receive client requests (such as the System V print spooler). The daemon opens the FIFO for read-only and its typical state is waiting

---

† Neither the System V Release 2 nor the System V Release 3 manuals note that this signal is generated for *both* pipes and FIFOs—they mention only pipes. As stated at the beginning of this section, FIFOs are the forgotten (and undocumented) child of IPC.

in a read system call for a client request. Client processes are started and they open the FIFO for writing, write their request, and exit. What happens is the read returns zero (end of file) to the daemon every time a client process terminates, if no other clients have the FIFO open for writing. The daemon has to then open the FIFO again (for read-only) and it waits here until a client process opens the FIFO for writing. To avoid this, a useful technique is for the daemon to open the FIFO two times—once for reading and once for writing. The file descriptor returned for reading is used to read the client requests, and the file descriptor for writing is never used. By having the FIFO always open for writing (as long as the daemon process exists) the reads do not return an EOF, but wait for the next client request.

We can write our simple client–server example using FIFOs. The client function and the server function don't change—their use of read and write doesn't change between pipes and FIFOs. The main function does change.

```
#include     <sys/types.h>
#include     <sys/stat.h>
#include     <sys/errno.h>
extern int   errno;

#define FIFO1   "/tmp/fifo.1"
#define FIFO2   "/tmp/fifo.2"
#define PERMS   0666

main()
{
    int     childpid, readfd, writefd;

    if ( (mknod(FIFO1, S_IFIFO | PERMS, 0) < 0) && (errno != EEXIST))
            err_sys("can't create fifo 1: %s", FIFO1);
    if ( (mknod(FIFO2, S_IFIFO | PERMS, 0) < 0) && (errno != EEXIST)) {
            unlink(FIFO1);
            err_sys("can't create fifo 2: %s", FIFO2);
    }

    if ( (childpid = fork()) < 0) {
            err_sys("can't fork");

    } else if (childpid > 0) {                       /* parent */
            if ( (writefd = open(FIFO1, 1)) < 0)
                    err_sys("parent: can't open write fifo");
            if ( (readfd = open(FIFO2, 0)) < 0)
                    err_sys("parent: can't open read fifo");

            client(readfd, writefd);

            while (wait((int *) 0) != childpid)      /* wait for child */
                    ;

            close(readfd);
            close(writefd);

            if (unlink(FIFO1) < 0)
```

```
                                err_sys("parent: can't unlink %s", FIFO1);
                        if (unlink(FIFO2) < 0)
                                err_sys("parent: can't unlink %s", FIFO2);
                        exit(0);

        } else {                                        /* child */
                if ( (readfd = open(FIFO1, 0)) < 0)
                        err_sys("child: can't open read fifo");
                if ( (writefd = open(FIFO2, 1)) < 0)
                        err_sys("child: can't open write fifo");

                server(readfd, writefd);

                close(readfd);
                close(writefd);
                exit(0);
        }
}
```

We first call `mknod` to create the FIFOs, realizing that they might already exist. After the `fork` both processes must open each of the two FIFOs as desired. The parent process removes the FIFOs with the `unlink` system call, after `waiting` for the child to terminate.

The order of the `open` calls is important, and avoids a deadlock condition. When the parent opens `FIFO1` for writing, it waits until the child opens it for reading. If the first call to `open` in the child were for `FIFO2` instead of `FIFO1`, then the child would wait for the parent to open `FIFO2` for writing. Each process would be waiting for the other, and neither would proceed. This is called a *deadlock*. The solution is either to code the calls to `open` as shown, or to specify the `O_NDELAY` option to `open`.

When we used pipes to implement this example, the client and server had to originate from the same process, since pipes cannot be shared between unrelated processes. With FIFOs, however, we do not have this restriction. Nevertheless, we used the same program structure for the FIFO example above as we used for the pipe example. We now rewrite the FIFO example, splitting it into two separate programs—one for the client and one for the server.

The `main` function for the client is

```
#include         "fifo.h"

main()
{
        int      readfd, writefd;

        /*
         * Open the FIFOs.  We assume the server has already created them.
         */

        if ( (writefd = open(FIFO1, 1)) < 0)
                err_sys("client: can't open write fifo: %s", FIFO1);
        if ( (readfd = open(FIFO2, 0)) < 0)
                err_sys("client: can't open read fifo: %s", FIFO2);
```

```
        client(readfd, writefd);

        close(readfd);
        close(writefd);

        /*
         * Delete the FIFOs, now that we're finished.
         */

        if (unlink(FIFO1) < 0)
                err_sys("client: can't unlink %s", FIFO1);
        if (unlink(FIFO2) < 0)
                err_sys("client: can't unlink %s", FIFO2);

        exit(0);
}
```

The server `main` function is

```
#include      "fifo.h"

main()
{
        int     readfd, writefd;

        /*
         * Create the FIFOs, then open them - one for reading and one
         * for writing.
         */

        if ( (mknod(FIFO1, S_IFIFO | PERMS, 0) < 0) && (errno != EEXIST))
                err_sys("can't create fifo: %s", FIFO1);
        if ( (mknod(FIFO2, S_IFIFO | PERMS, 0) < 0) && (errno != EEXIST)) {
                unlink(FIFO1);
                err_sys("can't create fifo: %s", FIFO2);
        }

        if ( (readfd = open(FIFO1, 0)) < 0)
                err_sys("server: can't open read fifo: %s", FIFO1);
        if ( (writefd = open(FIFO2, 1)) < 0)
                err_sys("server: can't open write fifo: %s", FIFO2);

        server(readfd, writefd);

        close(readfd);
        close(writefd);

        exit(0);
}
```

To run this program we first start the server process in the background

```
server &
```

and then run the client in the foreground (since the client reads from the standard input and writes to the standard output):

```
client
```

Alternatively, we could just start the client program by hand, and have it invoke the server program. If the two programs are on the same computer system (as they must be if a FIFO is being used for IPC), the client can `fork` and `exec` the server process. We will see examples later when the client process invokes the required server process automatically. Indeed, when we invoke a client program, we should not need to worry about starting the server process that the client needs—this should be done automatically by the client.

3.6 Streams and Messages

The examples shown so far, for pipes and FIFOs, have used the stream I/O model, which is natural for Unix. There are no record boundaries—reads and writes do not examine the data at all. A process reading 100 bytes from a pipe, for example, cannot tell if the process that wrote the data into the pipe did a single write of 100 bytes, five writes of 20 bytes, or two writes of 50 bytes. It could also happen that one process writes 55 bytes into the pipe, followed by another process writing 45 bytes. The data is a *stream* of bytes with no interpretation done by the system. If any interpretation is desired, the writing process and the reading process must agree to it and do it themselves.

There are times, however, when a process wants to impose some structure on the data being transferred. This can happen when the data consists of variable-length messages and it is required that the reader know where the message boundaries are so that it knows when a single message has been read. Many Unix processes that need to impose a message structure on top of a stream based IPC facility do it using the newline character to separate each message. The writing process appends a newline to each message and the reading process reads from the IPC channel, one line at a time. In Chapter 13 we will see that both the 4.3BSD line printer spooler and the System V line printer spooler use this method of delineating messages on an IPC stream.

The standard I/O library can also be used to read or write a pipe or FIFO. Since the only way to open a pipe is with the `pipe` system call, which returns a file descriptor, the standard I/O function `fdopen` must be used to associate an open file descriptor with a standard I/O *stream*. Since a FIFO has a name, it can be opened using the standard I/O `fopen` function.

More structured messages can also be built, and this is what the Unix message queue form of IPC does. We can also add more structure to either a pipe or FIFO. We define a message in our `mesg.h` header file as

```
/*
 * Definition of "our" message.
 *
 * You may have to change the 4096 to a smaller value, if message queues
 * on your system were configured with "msgmax" less than 4096.
 */

#define MAXMESGDATA      (4096-16)
                              /* we don't want sizeof(Mesg) > 4096 */

#define MESGHDRSIZE      (sizeof(Mesg) - MAXMESGDATA)
                              /* length of mesg_len and mesg_type */

typedef struct {
  int   mesg_len;       /* #bytes in mesg_data, can be 0 or > 0 */
  long  mesg_type;      /* message type, must be > 0 */
  char  mesg_data[MAXMESGDATA];
} Mesg;
```

Each message has a *type* which we define as a long integer whose value must be greater than zero. We ignore the type field for now, but return to it in Section 3.9 when we describe message queues. We also specify a *length* for each message, and allow the length to be zero. If we use the stream format for messages, with newlines separating each message, the length is implied by the newline character at the end of each message. What we are doing with the `Mesg` definition is to precede each message with its length, instead of using newlines to separate the messages. The only advantage this has over the newline separation is if binary messages are being exchanged—with the length preceding the message the actual content of the message does not have to be scanned to find the end. We define two functions to send and receive messages.

```
#include        "mesg.h"

/*
 * Send a message by writing on a file descriptor.
 * The mesg_len, mesg_type and mesg_data fields must be filled
 * in by the caller.
 */

mesg_send(fd, mesgptr)
int     fd;
Mesg    *mesgptr;
{
        int     n;

        /*
         * Write the message header and the optional data.
         * First calculate the length of the length field, plus the
         * type field, plus the optional data.
```

```
        */

        n = MESGHDRSIZE + mesgptr->mesg_len;

        if (write(fd, (char *) mesgptr, n) != n)
                err_sys("message write error");
}

/*
 * Receive a message by reading on a file descriptor.
 * Fill in the mesg_len, mesg_type and mesg_data fields, and return
 * mesg_len as the return value also.
 */

int
mesg_recv(fd, mesgptr)
int     fd;
Mesg    *mesgptr;
{
        int     n;

        /*
         * Read the message header first.  This tells us how much
         * data follows the message for the next read.
         * An end-of-file on the file descriptor causes us to
         * return 0.  Hence, we force the assumption on the caller
         * that a 0-length message means EOF.
         */

        if ( (n = read(fd, (char *) mesgptr, MESGHDRSIZE)) == 0)
                return(0);                  /* end of file */
        else if (n != MESGHDRSIZE)
                err_sys("message header read error");

        /*
         * Read the actual data, if there is any.
         */

        if ( (n = mesgptr->mesg_len) > 0)
                if (read(fd, mesgptr->mesg_data, n) != n)
                        err_sys("data read error");
        return(n);
}
```

We now change the client and server functions to use the `mesg_send` and `mesg_recv` functions.

```
#include        <stdio.h>
#include        "mesg.h"

Mesg    mesg;

client(ipcreadfd, ipcwritefd)
int     ipcreadfd;
```

```
int     ipcwritefd;
{
        int     n;

        /*
         * Read the filename from standard input, write it as
         * a message to the IPC descriptor.
         */

        if (fgets(mesg.mesg_data, MAXMESGDATA, stdin) == NULL)
                err_sys("filename read error");

        n = strlen(mesg.mesg_data);
        if (mesg.mesg_data[n-1] == '\n')
                n--;                        /* ignore newline from fgets() */
        mesg.mesg_len = n;
        mesg.mesg_type = 1L;
        mesg_send(ipcwritefd, &mesg);

        /*
         * Receive the message from the IPC descriptor and write
         * the data to the standard output.
         */

        while ( (n = mesg_recv(ipcreadfd, &mesg)) > 0)
                if (write(1, mesg.mesg_data, n) != n)
                        err_sys("data write error");

        if (n < 0)
                err_sys("data read error");
}

#include        <stdio.h>
#include        "mesg.h"

extern int      errno;

Mesg    mesg;

server(ipcreadfd, ipcwritefd)
int     ipcreadfd;
int     ipcwritefd;
{
        int     n, filefd;
        char    errmesg[256], *sys_err_str();

        /*
         * Read the filename message from the IPC descriptor.
         */

        mesg.mesg_type = 1L;
        if ( (n = mesg_recv(ipcreadfd, &mesg)) <= 0)
                err_sys("server: filename read error");
        mesg.mesg_data[n] = '\0';       /* null terminate filename */
```

```
        if ( (filefd = open(mesg.mesg_data, 0)) < 0) {
                /*
                 * Error.  Format an error message and send it back
                 * to the client.
                 */

                sprintf(errmesg, ": can't open, %s\n", sys_err_str());
                strcat(mesg.mesg_data, errmesg);
                mesg.mesg_len = strlen(mesg.mesg_data);
                mesg_send(ipcwritefd, &mesg);

        } else {
                /*
                 * Read the data from the file and send a message to
                 * the IPC descriptor.
                 */

                while ( (n = read(filefd, mesg.mesg_data, MAXMESGDATA)) > 0) {
                        mesg.mesg_len = n;
                        mesg_send(ipcwritefd, &mesg);
                }
                close(filefd);

                if (n < 0)
                        err_sys("server: read error");
        }

        /*
         * Send a message with a length of 0 to signify the end.
         */

        mesg.mesg_len = 0;
        mesg_send(ipcwritefd, &mesg);
}
```

The `main` functions that call the `client` and `server` functions don't change at all. We can use either the pipe version or the FIFO version.

3.7 Name Spaces

Pipes do not have names but FIFOs have a Unix pathname to identify them. As we move to other forms of IPC in the following sections, additional naming conventions are used. The set of possible names for a given type of IPC is called its *name space*. The name space is important because for all forms of IPC other than plain pipes, the name is how the client and server "connect" to exchange messages. All forms of IPC that we cover in this chapter are restricted to use on a single computer system. When we describe methods for IPC between processes on *different* systems, the choice of names from the available name space becomes important.

Figure 3.10 summarizes the naming conventions used by the different forms of IPC. The last column specifies how a process accesses a particular form of IPC.

IPC type	Name space	Identification
pipe	(no name)	file descriptor
FIFO	pathname	file descriptor
message queue	key_t key	identifier
shared memory	key_t key	identifier
semaphore	key_t key	identifier
socket—Unix domain	pathname	file descriptor
socket—other domains	(domain dependent)	file descriptor

Figure 3.10 Name spaces for IPC.

key_t **Keys**

The function `ftok` is provided by the System V standard C library to convert a pathname and project identifier into a System V IPC key.† These System V IPC keys are used to identify message queues, shared memory, and semaphores, all of which are described in the following sections:

```
#include <sys/types.h>
#include <sys/ipc.h>

key_t ftok(char *pathname, char proj);
```

The file `<sys/types.h>` defines the `key_t` datatype, which is typically a 32-bit integer.

An IPC application should have the server and clients all agree on a single pathname that has some meaning to the application. It could be the pathname of the server daemon, the pathname of a common data file used by the server, or some other pathname on the system. If the client and server only need a single IPC channel between them, a *proj* of one, say, can be used. If multiple IPC channels are needed, say one from the client to the server and another from the server to the client, then one channel can use a *proj* of one, and the other a *proj* of two, for example. Once the *pathname* and *proj* are agreed on by the client and server, then both can call the `ftok` function to convert these into the same IPC key.

If the *pathname* does not exist, or is not accessible to the calling process, `ftok` returns −1. Be aware that the file whose *pathname* is used to generate the key must not be a file that is created and deleted by the server during its existence, since each time it is created it can assume a new i-node number which can change the key returned by `ftok` to the next caller.

---

† For some reason this function is found in the System V manual under *stdipc*(3C), instead of its real name.

Note that the *proj* argument to `ftok` is an 8-bit character, not a pointer to a character string.

The normal implementation of the `ftok` function is as follows. It combines the 8-bit *proj* value, along with the numeric i-node number of the disk file corresponding to the specified *pathname*, along with the minor device number of the filesystem on which the disk file resides. The combination of these three values produces a 32-bit key. By using the i-node number of the file within the filesystem that it resides on, along with the minor device number of that filesystem (which corresponds to the disk partition of a single disk controller), this function attempts to generate a unique key value. To *guarantee* a unique key for every possible pathname on a system, we need to combine the 32-bit i-node number, the 8-bit major device number, and the 8-bit minor device number. The algorithm chosen by `ftok` is a compromise, since there is a nonzero (but small) chance that two different pathnames can generate the same key value. But few real i-node numbers are larger than 16 bits and to have two different pathnames generate the same key, both files must have the same i-node number and the same minor device number, but have different major device numbers.

3.8 System V IPC

The three types of IPC

- message queues
- semaphores
- shared memory

are collectively referred to as "System V IPC." They share many similarities in the system calls that access them, and in the information that the kernel maintains on them. A summary of their system calls is shown in Figure 3.11.

	Message queue	Semaphore	Shared memory
include file	`<sys/msg.h>`	`<sys/sem.h>`	`<sys/shm.h>`
system call to create or open	msgget	semget	shmget
system call for control operations	msgctl	semctl	shmctl
system calls for IPC operations	msgsnd	semop	shmat
	msgrcv		shmdt

Figure 3.11 Summary of System V IPC system calls.

The kernel maintains a structure of information for each IPC channel, similar to the information it maintains for files.

```
struct ipc_perm {
    ushort   uid;      /* owner's user id */
    ushort   gid;      /* owner's group id */
    ushort   cuid;     /* creator's user id */
```

```
    ushort   cgid;     /* creator's group id */
    ushort   mode;     /* access modes */
    ushort   seq;      /* slot usage sequence number */
    key_t    key;      /* key */
};
```

This structure, and other manifest constants for the System V IPC system calls, are defined in `<sys/ipc.h>`. The three `ctl` system calls are used to access this structure and modify it.

The three `get` system calls that create or open an IPC channel, all take a *key* value, whose type is `key_t`, and return an integer identifier. The sequence of steps is shown in Figure 3.12.

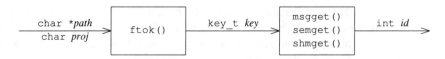

Figure 3.12 Generating IPC *ids* using `ftok`.

All three of the `get` system calls also take a *flag* argument that specifies the low-order 9 bits of the `mode` for the IPC channel, and whether a new IPC channel is being created, or if an existing one is being referenced. The rules for whether a new IPC channel is created or whether an existing one is referenced are

- Specifying a *key* of `IPC_PRIVATE` guarantees that a unique IPC channel is created. There are no combinations of *pathname* and *proj* that cause `ftok` to generate a *key* value of `IPC_PRIVATE`.

- Setting the `IPC_CREAT` bit of the *flag* word creates a new entry for the specified *key*, if it does not already exist. If an existing entry is found, that entry is returned.

- Setting both the `IPC_CREAT` and `IPC_EXCL` bits of the *flag* word creates a new entry for the specified *key*, only if the entry does not already exist. If an existing entry is found, an error occurs, since the IPC channel already exists.

  Note that the `IPC_EXCL` bit does *not* guarantee the caller exclusive access to the IPC channel. Its only function is to guarantee that a new IPC channel is created, or else an error is returned. Even if we create a new IPC channel by specifying both `IPC_CREAT` and `IPC_EXCL`, other users can also access that channel, if they have adequate permission as specified by the low-order 9 bits of the channel's `mode` word.

- Setting the `IPC_EXCL` bit, without setting the `IPC_CREAT` bit, has no meaning.

The actual logic flow for opening an IPC channel is shown in Figure 3.13.

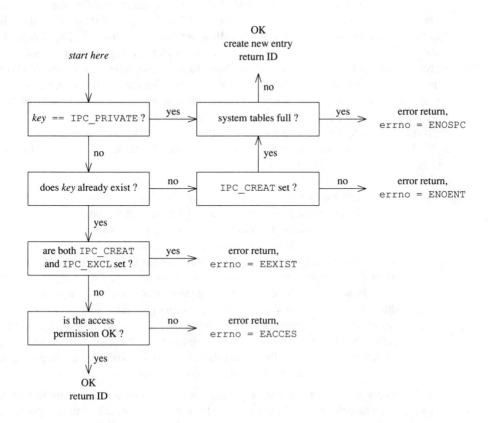

Figure 3.13 Logic for opening or creating an IPC channel.

Another way of looking at Figure 3.13 is shown in Figure 3.14.

flag argument	*key* does not exist	*key* already exists
no special flags	error, errno = ENOENT	OK
IPC_CREAT	OK, creates new entry	OK
IPC_CREAT | IPC_EXCL	OK, creates new entry	error, errno = EEXIST

Figure 3.14 Logic for creating or opening an IPC channel.

One thing to note is that for the middle line of Figure 3.14, the IPC_CREAT flag without IPC_EXCL, we do not get an indication whether a new entry has been created or if we are referencing an existing entry.

Whenever a new IPC channel is created, using one of the `get` system calls with the `IPC_CREAT` flag, the low-order 9 bits of the *flag* argument initialize the `mode` word in the `ipc_perm` structure. Additionally the `cuid` and `cgid` fields are set to the effective user ID and effective group ID of the calling process, respectively. The two fields `uid` and `gid` in the `ipc_perm` structure are also set to the effective user ID and effective group ID of the calling process. These latter two IDs are called the "owner" IDs, while the `cuid` and `cgid` are called the "creator" IDs. The creator IDs never change, while a process can change the owner IDs, by calling the `ctl` system call for the IPC mechanism—`msgctl`, `semctl`, or `shmctl`. These three `ctl` system calls also allow a process to change the low-order 9 bits of the `mode` word for the IPC channel.

Two levels of checking are done whenever an IPC channel is accessed by any process.

1. Whenever a process accesses an existing IPC channel with one of the `get` system calls, an initial check is made that the caller's *flag* argument does not specify any access bits that are not in the `mode` word. For example, a server process can set the `mode` word for its input message queue so that the group-read and world-read permission bits are off. Any process that tries to specify a *flag* argument that includes these bits gets an error return from the `msgget` system call. But this test that's done by the `get` system calls is of little use. It implies that the caller knows which permission category it falls into—owner, group, or world. If the creator specifically turns off certain permission bits, and if the caller specifies these bits, the error is detected by the `get` system call. Any process, however, can totally bypass this check by just specifying a *flag* argument of zero if it knows that the IPC channel already exists.

2. Every IPC operation does a permission test for the process using the operation. For example, every time a process tries to put a message onto a message queue with the `msgsnd` system call, tests similar to those done for filesystem access are performed.

   - The superuser is always granted access.
   - If the effective user ID equals either the `uid` value or the `cuid` value for the IPC channel, and if the appropriate access bit is on in the `mode` word for the IPC channel, permission is granted. By "appropriate access bit" we mean the read-bit must be set if the caller wants to do a read operation on the IPC channel (receiving a message from a message queue, for example), or the write-bit must be set for a write operation.
   - If the effective group ID equals either the `gid` value or the `cgid` value for the IPC channel, and if the appropriate access bit is on in the `mode` word for the IPC channel, permission is granted.
   - If none of the above tests are "true," the appropriate world access bit must be on in the `mode` word for the IPC channel, for permission to be allowed.

The `ipc_perm` structure also contains a variable named `seq`, which is a slot usage sequence number. This is a counter that is maintained by the kernel for every potential IPC channel in the system. Every time an IPC channel is closed, the kernel increments the slot number, cycling it back to zero when it overflows.

This counter is needed for the following reasons. First consider the file descriptors maintained by the kernel for open files. They are small integers, but only have meaning within a single process—they are process specific numbers. If we try to read from file descriptor 4, say, in a process, this only works if the process has a file open on this descriptor. It has no effect whatsoever with a file that might be open on file descriptor 4 in some other unrelated process. IPC channels, however, are *systemwide* and not process specific. We obtain an IPC identifier (similar to a file descriptor) from one of the `get` system calls—`msgget`, `semget`, and `shmget`. These identifiers are also integers, but their meaning applies to *all* processes. If two unrelated processes, a client and server for example, use a single message queue, the message queue identifier returned by the `msgget` system call is the same integer value in both processes. This means that a devious process could try to read a message using different small integer identifiers, hoping to find one that is currently in use that allows world read access. If the potential values for these identifiers were small integers (like file descriptors) then the probability of finding a valid identifier would be about 1 in 50.

To avoid this potential problem, the designers of the System V IPC facilities decided to increase the possible range of identifier values to include *all* integers, not just small integers. This is implemented by incrementing the identifier value that is returned to the calling process, by the number of IPC table entries, each time a table entry is reused. For example, if the system is configured for a maximum of 50 message queues, then the first time the first message queue table entry in the kernel is used, the identifier returned to the process is zero. After this message queue is removed and the first table entry is reused, the identifier returned is 50. The next time the identifier is 100, and so on. Since `seq` is an unsigned short integer (see the `ipc_perm` structure shown earlier in this section) it cycles after the table entry has been used 65,535 times. An an example of this pattern, the following program prints the first 10 identifier values returned by `msgget`.

```
#include         <sys/types.h>
#include         <sys/ipc.h>
#include         <sys/msg.h>

#define KEY      ((key_t) 98765L)
#define PERMS    0666

main()
{
        int      i, msqid;

        for (i = 0; i < 10; i++) {
                if ( (msqid = msgget(KEY, PERMS | IPC_CREAT)) < 0)
                        err_sys("can't create message queue");

                printf("msqid = %d\n", msqid);
```

```
                    if (msgctl(msqid, IPC_RMID, (struct msqid_ds *) 0) < 0)
                        err_sys("can't remove message queue");
            }
    }
```

Its output is

```
    msqid = 0
    msqid = 50
    msqid = 100
    msqid = 150
    msqid = 200
    msqid = 250
    msqid = 300
    msqid = 350
    msqid = 400
    msqid = 450
```

3.9   Message Queues

Some form of message passing between processes is now part of many modern operating systems. Some operating systems restrict the passing of messages such that a process can only send a message to another specific process. System V has no such restriction. In the System V implementation of messages, all messages are stored in the kernel, and have an associated *message queue identifier*. It is this identifier, which we call an *msqid*, that identifies a particular queue of messages. Processes read and write messages to arbitrary queues. There is no requirement that any process be waiting for a message to arrive on a queue before some other process is allowed to write a message to that queue. This is in contrast to both pipes and FIFOs, where it made no sense to have a writer process unless a reader process also exists. It is possible for a process to write some messages to a queue, then exit, and have the messages read by another process at a later time.

Every message on a queue has the following attributes:

- long integer *type*;
- *length* of the data portion of the message (can be zero);
- *data* (if the *length* is greater than zero).

For every message queue in the system, the kernel maintains the following structure of information:

```
    #include  <sys/types.h>
    #include  <sys/ipc.h>          /* defines the ipc_perm structure */

    struct msqid_ds {
      struct ipc_perm msg_perm;   /* operation permission struct */
      struct msg      *msg_first; /* ptr to first message on q */
      struct msg      *msg_last;  /* ptr to last message on q */
```

```
    ushort            msg_cbytes; /* current # bytes on q */
    ushort            msg_qnum;   /* current # of messages on q */
    ushort            msg_qbytes; /* max # of bytes allowed on q */
    ushort            msg_lspid;  /* pid of last msgsnd */
    ushort            msg_lrpid;  /* pid of last msgrcv */
    time_t            msg_stime;  /* time of last msgsnd */
    time_t            msg_rtime;  /* time of last msgrcv */
    time_t            msg_ctime;  /* time of last msgctl
                                     (that changed the above) */
};
```

The `ipc_perm` structure was described in Section 3.8 and contains the access permissions for this particular message queue. The `msg` structures are the internal data structure used by the kernel to maintain the linked list of messages on a particular queue.

We can picture a particular message queue in the kernel as a linked list of messages, as shown in Figure 3.15. Assume that three messages are on a queue, with lengths of 1 byte, 2 bytes, and 3 bytes, and that the messages were written in that order. Also assume that these three messages were written with *types* of 100, 200, and 300, respectively.

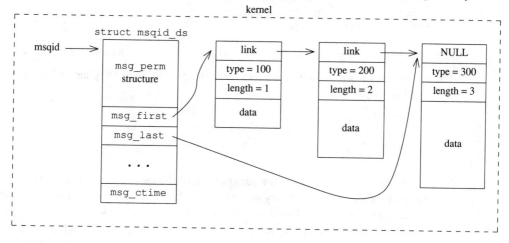

Figure 3.15 Message queue structures in kernel.

A new message queue is created, or an existing message queue is accessed with the `msgget` system call

```
#include  <sys/types.h>
#include  <sys/ipc.h>
#include  <sys/msg.h>

int msgget(key_t key, int msgflag);
```

The *msgflag* value is a combination of the constants shown in Figure 3.16.

Numeric	Symbolic	Description
0400	MSG_R	Read by owner
0200	MSG_W	Write by owner
0040	MSG_R >> 3	Read by group
0020	MSG_W >> 3	Write by group
0004	MSG_R >> 6	Read by world
0002	MSG_W >> 6	Write by world
	IPC_CREAT	(See Section 3.8)
	IPC_EXCL	(See Section 3.8)

Figure 3.16   *msgflag* values for msgget system call.

The value returned by msgget is the message queue identifier, *msqid*, or −1 if an error occurred.

Once a message queue is opened with msgget, we put a message on the queue using the msgsnd system call.

```
#include   <sys/types.h>
#include   <sys/ipc.h>
#include   <sys/msg.h>

int msgsnd(int msqid, struct msgbuf *ptr, int length, int flag);
```

The *ptr* argument is a pointer to a structure with the following template. (This template is defined in <sys/msg.h>.)

```
struct msgbuf {
  long   mtype;      /* message type, must be > 0 */
  char   mtext[1];   /* message data */
};
```

The name *mtext* is a misnomer—the data portion of the message is not restricted to text. Any form of data is allowed, binary data or text. The message type must be greater than zero, since a message type of zero is used as a special indicator to the msgrcv system call, which we describe later. By template we mean that the ptr argument must point to a long integer that contains the message type, followed by the message itself (if the length of the message is greater than zero bytes). The kernel does not interpret the contents of the message at all. If some cooperating processes wanted to exchange messages consisting of a short integer followed by an 8-byte character array, they can define their own structure:

```
typedef struct my_msgbuf {
  long    mtype;     /* message type */
  short   mshort;    /* start of message data */
  char    mchar[8];
} Message;
```

The *length* argument to `msgsnd` specifies the length of the message in bytes. This is the length of the user-defined data that follows the long integer message type. The length can be zero.

The *flag* argument can be specified as either `IPC_NOWAIT` or as zero. The `IPC_NOWAIT` value allows the system call to return immediately if there is no room on the message queue for the new message. This condition can occur if either there are too many messages on the specified queue, or if there are too many messages systemwide. If there is no room for the message, and if `IPC_NOWAIT` is specified, `msgsnd` returns −1 and `errno` is set to `EAGAIN`. If the system call is successful, `msgsnd` returns zero.

A message is read from a message queue using the `msgrcv` system call.

```
#include   <sys/types.h>
#include   <sys/ipc.h>
#include   <sys/msg.h>

int msgrcv(int msqid, struct msgbuf *ptr, int length, long msgtype,
           int flag);
```

The *ptr* argument is like the one for `msgsnd`, and specifies where the received message is stored. *len* specifies the size of the data portion of the structure pointed to by *ptr*. This is the maximum amount of data that is returned by the system call. If the `MSG_NOERROR` bit in the *flag* argument is set, this specifies that if the actual data portion of the received message is greater than *length*, just truncate the data portion and return without an error. Not specifying the `MSG_NOERROR` flag causes an error return if *length* is not large enough to receive the entire message.

The long integer *msgtype* argument specifies which message on the queue is desired.

- If *msgtype* is zero, the first message on the queue is returned. Since each message queue is maintained as a first-in, first-out list, a *msgtype* of zero specifies that the oldest message on the queue is to be returned.

- If *msgtype* is greater than zero, the first message with a type equal to *msgtype* is returned.

- If *msgtype* is less than zero, the first message with the *lowest* type that is less than or equal to the absolute value of *msgtype* is returned.

Consider the message queue example shown in Figure 3.15, which has three messages: the first message has a type of 100 and a length of 1, the next has a type of 200 and a length of 2, and the last message has a type of 300 and a length of 3. Figure 3.17 shows the message returned for different values of *msgtype*.

The *flag* argument specifies what to do if a message of the requested type is not on the queue. If the `IPC_NOWAIT` bit is set, the `msgrcv` system call returns immediately if a message is not available. In this case the system call returns a −1 with `errno` set to `ENOMSG`. Otherwise, the caller is suspended until one of the following occurs:

msgtype	Type of message returned
0L	100
100L	100
200L	200
300L	300
-100L	100
-200L	100
-300L	100

Figure 3.17 Messages returned by msgrcv for different values of *msgtype*.

- a message of the requested type is available,
- the message queue is removed from the system,
- the process receives a signal that is caught.

Additionally, the MSG_NOERROR bit of the *flag* argument can be set, as mentioned above.

On successful return, msgrcv returns the number of bytes of data in the received message. This does not include the long integer message size that is also returned through the *ptr* argument.

The msgctl system call provides a variety of control operations on a message queue.

```
#include   <sys/types.h>
#include   <sys/ipc.h>
#include   <sys/msg.h>

int msgctl(int msqid, int cmd, struct msqid_ds *buff);
```

Our only use will be a *cmd* of IPC_RMID to remove a message queue from the system.

We now show the code for our client–server example, using two message queues. One queue is for messages from the client to the server, and the other queue is for messages in the other direction. Our header file msgq.h is

```
#include       <sys/types.h>
#include       <sys/ipc.h>
#include       <sys/msg.h>

#include       <sys/errno.h>
extern int     errno;

#define MKEY1   1234L
#define MKEY2   2345L

#define PERMS   0666
```

The `main` function for the server is

```
#include        "msgq.h"

main()
{
        int     readid, writeid;

        /*
         * Create the message queues, if required.
         */

        if ( (readid = msgget(MKEY1, PERMS | IPC_CREAT)) < 0)
                err_sys("server: can't get message queue 1");
        if ( (writeid = msgget(MKEY2, PERMS | IPC_CREAT)) < 0)
                err_sys("server: can't get message queue 2");

        server(readid, writeid);

        exit(0);
}
```

The `main` function for the client is

```
#include        "msgq.h"

main()
{
        int     readid, writeid;

        /*
         * Open the message queues.  The server must have
         * already created them.
         */

        if ( (writeid = msgget(MKEY1, 0)) < 0)
                err_sys("client: can't msgget message queue 1");
        if ( (readid = msgget(MKEY2, 0)) < 0)
                err_sys("client: can't msgget message queue 2");

        client(readid, writeid);

        /*
         * Now we can delete the message queues.
         */

        if (msgctl(readid, IPC_RMID, (struct msqid_ds *) 0) < 0)
                err_sys("client: can't RMID message queue 1");
        if (msgctl(writeid, IPC_RMID, (struct msqid_ds *) 0) < 0)
                err_sys("client: can't RMID message queue 2");

        exit(0);
}
```

Both of these program use the `client` and `server` functions that were shown in Section 3.6. These two functions in turn call the following `mesg_send` and `mesg_recv` functions that use message queues.

```
#include        "mesg.h"

/*
 * Send a message using the System V message queues.
 * The mesg_len, mesg_type and mesg_data fields must be filled
 * in by the caller.
 */

mesg_send(id, mesgptr)
int     id;                /* really an msqid from msgget() */
Mesg    *mesgptr;
{
        /*
         * Send the message - the type followed by the optional data.
         */

        if (msgsnd(id, (char *) &(mesgptr->mesg_type),
                                        mesgptr->mesg_len, 0) != 0)
                err_sys("msgsnd error");
}

/*
 * Receive a message from a System V message queue.
 * The caller must fill in the mesg_type field with the desired type.
 * Return the number of bytes in the data portion of the message.
 * A 0-length data message implies end-of-file.
 */

int
mesg_recv(id, mesgptr)
int     id;                /* really an msqid from msgget() */
Mesg    *mesgptr;
{
        int     n;

        /*
         * Read the first message on the queue of the specified type.
         */

        n = msgrcv(id, (char *) &(mesgptr->mesg_type), MAXMESGDATA,
                                        mesgptr->mesg_type, 0);
        if ( (mesgptr->mesg_len = n) < 0)
                err_dump("msgrcv error");

        return(n);                /* n will be 0 at end of file */
}
```

Multiplexing Messages

The purpose of having a type associated with each message is to allow multiple processes to *multiplex* messages onto a single queue. Consider our simple example of a server process and a single client process. With either pipes or FIFOs, two IPC channels are required to exchange data in both directions, since these types of IPC are unidirectional. With a message queue, a single queue can be used, having the type of each message signify if the message is from the client to the server, or vice versa.

Consider the next complication, a server with multiple clients. Here we can use a type of 1, say, to indicate a message from any client to the server. If the client passes its process ID as part of the message, the server can send its messages to the client processes, using the client's process ID as the message type. Each client process specifies the *msgtype* argument to `msgrcv` as its process ID. Figure 3.18 shows how a single message queue can be used to multiplex these messages between multiple processes.

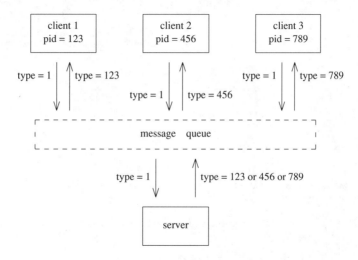

Figure 3.18 Multiplexing messages between three clients and one server.

Another feature provided by the type attribute of messages if the ability of the receiver to read the messages in an order other than first-in, first-out. With pipes and FIFOs, the data must be read in the order in which it was written. With message queues we can read the messages in any order that is consistent with the values we associate with the message types. We can, in essence, assign priorities to the messages by associating a priority to a type, or range of types. Furthermore, we can call `msgrcv` with the `IPC_NOWAIT` flag to read any messages of a given type from the queue, but return immediately if there are no messages of the specified type.

Now we can redo the client–server example using a single message queue. These programs use the convention that messages with a type of 1 are from the client to the server, and messages with a type of 2 are from the server to the client. The server program is

```
#include        <stdio.h>
#include        "mesg.h"
#include        "msgq.h"

Mesg    mesg;

main()
{
        int     id;

        /*
         * Create the message queue, if required.
         */

        if ( (id = msgget(MKEY1, PERMS | IPC_CREAT)) < 0)
                err_sys("server: can't get message queue 1");

        server(id);

        exit(0);
}

server(id)
int     id;
{
        int     n, filefd;
        char    errmesg[256], *sys_err_str();

        /*
         * Read the filename message from the IPC descriptor.
         */

        mesg.mesg_type = 1L;            /* receive messages of this type */
        if ( (n = mesg_recv(id, &mesg)) <= 0)
                err_sys("server: filename read error");
        mesg.mesg_data[n] = '\0';       /* null terminate filename */

        mesg.mesg_type = 2L;            /* send messages of this type */
        if ( (filefd = open(mesg.mesg_data, 0)) < 0) {
                /*
                 * Error.  Format an error message and send it back
                 * to the client.
                 */

                sprintf(errmesg, ": can't open, %s\n", sys_err_str());
                strcat(mesg.mesg_data, errmesg);
                mesg.mesg_len = strlen(mesg.mesg_data);
                mesg_send(id, &mesg);
```

```
                } else {
                        /*
                         * Read the data from the file and send a message to
                         * the IPC descriptor.
                         */

                        while ( (n = read(filefd, mesg.mesg_data, MAXMESGDATA)) > 0) {
                                mesg.mesg_len = n;
                                mesg_send(id, &mesg);
                        }
                        close(filefd);

                        if (n < 0)
                                err_sys("server: read error");
                }

                /*
                 * Send a message with a length of 0 to signify the end.
                 */

                mesg.mesg_len = 0;
                mesg_send(id, &mesg);
}
```

The client program is

```
#include        <stdio.h>
#include        "mesg.h"
#include        "msgq.h"

Mesg    mesg;

main()
{
        int     id;

        /*
         * Open the single message queue.  The server must have
         * already created it.
         */

        if ( (id = msgget(MKEY1, 0)) < 0)
                err_sys("client: can't msgget message queue 1");

        client(id);

        /*
         * Now we can delete the message queue.
         */

        if (msgctl(id, IPC_RMID, (struct msqid_ds *) 0) < 0)
                err_sys("client: can't RMID message queue 1");

        exit(0);
```

```
}

client(id)
int      id;
{
        int      n;

        /*
         * Read the filename from standard input, write it as
         * a message to the IPC descriptor.
         */

        if (fgets(mesg.mesg_data, MAXMESGDATA, stdin) == NULL)
                err_sys("filename read error");

        n = strlen(mesg.mesg_data);
        if (mesg.mesg_data[n-1] == '\n')
                n--;                        /* ignore the newline from fgets() */
        mesg.mesg_data[n] = '\0';           /* overwrite newline at end */
        mesg.mesg_len = n;
        mesg.mesg_type = 1L;                /* send messages of this type */
        mesg_send(id, &mesg);

        /*
         * Receive the message from the IPC descriptor and write
         * the data to the standard output.
         */

        mesg.mesg_type = 2L;     /* receive messages of this type */
        while( (n = mesg_recv(id, &mesg)) > 0)
                if (write(1, mesg.mesg_data, n) != n)
                        err_sys("data write error");

        if (n < 0)
                err_sys("data read error");
}
```

Both of these programs use the `mesg_send` and `mesg_recv` functions that were shown earlier in this section for the example that used two message queues.

Message Queue Limits

There are certain system limits on message queues. Some of these can be changed by a system administrator, by configuring a new kernel. Figure 3.19 shows the values for five different versions of Unix.†

----

† Note that three of these systems specify a per-queue maximum of 16,384 bytes when they only allow a systemwide maximum of 8,192 bytes. This doesn't make sense. Also, these three systems allow more total message queues (50) than messages (40), meaning we can't have one message per queue outstanding, at any point in time.

Parameter name	AT&T VAX Sys V Rel 2	DEC VAX Ultrix	AT&T Unix PC	Xenix 286	Xenix 386	Description
msgmax	8,192	8,192	8,192	8,192	8,192	max # of bytes per message
msgmnb	16,384	16,384	16,384	8,192	8,192	max # of bytes on any one message queue
msgmni	50	50	50	10	10	max # of message queues, systemwide
msgtql	40	40	40	60	60	max # of messages, systemwide
	8,192	8,192	8,192	8,192	8,192	max # of bytes of messages, systemwide

Figure 3.19 Typical limits for message queues.

The intent is to show some typical values, to aid in planning for portability. For example, if we write an application that uses messages that are 20,000 bytes long, it will not be portable. The magic number 8192 bytes for a maximum message size is similar to the magic number of 4096 bytes for a maximum write to a pipe of FIFO.

3.10 Semaphores

Semaphores are a synchronization primitive. As a form of IPC, they are not used for exchanging large amounts of data, as are pipes, FIFOs, and message queues, but are intended to let multiple processes synchronize their operations. Our main use of semaphores is to synchronize the access to shared memory segments, which we discuss in the next section. This section provides a general overview of the semaphore system calls.

Consider a semaphore as an integer valued variable that is a resource counter. The value of the variable at any point in time is the number of resource units available. If we have one resource, say a file that is shared, then the valid semaphore values are zero and one.

Since our use of semaphores is to provide resource synchronization between different processes, the actual semaphore value must be stored in the kernel. We show this in Figure 3.20.

To obtain a resource that is controlled by a semaphore, a process needs to test its current value, and if the current value is greater than zero, decrement the value by one. If the current value is zero, the process must wait until the value is greater than zero (i.e., wait for some other process to release the resource). To release a resource that is controlled by a semaphore, a process increments the semaphore value. If some other process has been waiting for the semaphore value to become greater than zero, that other process can now obtain the semaphore. We can show this in pseudocode as

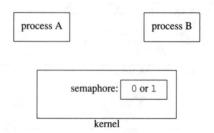

Figure 3.20 Semaphore value stored in kernel.

```
for ( ; ; ) {
        if (semaphore_value > 0) {
                semaphore_value--;
                break;
        }
}

/* we've obtained the semaphore */
```

The pitfall in this implementation of semaphores is that the test of the semaphore's current value, followed by the decrement of that value, is not an atomic operation. It must not be possible for one process to do the test and then be interrupted by another process that does the same test and then decrements the value. The System V implementation of semaphores is done in the kernel, where it is possible to guarantee that a group of operations on a semaphore is done atomically, with respect to other processes.

What we have described as a semaphore is a single *binary semaphore*—a semaphore with a single value that can be either zero or one. The System V implementation expands this in two directions.

1. A semaphore is not a single value but a *set* of nonnegative integer values. The number of nonnegative integer values in the set can be from one to some system defined maximum.

2. Each value in the set is not restricted to zero and one. Instead each value in the set can assume any nonnegative value, up to a system defined maximum value.

For every set of semaphores in the system, the kernel maintains the following structure of information.

```
#include  <sys/types.h>
#include  <sys/ipc.h>          /* defines the ipc_perm structure */

struct semid_ds {
  struct ipc_perm sem_perm;  /* operation permission struct */
  struct sem      *sem_base; /* ptr to first semaphore in set */
```

```
    ushort               sem_nsems; /* # of semaphores in set */
    time_t               sem_otime; /* time of last semop */
    time_t               sem_ctime; /* time of last change */
};
```

The `ipc_perm` structure was described in Section 3.8 and contains the access permissions for this particular semaphore. The `sem` structure is the internal data structure used by the kernel to maintain the set of values for a given semaphore. Every member of a semaphore set is described by the following structure:

```
struct sem {
    ushort   semval;    /* semaphore value, nonnegative */
    short    sempid;    /* pid of last operation */
    ushort   semncnt;   /* # awaiting semval > cval */
    ushort   semzcnt;   /* # awaiting semval = 0 */
};
```

In addition to maintaining the actual set of values for a semaphore, the kernel also maintains three other pieces of information for each value in the set—the process ID of the process that did the last operation on the value, a count of the number of processes waiting for the value to increase, and a count of the number of processes waiting for the value to become zero.

We can picture a particular semaphore in the kernel as being a `semid_ds` structure that points to an array of `sem` structures. If the semaphore has two members in its set, we would have the picture shown in Figure 3.21.

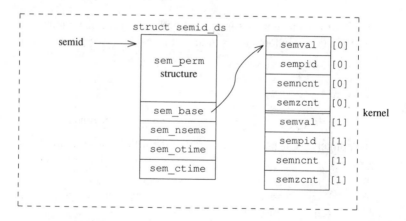

Figure 3.21   Kernel data structures for a semaphore set.

In Figure 3.21, the variable `sem_nsems` has a value of two and we have denoted each member of the set with the subscripts `[0]` and `[1]`.

A semaphore is created, or an existing semaphore is accessed with the `semget` system call.

```
#include   <sys/types.h>
#include   <sys/ipc.h>
#include   <sys/sem.h>

int semget(key_t key, int nsems, int semflag);
```

The value returned by `semget` is the semaphore identifier, *semid*, or −1 if an error occurred.

The *nsems* argument specifies the number of semaphores in the set. If we are not creating a new semaphore set, but only accessing an existing set (i.e., we did not specify the `IPC_CREAT` flag for the *semflag* argument), we can specify this argument as zero. We cannot change the number of semaphores in a set once it is created.

The *semflag* value is a combination of the constants shown in Figure 3.22.

Numeric	Symbolic	Description
0400	SEM_R	Read by owner
0200	SEM_A	Alter by owner
0040	SEM_R >> 3	Read by group
0020	SEM_A >> 3	Alter by group
0004	SEM_R >> 6	Read by world
0002	SEM_A >> 6	Alter by world
	IPC_CREAT	(See Section 3.8)
	IPC_EXCL	(See Section 3.8)

Figure 3.22 *semflag* values for `semget` system call.

Once a semaphore set is opened with `semget`, operations are performed on one or more of the semaphore values in the set using the `semop` system call.

```
#include   <sys/types.h>
#include   <sys/ipc.h>
#include   <sys/sem.h>

int semop(int semid, struct sembuf **opsptr, unsigned int nops);
```

The pointer *opsptr* points to an array of the following structures:

```
struct sembuf {
  ushort  sem_num;   /* semaphore # */
  short   sem_op;    /* semaphore operation */
  short   sem_flg;   /* operation flags */
};
```

The number of elements in the array of `sembuf` structures pointed to by *opsptr* is specified by the *nops* argument. Each element in this array specifies an operation for one particular semaphore value in the set. The particular semaphore value is specified by the `sem_num` value, which is zero for the first element, one for the second, and so on, up to *nsems−1*, where *nsems* is the number of semaphore values in the set (the second argument in the call to `semget` when the semaphore set was created).

The array of operations passed to the `semop` system call are guaranteed to be done atomically by the kernel. The kernel either does all the operations that are specified, or it doesn't do any of them. Each particular operation is specified by a `sem_op` value, which can be negative, zero, or positive.

1. If `sem_op` is positive, the value of `sem_val` is added to the semaphore's current value. This corresponds to the release of resources that a semaphore controls.

2. If `sem_op` is zero, the caller wants to wait until the semaphore's value becomes zero.

3. If `sem_op` is negative, the caller wants to wait until the semaphore's value becomes greater than or equal to the absolute value of `sem_op`. This corresponds to the allocation of resources.

The return value from `semop` is zero if all is OK, or −1 if an error occurred.†

There are a multitude of options available to the `semop` system call. We can specify, for example, the `IPC_NOWAIT` flag for the `sem_flg` value associated with an operation. This tells the system we don't want to wait if that operation can't be completed. There is also the capability of having the system remember adjustment values for a given semaphore so that if a process exits before releasing a semaphore, the system does the release for the process. We describe this option later in this section.

The `semctl` system call provides various control operations on a semaphore.

```
#include    <sys/types.h>
#include    <sys/ipc.h>
#include    <sys/sem.h>

int semctl(int semid, int semnum, int cmd, union semun arg);

union semun {
    int             val;    /* used for SETVAL only */
    struct semid_ds *buff;  /* used for IPC_STAT and IPC_SET */
    ushort          *array; /* used for IPC_GETALL & IPC_SETALL */
} arg;
```

We'll use a *cmd* of `IPC_RMID` to remove a semaphore from the system. We'll also use the `GETVAL` and `SETVAL` commands, to fetch and set a specific semaphore value. These two commands use the *semnum* argument to specify one member of the semaphore set. The `GETVAL` command returns the semaphore's value as the value of the system call. The `SETVAL` command sets the semaphore's value to *arg.val*.

---

† Both the System V Release 2 manual page for *semop*(2) and Bach [1986] say that the return value is the value of the last semaphore that was operated on, before it was changed. This is an error. The System V Release 3 manual page correctly states that the return value from a successful call is zero.

File Locking with Semaphores

Since semaphores can be thought of as a synchronization facility, we can return to the file locking examples from Section 3.2 and provide yet another implementation, using semaphores.

We create a binary semaphore—a single semaphore value that is either zero or one. To lock the semaphore we call `semop` to do two operations atomically. First, wait for the semaphore value to become zero (a `sem_op` value of zero), then increment the value to one. This is an example where multiple semaphore operations must be done atomically by the kernel. If it took two system calls to do this—one to test the value and wait for it to become zero, and another to increment the value—the operation would not work.

To unlock the resource, we call `semop` to decrement the semaphore value. Since we have the lock on the resource, we know that the semaphore value is one before the call, so the call cannot wait. We explicitly set `sem_flg` to `IPC_NOWAIT` so that if this "impossible condition" does happen, an error return occurs and the process aborts.

You might wonder why we don't initialize the semaphore value to one and use it as a resource counter, as we described earlier. Then, to allocate the resource we wait for its value to become greater than zero, and decrement it. The release of the resource would be done by incrementing the semaphore value. The reason we use the semaphore in our "backwards" fashion has to do with an initialization problem with System V semaphores. It is hard to initialize a semaphore to a value other than zero, as we soon see.

```
/*
 * Locking routines using semaphores.
 */

#include        <sys/types.h>
#include        <sys/ipc.h>
#include        <sys/sem.h>

#define SEMKEY  123456L /* key value for semget() */
#define PERMS   0666

static struct sembuf    op_lock[2] = {
        0, 0, 0,        /* wait for sem#0 to become 0 */
        0, 1, 0         /* then increment sem#0 by 1 */
};

static struct sembuf    op_unlock[1] = {
        0, -1, IPC_NOWAIT       /* decrement sem#0 by 1 (sets it to 0) */
};

int     semid = -1;     /* semaphore id */

my_lock(fd)
int     fd;
{
        if (semid < 0) {
```

```
                   if ( (semid = semget(SEMKEY, 1, IPC_CREAT | PERMS)) < 0)
                        err_sys("semget error");
        }
        if (semop(semid, &op_lock[0], 2) < 0)
                err_sys("semop lock error");
}

my_unlock(fd)
int     fd;
{
        if (semop(semid, &op_unlock[0], 1) < 0)
                err_sys("semop unlock error");
}
```

There is a slight problem with this implementation—if the process aborts for some reason while it has the lock, the semaphore value is left at one. Any other process that tries to obtain the lock waits forever when it does the locking semop that first waits for the value to become zero. There are some ways around this.

- A process that has a lock can set up signal handlers to catch all possible signals, and remove the lock before terminating. The only problem with this is that there are some signals that a process can't catch, such as SIGKILL.

- The my_lock function can become more sophisticated. It can specify the IPC_NOWAIT flag on the first operation in the op_lock array. If the semop returns an error with errno equal to EAGAIN, the process can call the semctl system call and look at the sem_ctime value for the semaphore. If some long amount of time has passed since the last change to the semaphore (a few minutes, perhaps) the process can assume that the lock has been abandoned by some other process and can go ahead and remove the lock. The problem with this solution is that it takes an additional system call every time the resource is locked, and we have to guess what amount of time implies that the lock has been left around.

- The third solution is to tell the kernel when we obtain the lock that if this process terminates before releasing the lock, release it for the process.

This third solution is provided by the System V implementation of semaphores. Every semaphore value in the system can optionally have another value associated with it. This other value is maintained by the kernel and is called the *semaphore adjustment value*. The rules for this adjustment value are simple.

1. When a semaphore value is initialized, whether created by semget, or specifically set by semctls SETVAL or SETALL commands, the adjustment value for that particular semaphore value is set to zero. Similarly, when a semaphore is deleted, any adjustment values associated with it are also deleted.

2. For every `semop` operation that specifies the `SEM_UNDO` flag, if the semaphore value goes up, the adjustment value goes down by the same amount. If the semaphore value goes down, the adjustment value goes up by the same amount.

3. When a process `exits`, the kernel automatically applies any adjustment values for that process.

Note that to take advantage of this feature, we must specify the `SEM_UNDO` flag for the corresponding operation. Also, we have to specify the `SEM_UNDO` flag consistently, that is, for both the allocation and deallocation, so that the corresponding adjustment value mirrors the semaphore's value.

We can change our file locking example to use this feature.

```
/*
 * Locking routines using semaphores.
 * Use the SEM_UNDO feature to have the kernel adjust the
 * semaphore value on premature exit.
 */

#include        <sys/types.h>
#include        <sys/ipc.h>
#include        <sys/sem.h>

#define SEMKEY   123456L /* key value for semget() */
#define PERMS    0666

static struct sembuf    op_lock[2] = {
        0, 0, 0,        /* wait for sem#0 to become 0 */
        0, 1, SEM_UNDO  /* then increment sem#0 by 1 */
};

static struct sembuf    op_unlock[1] = {
        0, -1, (IPC_NOWAIT | SEM_UNDO)
                        /* decrement sem#0 by 1 (sets it to 0) */
};

int     semid = -1;     /* semaphore id */

my_lock(fd)
int     fd;
{
        if (semid < 0) {
                if ( (semid = semget(SEMKEY, 1, IPC_CREAT | PERMS)) < 0)
                        err_sys("semget error");
        }
        if (semop(semid, &op_lock[0], 2) < 0)
                err_sys("semop lock error");
}

my_unlock(fd)
int     fd;
{
        if (semop(semid, &op_unlock[0], 1) < 0)
```

```
                       err_sys("semop unlock error");
}
```

There is still a problem with this implementation, the semaphore is never removed from the system. The `main` function that calls our locking functions should call the `semctl` system call with a command argument of `IPC_RMID` before exiting, if it is the last process using the semaphore. Note that the undo feature that we described earlier only assures that the actual semaphore value gets adjusted as required if the process exits prematurely. It does not remove a semaphore that is not used by any active processes.

Simpler Semaphore Operations

The semaphore facility provided by System V is not simple to understand or use. There are some fundamental problems with its implementation.

- The creation of a semaphore with `semget` is independent of its initialization using `semctl`. This can easily lead to race conditions if we are not careful. As we saw in the file locking section of this chapter, when it takes two system calls to do what is logically a single operation, problems arise.

- Unless a semaphore is explicitly removed, it exists within the system, using system resources, until the system is rebooted. It is a remote condition where a semaphore that is not being used by any processes can be of any real use.

To get around these problems, the following functions provide an easier interface to the semaphore system calls. These functions handle the potential race conditions and also remove semaphores when they are no longer used (most of the time—see the comments in the code). We use these functions in the next section, to synchronize the access to shared memory. The technique used by these functions is to create a semaphore set made up of three members.

- The first member is the actual semaphore value that the user initializes, increments, and decrements. Functions are provided to increment and decrement by one, or by some other integer value.

- The second member of the set is used as a counter of the number of processes currently using the semaphore. This is so that the semaphore can be deleted when no more processes use it. Instead of being an actual counter of the number of processes, this member is initialized to a large value (10,000) and decremented every time a new process opens it, and incremented every time a process closes it. By always keeping the value of this member greater than zero, we don't have to worry about any operation on it blocking.

- The third member of the set is a lock variable for the semaphore. This is required to protect from race conditions when the semaphore is being initialized and closed. This lock variable is a binary semaphore that we handle in the same way as the lock variable in the example shown previously in this section. Note that the lock variable is *not* needed when the value of the semaphore is being incremented or decremented. The kernel's `semop` system call handles this just fine. The problems arise in the creation, initialization, and closing of the semaphore.

```
/*
 * Provide an simpler and easier to understand interface to the System V
 * semaphore system calls.  There are 7 routines available to the user:
 *
 *      id = sem_create(key, initval);  # create with initial value or open
 *      id = sem_open(key);             # open (must already exist)
 *      sem_wait(id);                   # wait = P = down by 1
 *      sem_signal(id);                 # signal = V = up by 1
 *      sem_op(id, amount);             # wait    if (amount < 0)
 *                                      # signal if (amount > 0)
 *      sem_close(id);                  # close
 *      sem_rm(id);                     # remove (delete)
 *
 * We create and use a 3-member set for the requested semaphore.
 * The first member, [0], is the actual semaphore value, and the second
 * member, [1], is a counter used to know when all processes have finished
 * with the semaphore.  The counter is initialized to a large number,
 * decremented on every create or open and incremented on every close.
 * This way we can use the "adjust" feature provided by System V so that
 * any process that exit's without calling sem_close() is accounted
 * for.  It doesn't help us if the last process does this (as we have
 * no way of getting control to remove the semaphore) but it will
 * work if any process other than the last does an exit (intentional
 * or unintentional).
 * The third member, [2], of the semaphore set is used as a lock variable
 * to avoid any race conditions in the sem_create() and sem_close()
 * functions.
 */

#include         <sys/types.h>
#include         <sys/ipc.h>
#include         <sys/sem.h>

#include         <errno.h>
extern int       errno;

#define BIGCOUNT         10000              /* initial value of process counter */

/*
 * Define the semaphore operation arrays for the semop() calls.
 */

static struct sembuf    op_lock[2] = {
        2, 0, 0,        /* wait for [2] (lock) to equal 0 */
        2, 1, SEM_UNDO  /* then increment [2] to 1 - this locks it */
                        /* UNDO to release the lock if processes exits
                           before explicitly unlocking */
};
```

```
static struct sembuf   op_endcreate[2] = {
        1, -1, SEM_UNDO,/* decrement [1] (proc counter) with undo on exit */
                        /* UNDO to adjust proc counter if process exits
                            before explicitly calling sem_close() */
        2, -1, SEM_UNDO /* then decrement [2] (lock) back to 0 */
};

static struct sembuf   op_open[1] = {
        1, -1, SEM_UNDO /* decrement [1] (proc counter) with undo on exit */
};

static struct sembuf   op_close[3] = {
        2, 0, 0,        /* wait for [2] (lock) to equal 0 */
        2, 1, SEM_UNDO, /* then increment [2] to 1 - this locks it */
        1, 1, SEM_UNDO  /* then increment [1] (proc counter) */
};

static struct sembuf   op_unlock[1] = {
        2, -1, SEM_UNDO /* decrement [2] (lock) back to 0 */
};

static struct sembuf   op_op[1] = {
        0, 99, SEM_UNDO /* decrement or increment [0] with undo on exit */
                        /* the 99 is set to the actual amount to add
                            or subtract (positive or negative) */
};

/***************************************************************************
 * Create a semaphore with a specified initial value.
 * If the semaphore already exists, we don't initialize it (of course).
 * We return the semaphore ID if all OK, else -1.
 */

int
sem_create(key, initval)
key_t   key;
int     initval;        /* used if we create the semaphore */
{
        register int         id, semval;
        union semun {
                int          val;
                struct semid_ds *buf;
                ushort       *array;
        } semctl_arg;

        if (key == IPC_PRIVATE)
                return(-1);     /* not intended for private semaphores */

        else if (key == (key_t) -1)
                return(-1);     /* probably an ftok() error by caller */

again:
        if ( (id = semget(key, 3, 0666 | IPC_CREAT)) < 0)
                return(-1);     /* permission problem or tables full */
```

```
        /*
         * When the semaphore is created, we know that the value of all
         * 3 members is 0.
         * Get a lock on the semaphore by waiting for [2] to equal 0,
         * then increment it.
         *
         * There is a race condition here.  There is a possibility that
         * between the semget() above and the semop() below, another
         * process can call our sem_close() function which can remove
         * the semaphore if that process is the last one using it.
         * Therefore, we handle the error condition of an invalid
         * semaphore ID specially below, and if it does happen, we just
         * go back and create it again.
         */

        if (semop(id, &op_lock[0], 2) < 0) {
                if (errno == EINVAL)
                        goto again;
                err_sys("can't lock");
        }

        /*
         * Get the value of the process counter.  If it equals 0,
         * then no one has initialized the semaphore yet.
         */

        if ( (semval = semctl(id, 1, GETVAL, 0)) < 0)
                err_sys("can't GETVAL");

        if (semval == 0) {
                /*
                 * We could initialize by doing a SETALL, but that
                 * would clear the adjust value that we set when we
                 * locked the semaphore above.  Instead, we'll do 2
                 * system calls to initialize [0] and [1].
                 */

                semctl_arg.val = initval;
                if (semctl(id, 0, SETVAL, semctl_arg) < 0)
                        err_sys("can SETVAL[0]");

                semctl_arg.val = BIGCOUNT;
                if (semctl(id, 1, SETVAL, semctl_arg) < 0)
                        err_sys("can SETVAL[1]");
        }

        /*
         * Decrement the process counter and then release the lock.
         */

        if (semop(id, &op_endcreate[0], 2) < 0)
                err_sys("can't end create");

        return(id);
```

```
}

/************************************************************************
 * Open a semaphore that must already exist.
 * This function should be used, instead of sem_create(), if the caller
 * knows that the semaphore must already exist.  For example a client
 * from a client-server pair would use this, if its the server's
 * responsibility to create the semaphore.
 * We return the semaphore ID if all OK, else -1.
 */

int
sem_open(key)
key_t   key;
{
        register int    id;

        if (key == IPC_PRIVATE)
                return(-1);     /* not intended for private semaphores */

        else if (key == (key_t) -1)
                return(-1);     /* probably an ftok() error by caller */

        if ( (id = semget(key, 3, 0)) < 0)
                return(-1);     /* doesn't exist, or tables full */

        /*
         * Decrement the process counter.  We don't need a lock
         * to do this.
         */

        if (semop(id, &op_open[0], 1) < 0)
                err_sys("can't open");

        return(id);
}

/************************************************************************
 * Remove a semaphore.
 * This call is intended to be called by a server, for example,
 * when it is being shut down, as we do an IPC_RMID on the semaphore,
 * regardless whether other processes may be using it or not.
 * Most other processes should use sem_close() below.
 */

sem_rm(id)
int     id;
{
        if (semctl(id, 0, IPC_RMID, 0) < 0)
                err_sys("can't IPC_RMID");
}

/************************************************************************
 * Close a semaphore.
```

```
 * Unlike the remove function above, this function is for a process
 * to call before it exits, when it is done with the semaphore.
 * We "decrement" the counter of processes using the semaphore, and
 * if this was the last one, we can remove the semaphore.
 */

sem_close(id)
int     id;
{
        register int    semval;

        /*
         * The following semop() first gets a lock on the semaphore,
         * then increments [1] - the process counter.
         */

        if (semop(id, &op_close[0], 3) < 0)
                err_sys("can't semop");

        /*
         * Now that we have a lock, read the value of the process
         * counter to see if this is the last reference to the
         * semaphore.
         * There is a race condition here - see the comments in
         * sem_create().
         */

        if ( (semval = semctl(id, 1, GETVAL, 0)) < 0)
                err_sys("can't GETVAL");

        if (semval > BIGCOUNT)
                err_dump("sem[1] > BIGCOUNT");
        else if (semval == BIGCOUNT)
                sem_rm(id);
        else
                if (semop(id, &op_unlock[0], 1) < 0)
                        err_sys("can't unlock");        /* unlock */
}

/*******************************************************************************
 * Wait until a semaphore's value is greater than 0, then decrement
 * it by 1 and return.
 * Dijkstra's P operation.  Tanenbaum's DOWN operation.
 */

sem_wait(id)
int     id;
{
        sem_op(id, -1);
}

/*******************************************************************************
 * Increment a semaphore by 1.
 * Dijkstra's V operation.  Tanenbaum's UP operation.
```

```
      */

sem_signal(id)
int     id;
{
        sem_op(id, 1);
}


/***********************************************************************
 * General semaphore operation.  Increment or decrement by a user-specified
 * amount (positive or negative; amount can't be zero).
 */

sem_op(id, value)
int     id;
int     value;
{
        if ( (op_op[0].sem_op = value) == 0)
                err_sys("can't have value == 0");

        if (semop(id, &op_op[0], 1) < 0)
                err_sys("sem_op error");
}
```

File Locking with Semaphores (Again)

We can use these simpler semaphore functions in our locking example. Here we have
changed the main function from the version that was used in all the previous locking
examples, so that here we call sem_create and sem_close outside the main loop.

```
/*
 * Locking example using the simpler semaphore operations.
 */

#include         <sys/types.h>

#define SEQFILE         "seqno"
#define SEMKEY          ((key_t) 23456L)
#define MAXBUFF         100

main()
{
        int     fd, i, n, pid, seqno, semid;
        char    buff[MAXBUFF];

        pid = getpid();
        if ( (fd = open(SEQFILE, 2)) < 0)
                err_sys("can't open %s", SEQFILE);
        if ( (semid = sem_create(SEMKEY, 1)) < 0)
                err_sys("can't open semaphore");

        for (i = 0; i < 20; i++) {
                sem_wait(semid);                        /* get the lock */
```

```
            lseek(fd, 0L, 0);                        /* rewind before read */
            if ( (n = read(fd, buff, MAXBUFF)) <= 0)
                    err_sys("read error");
            buff[n] = '\0';                /* null terminate for sscanf */

            if ( (n = sscanf(buff, "%d\n", &seqno)) != 1)
                    err_sys("sscanf error");
            printf("pid = %d, seq# = %d\n", pid, seqno);

            seqno++;

            sprintf(buff, "%03d\n", seqno);
            n = strlen(buff);
            lseek(fd, 0L, 0);                        /* rewind before write */
            if (write(fd, buff, n) != n)
                    err_sys("write error");

            sem_signal(semid);                       /* release the lock */
        }
        sem_close(semid);
}
```

Semaphore Limits

As with message queues, there are certain system limits with semaphores, some of which can be changed by reconfiguring the kernel. These are shown in Figure 3.23.

Parameter name	AT&T VAX Sys V Rel 2	DEC VAX Ultrix	AT&T Unix PC	Xenix 286	Xenix 386	Description
semmni	10	10	10	10	10	max # of unique semaphore sets, systemwide
semmns	60	60	60	40	40	max # of semaphores, systemwide
semmsl	25	25	25	10	10	max # of semaphores per semaphore set
semopn	10	10	10	5	5	max # of operations per semop call
semmnu	30	30	30	20	20	max # of undo structures, systemwide
semume	10	10	10	5	5	max # of undo entries per undo structure
semvmx	32,767	32,767	32,767	32,766	32,766	max value of any semaphore
semaem	16,384	16,384	16,384	16,384	16,384	max value of any semaphore's adjust-on-exit value

Figure 3.23 Typical limits for semaphores.

3.11 Shared Memory

Consider the normal steps involved in the client–server file copying program that we have been using for the example throughout this chapter.

- The server reads from the input file. Typically the data is read by the kernel into one of its internal block buffers and copied from there to the server's buffer (the second argument to the `read` system call). It should be noted that most Unix systems detect sequential reading, as is done by the server, and try to keep one block ahead of the `read` requests. This helps reduce the clock time required to copy a file, but the data for every `read` is still copied by the kernel from its block buffer to the caller's buffer.

- The server writes this data in a message, using one of the techniques described in this chapter—a pipe, FIFO or message queue. Any of these three forms of IPC require the data to be copied from the user's buffer into the kernel.

- The client reads the data from the IPC channel, again requiring the data be copied from the kernel's IPC buffer to the client's buffer.

- Finally the data is copied from the client's buffer, the second argument to the `write` system call, to the output file. This might involve just copying the data into a kernel buffer and returning, with the kernel doing the actual write operation to the device at some later time.

A total of four copies of the data are required. Additionally, these four copies are done between the kernel and a user process—an *intercontext* copy. While most Unix implementations try to speed up these copies as much as possible, they can still be expensive. Figure 3.24 depicts this data movement between the two processes.

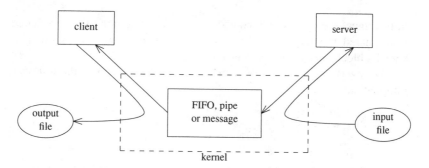

Figure 3.24 Typical movement of data between client and server.

The problem with these forms of IPC—pipes, FIFOs, and message queues—is that for two processes to exchange information, the information has to go through the kernel. Shared memory provides a way around this by letting two or more processes share a memory segment. There is, of course, a problem involved in multiple processes sharing a piece of memory: the processes have to coordinate the use of the memory among themselves. (Sharing a common piece of memory is similar to sharing a disk file, such as the sequence number file used in all the file locking examples.) If one process is reading into some shared memory, for example, other processes must wait for the read to finish before processing the data. Fortunately this is an easy problem to solve, using semaphores for the synchronization.

The steps for the client–server example now become

- The server gets access to a shared memory segment using a semaphore.
- The server reads from the input file into the shared memory segment. The address to read into, the second argument to the `read` system call, points into shared memory.
- When the read is complete the server notifies the client, again using a semaphore.
- The client writes the data from the shared memory segment to the output file.

This is depicted in Figure 3.25.

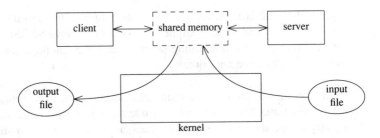

Figure 3.25 Movement of data between client and server using shared memory.

In this figure the data is only copied twice—from the input file into shared memory and from shared memory to the output file. Both of these copies probably involve the kernel's block buffers, as mentioned earlier.

For every shared memory segment, the kernel maintains the following structure of information:

```
#include    <sys/types.h>
#include    <sys/ipc.h>             /* defines the ipc_perm structure */

struct shmid_ds {
    struct ipc_perm shm_perm;       /* operation permission struct */
    int             shm_segsz;      /* segment size */
    struct XXX      shm_YYY;        /* implementation dependent info */
    ushort          shm_lpid;       /* pid of last operation */
    ushort          shm_cpid;       /* creator pid */
    ushort          shm_nattch;     /* current # attached */
    ushort          shm_cnattch;    /* in-core # attached */
```

```
    time_t          shm_atime;   /* last attach time */
    time_t          shm_dtime;   /* last detach time */
    time_t          shm_ctime;   /* last change time */
};
```

The `ipc_perm` structure was described in Section 3.8 and contains the access permissions for the shared memory segment. Unlike message queues and semaphores, we can't describe the actual data structures used by the kernel to point to the shared memory segment, since it is hardware and implementation dependent. The notation XXX and YYY is used in the structure above to note this fact.

A shared memory segment is created, or an existing one is accessed with the `shmget` system call.

```
#include    <sys/types.h>
#include    <sys/ipc.h>
#include    <sys/shm.h>

int shmget(key_t key, int size, int shmflag);
```

The value returned by `shmget` is the shared memory identifier, *shmid*, or −1 if an error occurs. The *size* argument specifies the size of the segment, in bytes. The *shmflag* argument is a combination of the constants shown in Figure 3.26.

Numeric	Symbolic	Description
0400	SHM_R	Read by owner
0200	SHM_W	Write by owner
0040	SHM_R >> 3	Read by group
0020	SHM_W >> 3	Write by group
0004	SHM_R >> 6	Read by world
0002	SHM_W >> 6	Write by world
	IPC_CREAT	(See Section 3.8)
	IPC_EXCL	(See Section 3.8)

Figure 3.26 *shmflag* values for `shmget` system call.

Note that the `shmget` call creates or opens a shared memory segment, but does not provide access to the segment for the calling process. We must attach the shared memory segment by calling the `shmat` system call.

```
#include    <sys/types.h>
#include    <sys/ipc.h>
#include    <sys/shm.h>

char *shmat(int shmid, char *shmaddr, int shmflag);
```

This system call returns the starting address of the shared memory segment. The rules for determining this address are as follows:

- If the *shmaddr* argument is zero, the system selects the address for the caller.

- If the *shmaddr* argument is nonzero, the returned address depends whether the caller specifies the SHM_RND value for the *shmflag* argument:

  - If the SHM_RND value is not specified, the shared memory segment is attached at the address specified by the *shmaddr* argument.

  - If the SHM_RND value is specified, the shared memory segment is attached at the address specified by the *shmaddr* argument, rounded down by the constant SHMLBA (LBA stands for ''lower boundary address'').

For all practical purposes, the only portable calls to shmat specify the *shmaddr* of zero, and let the kernel select the address.

By default, the shared memory segment is attached for both reading and writing by the calling process. The SHM_RDONLY value can also be specified for the *shmflag* argument, specifying ''read-only'' access.

When a process is finished with a shared memory segment, it detaches the segment by calling the shmdt system call.

```
#include   <sys/types.h>
#include   <sys/ipc.h>
#include   <sys/shm.h>

int shmdt(char *shmaddr);
```

This call does not delete the shared memory segment. To remove a shared memory segment, the shmctl system call is used.

```
#include   <sys/types.h>
#include   <sys/ipc.h>
#include   <sys/shm.h>

int shmctl(int shmid, int cmd, struct shmid_ds *buf);
```

A *cmd* of IPC_RMID removes a shared memory segment from the system.

We can now redo our client–server example using shared memory and the simpler semaphore operations developed in the previous section. This code uses a single shared memory segment and two binary semaphores—one named clisem and one named servsem. The server waits until it has control of servsem and then reads from the file directly into the shared memory segment. When the client gets control of its semaphore, it writes from the shared memory to the standard output. The server creates the shared memory segment and the two semaphores, with clisem initialized to one, to allow the client to start things off by reading a filename into the shared memory segment. The two semaphores then alternate between zero and one (when one semaphore value is zero the other value is one, and vice versa) as control of the shared memory toggles between the two processes.

Our header file `shm.h` is

```
#include        "mesg.h"

#define NBUFF   4       /* number of buffers in shared memory */
                        /* (for multiple buffer version) */

#define SHMKEY  ((key_t) 7890) /* base value for shmem key */

#define SEMKEY1 ((key_t) 7891) /* client semaphore key */
#define SEMKEY2 ((key_t) 7892) /* server semaphore key */

#define PERMS   0666
```

The file `mesg.h` is the same file shown earlier that defined the `Mesg` structure. (We'll discuss the NBUFF variable later in this section.)

Here is the server program.

```
#include        <stdio.h>
#include        <sys/types.h>
#include        <sys/ipc.h>
#include        <sys/shm.h>

#include        "shm.h"

int     shmid, clisem, servsem; /* shared memory and semaphore IDs */
Mesg    *mesgptr;               /* ptr to message structure, which is
                                   in the shared memory segment */

main()
{
        /*
         * Create the shared memory segment, if required,
         * then attach it.
         */

        if ( (shmid = shmget(SHMKEY, sizeof(Mesg), PERMS | IPC_CREAT)) < 0)
                err_sys("server: can't get shared memory");
        if ( (mesgptr = (Mesg *) shmat(shmid, (char *) 0, 0)) == (Mesg *) -1)
                err_sys("server: can't attach shared memory");

        /*
         * Create two semaphores.  The client semaphore starts out at 1
         * since the client process starts things going.
         */

        if ( (clisem = sem_create(SEMKEY1, 1)) < 0)
                err_sys("server: can't create client semaphore");
        if ( (servsem = sem_create(SEMKEY2, 0)) < 0)
                err_sys("server: can't create server semaphore");

        server();
```

```
        /*
         * Detach the shared memory segment and close the semaphores.
         * The client is the last one to use the shared memory, so
         * it'll remove it when it's done.
         */

        if (shmdt(mesgptr) < 0)
                err_sys("server: can't detach shared memory");

        sem_close(clisem);
        sem_close(servsem);

        exit(0);
}

server()
{
        int     n, filefd;
        char    errmesg[256], *sys_err_str();

        /*
         * Wait for the client to write the filename into shared memory.
         */

        sem_wait(servsem);        /* we'll wait here for client to start things */

        mesgptr->mesg_data[mesgptr->mesg_len] = '\0';
                                        /* null terminate filename */

        if ( (filefd = open(mesgptr->mesg_data, 0)) < 0) {
                /*
                 * Error.  Format an error message and send it back
                 * to the client.
                 */

                sprintf(errmesg, ": can't open, %s\n", sys_err_str());
                strcat(mesgptr->mesg_data, errmesg);
                mesgptr->mesg_len = strlen(mesgptr->mesg_data);
                sem_signal(clisem);            /* send to client */
                sem_wait(servsem);             /* wait for client to process */

        } else {
                /*
                 * Read the data from the file right into shared memory.
                 * The -1 in the number-of-bytes-to-read is because some
                 * Unices have a bug if you try and read into the final byte
                 * of a shared memory segment.
                 */

                while ( (n = read(filefd, mesgptr->mesg_data,
                                                MAXMESGDATA-1)) > 0) {
                        mesgptr->mesg_len = n;
                        sem_signal(clisem);     /* send to client */
                        sem_wait(servsem);      /* wait for client to process */
```

```
                    }
                    close(filefd);
                    if (n < 0)
                            err_sys("server: read error");
          }

          /*
           * Send a message with a length of 0 to signify the end.
           */

          mesgptr->mesg_len = 0;
          sem_signal(clisem);
}
```

Note that unlike the earlier versions of this program, the shared memory version defines a pointer to a Mesg structure (the mesgptr variable), not a structure itself. The actual structure is allocated by the system in the shared memory segment.

Here is the client program.

```
#include         <stdio.h>
#include         <sys/types.h>
#include         <sys/ipc.h>
#include         <sys/shm.h>

#include         "shm.h"

int     shmid, clisem, servsem; /* shared memory and semaphore IDs */
Mesg    *mesgptr;                       /* ptr to message structure, which is
                                           in the shared memory segment */

main()
{
          /*
           * Get the shared memory segment and attach it.
           * The server must have already created it.
           */

          if ( (shmid = shmget(SHMKEY, sizeof(Mesg), 0)) < 0)
                  err_sys("client: can't get shared memory segment");
          if ( (mesgptr = (Mesg *) shmat(shmid, (char *) 0, 0)) == (Mesg *) -1)
                  err_sys("client: can't attach shared memory segment");

          /*
           * Open the two semaphores.  The server must have
           * created them already.
           */

          if ( (clisem = sem_open(SEMKEY1)) < 0)
                  err_sys("client: can't open client semaphore");
          if ( (servsem = sem_open(SEMKEY2)) < 0)
                  err_sys("client: can't open server semaphore");

          client();
```

```
        /*
         * Detach and remove the shared memory segment and
         * close the semaphores.
         */

        if (shmdt(mesgptr) < 0)
                err_sys("client: can't detach shared memory");
        if (shmctl(shmid, IPC_RMID, (struct shmid_ds *) 0) < 0)
                err_sys("client: can't remove shared memory");

        sem_close(clisem);      /* will remove the semaphore */
        sem_close(servsem);     /* will remove the semaphore */

        exit(0);
}

client()
{
        int     n;

        /*
         * Read the filename from standard input, write it to shared memory.
         */

        sem_wait(clisem);                       /* get control of shared memory */
        if (fgets(mesgptr->mesg_data, MAXMESGDATA, stdin) == NULL)
                err_sys("filename read error");

        n = strlen(mesgptr->mesg_data);
        if (mesgptr->mesg_data[n-1] == '\n')
                n--;                            /* ignore newline from fgets() */
        mesgptr->mesg_len = n;
        sem_signal(servsem);                    /* wake up server */

        /*
         * Wait for the server to place something in shared memory.
         */

        sem_wait(clisem);                       /* wait for server to process */
        while( (n = mesgptr->mesg_len) > 0) {
                if (write(1, mesgptr->mesg_data, n) != n)
                        err_sys("data write error");
                sem_signal(servsem);    /* wake up server */
                sem_wait(clisem);       /* wait for server to process */
        }

        if (n < 0)
                err_sys("data read error");
}
```

The two processes wait for access to the shared memory by waiting for a semaphore's value to become greater than zero. This is the most efficient way to wait for the resource, since it is the kernel that does all semaphore operations and the kernel puts a process to sleep when it has to wait for a semaphore. While the process is asleep, the kernel can allocate the CPU to other processes that are ready to run. Some books show what is called *busy–waiting* when a process needs to wait for an event. The process doesn't go to sleep, it just keeps trying to obtain the resource, over and over again, until it gets it. For example, we could add another variable to the `Mesg` structure and use this as a flag to indicate which process has control of the shared memory segment. If the flag were zero, perhaps, the client is using it, while if it were one the server could use it. Instead of executing

```
sem_signal(clisem);
sem_wait(servesm);
```

in the server loop, it could execute

```
mesgptr->mesg_flag = 0;          /* signal client */
while (mesgptr->mesg_flag == 0)
        ;                        /* wait for client to process */
```

if `mesg_flag` were the busy–wait flag in the `Mesg` structure. The corresponding code in the client loop becomes

```
mesgptr->mesg_flag = 1;          /* signal server */
while (mesgptr->mesg_flag == 1)
        ;                        /* wait for server to process */
```

While this approach works, semaphores should always be used for this type of synchronization. A busy–wait loop is a waste of CPU resources.

Multiple Buffers

In a typical program that processes some data we find a loop of the form

```
while ( (n = read(fdin, buff, BUFFSIZE)) > 0) {
        /* process the data */
        write(fdout, buff, n);
}
```

Many programs that process a text file, for example, read a line of input, process that line, and write a line of output. For text files, the calls to `read` and `write` are normally replaced with calls to the standard I/O functions `fgets` and `fputs`.

If we look at a process that reads data and then writes it out we have the time line shown in Figure 3.27. We have labeled the time line with numbers on the left, designating some arbitrary units of time.

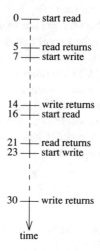

Figure 3.27 Time line for single-process read–write example.

Time increases downward. We have assumed that a read operation takes 5 units of time, a write takes 7 units of time, and the processing time between the read and write consumes 2 units of time.

If we divide the processing into two processes, as we've done with the client–server example in this chapter, we have the time line shown in Figure 3.28.

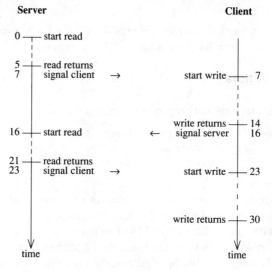

Figure 3.28 Time line for two processes doing read–write example.

This time line assumes that there is a single shared memory segment for the client and server processes. We assume here that the time to process the data in the buffer, along with the signaling of the other process takes 2 units of time. The important thing to note is that dividing the reading and writing into two processes does not affect the total amount of time required to do the operation. We have not gained any speed advantage.

There are many fine points that we are ignoring in these time lines. For example, Unix systems detect sequential reading of a file and do asynchronous *read ahead* of the next disk block for the reading process. This can improve the actual amount of time, called "clock time," that it takes to perform this type of operation. We are also ignoring the effect of other processes on our reading and writing processes, and the effects of the operating system's scheduling algorithms. Our goal is to describe the concept of double buffering and see how it affects the clock time for a typical process.

Unix I/O is termed *synchronous*. A `read` or `write` system call does not return to the calling process until the operation is complete and the requested data has been copied by the kernel, either into the buffer for a `read`, or from the buffer for a `write`. The data might only be copied to or from a buffer in the kernel. There is no guarantee for typical disk I/O that the data is really read from the disk or written to the disk. Indeed, the read ahead mechanism mentioned above often causes the kernel to already have the data in one of its buffers. A similar operation on `writes`, termed *write behind*, allows the kernel to write the data to the disk at some later time.

Some operating systems provide *asynchronous I/O*. This allows a process to execute a system call to start an I/O operation and have the system call return immediately after the operation is started or queued. Another system call is required to wait for the operation to complete (or return immediately if the operation is already finished). The advantage of asynchronous I/O is that a process can overlap its execution with its I/O, or it can overlap I/O between different devices. While this typically doesn't have a great effect on a process that is reading from a disk file and writing to another disk file, asynchronous I/O can provide significant performance improvements for other types of I/O driven programs—a program that dumps a disk to a magnetic tape, a program that displays an image on an image display. Even though Unix does not provide asynchronous I/O we can gain the same performance improvements by splitting our processing into multiple processes and have them share more than one buffer.

Now consider the example from above, but with the client and server using two buffers. This is shown in Figure 3.29. The server first reads into buffer 1, then signals the client that buffer 1 is ready for processing. The server then starts reading into buffer 2, while the client is writing buffer 1. Note that we can't go any faster than the slowest operation, which in our example is the write. Once the server has completed the first two reads, it has to wait the additional 2 units of time that is the time difference between the write (7) and the read (5). The total clock time, however, will be almost halved for the double buffer case, compared to the single buffered case, for our hypothetical example.

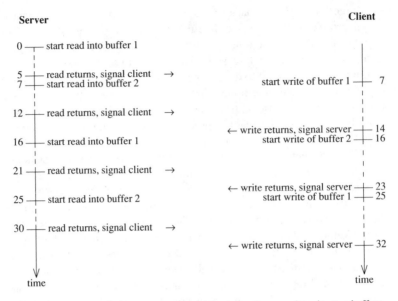

Figure 3.29 Time line for two processes doing read–write example, using two buffers.

We now show the client–server example using multiple buffers. The code was written for NBUFF buffers, not just for two buffers. Typically it is wise, when converting a single resource program to a 2-resource program, to develop an N-resource solution instead. The extra effort required to develop a solution to the N-resource case is often worth it, as many times generalizing a problem makes the solution "cleaner." By this we mean the solution is often more general and avoids magic numbers and special case handling.

The server program is

```
#include        <stdio.h>
#include        <sys/types.h>
#include        <sys/ipc.h>
#include        <sys/shm.h>

#include        "shm.h"

int     clisem, servsem;        /* semaphore IDs */

int     shmid[NBUFF];           /* shared memory IDs */
Mesg    *mesgptr[NBUFF];        /* ptr to message structures, which are
                                   in the shared memory segment */

main()
{
        register int    i;

        /*
         * Get the shared memory segments and attach them.
```

```
         */

        for (i = 0; i < NBUFF; i++) {
                if ( (shmid[i] = shmget(SHMKEY + i, sizeof(Mesg),
                                                PERMS | IPC_CREAT)) < 0)
                        err_sys("server: can't get shared memory %d", i);
                if ( (mesgptr[i] = (Mesg *) shmat(shmid[i], (char *) 0, 0))
                                                        == (Mesg *) -1)
                        err_sys("server: can't attach shared memory %d", i);
        }

        /*
         * Create the two semaphores.
         */

        if ( (clisem = sem_create(SEMKEY1, 1)) < 0)
                err_sys("server: can't create client semaphore");
        if ( (servsem = sem_create(SEMKEY2, 0)) < 0)
                err_sys("server: can't create server semaphore");

        server();

        /*
         * Detach the shared memory segments and close the semaphores.
         * We let the client remove the shared memory segments,
         * since it'll be the last one to use them.
         */

        for (i = 0; i < NBUFF; i++) {
                if (shmdt(mesgptr[i]) < 0)
                        err_sys("server: can't detach shared memory %d", i);
        }

        sem_close(clisem);
        sem_close(servsem);

        exit(0);
}

server()
{
        register int    i, n, filefd;
        char            errmesg[256], *sys_err_str();

        /*
         * Wait for the client to write the filename into shared memory,
         * then try to open the file.
         */

        sem_wait(servsem);
        mesgptr[0]->mesg_data[mesgptr[0]->mesg_len] = '\0';
                                        /* null terminate filename */
        if ( (filefd = open(mesgptr[0]->mesg_data, 0)) < 0) {
                /*
```

```
                        * Error.  Format an error message and send it back
                        * to the client.
                        */

                       sprintf(errmesg, ": can't open, %s\n", sys_err_str());
                       strcat(mesgptr[0]->mesg_data, errmesg);
                       mesgptr[0]->mesg_len = strlen(mesgptr[0]->mesg_data);
                       sem_signal(clisem);     /* wake up client */

                       sem_wait(servsem);      /* wait for client to process */
                       mesgptr[1]->mesg_len = 0;
                       sem_signal(clisem);     /* wake up client */

            } else {
                       /*
                        * Initialize the server semaphore to the number
                        * of buffers.  We know its value is 0 now, since
                        * it was initialized to 0, and the client has done a
                        * sem_signal(), followed by our sem_wait() above.
                        * What we do is increment the semaphore value
                        * once for every buffer (i.e., the number of resources
                        * that we have).
                        */

                       for (i = 0; i < NBUFF; i++)
                               sem_signal(servsem);

                       /*
                        * Read the data from the file right into shared memory.
                        * The -1 in the number-of-bytes-to-read is because some
                        * Unices have a bug if you try and read into the final byte
                        * of a shared memory segment.
                        */

                       for ( ; ; ) {
                               for (i = 0; i < NBUFF; i++) {
                                       sem_wait(servsem);
                                       n = read(filefd, mesgptr[i]->mesg_data,
                                                               MAXMESGDATA-1);
                                       if (n < 0)
                                               err_sys("server: read error");
                                       mesgptr[i]->mesg_len = n;
                                       sem_signal(clisem);
                                       if (n == 0)
                                               goto alldone;
                               }
                       }
alldone:
                       /* we've already written the 0-length final buffer */
                       close(filefd);
            }
}
```

The client program is

```
#include        <stdio.h>
#include        <sys/types.h>
#include        <sys/ipc.h>
#include        <sys/shm.h>

#include        "shm.h"

int     clisem, servsem;        /* semaphore IDs */

int     shmid[NBUFF];           /* shared memory IDs */
Mesg    *mesgptr[NBUFF];        /* ptr to message structures, which are
                                   in the shared memory segment */

main()
{
        register int    i;

        /*
         * Get the shared memory segments and attach them.
         * We don't specify IPC_CREAT, assuming the server creates them.
         */

        for (i = 0; i < NBUFF; i++) {
                if ( (shmid[i] = shmget(SHMKEY + i, sizeof(Mesg), 0)) < 0)
                        err_sys("client: can't get shared memory %d", i);
                if ( (mesgptr[i] = (Mesg *) shmat(shmid[i], (char *) 0, 0))
                                                        == (Mesg *) -1)
                        err_sys("client: can't attach shared memory %d", i);
        }

        /*
         * Open the two semaphores.
         */

        if ( (clisem = sem_open(SEMKEY1)) < 0)
                err_sys("client: can't open client semaphore");
        if ( (servsem = sem_open(SEMKEY2)) < 0)
                err_sys("client: can't open server semaphore");

        client();

        /*
         * Detach and remove the shared memory segments and
         * close the semaphores.
         */

        for (i = 0; i < NBUFF; i++) {
                if (shmdt(mesgptr[i]) < 0)
                        err_sys("client: can't detach shared memory %d", i);
                if (shmctl(shmid[i], IPC_RMID, (struct shmid_ds *) 0) < 0)
                        err_sys("client: can't remove shared memory %d", i);
        }
```

```
        sem_close(clisem);
        sem_close(servsem);

        exit(0);
}

client()
{
        int     i, n;

        /*
         * Read the filename from standard input, write it to shared memory.
         */

        sem_wait(clisem);                   /* wait for server to initialize */
        if (fgets(mesgptr[0]->mesg_data, MAXMESGDATA, stdin) == NULL)
                err_sys("filename read error");

        n = strlen(mesgptr[0]->mesg_data);
        if (mesgptr[0]->mesg_data[n-1] == '\n')
                n--;                        /* ignore newline from fgets() */
        mesgptr[0]->mesg_len = n;
        sem_signal(servsem);                /* wake up server */

        for ( ; ; ) {
                for (i = 0; i < NBUFF; i++) {
                        sem_wait(clisem);
                        if ( (n = mesgptr[i]->mesg_len) <= 0)
                                goto alldone;
                        if (write(1, mesgptr[i]->mesg_data, n) != n)
                                err_sys("data write error");
                        sem_signal(servsem);
                }
        }

alldone:
        if (n < 0)
                err_sys("data read error");
}
```

One change that could be made is to allocate a single shared memory segment whose size is NBUFF `*` `sizeof(Mesg)`, instead of NBUFF segments.

Shared Memory Limits

As with message queues and semaphores, there are certain system limits on shared memory. Typical values are shown in Figure 3.30. Some of these can be changed by a system administrator, by configuring a new kernel. Compared to the other forms of IPC described in this chapter (pipes, FIFOs, message queues, and semaphores), there is a greater potential for writing nonportable code when using shared memory, so portability must be kept in mind.

Parameter name	AT&T VAX Sys V Rel 2	DEC VAX Ultrix	AT&T Unix PC	Xenix 386	Description
shmmax	131,072	131,072	65,536	4,194,304	maximum size in bytes of a shared memory segment
shmmin	1	1	1	1	minimum size in bytes of a shared memory segment
shmmni	100	100	100	25	max # of shared memory segments, systemwide
shmseg	6	6	6	6	max # of shared memory segments attached per process
shmbrk	8,192	32,768	8,192	0	(see text)

Figure 3.30 Typical limits for shared memory.

The shmbrk value needs some additional explanation. Referring to Figure 2.2, shared memory is normally allocated by the system above the heap. If shared memory starts too close to the heap, we won't be able to obtain additional memory dynamically, using either the malloc function in the standard C library or the brk or sbrk system calls. The shmbrk value specifies the number of bytes between the end of the heap (when the first shared memory segment is allocated) and the start of the first shared memory segment. If a process wants to increase the distance between the top of the heap and the first shared memory segment (to allow for future calls to malloc after the shared memory has been created), it can call malloc before creating the first shared memory segment.

3.12 Sockets and TLI

Sockets are a form of IPC provided by 4.3BSD that provide communication between processes on a single system and between processes on different systems. One type of socket—the Unix domain socket—is used for IPC between processes on a single system. Pipes are implemented in 4.3BSD using a Unix domain socket.

Describing the system calls that pertain to sockets requires additional understanding of the communication protocols that are available to the socket, so we defer our description of sockets until Chapter 6.

TLI stands for *transport layer interface* and is a form of IPC provided with System V Release 3.0. As a form of IPC, TLI is similar to Berkeley sockets in that it provides communication between processes on the same system or on different systems. We defer our discussion of TLI until Chapter 7.

3.13 Summary

IPC has traditionally been a messy area in Unix. Various solutions have been implemented, none of which are perfect. We first covered record locking and file locking, since the sharing of a single file between multiple processes is a common occurrence. We then examined numerous IPC techniques—pipes, FIFOs, message queues, semaphores, and shared memory—and will cover two more in Chapters 6 and 7. You must evaluate your needs for both IPC and portability, and choose the best technique available.

In Chapter 17 we'll examine some typical performance values for the various IPC techniques.

We'll encounter IPC in many of the examples later in the text. For example, IPC, record locking, and network programming will all come together in our discussion of the 4.3BSD line printer spooler in Chapter 13.

Exercises

3.1 Implement one of the filesystem based locking techniques from Section 3.2, say the technique that uses the `link` system call, and compare the amount of time required for this, versus actual file locking.

3.2 Under System V Release 3.2 or later, write a program that uses record locking. Use the program to verify that advisory locking is only advisory. Then modify the file's access bits to enable mandatory record locking and use the program to verify that the locking is now mandatory.

3.3 Why is a signal generated for the writer of a pipe or FIFO when the other end disappears, and not for the reader of a pipe or FIFO when its writer disappears?

3.4 Use the multiple buffer technique in Section 3.11 to write a program that copies between two different devices—a disk file and a tape drive, for example. First measure the operation when only a single buffer is used, then measure the operation for different values of NBUFF, say 2, 3, and 4. Compare the results. Where do you think most of the overhead is when multiple buffers are used?

3.5 What happens with the client–server example using message queues, if the file to be copied is a binary file? What happens to the version that uses the `popen` function if the file is a binary file?

3.6 For the multiple buffer, shared memory example in Section 3.11, draw a time line showing which process (client or server) is using which buffer, along with the values of the two semaphores. Assume NBUFF is 3.

4

A Network Primer

We have to define some basic networking terms and concepts before they are used in later chapters. When necessary, we jump ahead and use specific examples from the next chapter, to provide actual network examples, instead of trying to describe everything in a generic, abstract sense. Tanenbaum [1989] provides additional details on many of the networking topics discussed in this chapter.

Internetworking

A *computer network* is a communication system for connecting end-systems. We often refer to the end-systems as *hosts*. The hosts can range in size from small microcomputers to the largest supercomputers. Some hosts on a computer network are dedicated systems, such as print servers or file servers, without any capabilities for interactive users. Other hosts might be single-user personal computers, while others might be general purpose time-sharing systems.

A *local area network*, or *LAN*, connects computer systems that are close together—typically within a single building, but possibly up to a few kilometers apart. Popular technologies today for LANs are Ethernet and token ring. LANs typically operate at high speeds—an Ethernet operates at 10 Mbps (million bits per second) while IBM's token ring operates at both 4 and 16 Mbps. Newer LAN technologies, such as FDDI (Fiber Distributed Data Interface), use fiber optics and have a data rate of 100 Mbps. Each computer on a LAN has an interface card of some form that connects it to the actual network hardware. (Be aware that these raw network speeds are usually not realized in actual data transfers. In Chapter 17 we'll discuss some actual performance measurements.)

A *wide area network* or *WAN* connects computers in different cities or countries. These networks are sometimes referred to as *long haul networks*. A common technology for WANs is leased telephone lines operating between 9600 bps (bits per second) and 1.544 Mbps (million bits per second).

Between the LAN and WAN is the *metropolitan area network* or *MAN*. These cover an entire city or metropolitan area and frequently operate at LAN speeds. Common technologies are coaxial cable (similar to cable TV) and microwave.

An *internet* or *internetwork* is the connection of two or more distinct networks so that computers on one network are able to communicate with computers on another network. The goal of internetworking is to hide the details of what might be different physical networks, so that the internet functions as a coordinated unit. One way to connect two distinct physical networks is to have a *gateway* that is attached to both networks. This gateway must pass information from one network to the other. It is sometimes called a *router*. As an example, Figure 4.1 shows an internet formed from two distinct networks.

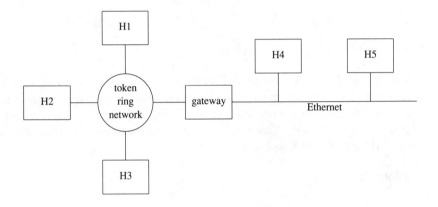

Figure 4.1   Internet example with two networks joined by a gateway.

There are three hosts on the token ring, H1, H2, and H3, and two hosts on the Ethernet, H4 and H5. There is a gateway between the two physical networks, and it must contain an interface card to attach to the token ring network and another interface card to attach to the Ethernet. It must also determine when information arriving on the Ethernet is destined for a host on the token ring (and vice versa), and handle it appropriately.

There are more ways to connect networks together. The term we use to describe the interconnection depends on the layer in the OSI model at which the connection takes place.

- *Repeaters* operate at the physical layer (layer 1) and typically just copy electrical signals (including noise) from one segment of a network to the next. Repeaters are often used with Ethernets, for example, to connect two cable segments together to form a single network.

- *Bridges* often operate at the data-link layer (layer 2) and they copy frames from one network to the next. Bridges often contain logic so that they only copy a subset of the frames they receive.

- *Routers* operate at the network layer (layer 3). The term router implies that this entity not only moves information (packets) from one network to another, but it can also make decisions about what route the information should take. (We talk more about routing later in this chapter.)

- *Gateway* is a generic term that refers to an entity used to interconnect two or more networks. In the TCP/IP community, for example, the term gateway refers to a network level router. The term gateway is sometimes used to describe software that performs specific conversions at layers above the network layer. For example, there are various mail gateways that convert electronic mail from one format to another. We mention an application-gateway in Section 5.6 that converts file transfer requests between the OSI FTAM protocol and the TCP/IP FTP protocol. We'll use the term gateway to describe a network level router, unless stated otherwise.

Repeaters are usually hardware devices, while bridges and routers can be implemented in either hardware or software. A router (gateway) is usually a dedicated system that only does this function. 4.2BSD, however, was the first general-purpose system that could also operate as a gateway.

A host is said to be *multihomed* if it has more than one network interface. For example, a host with an Ethernet interface and a token ring interface would be multihomed.

Looking at the different levels of abstraction, we go from a user sitting at a terminal to an internet.

- *Users* login to a host computer.

- *Host* computers are connected to a network.

- *Networks* are connected together to form an internet.

An internet of computer networks is similar in principle to the international long distance telephone service that is available today. Telephones are connected to a local phone company, which in turn is connected into a national long distance network, which is then connected into an international network. When you direct dial an international call, this "telephone internet" hides all the details and connects all the telephones into a coordinated unit. This is the goal of an internet of computer networks.

OSI Model, Protocols, and Layering

The computers in a network use well-defined *protocols* to communicate. A protocol is a set of rules and conventions between the communicating participants. Since these protocols can be complex, they are designed in layers, to make their implementation more manageable. Figure 4.2 shows the OSI model that was introduced in Section 1.3.

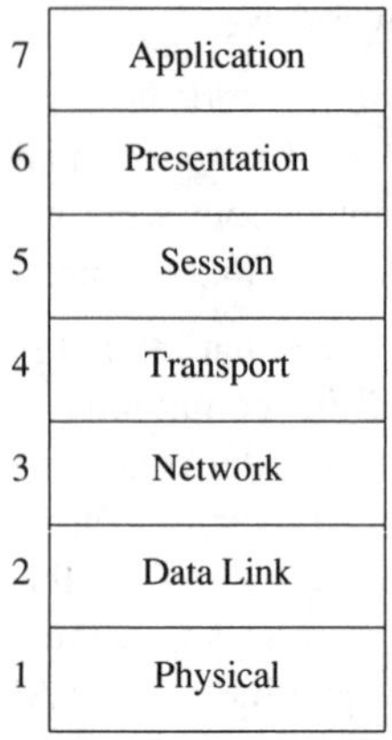

7	Application
6	Presentation
5	Session
4	Transport
3	Network
2	Data Link
1	Physical

Figure 4.2 OSI model.

This model, developed between 1977 and 1984, is a guide, not a specification. It provides a framework in which standards can be developed for the services and protocols at each layer. Indeed, the networks that we consider in this text (TCP/IP, XNS, and SNA) were developed before the OSI model. We will compare the layers for these actual networks against the OSI model, but realize that no network is implemented exactly as the OSI model shows.

One advantage of layering is to provide well-defined interfaces between the layers, so that a change in one layer doesn't affect an adjacent layer. It is important to understand that protocols exist at each layer. A *protocol suite* is a collection of protocols from more than one layer that forms the basis of a useful network. This collection is also referred to as a *protocol family*. The protocol suites that we describe in Chapter 5 are

- the TCP/IP protocol suite (the DARPA Internet protocols),
- Xerox Network Systems (Xerox NS or XNS),
- IBM's Systems Network Architecture (SNA),
- IBM's NetBIOS,
- the OSI protocols,
- UUCP.

Each of these protocol suites define different protocols at different layers, as we see in the next chapter.

Recall from Section 1.5 that we simplified the OSI model into a 4-layer model that we use in the text. Figure 4.3 shows this model for two systems that are connected with a network.

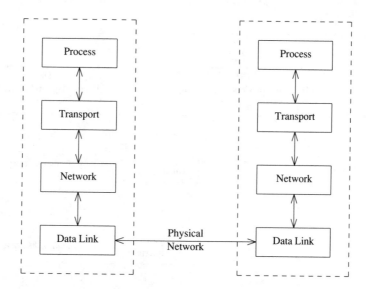

Figure 4.3 Simplified 4-layer model connecting two systems.

The layers that define a protocol suite are the two boxes called the *transport layer* and the *network layer*. The multiple layers that define the network and hardware characteristics (Ethernet, token ring, etc.) are grouped together into our *data-link* layer. Application programs exist at the *process layer*. It is the interface between the transport layer and the process layer that we describe in Chapters 6 and 7.

Let's jump ahead to provide a concrete example for layering and some of the other concepts described in this chapter. Figure 4.4 shows the layering used by the TCP/IP protocol suite.

Consider one specific user process whose protocol is defined by the TCP/IP protocol suite, TFTP, the Trivial File Transfer Protocol. This application allows a user on one system to send and receive files to and from another system. TFTP uses UDP (User Datagram Protocol), which in turn uses IP (Internet Protocol), to exchange data with the other host.

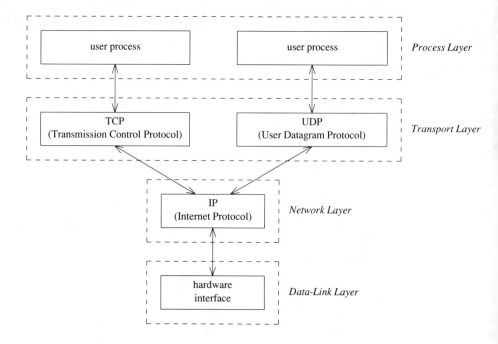

Figure 4.4 TCP/IP protocol suite using 4-layer model.

If we consider two hosts connected with an Ethernet, Figure 4.5 shows the four layers.

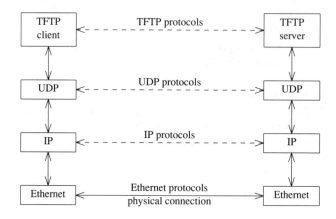

Figure 4.5 4-layer model for TFTP over UDP/IP on an Ethernet.

We show the protocols between the top three boxes with dashed lines to indicate that the boxes at these three layers communicate ''virtually'' with each other using the indicated protocols. Realize that only the boxes at the lowest layer physically communicate with each other. We call these horizontal lines between layers at the same level *peer-to-peer protocols*. The actual flow of data is from the TFTP box on one side, down to the UDP box, down to the IP box, down to the Ethernet box, then across the physical link to the other side and up.

Another goal of layering, besides making the protocol suite easier to understand, is to allow us to replace the contents of a layer with something else that provides the same functionality. With the example shown in Figure 4.5, if we are able to connect the two computer systems with a token ring network, we would have the layers shown in Figure 4.6.

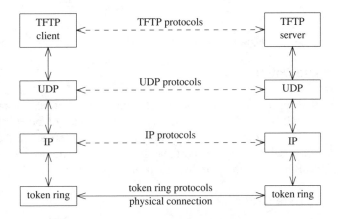

Figure 4.6 4-layer model for TFTP over UDP/IP on a token ring.

The TFTP protocols do not have to change at all between this network and the previous one that used an Ethernet. Similarly, the UDP/IP protocols do not have to change either.

We can take this example one step further and replace the middle two boxes that use the UDP/IP protocols from the TCP/IP protocol suite, with boxes that use the PEX/IDP protocols from the Xerox NS protocol suite. If this were done using an Ethernet connection between the two systems, we would have the layers shown in Figure 4.7. Again, the TFTP protocols do not have to change at all between the version that uses the UDP/IP protocols and the version that uses the Xerox PEX/IDP protocols.

In Chapter 12 we develop a complete implementation of a TFTP client and server and implement it using different transport protocols.

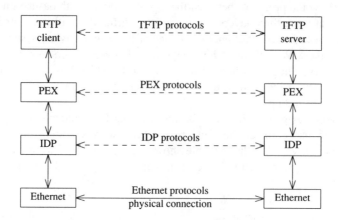

Figure 4.7   4-layer model for TFTP over PEX/IDP on an Ethernet.

Bytes and Octets

A term that appears in the networking literature is *octet*, which means an 8-bit quantity of data. We will consistently use the term *byte* instead of octet. The term octet arose because some computer systems, notably the DEC-10 series and the Control Data Cyber series, don't use 8-bit bytes. Fortunately, however, virtually all modern computers use 8-bit bytes, so we use the term byte to mean an 8-bit byte.

Network Byte Order

Unfortunately, not all computers store the bytes that comprise a multibyte value in the same order. While the problems with systems that don't use 8-bit bytes are slowly disappearing, as these older systems fade into history, the problems with byte ordering will be with us for a long time, as there is no clear standard.

Consider a 16-bit integer that is made up of 2 bytes. There are two ways to store this value: with the low-order byte at the starting address, known as *little endian*, or with the high-order byte at the starting address, known as *big endian*. The first case is shown in Figure 4.8.

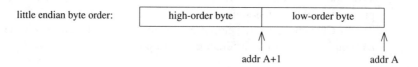

Figure 4.8   Little endian byte order for a 16-bit quantity.

Here we are looking at increasing memory addresses going from *right to left*. The reasoning behind this byte ordering is that a lower address implies a lower order byte.

The big endian format can be pictured as in Figure 4.9.

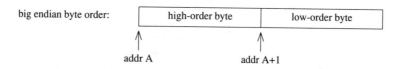

Figure 4.9 Big endian byte order for a 16-bit quantity.

Here we are looking at increasing memory addresses going from *left to right*.

The byte ordering used by some current computer systems is shown in Figure 4.10.

big endian:	IBM 370, Motorola 68000, Pyramid
little endian:	Intel 80x86 (IBM PC), DEC VAX, DEC PDP-11

Figure 4.10 Byte ordering used by different systems.

The byte ordering with 32-bit integers is even worse, as some systems swap the two 16-bit pieces of the 32-bit integer.

The solution to this problem is for a network protocol to specify its *network byte order*. The TCP/IP, XNS, and SNA protocols all use the big endian format for the 16-bit integers and 32-bit integers that they maintain in the protocol headers. (Fortunately the protocols maintain only integer fields, as the differences in the internal formats for floating point data are even worse.) The protocol has no control over the format of the data that the applications transfer across the network—the protocol only specifies the format for the fields that it maintains. We will be concerned with the network byte ordering of multibyte integer fields in Chapter 6 when we discuss the interface between a user process and the networking software. We also return to the problem of application data format in Chapter 18 when we discuss remote procedure calls.

Encapsulation

Let's again consider the TFTP application, using the UDP/IP protocols, between two systems connected with an Ethernet. If there are 400 bytes for the TFTP client process to transfer to the TFTP server process, the TFTP client process adds 4 bytes of control information to the beginning of the data buffer, before passing the data down one layer to the UDP layer. This addition of control information to data is called *encapsulation* and is shown in Figure 4.11.

The UDP layer does not interpret the 4-byte TFTP header at all. The task of the UDP layer is to transfer 404 bytes of data to the other UDP layer. The UDP layer then prepends its own 8-byte header and passes the 412-byte buffer to the IP layer. The IP

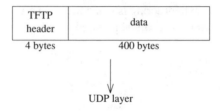

Figure 4.11   Encapsulation of user data by TFTP.

layer prepends its 20-byte header and passes the 432-byte buffer to the data-link layer for the Ethernet. At this layer a 14-byte header and a 4-byte trailer are added to the buffer of information. Figure 4.12 shows this encapsulation by each layer.

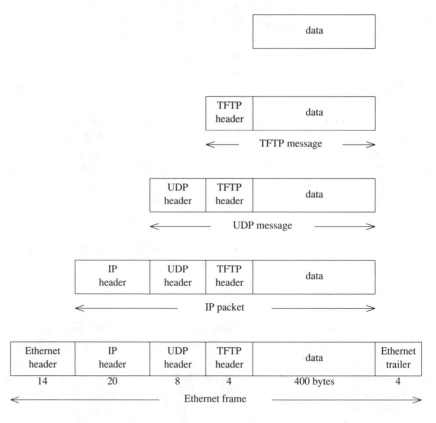

Figure 4.12   Encapsulation of TFTP over UDP/IP on an Ethernet.

The final diagram shows the Ethernet frame that is physically transmitted across the Ethernet, along with the sizes of each of the headers and trailers, in bytes.

We define the units of information that are passed along a network according to the layer at which the transfer is taking place. This is shown in Figure 4.13.

7	Application	*message*
6	Presentation	*message*
5	Session	*message*
4	Transport	*message*
3	Network	*packets*
2	Data Link	*frames*
1	Physical	*bits*

Figure 4.13 OSI model with units of information exchanged at each layer.

We call the unit of interchange at the network layer *packets*. At the data-link layer we call them *frames*, and at the lowest layer, the physical layer, *bits* are exchanged.

Multiplexing and Demultiplexing

Multiplexing means to combine many into one, and we have examples of this happening at most layers in a network. Consider the multihomed, multiuser computer system shown in Figure 4.14. This figure shows applications using both UDP and TCP from the TCP/IP protocol suite along with PEX and SPP from the Xerox NS protocol suite. Both of these protocol suites can use a single Ethernet. There are many points to be made from Figure 4.14.

- A user process can use different protocols at the same time. For example, process B is using both UDP and TCP at the same time. Similarly, process D is using TCP and PEX.

- More than one user process at a time can be using any of the user-accessible protocols (UDP, TCP, PEX, or SPP). This requires that a given protocol box, the UDP box for example, must identify the user process (A or B) that is sending data when the UDP software passes this data down to the IP layer. This is one example of *multiplexing*. Conversely, when the UDP software receives data from the IP layer, it must be able to identify the user process to receive the data. This is *demultiplexing*. For these examples, both UDP and TCP have a 16-bit port number that identifies the user process. We discuss this field in the next chapter.

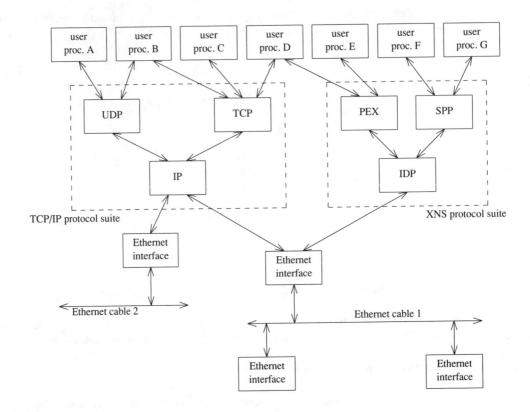

Figure 4.14 Multiplexing and demultiplexing.

- The IP module must determine if data that it receives from the Ethernet interface is for the UDP module or the TCP module. The IP header contains an 8-bit protocol field that is used for this purpose.

- We show the computer system with two Ethernet interfaces. This system is a gateway between the two networks. The IP module must determine which interface is to be used for packets from either the UDP module or the TCP module.

- The software (the device driver) for the interface connected to Ethernet cable 1 must determine if a received Ethernet frame is for the IP module or the IDP module. There is a 16-bit field in the Ethernet header that identifies the frame type. This allows multiple protocol suites, such as the TCP/IP suite and the XNS suite, to share the same Ethernet.

- An Ethernet interface must determine if a frame that is being transmitted across the physical cable is for it, or for another interface. This determination is done by the Ethernet hardware. Each Ethernet frame contains a 6-byte address in its header that identifies the destination interface. Ethernet addresses are usually supplied by the hardware vendor so that every interface has a unique 6-byte address.

Packet Switching

Communication networks can be divided into two basic types: *circuit-switched* and *packet-switched*. The classic example of a circuit-switched network is the public telephone system. When you place a telephone call, either local or long distance, a dedicated circuit is established for you by the telephone switching offices, from your telephone to the other telephone. Every telephone is directly connected to a local office, typically within a few miles of the phone. The local offices are then connected to toll centers, and these toll centers are connected together through sectional centers and regional centers. Once this circuit is established, the only delay involved in the communication is the time required for the propagation of the electromagnetic signal through all the wires and switches. While it might be hard to obtain a circuit sometimes (such as calling long distance on Christmas day), once the circuit is established you are guaranteed exclusive access to it.

A leased telephone line, which is common for WANs, is a special case of a circuit-switched network. But there is no setup required to establish a dedicated circuit between the two telephones.

An internet, on the other hand, typically uses packet-switching techniques. Instead of trying to establish a dedicated communication line between one computer and another, the computers share communication links. Instead, the information is divided into pieces and each piece is transmitted on its own through the connection of networks. These pieces are called *packets*.

A packet is the smallest unit that can be transferred through the networks by itself. A packet must contain the address of its final destination, so that it can be sent on its way through the internet. Most protocols also specify that a packet contain the sender's address, too. (We describe these addresses later in the chapter.) Recall from earlier in this chapter that we defined the unit of information that is exchanged at the network layer is a packet. Indeed, it is the network layer that is involved in transferring packets around the networks.

With a circuit-switched network, we are guaranteed that once a circuit is established, we can use the full capacity of the circuit. With a packet-switched network, however, we are sharing the communication bandwidth with other computers.

Packet switching on a local area network refers to multiple computers sharing a single communications channel, such as an Ethernet or a token ring. A dedicated link is not used between each computer. All the computers on the LAN share the available capacity of the network.

A WAN can also use packet switching. We'll show an example of this, after discussing gateways.

Consider the internet shown in Figure 4.15.

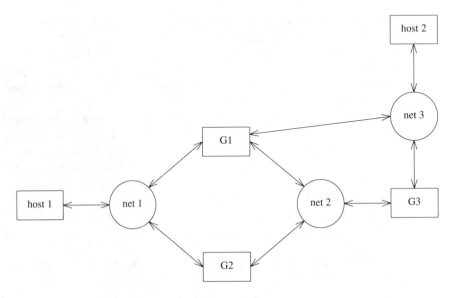

Figure 4.15 Internet example for routing.

For a packet to go from host 1 to host 2, there are four possible acyclic paths.

- host 1, net 1, G1, net 3, host 2;
- host 1, net 1, G1, net 2, G3, net 3, host 2;
- host 1, net 1, G2, net 2, G3, net 3, host 2;
- host 1, net 1, G2, net 2, G1, net 3, host 2.

Each of these paths is called a *route*. Routing decisions are usually made at the network layer in the OSI model. We'll consider routing in more detail later in this chapter.

In a packet-switched network, there is no guarantee how long it takes a packet to go from one host to another. The time taken for each packet depends on the route chosen for that packet, along with the volume of data being transferred along that route.

Gateways

Earlier we defined a *gateway* as a system that interconnects two or more networks. The function of a gateway is to pass along information from one network to another.

The layer at which a gateway operates depends on the type of translation and forwarding done by the gateway. For example, if we have an internet of networks that all use the TCP/IP protocols, no translation of protocols is required. Instead, each gateway only needs to forward packets from one network to another. The IP layer is responsible for this forwarding of packets. An example of this is shown in Figure 4.16.

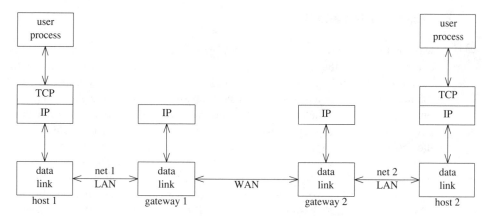

Figure 4.16 Gateway example.

Each IP packet contains enough information (i.e., its final destination address) for it to be routed through the TCP/IP internet by itself.

Things become more complicated, if we want a gateway between networks that use different protocol suites. The conversion is often done in layers above the network layer.

Notice in Figure 4.16 that the TCP layer is not needed on the intermediate gateways. This is why we distinguished between the transport layer and the network layer, in Figures 4.3 and 4.4. You might think we could combine them, since they often appear as a single entity within the operating system, to the application programmer. Our reason for separating them is because of the different roles they each play in an internet. The transport layer is the lowest layer that provides the virtual connection between the two hosts on which the user processes are running.

To understand packet switching in a WAN, let's look at Figure 4.16 again. Assume the two LANs are Ethernets and assume that the two gateways are separated by thousands of miles but are connected with a leased phone line. Even though this leased phone line is a circuit-switched connection, we still consider this a packet-switched network. The reason is there are usually many hosts that share the Ethernets connecting each host and its gateway. (The number of hosts on an internet typically exceeds the number of gateways on the internet by a factor of 10 or more. For example, the TCP/IP Internet is currently estimated to have over 150,000 hosts and 850 networks.) All the hosts on one of these Ethernets compete with the other hosts on that same Ethernet for the single link between the two gateways. Nevertheless, this arrangement is more reasonable than a leased phone line between every host on network 1 and every host on network 2.

Fragmentation and Reassembly

Most network layers have a maximum packet size that they can handle, based on the characteristics of the data-link layer that they are sending its packets through. This is called the network's *maximum transmission unit* or *MTU*. (This term can be applied to the maximum size of a protocol message exchanged by any two layers in a protocol suite, not just the network layer.) For example, part of the Ethernet standard is that the data portion of a frame (the data between, but not including, the 14-byte Ethernet header and the 4-byte Ethernet trailer) cannot exceed 1500 bytes. The maximum for a token ring network is typically 4464 bytes, while some networks have small MTUs. Consider the example shown in Figure 4.16 and assume that the two LANs are Ethernets. But, if the WAN between the two gateways uses a data link with a maximum packet size of 128 bytes, then something has to be done when IP packets are sent from host 1 to host 2.

Fragmentation is the breaking up of a data stream into smaller pieces. Some networks use the term *segmentation* instead of fragmentation. The reverse of fragmentation is *reassembly*. Using the layering concept that we've already talked about, fragmentation should happen at the lowest layer possible, so that upper layers need not be concerned with it. For example, using the gateway example in Figure 4.16, we would like fragmentation to take place at the IP layer, without the TCP layer even knowing that it was taking place. Indeed, with the TCP/IP protocols, it is the IP layer that handles fragmentation and reassembly, as required by the different data-link layers that are used by TCP/IP.

Modes of Service

There are several parameters that describe the type of communication service provided between two peer entities at any layer of the OSI model. In this text we are interested in the service provided to an application program, typically by the transport layer. These parameters are

- connection-oriented (virtual circuit) or connectionless,
- sequencing,
- error control,
- flow control,

- byte stream or messages,
- full-duplex or half-duplex.

A *connection-oriented* service requires that the two application programs establish a logical connection with each other before communication can take place. There is some overhead involved in establishing this connection. We also use the term *virtual circuit* to describe this service, since it appears to the application programs that they have a dedicated circuit between them, even though the actual data flow usually takes place using a packet-switched network. A connection-oriented service is often used when more than one message is to be exchanged between the two peer entities. A connection-oriented exchange involves three steps:

- connection establishment,
- data transfer (can be lengthy),
- connection termination.

The converse of a connection-oriented service is a *connectionless* service, also called a *datagram* service. In this type of service, messages called datagrams are transmitted from one system to the other. Since each message is transmitted independently, each must contain all the information required for its delivery. In the TCP/IP protocol suite, TCP provides a connection-oriented virtual circuit, while UDP provides a connectionless datagram facility.

Sequencing describes the property that the data is received by the receiver in the same order as it is transmitted by the sender. In a packet-switched network, it is possible for two consecutive packets to take different routes from the source computer to the destination computer, and thus arrive at their destination in a different order from the order in which they were sent.

Error control guarantees that error-free data is received by the application programs. There are two conditions that can generate errors: the data gets corrupted (modified during transmission), or the data gets lost. A technique to detect data corruption is for the sender to include a checksum so the receiver can verify, with a high probability, that the data does not get modified. If the data does get corrupted, the receiver has to ask the sender to retransmit the data. Therefore, checksums are usually combined with a technique called positive acknowledgment—the receiver notifies the sender each time a data message is received, either correctly or with errors. If the data was received correctly the sender can discard it, otherwise the data must be retransmitted. To handle the loss of data somewhere in the network requires that the sender start a timer after it has sent a data message, and if the timer expires (called a timeout) the sender must retransmit the data. Note that when positive acknowledgments and timeouts are being used, it is possible not only for data to get lost but for acknowledgments to be lost as well. If this happens, the original sender will retransmit the data, causing the other end to receive the same data twice. This requires the receiver to perform duplicate detection—determine when data has already been received and ignore (but acknowledge) the duplicate message.

Flow control assures that the sender does not overwhelm the receiver by sending data at a rate faster than the receiver can process the data. This is also called *pacing*. If flow control is not provided, it is possible for the receiver to lose data because of a lack of resources. Both TCP and SNA LU 6.2 provide sequencing, error control, and flow control. UDP, however, does not provide any of these services.

A *byte-stream* service does not provide any record boundaries to the data stream. The converse of this feature is a message-oriented service that preserves the sender's message boundaries for the receiver. These features were described in Section 3.6. TCP is a byte-stream protocol, while UDP and the XNS SPP (Sequenced Packet Protocol) provide message boundaries.

A *full-duplex* connection allows data to be transferred in both directions at the same time between the two peer entities. Some protocols are *half-duplex* and only allow one side to transfer at a time. TCP is full-duplex, while SNA LU 6.2 is a half-duplex protocol.

Many of these parameters occur together. For example, sequencing and error control are usually provided together and the protocol is then termed *reliable*. It is also unusual to find a reliable protocol that does not provide flow control. It is unusual to have a connectionless protocol that provides sequencing, since the datagrams in such a protocol are usually unrelated to previous or future datagrams. We see an example of sequencing, positive acknowledgment, and retransmission after timeout in Chapter 12, when we develop an implementation of the Trivial File Transfer Protocol.

Tanenbaum [1989] provides an excellent analogy between virtual circuits and datagrams: A telephone call is similar to a virtual circuit. You establish a connection with the other party, exchange data for a while, then close the connection. The postal service resembles a datagram delivery service. Every letter contains the complete address of the destination. Every letter that you mail to the same address can follow a different route to the destination. (No doubt everyone has mailed two letters to the same destination, one or two days apart, only to have them arrive out of order.) There is no guarantee that a letter arrives at the destination. To receive an acknowledgment of delivery you must add extra processing to the normal mailing of a letter (i.e., pay extra for a ''return receipt'' if you're using the U.S. Postal Service). If you are expecting a response from your letter, you must also add extra processing—wait for some period and if a response is not received (timeout), retransmit the letter.

End-to-End versus Hop-by-Hop

When describing protocol features such as flow control, error control, and the like, we must differentiate between those features that are done on an *end-to-end* basis and those that are done on a *hop-by-hop* basis. End-to-end flow control, for example, regulates the flow of data between the two user processes that are exchanging data. Hop-by-hop flow control, on the other hand, worries about the flow of data at each hop of the communication link (i.e., all the gateways between the two end systems). As we'll see in the next chapter, TCP provides end-to-end flow control, while IP provides an elementary type of hop-by-hop flow control.

As another example, error control is usually handled on a hop-by-hop basis by the data-link layer. An Ethernet frame, a token ring frame, or an SDLC frame, all contain a checksum that detects any modifications to the data as it travels across the physical link. This is a hop-by-hop form of error detection. Some protocols also provide some form of end-to-end error control also. The TCP layer in the TCP/IP suite provides this—the source TCP layer calculates and stores a checksum in the TCP message header which is then checked by the receiving TCP layer.

Looking at Figure 4.16 again, we see that any feature that is to be implemented in the TCP/IP protocol suite on an end-to-end basis, has to be handled by the TCP layer, or the user process above TCP. Similarly, any hop-by-hop feature must be handled by the IP layer or the data-link layer.

Buffering and Out-of-Band Data

Consider a byte-stream service. The user process can read or write any number of bytes at a time, since there are no message boundaries. What typically happens is that the byte-stream service layer (TCP, for example) buffers this data internally and then passes it to the next lower layer for transmission to the other end. Buffering can also take place if the protocol does flow control (as most byte-stream service protocols do) since the sending side can be generating data faster than the receiving end can process the data. Also, a reliable protocol can be buffering data on the sending side while it is waiting for an acknowledgment of previously sent data from the other end. Note that buffering can be taking place on both ends, as the receiving byte-stream service can be receiving data from the network faster than the user process is reading the data. Figure 4.17 shows this buffering on both hosts.

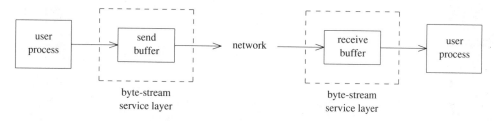

Figure 4.17 Normal buffering that takes place with a byte-stream service.

Sometimes a user process wants to disable this buffering. For instance, consider a terminal emulation program. The process that is reading the keystrokes wants to send each keystroke to the other end, one byte at a time, since the other end might be operating on each character as it is entered. This is how full screen editors under Unix operate, for example. Similarly, the process that is sending terminal output also wants to force the data to be transferred, perhaps at the end of every line. What we would like is the ability for a user process to tell its byte-stream service layer (e.g., TCP) to flush any data that is has buffered and send it to the other end. TCP, for example, supports this option, which it calls a *push*.

This type of buffering sounds like the type done by the standard I/O library, but network buffering quickly becomes more complex. The complicating factors are that some network applications are interactive (e.g., remote echoing in a remote login application), which makes us want to buffer as little as possible, while performance considerations make us want to buffer as much as possible. Also, congestion can quickly become a problem if we send many small packets through a busy network, since there is a fixed overhead for every packet, no matter how much data it contains. The techniques used by the TCP implementation in 4.3BSD are covered in Section 12.7 of Leffler et al. [1989]. (We consider the buffering techniques of the 4.3BSD TCP implementation in more detail in Section 6.11 when we describe the TCP_NODELAY socket option.)

Similarly, when a user at a terminal presses the attention key, it needs to be operated on as soon as possible. The Unix interrupt key (typically the Delete key or Control-C) is one example of this, as are the terminal flow control characters (typically Control-S and Control-Q). This type of information is termed *out-of-band data* or *expedited data*. With out-of-band data we want the byte-stream service layer on the sending side to send this data before any other data that it has buffered. Similarly we want the receiving end to pass this data to its user process ahead of any data that it might have buffered. Some method is also desired for the receiving byte-stream service layer to notify the user process asynchronously that out-of-band data has arrived. As you might guess, a Unix signal can be used for this notification. The term *out of band* is used because it appears to the user processes that a separate communication channel is being used for this data, in addition to the normal data channel (band). This is shown in Figure 4.18.

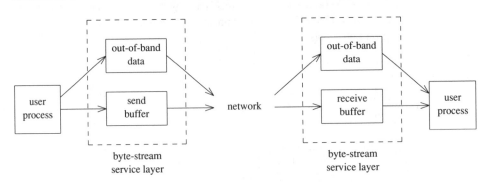

Figure 4.18 In-band data and out-of-band data.

Some byte-stream layers provide out-of-band data and some don't. Those that do provide it allow differing amounts. For example, SPP provides a single byte of out-of-band data, while TCP allows an unlimited amount. We return to both of these features, buffer flushing and out-of-band data, in the next three chapters when we examine each specific protocol family and then examine the user process interface to the transport layer.

Services and Protocols

It is necessary to differentiate between *services* and *protocols* in a layered model such as the OSI model. A layer provides one or more services to the layer above it. As mentioned earlier, this text is mainly concerned with the services provided by the transport layer to an application. Earlier we defined a protocol as a set of rules and conventions that the communicating participants must follow, to exchange information.

In many of the protocol suites that preceded the OSI model, the services provided by the different layers are not distinguished from the protocols that implement these services. Most of the OSI protocols, however, separate the two, as we'll see in Section 5.6. The advantage in separating the service from the protocol is that multiple protocols can be developed over time to provide a given service.

Chapter 5 is concerned mainly with protocols, although there will be some implied service features for those protocols that don't differentiate between services and protocols. Chapters 6 and 7, however, deal with the services provided by the transport layer to a user process—Berkeley sockets and System V TLI.

Addresses

Recall that the end points for communication are two user processes, one on each system. With an internet, the two systems can be located on different networks, connected by one or more gateways. This requires three levels of addressing.

- A particular network must be specified. As we've seen earlier in this chapter, a given host can be connected to more than one network.

- Each host on a network must have a unique address.

- Each process on a host must have a unique identifier on that host.

Typically a host address consists of a network ID and a host ID on that network. The identification of the user process on a host is often done with an integer value assigned by the protocol. For example, the TCP/IP protocol suite uses a 32-bit integer to specify a combined network ID and host ID, and both TCP and UDP use 16-bit port numbers to identify specific user processes. The XNS protocol suite uses a 32-bit network ID, a 48-bit host ID, and a 16-bit port number. In the next chapter we'll examine the specific address formats used by each protocol suite in more detail.

Most protocol suites define a set of *well-known addresses* that are used to identify the well-known services that a host can provide. For example, most TCP/IP implementations provide a file transfer server named FTP that a client can contact to transfer a file. The 16-bit integer port for FTP is 21. In Chapter 8 we discuss how a service name such as FTP is mapped into a protocol-specific address, since it differs between protocol suites and between implementations.

Broadcast and Multicast

Consider a single network without any gateways. A *unicast* message is sent by a host to one specific host on the network. A *broadcast* message is one that is transmitted by a host to every host on the network. A *multicast* message is one that is transmitted by a host to a specified group of hosts on the network. Some types of local area network technology support broadcast messages at the data-link layer—Ethernet and token ring, for example. A special destination address specifies a broadcast message. An Ethernet destination address of all 1-bits, for example, specifies a broadcast. Other forms of network connections, such as point-to-point phone lines, require some form of software implementation of broadcast.

A multicast message implies that some subset of the host systems belong to a multicast group. Some forms of network hardware provide support for multicast addresses, but this is more product specific than support for broadcast messages. For example, some (but not all) Ethernet interfaces allow the host to specify those multicast groups to which it belongs to.

When a network is connected to another network through a gateway, should broadcast messages generated on the local network be passed along by the gateway to the next network? In normal practice, broadcast messages are not forwarded.

We will see examples of broadcast messages in the next chapter. Multicasting is not as widely supported as broadcasting.

Routing

The topic of network routing is complex and could consume an entire text of its own. Here we'll provide a brief overview. Note that the applications programmer typically has little control over routing.

When a node, either a host or a gateway, has a packet to send to some other host, there are four possible cases.

1. The destination host is either directly connected to the node (with a leased phone line, for example), or the destination host and the node are on the same network (an Ethernet, for example). In either case the node can send the packet directly to the destination host—no routing decision has to be made.

2. The arriving packet can contain the address of the next node to send the packet to. This is called *source routing* since the list of addresses for the packet to follow is established by the source host. No decisions have to be made by the current node about where to send the received packet. This technique is used by the IBM token ring [Dixon and Pitt 1988]. Additionally, the TCP/IP protocol suite has an option that allows source routing to be used, however, this is typically used only by network administrators for testing. See Section 7.8.2 of Comer [1988].

3. The current node can already know the route that packets from this source are to follow to reach the specified destination. There are some packet-switched networks in which every packet from a given source to a given destination follow the same route. In this case there are no decisions to be made by the current node. The commercial TYMNET network, for example, uses this technique, as does the IBM SNA/LEN product [Baratz et al. 1985].

4. None of the three cases above apply. A routing decision must be made by the current node. This, for example, is the normal mode of operation for a gateway on the TCP/IP Internet. Source routing is not typically used and two consecutive datagrams from a given host to the same destination can follow different paths.

Note that some routing decision has to be made for cases 2, 3, and 4 above. In cases 2 and 3 the decision is made before the node receives the packet, so the node itself doesn't have to make a decision. Nevertheless, someone had to make a routing decision for this packet. In case 4 the routing decision is made on-the-fly by the node, which is typically a gateway.

When routing decisions have to be made, there are four different types of algorithms that can be used.

- static routing,
- isolated dynamic routing,
- centralized dynamic routing,
- distributed dynamic routing.

The routing algorithm can be applied by the source host (case 2), by a central authority (case 3), or by the gateway itself (case 4).

Static routing chooses a route based on precomputed information. There is no consideration of the current network dynamics—the load between gateways, for example. The Unix `pathalias` program generates static routing tables that are used by the Unix mailers. Sites typically run this program at some interval (every night or every week) to compute the routes that UUCP mail will follow.

Dynamic routing takes into account the current load on the network. The first dynamic technique, isolated dynamic routing, bases its decisions on local information only. Typically this is the amount of data that the gateway currently has to send, or has recently sent, out each of its interfaces. This technique is rarely used.

Centralized dynamic routing has a central authority that makes all routing decisions based on current network information. The commercial TYMNET network, for example, uses this technique. Each gateway regularly reports its traffic information to a central node and this central node uses all this information to choose routes. Since a source host must contact the central node each time a routing decision is made, realistically this technique is only applicable to networks that use virtual circuits at the network layer—all packets from a given host to a given destination follow the same path. This way the central node only has to be contacted when a new virtual circuit is established.

Distributed dynamic routing uses a mixture of global and local information to make routing decisions. In order for a gateway to obtain global information, the gateways must have some way of exchanging this information. The TCP/IP Internet, for example, uses distributed dynamic routing. Narten [1989] discusses the history of the routing protocols used in the TCP/IP Internet.

Connections and Associations

We use the term *connection* to define the communication link between two processes. The term *association* is used for the 5-tuple that completely specifies the two processes that make up a connection:

   {protocol, local-addr, local-process, foreign-addr, foreign-process}

The *local-addr* and *foreign-addr* specify the network ID and host ID of the local host and the foreign host, in whatever format is defined by the protocol suite. The *local-process* and *foreign-process* are used to identify the specific processes on each system that are involved in the connection, again in whatever format is defined by the protocol suite. In the TCP/IP suite, for example,

   `{tcp, 192.43.235.2, 1500, 192.43.235.6, 21}`

could be a valid association, where the protocol is TCP, the local-address is 192.43.235.2, the local-process is 1500, the foreign-address is 192.43.235.6, and the foreign-process is 21. When we cover each protocol suite in the next chapter, we will see other examples of this 5-tuple.

We also define a *half association* as either *{protocol, local-addr, local-process}* or *{protocol, foreign-addr, foreign-process}*, which specify each half of a connection. This half association is also called a *socket* or a *transport address*. The term socket has been popularized by the Berkeley Unix networking system, where it is "an end point of communication," which corresponds to our definition of a half association. A socket pair then corresponds to our definition of an association. Unfortunately the XNS protocol suite uses the term socket to refer to what we called the 16-bit port above.

Client–Server Model

In Section 1.6 we briefly described the client–server model that is prevalent in computer networking. We defined *iterative servers* and *concurrent servers*. The former knows ahead of time about how long it takes to handle each request and the server process handles each request itself. In the latter case, the amount of work required to handle a request is unknown, so the server starts another process to handle each request.

Notice that the roles of the client and server processes are *asymmetric*. This means that both halves are coded differently. The server is started first and typically does the following steps:

1. Open a communication channel and inform the local host of its willingness to accept client requests on some well-known address.

2. Wait for a client request to arrive at the well-known address.

3. For an iterative server, process the request and send the reply. Iterative servers are typically used when a client request can be handled with a single response from the server.

   For a concurrent server, a new process is spawned to handle this client request. This requires a `fork` and possibly an `exec` under Unix, to start the new process. This new process then handles this client's request, and does not have to respond to other client requests. When this new process is finished, it closes its communication channel with the client, and terminates.

4. Go back to step 2: wait for another client request.

Implicit in the steps above is that the system somehow queues client requests that arrive while the server is processing a previous client's request. For example, with a concurrent server it is possible for additional requests to arrive during the time it takes for the server to spawn a new process to handle a request. Also implicit above is that the main server process exists as long as the host system is running—server processes never terminate unless forced to (such as when the system is being shut down).

The client process performs a different set of actions.

1. Open a communication channel and connect to a specific well-known address on a specific host (i.e., the server).

2. Send service request messages to the server, and receive the responses. Continue doing this as long as necessary.

3. Close the communication channel and terminate.

When the server opens a communication channel and waits for a client request, we call this a *passive open*. The client, on the other hand, executes what is called an *active open* since it expects the server to be waiting.

Who's Who in Networking Standards

There are many different organizations involved in the development of networking standards. Both the organizations and the standards are referred to by acronyms in most of the networking literature.

ISO, the *International Standards Organization*, was founded in 1946 and develops standards on a wide variety of subjects. The members of ISO are the national standards organizations from the member countries. The U.S. member of ISO is *ANSI*, the *American National Standards Institute*. The open systems interconnection model (OSI model) was adopted by ISO in 1984.

CCITT, the *Consultative Committee for International Telephony and Telegraphy*, develops standards for telephony and telegraphy. CCITT standards tend to be identified by a letter, followed by a period, followed by a number. For example, X.25 is a CCITT standard for packet-switched networks, and X.400 is a CCITT standard for electronic mail.

IEEE (pronounced "I triple-E"), the *Institute for Electrical and Electronic Engineers*, also issues standards. Its 802 standards are used for local area networks and provide standardization at the two lowest layers of the OSI model. The 802.2 standard defines the logical link control (LLC) used by the data-link layer. The 802.3, 802.4, and 802.5 standards define the media access control used by the data-link layer and the physical layer, for Ethernet†, token bus, and token ring networks, respectively.

EIA, the *Electronics Industry Association*, is a trade association concerned primarily with the physical layer of the OSI model. EIA developed the RS-232 standard that is used widely for connecting terminals to computers.

IAB, the *Internet Activities Board*, is a small group of researchers who direct most of the work on the TCP/IP protocols. It functions as a board of directors of the Internet.

Some networking standards originate with one organization and are then adopted by others. For example, the IEEE 802.2−1985 standard is also ISO Draft International Standard (DIS) 8802/2. The EIA RS-232 standard is also the CCITT V.24/V.28 standard.

Exercises

4.1 Draw a diagram of the local area network that you have access to. Include hosts, repeaters, bridges, routers, and gateways. Indicate what equipment (token ring, Ethernet, etc.) is being used at the physical layer.

---

† The original Ethernet standard was developed at Xerox Corp. in the 1970s and then standardized by DEC, Intel, and Xerox in 1981. The newest version is the IEEE 802.3 standard, dated 1985. It differs slightly from the original Ethernet.

5

Communication Protocols

5.1   Introduction

In this chapter we provide an overview of several communication protocol families. Our goal is to provide enough of an overview so that we understand how to use the protocols, and to provide references to more detailed descriptions of the actual design and implementation of the protocols.

   We cover the following protocol suites, in the order shown:

- the TCP/IP protocol suite (the Internet protocols),
- Xerox Networking Systems (Xerox NS or XNS),
- IBM's Systems Network Architecture (SNA),
- IBM's NetBIOS,
- the OSI protocols,
- Unix-to-Unix Copy (UUCP).

For each protocol suite we give an overview, and then discuss the relevant portions for the protocol's layers. We start from the bottom layer and work our way up. Note that we cover each protocol family in its entirety, and we cover them in order of their importance in the remainder of this text.

5.2   TCP/IP—the Internet Protocols

5.2.1   Introduction

During the late 1960s and the 1970s the Advanced Research Projects Agency (ARPA) of the Department of Defense (DoD) sponsored the development of the ARPANET. The ARPANET included military, university, and research sites, and was used to support computer science and military research projects. (ARPA is now called DARPA, with the first letter of the acronym standing for ''Defense.'') In 1984 the DoD split the ARPANET into two networks—the ARPANET for experimental research, and the MILNET for military use. In the early 1980s a new family of protocols was specified as the standard for the ARPANET and associated DoD networks. Although the accurate name for this family of protocols is the ''DARPA Internet protocol suite,'' it is commonly referred to as the TCP/IP protocol suite, or just TCP/IP.

In 1987 the National Science Foundation (NSF) funded a network that connects the six national supercomputer centers together. This network is called the *NSFNET*. Physically this network connects 13 sites using high-speed leased phone lines and this is called the NSFNET backbone. About eight more backbone nodes are currently planned. Additionally the NSF has funded about a dozen regional networks that span almost every state. These regional networks are connected to the NSFNET backbone, and the NSFNET backbone is also connected to the DARPA Internet. The NSFNET backbone and the regional networks all use the TCP/IP protocol suite.

There are several interesting points about TCP/IP.

- It is not vendor-specific.

- It has been implemented on everything from personal computers to the largest supercomputers.

- It is used for both LANs and WANs.

- It is used by many different government agencies and commercial sites, not just DARPA-funded research projects.

The DARPA-funded research has led to the interconnection of many different individual networks into what appears as a single large network—an *internet*, as described in the previous chapter. We refer to this internet as just the Internet (capitalized).

It is important to realize that while sites on the Internet use the TCP/IP protocols, many other organizations (with no government affiliation whatsoever) have established their own internets using the same TCP/IP protocols. At one extreme we have the Internet using TCP/IP to connect more than 150,000 computers throughout the United States, Europe and Asia, and at the other extreme we could have a network consisting of only two personal computers in the same room connected by an Ethernet using the same TCP/IP protocols.

To avoid having to qualify everything with "the TCP/IP protocol suite" or "the DARPA Internet protocol suite," we use the capitalized word *Internet*, as in "an Internet address," or "the Internet protocols," to refer to the TCP/IP protocol suite. This is to avoid confusion with internets that use protocols other than TCP/IP.

One reason for the increased use of the TCP/IP protocols during the 1980s was their inclusion in the BSD Unix system around 1982. This, along with the use of BSD Unix in technical workstations, allowed many organizations and university departments to establish their own LANs.

5.2.2 Overview

Although the protocol family is referred to as TCP/IP, there are more members of this family than TCP and IP. Figure 5.1 shows the relationship of the protocols in the protocol suite along with their approximate mapping into the OSI model.

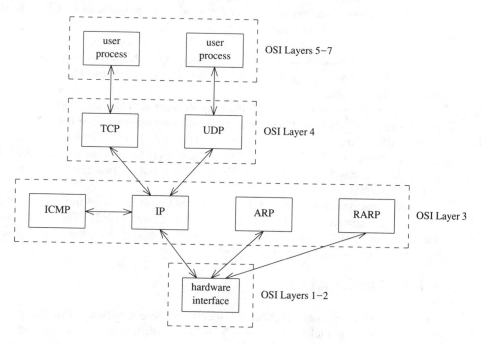

Figure 5.1 Layering in the Internet protocol suite.

TCP *Transmission Control Protocol.* A connection-oriented protocol that provides a reliable, full-duplex, byte stream for a user process. Most Internet application programs use TCP. Since TCP uses IP (as shown in Figure 5.1) the entire Internet protocol suite is often called the TCP/IP protocol family.

UDP   *User Datagram Protocol.* A connectionless protocol for user processes. Unlike TCP, which is a reliable protocol, there is no guarantee that UDP datagrams ever reach their intended destination.

ICMP   *Internet Control Message Protocol.* The protocol to handle error and control information between gateways and hosts. While ICMP messages are transmitted using IP datagrams, these messages are normally generated by and processed by the TCP/IP networking software itself, not user processes.

IP   *Internet Protocol.* IP is the protocol that provides the packet delivery service for TCP, UDP, and ICMP. Note from the Figure 5.1 that user processes normally do not need to be involved with the IP layer.

ARP   *Address Resolution Protocol.* The protocol that maps an Internet address into a hardware address. This protocol and the next, RARP, are not used on all networks. Only some networks need it.

RARP   *Reverse Address Resolution Protocol.* The protocol that maps a hardware address into an Internet address.

There are other protocols in the Internet protocol suite that we do not consider in this text—GGP (Gateway-to-Gateway Protocol) and VMTP (Versatile Message Transaction Protocol), for example.

All the Internet protocols are defined by *Request for Comments (RFCs)*, which are their formal specifications. Corrections and explanations for many of the RFCs are found in RFC 1009 [Braden and Postel 1987], RFC 1122 [Braden 1989a], and RFC 1123 [Braden 1989b]. RFC 1118 [Krol 1989] provides hints for new members of the Internet community. It also describes how to obtain on-line information and how to be a good Internet neighbor.

Additional details on the TCP/IP protocol suite can be found in Comer [1988]. A sample implementation of UDP and IP is given in Comer [1987]. The source code for the complete 4.3BSD implementation of TCP/IP is provided on the BSD Networking Software release—refer to the Bibliography.

5.2.3 Data-Link Layer

The ARPANET consists of about 50 special purpose computers that are connected together using leased telephone lines at 57.6 Kbps. The host computers and gateways on the ARPANET are then connected to these special purpose computers. The 13 backbone sites of the NSFNET are connected with T1 leased phone lines, which operate at 1.544 Mbps. Most 4.3BSD systems using the TCP/IP suite for a LAN use Ethernet technology. Products also exist that use a token ring for a LAN using TCP/IP. There also exist implementations using an RS-232 serial line protocol (at speeds from 1200 bps to 19.2 Kbps) called the Serial Line Internet Protocol (SLIP). There are a variety of other data-link connections in use by TCP/IP networks: satellite links and packet radio, for example.

5.2.4 Network Layer—IP

IP Datagrams

The IP layer provides a connectionless and unreliable delivery system. It is connectionless because it considers each IP datagram independent of all others. Any association between datagrams must be provided by the upper layers. Every IP datagram contains the source address and the destination address (described below) so that each datagram can be delivered and routed independently. The IP layer is unreliable because it does not guarantee that IP datagrams ever get delivered or that they are delivered correctly. Reliability must also be provided by the upper layers. The IP layer computes and verifies a checksum that covers its own 20-byte header (that contains, for example, the source and destination addresses). This allows it to verify the fields that it needs to examine and process. But if an IP header is found in error, it is discarded, with the assumption that a higher layer protocol will retransmit the packet.

As we saw in the gateway examples from the previous chapter, it is the IP layer that handles routing through an Internet. The IP layer is also responsible for fragmentation, as described in the previous chapter. For example, if a gateway receives an IP datagram that is too large to transmit across the next network, the IP module breaks up the datagram into fragments and sends each fragment as an IP packet. (Technically, the protocol unit exchanged by the end-to-end IP layers is an IP datagram. An IP datagram can be fragmented into smaller IP packets. When fragmentation does occur, the IP layer duplicates the source address and destination address into each IP packet, so the resulting IP packets can be delivered independently of each other.) The fragments are reassembled into an IP datagram only when they reach their final destination. If any of the fragments are lost or discarded, the entire datagram is discarded by the destination host.

The IP layer provides an elementary form of flow control. When IP packets arrive at a host or gateway so fast that they are discarded, the IP module sends an ICMP source quench message to the original source informing that system that the data is arriving too fast. With 4.3BSD, for example, the ICMP source quench is passed to the TCP module (assuming it was a TCP message that caused the source quench), which then decreases the amount of data being sent on that connection.

The reference for IP is RFC 791 [Postel 1981a].

Internet Addresses

Every protocol suite defines some type of addressing that identifies networks and computers. An Internet address occupies 32 bits and encodes both a network ID and a host ID. The host ID is relative to the network ID. Every host on a TCP/IP internet must have a unique 32-bit address. TCP/IP addresses on the Internet are assigned by a central authority—the Network Information Center (NIC) located at SRI International. Even if you are establishing your own internet, and don't plan to join the Internet, you can still get an assigned Internet address by contacting SRI. (See Appendix M of Nemeth, Snyder, and Seebas [1989] for the details on how to do this.)

A 32-bit Internet address has one of the four formats shown in Figure 5.2.

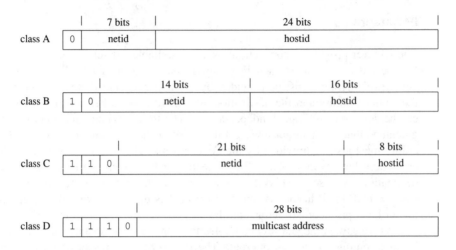

Figure 5.2 Internet address formats.

Class A addresses are used for those networks that have a lot of hosts on a single net-work, while Class C addresses allow for more networks but fewer hosts per network. For network addresses assigned by the NIC, only the type of address (Class A, B, or C) and the network ID is assigned. The requesting organization then has responsibility for assigning individual host addresses on that network. We won't consider multicast addresses (Class D) any further.

Internet addresses are usually written as four decimal numbers, separated by decimal points. Each decimal digit encodes one byte of the 32-bit Internet address. For example, the 32-bit hexadecimal value 0x0102FF04 is written as 1.2.255.4. This example is a Class A address with a network ID of 1 and a host ID of 0x02FF04. A sample Class B address is 128.3.0.5, and a sample class C address is 192.43.235.6.

Every IP datagram contains the 32-bit Internet address of the source host and the 32-bit Internet address of the destination host, in every 20-byte IP header. Since an Inter-net address is comprised of a network ID and a host ID, gateways can easily extract the network ID field from a 32-bit address and route IP datagrams based solely on the net-work ID. This is an important concept for routing, as it means that a gateway needs only to know the location of other networks, and does not to need to know the location of every host on an Internet.

Recall that a multihomed host is connected to two or more networks. This implies that it must have two or more Internet addresses, one for each network that it is con-nected to. This means that every Internet address specifies a unique host, but each host does not have a unique address.

Subnet Addresses

Any organization with an Internet address of any class can subdivide the available host address space in any way it desires, to provide subnetworks. For example, if you have a Class B address, there are 16 bits allocated for the host ID. If your organization wants to assign host IDs to its 150 hosts, that are in turn organized into 10 physical networks, there are two different ways to do this.

- You can allocate host IDs of 1 through 150, ignoring the physical network structure. This requires that all the gateway systems among the 150 hosts know where each individual host is located, for routing purposes. Adding a new host requires that each gateway's routing table be updated.

- You can allocate some of the high-order bits from the host ID, say the high-order 8 bits, for the network ID within your subnetwork. These 8 bits are independent of the Class B network ID. The remaining 8 bits of the Class B host ID you then use to identify the individual hosts on each internal network. Using this technique, your gateway systems can extract the 8-bit internal network ID and use it for routing, instead of having to know where each of the 150 hosts are located. Adding a new host on an existing internal network doesn't require any changes to the internal gateways.

A picture of what the second option is doing is given in Figure 5.3.

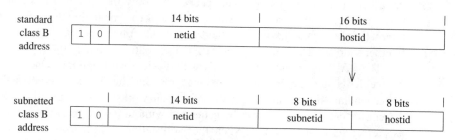

Figure 5.3 Class B Internet address with subnetting.

This feature adds another level to the Internet address hierarchy.

- network ID
- subnet ID within network
- host ID within subnet

The reference for subnetting is RFC 950 [Mogul and Postel 1985].

Address Resolution

If we have an Ethernet LAN consisting of hosts using the TCP/IP protocols, we have two types of addresses: 32-bit Internet addresses and 48-bit Ethernet addresses. Recall from the previous chapter that the 48-bit Ethernet addresses are typically assigned by the manufacturer of the interface board and are all unique. We have the following address resolution problems:

- If we know the Internet address of the other host that we want to communicate with, how does the IP layer determine which Ethernet address corresponds to that host? This is the *address resolution problem*.

- When a diskless workstation is initialized (bootstrapped), the operating system can usually determine its own 48-bit Ethernet address from its interface hardware. But we do not want to embed the workstation's 32-bit Internet address into the operating system image, as this prevents us from using the same image for multiple workstations. How can the diskless workstation determine its Internet address at bootstrap time? This is the *reverse address resolution problem*.

The first problem is solved using the Internet *Address Resolution Protocol (ARP)*, and the second uses the Internet *Reverse Address Resolution Protocol (RARP)*.

The ARP allows a host to broadcast a special packet on the Ethernet that asks the host with a specified Internet address to respond with its Ethernet address. Every host on the Ethernet receives this broadcast packet, but only the specified host should respond. Once the requesting host receives the response it can maintain the mapping between the Internet address and the Ethernet address for all future packets destined for the same Internet address. The reference for ARP is RFC 826 [Plummer 1982].

The RARP is intended for a LAN with diskless workstations. One or more systems on the LAN are the RARP servers and contain the 32-bit Internet address and its corresponding 48-bit Ethernet address for each workstation. This allows the operating system for each workstation to be generated without having to have its Internet address as part of its configuration. When the workstation is initialized, it obtains its 48-bit Ethernet address from the interface hardware and broadcasts an Ethernet RARP packet containing its Ethernet address and asking for its Internet address. Every host on the Ethernet LAN receives this broadcast, but only the RARP servers should respond. The reference for RARP is RFC 903 [Finlayson et al. 1984a].

5.2.5 Transport Layer—UDP and TCP

User processes interact with the TCP/IP protocol suite by sending and receiving either TCP data or UDP data. The relationship of TCP and UDP to our simplified 4-layer model from Section 1.5 is shown in Figure 5.4.

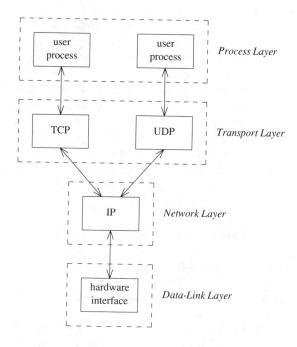

Figure 5.4 4-layer model showing UDP, TCP, and IP.

These two protocols are sometimes referred to as TCP/IP or UDP/IP, to indicate that both use IP also.

TCP provides a connection-oriented, reliable, full-duplex, byte-stream service to an application program. UDP, on the other hand, provides a connectionless, unreliable datagram service. Figure 5.5 compares IP, UDP, and TCP against the modes of service that we described in the previous chapter.

	IP	UDP	TCP
connection-oriented ?	no	no	yes
message boundaries ?	yes	yes	no
data checksum ?	no	opt.	yes
positive ack. ?	no	no	yes
timeout and rexmit ?	no	no	yes
duplicate detection ?	no	no	yes
sequencing ?	no	no	yes
flow control ?	no	no	yes

Figure 5.5 Comparison of protocol features for IP, UDP, and TCP.

Notice that we list IP as not having flow control, since the source quench feature described earlier is not an end-to-end flow control technique.

Since the IP layer provides an unreliable, connectionless delivery service for TCP, it is the TCP module that contains the logic necessary to provide a reliable, virtual circuit for a user process. TCP handles the establishment and termination of connections between processes, the sequencing of data that might be received out of order, the end-to-end reliability (checksums, positive acknowledgments, timeouts), and the end-to-end flow control. RFC 793 [Postel 1981c] is the standard reference for TCP.

UDP provides only two features that are not provided by IP: port numbers (described below) and an optional checksum to verify the contents of the UDP datagram. But these two features are enough reason for a user process to use UDP instead of trying to use IP directly, when a connectionless datagram protocol is required. The reference for UDP is RFC 768 [Postel 1980].

Port Numbers

Figure 4.14 shows that it is possible for more than one user process at a time to be using either TCP or UDP. This requires some method for identifying the data associated with each user process. Both TCP and UDP use 16-bit integer *port numbers* for this identification.

When a client process wants to contact a server, the client must have a way of identifying the server that it wants. If the client knows the 32-bit Internet address of the host on which the server resides it can contact that host, but how does the client identify the particular server process? To solve this problem, both TCP and UDP have defined a group of *well-known ports*. (These are the Internet-specific *well-known addresses* that we described in the previous chapter.) For example, every TCP/IP implementation that supports FTP, the File Transfer Protocol, assigns the well-known port of 21 (decimal) to it. TFTP, the Trivial File Transfer Protocol, is assigned the UDP port of 69.

Let's take this client–server interaction to the next step and assume that a client sends a message to the FTP server on some host by sending a message to port 21 on that host. How does the FTP server know where to send its response? First, the server can obtain the 32-bit Internet address of the client from the IP datagram, since these datagrams contain the source and destination Internet addresses in the 20-byte IP header. The client process also requests an unused port number from the TCP module on its local host. The server can obtain the 16-bit port number from the TCP header. As long as the client's TCP module does not reassign this port number to some other process before the first client is finished, there won't be any conflict. When TCP or UDP assign unique port numbers for user processes, they are called *ephemeral port numbers* (short lived). The process that receives the ephemeral port number (the client process in this example) doesn't care what value it is. It is the other end of the communication link (the server) that needs it. TCP and UDP port numbers in the range 1 through 255 are reserved. All the well-known ports are in this range. Some operating systems reserve additional ports for privileged programs (4.3BSD reserves the ports 1−1023 for superuser processes as we describe in Section 6.8), and the ephemeral ports are above these reserved ports.

We have described a hierarchical addressing scheme that involves multiple layers.

- The IP datagram contains the source and destination Internet addresses in its IP header. These two 32-bit values uniquely identify the two host systems that are communicating.

- Also contained in the IP header is a protocol identifier, so that the IP module can determine if an IP datagram is for TCP, UDP, or some other protocol module that uses IP, which isn't discussed in this text.

- The UDP header and the TCP header both contain the source port number and the destination port number. These two 16-bit integer values are used by the protocol modules to identify a particular user process. Note that the TCP ports are independent of the UDP ports, since the IP header specifies the protocol. TCP port 1035, for example, is independent of UDP port 1035.

As described in the previous chapter, the addition of this control information by the different protocol modules is *encapsulation*. The combination of information from different sources using identifiers such as port numbers, protocol types, and Internet addresses is called *multiplexing*.

The 5-tuple that defines an *association* in the Internet suite consists of

- the protocol (TCP or UDP),
- the local host's Internet address (a 32-bit value),
- the local port number (a 16-bit value),
- the foreign host's Internet address (a 32-bit value),
- the foreign port number (a 16-bit value).

An example could be

```
{tcp, 128.10.0.3, 1500, 128.10.0.7, 21}
```

Figure 5.6 diagrams the encapsulation that takes place with UDP data on an Ethernet.

If the length of the IP datagram (the data, plus the UDP header, plus the IP header) is greater than the MTU of the network access layer, then the IP layer has to fragment the datagram before it is passed to the network access layer. If this happens, the receiving IP layer has to reassemble the fragments into a single datagram before it is passed to the upper layers (e.g., UDP). Whether fragmentation takes place or not, the size of the data message (the datagram) exchanged by the two UDP layers is the same.

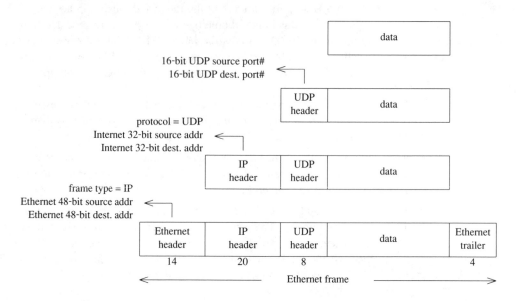

Figure 5.6 Encapsulation of UDP data on an Ethernet.

Similarly, the encapsulation that takes place with TCP data is shown in Figure 5.7.

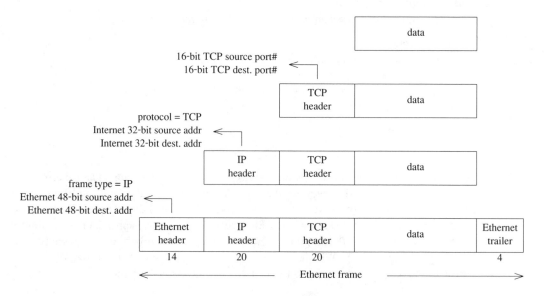

Figure 5.7 Encapsulation of TCP data on an Ethernet.

As with UDP, it is also possible for the TCP layer to pass messages to the IP layer that exceed the underlying network's MTU. If this happens, the sending IP layer does fragmentation and the receiving IP layer does reassembly. For performance reasons, however, most TCP implementations try to prevent IP fragmentation.

Concurrent Servers

With a concurrent server, what happens if the child process that is spawned by the main server continues to use its well-known port number while servicing a long request? Let's examine a typical sequence. First, the server is started on the host `orange` and it does a passive open using its well-known port number (21, for this example). It is now waiting for a client request.

```
    server
{tcp, *, 21}
```

We use the notation {`tcp`, `*`, `21`} to indicate that the server is waiting for a TCP connection on any connected network (i.e., interface), on port 21. If the host on which the server is running is connected to more than one TCP/IP network, the server can specify that it only wants to accept a connection from a client on one specific network. Our asterisk notation indicates that a connection will be accepted on any network.

At some later time a client starts up and executes an active open to the server. The client has an ephemeral port number assigned to it by the protocol module (TCP, in this example). Assume the ephemeral port number is 1500 for this example, and assume that the name of the client's host is `apple`. This is shown in Figure 5.8.

Figure 5.8 Connection from client to server.

The notation {`tcp`, `apple`, `1500`} is the client's *half association* or *socket*. Here we are designating the Internet address as `apple`, using the name of the host instead of its 4-digit notation. When the server receives the client's connection request, it `forks` a copy of itself, passing the connection to the child process, as shown in Figure 5.9.

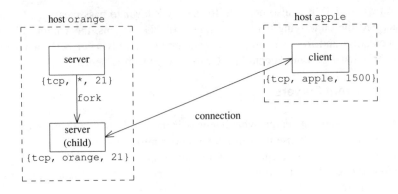

Figure 5.9 Concurrent server passes connection to child.

The association is {tcp, orange, 21, apple, 1500}. The server process that was waiting for the client connection now returns to its wait loop, letting the child process handle the client's request.

Assume that another client process on the host apple requests a connection to the same server. The client's TCP module assigns it a new ephemeral port number, say 1501, so that the half association {tcp, apple, 1501} is unique on the host apple. This gives us the picture shown in Figure 5.10.

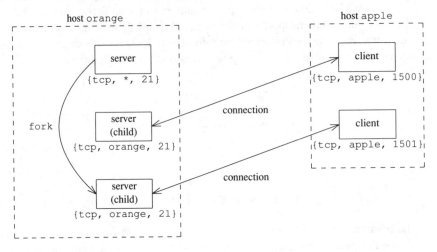

Figure 5.10 Second client connection passed to another child.

Note that even though there are two identical half associations on the `orange` host, `{tcp, orange, 21}`, the two complete associations are unique.

```
{tcp, orange, 21, apple, 1500}
{tcp, orange, 21, apple, 1501}
```

The TCP module on the `orange` system is able to determine which server child process is to receive a given data message, based on the source Internet address and the source TCP port number.

    We assumed in the examples above that the TCP module assigns a unique ephemeral port number to a process (e.g., a client) if the process does not need to assign a well-known port to itself (e.g., a server). This is what normally happens. There are instances, however, when a process can request that a specific port be used. The Internet FTP has this requirement, and it is interesting to examine this as another example of Internet addressing and port assignment.

    FTP normally runs using the standard client and concurrent-server relationship, as shown above. User commands are passed from the client to the server across the TCP connection, with the server's responses being returned on the connection. But when we request a file to be transferred between the client and server, another TCP connection is established between the two processes. This provides one connection for commands and one connection for data. The client initiates the transfer by sending a command across the existing connection to the server. The client also creates a new communication channel, using the same port number that it is using for the control connection. The client does a passive open on this new channel, waiting for the server to complete the connection. This is different from the previous examples, as the client now has to tell its TCP module that it is OK to use the same port number, even though the half association, `{tcp, apple, 1500}`, for example, is not unique on the client's host. (This is done using the `SO_REUSEADDR` socket option, as we'll describe in Section 6.11.) To guarantee a unique association when the server completes the connection with this new client port, the server must use some other port. FTP dictates that the server use the well-known port 20 for this purpose. If we assume that both the client processes in our previous examples are FTP clients, and both have established a data connection with their respective servers, we have the picture shown in Figure 5.11. All four associations are unique, as required by the Internet protocol suite.

```
{tcp, orange, 20, apple, 1500}
{tcp, orange, 21, apple, 1500}
{tcp, orange, 20, apple, 1501}
{tcp, orange, 21, apple, 1501}
```

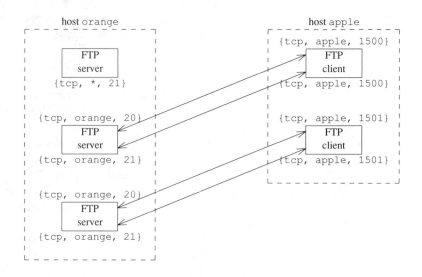

Figure 5.11   FTP example with two clients and two servers.

Buffering and Out-of-Band Data

UDP is a datagram service. Every datagram written by a user process has a header
encapsulated by the UDP layer, then the datagram is passed to the IP layer for transmission. There is no reason for the UDP layer to let the user's data hang around in the UDP
layer. The data is transmitted as soon as the IP layer can get to it, so the concepts of
buffering and out-of-band data do not apply to UDP.

TCP, however, presents a byte-stream service to the user process, and provides both
of these features. In TCP terminology the flush output command is called the *push* flag,
and out-of-band data is called *urgent data*. By definition, TCP supports any amount of
out-of-band data, but not all implementations support more than one byte at a time of
urgent data.

We show how a user process can set the TCP push flag with a socket option in Section 6.11, and we return to TCP out-of-band data in Section 6.14.

Buffer Sizes and Limitations

By definition the maximum size of an IP datagram is 65,536 bytes. Assuming a 20-byte
IP header, this leaves up to 65,516 bytes for other data in the datagram. Realize, however, that as soon as the size of an IP datagram exceeds the size of the underlying
network's MTU, fragmentation occurs. Furthermore, not all TCP/IP implementations
support IP fragmentation, let alone fragmentation of a 65,536-byte datagram. Every
TCP/IP implementation must support a minimum IP datagram size of 576 bytes. Note
that a network can have an MTU smaller than 576, but any host must be able to

reassemble the fragmented IP packets into at least a 576-byte IP datagram. The actual maximum size of an IP datagram depends on the IP software on both ends, as well as the software on every gateway between the two ends.

Since UDP packets are transmitted using IP, if the result of adding the UDP header and the IP header causes the datagram to exceed the network's MTU, fragmentation occurs. This means, for example, that sending 2048-byte UDP packets on an Ethernet guarantees fragmentation.

TCP is different, since it breaks up the data into what it calls *segments*. The segment size used by TCP is agreed on between the two ends when a connection is established. In Section 6.11 we describe a socket option that allows a user process to determine the segment size being used by TCP.

Cabrera et al. [1988] show the effects of IP fragmentation on network performance. Kent and Mogul [1987] provide arguments for not allowing fragmentation at all.

5.2.6 Application Layer

There are several application programs that are provided by almost every TCP/IP implementation. One strength of the TCP/IP protocol suite is the availability of these standard applications for a variety of operating environments.

Additional details on FTP, TELNET, and SMTP are given in Stallings et al. [1988], in addition to the RFCs referenced below.

FTP—File Transfer Protocol

FTP is a program used to transfer files from one system to another. It provides a rich set of features and options, such as user authentication, data conversion, directory listings, and the like. Its standard definition is RFC 959 [Postel and Reynolds 1985].

A typical sequence of events is for an interactive user to invoke an FTP client process on the local system. This client process establishes a connection with an FTP server process on the remote system using TCP. FTP establishes two connections between the client and server processes—one for control information (commands and responses) and the other for the data being transferred. The interactive user is prompted for access information on the remote system (login name and password, if required), and files can then be transferred in both directions. FTP handles both binary and text files.

TFTP—Trivial File Transfer Protocol

TFTP is a simpler protocol than FTP. While it provides for file transfer between a client process and a server process, it does not provide user authentication or some of the other features of FTP (listing directories, moving between directories, etc.). TFTP uses UDP, not TCP. The reference for TFTP is RFC 783 [Sollins 1981].

We develop a complete client and server implementation of TFTP in Chapter 12.

TELNET—Remote Login

TELNET provides a remote login facility. It allows an interactive user on a client system to start a login session on a remote system. Once a login session is established, the client process passes the user's keystrokes to the server process. As with the FTP program, TELNET uses TCP. The standard for TELNET is RFC 854 [Postel and Reynolds 1983].

We consider the design of a remote login facility in Chapter 15 when we discuss the 4.3BSD remote login command.

SMTP—Simple Mail Transfer Protocol

SMTP provides a protocol for two systems to exchange electronic mail using a TCP connection between the two systems. The protocol definition for SMTP is RFC 821 [Postel 1982]. The standard for the format of the mail messages is RFC 822 [Crocker 1982]. RFC 974 [Partridge 1986] specifies how mail is routed.

5.3   XNS—Xerox Network Systems

5.3.1 Introduction

Xerox Network Systems (also called Xerox NS, or XNS) is the network architecture developed by Xerox Corporation in the late 1970s for integrating their office products and computer systems. XNS is an *open* system, in that Xerox has published and made available the protocols used by XNS. Other vendors also provide hardware and software that supports the XNS protocols. Most 4.3BSD systems provide support for the XNS protocol suite. XNS is similar in structure to the TCP/IP protocol suite, so the presentation in this section assumes the reader has read the TCP/IP description in the previous section.

5.3.2 Overview

The arrangement of the layers in the XNS protocol suite, and their approximate mapping into the OSI model is shown in Figure 5.12.

ECHO   *Echo Protocol.* A simple protocol that causes a host to echo the packet that it receives. Most XNS implementations support this protocol.

RIP   *Routing Information Protocol.* A protocol used to maintain a routing database for use on a host in the forwarding of IDP packets to another host. Typically a routing process exists on the host, and this process uses RIP to maintain the database.

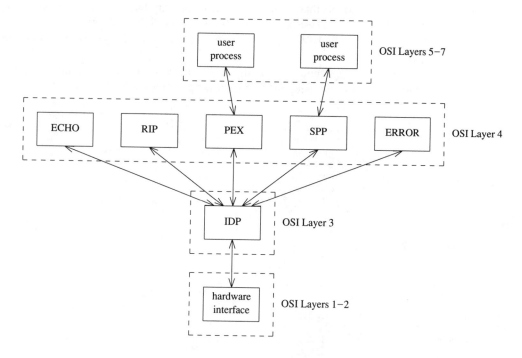

Figure 5.12 Layering in the XNS protocol suite.

PEX   *Packet Exchange Protocol.* An unreliable, connectionless, datagram proto-
           col for user processes. Although PEX is not a reliable protocol, it does
           retransmission but does not perform duplicate detection. We describe PEX
           later in this section.

SPP   *Sequenced Packet Protocol.* A connection-oriented, reliable protocol for
           user processes. It provides a byte stream for the user process with optional
           message boundaries. SPP is the most commonly used protocol in the XNS
           suite, similar to TCP in the Internet suite. We describe SPP in more detail
           later in this section.

ERROR   *Error Protocol.* A protocol that can be used by any process to report that it
           has discovered an error and therefore discarded a packet.

IDP   *Internet Datagram Protocol.* IDP is the connectionless, unreliable data-
           gram protocol that provides the packet delivery service for all the above
           protocols. We describe IDP later in this section.

The five protocols that we show at OSI layer 4 are termed the ''Internet'' Transport Protocols by Xerox. These are defined by Xerox [1981b], with additional details given in O'Toole, Torek, and Weiser [1985]. Boggs et al. [1980] gives some insight into the design of XNS.

Most Xerox applications are built using the Courier remote procedure call protocol. Courier, in turn, is built using SPP. We show this in Figure 5.13.

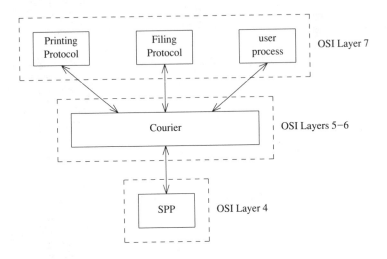

Figure 5.13 Typical XNS applications that use Courier.

A user process has the choice of interacting directly with SPP or using Courier. We return to Courier in Chapter 18 when we describe remote procedure calls in more detail.

Note that all XNS protocols use IDP. Recall from the TCP/IP protocol suite that ARP and RARP did not use IP.

5.3.3 Data-Link Layer

The typical XNS network is an Ethernet, although other technologies such as leased or switched telephone lines using SDLC are possible.

5.3.4 Network Layer—IDP

XNS Addresses

An XNS address occupies 12 bytes and is comprised of three parts:

- a 32-bit network ID,
- a 48-bit host ID,
- a 16-bit port number.

(Unfortunately, the XNS literature calls the 16-bit port number a *socket*. To avoid confusion with the term socket that we defined in the previous chapter, we call this XNS field a *port*.) In our definition of a socket from the previous chapter, *{protocol, local-addr, local-process}*, the *protocol* is `xns`, the *local-addr* is the combination of the network ID and the host ID, and the *local-process* is the port number. Note that an association in the TCP/IP protocol suite interprets the *local-process* relative to the *protocol*, which is why we have to differentiate between TCP and UDP. With XNS, however, that distinction isn't required since the *local-process* (the port number) does not depend on any specific transport protocol within XNS.

The host ID is an absolute number that must be unique across all XNS internets. Typically the 48-bit host ID is set to the 48-bit Ethernet address, as most Xerox internets are built using Ethernets. (Recall from the previous chapter that all Ethernet interfaces are provided by their manufacturer with a unique 48-bit Ethernet address.) With unique host IDs, the network ID is redundant, but it is required for routing purposes. Like the host ID, the network ID must also be unique across all XNS internets. Both host IDs and network IDs are assigned by Xerox Corp. to guarantee their uniqueness. Host IDs are typically written as six hexadecimal digits separated by periods, as in 2.7.1.0.2a.19. The network ID is typically written as a decimal integer.

Recall that TCP/IP host IDs are relative to the network ID, not absolute. For example, the host ID in both of the Class B addresses 128.1.0.3 and 128.2.0.3 is 3, but the first network ID is 1 and the second is 2. XNS host addresses, on the other hand, form a flat address space.

IDP Packets

Everything in XNS is eventually transmitted in an IDP packet. IDP provides a connectionless and unreliable delivery service, similar to the IP layer in the TCP/IP protocol suite. Every IDP packet contains a 30-byte header with the following fields:

- source XNS address (host ID, network ID, port),
- destination XNS address (host ID, network ID, port),
- checksum,
- length of data (typically 0–546 bytes),
- higher layer packet type (SPP, PEX, etc.).

The differences between IP and IDP are as follows:

- The IDP packet contains a checksum that includes the entire IDP packet. Recall that the IP checksum is only for the IP header, and does not include the data in the IP datagram. IP forces the upper layers (UDP and TCP) to add their own checksums, if desired.

- IDP packets contain a 16-bit port number. In the TCP/IP suite, both UDP and TCP are required to define their own port numbers, which are stored in their own headers. The IDP port number is in the IDP header.

- IDP demultiplexes the incoming datagrams based on the port number, since the IDP port number is independent of the actual protocol. The IP layer, on the other hand, demultiplexes the incoming datagrams based on their protocol field— usually TCP or UDP. The TCP and UDP layers then demultiplex the data based on the port numbers in the TCP and UDP headers.

Given the first two points, it is more reasonable for a user process to use IDP directly, when an unreliable datagram protocol is required, than for a user process to use IP directly.

Since the IDP layer demultiplexes the incoming datagrams based on the local port number, and not the packet type, it is possible for a protocol module to receive packets of another protocol. For example, it is possible for the SPP protocol module to receive an ERROR protocol packet whose destination is the port using SPP. Each protocol package in the XNS suite must be prepared to receive ERROR protocol packets. Again, this differs from the TCP/IP suite.

5.3.5 Transport Layer—SPP and PEX

SPP—Sequenced Packet Protocol

SPP, the predominant transport layer protocol in XNS, is similar to TCP. It provides a connection-oriented, reliable, full-duplex service to an application program. Unlike TCP, which provides only a byte-stream interface, there is a three-level hierarchy in the data being transferred using SPP.

- Bytes are the basic entity.
- A packet is composed of zero or more bytes.
- A message is composed of one or more packets.

Using these data forms, SPP can present three different interfaces to a user process.

- A *byte-stream* interface: the bytes are delivered to the user process in order. The user process reads or writes the data using any convenient buffer size. Message boundaries are preserved, but there are no packet boundaries seen by the user process.

- A *packet-stream* interface: the packets are delivered to the user process in order. The user process reads or writes entire packets, each of which is passed on to the IDP layer. The user process has to know more details, such as the format of the

12-byte SPP header, to set and detect message boundaries. The user process is
not to associate any semantics with the physical packet boundaries that it reads
and writes; instead the message boundaries available through SPP are to be used
for message demarcation.

- A *reliable-packet* interface: the packets are delivered to the user process, but they
  might be out of order. This interface presents the packets to the user process as
  they arrive, which might be out of order, since two consecutive IDP packets might
  travel from the source to the destination following different routes. Duplicate
  packets are removed by the SPP software.

The first two interfaces are typically provided, while the reliable-packet interface is an
option. Also, it is possible for both ends of a connection to be using a different interface.
For example, there is nothing to prevent a client from using the byte-stream interface
when communicating with a server that is using the packet-stream interface. We compare these three interfaces in Figure 5.14.

	SPP		
	byte-stream	packet-stream	reliable-packet
connection-oriented ?	yes	yes	yes
message boundaries ?	yes	yes	no
packet boundaries ?	no	yes	yes
data checksum ?	yes	yes	yes
positive ack. ?	yes	yes	yes
timeout and rexmit ?	yes	yes	yes
duplicate detection ?	yes	yes	yes
sequencing ?	yes	yes	no
flow control ?	yes	yes	yes

Figure 5.14 Comparison of interfaces provided by SPP.

In this figure we have added the line ''packet boundaries'' to differentiate between the
byte-stream interface and the packet-stream interface. In future figures we show only the
SPP byte-stream interface, since it supports message boundaries. Since the reliable-
packet interface is not common, we do not consider it any further in this text.

In Figure 5.15 we diagram the encapsulation that takes place with SPP data on an
Ethernet.

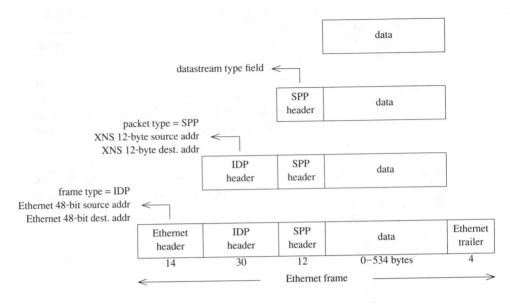

Figure 5.15 Encapsulation of SPP data on an Ethernet.

The datastream type field and the packet type field are termed *bridge fields* and we describe them later in this section. The 12-byte XNS address fields contain the 48-bit host address, the 32-bit network address and the 16-bit port number.

PEX—Packet Exchange Protocol

Another transport layer protocol is PEX the Packet Exchange Protocol. PEX is a datagram oriented protocol, similar to UDP, but PEX retransmits a request when necessary (requiring a timeout and retransmission) and PEX does not do duplicate detection. PEX has a 6-byte header that includes a 32-bit ID field and a 16-bit client type. The protocol operates as follows:

1. The client sets the ID field to some value that it chooses and sets the client type field to a value that specifies the type of service requested. The packet is sent to the server.

2. The server performs the service specified by the client type.

3. When the server forms its response packet, it must return the same ID field that was sent by the client. This way, when the client receives the response it knows which request the server is responding to. The client must then use a different ID field for its next request.

The purpose of the client type field in the PEX header is to allow a single server to handle multiple service requests, each service corresponding to a different client type. The PEX module on the client end will retransmit the request if a response if not received in a specified amount of time, obviating the user's client process from having to do this.

The encapsulation that takes place with PEX data on an Ethernet is shown in Figure 5.16.

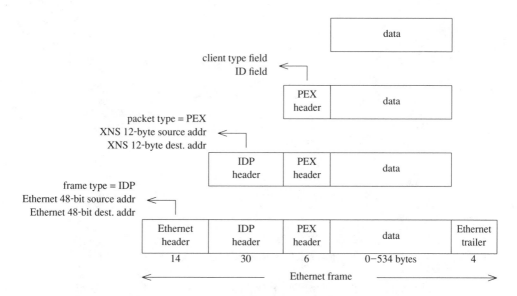

Figure 5.16 Encapsulation of PEX data on an Ethernet.

The relationship of the XNS protocols that we have described to our simplified 4-layer model is shown in Figure 5.17.

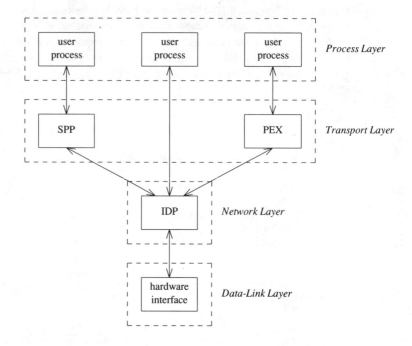

Figure 5.17   4-layer model showing SPP, PEX, and IDP.

In Figure 5.18 we add IDP, PEX, and SPP to our table of protocol services from the previous section.

	IP	IDP	UDP	PEX	TCP	SPP
connection-oriented ?	no	no	no	no	yes	yes
message boundaries ?	yes	yes	yes	yes	no	yes
data checksum ?	no	yes	opt.	yes	yes	yes
positive ack. ?	no	no	no	no	yes	yes
timeout and rexmit ?	no	no	no	yes	yes	yes
duplicate detection ?	no	no	no	no	yes	yes
sequencing ?	no	no	no	no	yes	yes
flow control ?	no	no	no	no	yes	yes

Figure 5.18   Comparison of protocol features: Internet protocols and XNS protocols.

As mentioned earlier in this section, the column for SPP is for either the byte-stream interface or the packet-stream interface, since both provide the same features for the services listed.

XNS Bridge Fields

The XNS protocols define *bridge fields* in the headers that are encapsulated by each layer. These fields are not used by a particular layer, but are set and interpreted by the next higher layer. There are three bridge fields.

1. The *packet type* field in the IDP header is not used by the IDP layer. It specifies the protocol of the data in the IDP packet. This is how, for example, the SPP module knows that a received packet is an ERROR protocol packet and not an SPP data packet.

2. The *datastream type* field in the SPP header is not used by the SPP module, but is available for the user process that is using SPP. The XNS reference, Xerox [1981b], provides an example use of this field in shutting down an SPP connection between two user processes.

3. The *client type* field in the PEX header is not used by the PEX protocol module. Again, it is intended for the user process that is using PEX.

The complication imposed by these bridge fields is that they are in the headers that are encapsulated and decapsulated by the protocol software—they are not in the normal data area that the user reads and writes. This requires some form of interface between the protocol modules (SPP and PEX) and the user process, to allow us to set and examine these bridge fields.

We'll examine the 4.3BSD socket options that allow a user process to examine and set these bridge fields in Section 6.11. Additionally, the XNS echo client that we develop in Section 11.3 uses one of these socket options to set the packet type field in the IDP header.

Buffering and Out-of-Band Data

PEX is a datagram service, so the concepts of buffering and out-of-band data don't apply. SPP, however, provides a single byte of out-of-band data. The Xerox specification states that this byte of data is to be made available to the user process as quickly as possible, and furthermore it is presented to the user process again according to its normal sequence. This means that the receiving SPP layer makes a copy of the out-of-band byte in some special location and also puts the byte into its sequential position in the receiver's input buffer.

We'll return to SPP out-of-band data in Section 6.14.

Buffer Sizes and Limitations

IDP packets are not fragmented as Internet IP datagrams might be. Most Xerox systems enforce a maximum IDP packet size of 576 bytes. Allocating 30 bytes for the IDP header, this allows up to 546 bytes of data in an IDP packet. Allowing 12 bytes for an SPP header, the maximum SPP packet size is 534 bytes.

5.3.6 Application Layer

The main use of XNS today is to communicate with Xerox hardware. As mentioned earlier, most of these applications use the Courier remote procedure facility, which we describe in Chapter 18. Xerox standards are available for the predominant application protocols—printing protocol (sending files to a Xerox printer), and filing protocol (sending and receiving files from a Xerox file server), for example. Xerox [1985] provides additional information on some of these applications.

5.4   SNA—Systems Network Architecture

5.4.1 Introduction

SNA, Systems Network Architecture, was originally released by IBM in 1974. It has since been enhanced many times and is now the predominant method used to form internets of various IBM computers. Additionally, many vendors other than IBM provide various levels of SNA support, allowing many non-IBM systems to participate in SNA networks. SNA is an architecture, not a product. There exist software and hardware products from both IBM and other vendors that implement different portions of SNA.

   Our reason for covering SNA in a book on Unix networking, is that most vendors of Unix systems now support SNA, in one form or another. Frequently the support is for LU 6.2, which is the emphasis of this section. Unfortunately there is no common programming interface across all these products, so we won't be able to say much about the C interface to an SNA implementation.

   SNA was originally designed to support the networking of nonprogrammable devices, such as terminals (termed ''workstations'' by IBM) and printers, to IBM mainframes. (An IBM ''mainframe'' is a system based on the System/370 architecture, as opposed to other IBM systems, both large and small.) Because of this non peer-to-peer evolution, where one system (the mainframe) is always the master in the communication relationship, SNA appears more complicated than the other communication architectures that we've discussed (TCP/IP, for example). SNA has always had a terminology all its own, and has been confounded by the mainframe requirements just to implement and configure an SNA network—CICS, VTAM, NCP, cluster controllers, and the like. Only in the past five years has SNA adopted the protocols and implementations that allow two user processes to communicate easily with each other, and without the requirement of a mainframe in the communication link.

The user of a network is defined to be an *end user*, which is either a user at a terminal or an application program (process). An end user interacts with a *logical unit* (referred to as an *LU*) to access the network. The type of services provided by the LU to the end user differs for each type of LU. LU types 2, 3, 4, and 7 support communication between processes and terminals, while LU types 1, 6.1, and 6.2 are for communication between two processes. The LU in turn interacts with a *physical unit* (referred to as a *PU*). The PU is, in essence, the operating system of the node, and it controls the data-link connections between the node and the network. We picture this in Figure 5.19.

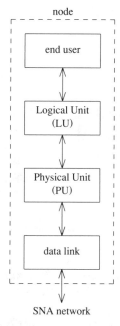

Figure 5.19 SNA node with logical unit and physical unit.

If we consider the PU as the operating system of the node, then the data-link portion is the device driver of the node. The type of node is specified by the PU type. Five types of nodes are currently supported—1, 2.0, 2.1, 4, and 5. These are referred to, for example, as a "Type 2.1 node," or "T2.1 node," or as PU 2.1. What we have called earlier in this text a "network host" or a "system on a network," is referred to by IBM as a *node*—an addressable unit on a network. IBM uses the term node, since an SNA node can be a nonprogrammable device such as a terminal or printer.

Our interest in this text is only with LU 6.2 and PU 2.1, as these are the strategic IBM products, and the only SNA implementations that adequately support communication between processes.

The bibliography lists several SNA manuals available from IBM that provide additional details on all the features mentioned here.

5.4.2 Overview

SNA was developed in a layered approach that is similar to the OSI model. The seven
SNA layers are shown in Figure 5.20.

SNA functions	SNA layers	OSI layers
user process	Transaction Services	Application
Logical Unit	Presentation Services	Presentation
	Data-Flow Control	Session
	Transmission Control	
Path Control	Path Control	Transport
		Network
Data Link	Data-Link Control	Data Link
	Physical Control	Physical

Figure 5.20 7-layer SNA model and approximate mapping between SNA layers and OSI model.

Since SNA predates the OSI model, there is no exact mapping from the seven SNA
layers into the seven OSI layers. An approximate mapping between the two, along with a
consolidation of the seven SNA layers into the corresponding SNA functions, is also
shown in Figure 5.20.

In the seven SNA layers, the LU performs the functions of layers 4, 5, and 6—
transmission control, data-flow control, and presentation services. The top layer, transaction services, is what we have called the user process. The bottom two layers are combined into what we have called the network access layer, as these are the two layers that
change depending on the interface types supported by the node (SDLC, token ring, etc.).

Note that the four SNA functions in Figure 5.20 correspond to our simplified 4-layer
model. What we call a user process is called a transaction program (TP) by IBM.

Two forms of SNA networks have evolved.

- *Subarea SNA networks.*
  These networks are built around IBM mainframes that maintain centralized control over the network. Internets of independent SNA subarea networks can be formed using the SNA network interconnect (SNI) facility.

- *APPN networks.*
  APPN stands for "Advanced Peer-to-Peer Networking" and was introduced by IBM in 1986 for the System/36. It has also been called SNA/LEN (low entry networking). In 1988 the capability was introduced for APPN networks to be connected together through an SNA subarea network. APPN is limited to PU Type 2.1 nodes and supports LU 6.2. APPN has features not found in subarea networks, such as dynamic routing. Baratz et al. [1985] describe the prototype implementation of APPN.

Today most of the more than 20,000 SNA networks in existence are subarea networks based on IBM mainframes. But the increased shift towards smaller systems and the increased capabilities of APPN should lead to the creation of many APPN-based networks.

5.4.3 Data-Link Layer

The predominant form of network access used in SNA networks is SDLC—synchronous data-link control. Typical SDLC links operate between 4.8 Kbps and 57.6 Kbps over leased or switched telephone lines. The token ring is now starting to be used for LANs. One IBM product, the RT, supports LU 6.2 over an Ethernet. IBM mainframes can communicate with each other using SNA over a System/370 data channel.

5.4.4 Path-Control Layer

In the TCP/IP and XNS protocol suites, the IP layer and the IDP layer both provided an unreliable datagram delivery service to the layers above. In SNA we encounter a different scenario where the SNA path-control layer provides a virtual circuit service to its upper layer (the LU). This means that the path-control layer, and the data-link layer beneath it, provide error control, flow control, and sequencing.

Path control is the layer responsible for moving packets around in an SNA network. Figure 5.21 shows the encapsulation that each layer applies to a message of user data being transmitted by an SNA node, assuming an SDLC data link.

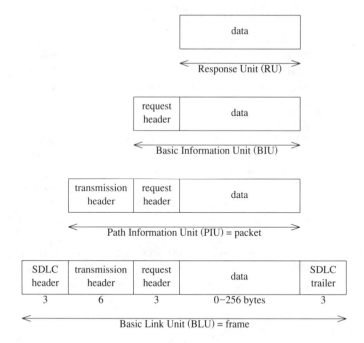

Figure 5.21   Encapsulation of SNA data on an SDLC link.

The request header is the LU header, and the transmission header is the PC (path control) header, if we follow the conventions from the TCP/IP and XNS protocol suites where the name of an encapsulated header is the name of the layer that adds the header. There is another header that is sometimes added by the LU—a function management header (FMH) that carries control information between LUs. This header is placed between the request header and the data, with a bit turned on in the request header specifying that a function management header is present.

In Figure 5.21 we show the data portion as being from 0 to 256 bytes in length. The maximum response unit size is typically 256 or 512 bytes, but this size can be negotiated to other values by the two LUs.

Every LU in a given SNA network must have a unique name, from 1 to 8 characters. In an internet of SNA networks, every network must have a unique name, also from 1 to 8 characters. A particular LU in an internet is identified by its *network-qualified LU name*. This consists of

- network name,
- LU name within the network.

The network-qualified LU name is written as *netname.LUname* using a period between the two names. The actual mapping of this network-qualified LU name to a physical address is handled by a portion of the LU called *directory services*.

The size of the transmission header that path control uses for moving packets through a network ranges from 6 to 26 bytes, depending on the node types. We showed a 6-byte transmission header Figure 5.21. These 6-byte headers are used for traffic between two adjacent Type 2.1 nodes. The 26-byte transmission header is used for data exchanges between two adjacent subarea nodes that support explicit routing and virtual routing. A complete treatment of SNA routing and SNA address formats is beyond the scope of this text. Fortunately, it is not a requisite to understanding the use of LU 6.2, which is the intent of our coverage of SNA.

Path control also does packet fragmentation and reassembly, termed *segmenting* in SNA, when a packet must be divided into pieces before being passed to the data-link layer. This is similar to the fragmentation and reassembly done by the IP layer in TCP/IP.

5.4.5 LU 6.2—APPC

LU 6.2 is also referred to as *APPC* for *Advanced Program-to-Program Communication* and was released by IBM in 1982. LU 6.2 can use either PU 2.0 or PU 2.1. The major difference is that PU 2.0 can only be used to communicate with an IBM mainframe, and has inherent in it the master–slave relationship, where the mainframe is the master. PU 2.1, however, is newer, and systems implementing PU 2.1 can communicate with each other, without the need for a mainframe in the communication path. All newer IBM implementations of SNA (System/36, System/38, AS/400, RT, PC) support PU 2.1.

LU 6.2 provides a connection-oriented, reliable, half-duplex service to an application program. Note that this is the first half-duplex service that we have encountered. Both TCP and SPP are full-duplex protocols. LU 6.2, however, allows data flow between the user processes only in a single direction at a time. In Figure 5.22 we add LU 6.2 to the table of protocol features that we have been building. This time, we'll add a row for the connection-oriented protocols indicating whether the protocol provides a full-duplex data stream to the user process.

	IP	IDP	UDP	PEX	TCP	SPP	LU6.2
connection-oriented ?	no	no	no	no	yes	yes	yes
message boundaries ?	yes	yes	yes	yes	no	yes	yes
data checksum ?	no	yes	opt.	yes	yes	yes	no
positive ack. ?	no	no	no	no	yes	yes	yes
timeout and rexmit ?	no	no	no	yes	yes	yes	yes
duplicate detection ?	no	no	no	no	yes	yes	yes
sequencing ?	no	no	no	no	yes	yes	yes
flow control ?	no	no	no	no	yes	yes	yes
full-duplex ?					yes	yes	no

Figure 5.22 Comparison of protocol features: Internet, XNS, and SNA.

Notice that LU 6.2 does not provide an end-to-end data checksum, which is different from the other connection-oriented protocols we've covered—TCP and SPP. The developers of SNA consider the hop-by-hop reliability of the data-link layer (the cyclic redundancy check provided by the SDLC protocol, for example) to be an adequate test for corrupted data. (We return to this topic in the last section of this chapter.) Yet LU 6.2 provides positive acknowledgments, timeout and retransmission, duplicate detection, and sequencing, so we still consider it a "reliable" protocol.

Sessions and Conversations

In SNA terminology, the peer-to-peer connection between two user processes is called a *conversation*. The peer-to-peer connection between two LUs is called a *session*. A session is usually a long-term connection between two LUs, while a conversation is often of a shorter duration. This is shown in Figure 5.23.

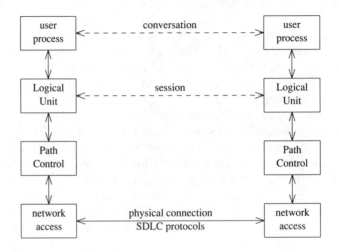

Figure 5.23 SNA sessions and conversations.

Using Figure 5.23 we can list some of the features provided by a Type 2.1 node that are not available with a Type 2.0 node.

- A T2.1 node supports multiple hardware links.
- A T2.1 node supports *parallel sessions* for its LUs. This means that two LUs, each in a different node, can have multiple sessions with each other.
- A T2.1 node supports *multiple sessions* for its LUs. This means that a given LU can have sessions with more than one partner LU at the same time.

An example is shown in Figure 5.24.

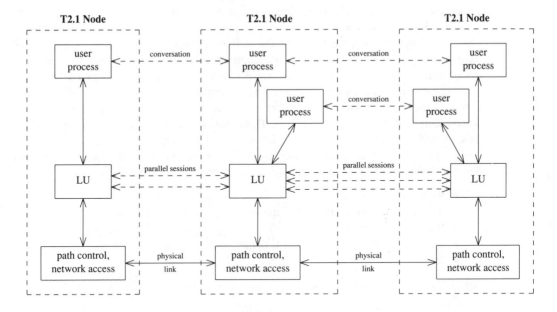

Figure 5.24 Example of sessions and conversations between Type 2.1 nodes.

Sessions are expensive to establish, so a typical LU establishes a certain number of sessions with its partner LUs. This forms a pool of active sessions for the LU to manage. When a user process wants to allocate a conversation, it requests the use of a session from the LU for the conversation. The LU picks an available session from its pool and dedicates this session to the conversation. The user process can use this conversation for a single transaction with its partner process, or it can hold on to the conversation for a long time. When the process is finished with the conversation, the process deallocates it. This allows the LU to put the conversation back into an available pool.

Using the terminology from the previous chapter we would call a conversation a *connection*, and ignore the fact that a conversation takes place over a session. Indeed, sessions are usually established by a network operator or when the system is initialized, so the typical user has no control over the session allocations. Note that LU 6.2 differs from both TCP and SPP in its explicit allocation and use of sessions. While a TCP connection between two user processes implies that the two TCP modules have a ''session'' of some form between them, we do not have to preallocate a certain number of sessions between two TCP modules. There is no inherent limit on the number of ''sessions'' that a TCP module can have with other TCP modules, other than any resource limits in its implementation (table sizes, number of processes allowed by the operating system, etc.). LU 6.2 requires more user control in specifying the number of sessions to allocate between LUs.

In our client–server model, we identified a server process as a process that had executed a passive open, awaiting a connection from a client process. This implied that the server process was already executing when it did the passive open. The server was identified by a well-known address that was protocol-dependent. LU 6.2 is different in that the client specifies the *name* of the partner program to execute—called the TP (transaction program) name. Furthermore, the target LU usually creates a new program instance (i.e., a new process) for every conversation that is started with a given TP name.

Each LU associates a conversation with a unique identifier, which we call a conversation ID, and this ID associates a packet with a particular process. (Since a conversation has exclusive use of a session, we can call this either a conversation ID or a session ID.) In an APPN network the conversation ID is a 16-bit integer. This 16-bit value is carried in the transmission header and is used by APPN to specify the user process. From our definition of an *association* from the previous chapter, for SNA it consists of

- the protocol (LU 6.2),
- the local network-qualified LU name,
- the local conversation ID,
- the foreign network-qualified LU name,
- the foreign conversation ID.

An example of this 5-tuple could be

```
{lu62, NET1.LUJOE, 5, NET1.LUMIKE, 3}
```

Again, we are not concerned with the conversion of a network-qualified LU name, such as NET1.LUJOE, into its internal representation as an SNA address.

LU 6.2 Protocol Boundary

The interface between a user process and the LU is called "presentation services" in SNA. There are two interfaces possible for a user process to LU 6.2:

- mapped conversations,
- unmapped conversations.

An unmapped conversation is also called a basic conversation. The major difference between the two types of conversations is in the format of the data that is exchanged between the process and the LU (which we discuss later in this section).

The interface between a user process and LU 6.2 is defined as a collection of *verbs* that a transaction program can execute to request a service from the LU. This defines the protocol boundary between the program and LU 6.2. The actual mapping of these verbs into an application program interface (API) depends on the specific LU 6.2 software being used. An API could be a set of functions that a user process can call. As mentioned earlier, there is no standard API for LU 6.2, not even among different IBM products. Therefore, instead of describing an actual API, we'll describe the different LU 6.2 verbs that most LU 6.2 implementations provide to an application program.

Here we provide a brief summary of the LU 6.2 verbs. We list only the names of the mapped conversation verbs—unless otherwise noted, a basic verb that does a similar function is available, and its name is formed by removing the MC_ prefix. For example, ALLOCATE is the basic conversation equivalent of MC_ALLOCATE.

MC_ALLOCATE	Allocates a conversation with another program. Required arguments are the name of the program to execute and the name of the LU where that program is located. The process issuing the ALLOCATE starts in the send state and the partner process starts in the receive state.
MC_CONFIRM	Sends a confirmation request to the remote process and waits for a reply. This allows the two processes in a conversation to synchronize their processing with each other.
MC_CONFIRMED	Sends a confirmation reply to the remote process.
MC_DEALLOCATE	Deallocates a conversation.
MC_FLUSH	Forces the transmission of the local send buffer to the other LU. In general, LU 6.2 waits until a full buffer is available before sending anything to the other process.
MC_GET_ATTRIBUTES	Obtains information about a conversation, such as the name of the partner LU.
MC_PREPARE_TO_RECEIVE	Changes the conversation from send to receive state. Recall that LU 6.2 is a half-duplex protocol, not full-duplex.
MC_RECEIVE_AND_WAIT	Waits for information to be received from the partner process. The information returned can be user data or a confirmation request.
MC_RECEIVE_IMMEDIATE	Receives any information that is available in the local LU's buffer, but does not wait for information to arrive.
MC_REQUEST_TO_SEND	Notifies the partner process that this process wants to send data. When the local process receives a ''send'' indication from the partner process, the state of the conversation changes.

MC_SEND_DATA   Sends one data record to the partner process. For a
                                mapped conversation, one user data record is option-
                                ally mapped into a mapped conversation record
                                (MCR), as described below. For an unmapped
                                conversation, some portion of a logical record is sent.
                                Note that regardless of the conversation type, this
                                verb might not cause any data to be sent to the other
                                process, depending on the buffering in the local LU.
                                See the MC_FLUSH verb above.

MC_SEND_ERROR   Informs the partner process that the local process has
                                detected an application error of some form.

There are additional verbs defined by LU 6.2 that are considered ''control operator
verbs.'' These are used to start sessions, change the number of sessions, stop sessions,
and the like. Their usage is product dependent and we don't consider them in this text.

The LU 6.2 protocol boundary defines numerous return codes from each of the
verbs. For example, the SEND_DATA verb can return that all is OK and additionally it
can indicate that the partner process has issued a REQUEST_TO_SEND.

Logical Records and GDS Variables

All user process data consists of a 2-byte length field (LL) followed by zero or more
bytes of data. This is called a *logical record* and is shown in Figure 5.25.

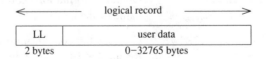

Figure 5.25 SNA logical record.

The length includes the two bytes occupied by the length field, so its value is always
greater than or equal to two.†

Two processes using the basic conversation verbs exchange logical records. A process that is writing logical records need not write a complete logical record with every
SEND_DATA verb. That is, a logical record consisting of 500 bytes (an LL field of 500,
followed by 498 bytes of user data) can be written in three pieces—100 bytes, followed
by a SEND_DATA of 250 bytes, followed by a SEND_DATA of 150 bytes. Similarly, the
receiving process can read the logical record (RECEIVE_AND_WAIT) in whatever sized
chunks it desires. A process must write a complete logical record, based on the LL value.

---

† Some internal LU components exchange control information for a session with the partner LU
using length fields less than two. This ''invalid'' length field informs the LU that the record is a
control record and not user data. We don't consider these control records in this text.

In the above example with an LL of 500, the process cannot write 400 bytes and then do a read. Not writing a complete logical record is called *truncation* and generates an error indication for the receiving process.

For mapped conversations each MC_SEND_DATA verb executed by the process generates a single *user data record*. If a mapping is being done, the mapping is applied to the user data record, generating the *mapped conversation record (MCR)*. A 2-byte LL field and a 2-byte ID field are prepended to the beginning of the MCR, generating a logical record. This is shown in Figure 5.26.

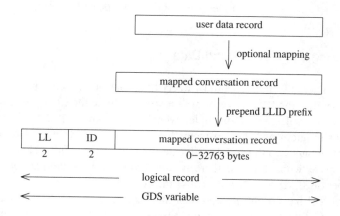

Figure 5.26 SNA mapped conversation record.

This logical record is the same as the logical record that is written using the basic conversation verbs, except a 2-byte ID field follows the LL field. This guarantees that the length of a logical record from an MC_SEND_DATA verb is greater than or equal to 4 bytes (since the lengths of the LL field and the ID field are include in the length). For all user process data, the ID field is set to 0x12FF by LU 6.2. Other values of the ID field are used by IBM applications and by the LU for special purposes.

A logical record containing an ID field is also called a *GDS variable*. GDS is an acronym for Generalized Data Stream. A GDS variable can be comprised of multiple logical records, if the length of the MCR exceeds 32,763 bytes. But the utility of writing such large records is questionable, so we won't confuse the diagrams to show this general case.†

No matter how the data was written, using either the basic conversation write or the mapped conversation write, the LU is free to break up the logical records into *response units (RUs)* as it wishes. The maximum response unit size is negotiated by the two partner LUs when the session is started and its value is typically 256 bytes for an SDLC data link. The LU appends the *request header (RH)* to the response unit and passes the buffer to path control, as shown earlier.

---

† Indeed, a conforming LU 6.2 implementation need handle only 2048-byte logical records.

Confirmation

One parameter for the ALLOCATE verbs is the synchronization level. This can be set to NONE or CONFIRM.† Specifying the confirmation option allows the user processes to use the CONFIRM and CONFIRMED verbs, which were described earlier. This provides an end-to-end confirmation that is built into the LU 6.2 protocol itself. Note that the same type of feature can be built into any protocol, if the two user processes agree on a convention for indicating a confirmation. We'll see in Section 13.2 how the 4.3BSD line printer spooler uses a single byte message to provide a confirmation message to its partner process.

Buffering and Out-of-Band Data

LU 6.2 internally buffers almost everything that one process sends to another. To circumvent this, the FLUSH verbs are provided to force the LU to send what is has accumulated in its buffer. For example, when a program ALLOCATEs a conversation with another program and then executes a SEND_DATA to transfer data to that process, the LU, by default, won't send the allocate until its buffer is full. This means that the initiating process won't know if there was an error invoking the partner program until some number of SEND_DATA verbs cause the allocate to be sent to the other side.

LU 6.2 has no out-of-band data mechanism, comparable to what we described with TCP and SPP. A user process must issue a SEND_ERROR verb to notify the other process that attention is required. It is then up to the user processes to determine how to handle things.

Well-Known Addresses

If the first character of the remote transaction program name (TP name) in an ALLOCATE is a special character (0x00−0x0D or 0x10−0x3F), then the remote TP is a *service transaction program*. These programs are typically supplied by IBM and only privileged processes can allocate conversations with them. Three service TPs are DIA, DDM, and SNADS, described in the next section. This feature corresponds to the privileged port feature of 4.3BSD for ports in the Internet domain and in the XNS domain.

---

† A third option, SYNCPT is specified in the LU 6.2 protocol definition. This option allows conversations to specify synchronization points for potentially backing out changes that it has made. This option appears to have been discarded by IBM [IBM 1988]. This feature is similar to the Commitment, Concurrency, and Recovery feature of the OSI Common Application Service Element, which we describe in Section 5.6.7.

Option Sets

The LU 6.2 specification provides a base set of features that any implementation must provide, along with 41 optional features that can also be provided by a given product. For example, one option allows conversations between programs at the same LU. Another option allows a process to flush the LU's buffer using the FLUSH verbs.

Unfortunately, this laxness in the "official" specification of the protocol makes portability of LU 6.2 applications less than desired. But most real-world implementations of LU 6.2 on computer systems of general interest (i.e., ignoring special purpose systems that weren't intended to be programmed by end users) tend to support options that should have been in the base set. Furthermore, the publication by IBM of their CPI-Communications API [IBM 1988] gives some indication about the features in LU 6.2 which will be supported in the future.

5.4.6 Application Layer

IBM is building distributed applications using LU 6.2. IBM differentiates between two types of user processes that are at the layer above the LU:

- application transaction programs,
- service transaction programs.

The only real difference is that service TPs are supplied by IBM and a service TP can provide a service for an application TP. Application TPs are user processes. Service TPs can only be invoked by privileged processes, as described above. From a network programming perspective the difference is negligible. Both types of TPs access the network in the same way through the LU.

DIA—Document Interchange Architecture

DIA defines the functions required for interchanging documents between different IBM office systems. DIA is implemented on top of LU 6.2. That is, DIA uses LU 6.2 for communicating between different computer systems. DIA provides the following functions: document library services (storing and retrieving documents), document distribution (delivering documents to others in the network), and file transfer. DIA specifies the protocols and data structures used to exchange information between two DIA processes—a DIA client process and a DIA server process. An implementation of DIA usually provides a command language for an interactive user to execute DIA commands. These user commands (such as sign on, sign off, search, retrieve, deliver, delete, etc.) are translated into the appropriate DIA functions that are exchanged between the user's DIA client process and the DIA server process, using LU 6.2. *DISOSS* (Distributed Office Support System) is the IBM mainframe implementation of DIA that runs under CICS.

One type of document that is exchanged using DIA is one whose format is specified by DCA. DCA (Document Content Architecture) specifies the internal format of a document that can be exchanged between IBM office systems—the data stream and how it is to be interpreted. There are two forms of DCA, revisable form and final form. The revisable form specifies the structure of the document while it can be edited or formatted. The final form specifies the structure of the completed document in a device independent format. The intent of DCA is to allow a document to be moved between different IBM office systems, in either a revisable form or a final format.

SNADS—SNA Distribution Services

SNADS is an *asynchronous* distribution service for moving distribution objects (such as a document or an electronic mail message) from a source node to a destination node. By asynchronous we mean that it initiates the sending of the object, but the actual delivery might take place later. Furthermore, the delivery might require temporary storage in one or more intermediate nodes. The asynchronous nature of SNADS is similar to the Unix electronic mail delivery service provided by the Unix `uucp` program, which we describe in Section 5.7.

Contrast this with a *synchronous* delivery service where the source and destination are connected together through an LU 6.2 conversation. This synchronous capability is similar to the TCP/IP SMTP application, which uses a TCP connection between the source host and the destination host.

DDM—Distributed Data Management

DDM is another application available from IBM that uses LU 6.2. DDM is IBM's architecture for transparent remote file access in an SNA network. DDM allows an application program to access the records in a file on another system. To do this, the application program calls the local DDM interface to request a record from a file. If the interface recognizes the request as one for a local file, the local file is accessed. Otherwise, the local interface (the DDM client process) establishes an LU 6.2 session with the DDM server process on the remote system, and the server accesses the record and returns it to the client.

5.5   NetBIOS

5.5.1   History

In 1984 IBM released its first LAN, the IBM PC Network. It was similar in concept to an Ethernet, but ran at 2 Mbps, whereas most Ethernets operate at 10 Mbps. The interface card for the IBM PC (called an ''adapter card'' by IBM) was developed by Sytek, Inc., and contained on it the first implementation of NetBIOS. The name *NetBIOS* is derived from the name BIOS for the ''basic input output system'' for the IBM PC. The BIOS was contained in read-only memory on the PC and provided an interface between a program on the PC and the actual hardware. Similarly, NetBIOS provides an interface between a program and the actual hardware on the interface card.

When IBM introduced its token ring LAN in 1985, it provided an implementation of NetBIOS for the token ring. The original PC Network implementation of NetBIOS was implemented in read-only memory on the interface card, while the token ring version was a software module. Despite the implementation differences, the token ring version provided the same interface to an application program as was provided by the original PC network.

The third implementation of NetBIOS by IBM occurred when the IBM PS/2 systems were introduced and the IBM LAN Support Program was available. This software package consists of device drivers and interface support for all of IBM's LAN interfaces.

NetBIOS is a software interface, not a network protocol. For example, the data packets that are exchanged across the IBM PC Network differ from those on a token ring network. We expect the actual frame that is transmitted by two different data-link layers to be different, since the data link header and trailer are different for each type of data link (token ring, Ethernet, SDLC, etc.). But the packet that is passed to the data-link layer should not change for a given protocol. For example, in the TCP/IP protocol suite, the IP datagram that starts with the IP header is the same, regardless of the data link being used. With NetBIOS this packet equivalency is not true. Nevertheless, the interfaces provided by all IBM implementations of NetBIOS are equivalent, providing a consistent software interface that has become a de facto standard for personal computers. In addition, there exist implementations of NetBIOS that use TCP and UDP as the underlying transport protocols, and standards exist for this in the Internet (RFC 1001 and RFC 1002).

Even though NetBIOS is not a protocol, we give an overview of the services that it provides here. Schwaderer [1988] provides details on using NetBIOS under the MS-DOS system. IBM [1987] provides additional details.

5.5.2 Overview

NetBIOS was designed for a group of personal computers, all sharing a common broadcast medium (the IBM PC Network, which we said earlier is like an Ethernet). It provides both a connection-oriented service (virtual circuit) and a connectionless (datagram) service. It supports both broadcast and multicast.

Four types of service are provided by NetBIOS:

- name service,
- session service,
- datagram service,
- general commands.

Figure 5.27 shows the relationship of these four services. Note that we do not indicate how these four services interact. In most implementations, a single box providing some form of datagram delivery (similar to the IP layer in the TCP/IP suite) is probably used.

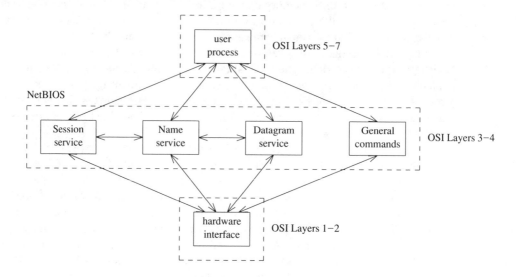

Figure 5.27 Relationship of NetBIOS services.

But unlike the IP layer, with NetBIOS the user process has no access to any services other than the ones described in the following sections, so the actual implementation need not concern us.

In many PC environments the application that NetBIOS is being used for is file sharing. In this case, another protocol interface exists above NetBIOS. This interface is called the Server Message Block protocol (SMB) and we show it in Figure 5.28.

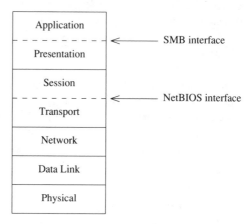

Figure 5.28 Relationship of NetBIOS and SMB to OSI model.

Dunsmuir [1989] shows the format of the SMB header and gives a listing of all the SMB functions: create directory, open file, read from file, and so on. Line printer access is automatically handled by this software interface by providing three SMB operations that are for print files, not regular files. These open, write, and close a print spool file.

5.5.3 Name Service

Names are used to identify resources in NetBIOS. For example, for two processes to participate in a conversation, each must have a name. The client process identifies the specific server by the server's name, and the server can determine the name of the client. The name space is flat (that is, it is not hierarchical) and each name consists of from 1 to 16 alphanumeric characters. Upper case is different from lower case and names cannot start with an asterisk or with the three characters ''IBM.''

There are two types of names: *unique names* and *group names*. A unique name must be unique across the network. (As stated earlier, NetBIOS was designed for a LAN, so the name must typically be unique on the local network.) A group name does not have to be unique and all processes that have a given group name belong to the group.

There are four commands pertaining to name service.

ADD_NAME	Add a unique name
ADD_GROUP_NAME	Add a group name
DELETE_NAME	Delete name
FIND_NAME	Determine if a name is registered

To obtain a unique name or a group name, a process must bid for the use of the name. This is done by broadcasting a notice that the process wants to use the name, as either a unique name or a group name—by issuing either the ADD_NAME command or the ADD_GROUP_NAME command, respectively. If no objections are received from any other NetBIOS node, the name is considered registered by the requesting node. An objection occurs for an ADD_NAME if some other node responds that the name is currently in use on that node as either a unique name or a group name. The only restriction on the ADD_GROUP_NAME command is that no other node can be using the name as a unique name.

Implied in the NetBIOS specification is that each NetBIOS node maintains a table of all names that processes on that node currently own. These names continue to be owned by the NetBIOS node, until the names are specifically deleted, or until the node is powered off or reset. Realize that names are handled by two different entities: name registration is done by NetBIOS for a process that issues a ADD_NAME command, but it is NetBIOS that maintains the name table. Even though the process that registered the name might cease to exist, unless the name is specifically deleted with the DELETE_NAME command, the node's NetBIOS name table continues to know the name.

Both the ADD_NAME and ADD_GROUP_NAME commands return a *local name number* that is a small integer identifying the name. This number is used for the datagram commands and for the RECEIVE_ANY command (both described below).

By default, the IBM PC LAN Support Program transmits a name registration request

six times, at half-second intervals, until it considers the name registered by itself. This
implies a 3-second delay every time an application that requires a new name is started for
the first time.

The FIND_NAME command was added with the token ring implementation of Net-
BIOS and determines if a particular name has been registered by any other NetBIOS
node.

5.5.4 Session Service

The NetBIOS session service provides a connection-oriented, reliable, full-duplex message service to a user process. The data is organized into messages and each message
can be between 0 and 131,071 bytes. NetBIOS does not provide any form of out-of-band
data.

The following commands provide session service:

CALL	Call—active open
LISTEN	Listen—passive open
SEND	Send session data
SEND_NO_ACK	Send session data, no acknowledgment
RECEIVE	Receive session data
RECEIVE_ANY	Receive session data
HANG_UP	Terminate session
SESSION_STATUS	Retrieve session status

NetBIOS requires one process to be the client and another to be the server. The
server first issues a passive open with the LISTEN command. The client then connects
with the server when the client executes the CALL command.

The LISTEN command requires the caller (typically a server process) to specify
both the local name (which must be in the local NetBIOS name table) and the remote
name. The local name is the *well-known address* that the server is known by. The
remote name is the name of the specific client with which a session can be established.
The caller can specify the remote name as an asterisk, allowing any remote process that
specifies the local name to establish a connection. Since most servers are willing to
accept a connection from any process (perhaps doing some form of authentication once
the session is established), specifying the remote name as an asterisk is the typical
scenario. Both ends of the session can access the name of the other end.

Both the LISTEN command and the CALL command return a *local session number*
to the calling process. This small integer is then used for SEND and RECEIVE commands to specify a particular session (since a process can have more than one session
active at any time). The local session number is also used by the HANG_UP command to
specify which session is to be terminated. When a session is terminated, all pending data
is first transferred.

In the normal SEND operation, the NetBIOS module waits for a positive acknowledgment from the other system before returning to the caller. Similarly, the RECEIVE
command sends an acknowledgment to the other system before passing the received data

to the caller. This provides an end-to-end verification that the data was received. When the token ring implementation of NetBIOS appeared, IBM introduced the SEND_NO_ACK command, which does not perform the acknowledgments between the NetBIOS modules. The reason for this is that the data-link layer of the token ring network performs acknowledgments between the two data-link layers.

The IBM PC implementations provide a CHAIN_SEND command that combines two user buffers into a single message. The reason for this command is that the count associated with a normal SEND command is a 16-bit integer, which allows values between 0 and 65535. By combining two sends into a single operation, messages up to 131,071 bytes can be exchanged. This command, however, is an interface issue between the NetBIOS implementation and the user process, and we won't consider it any more in this text.

The RECEIVE command receives data for a particular session that the process has open. The local session number that was returned by the CALL or LISTEN specifies the session. The RECEIVE_ANY command allows a process to receive the next message from any of its current session partners. NetBIOS returns the actual session number corresponding to the received data.

5.5.5 Datagram Service

NetBIOS supports datagrams up to 512 bytes in length.† Datagrams can be sent to a specific name (either a unique name or a group name) or can be broadcast to the entire local area network. As with other datagram services, such as UDP/IP, the NetBIOS datagrams are connectionless and unreliable.

There are four datagram commands.

SEND_DATAGRAM	Send datagram
SEND_BROADCAST_DATAGRAM	Send broadcast datagram
RECEIVE_DATAGRAM	Receive datagram
RECEIVE_BROADCAST_DATAGRAM	Receive broadcast datagram

The SEND_DATAGRAM command requires the caller to specify the name of the destination. The name can be either a unique name or a group name. If the destination is a group name, then every member of the group receives the datagram. The caller of the RECEIVE_DATAGRAM command must specify the local name for which it wants to receive datagrams. Datagrams addressed to this name are received by the caller. The RECEIVE_DATAGRAM command also returns the name of the sender, in addition to the actual datagram data. If NetBIOS receives a datagram (i.e., the NetBIOS module has previously registered the name to which the datagram was addressed), but there are no RECEIVE_DATAGRAM commands pending, then the datagram is discarded.

The SEND_BROADCAST_DATAGRAM command sends the message to every

---

† The NetBIOS device driver supplied with the PC LAN Support Program allows a configuration option to specify a maximum datagram length other than 512 bytes.

NetBIOS system on the local network. When a broadcast datagram is received by a Net-
BIOS node, every process that has issued a `RECEIVE_BROADCAST_DATAGRAM` command receives the datagram. If none of these commands are outstanding when the
broadcast datagram is received, the datagram is discarded. As with a normal datagram,
the name of the broadcast datagram source is also returned to the receiver.

5.5.6 General Commands

There are four general commands.

`RESET`	Reset NetBIOS
`CANCEL`	Cancel an asynchronous command
`ADAPTER_STATUS`	Fetch adapter status
`UNLINK`	Unlink from bootstrap server

The `RESET` command clears the NetBIOS name and session tables, and also aborts any
existing sessions.

The `CANCEL` command assumes that NetBIOS commands can be issued
asynchronously by a user process. That is, the user process starts a command but does
not wait for it to complete. Some method is required for the process to be notified when
the command completes or for the process to check if a specific command is done or not.
If asynchronous commands are supported by the NetBIOS implementation, then the
`CANCEL` command cancels a specific outstanding command. If the command being cancelled is a `SEND`, then the associated session is aborted.

The `STATUS` command returns interface-specific status associated with either a local
name or a remote name. Additionally, it returns the NetBIOS name table for that Net-
BIOS node (either the local node or a remote node). Unfortunately, for the IBM PC
implementations of NetBIOS, the actual contents of the adapter status information that is
returned to the caller depends on the adapter type (PC Network or token ring).

The `UNLINK` command was used with the original PC Network interface when a
diskless workstation was bootstrapped from a remote disk drive.

5.5.7 NetBIOS Summary

In Figure 5.29 we add the two NetBIOS services to the table that we have been building.
We use the terms **NbS** for the NetBIOS session services and **NbD** for the datagram services. Note that the NetBIOS session service is like LU 6.2—both assume the underlying data link provides reliability.

	IP	IDP	UDP	PEX	NbD	TCP	SPP	LU6.2	NbS
connection-oriented ?	no	no	no	no	no	yes	yes	yes	yes
message boundaries ?	yes	yes	yes	yes	yes	no	yes	yes	yes
data checksum ?	no	yes	opt.	yes	no	yes	yes	no	no
positive ack. ?	no	no	no	no	no	yes	yes	yes	yes
timeout and rexmit ?	no	no	no	yes	no	yes	yes	yes	yes
duplicate detection ?	no	no	no	no	no	yes	yes	yes	yes
sequencing ?	no	no	no	no	no	yes	yes	yes	yes
flow control ?	no	no	no	no	no	yes	yes	yes	yes
full-duplex ?						yes	yes	no	yes

Figure 5.29 Comparison of protocol features: Internet, XNS, SNA, and NetBIOS.

Using our definition of an *association* from the previous chapter, for the NetBIOS session service it consists of

- the protocol (NetBIOS session service),
- the source name,
- the source session number,
- the destination name,
- the destination session number.

An example could be

```
{NbS, JOESXT, 4, PRINTER, 7}
```

For the NetBIOS datagram service, only the protocol and the names are required, as there is no concept of a session for a datagram. Note also that the name of a partner process implies both the host name and the server's name.

5.6   OSI Protocols

5.6.1   Introduction

As stated in the previous chapter, the OSI model provides a framework within which standards can be developed for protocols at each layer. We refer to the protocol standards developed by ISO and other related organizations (CCITT, for example) as *OSI protocols*. This is in contrast to other networking protocols, most of which predate the OSI model, which have been developed by organizations other than ISO or CCITT. TCP/IP, XNS, and SNA, for example, are protocol suites that are not based on ISO standards.

OSI protocols have become popular lately as many organizations (such as the U.S. Government) have stated their intentions to move towards networks based on ISO standards. Unfortunately, networks based on OSI protocols are still in their infancy. Working examples of the lower layers exist, but most of the standards at these lower layers (layers 1–3) were developed before the OSI model. Standards exist and are currently being developed for the upper layers and for specific applications (see the description of the ISODE package below). In the remainder of this section we describe the existing ISO standards at each layer. We refer to the actual ISO standard documents by their 4-digit number.

As we mentioned in Chapter 4, the ISO standards differentiate between the services provided by a layer (for the layer above it) and the actual protocol used to provide the service. The protocol definitions describe the actual formats of the protocol packets, the header fields, and the like. Most layers or applications have both a standard for the service that it provides, along with a standard for the protocol used to provide that service.

A nonproprietary implementation of many of the OSI protocols is available as the ISODE software package. This package runs under 4.2BSD, 4.3BSD, System V Releases 2 and 3, along with other variants of these Unix systems. Refer to the Bibliography or Appendix A of Rose [1990] for ordering information. Version 5.0 of this package provides support for the following features:

- Transport services: TP0 and TP4,
- Session services,
- Presentation services,
- Association control services,
- Remote operation services (similar to the RPC techniques described in Chapter 18),
- ASN.1 abstract syntax notation tools,
- FTAM (transfer of text and binary files, directory listings, file management),
- FTAM/FTP gateway,
- VT (virtual terminal: basic class with TELNET profile),
- Directory services.

Future releases might provide the OSI electronic mail service (X.400) and a gateway between this and the Internet SMTP application. All these features and acronyms are described in the following sections.

Many people predict a gradual shift from non-OSI protocols to the OSI protocols between 1990 and 1995. The next major release of 4.xBSD should have support for some of the OSI protocols. The implementation of the upper layers in this release should be based on the ISODE package.

One confusing feature of the ISO standards is that their terminology differs from existing networking terminology. For example, what we call a client and server are termed an initiator and responder, respectively, in the ISO-world. The concepts of an iterative server and a concurrent server, which we introduced in Section 1.6, are called a static responder and a dynamic responder. The packets or messages that are exchanged by peer layers (see Figure 4.13, for example) are termed protocol data units in the OSI model.

For additional information on the OSI protocols, refer to Rose [1990], Henshall and Shaw [1988], Stallings [1987a], and Knightson, Knowles, and Larmouth [1988]. A detailed listing of all relevant ISO standards is in Chapin [1989].

5.6.2 Data-Link Layer

The data-link layer provides services to the network layer. LANs that use the OSI protocols typically use the IEEE 802 standards for the data-link layer and the physical layer. This provides for the IEEE 802.2 logical link control as the interface between the network layer and the data-link layer. The lower portion of the data-link layer, along with the physical layer, is then Ethernet (802.3), token bus (802.4), or token ring (802.5). These four IEEE standards have comparable ISO standards: 8802/2, 8802/3, 8802/4, and 8802/5. The 802.2 standard allows either a connection-oriented service or a connectionless service to be provided to the network layer. Stallings [1987b] provides additional details on the IEEE 802 standards.

Networks that use the OSI protocols with point-to-point connections typically use the link access procedure (LAP) that is part of the X.25 standard. (We mention X.25 below when we describe the network layer.) This protocol is similar to the SDLC protocol used by SNA for point-to-point links.

5.6.3 Network Layer

ISO standard 8348 defines the services provided by the network layer for the presentation layer. The original version of the standard provided only for a connection-oriented network service (CONS). An addendum provides for a connectionless network service (CLNS) also.

X.25 is the name used to describe the widely used connection-oriented protocol network layer protocol. X.25 is a CCITT standard that first appeared in 1974. X.25 encompasses layers 1, 2, and 3, not just the network layer. ISO standard 8878 describes how X.25 can be used to provide a connection-oriented network service.

ISO standard 8473 defines the protocol used to provide the connectionless network service. This protocol is similar to the Internet Protocol, IP, which we discussed in Section 5.2.4. One difference is that the Internet IP uses fixed-length address fields in its IP header (the 32-bit network ID and host ID value) while the OSI IP uses variable-length address fields.

5.6.4 Transport Layer

The task of the transport layer is to provide reliable, end-to-end data transfer for users of the transport layer. ISO standard 8072 provides the definition of the services provided by the transport layer. As with the network layer, the original standard only defined the services for a connection-oriented transmission, with an addendum specifying the services for connectionless transmission.

One service that the connection-oriented transport layer must provide is expedited data, which we called out-of-band data in Chapter 4. Few specifics are given, however, other than the requirement that up to 16 bytes of expedited data be sent in a single operation. Additionally, the service definition requires that normal data sent after expedited data must not be delivered to the peer before the expedited data.

The definition of the transport layer services also includes features such as establishing a connection between two endpoints, and the negotiation of parameters during connection establishment.

The specification of the actual connection-oriented transport layer protocols is given in ISO standard 8073. Included in this standard is the definition of three different types of network services that are provided to the transport layer, types A, B, and C.

Type A   A reliable network service. The network layer and the data-link layer handle all error conditions.

Type B   A reliable network service with error notification. Although most error conditions are handled by the network layer and the data-link layer for this type of service, there can be some notifications to the transport layer that something has gone wrong. A reset notification from the network layer requires that both transport ends resynchronize. A restart notification requires that both transport ends establish a new connection.

Type C   An unreliable network service. This is the type of service provided by datagram-oriented networks.

X.25 networks provide a type B network service, since both resets and restarts are possible. But, it is often assumed that an X.25 network provides a reliable type A service.

Given these three types of network services, there are five different classes of connection-oriented transport protocols: classes 0 through 4. We can classify the five protocol classes by the type of network service they are intended to be used with (A, B, or C), whether they can detect errors on their own, whether they can recover from errors that are signaled by the network layer, and whether they do multiplexing. We show this in Figure 5.30. Multiplexing here means the ability to have two or more transport connections over a single network connection.

Transport protocol class	Network service type	Error detection ?	Error recovery ?	Multiplexing ?
0	A	no	no	no
1	B	no	yes	no
2	A	no	no	yes
3	B	no	yes	yes
4	C	yes	yes	yes

Figure 5.30   ISO connection-oriented transport protocol classes.

(Figure 5.30 is a simplified description of these five classes. We could show over 20 different criteria, such as flow control, multiplexing, retransmission and timeout, and then note whether each of the five classes supports that feature.) These five classes are sometimes called TP0 through TP4. TP0 is a simple protocol—everything is handled by the lower layers. TP1 can be used with an X.25 network service, although if a reliable X.25 service is assumed, TP0 can be used instead. TP4 is similar to the Internet TCP, since TP4 assumes an unreliable network layer. TP4 could be used with the ISO connectionless network layer.

The ISO connectionless transport protocol is similar to UDP. It is defined in ISO standard 8602. A single packet format is defined and each packet contains the source address, destination address, an optional checksum, and the user data. The addresses can be used to identify user processes, similar to the port numbers used by UDP. Similar to UDP, if a checksum error is detected by the receiving transport layer, the packet is discarded.

5.6.5 Session Layer

The session layer provides services to a user process, in addition to the services provided by the transport layer. ISO standard 8326 defines the services to be provided by the session layer and ISO standard 8327 defines the session layer protocol.

Two of the services provided by the session layer to the layers above it are session establishment and session release. A session is similar in concept to a transport connection. During the life of a session there are two possible ways for the session layer to handle the transport connection that it needs for the session: a single transport connection can be used for the entire session, or two or more transport connections can be used for the entire session. In the latter case, it must be transparent to the user of the session layer that the actual transport connection has changed. It is also possible for a session layer to have consecutive sessions use a single transport connection. One restriction, however, is that the session layer cannot multiplex several sessions on a single transport connection.

Another service that can be provided by the session layer is dialog management. This feature provides a half-duplex, flip-flop form of data exchange. To manage this feature, an imaginary token is maintained by the two session layers. Only the end that holds the token can transmit data. During the session establishment, it is determined which end gets the token to start. One end can also ask the other end for the token when it wants to transmit data. This half-duplex, flip-flop mode of operation is similar to the SNA LU 6.2 protocol which we described in Section 5.4.5.

There are other services that the session layer can provide: synchronization, activity management, and exception reporting. Furthermore, the ISO standard defines four subsets of the session services, realizing that few applications, if any, need all the features that the session layer can provide. These four subsets are called kernel, BCS (basic combined subset), BSS (basic synchronized subset), and BAS (basic activity subset). The simplest of these, the kernel, must be provided with any implementation. All the kernel subset provides is session establishment and data transfer.

There is nothing similar to the session layer in the TCP/IP protocol suite.

5.6.6 Presentation Layer

The presentation layer is concerned with the representation of the data that is being exchanged. This can include conversion of the data between different formats (ASCII, EBCDIC, binary), data compression, and encryption. Additionally, the presentation layer must make the services of the session layer available to the application. Much of the presentation layer, therefore, is just a pass-through of application requests (establish a session, terminate a session, etc.) to the session layer.

ISO standard 8822 defines the services for the presentation layer and ISO standard 8823 defines the protocols.

One task of the presentation layer is to convert the application data into some standard form. To explain this we'll introduce the ISO terminology of *abstract syntax* and *transfer syntax*. The application layer deals with an abstract syntax. This includes items such as "an integer whose value is 1." This is an abstract description that does not say how the data value is represented. A transfer syntax, however, specifies exactly how this data value is represented. For example, it could be represented as 16-bit integer in twos complement binary format with the most significant bit transferred first. To convert from an abstract syntax to a transfer syntax, *encoding rules* are applied by the presentation layer. Two presentation layers exchange data in the transfer format, while the two application layers exchange data in the abstract format.

ISO standard 8824 specifies an abstract syntax called ASN.1. This stands for "abstract syntax notation 1." The encoding rules for converting ASN.1 data structures into a bit stream for transmission are contained in ISO standard 8825. A full description of ASN.1 is beyond the scope of this text. Refer to Section 8.2 of Tanenbaum [1989] for additional details. We'll discuss some other standards for data representation in Section 18.2 when we discuss remote procedure calls.

SNA supports some features that resemble the presentation layer. For example, the mapping of user data into a mapped conversation record, which we described in Section 5.4.5, is similar in concept.

5.6.7 Application Layer

Common Application Service Elements

CASE stands for "common application service elements." It is intended to provide capabilities that are useful to a variety of applications. Currently there are only two CASEs.

- Association Control Service Elements (ACSE).
  This element allows the user process to establish and release associations with a peer. There is a one-to-one relationship between associations and presentation layer connections.

- Commitment, Concurrency, and Recovery (CCR).
  CCR provides atomic actions between application entities. An atomic action is a set of operations, with either all operations being done or none of the operations being done—there is no in-between. Atomic operations and the techniques used by CCR have been used by distributed database systems and transaction processing systems for many years. This feature is similar to the syncpoint feature that we mentioned with the LU 6.2 `ALLOCATE` verb in Section 5.4.5.

ISO standard 8649 defines the CASE services and ISO standard 8650 defines the CASE protocols.

Electronic Mail

In 1984 CCITT defined a set of protocols for what it calls MHS (message handling system). The CCITT recommendations are defined in their X.400-series. These were incorporated in the OSI model at the application layer where they are called MOTIS (message-oriented text interchange system). X.400 provides for more than simple text-oriented electronic mail. It provides for a variety of message types, including text, facsimile, and digitized voice, for example.

Electronic mail under Unix is usually divided into two pieces. The user agent (UA) is the program the user interacts with the interactive user to send or receive mail. The user agent then communicates with a message transfer agent (MTA) that delivers the mail. Typical user agents are `/usr/ucb/Mail` on 4.3BSD, `/bin/mail` and `mailx` on System V, and a variety of other programs. The typical message transfer agent on 4.3BSD is `sendmail`. X.400 is concerned with all aspects of message handling—the user agent and the message transfer agent.

Directory Services

Directory services (DS) are similar to a telephone book. It maps names of people and services into their corresponding attributes (addresses, etc.). It is intended that the directory services be usable by the message handling systems (MHS) and other OSI applications. Directory services are sometimes classified as ''white pages'' or ''yellow pages,'' similar to a telephone book, depending whether you are searching for a name or a service.

ISO standard 9594 and the CCITT X.500 recommendation specify all the details of the OSI directory.

Virtual Terminal

The OSI virtual terminal (VT) allows various terminals to be used. The intent is to isolate applications from the differences in terminal characteristics. ISO standards 9040 and 9041 describe the virtual terminal services and protocols, respectively.

When a virtual terminal connection is started, the two peer entities negotiate the parameters of the terminal that can be supported. An example of the types of parameters that can be specified for the virtual terminal are: number of dimensions (two for a standard CRT, three for a bit-mapped display), maximum coordinate in each dimension, allowable character sets, and so on. Some example operations that can be done are: move cursor to absolute position, enter characters starting at current position, and erase this line from cursor to end.

The ISO virtual terminal can be used to provide a remote login client and server, similar to the Internet TELNET application.

File Transfer, Access, and Management

The OSI file transfer, access, and management application (FTAM) is built around the concept of a virtual filestore. This virtual filestore presents a standard interface to its users. It is up to the software to map this virtual filestore into the actual filesystem being used. ISO standard 8571 specifies the services and protocols used by FTAM.

5.7   UUCP—Unix-to-Unix Copy

UUCP is the generic name used to describe a set of programs that can be used to copy files between different systems and to execute commands on other systems. An early version was made available with Version 7 Unix in 1978 and was intended for communication between systems using dial-up telephone lines. Today there are two major flavors of UUCP in use, the version distributed with 4.3BSD, which is derived from the Version 7 software, and a version known as Honey DanBer UUCP. (This name is derived from the login names of its three authors, Peter Honeyman, David A. Nowitz, and Brian E. Redman.) The Honey DanBer version is distributed with System V Release 3 where it is officially called BNU—Basic Networking Utilities. All versions of UUCP communicate with each other, so for our purposes it doesn't matter which specific version we describe. Details on the 4.3BSD version of UUCP can be found in Chapter 16 of Nemeth, Synder, and Seebas [1989]. Redman [1989] gives details on the Honey DanBer version, along with a history of UUCP.

UUCP is a collection of programs. The four that we're interested in are as follows:

uucp   This program can be invoked by users to copy a file from one system to another. We'll use the term uucp to refer to this specific program, and the term UUCP to refer to the collection of programs. uucp is patterned after the Unix cp command, which copies one or more files. A typical use of uucp is

```
uucp main.c apple!~uucp
```

This command says to copy the file `main.c` in the current directory to the login directory of `uucp` on the system named `apple`.

uux   This program spools a command for execution on another system. Although a user can execute this command, frequently this command is generated automatically by the mail software or the news software. (For additional details on the Usenet news system, refer to Tanenbaum [1989].)

uucico This program is usually run as a daemon process to perform the actions that have been requested by previous `uucp` or `uux` commands. Most Unix systems invoke the `uucico` program automatically at various times of the day from the `/usr/lib/crontab` file. This is one fundamental feature of the UUCP system—it is a batch mode system. The `uucp` and `uux` commands just queue work, and the work is executed at some later time by the `uucico` process.

uuxqt   Executes files that were generated by `uux`. Normally `uuxqt` is invoked by `uux` or it is spawned by `uucico` to process execution files that have been received from another system.

Other programs exist in a typical UUCP software package—a program to display the jobs queued for transmission, one to remove a job that's been queued, and so on.

Figure 5.31 shows the typical operation of UUCP. Note that it is the `uucico` processes that communicate with each other across the network. There is no capability for a user process to use the UUCP protocols to communicate with some other user process.

The original `uucico` process supported a single data-link protocol known as the 'g' protocol. This was developed for dial-up or hardwired terminal lines and typically uses 64-byte packets. Its throughput is limited to around 9000 baud, even with higher line speeds. The 4.3BSD version supports two additional protocols. The 't' protocol assumes that the communication channel is error-free and no checksums are used. This protocol is typically used with TCP links. The 'f' protocol is used for X.25 links and relies on the flow control provided by the data stream. The 'f' protocol also applies a checksum only to the entire file (not to each packet) and uses a 7-bit data path, instead of the usual 8-bit data path.

Our overview of UUCP is to show where it belongs in relation to the other protocols described in this chapter. Since there is no ability for user processes to communicate across the network using UUCP, we don't describe it further in this text. Nevertheless, UUCP is an important piece of the networking tools used by most Unix sites.

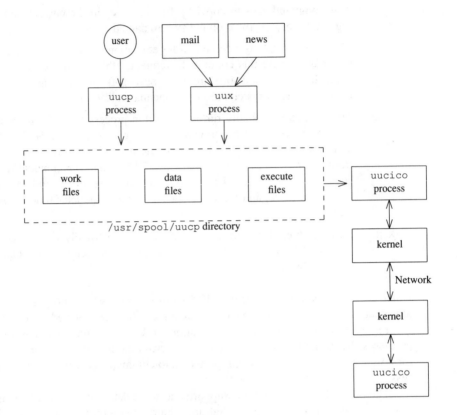

Figure 5.31 Overview of UUCP processes.

5.8   Protocol Comparisons

It is interesting to compare the types of services provided by the protocols we have discussed.

Fragmentation and Reassembly

TCP/UDP/IP   IP handles this. TCP and UDP need not worry about it, other than performance implications. Once a packet is fragmented, it is not reassembled until it reaches the destination host.

XNS   Never done. If a packet must be fragmented by some data-link layer, then it must be reassembled by the other end of the link, to prevent any other systems from knowing that it happened. The packet size is almost always 576 bytes, which is less than optimal for an Ethernet.

SNA   Done by path control.

NetBIOS   An implementation detail that is not specified.

Flow Control

IP   The IP layer sends ICMP source quench messages to a host when packets
             are arriving too quickly from that host. This is a form of hop-by-hop flow
             control.

TCP   Provides end-to-end flow control whereby the receiver tells the sender
             how much data it can accept.

UDP   No flow control is provided by UDP (other than the ICMP source quench
             feature of the underlying IP layer).

IDP   The error protocol can be used to notify a host when a packet from that
             host has been discarded because of resource limitations. This is similar to
             the ICMP source quench.

SPP   Provides end-to-end flow control, similar to TCP.

PEX   No flow control is provided (other than the error control packets provided
             by the underlying IDP layer).

SNA   Link-to-link flow control is provided by the data-link layer for most SNA
             data links (SDLC, token ring). Additionally, an end-to-end flow control is
             also provided by the LU.

NetBIOS   An implementation detail that is not specified.

Reliability

The issue of reliability is a touchy area when talking about whether some form of end-to-end reliability is needed. (This is one of the "religious topics" of networking.) Obviously, if the underlying data-link and network layers are unreliable, the transport layer must provide an end-to-end check. This is how TCP and UDP operate. But with UDP the end-to-end reliability is optional and there are some implementations that disable it when running on a "reliable" LAN such as an Ethernet.† The reason we say that an Ethernet is reliable is that every Ethernet frame has a 32-bit CRC appended to it, to verify that the data is exchanged without any errors between the two Ethernet interface cards. Other LAN technology, such as the token ring, also provides a 32-bit CRC to provide link-to-link reliability.

 If the data-link layer is reliable, do we still need an end-to-end reliability check?

---

† If you're running some form of BSD Unix, and if you have adequate permission and knowledge, look at the global variable `udpcksum` in the kernel with a debugger. If its value is zero, UDP checksums are not calculated for outgoing UDP packets. A value of one enables the checksum calculation for outgoing packets.

Without answering this touchy question we should point out where the data could be corrupted, even if it is transferred between the two interface cards without any errors. First, the interface card contains memory in which the incoming and outgoing frames are stored. This memory can be a source of errors. The data is also transferred between the interface card and the computer's memory, typically along an input/output bus of some form. On some LANs there might also be bridges or repeaters, which can also be the source of errors.

IP	Provides a 16-bit checksum that covers the IP header only. The upper layers (TCP and UDP) are left to do their own checksum of the actual message, if desired.
TCP	Assumes the IP layer is unreliable and provides a 16-bit checksum of the entire message.
UDP	As with TCP, it provides a 16-bit checksum of the entire message.
XNS	IDP provides a 16-bit checksum of the entire packet, therefore no additional end-to-end reliability checks are required by the upper layers (SPP and PEX).
SNA	Assumes the data-link layer provides the reliability. No form of end-to-end checksum is provided.
NetBIOS	Both the datagram service and the session service assume the data link layer is reliable, with no additional checksums provided.

Sequencing

The datagram protocols do not perform sequencing—IP, UDP, IDP, PEX, and NetBIOS datagram. The connection-oriented protocols all provide this feature—TCP, SPP, LU 6.2, and NetBIOS session. SNA assumes that the data-link layer does the sequencing, with a verification of this taking place in the LU. NetBIOS also assumes the data link does the sequencing. TCP and SPP both do the sequencing themselves, assuming the underlying layers do not sequence the data.

Timeout and Retransmission

Most datagram protocols do not provide this service (IP, UDP, IDP, and NetBIOS). PEX, however, is a datagram service that provides a timeout and retransmission. As expected, the connection-oriented protocols do provide this service—TCP, SPP, LU 6.2, and NetBIOS. As with sequencing, both SNA and NetBIOS require the data link to handle this.

5.9   Summary

We have covered five protocol suites in this chapter.

- TCP/IP
- XNS
- SNA
- NetBIOS
- OSI
- UUCP

Our emphasis has been the TCP/IP protocol suite, as that is the one used for most of the examples in the later chapters. We'll also show examples using XNS in Chapters 6 and 11. Protocol comparisons are worthwhile, to help put things into perspective.

We've covered many protocols in this chapter, not all of which are essential for network programming. For example, although you probably won't use the ARP or RARP protocols directly (compared to UDP or TCP), you will encounter RARP as soon as you connect a diskless workstation to a TCP/IP internet.

In the next two chapters we'll cover two application program interfaces (APIs) between a user process and a networking protocol: Berkeley sockets and the System V Transport Layer Interface.

Exercises

5.1   What is the maximum number of hosts on a TCP/IP internet?

5.2   What is the maximum number of hosts on a XNS internet?

5.3   Given the addressing structure of TCP/IP and XNS, would it be feasible for every home in the U.S. to have a unique network address? How about every home in the world?

5.4   Compare the OSI connectionless network service (Section 5.6.3) with IP.

6

Berkeley Sockets

6.1   Introduction

This chapter describes the first of several *application program interfaces (APIs)* to the communication protocols. The API is the interface available to a programmer. The availability of an API depends on both the operating system being used, and the programming language. The two most prevalent communication APIs for Unix systems are Berkeley sockets and the System V Transport Layer Interface (TLI). Both of these interfaces were developed for the C language. This chapter describes the Berkeley socket interface, and the next chapter describes TLI.

First, let's compare network I/O to file I/O. For a Unix file, there are six system calls for input and output: `open`, `creat`, `close`, `read`, `write`, and `lseek`. All these system calls work with a file descriptor, as described in Section 2.3. It would be nice if the interface to the network facilities maintained the file descriptor semantics of the Unix filesystem, but network I/O involves more details and options than file I/O.† For example, the following points must be considered:

---

† The original TCP/IP implementation for the BSD version of Unix was developed by Bolt, Beranek, and Newman (BBN) under a DARPA contract in 1981 [Walsh and Gurwitz 1984]. It is interesting to note that this version used these six system calls for both file I/O and network I/O. The socket interface and the interprocess communication facilities, which we describe in this chapter, were then added by Berkeley with the 4.1cBSD release.

- The typical client–server relationship is not symmetrical. To initiate a network connection requires that the program know which role (client or server) it is to play.

- A network connection can be connection-oriented or connectionless. The former case is more like file I/O than the latter, since once we open a connection with another process, the network I/O on that connection is always with the same peer process. With a connectionless protocol, there is nothing like an "open" since every network I/O operation could be with a different process on a different host.

- Names are more important in networking than for file operations. For example, a program that is passed a file descriptor by a parent process can do file I/O on it without ever needing to know the original name that the file was opened under. The file descriptor is all the process needs. A networking application, however, might need to know the name of its peer process to verify that the process has authority to request the services.

- Recall our definition of an association in Chapter 4

  {protocol, local-addr, local-process, foreign-addr, foreign-process}

  There are more parameters that must be specified for a network connection, than for file I/O. Also, as we saw in Chapter 5, each of the parameters can differ from one protocol to the next. Compare, for example, the format of either the *local-addr* or the *foreign-addr* between the Internet and XNS: the Internet address is 4 bytes while the XNS address is 10 bytes.

- For some communication protocols, record boundaries have significance. The Unix I/O system is stream oriented, not message oriented, as discussed in Section 3.6.

- The network interface should support multiple communication protocols. For example, the network functions can't use a 32-bit integer to hold network addresses, since even though this is adequate for Internet addresses, it is inadequate for XNS addresses. Generic techniques must be used to handle features that can change from one protocol to another, such as addresses. Supporting multiple communication protocols is almost akin to having Unix support multiple file access techniques. Imagine the Unix I/O system if the kernel had to support Unix I/O along with three or four other techniques (DEC's RMS, IBM's VSAM, etc.).

As another comparison between network I/O and file I/O, Figure 6.1 shows some of the steps required to use sockets, TLI, System V message queues, and FIFOs, for a connection-oriented transfer. We'll cover the details in Figure 6.1 as we proceed through this chapter and the next. Our purpose now is to show the added complexity imposed by the networking routines, compared to message queues and FIFOs.

		Sockets	TLI	Messages	FIFOs
Server:	allocate space		t_alloc()		
	create endpoint	socket()	t_open()	msgget()	mknod() open()
	bind address	bind()	t_bind()		
	specify queue	listen()			
	wait for connection	accept()	t_listen()		
	get new fd		t_open() t_bind() t_accept()		
Client:	allocate space		t_alloc()		
	create endpoint	socket()	t_open()	msgget()	open()
	bind address	bind()	t_bind()		
	connect to server	connect()	t_connect()		
	transfer data	read() write() recv() send()	read() write() t_rcv() t_snd()	msgrcv() msgsnd()	read() write()
	datagrams	recvfrom() sendto()	t_rcvudata() t_sndudata()		
	terminate	close() shutdown()	t_close() t_sndrel() t_snddis()	msgctl()	close() unlink()

Figure 6.1   Comparison of sockets, TLI, message queues, and FIFOs.

In the examples that we show in this chapter we must specify the type of process (client or server) and the type of protocol (connection-oriented or connectionless). Furthermore, for the server examples we have to specify if the server is a concurrent server or an iterative server. (Usually it doesn't matter to the client whether it is communicating with a concurrent server or an iterative server.) This gives four potential combinations.

	iterative server	concurrent server
connection-oriented protocol	infrequent (Daytime)	typical
connectionless protocol	typical	infrequent (TFTP)

The Internet Daytime protocol, which we describe in Section 10.2, is an example of a connection-oriented protocol whose server is usually implemented using an iterative server. Indeed, the 4.3BSD Internet superserver which we describe in Section 6.16 provides an iterative server for this protocol. We provide an example of a concurrent server using a connectionless protocol in Chapter 12—the TFTP server.

6.2   Overview

The socket interface was first provided with the 4.1cBSD system for the VAX, circa 1982. The interface that we describe here corresponds to the original 4.3BSD VAX release from 1986. This release supported the following communication protocols:

- Unix domain (described in Section 6.3)
- Internet domain (TCP/IP)
- Xerox NS domain

Be aware that some vendors who provide 4.3BSD-based systems do not provide the XNS support that was provided by Berkeley. Nevertheless, we show examples using XNS, since it provides a good working example, in addition to TCP/IP, for some of the portability problems in network programming.

Figure 6.2 shows a time line of the typical scenario that takes place for a connection-oriented transfer—first the server is started, then sometime later a client is started that connects to the server.

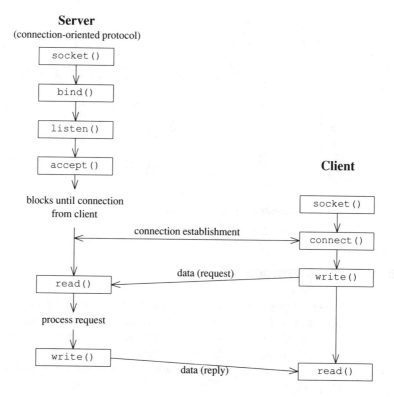

Figure 6.2   Socket system calls for connection-oriented protocol.

For a client–server using a connectionless protocol, the system calls are different. Figure 6.3 shows these system calls. The client does not establish a connection with the server. Instead, the client just sends a datagram to the server using the `sendto` system call, which requires the address of the destination (the server) as a parameter. Similarly, the server does not have to accept a connection from a client. Instead, the server just issues a `recvfrom` system call that waits until data arrives from some client. The `recvfrom` returns the network address of the client process, along with the datagram, so the server can send its response to the correct process.

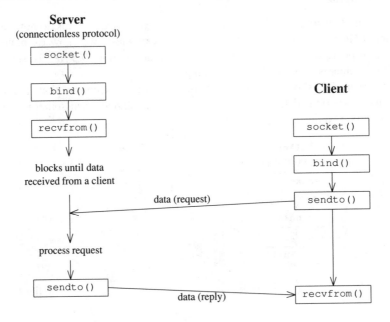

Figure 6.3 Socket system calls for connectionless protocol.

6.3   Unix Domain Protocols

4.3BSD provides support for what it calls the ''Unix domain'' protocols. But unlike other domains, such as the Internet domain and the XNS domain, sockets in the Unix domain can only be used to communicate with processes on the same Unix system. We did not provide a description of the Unix domain protocols in the previous chapter, as they are limited to 4.3BSD, and are not ''communication protocols'' in the true sense of the term. They are a form of IPC, but their implementation has been built into the 4.3BSD networking system in the same fashion as other true communication protocols.

4.3BSD provides both a connection-oriented interface and a connectionless interface to the Unix domain protocols. Both can be considered reliable, since they exist only within the kernel and are not transmitted across external facilities such as a communication line between systems. Checksums and the like are not needed. As with other connection-oriented protocols (TCP and SPP, for example), the connection-oriented Unix version provides flow control. In a similar fashion, as with other connectionless protocols (UDP and IDP, for example), the Unix domain datagram facility does *not* provide flow control. This has implications for user programs, since it is possible for a datagram client to send data so fast that buffer starvation can occur. If this happens, the sender must try to send the data repeatedly. For this reason alone, it is recommended that you use the connection-oriented Unix domain protocol.

The Unix domain protocols provide a feature that is not currently provided by any other protocol family: the ability to pass access rights from one process to another. We'll discuss this feature in more detail in Section 6.10 when we describe the passing of file descriptors between processes.

Unlike the other protocols we've covered, there is nothing like encapsulation performed on the Unix domain messages—their actual implementation is a kernel detail that need not concern us. As it turns out, 4.3BSD implements pipes using the connection-oriented Unix domain protocol.

The name space used by the Unix domain protocols consists of pathnames. A sample association could be

```
{unixstr, 0, /tmp/log.01528, 0, /dev/logfile}
```

The *protocol* here is `unixstr`, which stands for "Unix stream," the connection-oriented protocol. The *local-process* in this example is `/tmp/log.01528` and the *foreign-process* is `/dev/logfile`. We show both the *local-addr* and the *foreign-addr* as zero, since the pathnames on the local host are the only addresses used in this domain.† An association using the connectionless Unix protocol is similar, except that we use the term `unixdg` to specify the datagram protocol, the first member of the 5-tuple.

The 4.3BSD implementation creates a file in the filesystem with the specified pathname, although there are comments in the 4.3BSD manuals indicating that future versions might not create these files. This is somewhat misleading, however, because these filesystem entries are not true "files." For example, we cannot open these files with the `open` system call. These files have a type of `S_IFSOCK` as reported by the `stat` or `fstat` system calls.

---

† We could define the *local-addr* and the *foreign-addr* to be the pathnames, with the *local-process* and *foreign-process* both being zero. Our reason for specifying the association as we did is to reiterate that a host address is not required since the association is limited to processes on the local host.

6.4   **Socket Addresses**

Many of the BSD networking system calls require a pointer to a socket address structure as an argument. The definition of this structure is in <sys/socket.h>:

```
struct sockaddr {
  u_short  sa_family;    /* address family: AF_xxx value */
  char     sa_data[14];  /* up to 14 bytes of protocol-specific
                            address */
};
```

The contents of the 14 bytes of protocol-specific address are interpreted according to the type of address. For the Internet family, the following structures are defined in <netinet/in.h>:

```
struct in_addr {
  u_long   s_addr;              /* 32-bit netid/hostid */
                                /* network byte ordered */
};

struct sockaddr_in {
  short          sin_family;    /* AF_INET */
  u_short        sin_port;      /* 16-bit port number */
                                /* network byte ordered */
  struct in_addr sin_addr;      /* 32-bit netid/hostid */
                                /* network byte ordered */
  char           sin_zero[8];   /* unused */
};
```

As we'll see throughout this chapter, almost every code example has

```
#include <sys/types.h>
```

at the beginning. This header file provides C definitions and data type definitions (typedefs) that are used throughout the system. We will mainly use the names defined for the four unsigned integer datatypes, which we show in Figure 6.4. Unfortunately these four names differ between 4.3BSD and System V.

C Data type	4.3BSD	System V
unsigned char	u_char	unchar
unsigned short	u_short	ushort
unsigned int	u_int	uint
unsigned long	u_long	ulong

Figure 6.4 Unsigned data types defined in <sys/types.h>.

For the Xerox NS family, the following structures are defined in <netns/ns.h>:

```
union ns_host {
  u_char          c_host[6]; /* hostid addr as six bytes */
  u_short         s_host[3]; /* hostid addr as three 16-bit shorts */
                             /* network byte ordered */
};

union ns_net {
  u_char          c_net[4];  /* netid as four bytes */
  u_short         s_net[2];  /* netid as two 16-bit shorts */
                             /* network byte ordered */
};

struct ns_addr {    /* here is the combined 12-byte XNS address */
  union ns_net   x_net;    /* 4-byte netid */
  union ns_host  x_host;   /* 6-byte hostid */
  u_short        x_port;   /* 2-byte port (XNS "socket") */
                           /* network byte ordered */
};

struct sockaddr_ns {
  u_short          sns_family;  /* AF_NS */
  struct ns_addr   sns_addr;    /* the 12-byte XNS address */
  char             sns_zero[2]; /* unused */
};
#define   sns_port   sns_addr.x_port
```

Things are more complicated with XNS, as some of the network code wants to get at the hostid and netid fields in different ways.

For the Unix domain, the following structure is defined in <sys/un.h>:

```
struct sockaddr_un {
  short   sun_family;     /* AF_UNIX */
  char    sun_path[108];  /* pathname */
};
```

(You may have noticed the discrepancies in the declarations of the first two bytes of these address structures, the XX_family members. The Internet and Unix domain members are declared as short integers, while the XNS member and the generic sockaddr member are unsigned short integers. Fortunately the values stored in these variables, the AF_xxx constants that we define in the next section, all have values between 1 and 20, so this discrepancy in the data types doesn't matter.)

Unlike most Unix system calls, the BSD network system calls don't assume that the Unix pathname in sun_path is terminated with a null byte. Notice that this protocol-specific structure is larger than the generic sockaddr structure, while the sockaddr_in and sockaddr_ns structures were both identical in size (16 bytes) to the generic structure. The system interface currently supports structures up to 110 bytes, but some of the generic system network routines (the routing tables in the kernel, for example) only support the 16-byte structures. The Unix domain protocols, however, can be larger than 16 bytes since they don't use these facilities. To handle socket address structures of different sizes, the system interface always passes the size of the address structure, in addition to a pointer to the structure, as we describe in the next paragraph.

A picture of these socket address structures is shown in Figure 6.5.

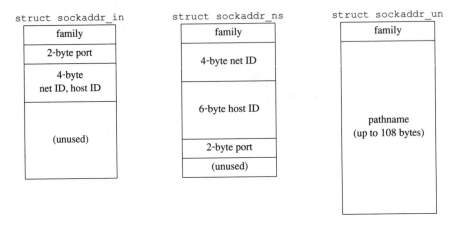

Figure 6.5 Socket address structures for Internet, XNS and Unix families.

The network system calls, such as `connect` and `bind`, work with any of the supported domains, so a technique must be used to pass any of the socket address structures shown in Figure 6.5, `sockaddr_in`, `sockaddr_ns`, or `sockaddr_un`, to these generic system calls. The network system calls take two arguments: the address of the generic `sockaddr` structure and the size of the actual protocol-specific structure. What the caller must do is provide the address of the protocol-specific structure as an argument, casting this pointer into a pointer to a generic `sockaddr` structure. For example, to invoke the `connect` system call for an Internet domain socket, we write

```
struct sockaddr_in  serv_addr; /* Internet-specific addr struct */
    . . .
(fill in Internet-specific information)
    . . .
connect(sockfd, (struct sockaddr *) &serv_addr, sizeof(serv_addr));
```

The second argument is a pointer to the Internet address structure and the third argument is its size (16 bytes).

The designers of the socket interface could have also chosen to use a C union to define the socket address structure. The declaration could look like

```
struct sock_addr {
  short  sa_family;        /* AF_xxx value */
  union {
    struct sockaddr_in  sa_in;    /* Internet address */
    struct sockaddr_ns  sa_ns;    /* XNS address */
    struct sockaddr_un  sa_un;    /* Unix address */
  } sa_val;
};
```

The problem with this approach is that the size of the union is determined by the size of the largest member, which is the Unix domain address. This would cause every `sock_addr` structure to be 110 bytes in size, even though Internet and XNS addresses need only 8 bytes and 14 bytes, respectively. (Note that in this case the 8 bytes of zero at the end of an Internet `sockaddr_in` and the 2 bytes of zero at the end of an XNS `sockaddr_ns` are not needed.) One advantage of a union is that the size of the structure would not have to be an argument (and sometimes a result) to the system calls, as we'll see below. The actual interface design and the choice of a generic `sockaddr` structure along with the protocol-specific socket address structures, was a compromise.

6.5   Elementary Socket System Calls

We now describe the elementary system calls required to perform network programming. In the following section we use these system calls to develop some networking examples.

`socket` System Call

To do network I/O, the first thing a process must do is call the `socket` system call, specifying the type of communication protocol desired (Internet TCP, Internet UDP, XNS SPP, etc.).

```
#include <sys/types.h>
#include <sys/socket.h>

int socket(int family, int type, int protocol);
```

The *family* is one of

AF_UNIX	Unix internal protocols
AF_INET	Internet protocols
AF_NS	Xerox NS protocols
AF_IMPLINK	IMP link layer

The `AF_` prefix stands for ''address family.'' There is another set of terms that is defined, starting with a `PF_` prefix, which stands for ''protocol family'': `PF_UNIX`, `PF_INET`, `PF_NS`, and `PF_IMPLINK`. Either term for a given family can be used, as they are equivalent.

An IMP is an *Interface Message Processor*. This is an intelligent packet switching node that was referred to in our description of the ARPANET in the previous chapter. These nodes are connected with point-to-point links, typically leased telephone lines. The BSD system provides a raw socket interface to the IMP, which is what the `AF_IMPLINK` address family is used for. We won't concern ourselves further with this special purpose network interface.

The socket *type* is one of the following:

SOCK_STREAM	stream socket
SOCK_DGRAM	datagram socket
SOCK_RAW	raw socket
SOCK_SEQPACKET	sequenced packet socket
SOCK_RDM	reliably delivered message socket (not implemented yet)

Not all combinations of socket *family* and *type* are valid. Figure 6.6 shows the valid combinations, along with the actual protocol that is selected by the pair.

	AF_UNIX	AF_INET	AF_NS
SOCK_STREAM	Yes	TCP	SPP
SOCK_DGRAM	Yes	UDP	IDP
SOCK_RAW		IP	Yes
SOCK_SEQPACKET			SPP

Figure 6.6 Protocols corresponding to socket *family* and *type*.

The boxes marked "Yes" are valid, but don't have handy acronyms. The empty boxes are not implemented.

The *protocol* argument to the `socket` system call is typically set to 0 for most user applications. There are specialized applications, however, that specify a *protocol* value, to use a specific protocol. The valid combinations are shown in Figure 6.7.

family	*type*	*protocol*	Actual protocol
AF_INET	SOCK_DGRAM	IPPROTO_UDP	UDP
AF_INET	SOCK_STREAM	IPPROTO_TCP	TCP
AF_INET	SOCK_RAW	IPPROTO_ICMP	ICMP
AF_INET	SOCK_RAW	IPPROTO_RAW	(raw)
AF_NS	SOCK_STREAM	NSPROTO_SPP	SPP
AF_NS	SOCK_SEQPACKET	NSPROTO_SPP	SPP
AF_NS	SOCK_RAW	NSPROTO_ERROR	Error protocol
AF_NS	SOCK_RAW	NSPROTO_RAW	(raw)

Figure 6.7 Combinations of *family*, *type*, and *protocol*.

The `IPPROTO_xxx` constants are defined in the file `<netinet/in.h>` and the `NSPROTO_xxx` constants are defined in the file `<netns/ns.h>`. In Section 11.2 we'll show the Internet `ping` program, which uses the ICMP protocol.

The `socket` system call returns a small integer value, similar to a file descriptor. We'll call this a socket descriptor, or a *sockfd*. To obtain this socket descriptor, all we've specified is an address family and the socket type (stream, datagram, etc.). For an association

{protocol, local-addr, local-process, foreign-addr, foreign-process}

all the `socket` system call specifies is one element of this 5-tuple, the *protocol*. Before the socket descriptor is of any real use, the remaining four elements of the association must be specified. To show what a typical process does next, we'll differentiate between both client and server, and between a connection-oriented protocol and a connectionless protocol. Figure 6.8 shows the typical system calls for each case.

	protocol	*local-addr, local-process*	*foreign-addr, foreign-process*
connection-oriented server	`socket()`	`bind()`	`listen()`, `accept()`
connection-oriented client	`socket()`	`connect()`	
connectionless server	`socket()`	`bind()`	`recvfrom()`
connectionless client	`socket()`	`bind()`	`sendto()`

Figure 6.8 Socket system calls and association elements.

`socketpair` **System Call**

This system call is implemented only for the Unix domain.

```
#include <sys/types.h>
#include <sys/socket.h>

int socketpair(int family, int type, int protocol, int sockvec[2]);
```

This returns two socket descriptors, *sockvec[0]* and *sockvec[1]*, that are unnamed and connected. This system call is similar to the `pipe` system call, but `socketpair` returns a pair of socket descriptors, not file descriptors. Additionally, the two socket descriptors returned by `socketpair` are bidirectional, unlike pipes, which are unidirectional. Recalling our pipe examples from Section 3.4, we had to execute the `pipe` system call twice, obtaining four file descriptors, to get a bidirectional flow of data between two processes. With sockets this isn't required. We'll call these bidirectional, connection-oriented, Unix domain sockets *stream pipes*. We return to these stream pipes in Section 6.9.

Since this system call is limited to the Unix domain, there are only two allowable versions of it

```
int      rc, sockfd[2];

rc = socketpair(AF_UNIX, SOCK_STREAM, 0, sockfd);
```

or

```
rc = socketpair(AF_UNIX, SOCK_DGRAM, 0, sockfd);
```

bind **System Call**

The bind system call assigns a name to an unnamed socket.

```
#include <sys/types.h>
#include <sys/socket.h>

int bind(int sockfd, struct sockaddr *myaddr, int addrlen);
```

The second argument is a pointer to a protocol-specific address and the third argument is the size of this address structure. There are three uses of bind.

1. Servers register their well-known address with the system. It tells the system "this is my address and any messages received for this address are to be given to me." Both connection-oriented and connectionless servers need to do this before accepting client requests.

2. A client can register a specific address for itself.

3. A connectionless client needs to assure that the system assigns it some unique address, so that the other end (the server) has a valid return address to send its responses to. This corresponds to making certain an envelope has a valid return address, if we expect to get a reply from the person we send the letter to.

The bind system call fills in the *local-addr* and *local-process* elements of the association 5-tuple.

connect **System Call**

A client process connects a socket descriptor following the socket system call to establish a connection with a server.

```
#include <sys/types.h>
#include <sys/socket.h>

int connect(int sockfd, struct sockaddr *servaddr, int addrlen);
```

The *sockfd* is a socket descriptor that was returned by the `socket` system call. The second and third arguments are a pointer to a socket address, and its size, as described earlier.

For most connection-oriented protocols (TCP and SPP, for example), the `connect` system call results in the actual establishment of a connection between the local system and the foreign system. Messages are typically exchanged between the two systems and specific parameters relating to the conversation might be agreed on (buffer sizes, amount of data to exchange between acknowledgments, etc.). In these cases the `connect` system call does not return until the connection is established, or an error is returned to the process. Section 12.15 of Comer [1988] discusses the three-way handshake used by TCP to establish a connection. Section 7.4 of Xerox [1981b] discusses a similar technique used by SPP.

The client does not have to `bind` a local address before calling `connect`. The connection typically causes these four elements of the association 5-tuple to be assigned: *local-addr*, *local-process*, *foreign-addr*, and *foreign-process*. In all the connection-oriented client examples that we'll show, we'll let `connect` assign the local address. This is what we diagramed in Figure 6.2 and Figure 6.8.

A connectionless client can also use the `connect` system call, but the scenario is different from what we just described. For a connectionless protocol, all that is done by the `connect` system call is to store the *servaddr* specified by the process, so that the system knows where to send any future data that the process writes to the *sockfd* descriptor. Also, only datagrams from this address will be received by the socket. In this case the `connect` system call returns immediately and there is not an actual exchange of messages between the local system and the foreign system.

One advantage of `connect`ing a socket associated with a connectionless protocol is that we don't need to specify the destination address for every datagram that we send. We can use the `read`, `write`, `recv`, and `send` system calls. (We describe the system calls used for socket I/O later in this section.)

There is another feature provided for connectionless clients that call `connect`. If the datagram protocol supports notification for invalid addresses, then the protocol routine can inform the user process if it sends a datagram to an invalid address. For example, the Internet protocols specify that a host should generate an ICMP port unreachable message if it receives a UDP datagram specifying a UDP port for which no process is waiting to read from. The host that sent the UDP datagram and receives this ICMP message can try to identify the process that sent the datagram, and notify the process. 4.3BSD, for example, notifies the process with a "connection refused" error (ECONNREFUSED) on the next system call for this socket, only if the process had `connect`ed the socket to the destination address. We'll see an example of this with our Internet time client in Section 10.2.

Note that the `connect` and `bind` system calls require only the pointer to the address structure and its size as arguments, not the protocol. This is because the protocol is available from two places: first, the AF_xxx value is always contained in the first two bytes of the socket address structure; second, these system calls all require a socket descriptor as an argument, and this descriptor is always associated with a single protocol family, from the `socket` system call that created the descriptor.

`listen` **System Call**

This system call is used by a connection-oriented server to indicate that it is willing to receive connections.

```
int listen(int sockfd, int backlog);
```

It is usually executed after both the `socket` and `bind` system calls, and immediately before the `accept` system call. The *backlog* argument specifies how many connection requests can be queued by the system while it waits for the server to execute the `accept` system call. This argument is usually specified as 5, the maximum value currently allowed.

Recall our description of a concurrent connection-oriented server in Chapter 4. In the time that it takes a server to handle the request of an `accept` (the time required for the server to `fork` a child process and then have the parent process execute another `accept`), it is possible for additional connection requests to arrive from other clients. What the *backlog* argument refers to is this queue of pending requests for connections.

`accept` **System Call**

After a connection-oriented server executes the `listen` system call described above, an actual connection from some client process is waited for by having the server execute the `accept` system call.

```
#include <sys/types.h>
#include <sys/socket.h>

int accept(int sockfd, struct sockaddr *peer, int *addrlen);
```

`accept` takes the first connection request on the queue and creates another socket with the same properties as *sockfd*. If there are no connection requests pending, this call blocks the caller until one arrives. (We discuss how a socket can be specified as non-blocking in Section 6.11.)

The *peer* and *addrlen* arguments are used to return the address of the connected peer process (the client). *addrlen* is called a value–result argument: the caller sets its value before the system call, and the system call stores a result in the variable. Often these value–result arguments are integers that the caller sets to the size of a buffer, with the system call changing this value on the return to the actual amount of data stored in the buffer. For this system call the caller sets *addrlen* to the size of the `sockaddr` structure whose address is passed as the *peer* argument. On return, *addrlen* contains the actual number of bytes that the system call stores in the *peer* argument. For the Internet and XNS address structures, since their sizes are constant (16 bytes), the value that we store in the *addrlen* argument (16) is the actual number of bytes that the system call returns in the *peer* argument. The size of the structure can differ from the actual size of the address returned with Unix domain addresses.

This system call returns up to three values: an integer return code that is either an error indication or a new socket descriptor, the address of the client process (*peer*), and the size of this address (*addrlen*).

`accept` automatically creates a new socket descriptor, assuming the server is a concurrent server. If this is the case, the typical scenario is

```
int     sockfd, newsockfd;

if ( (sockfd = socket ( ... )) < 0)
        err_sys ("socket error");
if (bind(sockfd, ... ) < 0)
        err_sys ("bind error");
if (listen(sockfd, 5) < 0)
        err_sys ("listen error");

for ( ; ; ) {
        newsockfd = accept(sockfd, ... );    /* blocks */
        if (newsockfd < 0)
                err_sys ("accept error");

        if (fork() == 0) {
                close(sockfd);       /* child */
                doit (newsockfd);    /* process the request */
                exit (0);
        }

        close (newsockfd);           /* parent */
}
```

When a connection request is received and accepted, the process `forks`, with the child process servicing the connection and the parent process waiting for another connection request. The new socket descriptor returned by `accept` refers to a complete association

{*protocol, local-addr, local-process, foreign-addr, foreign-process*}

All five elements of the 5-tuple associated with `newsockfd` have been filled in on return from `accept`. On the other hand, the `sockfd` argument that is passed to `accept` only has three elements of the 5-tuple filled in. The *foreign-addr* and *foreign-process* are still unspecified, and remain so after `accept` returns. This allows the original process (the parent) to `accept` another connection using `sockfd`, without having to create another socket descriptor. Since most connection-oriented servers are concurrent servers, and not iterative servers, the system goes ahead and creates a new socket automatically as part of the `accept` system call. If we wanted an iterative server, the scenario would be

```
int    sockfd, newsockfd;

if ( (sockfd = socket( ... ) < 0)
        err_sys("socket error");
bind(sockfd, ... ) < 0)
        err_sys("bind error");
listen(sockfd, 5) < 0)
        err_sys("listen error");

for ( ; ; ) {
        newsockfd = accept(sockfd, ... );    /* blocks */
        if (newsockfd < 0)
                err_sys("accept error");

        doit(newsockfd);      /* process the request */
        close(newsockfd);
}
```

Here the server handles the request using the connected socket descriptor, `newsockfd`. It then terminates the connection with a `close` and waits for another connection using the original descriptor, `sockfd`, which still has its *foreign-addr* and *foreign-process* unspecified.

send, sendto, recv **and** recvfrom System Calls

These system calls are similar to the standard `read` and `write` system calls, but additional arguments are required.

```
#include <sys/types.h>
#include <sys/socket.h>

int send(int sockfd, char *buff, int nbytes, int flags);

int sendto(int sockfd, char *buff, int nbytes, int flags,
           struct sockaddr *to, int addrlen);

int recv(int sockfd, char *buff, int nbytes, int flags);

int recvfrom(int sockfd, char *buff, int nbytes, int flags,
             struct sockaddr *from, int *addrlen);
```

The first three arguments, *sockfd*, *buff*, and *nbytes*, to the four system calls are similar to the first three arguments for `read` and `write`.

The *flags* argument is either zero, or is formed by or'ing one of the following constants:

`MSG_OOB`	send or receive out-of-band data
`MSG_PEEK`	peek at incoming message (`recv` or `recvfrom`)
`MSG_DONTROUTE`	bypass routing (`send` or `sendto`)

The `MSG_PEEK` flag lets the caller look at the data that's available to be read, without having the system discard the data after the `recv` or `recvfrom` returns. We'll discuss the `MSG_OOB` option in Section 6.14 and the `MSG_DONTROUTE` option in Section 6.11. The *to* argument for `sendto` specifies the protocol-specific address of where the data is to be sent. Since this address is protocol-specific, its length must be specified by *addrlen*. The `recvfrom` system call fills in the protocol-specific address of who sent the data into *from*. The length of this address is also returned to the caller in *addrlen*. Note that the final argument to `sendto` is an integer value, while the final argument to `recvfrom` is a pointer to an integer value (a value–result argument).

All four system calls return the length of the data that was written or read as the value of the function. In the typical use of `recvfrom`, with a connectionless protocol, the return value is the length of the datagram that was received.

`close` **System Call**

The normal Unix `close` system call is also used to close a socket.

```
int close(int fd);
```

If the socket being closed is associated with a protocol that promises reliable delivery (e.g., TCP or SPP), the system must assure that any data within the kernel that still has to be transmitted or acknowledged, is sent. Normally the system returns from the `close` immediately, but the kernel still tries to send any data already queued.

Later in this chapter we'll describe the `SO_LINGER` socket option. This socket option allows a process to specify that either: (a) the `close` should try to send any queued data, or (b) any data queued to be sent should be flushed.

Byte Ordering Routines

The following four functions handle the potential byte order differences between different computer architectures and different network protocols. We detailed some of the differences in Chapter 4.

```
#include <sys/types.h>
#include <netinet/in.h>

u_long htonl(u_long hostlong);

u_short htons(u_short hostshort);

u_long ntohl(u_long netlong);

u_short ntohs(u_short netshort);
```

These functions were designed for the Internet protocols. Fortunately, the XNS protocols use the same byte ordering as the Internet. On those systems that have the same byte ordering as the Internet protocols (Motorola 68000-based systems, for example), these four functions are null macros. The conversions done by these functions are shown in Figure 6.9.

`htonl`	convert host–to–network, long integer
`htons`	convert host–to–network, short integer
`ntohl`	convert network–to–host, long integer
`ntohs`	convert network–to–host, short integer

Figure 6.9 Byte ordering functions.

These four functions are operate on unsigned integer values, although they work just as well on signed integers. Implicit in these functions is that a short integer occupies 16 bits and a long integer 32 bits.

Byte Operations

There are multibyte fields in the various socket address structures that need to be manipulated. Some of these fields, however, are not C integer fields, so some other technique must be used to operate on them portably.

4.3BSD defines the following three routines that operate on user-defined byte strings. By user-defined we mean they are not the standard C character strings (which are always terminated by a null byte). The user-defined byte strings can have null bytes within them and these do *not* signify the end of the string. Instead, we must specify the length of each string as an argument to the function.

```
bcopy(char *src, char *dest, int nbytes);

bzero(char *dest, int nbytes);

int bcmp(char *ptr1, char *ptr2, int nbytes);
```

bcopy moves the specified number of bytes from the source to the destination. Note that the order of the two pointer arguments is different from the order used by the standard I/O `strcpy` function. The `bzero` function writes the specified number of null bytes to the specified destination. `bcmp` compare two arbitrary byte strings. The return value is zero if the two user-defined byte strings are identical, otherwise its nonzero. Note that this differs from the return value from the standard I/O `strcmp` function.

We'll use these three functions throughout the remaining chapters, usually to operate on socket address structures.

System V has three similar functions, `memcpy`, `memset`, and `memcmp`. But most socket libraries for System V supply functions with the 4.3BSD names, for compatibility. Details of the System V functions are on the *memory*(3) manual page.

Address Conversion Routines

As mentioned in Section 5.2, an Internet address is usually written in the dotted-decimal format, for example `192.43.235.1`. The following functions convert between the dotted-decimal format and an `in_addr` structure.

```
#include <sys/socket.h>
#include <netinet/in.h>
#include <arpa/inet.h>

unsigned long inet_addr(char *ptr);

char *inet_ntoa(struct in_addr inaddr);
```

The first of these, `inet_addr` converts a charter string in dotted-decimal notation to a 32-bit Internet address.† The `inet_ntoa` function does the reverse conversion.

Similar functions exist for handling XNS addresses, but there is not as clear a standard for representing XNS addresses in a readable form. The format of an XNS address is typically three fields, delimited by a separator character:

<network-ID><separator><host-ID><separator><port#>

For example, we write

```
123:02.07.01.00.a1.62:6001
```

using a colon as the field separator and a period as the byte separator for the host ID field. The function `ns_addr` defined below is lenient in what it accepts. First it tries to divide the character string into one to three fields, accepting either a period, colon, or pound sign as the separator. Each field is then scanned for byte separators, either a colon or a period. (Obviously you can't use the same character as the field separator and the byte separator.)

---

† Note that this function returns an unsigned long integer, when it should return an `in_addr` structure. Some systems that are based on 4.3BSD have corrected this.

```
#include <sys/types.h>
#include <netns/ns.h>

struct ns_addr ns_addr(char *ptr);

char *ns_ntoa(struct ns_addr ns);
```

The first of these converts a character string representation of an XNS network ID, host ID, and port number into an `ns_addr` structure. The second function does the reverse conversion. This function generates strings using a period to separate the three fields, with each field in hexadecimal.

6.6   A Simple Example

Now we'll use the elementary system calls from the previous section to provide 12 complete programs, showing examples of client–servers using each of the three protocol families available with 4.3BSD. We have 12 programs since we have a connection-oriented server, a connection-oriented client, a connectionless server and a connectionless client for each of the three protocol families (Internet, XNS, and Unix domain). The programs do the following:

1. The client reads a line from its standard input and writes the line to the server.

2. The server reads a line from its network input and echoes the line back to the client.

3. The client reads the echoed line and prints it on its standard output.

This is an example of what is called an echo server. While we develop our own implementation of an echo server, most TCP/IP implementations provide such a server, using both TCP and UDP. See RFC 862 [Postel 1983a] for the official specification. Similarly, most XNS implementations also provide an echo server that is different from our implementation. We'll present a client for the standard XNS echo server in Section 11.3.

A pair of client–server programs to echo input lines is a good example of a network application. All the steps normally required to implement any client–server are illustrated by this example. All you need to do with this echo example, to expand it into your own application, is change what the server does with the input it receives from its clients.

In all these examples, we have "hard-coded" protocol-specific constants such as addresses and ports. There are two reasons for this. First, you should understand exactly what needs to be stored in the protocol-specific address structures. Second, we have not yet covered the library functions provided by 4.3BSD that make this more portable. These functions are covered in Section 8.2.

In these examples we have coded the connection-oriented Internet and Unix servers as concurrent servers, and the connection-oriented XNS server as an iterative server. This is to show examples of both types of servers.

Utility Routines

Stream sockets exhibit a behavior with the `read` and `write` system calls that differs from normal file I/O. A `read` or `write` on a socket might input or output fewer bytes than requested, but this is not an error condition. The reason is that buffer limits might be reached for the socket in the kernel and all that is required is for the caller to invoke the `read` or `write` system call again, to input or output the remaining bytes. Some versions of Unix also exhibit this behavior when writing more than 4096 bytes to a pipe.

We show three functions below that we'll use whenever we read or write to or from a stream socket. A datagram socket does not have this problem, since each I/O operation corresponds to a single packet.

```
/*
 * Read "n" bytes from a descriptor.
 * Use in place of read() when fd is a stream socket.
 */

int
readn(fd, ptr, nbytes)
register int    fd;
register char   *ptr;
register int    nbytes;
{
        int     nleft, nread;

        nleft = nbytes;
        while (nleft > 0) {
                nread = read(fd, ptr, nleft);
                if (nread < 0)
                        return(nread);              /* error, return < 0 */
                else if (nread == 0)
                        break;                  /* EOF */

                nleft -= nread;
                ptr   += nread;
        }
        return(nbytes - nleft);         /* return >= 0 */
}
```

The following function writes to a stream socket:

```
/*
 * Write "n" bytes to a descriptor.
 * Use in place of write() when fd is a stream socket.
 */

int
writen(fd, ptr, nbytes)
register int    fd;
register char   *ptr;
register int    nbytes;
{
```

```
int     nleft, nwritten;

nleft = nbytes;
while (nleft > 0) {
        nwritten = write(fd, ptr, nleft);
        if (nwritten <= 0)
                return(nwritten);                   /* error */

        nleft -= nwritten;
        ptr   += nwritten;
}
return(nbytes - nleft);
}
```

We use the following function to read a line from a stream socket. In our examples we'll be exchanging Unix text lines between the client and server.

```
/*
 * Read a line from a descriptor.  Read the line one byte at a time,
 * looking for the newline.  We store the newline in the buffer,
 * then follow it with a null (the same as fgets(3)).
 * We return the number of characters up to, but not including,
 * the null (the same as strlen(3)).
 */

int
readline(fd, ptr, maxlen)
register int    fd;
register char   *ptr;
register int    maxlen;
{
        int     n, rc;
        char    c;

        for (n = 1; n < maxlen; n++) {
                if ( (rc = read(fd, &c, 1)) == 1) {
                        *ptr++ = c;
                        if (c == '\n')
                                break;
                } else if (rc == 0) {
                        if (n == 1)
                                return(0);        /* EOF, no data read */
                        else
                                break;            /* EOF, some data was read */
                } else
                        return(-1);     /* error */
        }

        *ptr = 0;
        return(n);
}
```

Note that our `readline` function issues one `read` system call for every byte of data. This is inefficient. Section 7.1 of Kernighan and Pike [1984], for example, shows that this requires about ten times more CPU time than issuing a system call for every 10 bytes of data. What we would like to do is buffer the data by issuing a `read` system call to read as much data as we can, and then examine the buffer one byte at a time. Indeed, this is what the standard I/O library does. But to avoid having to worry about the possible interactions of the standard I/O library with a socket, we'll use the system call directly. It is possible to use the standard I/O library with a socket, but we have to be cognizant about the buffering that is taking place, and any interactions that can have with our application.

The three functions shown above are used throughout the text. We'll now present four functions that are common to the clients and servers shown in this section.

The following function is used by the three connection-oriented servers. It is an echo function that reads a line from the stream socket and writes it back to the socket.

```
/*
 * Read a stream socket one line at a time, and write each line back
 * to the sender.
 *
 * Return when the connection is terminated.
 */

#define MAXLINE 512

str_echo(sockfd)
int     sockfd;
{
        int     n;
        char    line[MAXLINE];

        for ( ; ; ) {
                n = readline(sockfd, line, MAXLINE);
                if (n == 0)
                        return;            /* connection terminated */
                else if (n < 0)
                        err_dump("str_echo: readline error");

                if (writen(sockfd, line, n) != n)
                        err_dump("str_echo: writen error");
        }
}
```

The following function is used by the three connection-oriented clients:

```
/*
 * Read the contents of the FILE *fp, write each line to the
 * stream socket (to the server process), then read a line back from
 * the socket and write it to the standard output.
 *
 * Return to caller when an EOF is encountered on the input file.
 */

#include         <stdio.h>
#define MAXLINE 512
```

```
str_cli(fp, sockfd)
register FILE    *fp;
register int     sockfd;
{
        int    n;
        char   sendline[MAXLINE], recvline[MAXLINE + 1];

        while (fgets(sendline, MAXLINE, fp) != NULL) {
                n = strlen(sendline);
                if (writen(sockfd, sendline, n) != n)
                        err_sys("str_cli: writen error on socket");

                /*
                 * Now read a line from the socket and write it to
                 * our standard output.
                 */

                n = readline(sockfd, recvline, MAXLINE);
                if (n < 0)
                        err_dump("str_cli: readline error");
                recvline[n] = 0;          /* null terminate */
                fputs(recvline, stdout);
        }

        if (ferror(fp))
                err_sys("str_cli: error reading file");
}
```

The following function is used by the three connectionless servers. By passing the address of the actual socket address structure to this function, it works with all three protocol families. Since the size of the structure can differ between protocol families, we also pass its size to this function, as it is needed for the recvfrom system call.

```
/*
 * Read a datagram from a connectionless socket and write it back to
 * the sender.
 *
 * We never return, as we never know when a datagram client is done.
 */

#include        <sys/types.h>
#include        <sys/socket.h>

#define MAXMESG 2048

dg_echo(sockfd, pcli_addr, maxclilen)
int             sockfd;
struct sockaddr *pcli_addr;    /* ptr to appropriate sockaddr_XX structure */
int             maxclilen;     /* sizeof(*pcli_addr) */
{
        int    n, clilen;
        char   mesg[MAXMESG];

        for ( ; ; ) {
```

```
            clilen = maxclilen;
            n = recvfrom(sockfd, mesg, MAXMESG, 0, pcli_addr, &clilen);
            if (n < 0)
                    err_dump("dg_echo: recvfrom error");

            if (sendto(sockfd, mesg, n, 0, pcli_addr, clilen) != n)
                    err_dump("dg_echo: sendto error");
    }
}
```

The following function is for the connectionless clients. It is similar to the one for a connection-oriented client, with the `writen` calls replaced by `sendto` and the `readn` calls replaced by `recvfrom`. Also, we need the address of the actual socket address structure and its size for the datagram system calls.

```
/*
 * Read the contents of the FILE *fp, write each line to the
 * datagram socket, then read a line back from the datagram
 * socket and write it to the standard output.
 *
 * Return to caller when an EOF is encountered on the input file.
 */

#include         <stdio.h>
#include         <sys/types.h>
#include         <sys/socket.h>

#define MAXLINE 512

dg_cli(fp, sockfd, pserv_addr, servlen)
FILE            *fp;
int             sockfd;
struct sockaddr *pserv_addr;     /* ptr to appropriate sockaddr_XX structure */
int             servlen;         /* actual sizeof(*pserv_addr) */
{
        int     n;
        char    sendline[MAXLINE], recvline[MAXLINE + 1];

        while (fgets(sendline, MAXLINE, fp) != NULL) {
                n = strlen(sendline);
                if (sendto(sockfd, sendline, n, 0, pserv_addr, servlen) != n)
                        err_dump("dg_cli: sendto error on socket");

                /*
                 * Now read a message from the socket and write it to
                 * our standard output.
                 */

                n = recvfrom(sockfd, recvline, MAXLINE, 0,
                                (struct sockaddr *) 0, (int *) 0);
                if (n < 0)
                        err_dump("dg_cli: recvfrom error");
                recvline[n] = 0;        /* null terminate */
                fputs(recvline, stdout);
```

```
        }

        if (ferror(fp))
                err_dump("dg_cli: error reading file");
}
```

TCP Example

Our TCP example follows the flow of system calls that we diagramed in Figure 6.2 for a connection-oriented client and server. First we show the header file that we use for both the TCP and UDP examples, inet.h.

```
/*
 * Definitions for TCP and UDP client/server programs.
 */

#include         <stdio.h>
#include         <sys/types.h>
#include         <sys/socket.h>
#include         <netinet/in.h>
#include         <arpa/inet.h>

#define SERV_UDP_PORT    6000
#define SERV_TCP_PORT    6000
#define SERV_HOST_ADDR   "192.43.235.6"  /* host addr for server */

char    *pname;
```

Our choice of the TCP port number is arbitrary. It must be greater than 1023, should be greater than 5000, and must not conflict with any other TCP server's port. (We describe the 4.3BSD port number conventions in more detail in Section 6.8.) The SERV_HOST_ADDR constant corresponds to the host being used by the author. As mentioned earlier, there are better ways of handling these magic numbers and constants, but for now we want to concentrate on the socket system calls themselves.

The server program is as follows:

```
/*
 * Example of server using TCP protocol.
 */

#include         "inet.h"

main(argc, argv)
int     argc;
char    *argv[];
{
        int                     sockfd, newsockfd, clilen, childpid;
        struct sockaddr_in      cli_addr, serv_addr;

        pname = argv[0];

        /*
```

```
 * Open a TCP socket (an Internet stream socket).
 */

if ( (sockfd = socket(AF_INET, SOCK_STREAM, 0)) < 0)
        err_dump("server: can't open stream socket");

/*
 * Bind our local address so that the client can send to us.
 */

bzero((char *) &serv_addr, sizeof(serv_addr));
serv_addr.sin_family      = AF_INET;
serv_addr.sin_addr.s_addr = htonl(INADDR_ANY);
serv_addr.sin_port        = htons(SERV_TCP_PORT);

if (bind(sockfd, (struct sockaddr *) &serv_addr, sizeof(serv_addr)) < 0)
        err_dump("server: can't bind local address");

listen(sockfd, 5);

for ( ; ; ) {
        /*
         * Wait for a connection from a client process.
         * This is an example of a concurrent server.
         */

        clilen = sizeof(cli_addr);
        newsockfd = accept(sockfd, (struct sockaddr *) &cli_addr,
                                                      &clilen);
        if (newsockfd < 0)
                err_dump("server: accept error");

        if ( (childpid = fork()) < 0)
                err_dump("server: fork error");

        else if (childpid == 0) {       /* child process */
                close(sockfd);          /* close original socket */
                str_echo(newsockfd);    /* process the request */
                exit(0);
        }

        close(newsockfd);               /* parent process */
   }
}
```

We specify the Internet address for the server's bind as the constant INADDR_ANY.
This tells the system that we will accept a connection on any Internet interface on the
system, if the system is a multihomed.

The client program is as follows:

```
/*
 * Example of client using TCP protocol.
 */
```

```
#include        "inet.h"

main(argc, argv)
int     argc;
char    *argv[];
{
        int                     sockfd;
        struct sockaddr_in      serv_addr;

        pname = argv[0];

        /*
         * Fill in the structure "serv_addr" with the address of the
         * server that we want to connect with.
         */

        bzero((char *) &serv_addr, sizeof(serv_addr));
        serv_addr.sin_family      = AF_INET;
        serv_addr.sin_addr.s_addr = inet_addr(SERV_HOST_ADDR);
        serv_addr.sin_port        = htons(SERV_TCP_PORT);

        /*
         * Open a TCP socket (an Internet stream socket).
         */

        if ( (sockfd = socket(AF_INET, SOCK_STREAM, 0)) < 0)
                err_sys("client: can't open stream socket");

        /*
         * Connect to the server.
         */

        if (connect(sockfd, (struct sockaddr *) &serv_addr,
                                        sizeof(serv_addr)) < 0)
                err_sys("client: can't connect to server");

        str_cli(stdin, sockfd);         /* do it all */

        close(sockfd);
        exit(0);
}
```

UDP Example

Our UDP client and server programs follow the system call flow that we diagramed in Figure 6.3 for a connectionless protocol.

The client calls `bind` after creating its socket, to have the system assign any local address to the client's socket. In some instances this specific step isn't required, if the system automatically assigns a local address when the `sendto` system call is used for the first time. But some connectionless protocols, such as the Unix domain datagram protocol, don't do this (for reasons which we discuss later in this section). Therefore, as both a good programming habit, and to provide consistency between protocols, we'll always call `bind` for connectionless clients.

This UDP example is not reliable. If a datagram disappears, neither the client or server are aware of it. To provide reliability for UDP requires additional user-level code that we'll develop in Section 8.4.

First the server program.

```
/*
 * Example of server using UDP protocol.
 */

#include        "inet.h"

main(argc, argv)
int     argc;
char    *argv[];
{
        int                     sockfd;
        struct sockaddr_in      serv_addr, cli_addr;

        pname = argv[0];

        /*
         * Open a UDP socket (an Internet datagram socket).
         */

        if ( (sockfd = socket(AF_INET, SOCK_DGRAM, 0)) < 0)
                err_dump("server: can't open datagram socket");

        /*
         * Bind our local address so that the client can send to us.
         */

        bzero((char *) &serv_addr, sizeof(serv_addr));
        serv_addr.sin_family      = AF_INET;
        serv_addr.sin_addr.s_addr = htonl(INADDR_ANY);
        serv_addr.sin_port        = htons(SERV_UDP_PORT);

        if (bind(sockfd, (struct sockaddr *) &serv_addr, sizeof(serv_addr)) < 0)
                err_dump("server: can't bind local address");

        dg_echo(sockfd, (struct sockaddr *) &cli_addr, sizeof(cli_addr));

                /* NOTREACHED */
}
```

As with the TCP server example, the Internet address for the `bind` is specified as `INADDR_ANY`.

The client program:

```
/*
 * Example of client using UDP protocol.
 */

#include        "inet.h"

main(argc, argv)
int     argc;
char    *argv[];
{
        int                     sockfd;
        struct sockaddr_in      cli_addr, serv_addr;

        pname = argv[0];

        /*
         * Fill in the structure "serv_addr" with the address of the
         * server that we want to send to.
         */

        bzero((char *) &serv_addr, sizeof(serv_addr));
        serv_addr.sin_family      = AF_INET;
        serv_addr.sin_addr.s_addr = inet_addr(SERV_HOST_ADDR);
        serv_addr.sin_port        = htons(SERV_UDP_PORT);

        /*
         * Open a UDP socket (an Internet datagram socket).
         */

        if ( (sockfd = socket(AF_INET, SOCK_DGRAM, 0)) < 0)
                err_dump("client: can't open datagram socket");

        /*
         * Bind any local address for us.
         */

        bzero((char *) &cli_addr, sizeof(cli_addr));    /* zero out */
        cli_addr.sin_family      = AF_INET;
        cli_addr.sin_addr.s_addr = htonl(INADDR_ANY);
        cli_addr.sin_port        = htons(0);
        if (bind(sockfd, (struct sockaddr *) &cli_addr, sizeof(cli_addr)) < 0)
                err_dump("client: can't bind local address");

        dg_cli(stdin, sockfd, (struct sockaddr *) &serv_addr, sizeof(serv_addr));

        close(sockfd);
        exit(0);
}
```

In assigning a local address for the client using bind, we set the Internet address to
INADDR_ANY and the 16-bit Internet port to zero. Setting the port to zero causes the
system to assign the client some unused port in the range 1024 through 5000. The system

guarantees that the assigned port is unique on the local system, so that the datagrams returned by the server to this port are delivered to the correct client. When we send a datagram to the server, the system determines which Internet interface to use to contact the server, and sets the client's 32-bit Internet address accordingly.

SPP Example

The XNS examples are similar to the Internet examples, the only exception being the handling of the XNS address structures.

First we show the header file used by both the SPP and IDP programs, `xns.h`.

```
/*
 * Definitions for SPP and IDP client/server programs.
 */

#include         <stdio.h>
#include         <sys/types.h>
#include         <sys/socket.h>
#include         <netns/ns.h>

#define SPP_SERV_ADDR    "123:02.07.01.00.a1.62:6001"
#define IDP_SERV_ADDR    "123:02.07.01.00.a1.62:6000"
                                /* <netid>:<hostid>:<port> */
#define SERV_SPP_PORT    6001
#define SERV_IDP_PORT    6000

char            *pname;
struct ns_addr  ns_addr();        /* BSD library routine */
```

Our choice of port numbers is arbitrary. Note that the SPP and IDP port numbers are different, while our Internet example used the same port number for the TCP port and the UDP port. Recall from Section 5.2 that TCP and UDP ports are independent on a system (they are demultiplexed at the transport layer). XNS port numbers, however, are not independent as they are demultiplexed at the network layer.

The `SPP_SERV_ADDR` and `IDP_SERV_ADDR` values correspond to the XNS addresses of the systems used for this example.

As mentioned at the beginning of this section, we have coded this server as an iterative server. It completely handles one client before accepting another connection. You should compare this with the TCP example shown earlier in this section, which we coded as a concurrent server.

```
/*
 * Example of server using SPP protocol.
 */

#include         "xns.h"

main(argc, argv)
int     argc;
char    *argv[];
```

```
{
        int                     sockfd, newsockfd, clilen;
        struct sockaddr_ns      cli_addr, serv_addr;

        pname = argv[0];

        /*
         * Open a SPP socket (an XNS stream socket).
         */

        if ( (sockfd = socket(AF_NS, SOCK_STREAM, 0)) < 0)
                err_dump("server: can't open stream socket");

        /*
         * Bind our local address so that the client can send to us.
         */

        bzero((char *) &serv_addr, sizeof(serv_addr));
        serv_addr.sns_family       = AF_NS;
        serv_addr.sns_addr.x_port = htons(SERV_SPP_PORT);

        if (bind(sockfd, (struct sockaddr *) &serv_addr, sizeof(serv_addr)) < 0)
                err_dump("server: can't bind local address");

        listen(sockfd, 5);

        for ( ; ; ) {
                /*
                 * Wait for a connection from a client process,
                 * then process it without fork()'ing.
                 * This is an example of an iterative server.
                 */

                clilen = sizeof(cli_addr);
                newsockfd = accept(sockfd, (struct sockaddr *) &cli_addr,
                                                            &clilen);
                if (newsockfd < 0)
                        err_dump("server: accept error");

                str_echo(newsockfd);     /* returns when connection is closed */

                close(newsockfd);
        }
}
```

Before binding its well-known address, the server zeroes its address structure and then stores its family and port, leaving the network ID and host ID as zero. This is similar to setting the 32-bit Internet network ID and host ID to INADDR_ANY. It tells the system that the server is willing to accept a connection from any host.

The client program:

```
/*
 * Example of client using SPP protocol.
 */

#include        "xns.h"

main(argc, argv)
int     argc;
char    *argv[];
{
        int                     sockfd;
        struct sockaddr_ns      serv_addr;

        pname = argv[0];

        /*
         * Fill in the structure "serv_addr" with the XNS address of the
         * server that we want to connect with.
         */

        bzero((char *) &serv_addr, sizeof(serv_addr));
        serv_addr.sns_family = AF_NS;
        serv_addr.sns_addr   = ns_addr(SPP_SERV_ADDR);
                                /* stores net-ID, host-ID and port */

        /*
         * Open a SPP socket (an XNS stream socket).
         */

        if ( (sockfd = socket(AF_NS, SOCK_STREAM, 0)) < 0)
                err_sys("client: can't open stream socket");

        /*
         * Connect to the server.
         */

        if (connect(sockfd, (struct sockaddr *) &serv_addr,
                                        sizeof(serv_addr)) < 0)
                err_sys("client: can't connect to server");

        str_cli(stdin, sockfd);         /* do it all */

        close(sockfd);
        exit(0);
}
```

IDP Example

As with our UDP example, the IDP programs that follow are not reliable. The IDP
server program:

```
/*
 * Example of server using XNS IDP protocol.
 */

#include        "xns.h"

main(argc, argv)
int     argc;
char    *argv[];
{
        int                     sockfd;
        struct sockaddr_ns      serv_addr, cli_addr;

        pname = argv[0];

        /*
         * Open an IDP socket (an XNS datagram socket).
         */

        if ( (sockfd = socket(AF_NS, SOCK_DGRAM, 0)) < 0)
                err_dump("server: can't open datagram socket");

        /*
         * Bind our local address so that the client can send to us.
         */

        bzero((char *) &serv_addr, sizeof(serv_addr));
        serv_addr.sns_family     = AF_NS;
        serv_addr.sns_addr.x_port = htons(SERV_IDP_PORT);

        if (bind(sockfd, (struct sockaddr *) &serv_addr, sizeof(serv_addr)) < 0)
                err_dump("server: can't bind local address");

        dg_echo(sockfd, (struct sockaddr *) &cli_addr, sizeof(cli_addr));
                /* NOTREACHED */
}
```

The IDP client program:

```
/*
 * Example of client using XNS IDP protocol.
 */

#include        "xns.h"

main(argc, argv)
int     argc;
char    *argv[];
{
```

```
        int                     sockfd;
        struct sockaddr_ns      cli_addr, serv_addr;

        pname = argv[0];

        /*
         * Fill in the structure "serv_addr" with the address of the
         * server that we want to send to.
         */

        bzero((char *) &serv_addr, sizeof(serv_addr));
        serv_addr.sns_family = AF_NS;
        serv_addr.sns_addr   = ns_addr(IDP_SERV_ADDR);
                                /* stores net-ID, host-ID and port */

        /*
         * Open an IDP socket (an XNS datagram socket).
         */

        if ( (sockfd = socket(AF_NS, SOCK_DGRAM, 0)) < 0)
                err_dump("client: can't open datagram socket");

        /*
         * Bind any local address for us.
         */

        bzero((char *) &cli_addr, sizeof(cli_addr));    /* zero out */
        cli_addr.sns_family = AF_NS;
        if (bind(sockfd, (struct sockaddr *) &cli_addr, sizeof(cli_addr)) < 0)
                err_dump("client: can't bind local address");

        dg_cli(stdin, sockfd, (struct sockaddr *) &serv_addr, sizeof(serv_addr));

        close(sockfd);
        exit(0);
}
```

Unix Stream Example

The Unix stream protocol example is similar to both the TCP and SPP examples. Here is
the header file that we use for both the stream and datagram examples, `unix.h`.

```
/*
 * Definitions for UNIX domain stream and datagram client/server programs.
 */

#include         <stdio.h>
#include         <sys/types.h>
#include         <sys/socket.h>
#include         <sys/un.h>

#define UNIXSTR_PATH    "./s.unixstr"
#define UNIXDG_PATH     "./s.unixdg"
```

```
#define UNIXDG_TMP      "/tmp/dg.XXXXXX"

char    *pname;
```

The server program:

```
/*
 * Example of server using UNIX domain stream protocol.
 */

#include        "unix.h"

main(argc, argv)
int     argc;
char    *argv[];
{
        int                     sockfd, newsockfd, clilen, childpid, servlen;
        struct sockaddr_un      cli_addr, serv_addr;

        pname = argv[0];

        /*
         * Open a socket (a UNIX domain stream socket).
         */

        if ( (sockfd = socket(AF_UNIX, SOCK_STREAM, 0)) < 0)
                err_dump("server: can't open stream socket");

        /*
         * Bind our local address so that the client can send to us.
         */

        bzero((char *) &serv_addr, sizeof(serv_addr));
        serv_addr.sun_family = AF_UNIX;
        strcpy(serv_addr.sun_path, UNIXSTR_PATH);
        servlen = strlen(serv_addr.sun_path) + sizeof(serv_addr.sun_family);

        if (bind(sockfd, (struct sockaddr *) &serv_addr, servlen) < 0)
                err_dump("server: can't bind local address");

        listen(sockfd, 5);

        for ( ; ; ) {
                /*
                 * Wait for a connection from a client process.
                 * This is an example of a concurrent server.
                 */

                clilen = sizeof(cli_addr);
                newsockfd = accept(sockfd, (struct sockaddr *) &cli_addr,
                                                        &clilen);

                if (newsockfd < 0)
                        err_dump("server: accept error");
```

```
                 if ( (childpid = fork()) < 0)
                         err_dump("server: fork error");

                 else if (childpid == 0) {      /* child process */
                         close(sockfd);         /* close original socket */
                         str_echo(newsockfd);   /* process the request */
                         exit(0);
                 }

                 close(newsockfd);              /* parent process */
         }
}
```

With a Unix domain address structure, we have to calculate the length of the structure for
the bind system call, since it depends on the length of the pathname specified. We
specify the length as the size of the sun_family variable plus the number of characters
in the pathname.

The client program:

```
/*
 * Example of client using UNIX domain stream protocol.
 */

#include        "unix.h"

main(argc, argv)
int     argc;
char    *argv[];
{
        int                     sockfd, servlen;
        struct sockaddr_un      serv_addr;

        pname = argv[0];

        /*
         * Fill in the structure "serv_addr" with the address of the
         * server that we want to send to.
         */

        bzero((char *) &serv_addr, sizeof(serv_addr));
        serv_addr.sun_family = AF_UNIX;
        strcpy(serv_addr.sun_path, UNIXSTR_PATH);
        servlen = strlen(serv_addr.sun_path) + sizeof(serv_addr.sun_family);

        /*
         * Open a socket (an UNIX domain stream socket).
         */

        if ( (sockfd = socket(AF_UNIX, SOCK_STREAM, 0)) < 0)
                err_sys("client: can't open stream socket");

        /*
         * Connect to the server.
         */
```

```
        if (connect(sockfd, (struct sockaddr *) &serv_addr, servlen) < 0)
                err_sys("client: can't connect to server");

        str_cli(stdin, sockfd);              /* do it all */

        close(sockfd);
        exit(0);
}
```

Unix Datagram Example

The Unix datagram protocol example presents an interesting problem that we haven't
encountered yet. Since Unix domain sockets are identified by pathnames of actual files
in the host's filesystem, the client has to form a unique pathname to use when it binds
its local address. When using UDP or IDP, the local port is specified by a 16-bit integer
that only has significance within the kernel. Therefore we let the system assign our local
port, leaving the responsibility to the system to guarantee its uniqueness on the local host.
But in the Unix domain we're dealing with pathnames that get turned into actual files by
the bind system call, so it is our responsibility to pick a local address and guarantee its
uniqueness on the local host. While this function could have been delegated to the kernel
(as is done with UDP and IDP), since side effects could occur (such as creating a file in a
directory in which the caller doesn't have permission to delete in), the designers chose to
leave this to the application.

   In this example we use the mktemp function in the standard C library to create a
name for the client's socket, based on the client's process ID. Note that we must try to
create a unique name for the client's socket, since there is a possibility that multiple
clients are using the same server at the same time. With unique client addresses, each
server response is returned to the correct client process.†

   The server program:

```
/*
 * Example of server using UNIX domain datagram protocol.
 */

#include        "unix.h"

main(argc, argv)
int     argc;
```

---

† There is a feature in the 4.3BSD implementation of Unix domain datagrams that limits the
number of characters of this filename that are transmitted along with the datagram, to 14 characters.
If the client binds a local address with more than 14 characters in the filename, that file, of type
socket, is correctly created in the filesystem, but only the first 14 characters of its name are sent to
the server. This means the server won't be able to respond to the client. Furthermore, if the filename is less than 14 characters, extraneous characters are usually appended to the name, which also
prevents the server from responding to the client. We have purposely chosen the pathname
/tmp/dg.XXXXXX to be exactly 14 characters.

```
char    *argv[];
{
        int                     sockfd, servlen;
        struct sockaddr_un      serv_addr, cli_addr;

        pname = argv[0];

        /*
         * Open a socket (a UNIX domain datagram socket).
         */

        if ( (sockfd = socket(AF_UNIX, SOCK_DGRAM, 0)) < 0)
                err_dump("server: can't open datagram socket");

        /*
         * Bind our local address so that the client can send to us.
         */

        unlink(UNIXDG_PATH);    /* in case it was left from last time */
        bzero((char *) &serv_addr, sizeof(serv_addr));
        serv_addr.sun_family = AF_UNIX;
        strcpy(serv_addr.sun_path, UNIXDG_PATH);
        servlen = sizeof(serv_addr.sun_family) + strlen(serv_addr.sun_path);

        if (bind(sockfd, (struct sockaddr *) &serv_addr, servlen) < 0)
                err_dump("server: can't bind local address");

        dg_echo(sockfd, (struct sockaddr *) &cli_addr, sizeof(cli_addr));
                /* NOTREACHED */
}
```

The client program:

```
/*
 * Example of client using UNIX domain datagram protocol.
 */

#include         "unix.h"

main(argc, argv)
int     argc;
char    *argv[];
{
        int                     sockfd, clilen, servlen;
        char                    *mktemp();
        struct sockaddr_un      cli_addr, serv_addr;

        pname = argv[0];

        /*
         * Fill in the structure "serv_addr" with the address of the
         * server that we want to send to.
         */
```

```
        bzero((char *) &serv_addr, sizeof(serv_addr));
        serv_addr.sun_family = AF_UNIX;
        strcpy(serv_addr.sun_path, UNIXDG_PATH);
        servlen = sizeof(serv_addr.sun_family) + strlen(serv_addr.sun_path);

        /*
         * Open a socket (a UNIX domain datagram socket).
         */

        if ( (sockfd = socket(AF_UNIX, SOCK_DGRAM, 0)) < 0)
                err_dump("client: can't open datagram socket");

        /*
         * Bind a local address for us.
         * In the UNIX domain we have to choose our own name (that
         * should be unique).  We'll use mktemp() to create a unique
         * pathname, based on our process id.
         */

        bzero((char *) &cli_addr, sizeof(cli_addr));      /* zero out */
        cli_addr.sun_family = AF_UNIX;
        strcpy(cli_addr.sun_path, UNIXDG_TMP);
        mktemp(cli_addr.sun_path);
        clilen = sizeof(cli_addr.sun_family) + strlen(cli_addr.sun_path);

        if (bind(sockfd, (struct sockaddr *) &cli_addr, clilen) < 0)
                err_dump("client: can't bind local address");

        dg_cli(stdin, sockfd, (struct sockaddr *) &serv_addr, servlen);

        close(sockfd);
        unlink(cli_addr.sun_path);
        exit(0);
}
```

6.7   Advanced Socket System Calls

We now proceed to the more advanced socket system calls, which we need in later sections of this chapter, and in some of the later chapters of this text.

`readv` and `writev` System Calls

4.3BSD provides what are called *scatter read* and *gather write* variants of the standard `read` and `write` system calls that we described in Section 2.3. What these two variants provide is the ability to read into or write from noncontiguous buffers.

```
#include <sys/types.h>
#include <sys/uio.h>

int writev(int fd, struct iovec iov[], int iovcount);

int readv(int fd, struct iovec iov[], int iovcount);
```

These two system calls use the following structure that is defined in `<sys/uio.h>`:

```
struct iovec {
  caddr_t  iov_base;    /* starting address of buffer */
  int      iov_len;     /* size of buffer in bytes */
};
```

The `writev` system call writes the buffers specified by *iov[0]*, *iov[1]*, through *iov[iovcount−1]*. The `readv` system call does the input equivalent. `readv` always fills one buffer (as specified by the `iov_len` value) before proceeding to the next buffer in the *iov* array. Both system calls return the total number of bytes read or written.

Consider, as an example, a hypothetical function named `write_hdr` that writes a buffer preceded by some header. The actual format of the header doesn't concern us.

```
int
write_hdr(fd, buff, nbytes)
int     fd;
char    *buff;
int     nbytes;
{
        int             n;
        struct hdr_info header;

        /* ... set up the header as required ... */

        if (write(fd, header, sizeof(header)) != sizeof(header))
                return(-1);

        if (write(fd, buff, nbytes) != nbytes)
                return(-1);

        return(nbytes);
}
```

Here two `write` system calls are used. Another way to do this is to allocate a temporary buffer, build the header in the beginning of the buffer, then copy the data into the buffer and do a single `write` of the entire buffer. A third way to do it (to avoid the extra `write` or to avoid the copy operation) is to force the caller to allocate space at the beginning of their buffer for the header. None of these three alternatives is optimal, which is why the `writev` system call (and its `readv` counterpart) were introduced.

The types of operation described here (adding information to either the beginning or end of a user's buffer) is just a form of encapsulation. The `writev` alternative for our example is

```
#include <sys/types.h>
#include <sys/uio.h>

int
write_hdr(fd, buff, nbytes)
int     fd;
char    *buff;
int     nbytes;
{
        struct hdr_info    header;
        struct iovec       iov[2];

        /* ... set up the header as required ... */

        iov[0].iov_base = (char *) &header;
        iov[0].iov_len  = sizeof(header);

        iov[1].iov_base = buff;
        iov[1].iov_len  = nbytes;

        if (writev(fd, &iovec[0], 2) != sizeof(header) + nbytes)
                return(-1);

        return(nbytes);
}
```

The `readv` and `writev` system calls can be used with any descriptor, not just sockets, although they are not portable beyond 4.3BSD. (One could write user functions named `readv` and `writev` that emulate these 4.3BSD system calls.)

The `writev` system call is an atomic operation. This is important if the descriptor refers to a record-based entity, such as a datagram socket or a magnetic tape drive. For example, a `writev` to a datagram socket produces a single datagram, whereas multiple `writes` would produce multiple datagrams. The only correct way to emulate `writev` is to copy all the data into a single buffer and then execute a single `write` system call.

`sendmsg` and `recvmsg` System Calls

These two system calls are the most general of all the read and write system calls.

```
#include <sys/types.h>
#include <sys/socket.h>

int sendmsg(int sockfd, struct msghdr msg[], int flags);

int recvmsg(int sockfd, struct msghdr msg[], int flags);
```

These use the `msghdr` structure that is defined in `<sys/socket.h>`

```
struct msghdr {
    caddr_t      msg_name;         /* optional address */
    int          msg_namelen;      /* size of address */
    struct iovec *msg_iov;         /* scatter/gather array */
    int          msg_iovlen;       /* # elements in msg_iov */
    caddr_t      msg_accrights;    /* access rights sent/recvd */
    int          msg_accrightslen;
};
```

The `msg_name` and `msg_namelen` fields are used when the socket is not connected, similar to the final two arguments to the `recvfrom` and `sendto` system calls. The `msg_name` field can be specified as a NULL pointer if a name is either not required or not desired. The `msg_iov` and `msg_iovlen` fields are used for scatter read and gather write operations, as described above for the `readv` and `writev` system calls. The final two elements of the structure, `msg_accrights` and `msg_accrightslen` deal with the passing and receiving of access rights between processes. We discuss this in Section 6.10 when we explain the passing of file descriptors between processes. The `flags` argument is the same as with the `send` and `recv` system calls, which we described in Section 6.5.

Figure 6.10 compares the five different read and write function groups.

System call	Any descriptor	Only socket descriptor	Single read/write buffer	Scatter/ gather read/write	Optional flags	Optional peer address	Optional access rights
read, write	●		●				
readv, writev	●			●			
recv, send		●	●		●		
recvfrom, sendto		●	●		●	●	
recvmsg, sendmsg		●		●	●	●	●

Figure 6.10   Read and write system call variants.

getpeername **System Call**

This system call returns the name of the peer process that is connected to a given socket.

```
#include <sys/types.h>
#include <sys/socket.h>

int getpeername(int sockfd, struct sockaddr *peer, int *addrlen);
```

When we say that this system call returns the "name" of the peer process, we mean that it returns the *foreign-addr* and *foreign-process* elements of the 5-tuple associated with *sockfd*. Note that the final argument is a value–result argument.

The original 4.3BSD release did not support this system call for Unix domain sockets, but fixes exist to correct this limitation.

`getsockname` **System Call**

This system call returns the name associated with a socket.

```
#include <sys/types.h>
#include <sys/socket.h>

int getsockname(int sockfd, struct sockaddr *peer, int *addrlen);
```

This call returns the *local-addr* and *local-process* elements of an association. As with the `getpeername` system call, the final argument is a value–result argument.

The original 4.3BSD release did not support this system call for Unix domain sockets, but fixes exist to correct this limitation.

`getsockopt` **and** `setsockopt` **System Calls**

These two system calls manipulate the options associated with a socket. We'll describe them in more detail in Section 6.11, along with two other system calls, `fcntl` and `ioctl`, that can modify the properties of a socket.

`shutdown` **System Call**

The normal way to terminate a network connection is to call the `close` system call. As we mentioned earlier, `close` normally attempts to deliver any data that is still to be sent. But the `shutdown` system call provides more control over a full-duplex connection.

```
int shutdown(int sockfd, int howto);
```

If the *howto* argument is 0, no more data can be received on the socket. A value of 1 causes no more output to be allowed on the socket. A value of 2 causes both sends and receives to be disallowed.

Remember that a socket is usually a *full-duplex* communication path. The data flowing in one direction is logically independent of the data going in the other direction. This is why `shutdown` allows either direction to be closed, independent of the other direction.

`select` **System Call**

This system call can be used when dealing with multiple descriptors. We'll discuss it in detail in Section 6.13.

6.8   Reserved Ports

There are two ways for a process to have an Internet port or an XNS port assigned to a socket.

- The process can request a specific port. This is typical for servers that need to assign a well-known port to a socket. All our server examples shown in Section 6.6 do this.

- The process can let the system automatically assign a port. For both the Internet domain and the XNS domain, specifying a port number of zero before calling `bind` requests the system to do this. Both our UDP and IDP client examples do this.

4.3BSD supports the concept of *reserved ports* in both the Internet and XNS domains. In the Internet domain, any TCP or UDP port in the range 1–1023 is reserved, and in the XNS domain ports in the range 1–2999 are reserved. A process is not allowed to `bind` a reserved port unless its effective user ID is zero (the superuser).

4.3BSD provides a library function that assigns a reserved TCP stream socket to its caller:

```
int rresvport(int *aport);
```

This function creates an Internet stream socket and `bind`s a reserved port to the socket. The socket descriptor is returned as the value of the function, unless an error occurs, in which case −1 is returned. Note that the argument to this function is the address of an integer (a value–result argument), not an integer value. The integer pointed to by *aport* is the first port number that the function attempts to `bind`. The caller typically initializes the starting port number to `IPPORT_RESERVED-1`. (The value of the constant `IPPORT_RESERVED` is defined to be 1024 in `<netinet/in.h>`.) If this `bind` fails with an `errno` of `EADDRINUSE`, then this function decrements the port number and tries again. If it finally reaches port 512 and finds it already in use, it sets `errno` to `EAGAIN`, and returns −1. If this function returns successfully, it not only returns the socket as the value of the function, but the port number is also returned in the location pointed to by *aport*.

Figure 6.11 summarizes the assignment of ports in the Internet and XNS domains.

	Internet	XNS
reserved ports	1–1023	1–2999
ports automatically assigned by system	1024–5000	3000–65535
ports assigned by `rresvport()`	512–1023	

Figure 6.11   Port assignment in the Internet and XNS domains.

Note that all ports assigned by standard Internet applications (FTP, TELNET, TFTP, SMTP, etc.) are between 1 and 255 and are therefore reserved. The servers for these applications must have superuser privileges when they create their socket and `bind` their well-known address. Also, the ports between 256 and 511 are considered reserved by 4.3BSD, but they are not currently used by any standard Internet application, and they are never allocated by the `rresvport` function.

The system doesn't automatically assign an Internet port greater than 5000. It leaves these ports for user-developed, nonprivileged servers. This provides a higher degree of certainty that a server can assign itself its well-known port, since any of the ports between 1024 and 5000 might be in use by some client.

Finally, note that any process that wants to obtain a privileged UDP, IDP, or SPP port has to do the same steps that `rresvport` does. There does not exist a standard library function similar to `rresvport` for these three protocols.

The concept of *reserved ports* as described above only handles the `binding` of ports to unbound sockets by the system. It is up to the application program (the server) that receives a request from a client with a reserved port, to consider the request as special or not. The server can obtain the address of the client using the `getpeername` system call. A connection-oriented server can also obtain the client's address from the *peer* argument of the `accept` system call, and a datagram server can obtain the address of the client from the *from* argument of the `recvfrom` system call. In Section 9.2 we consider reserved ports and their use by typical 4.3BSD servers for authentication.

6.9   Stream Pipes

We introduced the term *stream pipe* in Section 6.5 when describing the `socketpair` system call. We consider a stream pipe to be similar to a pipe, but a stream pipe is *bidirectional*. Furthermore, stream pipes are used in both 4.3BSD and in System V Release 3 for passing file descriptors between processes. Therefore we'll provide a function named `s_pipe` to create a stream pipe and have it look just like the `pipe` system call.

We also have the option of associating a name with a stream pipe, so we can provide two versions: *unnamed* stream pipes and *named* stream pipes. Figure 6.12 compares the four types of pipes that we've described.

	Unidirectional	Bidirectional	4.3BSD	System V
pipe	●		yes	yes
named pipe (FIFO)	●		some	yes
stream pipe		●	yes	yes
named stream pipe		●	yes	yes

Figure 6.12   Comparison of pipes, FIFOs, stream pipes, and named stream pipes.

Pipes and named pipes were described in Chapter 3.

A function to create an unnamed stream pipe is trivial for 4.3BSD.

```
/*
 * Create an unnamed stream pipe.
 */

#include        <sys/types.h>
#include        <sys/socket.h>

int                     /* returns 0 if all OK, -1 if error (with errno set) */
s_pipe(fd)
int     fd[2];          /* two file descriptors returned through here */
{
        return( socketpair(AF_UNIX, SOCK_STREAM, 0, fd) );

}
```

Our function to create a named stream pipe first creates an unnamed stream pipe, then associates a name with one end of it, using the bind system call. This function requires another argument: the name within the fileystem to be associated with the stream pipe.

```
/*
 * Create a named stream pipe.
 */

#include        <sys/types.h>
#include        <sys/socket.h>
#include        <sys/un.h>

int                     /* returns 0 if all OK, -1 if error (with errno set) */
ns_pipe(name, fd)
char    *name;          /* user-specified name to assign to the stream pipe */
int     fd[2];          /* two file descriptors returned through here */
{
        int                     len;
        struct sockaddr_un      unix_addr;

        if (s_pipe(fd) < 0)     /* first create an unnamed stream pipe */
                return(-1);

        unlink(name);   /* remove the name, if it already exists */

        bzero((char *) &unix_addr, sizeof(unix_addr));
        unix_addr.sun_family = AF_UNIX;
        strcpy(unix_addr.sun_path, name);
        len = strlen(unix_addr.sun_path) + sizeof(unix_addr.sun_family);

        if (bind(fd[0], (struct sockaddr *) &unix_addr, len) < 0)
                return(-1);

        return(0);

}
```

As we mentioned in Section 6.3, the filename that is specified for a socket that is created in the Unix domain (as we are doing to implement named stream pipes) refers to a socket, not a true Unix file. The only way another process can access this endpoint is through the socket system calls. We cannot, for example, use the `open` system call on these named stream pipes.

With stream pipes, both unnamed and named, the two descriptors returned by the functions `s_pipe` and `ns_pipe` are indistinguishable: both can be used for reading and writing, since these stream pipes are bidirectional. Recall with the `pipe` system call that only one descriptor is available for reading and the other is only available for writing.

6.10   Passing File Descriptors

Recall from Chapter 2 that for most Unix systems the only way to pass an open file from one process to another is for a parent process to open a file and then either `fork` or `exec` another process. There is normally no way for one process to pass an open file to some other, arbitrary (i.e., unrelated) process, or for a child to pass an open file to its parent process. 4.3BSD and System V Release 3 both provide a mechanism to do this. When we say "open file" we mean "open descriptor," since either a file descriptor or a socket descriptor can be passed. Since devices are handled using the same descriptors as files, descriptors that refer to devices can also be passed. When we use the term "file descriptor" in this section, realize that 4.3BSD descriptors are not restricted to actual files.

Recall our picture of the open file table in the kernel for a given process (Figure 2.12). It is a vector that is indexed by the file descriptor to obtain a pointer into the kernel's file table. When we say we want to pass an open file from one process to another, what we want to do is take an open file from the sending process and generate another pointer to the file table entry for that file. Pictorially, we want the data structures as shown in Figure 6.13.

Notice that the actual descriptor value is generally different between the sending process and the receiving process. Figure 6.13 shows, for example, that the descriptor could be 3 in the sending process, but the descriptor in the receiving process could be 4, if that is the first available value. Nevertheless, entry *fd[3]* in the sending process and entry *fd[4]* in the receiving process both point to the same file table entry in the kernel, allowing the two processes to share the same file. Typically the sending process closes the file after it has been sent to the receiving process.

To pass a descriptor from one process to another, the two processes must be connected with a Unix domain socket. This connection can be either a stream socket or a datagram socket. Given the comments we presented earlier about the potential buffer problems with a datagram protocol, we'll use a stream protocol in our examples. We'll use the `s_pipe` function from the previous section to create a stream pipe which is really a Unix domain stream socket. The only way to pass a descriptor is for the sending process to use the `sendmsg` system call and then the receiving process must use the

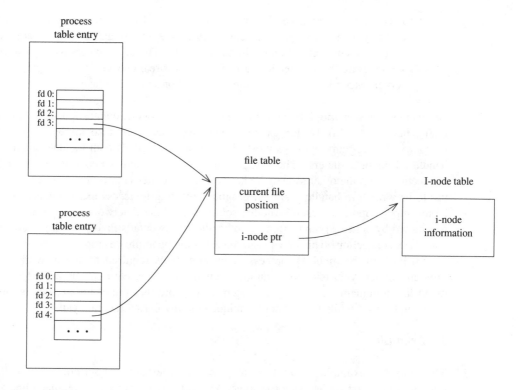

Figure 6.13 Sharing a file table entry between two processes.

`recvmsg` system call. These two system calls are the only ones that support the concept of ''access rights,'' which is how descriptors are passed.

The term ''access rights'' indicates that a process has the right to access a system-maintained object. In this case the object is a file, device, or socket that the system has granted access to by opening the object and returning a file descriptor to the process. The process that has this access right (the sending process that obtained the right from the kernel) passes it to another process. Although we can imagine other access rights that might be passed from one process to another (access to a portion of memory, for example), 4.3BSD only supports the passing of file descriptors.

There are two instances where the ability to pass a file descriptor can be useful. (These ideas come from Presotto and Ritchie [1985].)

1. A process `forks` a child process and the child then `execs` another process to open a particular file. The `execed` process does whatever it has to do to open the file and then passes the open file descriptor back to the original process. Since the `execed` process is a child process of the original process, there is no way for it to pass an open file back to the parent, other than passing an open file as we describe in this section.

2. A connection server can be invoked to handle all network connections. Instead of using `fork` and `exec` as described above, this scenario requires any client process to connect with a well-known server. The client writes its request to the server using this connection (a Unix domain stream socket, for example) and the server responds with an open file descriptor or an error indication.

An example of scenario 1 is the establishment of a network connection using an automatic dialer. In 4.3BSD, for example, the programs `tip` (also known as `cu`) and `uucico` (the program that does most of the work for UUCP) both include functions to handle all possible dialers. The `uucico` program also includes code to establish TCP connections with the other system. Whenever a new dialer is introduced, a new function has to be written to handle it and all programs wanting to access the new dialer have to be recompiled and link edited. Another solution is to have a network access program that is `exec`ed by both `tip` and `uucico` to handle all the details involved with establishing a network connection. This new program passes the open file descriptor (or an error indication) back to the invoking process. Any arguments required by the network access program (dialer type, telephone number, network address, etc.) can be passed as command line arguments in the `exec` system call. Note that this solution does involve a `fork` and `exec`, while the current technique only involves a function call.

An Example

The following example shows how to pass and receive file descriptors in a 4.3BSD environment. First we have a `main` function that takes zero or more command line arguments that specify files to be copied to the standard output. If the program is called `mycat` then it can be invoked as

```
mycat /etc/passwd
```

to print the password file on your terminal.

```
/*
 * Catenate one or more files to standard output.
 * If no files are specified, default to standard input.
 */

#define BUFFSIZE        4096

main(argc, argv)
int     argc;
char    *argv[];
{
        int             fd, i, n;
        char            buff[BUFFSIZE];
        extern char     *pname;

        pname = argv[0];
        argv++; argc--;
```

```
        fd = 0;            /* default to stdin if no arguments */
        i = 0;
        do {
                if (argc > 0 && (fd = my_open(argv[i], 0)) < 0) {
                        err_ret("can't open %s", argv[i]);
                        continue;
                }

                while ( (n = read(fd, buff, BUFFSIZE)) > 0)
                        if (write(1, buff, n) != n)
                                err_sys("write error");
                if (n < 0)
                        err_sys("read error");

        } while (++i < argc);
        exit(0);
}
```

If the call to the function `my_open` shown above is replaced with a call to the standard library function named `open`, the program works fine. It is similar to the standard Unix `cat` command. What we'll do, however, is provide our own function named `my_open`. Our version goes through the steps listed in scenario 1 above: it `fork`s a copy of itself and the child process `exec`s another program to do the actual `open` system call, returning a file descriptor to the parent process. Here is our version of the `open` function.

```
/*
 * Open a file, returning a file descriptor.
 *
 * This function is similar to the UNIX open() system call,
 * however here we invoke another program to do the actual
 * open(), to illustrate the passing of open files
 * between processes.
 */

int
my_open(filename, mode)
char    *filename;
int     mode;
{
        int             fd, childpid, sfd[2], status;
        char            argsfd[10], argmode[10];
        extern int      errno;

        if (s_pipe(sfd) < 0)             /* create an unnamed stream pipe */
                return(-1);              /* errno will be set */

        if ( (childpid = fork()) < 0)
                err_sys("can't fork");

        else if (childpid == 0) {        /* child process */
                close(sfd[0]);           /* close the end we don't use */
                sprintf(argsfd, "%d", sfd[1]);
                sprintf(argmode, "%d", mode);
                if (execl("./openfile", "openfile", argsfd, filename,
```

```
                              argmode, (char *) 0) < 0)
                                  err_sys("can't execl");
        }

        /* parent process - wait for the child's execl() to complete */

        close(sfd[1]);                          /* close the end we don't use */
        if (wait(&status) != childpid)
                err_dump("wait error");
        if ((status & 255) != 0)
                err_dump("child did not exit");
        status = (status >> 8) & 255;           /* child's exit() argument */
        if (status == 0) {
                fd = recvfile(sfd[0]);          /* all OK, receive fd */
        } else {
                errno = status; /* error, set errno value from child's errno */
                fd = -1;
        }

        close(sfd[0]);           /* close the stream pipe */
        return(fd);
}
```

The program that is execed by the parent is the one that does the open system call. Its
pathname was specified as ./openfile in the function shown above.

```
/*
 *       openfile <socket-descriptor-number> <filename> <mode>
 *
 * Open the specified file using the specified mode.
 * Return the open file descriptor on the specified socket descriptor
 * (which the invoker has to set up before exec'ing us).
 * We exit() with a value of 0 if all is OK, otherwise we pass back the
 * errno value as our exit status.
 */

main(argc, argv)
int     argc;
char    *argv[];
{
        int             fd;
        extern int      errno;
        extern char     *pname;

        pname = argv[0];

        if (argc != 4)
                err_quit("openfile <sockfd#> <filename> <mode>");

        /*
         * Open the file.
         */

        if ( (fd = open(argv[2], atoi(argv[3]))) < 0)
                exit( (errno > 0) ? errno : 255 );
```

```
        /*
         * And pass the descriptor back to caller.
         */

        exit( sendfile(atoi(argv[1]), fd) );
}
```

Both of the programs above use the following two functions to send and receive the file descriptor being passed. We have coded the actual calls to `sendmsg` and `recvmsg` as separate functions, to allow their inclusion into other programs that might want to pass descriptors.

```
/*
 * Pass a file descriptor to another process.
 * Return 0 if OK, otherwise return the errno value from the
 * sendmsg() system call.
 */

#include         <sys/types.h>
#include         <sys/socket.h>
#include         <sys/uio.h>

int
sendfile(sockfd, fd)
int     sockfd;         /* UNIX domain socket to pass descriptor on */
int     fd;             /* the actual fd value to pass */
{
        struct iovec    iov[1];
        struct msghdr   msg;
        extern int      errno;

        iov[0].iov_base = (char *) 0;                /* no data to send */
        iov[0].iov_len  = 0;
        msg.msg_iov         = iov;
        msg.msg_iovlen      = 1;
        msg.msg_name        = (caddr_t) 0;
        msg.msg_accrights   = (caddr_t) &fd;   /* address of descriptor */
        msg.msg_accrightslen = sizeof(fd);      /* pass 1 descriptor */

        if (sendmsg(sockfd, &msg, 0) < 0)
                return( (errno > 0) ? errno : 255 );

        return(0);
}

/*
 * Receive a file descriptor from another process.
 * Return the file descriptor if OK, otherwise return -1.
 */

#include         <sys/types.h>
#include         <sys/socket.h>
#include         <sys/uio.h>
```

```
int
recvfile(sockfd)
int     sockfd;          /* UNIX domain socket to receive descriptor on */
{
        int            fd;
        struct iovec   iov[1];
        struct msghdr  msg;

        iov[0].iov_base = (char *) 0;            /* no data to receive */
        iov[0].iov_len  = 0;
        msg.msg_iov          = iov;
        msg.msg_iovlen       = 1;
        msg.msg_name         = (caddr_t) 0;
        msg.msg_accrights    = (caddr_t) &fd;    /* address of descriptor */
        msg.msg_accrightslen = sizeof(fd);       /* receive 1 descriptor */

        if (recvmsg(sockfd, &msg, 0) < 0)
                return(-1);

        return(fd);
}
```

6.11 Socket Options

There are a multitude of ways to set options that affect a socket.

- the setsockopt system call
- the fcntl system call
- the ioctl system call

We mentioned the fcntl and ioctl system calls in Section 2.3, and describe their effect on sockets later in this section.

getsockopt **and** setsockopt **System Calls**

These two system calls apply only to sockets.

```
#include <sys/types.h>
#include <sys/socket.h>

int getsockopt(int sockfd, int level, int optname, char *optval, int *optlen);

int setsockopt(int sockfd, int level, int optname, char *optval, int optlen);
```

The *sockfd* argument must refer to an open socket descriptor. The *level* specifies who in the system is to interpret the option: the general socket code, the TCP/IP code, or the XNS code. Some options are protocol-specific and others are applicable to all sockets.

The *optval* argument is a pointer to a user variable from which an option value is set by `setsockopt`, or into which an option value is returned by `getsockopt`. Although this argument is type coerced into a `char *`, none of the supported options are character values. The "data type" column in Figure 6.14 shows the data type of what the *optval* pointer must point to for each option. The *optlen* argument to `setsockopt` specifies the size of the variable. The *optlen* argument to `getsockopt` is a value–result parameter that we set to the size of the *optval* variable before the call. This size is then set by the system on return to specify the amount of data stored into the *optval* variable. This ability to handle variable-length options is only used by a single option currently: `IP_OPTIONS`. All the other options described below pass a fixed amount of data between the kernel and the user process.

Figure 6.14 provides a summary of all options that can be queried by `getsockopt` or set by `setsockopt`. There are two types of options: binary options that enable or disable a certain feature (flags), and options that fetch and return specific values that we can either set or examine (values). The column labeled "flag" specifies if the option is a flag option. When calling `getsockopt` for these flag options, *optval* is an integer. The value returned in *optval* is zero if the option is disabled, or nonzero if the option is enabled. Similarly, `setsockopt` requires a nonzero *optval* to turn the option on, and a zero value to turn the option off. If the "flag" column does not contain a "•" then the option is used to pass a value of the specified data type between the user process and the system.

level	optname	get	set	Description	flag	Data type
IPPROTO_IP	IP_OPTIONS	•	•	options in IP header		
IPPROTO_TCP	TCP_MAXSEG	•		get TCP maximum segment size		int
	TCP_NODELAY	•	•	don't delay send to coalesce packets	•	int
NSPROTO_SPP	SO_HEADERS_ON_INPUT	•	•	pass SPP header on input	•	int
	SO_HEADERS_ON_OUTPUT	•	•	pass SPP header on output	•	int
	SO_DEFAULT_HEADERS	•	•	set default SPP header for output		struct sphdr
	SO_LAST_HEADER	•		fetch last SPP header		struct sphdr
	SO_MTU	•	•	SPP MTU value		u_short
NSPROTO_PE	SO_SEQNO	•		generate unique PEX ID		long
NSPROTO_RAW	SO_HEADERS_ON_INPUT	•	•	pass IDP header on input	•	int
	SO_HEADERS_ON_OUTPUT	•	•	pass IDP header on output	•	int
	SO_DEFAULT_HEADERS	•	•	set default IDP header for output		struct idp
	SO_ALL_PACKETS	•	•	pass all IDP packets to user	•	int
	SO_NSIP_ROUTE		•	specify IP route for XNS		struct nsip_req
SOL_SOCKET	SO_BROADCAST	•	•	permit sending of broadcast msgs	•	int
	SO_DEBUG	•	•	turn on debugging info recording	•	int
	SO_DONTROUTE	•	•	just use interface addresses	•	int
	SO_ERROR	•		get error status and clear		int
	SO_KEEPALIVE	•	•	keep connections alive	•	int
	SO_LINGER	•	•	linger on close if data present		struct linger
	SO_OOBINLINE	•	•	leave received OOB data in-line	•	int
	SO_RCVBUF	•	•	receive buffer size		int
	SO_SNDBUF	•	•	send buffer size		int
	SO_RCVLOWAT	•	•	receive low-water mark		int
	SO_SNDLOWAT	•	•	send low-water mark		int
	SO_RCVTIMEO	•	•	receive timeout		int
	SO_SNDTIMEO	•	•	send timeout		int
	SO_REUSEADDR	•	•	allow local address reuse	•	int
	SO_TYPE	•		get socket type		int
	SO_USELOOPBACK	•	•	bypass hardware when possible	•	int

Figure 6.14 Socket options for `getsockopt` and `setsockopt`.

Let's first show a simple program that both fetches an option and sets an option.

```
/*
 * Example of getsockopt() and setsockopt().
 */

#include        <sys/types.h>
#include        <sys/socket.h>          /* for SOL_SOCKET and SO_xx values */
#include        <netinet/in.h>          /* for IPPROTO_TCP value */
#include        <netinet/tcp.h>         /* for TCP_MAXSEG value */

main()
{
        int     sockfd, maxseg, sendbuff, optlen;

        if ( (sockfd = socket(AF_INET, SOCK_STREAM, 0)) < 0)
```

```
        err_sys("can't create socket");

    /*
     * Fetch and print the TCP maximum segment size.
     */

    optlen = sizeof(maxseg);
    if (getsockopt(sockfd, IPPROTO_TCP, TCP_MAXSEG, (char *) &maxseg,
                        &optlen) < 0)
            err_sys("TCP_MAXSEG getsockopt error");
    printf("TCP maxseg = %d\n", maxseg);

    /*
     * Set the send buffer size, then fetch it and print its value.
     */

    sendbuff = 16384;        /* just some number for example purposes */
    if (setsockopt(sockfd, SOL_SOCKET, SO_SNDBUF, (char *) &sendbuff,
                                        sizeof(sendbuff)) < 0)
            err_sys("SO_SNDBUF setsockopt error");

    optlen = sizeof(sendbuff);
    if (getsockopt(sockfd, SOL_SOCKET, SO_SNDBUF, (char *) &sendbuff,
                                        &optlen) < 0)
            err_sys("SO_SNDBUF getsockopt error");
    printf("send buffer size = %d\n", sendbuff);
}
```

If we compile and execute this program, its output is

```
TCP maxseg = 512
send buffer size = 16384
```

The most confusing thing about the getsockopt and setsockopt system calls is the handling of the final argument.

The following list gives additional details on the options that affect a socket. When we say *allows us to specify* we are referring to the setsockopt system call. We say *when requested* to refer to the getsockopt system call. When a given option can only be used with a specific type of socket, the socket type (such as SOCK_DGRAM) is listed in parentheses first. For example, the TCP_MAXSEG option only applies to an Internet SOCK_STREAM socket.

IP_OPTIONS   (Internet SOCK_STREAM or SOCK_DGRAM.) Allows us to set specific options in the IP header. Requires intimate knowledge of the IP header. See Section 7.8 of Comer [1988] for a description of the possible IP options. We'll use this option in our remote command server in Section 14.3 and our remote login server in Section 15.12. Both of these servers check for client connections that specify IP options, and if encountered, record the fact in the system log and disable the options.

TCP_MAXSEG   (Internet SOCK_STREAM.) Returns the maximum segment size in use for the socket. The typical value for a 4.3BSD socket using an Ethernet is 1024 bytes. Note that the value for this option can only be examined, it cannot be set by us, since the system decides what size to use.

Note in the example program shown above that the value printed for this option was 512 and not 1024. This is because the socket was not yet connected, so TCP does not know the type of interface being used. It defaults the size to 512 until the socket is connected when it decides on the size to use.

TCP_NODELAY   (Internet SOCK_STREAM.) When TCP is being used for a remote login (which we discuss in Chapter 15) there will be many small data packets sent from the client's system to the server. Each packet can contain a single character that the client enters, which is sent to the server for echoing and processing. On a fast LAN these small packets are not a problem, since the capacity of the network (its bandwidth) is usually adequate to handle all the packets. On a slower WAN, however, it is desirable to reduce the number of these small packets, to reduce the traffic on the network. The scheme used by 4.3BSD is to allow only a single small packet to be outstanding on a given TCP connection at any time. (For additional details on the 4.3BSD TCP output algorithms, see Section 12.7 of Leffler et al. [1989].) On a fast LAN this isn't a problem since the round-trip time for a 1-character packet is usually less than the time between a user entering successive characters on a terminal. On a slower WAN, what happens is the client's TCP buffers input characters until the previous small packet is acknowledged. One problem, however, is if the client is sending small packets that are not keystrokes being entered on a terminal to be echoed by the server. This can happen if the client is sending input from a mouse, for example, on a windowed terminal. The client's input can consist of small packets that are not echoed by the server. The TCP_NODELAY option is used for these clients, to defeat the buffering algorithm described above, to allow the client's TCP to send small packets as soon as possible.

SO_HEADERS_ON_INPUT

       (XNS SOCK_DGRAM.) When set, the first 30 bytes of the data returned by the read and receive system calls is the IDP header.

       (XNS SOCK_STREAM or SOCK_SEQPACKET.) When set, the first 12 bytes of the data returned by the read and receive system calls is the SPP header.

SO_HEADERS_ON_OUTPUT

> (XNS SOCK_DGRAM.) When set, the first 30 bytes of the data passed to the send and write system calls must be the IDP header.
>
> (XNS SOCK_STREAM or SOCK_SEQPACKET.) When set, the first 12 bytes of the data passed to the send and write system calls must be the SPP header.

SO_DEFAULT_HEADERS

> This option provides a way for a user process to set and examine the XNS bridge fields that we described in Section 5.3.
>
> (XNS SOCK_DGRAM.) Allows us to specify a default IDP header for outgoing packets. The actual variable pointed to by the *optval* argument must be a struct idp (the structure defining an IDP header). The only value used by the system from this header is the packet type field. When requested, the system returns its default IDP header, with the following fields filled in: packet type, local address, and foreign address. We'll show an example using this option in Section 11.3.
>
> (XNS SOCK_STREAM or SOCK_SEQPACKET.) Allows us to specify a default SPP header for outgoing packets. The actual variable pointed to by the *optval* argument must be a struct sphdr (the structure defining an SPP header). The only values used by the system from this header are the End-of-Message bit and the Data-stream Type. When requested, the system returns its default SPP header.

SO_LAST_HEADER

> (XNS SOCK_STREAM or SOCK_SEQPACKET.) When requested, returns the most recent SPP header received. The actual variable pointed to by the *optval* argument must be a struct sphdr (the structure defining an SPP header).

SO_MTU

> (XNS SOCK_STREAM or SOCK_SEQPACKET.) By default the SPP MTU is 534 bytes, the Xerox standard. This allows a maximum IDP packet size of 576 bytes, allowing 30 bytes for the IDP header and 12 bytes for the SPP header. Note that any value other than this default is frowned on by an actual Xerox system. This option applies only to SPP sockets, since the BSD implementation of XNS allows IDP packets up to the maximum size of the underlying interface. For an Ethernet, this maximum IDP packet size is 1500 bytes. Again, however, these larger than normal IDP packets can create problems with true Xerox systems.

SO_SEQNO   (XNS SOCK_DGRAM.) The XNS Packet Exchange protocol requires a unique 32-bit ID field, called the transaction ID, with every packet. This ID should be unique among different processes on the same system. This socket option allows the caller to obtain a unique value. The kernel allocates these IDs to any requesting process, incrementing the ID each time a process needs one. Furthermore, the kernel initializes its starting ID whenever the system is rebooted, from a random source (usually the time-of-day clock). This way individual processes can obtain unique IDs and, if the system is taken down and rebooted quickly (while a packet is possibly being retransmitted by some other host on the network), the IDs provided after rebooting are different from those used earlier. Note that the value for this option can only be examined, it cannot be set by us.

SO_ALL_PACKETS
                     (XNS SOCK_DGRAM.) When set, prevents the system from processing Error Protocol packets and SPP packets. Instead, these packets are passed to us.

SO_NSIP_ROUTE
                     (XNS SOCK_DGRAM.) NSIP is an option that can be enabled when the 4.3BSD kernel is configured. If enabled, it allows XNS packets to be sent to another 4.3BSD system, encapsulated in Internet IP datagrams. This allows us, for example, to share a single data link on a WAN between Internet applications and XNS applications. Using this feature any two cooperating systems that are connected on an Internet using the TCP/IP protocols can also exchange XNS packets. This socket option allows us to specify an Internet address to be associated with an XNS address. We won't discuss this option any further in this text.

SO_BROADCAST   (Internet or XNS SOCK_DGRAM.) Enables or disables the ability of the process to send broadcast messages. Broadcasting is only provided for datagram sockets and only on networks that support the concept of a broadcast message (the kernel does not provide a simulation of broadcasting through software).

SO_DEBUG   Enables or disables low-level debugging within the kernel. This option allows the kernel to maintain a history of the recent packets that have been received or sent. With adequate knowledge of the kernel, this history can either be examined (by looking at kernel memory with a debugger) or printed on the console.

SO_DONTROUTE   Specifies that outgoing messages are to bypass the normal routing mechanisms of the underlying protocol. Instead, the message is directed to the appropriate network interface, as specified by the network portion of the destination address. The equivalent of this option can also be applied to individual datagrams using the MSG_DONTROUTE flag with the send, sendto, or sendmsg system calls.

SO_ERROR   Returns to the caller the current contents of the variable so_error, which is defined in <sys/socketvar.h>. This variable holds the standard Unix error numbers (the same values found in the Unix errno variable) for the socket. This error variable is then cleared by the kernel.

SO_KEEPALIVE   (Internet or XNS SOCK_STREAM.) Enables periodic transmissions on a connected socket, when no other data is being exchanged. If the other end does not respond to these messages, the connection is considered broken and the so_error variable is set to ETIMEDOUT.

SO_LINGER   (Internet SOCK_STREAM.) This option determines what to do when unsent messages exist for a socket when the process executes a close on the socket. By default, the close returns immediately and the system attempts to deliver any unsent data. But if the linger option is set for the socket, the action taken depends on the linger time specified by the user. This option requires the following structure to be passed between the user process and the kernel. It is defined in <sys/socket.h>.

```
struct linger {
  int   l_onoff;   /* zero=off, nonzero=on */
  int   l_linger;  /* linger time, in seconds */
};
```

If the linger time is specified as zero, any remaining data to be sent is discarded when the socket is closed. If the linger time is nonzero, the system attempts to deliver any unsent data. Currently the actual value of a nonzero linger time is ignored, despite the comment in the structure definition.

SO_OOBINLINE   (Internet SOCK_STREAM.) When set, specifies that out-of-band data also be placed in the normal input queue (i.e., in-line). When the out-of-band data is placed in-line, the MSG_OOB flag to the receive system calls is not needed to read the out-of-band data. This option applies only to TCP sockets, since the XNS SPP protocol specifies that out-of-band data also be placed in the normal input queue by default. We discuss out-of-band data in more detail in Section 6.14.

SO_RCVBUF and SO_SNDBUF

Specifies the size of the receive queue buffer or the send queue buffer for the socket. These options are only needed when we would like more buffer space than is provided by default. These options are not required for these cases, but they can improve performance. For example, the BSD `rdump` command, which writes 32768-byte buffers using TCP, sets its `SO_SNDBUF` option value to 32768, overriding the default TCP send buffer of 4096 bytes. Similarly, the `/etc/rmt` daemon, which receives these buffers and writes them to tape, sets its `SO_RCVBUF` option to 32768 also. With 4.3BSD there is an upper limit of around 52,000 bytes for either of these buffer sizes. We'll see one use of these options when we look at the 4.3BSD remote tape server in Chapter 16.

`SO_RCVLOWAT` and `SO_SNDLOWAT`
These two options specify the sizes of the receive and send low-water marks. These values are currently unused.

`SO_RCVTIMEO` and `SO_SNDTIMEO`
These two options specify the receive and send timeout values. These values are not currently used for anything. Note that this does not imply that the reliable protocols do not use timers for detecting lost packets and lost connections. Timers are indeed used by TCP and SPP, for example, but these two socket options don't currently affect these timers.

`SO_REUSEADDR`   (Internet `SOCK_STREAM` or `SOCK_DGRAM`.) Instructs the system to allow local addresses, the *local-process* portion of an association 5-tuple, to be reused. Normally the system does not allow a local address to be reused. When `connect` is called for the socket, the system still requires that the complete association be unique, as discussed earlier. We mentioned this requirement in Section 5.2 when discussing the use of TCP port numbers by FTP.

`SO_TYPE`   Returns the socket type. The integer value returned is a value such as `SOCK_STREAM` or `SOCK_DGRAM`. This option is typically used by a process that inherits a process when it is started.

`SO_USELOOPBACK`
This option is unused.

`fcntl` **System Call**

This system call affects an open file, referenced by the *fd* argument.

```
#include <fcntl.h>

int fcntl(int fd, int cmd, int arg);
```

As mentioned in Section 2.3, the *cmd* argument specifies the operation to be performed. Regarding sockets we are interested in the *cmd* values of `F_GETOWN`, `F_SETOWN`, `F_GETFL`, and `F_SETFL`.

The `F_SETOWN` command sets either the process ID or the process group ID to receive the `SIGIO` or `SIGURG` signals for the socket associated with *fd*. Every socket has an associated process group number, similar to the terminal process group number that we discussed in Chapter 2. For a socket, its process group number is initialized to zero and can be set by calling `fcntl` with the `F_SETOWN` command. (It can also be set by both the `FIOSETOWN` and `SIOCSPGRP` `ioctl`s. As we said, there are many ways to set options that affect a socket.) The *arg* value for the `F_SETOWN` command can be either a positive integer, specifying a process ID, or a negative integer, specifying a process group ID. The `F_GETOWN` command returns, as the return value from the `fcntl` system call, either the process ID (a positive return value) or the process group ID (a negative value other than −1) associated with the socket. The difference between specifying a process or a process group to receive the signal is that the former causes only a single process to receive the signal, while the latter causes all processes in the process group (perhaps more than one) to receive the signal. This `fcntl` command is only available for terminals and sockets. We show an example of the `F_SETOWN` command in Section 6.12.

A file's flag bits are set and examined with the `F_SETFL` and `F_GETFL` commands. Figure 6.15 shows the *arg* values that can be used with the `F_GETFL` and `F_SETFL` commands.

arg	Meaning
FAPPEND	append on each write
FASYNC	signal process group when data ready
FCREAT	create if nonexistent
FEXCL	error if already created
FNDELAY	nonblocking I/O
FTRUNC	truncate to zero length

Figure 6.15 `fcntl` options for `F_GETFL` and `F_SETFL` commands.

Of these five values, only the following two are of interest to us now.

FNDELAY   This option designates the socket as "nonblocking." An I/O request that cannot complete on a nonblocking socket is not done. Instead, return is made to the caller immediately and the global `errno` is set to `EWOULDBLOCK`.

This option affects the following system calls: `accept`, `connect`, `read`, `readv`, `recv`, `recvfrom`, `recvmsg`, `send`, `sendto`, `sendmsg`, `write`, and `writev`. Note that a `connect` on a connectionless socket cannot block, since all the system does is record the peer address that is to be used for future output. On a connection-oriented socket, however, the `connect` can take a while to execute, since it usually involves the exchange of actual information with the peer system. In this case a nonblocking socket returns immediately from the `connect` system call, but the `errno` value is set to `EINPROGRESS` instead of `EWOULDBLOCK`.

Note also that the output system calls (the five starting with `send` in the list above) do partial writes on a nonblocking socket when it makes sense (e.g., if the socket is a stream socket). When the socket has record boundaries associated with it (e.g., a datagram socket), if the entire record cannot be written, nothing is written.

FASYNC   This option allows the receipt of asynchronous I/O signals. The `SIGIO` signal is sent to the process group of the socket when data is available to be read. We'll cover asynchronous I/O in the next section.

`ioctl` **System Call**

This system call affects an open file, referenced by the *fd* argument. The intent is for `ioctl`s to manipulate device options.

```
#include <sys/ioctl.h>

int ioctl(int fd, unsigned long request, char *arg);
```

System V defines the second argument to be an `int` instead of an `unsigned long`, but that is not a problem, since the header file `<sys/ioctl.h>` defines the constants that should be used for this argument.

We can divide the *request*s into four categories.

- file operations
- socket operations
- routing operations
- interface operations

Figure 6.16 lists the *request*s provided by 4.3BSD, along with the data type of what the *arg* address must point to. (Notice that none of the requests use the character-pointer data type specified in the function prototype.) We now give a brief description of these options.

FIOCLEX   Sets the close-on-`exec` flag for the file descriptor. Similar to the `F_SETFD` command of `fcntl` (with an *arg* of one).

FIONCLEX   Clears the close-on-`exec` flag for the file descriptor. Similar to the `F_SETFD` command of `fcntl` (with an *arg* of zero).

FIONBIO   Set or clear the nonblocking I/O flag for the file. This flag accomplishes the same affect as the `FNDELAY` argument for the `F_SETFL` command to the `fcntl` system call. Note one difference between the two system calls, however: with the `F_SETFL` command of `fcntl` we must specify all the flag values for the file each time we want to

Category	*request*	Description	Data type
file	FIOCLEX	set exclusive use on fd	
	FIONCLEX	clear exclusive use	
	FIONBIO	set/clear nonblocking i/o	int
	FIOASYNC	set/clear asynchronous i/o	int
	FIONREAD	get # bytes to read	int
	FIOSETOWN	set owner	int
	FIOGETOWN	get owner	int
socket	SIOCSHIWAT	set high-water mark	int
	SIOCGHIWAT	get high-water mark	int
	SIOCSLOWAT	set low-water mark	int
	SIOCGLOWAT	get low-water mark	int
	SIOCATMARK	at out-of-band mark ?	int
	SIOCSPGRP	set process group	int
	SIOCGPGRP	get process group	int
routing	SIOCADDRT	add route	struct rtentry
	SIOCDELRT	delete route	struct rtentry
interface	SIOCSIFADDR	set ifnet address	struct ifreq
	SIOCGIFADDR	get ifnet address	struct ifreq
	SIOCSIFFLAGS	set ifnet flags	struct ifreq
	SIOCGIFFLAGS	get ifnet flags	struct ifreq
	SIOCGIFCONF	get ifnet list	struct ifconf
	SIOCSIFDSTADDR	set point-to-point address	struct ifreq
	SIOCGIFDSTADDR	get point-to-point address	struct ifreq
	SIOCGIFBRDADDR	get broadcast addr	struct ifreq
	SIOCSIFBRDADDR	set broadcast addr	struct ifreq
	SIOCGIFNETMASK	get net addr mask	struct ifreq
	SIOCSIFNETMASK	set net addr mask	struct ifreq
	SIOCGIFMETRIC	get IF metric	struct ifreq
	SIOCSIFMETRIC	set IF metric	struct ifreq
	SIOCSARP	set ARP entry	struct arpreq
	SIOCGARP	get ARP entry	struct arpreq
	SIOCDARP	delete ARP entry	struct arpreq

Figure 6.16 ioctl options for networking.

turn a specific flag on or off. With this ioctl call, however, we can turn a flag on or off, by specifying a zero or nonzero value for *arg*.

FIOASYNC Set or clear the flag that allows the receipt of asynchronous I/O signals (SIGIO). This flag accomplishes the same affect as the FASYNC argument for the F_SETFL command to the fcntl system call.

FIONREAD Returns in *arg* the number of bytes available to read from the file descriptor. This feature works for files, pipes, terminals and sockets.

FIOSETOWN Set either the process ID or the process group ID to receive the SIGIO and SIGURG signals. This *request* works only for terminals and sockets. This command is identical to an fcntl of F_SETOWN.

FIOGETOWN   Get either the process ID or the process group ID that is set to receive the SIGIO and SIGURG signals. This *request* works only for terminals and sockets. This command is identical to an fcntl of F_GETOWN.

SIOCSHIWAT   Set the high-water mark. This command is not currently implemented.

SIOCGHIWAT   Get the high-water mark. This command is not currently implemented.

SIOCSLOWAT   Set the low-water mark. This command is not currently implemented.

SIOCGLOWAT   Get the low-water mark. This command is not currently implemented.

SIOCATMARK   Return a zero or nonzero value, depending whether the specified socket's read pointer is currently at the out-of-band mark. We describe out-of-band data in more detail in Section 6.14.

SIOCSPGRP   Equivalent to FIOSETOWN for a socket.

SIOCGPGRP   Equivalent to FIOGETOWN for a socket.

The following *request*s are for lower level operations, usually relating to the actual network interface being used. We briefly mention their purpose. The interested reader should consult both of the references by Leffler et al. [1986a, 1986b] for additional information. Several of these commands are used by the network configuration program, ifconfig, which is described in Section 8 of the 4.3BSD Programmer's Manual. This program is usually invoked on system startup to initialize all the network interfaces on the system. Some of the commands related to routing are used by the BSD routing daemon, routed, which is also described in Section 8 of the BSD manual.

SIOCADDRT   Add an entry to the interface routing table.

SIOCDELRT   Delete an entry from the interface routing table.

SIOCSIFADDR

     Set the interface address. Additionally the initialization function for the interface is also called.

SIOCGIFADDR

     Get the interface address.

SIOCSIFFLAGS

     Set the interface flags.

SIOCGIFFLAGS

     Get the interface flags. The flags indicate, for example, if the interface is a point-to-point interface, if the interface supports broadcast addressing, if the interface is running, and so on.

SIOCGIFCONF

     Get the interface configuration list. This command returns a list containing one ifreq structure for every interface currently is use by the system. This command allows a user program to determine at run time, the interfaces on the system. A program can then go through this list and determine which interfaces it is interested in (all interfaces that are point-to-point Internet interfaces, for example).

SIOCSIFDSTADDR

Set the point-to-point interface address.

SIOCGIFDSTADDR

Get the point-to-point interface address.

SIOCSIFBRDADDR

Set the broadcast address for the interface.

SIOCGIFBRDADDR

Get the broadcast address for the interface.

SIOCSIFNETMASK

Set the mask for the network portion of the interface address. For Internet addresses the network mask defines the netid portion of the 32-bit address. If this mask contains more bits that would normally be indicated by the class of Internet address (class A, B, or C) then subnets are being used. Refer to Section 5.2 for additional details on Internet addresses.

SIOCGIFNETMASK

Get the interface network mask for an Internet address.

SIOCGIFMETRIC

Get the interface routing metric. The routing metric is stored in the kernel for each interface, but is used by the routing protocol, the `routed` daemon.

SIOCSIFMETRIC

Set the interface routing metric. The 4.3BSD kernel does not make policy decisions for routing. Instead, this is left to a user process, which then uses this `ioctl` to modify the kernel's routing tables. Refer to Section 11.5 of Leffler et al. [1989] for additional details.

SIOCSARP   Set an entry in the Internet ARP (Address Resolution Protocol) table. The structure `arpreq` is defined in `<net/if_arp.h>`. Refer to the entry for `arp(4P)` in Section 4 of the BSD manual for additional information.

SIOCGARP   Get an entry from the Internet ARP entry. The caller specifies an Internet address and this system call returns the corresponding Ethernet address.

SIOCDARP   Delete an entry from the Internet ARP table. The caller specifies the Internet address for the entry to be deleted.

6.12 Asynchronous I/O

Asynchronous I/O allows the process to tell the kernel to notify it when a specified descriptor is ready for I/O. It is also called signal-driven I/O. The notification from the kernel to the user process takes place with a signal, the SIGIO signal.

To do asynchronous I/O, a process must perform the following three steps:

1. The process must establish a handler for the SIGIO signal. This is done by calling the signal system call, as described in Section 2.4.

2. The process must set the process ID or the process group ID to receive the SIGIO signals. This is done with the fcntl system call, with the F_SETOWN command, as described in Section 6.11.

3. The process must enable asynchronous I/O using the fcntl system call, with the F_SETFL command and the FASYNC argument.

To show an example of asynchronous I/O, let's first show a simple program that copies standard input to standard output.

```
/*
 * Copy standard input to standard output.
 */

#define BUFFSIZE        4096

main()
{
        int             n;
        char            buff[BUFFSIZE];

        while ( (n = read(0, buff, BUFFSIZE)) > 0)
                if (write(1, buff, n) != n)
                        err_sys("write error");

        if (n < 0)
                err_sys("read error");

        exit(0);
}
```

We now change this program to do the three steps listed, using asynchronous I/O.

```
/*
 * Copy standard input to standard output, using asynchronous I/O.
 */

#include         <signal.h>
#include         <fcntl.h>

#define BUFFSIZE        4096
```

```
int     sigflag;

main()
{
        int             n;
        char            buff[BUFFSIZE];
        int             sigio_func();

        signal(SIGIO, sigio_func);

        if (fcntl(0, F_SETOWN, getpid()) < 0)
                err_sys("F_SETOWN error");

        if (fcntl(0, F_SETFL, FASYNC) < 0)
                err_sys("F_SETFL FASYNC error");

        for ( ; ; ) {
                sigblock(sigmask(SIGIO));
                while (sigflag == 0)
                        sigpause(0);            /* wait for a signal */

                /*
                 * We're here if (sigflag != 0).  Also, we know that the
                 * SIGIO signal is currently blocked.
                 */

                if ( (n = read(0, buff, BUFFSIZE)) > 0) {
                        if (write(1, buff, n) != n)
                                err_sys("write error");
                } else if (n < 0)
                        err_sys("read error");
                else if (n == 0)
                        exit(0);                /* EOF */

                sigflag = 0;                    /* turn off our flag */

                sigsetmask(0);                  /* and reenable signals */
        }
}

int
sigio_func()
{
        sigflag = 1;            /* just set flag and return */

        /* the 4.3BSD signal facilities leave this handler enabled
           for any further SIGIO signals. */
}
```

This interrupt driven example works only for terminals (and would work for a socket too, if the appropriate code were added to create a socket) because of the restrictions of the 4.3BSD F_SETOWN command.

This example also shows the use of the reliable signals provided by 4.3BSD, which we described in Section 2.4.

Since a process can have only one signal handler for a given signal, if asynchronous I/O is enabled for more than one descriptor, the process doesn't know, when the signal occurs, which descriptor is ready for I/O. To do this, the `select` system call is used, which we describe in the next section.

6.13 Input/Output Multiplexing

Consider a process that reads input from more than one source. An actual example is the 4.3BSD line printer spooler that we cover in Section 13.2. It opens two sockets, a Unix stream socket to receive print requests from processes on the same host, and a TCP socket to receive print requests from processes on other hosts. Since it doesn't know when requests will arrive on the two sockets, it can't start a read on one socket, as it could block while waiting for a request on that socket, and in the mean time a request can arrive on the other socket. There are a few different techniques available to handle this multiplexing of different I/O channels.

1. It can set both sockets to nonblocking, using either the `FNDELAY` flag to `fcntl` or the `FIONBIO` request to `ioctl`. But the process has to execute a loop that reads from each socket, and if nothing is available to read, wait some amount of time before trying the reads again. This is called *polling*. The software polls each socket at some interval (every second, perhaps) and if no data is available to read, the process waits by calling the `sleep` function in the standard C library. Polling can waste computer resources, since most of the time there is no work to be done.

2. The process can `fork` one child process to handle each I/O channel. In this example it spawns two processes, one to read from the Unix socket and one to read from the TCP socket. Each child process calls `read` and blocks until data is available. When a child returns from its `read` it passes the data to the parent process using some form of IPC (that the parent must set up before spawning its children). Any of the techniques that we discussed in Chapter 3 can be used: pipes, FIFOs, message queues, shared memory with a semaphore, or another socket can also be used.

3. Asynchronous I/O can be used. The problem with this method is that signals are expensive to catch [Leffler et al. 1989]. Also, if more than one descriptor has been enabled for asynchronous I/O, the occurrence of the `SIGIO` signal doesn't tell us which descriptor is ready for I/O. Finally, as mentioned in Section 6.12, this technique is only available for terminals and sockets under 4.3BSD.

4. Another technique is provided by 4.3BSD with its `select` system call, which we describe below. This system call allows the user process to instruct the kernel to wait for any one of multiple events to occur and to wake up the process only when one of these events occurs. In this example the kernel can be instructed to notify the process only when data is available to be read from either of the two sockets that we're interested in.

The prototype for the system call is

```
#include <sys/types.h>
#include <sys/time.h>

int select(int maxfdp1, fd_set *readfds, fd_set *writefds, fd_set *exceptfds,
           struct timeval *timeout);

FD_ZERO(fd_set *fdset);       /* clear all bits in fdset */
FD_SET(int fd, fd_set *fdset);   /* turn the bit for fd on in fdset */
FD_CLR(int fd, fd_set *fdset);   /* turn the bit for fd off in fdset */
FD_ISSET(int fd, fd_set *fdset); /* test the bit for fd in fdset */
```

The structure pointed to by the *timeout* argument is defined in `<sys/time.h>` as

```
struct timeval {
  long   tv_sec;    /* seconds */
  long   tv_usec;   /* microseconds */
};
```

The C `typedef` for the `fd_set` structure, and the definitions of the `FD_xxx` macros are in the `<sys/types.h>` include file. The definition of this system call makes it look more complicated than it is.

A request to `select` could be: tell us if any of the file descriptors in the set {1, 4, 5} are ready for reading, or if any of the file descriptors in the set {2, 7} are ready for writing, or if any of the file descriptors in the set {1, 4} have an exceptional condition pending. Additionally we can tell the kernel to

- Return immediately after checking the descriptors. This is a poll. For this, the *timeout* argument must point to a `timeval` structure, and the timer value (the number of seconds and microseconds specified by the structure) must be zero.

- Return when one of the specified descriptors is ready for I/O, but don't wait beyond a fixed amount of time. For this, the *timeout* argument must point to a `timeval` structure, and its value (the number of seconds and microseconds specified by the structure members) must be the nonzero amount of time to wait.

- Return only when one of the specified descriptors is ready for I/O—wait indefinitely. For this, the *timeout* argument must be NULL. This wait can also be interrupted by a signal.

Before describing how to specify the file descriptors to be checked, let's first show an example where we are not interested in any file descriptors. We'll use `select` as a higher precision timer than is provided by the `sleep` function. (`sleep` provides a resolution of seconds, whereas `select` allows us to specify a resolution in microseconds.)

```
#include         <sys/types.h>
#include         <sys/time.h>

main(argc, argv)
int      argc;
char     *argv[];
{
        long                    atol();
        static struct timeval   timeout;

        if (argc != 3)
                err_quit("usage: timer <#seconds> <#microseconds>");
        timeout.tv_sec  = atol(argv[1]);
        timeout.tv_usec = atol(argv[2]);

        if (select(0, (fd_set *) 0, (fd_set *) 0, (fd_set *) 0, &timeout) < 0)
                err_sys("select error");
        exit(0);
}
```

Here we have specified the second, third and fourth arguments to `select` as NULL.

The *readfds*, *writefds*, and *exceptfds* arguments specify which file descriptors we're interested in checking for each of the conditions—descriptor ready for reading, descriptor ready for writing and exceptional condition on descriptor, respectively. There are only two exceptional conditions currently supported.

1. The arrival of out-of-band data for a socket. We describe this in more detail in the next section.

2. The presence of control status information to be read from the master side of a pseudo-terminal that has been put into packet mode. We cover this in Section 15.10.

The problem the designers of this system call had was how to specify one or more descriptor values for each of these three arguments. The decision was made to represent the set of all possible descriptors using an array of integers, where each bit corresponds to a descriptor. For example, using 32-bit integers, the first element of the array corresponds to descriptors 0 through 31, the second element of the array corresponds to descriptors 32 through 63, and so on. All this implementation detail is hidden through the `typedef` of the `fd_set` structure and the `FD_xxx` macros.

For example, to define a variable of type `fd_set` and then turn on the indicators for descriptors 1, 4, and 5

```
fd_set  fdvar;

FD_ZERO(&fdvar);        /* initialize the set - all bits off */
FD_SET(1, &fdvar);      /* turn on bit for fd 1 */
FD_SET(4, &fdvar);      /* turn on bit for fd 4 */
FD_SET(5, &fdvar);      /* turn on bit for fd 5 */
```

It is important to initialize the set, since unpredictable results can occur if the set is allocated as an automatic variable and not initialized. Any of the three arguments to `select`, *readfds*, *writefds*, or *exceptfds*, can be specified as NULL pointers, if we're not interested in that condition.

The *maxfdp1* argument specifies the number of file descriptors to be tested. Its value is the maximum file descriptor to be tested, plus one. The descriptors 0, 1, 2, up through and including *maxfdp1-1* are tested. The system allows for a potentially huge number of descriptors to be tested (currently 256), although most BSD kernels don't allow any single process to have that many open files. The *maxfdp1* argument lets us tell the system the largest descriptor that we're interested in, which is usually much less than 256. For example, given the example code above that turns on the indicators for descriptors 1, 4, and 5, a *maxfdp1* value of 6 can be specified. The reason it is 6 and not 5 is that we're specifying the number of descriptors, not the largest value, and descriptors start at zero.

This system call modifies the three arguments *readfds*, *writefds*, and *exceptfds* to indicate which descriptors are ready for the specified condition. These three arguments are value–result arguments. The caller should use the `FD_ISSET` macro to test a specific bit in an `fd_set` structure. The return value from this system call indicates the total number of descriptors that are ready. If the timer value expired before any of the descriptors were ready, a value of zero is returned. As usual, a return value of −1 indicates an error.

We have been talking about waiting for a file descriptor to become ready for I/O (reading or writing) or to have an exceptional condition pending on it. For sockets, this assumes that the process wants to do I/O on the socket. The `select` system call can also be used to await a connection on a socket. For example, if a process is awaiting a `connect` on more than one socket, if it doesn't want to execute the `accept` system call and potentially block, it can issue a `select` instead. If a `connect` is received by the system for a socket that is being waited for, the socket is then considered ready for reading, and the `select` returns.

6.14   Out-of-Band Data

We described the notion of out-of-band data in Chapter 4, and also mentioned it in Chapter 5 when we discussed the TCP and SPP protocols. Of all the protocols we've discussed so far, only TCP and SPP support out-of-band data. (Out-of-band data is only defined for stream sockets, and the Unix domain stream sockets don't support it.) Unfortunately, TCP and SPP treat out-of-band data differently. The designers of the socket interface tried to support out-of-band data in a generic way, but there are many programs that have been written using the TCP out-of-band data features that would be hard to port to SPP. The BSD socket abstraction calls for the protocol to support at least one outstanding out-of-band message at any time, and the out-of-band message must contain at least one byte of data.

   To send an out-of-band message, the `MSG_OOB` flag must be specified for the `send`, `sendto`, or `sendmsg` system calls. SPP only allows a single byte of out-of-band data to be sent, while TCP has no restriction.

SPP Out-of-Band Data

When out-of-band data is received by the other end, several possibilities exist about how it is handled. Let's first consider how SPP handles it, as it is less complicated than the TCP implementation.

- The out-of-band byte is received along with a special flag specifying that the byte contains out-of-band data. (This flag is the Attention bit in the SPP header.)

- If the socket has a process group, the `SIGURG` signal is generated for the process group of the socket.

- The socket option `SO_OOBINLINE` has no effect, since the Xerox protocol specifies that the out-of-band byte is to be delivered again to the receiving process, in its normal position in the data stream.

- The process can read the out-of-band byte by calling any one of the three receive system calls, specifying the `MSG_OOB` flag. Only the single out-of-band byte is returned. If there is no out-of-band data when the `MSG_OOB` flag is specified, an error of `EINVAL` is returned by these three system calls instead.

- Regardless whether the process reads the out-of-band byte or not, the position of the byte in the normal data stream is remembered.

- The process continues reading data from the socket. Since the system remembers the position of the out-of-band data byte, it does not read right past it in a single read request. That is, if there are 20 bytes from the current read position until the out-of-band byte, and if we execute a read or receive system call specifying a length of 30 bytes, the system only returns 20 bytes. This forced stopping at the out-of-band mark is to allow us to execute the `SIOCATMARK ioctl` to determine when we're at the mark. This allows us to ignore all the data up to the out-of-band byte. When this `ioctl` indicates that we're at the mark, the next byte we read is the out-of-band byte.

TCP Out-of-Band Data

All this gets more complicated with TCP because it can send the notification that out-of-band data exists (termed "urgent data" by TCP) *before* it sends the out-of-band data. In this case, if the process executes one of the three receive system calls, an error of `EWOULDBLOCK` is returned if the out-of-band data has not arrived. As with the SPP example above, an error of `EINVAL` is returned by these three system calls if the `MSG_OOB` flag is specified when there isn't any out-of-band data.

Still another option is provided with the TCP implementation, to allow for multiple bytes of out-of-band data. By default, only a single byte of out-of-band data is provided, and unlike SPP, this byte of data is not stored in the normal data stream. This data byte can only be read by specifying the `MSG_OOB` flag to the receive system calls. But if we set the `SO_OOBINLINE` option for the socket, using the `setsockopt` system call described in Section 6.11, the out-of-band data is left in the normal data stream and is read without specifying the `MSG_OOB` flag. If this socket option is enabled, we must use the `SIOCATMARK ioctl` to determine where in the data stream the out-of-band data occurs. In this case, if multiple occurrences of out-of-band data are received, all the data is left in-line (i.e., none of the data can be lost) but the mark returned by the `SIOCATMARK ioctl` corresponds to the final sequence of out-of-band data that was received. If the out-of-band data is not received in-line, it is possible to lose some intermediate out-of-band data when the out-of-band data arrives faster than it is processed by the user.

The remote login application in Chapter 15 uses TCP out-of-band data along with the `SIOCATMARK ioctl`.

6.15   Sockets and Signals

We have mentioned signals in relation to sockets a few times in this chapter, and its worth taking a moment to summarize the conditions under which signals are generated for a socket and all the related nuances. There are three signals that can be generated for a socket

`SIGIO`   This signal indicates that a socket is ready for asynchronous I/O. The signal is sent to the process group of the signal. This process group is established by calling `ioctl` with a command of either `FIOSETOWN` or `SIOCSPGRP`, or by calling `fcntl` with a command of `F_SETOWN`. This signal is sent to the process group only if the process has enabled asynchronous I/O on the socket by calling `ioctl` with a command of `FIOASYNC` or by calling `fcntl` with a command of `F_SETFL` and an argument of `FASYNC`.

SIGURG   This signal indicates that an urgent condition is present on a socket. An urgent condition is either the arrival of out-of-band data on the socket or the presence of control status information to be read from the master side of a pseudo-terminal that has been put into packet mode. (We discuss pseudo-terminal packet mode in Section 15.10.) The signal is sent to the process group of the signal. This process group is established by calling `ioctl` with a command of either `FIOSETOWN` or `SIOCSPGRP`, or by calling `fcntl` with a command of `F_SETOWN`.

SIGPIPE   This signal indicates that we can no longer write to a socket, pipe, or FIFO. Nothing special is required by a process to receive this signal, but unless the process arranges to catch the signal, the default action is to terminate the process. This signal is sent only to the process associated with the socket; the process group of the socket is not used for this signal.

We mentioned in Section 2.4 that certain system calls (termed the "slow" system calls) can be interrupted when the process handles a signal. This always has to be considered when handling signals. Although 4.3BSD tries automatically to restart certain system calls that are interrupted, the `accept` and `recvfrom` system calls are never restarted automatically by the kernel. Since both of these system calls can typically block, if you are using them and handling signals, be prepared to restart the system call if they're interrupted.

6.16 Internet Superserver

On a typical 4.3BSD system there can be many daemons in existence, just waiting for a request to arrive. For example, there could be an Internet FTP daemon, an Internet TELNET daemon, and Internet TFTP daemon, a remote login daemon, a remote shell daemon, and so on. With systems before 4.3BSD, each of these services had a process associated with it. This process was started at boot time from the `/etc/rc` startup file, and each process did nearly identical startup tasks: create a socket, `bind` the server's well-known address to the socket, wait for a connection, then `fork`. The child process performed the service while the parent waited for another request.

The 4.3BSD release simplified this by providing an Internet superserver: the `inetd` process. This daemon can be used by a server that uses either TCP or UDP. It does not handle either the XNS or Unix domain protocols. What this daemon provides is two features:

- It allows a single process (`inetd`) to be waiting to service multiple connection requests, instead of one process for each potential service. This reduces the total number of processes in the system.

- It simplifies the writing of the daemon processes to handle the requests, since many of the start-up details are handled by `inetd`. This obviates the need for the actual service process to call the `daemon_start` function that we developed in Section 2.6. All the details that we said had to be handled by a typical daemon, are done by `inetd`, before the actual server is invoked.

There is a price to pay for this, however, in that the `inetd` daemon has to execute both a `fork` and an `exec` to invoke the actual server process, while a self-contained daemon that did everything itself only has to execute a `fork` to handle each request. This additional overhead, however, is worth the simplification of the actual servers and the reduction in the total number of processes in the system.

The `inetd` process establishes itself as a daemon using many of the techniques that we described in Section 2.6. It then reads the file `/etc/inetd.conf` to initialize itself. This text file specifies the services that the superserver is to listen for, and what to do when a service request arrives. Each line contains the fields shown in Figure 6.17.

Field	Description
service-name	must be in `/etc/services`
socket-type	`stream` or `dgram`
protocol	must be in `/etc/protocols`: either `tcp` or `udp`
wait-flag	`wait` or `nowait`
login-name	from `/etc/passwd`: typically `root`
server-program	full pathname to `exec`
server-program-arguments	maximum of 5 arguments

Figure 6.17 Fields in `inetd` configuration file.

Some sample lines are

```
ftp       stream  tcp    nowait   root     /etc/ftpd      ftpd
telnet    stream  tcp    nowait   root     /etc/telnetd   telnetd
login     stream  tcp    nowait   root     /etc/rlogind   rlogind
tftp      dgram   udp    wait     nobody   /etc/tftpd     tftpd
```

The actual name of the server is always passed as the first argument to a program when it is `exec`ed.

A picture of what the daemon does is shown in Figure 6.18. Let's go through a typical scenario for this daemon.

1. On startup it reads the `/etc/inetd.conf` file and creates a socket of the appropriate type (stream or datagram) for all the services specified in the file. Realize that

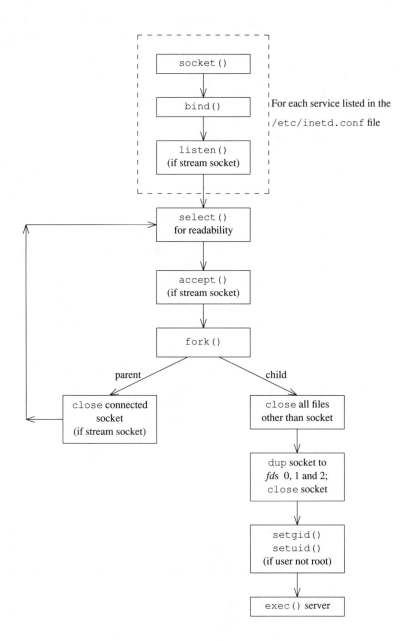

Figure 6.18 Steps performed by `inetd`.

there is a limit to the number of servers that `inetd` can be waiting for, as the total number of file descriptors used by `inetd` can't exceed the system's per-process limit. On most BSD systems this limit is 64, but it can be changed by reconfiguring the kernel.

2. As each socket is created, a `bind` is executed for every socket, specifying the well-known address for the server. This TCP or UDP port number is obtained by looking up the *service-name* field from the configuration file in the `/etc/services` file. Some typical lines in this file, corresponding to the example lines in the configuration file that we showed above, are

```
ftp          21/tcp
telnet       23/tcp
tftp         69/udp
login        513/tcp
```

Both the *service-name* (such as `telnet`) and the *protocol* from the `inetd` configuration file are passed as arguments to the library function `getservbyname`, to locate the correct port number for the `bind`. (We describe the `getservbyname` function in Section 8.2.)

3. For stream sockets, a `listen` is executed, specifying a willingness to receive connections on the socket and the queue length for incoming connections. This step is not done for datagram sockets.

4. A `select` is then executed, to wait for the first socket to become ready for reading. Recall from our description of this system call in Section 6.13, that a stream socket is considered ready for reading when a connection request arrives for that socket. A datagram socket is ready for reading when a datagram arrives. At this point the `inetd` daemon just waits for the `select` system call to return.

5. When a socket is ready for reading, if it is a stream socket, an `accept` system call is executed to accept the connection.

6. The `inetd` daemon `forks` and the child process handles the service request. The child closes all the file descriptors other than the socket descriptor that it is handling and then calls `dup2` to cause the socket to be duplicated on file descriptors 0, 1, and 2. The original socket descriptor is then closed. Doing this, the only file descriptors that are open in the child are 0, 1, and 2. It then calls `getpwnam` to get the password file entry for the *login-name* that is specified in the `/etc/inetd.conf` file. If this entry does not have a user ID of zero (the superuser) then the child becomes the specified user by executing the `setgid` and `setuid` system calls. (Since the `inetd` process is executing with a user ID of zero, the child process inherits this user ID across the `fork`, so it is able to become any user that it chooses.) The child process now does an `exec` to execute the appropriate *server-program* to handle the request, passing the arguments that are specified in the configuration file.

7. If the socket is a stream socket, the parent process must close the connected socket. The parent goes back and executes the `select` system call again, waiting for the next socket to become ready for reading.

The scenario we've described above handles the case where the configuration file specifies `nowait` for the server. This is typical for all TCP services. If another connection request arrives for the same server, it is returned to the parent process as soon as it executes the `select`. The steps listed above are executed again, and another child process handles this new service request.

Specifying the `wait` flag for a datagram service changes the steps done by the parent process. First, after the `fork` the parent saves the process ID of the child, so it can tell later when that specific child process terminates, by looking at the value returned by the `wait` system call. Second, the parent disables the current socket from future `select`s by using the `FD_CLR` macro to turn off the bit in the `fd_set` structure that it uses for the `select`. This means that the child process takes over the socket until it terminates. Once the child process terminates, the parent process is notified by a `SIGCLD` signal, and the parent's signal handler obtains the process ID of the terminating child and reenables the `select` for the corresponding socket by using the `FD_SET` macro. When the child process terminates, the parent is probably waiting for its `select` system call to return. As mentioned in Section 2.4, when a signal handler is invoked while a process is executing a "slow" system call, when the signal handler returns, the system call (the `select` in this case) returns with an error indication and an `errno` value of `EINTR`. The `inetd` process recognizes this and executes the `select` system call again. But by executing the system call again, it can now wait for the socket corresponding to the child process that terminated. If the occurrence of the signal did not interrupt the `select` system call, the parent would not be able to wait for the socket corresponding to the terminating child process. When we go through the TFTP example in Chapter 12 we'll see how a datagram server uses the `wait` mode.

It is worth going through a time sequence of the steps involved in the previous paragraph, making certain we understand the interaction of the parent and child processes, the `SIGCLD` signal, and how the `select` system call can be interrupted.

- The datagram request arrives on socket *N*, the `select` returns to the `inetd` process.

- A child process is `fork`ed and `exec`ed to handle the request.

- `inetd` disables socket descriptor *N* from its `fd_set` structure for the `select`. The child process takes over the socket.

- The child handles this request and `inetd` handles requests for other services.

- Eventually `inetd` calls `select` and blocks.

- The child terminates, the `SIGCLD` signal is generated for the `inetd` process.

- `inetd` handles the signal and obtains the process ID of the terminating child process from the `wait` system call. It figures out which socket descriptor corresponded to this child process and turns on the appropriate bit in its `fd_set` structure.

- When the signal handler returns, the `select` returns to the `inetd` process, with an `errno` of `EINTR`.

- `inetd` calls `select` again, this time with an `fd_set` structure that enables socket descriptor *N*.

While the `inetd` daemon is set up to handle both a TCP socket with the `wait` flag and a UDP socket with the `nowait` flag, there are no examples of this in the distributed 4.3BSD system.

The `inetd` daemon has several servers that are handled by the daemon itself. These internal servers handle some of the standard Internet services.

- Echo service—RFC 862 [Postel 1983a]
- Discard service—RFC 863 [Postel 1983b]
- Character generator service—RFC 864 [Postel 1983c]
- Daytime (human readable) service—RFC 867 [Postel 1983d]
- Machine time (binary) service—RFC 868 [Postel and Harrenstein 1983]

Each of these services can be contacted using either TCP or UDP. The TCP servers for these internal functions are handled as iterative servers if the amount of time to handle the request is fixed (the daytime and machine time servers), or as concurrent servers if the amount of time depends on the request (echo, discard and character generator).

Since `inetd` is the process that does the `accept` of a stream connection, the server that is invoked by `inetd` has to execute the `getpeername` system call to obtain the address of the client. This is done, for example, by servers that want to verify that the client is using a reserved port. For datagram servers, the address of the client is returned to the server when it executes one of the receive system calls.

6.17 Socket Implementation

Sockets, as implemented by 4.3BSD, are implemented within the Unix kernel. All the system calls that we discussed in this chapter are entry points into the kernel. All the algorithms and code to support the communication protocols (TCP, UDP, IDP, etc.) are completely within the kernel. Adding a new protocol (such as the OSI-related standards) requires changing the kernel. The overall networking design gets more modular with each release (the addition of XNS support in 4.3BSD required changes, as documented in O'Toole, Torek, and Weiser [1985], and the addition of OSI protocols in 4.4BSD will require additional changes that weren't anticipated in earlier releases), but it still requires kernel changes.

The actual kernel implementation separates the network system into three layers, as shown in Figure 6.19. See Leffler et al. [1989] for additional details.

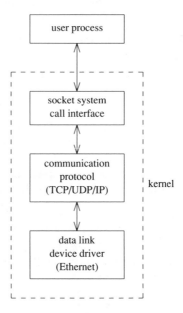

Figure 6.19   Networking implementation in 4.3BSD.

6.18 Summary

This has been a long chapter with many details. Our presentation was divided into four parts.

- Elementary socket system calls
- Examples using only the elementary socket system calls
- Advanced socket system calls
- Advanced socket features and options

One key point is that the simple examples presented in Section 6.6 can form the basis for any networking application. Just modify the client and server to do whatever you desire.

We'll present additional features for these examples in Chapter 8. For example, in Section 8.2 we show a better way of obtaining the address of a remote system (instead of hard coding it in a header file). Section 8.3 develops some functions that simplify the standard operations that most client applications execute when opening a socket. Section 8.4 shows how to add reliability to a datagram application.

The advanced features that we've described in this chapter are used in the examples that follow in the text. For example, the remote login example in Chapter 15 uses socket options, I/O multiplexing, out-of-band data and signals. You should review the later sections of this chapter as you encounter examples that use a particular feature.

Exercises

6.1 The example servers in Section 6.6 do not call the `daemon_start` function which we developed in Section 2.6. Modify one of these servers to call this function. What other changes do you have to make to the server?

6.2 Rewrite the SPP example from Section 6.6 to use the packet-stream interface, `SOCK_SEQPACKET`, and set the end-of-message bit at the end of every line.

6.3 What happens with the clients and servers in Section 6.6 if standard input is a binary file?

6.4 Code a function that is similar to `rresvport`, but for UDP sockets.

6.5 Print the value of `TCP_MAXSEG` after the socket has been connected to a peer process. If possible, connect to a peer process on a LAN and print value and then connect to a peer process on a WAN and compare the results.

6.6 Write a program that copies standard input to standard output using the `select` system call.

6.7 Now that we have covered asynchronous I/O and I/O multiplexing, compare the use of Unix domain stream sockets and message queues. If you had to write a server to handle multiple client requests on a single host, which would you use and why?

6.8 Write a simple client and server to verify that a single datagram is produced by the `writev` system call.

6.9 If your system supports file access across a network (such as Sun's NFS) test the Unix stream example from Section 6.6 with the client and server on different systems. Modify the pathname used by the client and server to be on a filesystem that is accessible to both.

7

System V
Transport Layer Interface

7.1 Introduction

TLI—Transport Layer Interface—was introduced with Release 3.0 of System V in 1986. Before this, the focal point of networking in the Unix community had been the BSD releases of Unix. TLI provides an interface to the transport layer of the OSI model, and was modeled after the ISO Transport Service Definition.

TLI is a library of functions that we have to instruct the link editor to search. A typical command is

```
cc main.c -lnsl_s
```

where "nsl" stands for "Network Services Library." We refer to the TLI functions as "functions" throughout this chapter, and not as system calls. The reason is that TLI is a set of user-callable functions that hides the actual streams interface to the networking system. We describe this streams interface in more detail in Section 7.7.

There are two terms used throughout TLI that we have not defined before:

> *transport endpoint,*
> *transport provider.*

The two processes that are communicating are called the *transport endpoints* by TLI. In Chapter 4 we termed this a *socket* or a *half association*. The *transport provider* is the set of routines on the host computer that provide communication support for a user process. A given Unix system, for example, could have a transport provider for the TCP/IP protocols and another transport provider for the XNS protocols. TLI provides the interface between the user process and the transport provider. Note that TLI is not a transport provider—it is an interface.

342

There was one deficiency in the release of TLI, and indeed with all the Release 3.x systems from AT&T: although they provide a networking interface (TLI), they don't supply a transport provider as part of the basic system. The networking software that is supplied, cu, UUCP, and RFS (Remote File System), can all use TLI if an appropriate transport provider is available. System V Release 4.0 is to contain a TCP/IP transport provider.

> 4.3BSD systems, on the other hand, provide not only a networking interface (sockets) but also provide the Internet protocols, the Unix domain protocols, and the XNS protocols.
>
> This is the method we'll use throughout this chapter to distinguish between TLI and sockets. After describing a TLI feature, we'll show the socket comparison indented, in smaller type, as we do here.

7.2   Overview

Figure 7.1 shows the typical time line of function calls for a connection-oriented client–server.

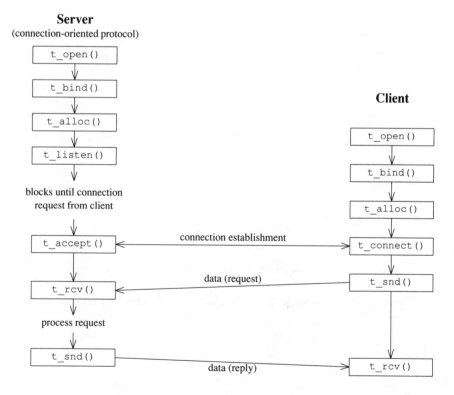

Figure 7.1 TLI function calls—connection-oriented protocol.

Unfortunately, there are some caveats we have to make about Figure 7.1. First, we're assuming an iterative server (as we defined in Section 1.6), otherwise additional system calls are required by the server to accept a connection request that can be handled concurrently. Second, we're using the TLI-specific receive and send functions, t_rcv and t_snd, instead of the standard read and write system calls. This is to avoid having to show the ioctl system calls that are required before being able to use read and write on a communication channel. We'll cover these details as we proceed through the chapter.

Figure 7.2 shows the TLI function calls for a client and server using a connectionless protocol.

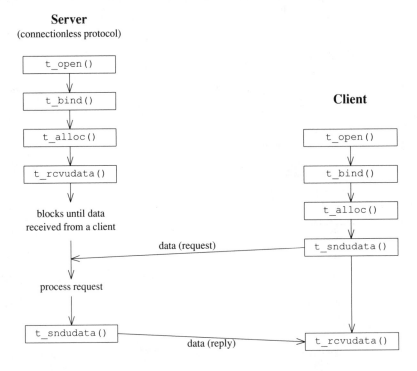

Figure 7.2   TLI function calls—connectionless protocol.

Figure 7.2 is similar to the connectionless example using sockets, which is shown in Figure 6.2.

7.3   Transport Endpoint Addresses

TLI imposes no restrictions on the structure of a transport address, leaving the interpretation of it to the transport provider. This allows new protocols to be supported without requiring any kernel changes. But, since there are no TLI-imposed standards for existing protocols (such as TCP/IP) it allows different implementations of these existing protocols (i.e., different transport providers) to support different address formats.

TLI defines a generic structure that passes various data between the TLI functions and the user code.

```
#include <tiuser.h>

struct netbuf {
  unsigned int  maxlen;   /* max size of buf */
  unsigned int  len;      /* actual amount of data in buf */
  char          *buf;     /* protocol-dependent data */
};
```

These structures are always passed between the user and the TLI function by reference. That is, we specify the address of the structure as an argument to a TLI function. The buf element points to a user buffer, and the amount of data currently in the buffer is specified by len. For those TLI functions that fill in the user's buf with information, the maxlen element specifies the size of the buffer, to prevent the TLI functions from overflowing the buffer. For those TLI functions that only look at the information in a netbuf structure, the maxlen variable is ignored.

> This structure is similar to the sockaddr structure. Since the address of the netbuf structure is always passed to a TLI function, and by having both the size of the buffer (maxlen) and the amount of data in the buffer (len) as part of the structure, there is no need in TLI for all the value–result arguments used with sockets.

7.4   Elementary TLI Functions

We first describe only those elementary TLI functions that we need to develop the same client–server example from Section 6.6. In Section 7.6 we describe additional advanced features available with TLI. The Unix manual pages for all the TLI functions are in AT&T [1989b].

t_error **Function**

The TLI functions set the variable t_errno on an error return. Additionally the array t_errlist can be indexed by t_errno to obtain an error message for a particular t_errno value.

```
#include <tiuser.h>

extern int    t_errno;       /* TLI error number */
extern char  *t_errlist[]; /* ptr to string, index by t_errno */
extern int    t_nerr;        /* # of entries in t_errlist[] */

void t_error(char *errmesg);
```

The function t_error prints the user's *errmesg* string, followed by the appropriate t_errlist value. If t_errno has the value TSYSERR this function prints the standard Unix error message associated with the variable errno.

> The socket system calls return all errors through the variable errno. All networking errors are identified by errno values. The TLI functions can't do this, since TLI is a user-level library and not a set of system calls.

Unless otherwise noted, all the TLI function calls return −1 on error, or zero if everything is OK.

t_open **Function**

The first step in establishing a transport endpoint is to open the Unix file that identifies the particular transport provider. This function returns a file descriptor (a small integer) that is used by the other TLI functions.

```
#include <tiuser.h>

int t_open(char *pathname, int oflag, struct t_info *info);

struct t_info {
  long  addr;    /* max size of transport protocol address */
  long  options; /* max #bytes of protocol-specific options */
  long  tsdu;    /* max size of transport service data unit (TSDU) */
  long  etsdu;   /* max size of expedited transport service data unit (ETSDU) */
  long  connect; /* max amount of data on conn. establishment */
  long  discon;  /* max amount of data on t_snddis() and t_rcvdis() */
  long  servtype; /* service type supported */
};
```

The actual *pathname* to use depends on the implementation details of the transport provider being used. For example, with the WIN/TCP package that is used for the examples in Section 7.5, the *pathname* can be /dev/tcp, /dev/udp, or /dev/ip.

The *oflag* argument specifies the flags, as we discussed in Section 2.3 for the open system call.

This TLI function is similar to the `socket` system call. Both return a file descriptor that is associated with a user specified protocol. Only one element of the association 5-tuple, the protocol, is set by both `t_open` and `socket`.

Information regarding the transport provider is returned to the caller in the *info* structure. If the caller is not interested in these values, a `NULL` argument can be specified. The values in the `t_info` structure are all long integers that specify particular characteristics of the transport provider. We're interested in three cases for each variable: ≥0, −1, and −2.

addr
: This specifies the maximum size of a protocol-specific address. A value of −1 indicates there is no limit to the size. A value of −2 indicates there is no user access to the protocol addresses.

options
: This specifies the size of the protocol-specific options. A value of −1 indicates there is no limit to the size. A value of −2 indicates there is no user access to the options.

tsdu
: TSDU stands for "transport service data unit." This variable specifies the maximum size of a TSDU. A value of zero indicates that the transport provider doesn't support the concept of a TSDU, although it does support a byte stream of data (i.e., record boundaries are not preserved, as we discussed in Section 3.6). A value of −1 indicates there is no limit to the size. A value of −2 indicates that the transport of normal data is not supported (a rare condition).

  For a stream-oriented protocol such as TCP, `tsdu` will be 0.

etsdu
: ETSDU stands for "expedited transport service data unit." This is what we've called urgent data, or out-of-band data. This variable specifies the maximum size of an ETSDU. A value of zero indicates that the transport provider doesn't support the concept of ETSDU, although it does support a byte stream of out-of-band data (i.e., record boundaries are not preserved in the out-of-band data). A value of −1 indicates there is no limit to the size. A value of −2 indicates that the transport of expedited data is not supported.

connect
: Some connection-oriented protocols support the transfer of user data along with a connection request. This variable specifies the maximum amount of this data. A value of −1 indicates there is no limit to the size. A value of −2 indicates that the transport provider doesn't support this feature.

discon
: Some connection-oriented protocols support the transfer of user data along with a disconnection request. We'll see the possibility of this when we discuss the `t_snddis` and `t_rcvdis` functions later in this section. This variable specifies the maximum amount of this data. A value of −1 indicates there is no limit to the size. A value of −2 indicates that the transport provider doesn't support this feature.

Neither TCP nor SPP support the transfer of data with a connection request or with a disconnect.

`servtype`   This specifies the type of service provided by the transport provider. There are three possibilities which we show in Figure 7.3.

servtype	Description
T_COTS	Connection-oriented service, without orderly release.
T_COTS_ORD	Connection-oriented service, with orderly release.
T_CLTS	Connectionless service.

Figure 7.3 Types of service that can be offered by a transport provider.

We describe the meaning of an "orderly release" later in this section. For a connectionless service, all three of the variables `etsdu`, `connect`, and `discon` will be set to −2, since these features are not provided by this service.

`t_alloc` and `t_free` Functions

Many of the data structures that are passed between the user code and the TLI functions are structures. Most of these structures, in turn, contain one or more `netbuf` structures, each of which contains a pointer to a buffer that is used for a particular purpose. For example, one buffer can be used to contain protocol-specific addresses, another protocol-specific options, another user data, and so on. The sizes of all these buffers are known once a specific transport provider is selected when we call `t_open`. These maximum buffer sizes are all available in the `t_info` structure returned by `t_open`. To simplify the dynamic allocation of these TLI structures, the `t_alloc` function is provided.

```
#include <tiuser.h>

char *t_alloc(int fd, int structtype, int fields);

int t_free(char *ptr, int structtype);
```

The *structtype* argument specifies the type of data structure and must be one of the constants shown in Figure 7.4.

structtype	Type of structure
T_BIND	struct t_bind
T_CALL	struct t_call
T_DIS	struct t_discon
T_INFO	struct t_info
T_OPTMGMT	struct t_optmgmt
T_UNITDATA	struct t_unitdata
T_UDERROR	struct t_uderr

Figure 7.4 *structtype* argument for t_alloc function.

We'll see as we describe the TLI functions that each of these structures, other than the t_info structure, contains one or more netbuf structures within it. The *fields* argument lets us specify that space for one or more netbuf structures should also be allocated and initialized appropriately. *fields* is the bitwise-OR of the constants shown in Figure 7.5.

fields	Allocate and initialize
T_ALL	all relevant fields of the given structure
T_ADDR	addr field of t_bind, t_call, t_unitdata, or t_uderr
T_OPT	opt field of t_optmgmt, t_call, t_unitdata, or t_uderr
T_UDATA	udata field of t_call, t_discon, or t_unitdata

Figure 7.5 *fields* argument for t_alloc function.

The reason for these different values of the *fields* argument is that some of the TLI structures contain more than one netbuf structure, and we may not want to allocate space for all the buffers. For example, the t_uderr structure, which we describe in Section 7.4 with the t_rcvuderr function, contains two netbuf structures.

```
struct t_uderr {
    struct netbuf   addr;    /* protocol-specific address */
    struct netbuf   opt;     /* protocol-specific options */
    long            error;   /* protocol-specific error code */
};
```

Specifying some combination of T_ADDR and T_OPT gives us complete control of the allocation. For our purposes, we'll use T_ALL for our examples.

The following example gives a clearer view of what the `t_alloc` function is doing. If we execute

```
#include <tiuser.h>

char    *ptr;
int     fd;

if ( (fd = t_open( ... )) < 0)
        err_sys( ... );
if ( (ptr = t_alloc(fd, T_UDERROR, T_ALL)) == NULL)
        err_sys( ... );
```

then given the definition of the `t_uderr` structure shown above, we get the picture shown in Figure 7.6.

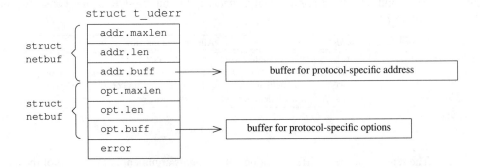

Figure 7.6   Example of `t_alloc` function.

The call to `t_alloc` above allocates space for the `t_uderr` structure, and for both buffers. It then initializes both `buf` pointers and their corresponding `maxlen` variables.

The `t_free` function frees a structure that was previously allocated by `t_alloc`. The *structtype* argument specifies the type of the structure, and the constants described earlier (`T_BIND`, etc.) are used for this. `t_free` not only frees the memory that was allocated for the structure specified by *structtype*, but it first checks any `netbuf` structures contained therein and releases the memory used by any buffers.

`t_bind` **Function**

This function assigns an address to a transport endpoint. It specifies the *local-addr* and *local-process* elements of the association 5-tuple.

```
#include <tiuser.h>

int t_bind(int fd, struct t_bind *request, struct t_bind *return);

struct t_bind {
  struct netbuf  addr;    /* protocol-specific address */
  unsigned int   qlen;    /* max# of outstanding connections */
};
```

The transport endpoint is specified by *fd*. There are three cases to consider for the *request* argument.

request == NULL
> The caller does not care what address gets assigned to the transport endpoint. The transport provider selects an address. The value of the qlen element is assumed to be zero (see below).

request != NULL, but *request->addr.len* == 0
> The caller does not care what address gets assigned to the transport endpoint, and again the transport provider selects an address. Unlike the previous case, however, the caller can now specify a nonzero value for the qlen element of the *request* structure.

request != NULL, and *request->addr.len* > 0
> The caller specifies an address for the transport provider to assign to the transport endpoint.

Whether the caller specifies the address or whether the provider selects an address, the provider returns the address that it assigns to the endpoint in the *return* structure. If we specify an address with the *request* argument, we should compare the returned address to verify that the desired address was really assigned by the provider. If we specify a NULL value for the *return* argument, the provider does not return the actual address.

> The TLI method for specifying that the caller wants the transport provider to select an appropriate address is more generic than the protocol-dependent method used by the bind system call. For example, recall that the BSD Internet protocols require the caller to specify an Internet address of INADDR_ANY and a port of zero, in order for the provider to select the local address. This is Internet-specific and not generic to the bind system call.

The qlen element of the request structure only applies to connection-oriented servers. It specifies the maximum number of outstanding connection requests the transport provider should support for this transport endpoint. It is possible for this value to be changed by the transport provider, in which case the qlen element of the return structure indicates the actual value supported by the transport provider.

The qlen value corresponds to the value specified by the listen system call. For a connection-oriented server, the TLI t_bind function does the same work as the bind and listen system calls.

In the examples we'll show, for both connection-oriented and connectionless clients, we specify both *request* and *return* arguments as NULL.

t_connect **Function**

A connection-oriented client initiates a connection with a server using the t_connect function. This completes the association 5-tuple by specifying the *foreign-addr* and *foreign-process*.

```
#include <tiuser.h>

int t_connect(int fd, struct t_call *sendcall, struct t_call *recvcall);

struct t_call {
    struct netbuf  addr;     /* protocol-specific address */
    struct netbuf  opt;      /* protocol-specific options */
    struct netbuf  udata;    /* user data */
    int            sequence; /* applies only to t_listen() func */
};
```

The *sendcall* structure specifies the information needed by the transport provider to establish the connection: the *addr* structure specifies the server's address, *opt* specifies any protocol-specific options desired by the caller, and *udata* contains any user data that is to be transferred to the server during connection establishment. The *sequence* variable has no significance. On return from this function, the *recvcall* structure contains information associated with the connection that is returned by the transport provider to the caller: the *addr* structure contains the address of the peer process, *opt* contains any protocol-dependent optional data associated with the connection, and *udata* contains any user data returned by the peer's transport provider during connection establishment. Again, the *sequence* variable has no meaning.

The contents of the *opt* structure are protocol-dependent. The caller can set the *len* field of this structure to zero, telling the transport provider to use default values for any connection options.

It is a protocol-dependent option whether user data is allowed to accompany a connection request. The connect field of the t_info structure returned by the t_open function specifies the maximum amount of user data allowed by the transport provider. If the caller of t_connect sets the len field of the udata structure to zero, no user data is transferred during connection establishment.

The caller can specify a *recvcall* value of NULL, if the return information regarding the connection is not desired.

By default, this function does not return until the specified connection is completed (synchronous), or an error occurs. We'll discuss an asynchronous version of this and other TLI functions Section 7.6.

The t_connect function is similar to the BSD connect system call. The TLI function can accomplish more in a single function, however, in that the options can be specified, along with user data, and values such as the peer address can also be returned. A BSD user has to call setsockopt and getpeername, for example, to specify an option and obtain the peer address.

t_listen **Function**

A connection-oriented server waits for a connection request from a client by calling the t_listen function.

```
#include <tiuser.h>

int t_listen(int fd, struct t_call *call);
```

We showed the elements of the t_call structure when we described the t_connect function. The structure returned by the *call* argument contains relevant parameters of the t_connect request: the addr structure contains the protocol address of the peer process, opt contains any protocol-specific options associated with the t_connect request, and udata contains any user data that was sent along with the connection request. The sequence variable contains a unique value that identifies this connection request.

> Although this function appears similar to the accept system call, it is different, as the t_listen function only waits for a connection request to arrive; it does not accept the connection. To do that, the TLI user has to call the t_accept function.

t_accept **Function**

Once the t_listen function indicates that a connection request has arrived, we choose whether to accept the request or not. To accept the request the t_accept function is called.

```
#include <tiuser.h>

int t_accept(int fd, int connfd, struct t_call *call);
```

The *fd* argument specifies the transport endpoint where the connection request arrived. This corresponds to the *fd* argument of the corresponding t_listen function. The *connfd* argument specifies the transport endpoint where the connection is to be established. For a concurrent server (the typical case), the caller creates a new transport endpoint, *connfd*, to receive the connection. This way the original transport endpoint, *fd*, is still available for listening for further connection requests. But for an iterative server, the value of *connfd* equals the value of *fd*.

Notice that it is our responsibility to create the new transport endpoint for a concurrent server. This is done by calling the t_open function after receiving the connection request. We show an example of this in the TCP server example in Section 7.5.

On return from this function, the transport endpoint corresponding to *connfd* has all five elements of its association 5-tuple filled in. If this transport endpoint differs from the one specified by *fd*, then the endpoint corresponding to *fd* still has two elements of its association 5-tuple empty: the *foreign-addr* and the *foreign-process*.

> The BSD accept system call combines the actions of the t_listen, t_open, and t_accept functions. The BSD system call assumes the typical case of a concurrent server and does all the work for us. The TLI functions, on the other hand, require additional work on the caller's part.

As with the t_listen function, the *call* argument returns information related to the connection.

t_snd **and** t_rcv **Functions**

These two functions send or receive either normal or expedited data.

```
int t_snd(int fd, char *buff, unsigned int nbytes, int flags);

int t_rcv(int fd, char *buff, unsigned int nbytes, int *flags);
```

The first three arguments are similar to the first three arguments of the standard read and write system calls. The *flags* argument to t_snd is either zero, or the bitwise-OR or the following constants:

T_EXPEDITED	send or receive expedited (out-of-band) data
T_MORE	there is more data to send or receive

The T_EXPEDITED flag is used with t_snd to send out-of-band data. This flag is set on return from t_rcv when out-of-band data is received. We'll discuss this flag in Section 7.13 when we describe out-of-band data.

The T_MORE flag is provided so that multiple t_snd or t_rcv function calls can be used to read or write what the protocol considers a logical record. This feature only applies to those connection-oriented protocols that support the concept of records. Recall that TCP is a byte-stream protocol and does not support records, while XNS provides SPP, which allows us to specify record boundaries in the data.

Note that the *flags* argument to t_snd is an integer value, while it is a pointer to an integer (a value–result argument) for t_rcv. Both of these functions return the actual number of bytes read or written.

> These two functions correspond to the 4.3BSD send and recv system calls.

t_sndudata, t_rcvudata, **and** t_rcvuderr **Functions**

The first two functions are used for connectionless protocols to send and receive datagrams.

```
#include <tiuser.h>

int t_sndudata(int fd, struct t_unitdata *unitdata);

int t_rcvudata(int fd, struct t_unitdata *unitdata, int *flags);

struct t_unitdata {
  struct netbuf  addr;       /* protocol-specific address */
  struct netbuf  opt;        /* protocol-specific options */
  struct netbuf  udata;      /* user data */
};
```

For the t_sndudata function, the *unitdata* argument specifies what data is to be sent and where it is to be sent: the udata structure specifies the data buffer and its size; the addr structure specifies the protocol address of the peer process. If the len field of the opt structure is not zero, this structure specifies protocol-specific options for the transport provider.

The t_rcvudata function receives a datagram, with the *unitdata* argument specifying where the datagram is to be stored (the udata structure), where to store the address of the sender (the addr structure), and where to store any protocol-specific options associated with the datagram (the opt structure). As mentioned earlier, the maxlen field of all three of these structures must be set by the caller, before the t_rcvudata function is called, so that the transport provider knows how much room is allocated in the corresponding buffer.

> These two functions correspond to the 4.3BSD sendto and recvfrom system calls.

Be aware that both of these functions return zero if everything was OK, or −1 on an error. This differs from most read and write functions that usually return the number of bytes transferred.

Recall that for a connectionless protocol, errors can be returned asynchronously. That is, a datagram can be correctly transmitted by the transport provider, only to have an error in it detected somewhere else in the network (invalid address, for example). This requires some form of notification from the transport provider to the user process and some means for us to determine just what happened. TLI provides this by setting t_errno to TLOOK after a call to t_rcvudata, to indicate that an error occurred on a previously sent datagram. We can then call the t_rcvuderr function to determine what happened and to clear the error status.

```
int t_rcvuderr(int fd, struct t_uderr *uderr);

struct t_uderr {
  struct netbuf  addr;       /* protocol-specific address */
  struct netbuf  opt;        /* protocol-specific options */
  long           error;      /* protocol-specific error */
};
```

On return from this function, the `addr` structure contains the protocol address of the erroneous datagram and the `opt` structure contains any protocol-specific options associated with the datagram. The `error` variable contains a protocol-specific error code.

If we don't care about the exact error indication, we can set the *uderr* argument to `NULL`, which clears the error status without returning any information.

An example of an asynchronous error with a connectionless protocol is sending a UDP datagram to a port on a host for which no process has issued a read from. As we saw in Section 6.5, an Internet host should send an ICMP port unreachable error to the sending host for this case.

`t_look` **Function**

Every transport endpoint has a current event associated with it. We can obtain this event from the transport provider by calling the `t_look` function.

```
#include <tiuser.h>

int t_look(int fd);
```

The integer value returned by this function corresponds to one of the events shown in Figure 7.7.

Current event	Description
`T_CONNECT`	connection confirmation received
`T_DATA`	normal data received
`T_DISCONNECT`	disconnect received
`T_ERROR`	fatal error indication
`T_EXDATA`	expedited data received
`T_LISTEN`	connection indication received
`T_ORDREL`	orderly release indication
`T_UDERR`	datagram error indication

Figure 7.7 Events returned by `t_look` function.

When a TLI function returns a `t_errno` value of `TLOOK`, we should call the `t_look` function to determine the current state of the transport endpoint. We'll use this function below in the processing of an orderly release.

`t_sndrel` **and** `t_rcvrel` **Functions**

TLI supports two ways of releasing a connection: an *abortive release* and an *orderly release*. The differences are that an abortive release does not guarantee the delivery of any outstanding data, while the orderly release does guarantee this. All transport providers must support an abortive release, while the support of an orderly release is optional.

Release type	TLI functions	TLI support ?	Service type
orderly release	t_sndrel(), t_rcvrel()	optional	T_COTS_ORD
abortive release	t_snddis(), t_rcvdis()	required	T_COTS

Figure 7.8 Types of connection release supported by TLI.

The "service type" column in Figure 7.8 refers to the servtype field of the t_info structure that we described with the t_open function earlier in this section. Note that there is nothing corresponding to the release of a connection for a connectionless protocol (T_CLTS). The orderly release functions are

```
#include <tiuser.h>

int t_sndrel(int fd);

int t_rcvrel(int fd);
```

To understand the semantics of an orderly release, we must remember that a connection-oriented protocol is usually a full-duplex connection between the two processes. The data transfer in each direction is independent of the data being transferred in the other direction. A picture of the two data paths between the processes is shown in Figure 7.9.

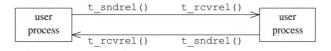

Figure 7.9 t_sndrel and t_rcvrel functions.

A process sends an orderly release indication by calling the t_sndrel function. This tells the other end that it is finished sending data—it is finished writing to the file descriptor. The process that calls t_sndrel can continue to receive data—it can still read from the file descriptor.

A process acknowledges the receipt of a connection release by calling the t_rcvrel function. But, how does a process know when to call this function? The receipt of a release connection by the transport provider is called an *asynchronous event*. The transport provider notifies the user process by returning an error on the next TLI function call. (Signals are also used, and we'll discuss them in Section 7.12.) What typically happens is the user process is expecting to receive normal data from its peer process, when a connection release is received instead. When this happens, the t_rcv function returns an error (−1) and t_errno is set to TLOOK. The current event for the transport endpoint is set to T_ORDREL to indicate that an orderly release was received from the other end.

A typical sequence of code is

```
while (t_rcv(fd, ... ) != -1) {

        /* ... process data ... */

}

if (t_errno == TLOOK && t_look(fd) == T_ORDREL) {
        t_rcvrel(fd);
        t_sndrel(fd);
        exit(0);
} else {
        t_error("t_rcv error");
        exit(1);
}
```

In this example we assume that the process receiving the connection release also wants to stop sending data, so it sends its own connection release after returning from the t_rcvrel function. There is nothing to stop this process from continuing to send data, if the other end is expecting it. It is an error, however, for the process that calls t_rcvrel to call t_rcv, since the call to t_rcv would block forever, as the other end is prevented from sending any more data after calling t_sndrel.

t_snddis **and** t_rcvdis **Functions**

These two functions do the abortive release that we discussed.

```
#include <tiuser.h>

int t_snddis(int fd, struct t_call *call);

int t_rcvdis(int fd, struct t_discon *discon);

struct t_discon {
  struct netbuf  udata;      /* user data */
  int            reason;     /* protocol-specific reason code */
  int            sequence;
};
```

The t_snddis function is used for two different purposes:

- to disconnect an established connection;
- to reject a connection request.

In the first case, the *call* argument can be NULL, in which case no information is sent to the peer process. Otherwise, the interpretation of the fields in the t_call structure is shown in Figure 7.10.

t_call structure	Disconnect	Reject connect
struct netbuf addr	Ignored	Ignored
struct netbuf opt	Ignored	Ignored
struct netbuf udata	*optional*	*optional*
int sequence	Ignored	*required*

Figure 7.10 Use of t_call structure by t_snddis function.

When a process has an established connection, a disconnect request is received as an asynchronous event, as described earlier for the orderly release case. If the process that called t_snddis sends data with the disconnect (the udata structure in the *call* argument), the receiving process has to pass a non NULL *discon* argument to the t_rcvdis function, to retrieve the data. Recall from our discussion of the t_open function that it is optional for the transport provider to support the transfer of data with a disconnect. The discon element of the t_info structure denotes if this is supported.

When a server is rejecting a connection request, it calls t_snddis instead of t_accept. The client that issued the connection request then receives an error return from its t_connect call. It can then issue a t_rcvdis call to fetch the t_discon structure associated with the connection rejection.

> 4.3BSD doesn't allow a server to reject a connection request. The request must be accepted (the accept system call) and then the server can examine any parameters relevant to the connection (such as the client's address, for example) and close the connection, if it chooses.

t_close **Function**

Unlike the orderly release and abortive release functions described, the t_close function can be used to close a transport endpoint, without terminating the connection.

```
#include <tiuser.h>

int t_close(int fd);
```

This function allows the transport provider to free any local resources that it has allocated for this endpoint, and the close system call is also called for this file descriptor.

The other actions done by this function depend on two conditions: (1) whether the calling process is the last one that has this endpoint open, (2) whether the endpoint is connected or not. If the transport endpoint is connected when this function is called, *and* if this is the last process to reference this endpoint, the connection is broken with an abortive disconnect. This is a quick and dirty way to close a connection instead of calling the t_snddis function. If the endpoint is connected, but some other process also has the endpoint open, a disconnect is not sent to the other end. Naturally, the calling process can't access the endpoint any more after calling t_close, but since some other process has the endpoint open also, that process continues to use the connection. This scenario corresponds to concurrent servers that pass a transport endpoint to another process (by the `fork` system call). The process calling `t_close` (the listening server) only wants to close its transport endpoint—it does *not* want to send a disconnect to the other end, since some other process is handling the connection.

The only error that can occur with this function is if the *fd* argument doesn't refer to a valid transport endpoint. In this case a −1 is returned.

7.5   A Simple Example

We now provide examples identical to the TCP and UDP client–server examples from the previous chapter. Indeed, one test of portability of the protocols is to make certain that the TCP server using sockets can communicate with the TCP client using TLI. The test should also switch the client and server between the socket code and the TLI code, and then do the same two tests using UDP.

At this point we have to mention some specifics about the actual TCP/IP transport provider being used. As we said at the beginning of this chapter, AT&T does not provide any transport providers with Unix System V Release 3—they are all provided by third-parties. The package used for all the examples in this chapter is "WIN/TCP for 386 Streams," Release 3.0, which is available from The Wollongong Group, Inc., Palo Alto, California. The examples were run on a Compaq 386/20 running AT&T UNIX System V/386, Release 3.2. The actual software package being used dictates the format of the many of the features we've described as "protocol-dependent." The WIN/TCP package, for example, requires that the local address specified with the `t_bind` function be represented in a `sockaddr_in` structure, identical to what we used with the `bind` system call in Chapter 6. The `t_connect` function also requires the address of the peer process in this format. The software package also dictates the device names to be used with the `t_open` function. The WIN/TCP package uses `/dev/tcp` for a TCP connection, and `/dev/udp` for UDP. It also supports other device names, such as `/dev/ip` which is similar to a 4.3BSD raw socket. Our examples use only TCP and UDP.

We use the same three utility functions that we showed in Section 6.6: `readn`, `writen`, and `readline`.

We also need a utility function for a connection-oriented server to use for accepting incoming connection requests. Recall that the TLI `t_accept` function does not create a new file descriptor as does the 4.3BSD `accept` system call. Hence we'll provide a standard function that a connection-oriented server can call to create the new descriptor.

```
/*
 * Accept an incoming connection request.
 *
 * Return the new descriptor that refers to the newly accepted connection,
 * or -1.  The only time we return -1 is if a disconnect arrives before
 * the accept is performed.
 */

#include        <stdio.h>
```

```
#include        <tiuser.h>
#include        <fcntl.h>
#include        <stropts.h>

int
accept_call(listenfd, callptr, name, rwflag)
int             listenfd;       /* the descriptor caller used for t_listen() */
struct t_call   *callptr;       /* from t_listen(), passed to t_accept() */
char            *name;          /* name of transport provider */
int             rwflag;         /* if nonzero, push read/write module */
{
        int             newfd;
        extern int      t_errno;

        /*
         * Open the transport provider to get a new file descriptor.
         */

        if ( (newfd = t_open(name, O_RDWR, (struct t_info *) 0)) < 0)
                err_sys("t_open error");

        /*
         * Bind any local address to the new descriptor.  Since this
         * function is intended to be called by a server after a
         * connection request has arrived, any local address will suffice.
         */

        if (t_bind(newfd, (struct t_bind *) 0, (struct t_bind *) 0) < 0)
                err_sys("t_bind error");

        /*
         * Accept the connection request on the new descriptor.
         */

        if (t_accept(listenfd, newfd, callptr) < 0) {
                if (t_errno == TLOOK) {
                        /*
                         * An asynchronous event has occurred.  We must have
                         * received a disconnect.  Go ahead and call t_rcvdis(),
                         * then close the new file descriptor that we opened
                         * above.
                         */

                        if (t_rcvdis(listenfd, (struct t_discon *) 0) < 0)
                                err_sys("t_rcvdis error");
                        if (t_close(newfd) < 0)
                                err_sys("t_close error");
                        return(-1);     /* return error to caller */
                }
                err_sys("t_accept error");
        }

        /*
         * If the caller requests, push the streams module "tirdwr" onto
```

```
        * the new stream, so that the read(2) and write(2) system calls
        * can be used.  We first have to pop the "timod" module (the
        * default).
        */

        if (rwflag) {
                if (ioctl(newfd, I_POP, (char *) 0) < 0)
                        err_dump("I_POP of timod failed");

                if (ioctl(newfd, I_PUSH, "tirdwr") < 0)
                        err_dump("I_PUSH of tirdwr failed");
        }

        return(newfd);
}
```

This function uses the streams `ioctl` operations of `I_POP` and `I_PUSH` to pop a
module from a stream and then push another module onto the stream. We discuss
streams in Section 7.7.

TCP Example

First we have the header file with all the definitions for the TCP and UDP clients and
servers.

```
/*
 * Definitions for TCP and UDP client/server programs.
 */

#include         <stdio.h>
#include         <fcntl.h>
#include         <tiuser.h>              /* System V R3.2 TLI definitions */
#include         <sys/types.h>
#include         <sys/socket.h>          /* WIN/TCP definitions */
#include         <sys/in.h>              /* WIN/TCP definitions */

#define DEV_UDP         "/dev/udp"       /* WIN/TCP names */
#define DEV_TCP         "/dev/tcp"       /* WIN/TCP names */

#define SERV_UDP_PORT   6000
#define SERV_TCP_PORT   6000
#define SERV_HOST_ADDR  "192.43.235.6"  /* host addr for server */

#define MAXLINE         255

char    *pname;
```

We'll write the server program as a concurrent server.

```
/*
 * Example of server using TCP protocol.
 */

#include        "inet.h"

main(argc, argv)
int     argc;
char    *argv[];
{
        int                     tfd, newtfd, clilen, childpid;
        struct sockaddr_in      cli_addr, serv_addr;
        struct t_bind           req;
        struct t_call           *callptr;

        pname = argv[0];

        /*
         * Create a TCP transport endpoint.
         */

        if ( (tfd = t_open(DEV_TCP, O_RDWR, (struct t_info *) 0)) < 0)
                err_dump("server: can't t_open %s", DEV_TCP);

        /*
         * Bind our local address so that the client can send to us.
         */

        bzero((char *) &serv_addr, sizeof(serv_addr));
        serv_addr.sin_family      = AF_INET;
        serv_addr.sin_addr.s_addr = htonl(INADDR_ANY);
        serv_addr.sin_port        = htons(SERV_TCP_PORT);

        req.addr.maxlen = sizeof(serv_addr);
        req.addr.len    = sizeof(serv_addr);
        req.addr.buf    = (char *) &serv_addr;
        req.qlen        = 5;

        if (t_bind(tfd, &req, (struct t_bind *) 0) < 0)
                err_dump("server: can't t_bind local address");

        /*
         * Allocate a t_call structure for t_listen() and t_accept().
         */

        if ( (callptr = (struct t_call *) t_alloc(tfd, T_CALL, T_ADDR)) == NULL)
                err_dump("server: t_alloc error for T_CALL");

        for ( ; ; ) {
                /*
                 * Wait for a connection from a client process.
                 * This is an example of a concurrent server.
                 */
```

```
        if (t_listen(tfd, callptr) < 0)
                err_dump("server: t_listen error");

        if ( (newtfd = accept_call(tfd, callptr, DEV_TCP, 1)) < 0)
                err_dump("server: accept_call error");

        if ( (childpid = fork()) < 0)
                err_dump("server: fork error");

        else if (childpid == 0) {       /* child process */
                t_close(tfd);           /* close original endpoint */
                str_echo(newtfd);       /* process the request */
                exit(0);
        }

        close(newtfd);                  /* parent process */
    }
}
```

Note that this TLI example uses the `str_echo` function that we defined in Section 6.6 for our stream socket examples. That function calls the `readline` and `writen` functions which were also defined in Section 6.6. These two functions then call the Unix `read` and `write` system calls to do the actual I/O. Since the server has the `accept_call` function push the `tirdwr` module onto the stream, these two system calls work with the transport endpoint.

Here is the client program.

```
/*
 * Example of client using TCP protocol.
 */

#include         "inet.h"

main(argc, argv)
int     argc;
char    *argv[];
{
        int                     tfd;
        char                    *t_alloc();      /* TLI function */
        struct t_call           *callptr;
        struct sockaddr_in      serv_addr;

        pname = argv[0];

        /*
         * Create a TCP transport endpoint and bind it.
         */

        if ( (tfd = t_open(DEV_TCP, O_RDWR, 0)) < 0)
                err_sys("client: can't t_open %s", DEV_TCP);

        if (t_bind(tfd, (struct t_bind *) 0, (struct t_bind *) 0) < 0)
                err_sys("client: t_bind error");
```

```
        /*
         * Fill in the structure "serv_addr" with the address of the
         * server that we want to connect with.
         */

        bzero((char *) &serv_addr, sizeof(serv_addr));
        serv_addr.sin_family      = AF_INET;
        serv_addr.sin_addr.s_addr = inet_addr(SERV_HOST_ADDR);
        serv_addr.sin_port        = htons(SERV_TCP_PORT);

        /*
         * Allocate a t_call structure, and initialize it.
         * Let t_alloc() initialize the addr structure of the t_call structure.
         */

        if ( (callptr = (struct t_call *) t_alloc(tfd, T_CALL, T_ADDR)) == NULL)
                err_sys("client: t_alloc error");
        callptr->addr.maxlen = sizeof(serv_addr);
        callptr->addr.len    = sizeof(serv_addr);
        callptr->addr.buf    = (char *) &serv_addr;
        callptr->opt.len     = 0;                    /* no options */
        callptr->udata.len   = 0;                    /* no user data with connect */

        /*
         * Connect to the server.
         */

        if (t_connect(tfd, callptr, (struct t_call *) 0) < 0)
                err_sys("client: can't t_connect to server");

        doit(stdin, tfd);        /* do it all */

        close(tfd);
        exit(0);
}

/*
 * Read the contents of the FILE *fp, write each line to the
 * transport endpoint (to the server process), then read a line back from
 * the transport endpoint and print it on the standard output.
 */

doit(fp, tfd)
register FILE    *fp;
register int     tfd;
{
        int     n, flags;
        char    sendline[MAXLINE], recvline[MAXLINE + 1];

        while (fgets(sendline, MAXLINE, fp) != NULL) {
                n = strlen(sendline);
                if (t_snd(tfd, sendline, n, 0) != n)
                        err_sys("client: t_snd error");
```

```
                /*
                 * Now read a line from the transport endpoint and write it to
                 * our standard output.
                 */

                n = t_rcv(tfd, recvline, MAXLINE, &flags);
                if (n < 0)
                        err_dump("client: t_rcv error");
                recvline[n] = 0;          /* null terminate */
                fputs(recvline, stdout);
        }

        if (ferror(fp))
                err_sys("client: error reading file");
}
```

For the client we did not push the `tirdwr` module onto the stream, so we are not able to use the `read` and `write` system calls. This was done to illustrate the TLI `t_snd` and `t_rcv` functions.

UDP Example

Our UDP example is unreliable, as we described in the previous chapter. Note that the client program and the server program both use the header file, `inet.h`, which we showed earlier in this section with our TCP example.

First, the server program.

```
/*
 * Example of server using UDP protocol.
 */

#include        "inet.h"

main(argc, argv)
int     argc;
char    *argv[];
{
        int                     tfd;
        struct sockaddr_in      serv_addr;
        struct t_bind           req;

        pname = argv[0];

        /*
         * Open a UDP endpoint.
         */

        if ( (tfd = t_open(DEV_UDP, O_RDWR, (struct t_info *) 0)) < 0)
                err_dump("server: can't t_open %s", DEV_UDP);

        /*
         * Bind our local address so that the client can send to us.
         */
```

```
            */

        bzero((char *) &serv_addr, sizeof(serv_addr));
        serv_addr.sin_family     = AF_INET;
        serv_addr.sin_addr.s_addr = htonl(INADDR_ANY);
        serv_addr.sin_port       = htons(SERV_UDP_PORT);

        req.addr.maxlen = sizeof(serv_addr);
        req.addr.len    = sizeof(serv_addr);
        req.addr.buf    = (char *) &serv_addr;
        req.qlen        = 5;

        if (t_bind(tfd, &req, (struct t_bind *) 0) < 0)
                err_dump("server: can't t_bind local address");

        echo(tfd);                  /* do it all */
                /* NOTREACHED */
}

/*
 * Read the contents of the socket and write each line back to
 * the sender.
 */

echo(tfd)
int     tfd;
{
        int                     n, flags;
        char                    line[MAXLINE];
        char                    *t_alloc();
        struct t_unitdata       *udataptr;

        /*
         * Allocate memory for the t_unitdata structure and the address field
         * in that structure.  This allows any size of address to be handled
         * by this function.
         */

        udataptr = (struct t_unitdata *) t_alloc(tfd, T_UNITDATA, T_ADDR);
        if (udataptr == NULL)
                err_dump("server: t_alloc error for T_UNITDATA");

        for ( ; ; ) {
                /*
                 * Read a message from the socket and send it back
                 * to whomever sent it.
                 */

                udataptr->opt.maxlen  = 0;       /* don't care about options */
                udataptr->opt.len     = 0;
                udataptr->udata.maxlen = MAXLINE;
                udataptr->udata.len   = MAXLINE;
                udataptr->udata.buf   = line;
                if (t_rcvudata(tfd, udataptr, &flags) < 0)
```

```
                        err_dump("server: t_rcvudata error");

            if (t_sndudata(tfd, udataptr) < 0)
                        err_dump("server: t_sndudata error");
        }
}
```

Here is the client program.

```
/*
 * Example of client using UDP protocol.
 */

#include        "inet.h"

main(argc, argv)
int     argc;
char    *argv[];
{
        int                     tfd;
        struct t_unitdata       unitdata;
        struct sockaddr_in      serv_addr;

        pname = argv[0];

        /*
         * Open a UDP endpoint.
         */

        if ( (tfd = t_open(DEV_UDP, O_RDWR, (struct t_info *) 0)) < 0)
                err_dump("client: can't t_open %s", DEV_UDP);

        /*
         * Bind any local address for us.
         */

        if (t_bind(tfd, (struct t_bind *) 0, (struct t_bind *) 0) < 0)
                err_dump("client: t_bind error");

        /*
         * Initialize a sockaddr_in structure with the address of the
         * the server we want to send datagrams to.
         */

        bzero((char *) &serv_addr, sizeof(serv_addr));
        serv_addr.sin_family      = AF_INET;
        serv_addr.sin_addr.s_addr = inet_addr(SERV_HOST_ADDR);
        serv_addr.sin_port        = htons(SERV_UDP_PORT);

        /*
         * Now initialize a unitdata structure for sending to the server.
         */

        unitdata.addr.maxlen = sizeof(serv_addr);        /* server's addr */
```

```
        unitdata.addr.len    = sizeof(serv_addr);
        unitdata.addr.buf    = (char *) &serv_addr;
        unitdata.opt.maxlen  = 0;                          /* no options */
        unitdata.opt.len     = 0;
        unitdata.opt.buf     = (char *) 0;

        doit(tfd, &unitdata, stdin);    /* do it all */

        t_close(tfd);
        exit(0);
}


/*
 * Read the contents of the FILE *fp, write each line to the transport
 * endpoint (to the server process), then read a line back from
 * the transport endpoint and print it on the standard output.
 */

doit(tfd, sudataptr, fp)
register int            tfd;
struct t_unitdata       *sudataptr;     /* unitdata for sends */
register FILE           *fp;
{
        int             n, flags;
        char            sendline[MAXLINE], recvline[MAXLINE + 1];
        char            *t_alloc();
        struct t_unitdata       *rudataptr;     /* unitdata for receives */

        /*
         * Allocate memory for the t_unitdata structure and the address field
         * in that structure.  This allows any size of address to be handled
         * by this function.
         */

        rudataptr = (struct t_unitdata *) t_alloc(tfd, T_UNITDATA, T_ADDR);
        if (rudataptr == NULL)
                err_dump("server: t_alloc error for T_UNITDATA");

        while (fgets(sendline, MAXLINE, fp) != NULL) {
                n = strlen(sendline);
                sudataptr->udata.len = n;
                sudataptr->udata.buf = sendline;
                if (t_sndudata(tfd, sudataptr) < 0)
                        err_dump("client: t_sndudata error");

                /*
                 * Now read a message from the transport endpoint and
                 * write it to our standard output.
                 */

                rudataptr->opt.maxlen = 0;       /* don't care about options */
                rudataptr->udata.maxlen = MAXLINE;
                rudataptr->udata.buf    = recvline;
                if (t_rcvudata(tfd, rudataptr, &flags) < 0)
```

```
                    err_dump("client: t_rcvudata error");
            recvline[rudataptr->udata.len] = 0;      /* null terminate */
            fputs(recvline, stdout);
    }

    if (ferror(fp))
            err_dump("client: error reading file");
}
```

7.6   Advanced TLI Functions

The TLI functions described in this section provide additional capabilities, beyond those
described in Section 7.4.

Nonblocking I/O

A transport endpoint can be put into a nonblocking state. This is done by specifying the
O_NDELAY flag in the call to t_open when the endpoint is created, or at a later time
with the fcntl system call. The format of the fcntl system call is almost identical to
what we described for a socket in Section 6.11: a *cmd* of F_SETFL and an *arg* that
includes O_NDELAY. (4.3BSD specifies the *arg* as FNDELAY.)
    When a transport endpoint is nonblocking, the following TLI functions can return
immediately, without blocking: t_connect, t_listen, t_rcv, t_rcvconnect,
t_rcvudata, t_snd, and t_sndudata. The first five of these return a value of −1
with t_errno set to TNODATA to indicate that the endpoint is nonblocking and the
requested operation can't be completed without blocking. The t_snd function returns
−1 with t_errno set to TFLOW if the endpoint is nonblocking and flow control restrictions prevent the provider from accepting any data. If the endpoint is nonblocking and
the transport provider can accept some data, t_snd returns the actual number of bytes
accepted and the TMORE *flags* value is returned to the caller. The t_sndudata function returns −1 and sets t_errno to TFLOW if the endpoint is nonblocking and the provider is unable to accept the data unit.

t_getinfo **Function**

Recall the t_info structure that is returned by the t_open function. The following
function also returns the same information to the caller.

```
    #include <tiuser.h>

    int t_getinfo(int fd, struct t_info *info);
```

Refer to the description of the t_open function in Section 6.5 for a description of the fields in the t_info structure. One reason for providing access to this information about the transport endpoint, in addition to returning it when t_open is called, is that some of the values might change after the endpoint is connected to a peer process.

t_getstate **Function**

Every transport endpoint has a *current state* associated with it. The following function returns the current state (an integer value) to the caller.

```
#include <tiuser.h>

int t_getstate(int fd);
```

The current state is specified by one of the constants shown in Figure 7.11.

State	Description	T_COTS	T_COTS_ORD	T_CLTS
T_DATAXFER	data transfer	•	•	
T_IDLE	bound, but idle	•	•	•
T_INCON	incoming connection pending for server	•	•	
T_INREL	incoming orderly release		•	
T_OUTCON	outgoing connection pending for client	•	•	
T_OUTREL	outgoing orderly release		•	
T_UNBIND	initialized but unbound	•	•	•

Figure 7.11 Possible current states of a transport endpoint.

The final three columns indicate which states are valid for the 3 different service types: T_COTS is the connection-oriented service, T_COTS_ORD is the connection-oriented service with orderly release, and T_CTLS is the connectionless service.

A state transition matrix can be developed to show exactly how the state of a transport endpoint changes as different TLI functions are called. For example, the state transition matrix shown in Figure 7.12 applies to all transport endpoints (connection oriented or connectionless).

TLI function	State before function call		
	T_UNINIT	T_UNBND	T_IDLE
t_open	T_UNBND		
t_bind		T_IDLE	
t_optmgmt			T_IDLE
t_unbind			T_UNBND
t_close		T_UNINIT	

Figure 7.12 State transition matrix for five TLI functions.

The blank entries for a given row and column mean that the function corresponding to the row cannot be called when the current state is given by the column value. The non-blank entries show what the state becomes *after* successful return from the function, when the state on entry to the function corresponds to that column. There is a state shown in Figure 7.12, T_UNINIT, that wasn't shown in the table of return values from the t_getstate function. The reason for this is because this state is never returned by the t_getstate function. This T_UNINIT state is an internal state used by the TLI functions. Whenever a file descriptor corresponds to a valid transport endpoint (i.e., it was returned by t_open), its state is one of the values shown in Figure 7.11.

The state transition matrix for a connectionless protocol is trivial. The three functions t_sndudata, t_rcvudata, and t_rcvuderr can only be called when the transport endpoint is in the T_IDLE state, and the state remains the same after the function returns.

The state transition matrix for a connection-oriented protocol is more complicated (17 rows by 6 columns). The interested reader is referred to Appendix A of the AT&T manual [1989d] for the matrix. Realize that we could build a single state transition matrix for every function call, instead of dividing it into three pieces as we've done: one matrix for the functions common to all three service types, one for the connectionless functions, and one for the connection-oriented functions. This yields a larger matrix (25 rows by 8 columns), which is harder to show on a single page.

t_optmgmt **Function**

The t_optmgmt function enables the caller to fetch or set protocol-dependent options.

```
#include <tiuser.h>

int t_optmgmt(int fd, struct t_optmgmt *request,
              struct t_optmgmt *return);

struct t_optmgmt {
  struct netbuf  opt;     /* protocol-specific options */
  long           flags;   /* action to take with options */
};
```

The options are protocol-specific and are stored in the opt.buf field of either the *request* or *return* arguments. The *flags* argument of the *request* structure specifies the action desired by the caller:

    T_DEFAULT   Requests the transport provider to return the default options in the *return−>opt* structure. The *request−>opt.len* field must be zero and the *request−>opt.buf* pointer may be NULL.

T_NEGOTIATE   Requests the transport provider to set the options specified by the
                 request->opt structure. The final values used by the provider are
                 returned to the caller in the *return->opt* structure. These final
                 values can differ from the requested values.

T_CHECK   Requests the transport provider to check the options specified by
                 the *request->opt* structure and return to the caller if these options
                 are supported. On return, the transport provider sets the
                 return->flags field to either T_SUCCESS or T_FAILURE.

> This TLI function corresponds to the 4.3BSD getsockopt and setsockopt socket calls.

t_rcvconnect **Function**

The following function allows a server to accept a connection request asynchronously.

```
#include <tiuser.h>

int t_rcvconnect(int fd, struct t_call *recvcall);
```

The sequence of steps to use this function are as follows:

1. A transport endpoint is created using t_open and placed in a nonblocking mode
    (as described at the beginning of this section).

2. A t_connect is issued. Since the transport endpoint is in nonblocking mode,
    this function returns a value of −1 immediately with t_errno set to TNODATA.

3. At some later point the process calls t_rcvconnect to determine if the con-
    nection has completed. (Recall that connection establishment can take some
    amount of time, as there are usually a few messages exchanged between the
    client and server transport providers.) If the endpoint is no longer in a non-
    blocking mode (the process has turned off the nonblocking flag since calling
    t_connect in step 2), then t_rcvconnect blocks until the connection is
    established. If the endpoint is still in a nonblocking mode, then this call to
    t_rcvconnect either: (a) returns immediately with a return value of zero if
    the connection is established, or (b) returns a value of −1 with t_errno set to
    TNODATA if the connection is not yet established.

Note that we specify the information required to establish the connection in the *sendcall*
to t_connect, but the information returned by the transport provider is returned by
t_rcvconnect in its *recvcall* argument.

t_sync **Function**

The t_sync function synchronizes the data structures maintained by the TLI library with the current state of the transport endpoint specified by *fd*.

```
#include <tiuser.h>

int t_sync(int fd);
```

This function also returns the current state of the endpoint as the value of the function. We listed the possible state values when we described the t_getstate function earlier in this section.

We'll return to this function and why it is needed, when we describe how TLI is implemented, in Section 7.8.

t_unbind **Function**

The effect of the t_bind function is reversed by the following function:

```
#include <tiuser.h>

int t_unbind(int fd);
```

This function disables the transport endpoint specified by *fd*. No further data will be accepted for this endpoint.

7.7   Streams

Before describing some of the advanced features available for System V networking, we need to understand some of its implementation details. TLI, as distributed with System V Release 3, is implemented using the stream I/O system. The stream I/O system was originally designed for the 8th Edition of Research Unix by Dennis Ritchie. See Ritchie [1984b] for the original article and Bach [1986] for an overview. Unix System V Release 3.0 provided the first commercially available version of streams.† The references for the System V implementation are AT&T [1989c] and AT&T [1989d].

Streams provide a full-duplex connection between a user process and a device driver, as shown in Figure 7.13. Although we describe the bottom box as a device driver, realize that this box can also be a pseudo-device driver. There is no requirement that it be associated with a hardware device.

---

† Although the System V Release 3 implementation of streams is similar to the original research version, there are differences. Some people refer to the System V Release 3 version as STREAMS and the research version as Streams. We'll call the concept streams.

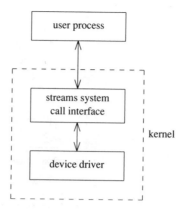

Figure 7.13 A stream shown between a user process and a device driver.

To emphasize the characteristics of a stream, we'll show the top portion of a stream in the kernel as the "stream head," as in Figure 7.14. We also show the connections from this box down to the driver using two arrows, reiterating the full-duplex nature of a stream.

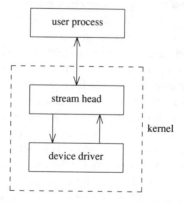

Figure 7.14 Stream showing full-duplex nature.

Before streams, the link between a process and most device drivers (other than disks) was the Unix character I/O system.

A nice feature of streams is that a process can add modules between the stream head (the system call interface) and the device driver. We show this in Figure 7.15.

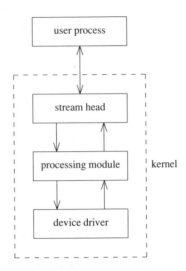

Figure 7.15 Stream with a processing module.

Any number of modules can be "pushed" onto a stream. When we say "push" we mean that each new module gets inserted just below the stream head (a LIFO stack). An example of a processing module is one to implement a terminal line discipline. The actual device driver for a terminal just inputs and outputs characters and it is the terminal line discipline module that implements features such as special character handling, forming complete lines of input, and so on. We return to terminal line disciplines in Section 15.2 when we discuss a remote login example.

Our interest in streams with networking is that the device driver becomes the network interface (Ethernet device driver, token ring device driver, etc.) and all the processing modules between the stream head and the device driver implement a communication protocol (TCP/IP, XNS). Streams provide a nice layered implementation of the networking system, similar in concept to the layering we described in Chapter 4. A streams module that accepts data from multiple sources is called a *multiplexor*. A streams-based implementation of the TCP/IP protocol suite, for example, could be as shown in Figure 7.16. Here the daemon process builds the multiplexor when it is started, typically at system initialization. Details on setting up a streams multiplexor such as this are given in Chapter 3 of AT&T [1989d].

Before the implementation of streams, if you didn't have the source code for Unix and wanted to add a new feature to the kernel, you wrote a character device driver to do what you wanted. You accessed the driver through the `open`, `close`, `read`, `write`, and `ioctl` system calls. This is how most third party networking software is implemented, on systems that don't support streams. This technique can also be used for purposes other than supporting new devices. For example, some sites implemented advisory

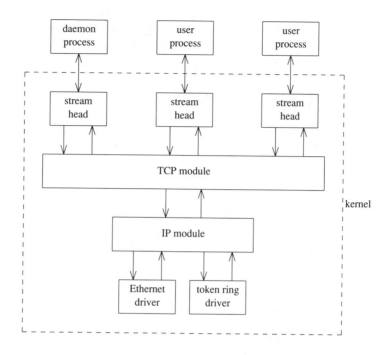

Figure 7.16 Possible streams implementation of TCP/IP.

record locking within the kernel by adding a device driver to handle all the locks. This was done to support some database systems before record locking was supported by System V Release 2.0.

The problem with this approach is that the existing Unix facility, the character I/O system, just isn't adequate or efficient enough for implementing networking protocols. Also, the modules required to implement networking protocols at layers above the device driver (such as the TCP module and the IP module shown in Figure 7.16) don't belong in the device driver. The availability of streams allows the efficient implementation of new features such as networking protocols. Using streams, a site without source code can add new stream modules to their system in a fashion similar to adding a new device driver.

Streams are accessed through the following standard system calls: `open`, `close`, `read`, `write`, and `ioctl`. Additionally, three new system calls were added to support streams: `putmsg`, `getmsg`, and `poll`. We describe the `poll` system call in Section 7.11 when we describe multiplexing of several I/O channels. We describe the other two system calls for streams below.

4.3BSD contains about 18 new system calls to support networking (`socket`, `bind`, etc.).

Additional information on the development of the streams facility, and specifics regarding its applicability for networking, is given in Olander, McGrath, and Israel [1986]. Rago [1989] details some enhancements made in System V Release 4.0 to provide better support for out-of-band data with streams.

getmsg and putmsg System Calls

The data transferred up and down a stream consists of *messages*. Each message contains a *control* part and a *data* part. To allow a user process to read and write these messages, two new system calls were added.

```
#include <stropts.h>

int getmsg(int fd, struct strbuf *cntlptr, struct strbuf *dataptr,
           int *flags);

int putmsg(int fd, struct strbuf *cntlptr, struct strbuf *dataptr,
           int flags);

struct strbuf {
  int    maxlen;     /* size of buffer */
  int    len;        /* amount of data in buffer */
  char   *buf;       /* buffer pointer */
};
```

(Note the similarity between the strbuf structure and the netbuf structure that's used by all the TLI functions. Even the names of the three elements in each structure are identical.)

These two system calls allow us to send and receive messages by specifying both the control part and the data part. Additionally, the *flags* can be set to zero or RS_HIPRI, the latter used for priority messages. These priority messages correspond to out-of-band data, as we'll describe in Section 7.13. There are many variations and special conditions that apply to these two system calls that we won't discuss. (Refer to their respective manual pages for all the gory details.) We will, however, use the getmsg system call in Section 7.9 with named stream pipes. In all our networking examples, the TLI library hides the actual stream system calls, other than the poll system call.

These two system calls are required because the read and write system calls don't allow optional flags to be specified. The read and write system calls also can't distinguish between control information and actual data. This is similar in concept to the additional input and output system calls that were added to support the 4.3BSD networking software: recv, send, recvmsg, and sendmsg.

7.8   TLI Implementation

TLI is a library of C functions that provides a user interface to the implementation of various networking protocols. TLI hides the actual streams interface from the user. A sample picture of the different layers is shown in Figure 7.17.

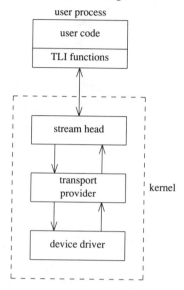

Figure 7.17   Implementation of TLI.

We could also draw an arrow between the user code and the stream head, as there are some instances where the user needs to access the stream I/O system directly. The actual implementation of the TLI functions, and how they invoke the system calls supported for streams, is an implementation detail that won't concern us.

Now that we understand how TLI is implemented, we return to the `t_sync` function that we mentioned briefly in Section 7.6. Assume that the process shown in Figure 7.17 `exec`s some other process that will handle a transport endpoint. We have the picture shown in Figure 7.18. Since the TLI functions are part of the user process, and not part of the kernel, the TLI data structures that were in process A for a given endpoint disappear after the `exec`. The TLI functions in process B know nothing about the endpoint. But the endpoint is a valid transport endpoint, since the file descriptor to the streams device was passed from process A to process B across the `exec` system call.

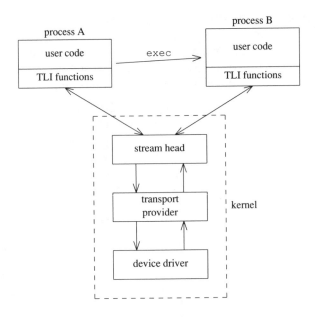

Figure 7.18 Effect of a `fork` on a transport endpoint.

What has to happen is for process B to call the `t_sync` function. This function queries the transport provider in the kernel for information about the endpoint, and initializes its appropriate TLI data structures accordingly. Process B can then use the file descriptor with the TLI functions appropriate for that endpoint. There are three conditions that require a process to call the `t_sync` function:

1. when a file descriptor is obtained from the `dup` system call,

2. when a file descriptor is obtained from the `open` system call,

3. after an `exec`.

We don't have to call `t_sync` after a `fork`, since the new process starts with a copy of the data area of the calling process. Also realize that with case 2 we can't `open` any file and have it become a transport endpoint—we still have to specify the same *pathname* as used in the `t_open` function, namely the pathname of the transport provider.

> Since the socket functions are all system calls, all appropriate data structures are maintained in the kernel, not in the user's process space. Therefore, nothing similar to the TLI `t_sync` function is required with sockets.

7.9   **Stream Pipes**

A *stream pipe* is a full-duplex connection between two processes. Stream pipes are used in System V for passing file descriptors between processes. Before showing an example of file descriptors being passed (in the next section) we show how to create and use stream pipes. An unnamed stream pipe can be used by a parent process that wants a stream pipe connection between itself and a child process that it creates at a later time, while a named stream pipe is used by unrelated processes that wish to communicate. Note that a named stream pipe is similar to a FIFO (which we described in Section 3.5) but the named stream pipe is full-duplex. Similarly an unnamed stream pipe is similar to a standard Unix pipe, but the unnamed stream pipe is full-duplex and the pipe is half-duplex.

> Stream pipes are similar to Unix domain sockets. As with Unix domain sockets, stream pipes can be named or unnamed. A named stream pipe corresponds to a Unix domain socket that has a name bound to it, while an unnamed stream pipe corresponds to the `socketpair` system call.

Stream pipes are implemented using a ''loop around'' driver. An example of this type of loop-around driver is shown in Section 10.4.1 of Bach [1986], where it is called a pseudo-terminal (pty). A complete implementation of a sample driver is given in Chapter 10 of AT&T [1989d]. The operation of a loop-around driver is simple: two streams are connected through the driver so that the output of one is the input of the other, and vice versa.

Stream pipes exist in System V Release 3.2, but are not documented. They appear to be provided for and used by AT&T's Remote File System (RFS). The *streamio*(7) manual page for System V/386 Release 3.2 mentions that stream pipes are required with the `I_SENDFD` and `I_RECVFD` stream commands, yet nowhere in the manuals do they describe how to create and use stream pipes. It is likely that stream pipes, both named and unnamed, will be provided in System V Release 4.0, perhaps in a different form from what we show here. Nevertheless, we need to use stream pipes to pass file descriptors between processes. If we develop a single function to create a stream pipe we can easily replace it later if something different is provided.

First a user process opens the loop device, `/dev/sxt`, two times, obtaining two file descriptors, *fd i* and *fd j*. We picture this in Figure 7.19.

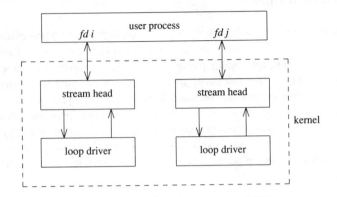

Figure 7.19   Stream pipe after opening /dev/sxt twice.

Next, the stream ioctl command I_FDINSERT connects the two file descriptors together. Once this is done we have the picture shown in Figure 7.20.

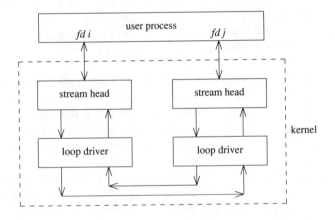

Figure 7.20   Stream pipe after connecting the two ends.

This example also provides an example of a *clone device*. A clone device is a streams device driver that does not require us to open a particular minor device. Instead, the clone device allocates an unused minor device and opens that device for us. This technique is useful when we are not interested in the particular device that is allocated, but we want a unique minor device. In the loop-around device driver, the caller doesn't care which two minor devices are allocated, it just wants two unique device entries so that they can be hooked together with the ioctl call.

4.3BSD does not have a feature like this. Instead, as we'll see in Section 15.4 when we describe pseudo-terminals, a user process has to open different minor devices, to find one that is not in use.

Here is the function for System V Release 3 that creates an unnamed stream pipe.

```
/*
 * Create an unnamed stream pipe.
 */

#include        <sys/types.h>
#include        <sys/stream.h>           /* defines queue_t */
#include        <stropts.h>              /* defines struct strfdinsert */
#include        <fcntl.h>

#define SPX_DEVICE      "/dev/spx"

int                                      /* return 0 if OK, -1 on error */
s_pipe(fd)
int     fd[2];           /* two file descriptors returned through here */
{
        struct strfdinsert      ins;
        queue_t                 *pointer;

        /*
         * First open the stream clone device "/dev/spx" twice,
         * obtaining the two file descriptors.
         */

        if ( (fd[0] = open(SPX_DEVICE, O_RDWR)) < 0)
                return(-1);

        if ( (fd[1] = open(SPX_DEVICE, O_RDWR)) < 0) {
                close(fd[0]);
                return(-1);
        }

        /*
         * Now link these two streams together with an I_FDINSERT ioctl.
         */

        ins.ctlbuf.buf    = (char *) &pointer; /* no ctl info, just the ptr */
        ins.ctlbuf.maxlen = sizeof(queue_t *);
        ins.ctlbuf.len    = sizeof(queue_t *);

        ins.databuf.buf    = (char *) 0;       /* no data to send */
        ins.databuf.len    = -1; /* magic: must be -1, not 0, for stream pipe */
        ins.databuf.maxlen = 0;

        ins.fildes = fd[1];     /* the fd to connect with fd[0] */
        ins.flags  = 0;         /* nonpriority message */
        ins.offset = 0;         /* offset of pointer in control buffer */

        if (ioctl(fd[0], I_FDINSERT, (char * ) &ins) < 0) {
                close(fd[0]);
```

```
                       close(fd[1]);
                       return(-1);
           }

           return(0);               /* all OK */
}
```

To create a named stream pipe we have to call the `mknod` system call. (Recall from Section 3.5 that we used this same system call to create a FIFO.) There is, however, a problem. While any user is able to invoke `mknod` to create a FIFO, only the superuser can call it for any other purpose. This means, unfortunately, that it requires superuser privileges to create a named stream pipe. Nevertheless, here is our function to do this.

```
/*
 * Create a named stream pipe.
 */

#include         <sys/types.h>
#include         <sys/stat.h>

int                                   /* return 0 if OK, -1 on error */
ns_pipe(name, fd)
char    *name;           /* user-specified name to assign to the stream pipe */
int     fd[2];           /* two file descriptors returned through here */
{
        int           omask;
        struct stat   statbuff;

        /*
         * First create an unnamed stream pipe.
         */

        if (s_pipe(fd) < 0)
                return(-1);

        /*
         * Now assign the name to one end (the first descriptor, fd[0]).
         * To do this we first find its major/minor device numbers using
         * fstat(2), then use these in a call to mknod(2) to create the
         * filesystem entry.  Beware that mknod(2) is restricted to root
         * (for everything other than FIFOs).
         * Under System VR3.2, the major value for the unnamed stream pipe
         * corresponds to the major for "/dev/spx" and the minor value is
         * whatever the "/dev/spx" clone driver assigned to make the
         * major/minor unique.
         */

        if (fstat(fd[0], &statbuff) < 0) {
                close(fd[0]);
                close(fd[1]);
                return(-1);
        }
```

```
            unlink(name);                    /* in case it already exists */
            omask = umask(0);                /* assure mode is 0666 */
            if (mknod(name, S_IFCHR | 0666, statbuff.st_rdev) < 0) {
                    close(fd[0]);
                    close(fd[1]);
                    umask(omask);
                    return(-1);
            }
            umask(omask);                     /* restore old umask value */

            return(0);               /* all OK */
    }
```

If we wanted to allow any user to create a named stream pipe, we could modify this function to invoke another program to do the mknod system call. This new program could be invoked from the ns_pipe function using the system function. This program that is invoked has to be set-user-ID to root so that it has the privilege to create the filesystem entry for the name. This program needs three arguments that can be passed as command line arguments: the name, the major device number, and the minor device number. We'll see in Section 15.4 that this technique is used by System V Release 3.2 to change the permissions on a pseudo-terminal device.

We can provide another example of the named stream pipe—the ability of another process to read or write this pipe. The following program creates a named stream pipe and then prints everything that is written to the pipe.

```
/*
 * Create a named stream pipe and read from it.
 */

#include        <sys/types.h>
#include        <stropts.h>

#define NSPIPENAME      "/tmp/nspipe.serv"
#define BUFFSIZE        1024

main()
{
        int             fd[2], flags;
        char            cntlbuff[BUFFSIZE], databuff[BUFFSIZE];
        struct strbuf   cntlstr, datastr;

        if (ns_pipe(NSPIPENAME, fd) < 0)
                err_sys("can't create named stream pipe");

        cntlstr.buf    = cntlbuff;
        cntlstr.maxlen = BUFFSIZE;
        cntlstr.len    = 0;

        datastr.buf    = databuff;
        datastr.maxlen = BUFFSIZE;
        datastr.len    = 0;
```

```
    flags = 0;

    for ( ; ; ) {
            /*
             * Since the ns_pipe() function associates the name with
             * fd[0], we have to read from fd[1] (the other end of
             * the pipe).
             */

            if (getmsg(fd[1], &cntlstr, &datastr, &flags) < 0)
                    err_sys("getmsg error");
            if (cntlstr.len > 0)
                    printf("received %d bytes of control information\n",
                                            cntlstr.len);
            if (datastr.len > 0)
                    printf("data: %.*s\n", datastr.len, datastr.buf);

    }
}
```

This program prints the control portion of each message and the data portion. If we start this program and then execute the following command on another terminal

```
    date  > /tmp/nspipe.serv
```

the output from the `date` command gets written to named stream pipe and output by our program. Since the named stream pipe can be accessed by any regular C program using the Unix `open` and `write` system calls, any program is able to write to the pipe.

> We are unable to do the same example using the 4.3BSD version of named stream pipes that we developed in the previous chapter. The reason is that to open the named stream pipe, as we implemented them using Unix domain stream sockets, requires a `socket` system call. Most Unix utilities, such as `date` and `cat` write to standard output, and there is no way to have the shell associate a socket with standard output.

7.10 Passing File Descriptors

We can now provide a System V equivalent to the file descriptor passing example from Chapter 6. Recall our example of a replacement for the Unix `cat` program from Section 6.10. All we have to do is replace the `sendfile` and `recvfile` functions, leaving the rest of the example intact. The call to the function s_pipe in the `my_open` function, refers, of course, to the System V version that we developed in the previous section. Here is the function that passes a file descriptor over an unnamed stream pipe.

```
/*
 * Pass a file descriptor to another process.
 * Return 0 if OK, otherwise return the errno value from the I_SENDFD ioctl.
 */

#include        <sys/types.h>
#include        <stropts.h>
```

```
int
sendfile(strfd, fd)
int      strfd;                /* stream pipe to pass descriptor on */
int      fd;                   /* the actual fd value to pass */
{
        if (ioctl(strfd, I_SENDFD, fd) < 0)
                return(-1);

        return(0);
}
```

Here is the corresponding function that receives the file descriptor.

```
/*
 * Receive a file descriptor from another process.
 * Return the file descriptor if OK, otherwise return -1.
 */

#include        <sys/types.h>
#include        <stropts.h>

int
recvfile(sfd)
int      sfd;                  /* stream pipe */
{
        int                    fd;
        struct strrecvfd       recv;

        if (ioctl(sfd, I_RECVFD, (char *) &recv) < 0)
                return(-1);

        return(recv.fd);        /* return the new file descriptor */
                /* we don't return the uid and gid that are available */
}
```

The structure that receives the file descriptor is defined in <stropts.h> as

```
struct strrecvfd {
   int                 fd;       /* new fd that was created */
   unsigned short      uid;      /* effective user ID of sender */
   unsigned short      gid;      /* effective group ID of sender */
   char                fill[8];
};
```

Note that System V provides the effective user ID and the effective group ID of the sending process. This can be used by the receiver to verify the identity of the sender.

> This information about the identity of the sender is not provided with the 4.3BSD recvmsg system call.

7.11   Input/Output Multiplexing

System V Release 3 provides the `poll` system call, which corresponds somewhat to the 4.3BSD `select` system call. There is, however, one fundamental limitation in the `poll` system call: it can only be used to determine the I/O status of a descriptor that refers to a streams device. It cannot be used on other descriptors. This has an effect on terminal devices. Since the terminal I/O system in all releases of System V, up through and including Release 3.2, is *not* streams based, we are not able to use the `poll` system call on descriptors that refer to terminal devices. (The implementation of the `poll` system call in Unix System V Release 4.0 is supposed to operate on any open descriptor. This version of Unix is also supposed to have a streams-based implementation of all terminal drivers.) Note that `poll` is a feature of System V streams, not TLI.

The format of the system call is

```
int poll(struct pollfd *fdarray, unsigned long nfds, int timeout);

struct pollfd {
   int    fd;         /* file descriptor to check */
   short  events;     /* events of interest on fd */
   short  revents;    /* events that occurred on fd */
};
```

The first argument is the address of the first element of an array of structures. Each element of the array is a `pollfd` structure that specifies the conditions to be tested for a given descriptor (*fd*). The conditions to be tested for are specified by the *events* field, and the system call returns its status for that descriptor in the corresponding *revents* field. Each of these two fields is comprised of one or more bits that specify a certain condition. Figure 7.21 shows the constants that are used to specify the *events* flag and to test the *revents* flag against.

Event name	Input to *events* ?	Result from *revents* ?	Description
POLLIN	●	●	nonpriority message present
POLLPRI	●	●	priority message present (out-of-band data)
POLLOUT	●	●	descriptor is writable (won't block)
POLLERR		●	an error message has arrived
POLLHUP		●	hangup has occurred
POLLNVAL		●	descriptor is not an open stream

Figure 7.21   Input and output events for `poll` system call.

The number of elements in the array of structures (i.e., the number of descriptors to check) is specified by the *nfds* argument. (Why this argument is specified as an unsigned long integer, and not a simple integer, is perplexing.)

The two return values `POLLIN` and `POLLPRI` are mutually exclusive for a given descriptor in the *revents* field. That is, on return from `poll`, if a given streams descriptor has both nonpriority messages and priority messages available, only `POLLPRI` is set in the *revents* field. We'll mention the `POLLPRI` event in Section 7.13 when we discuss out-of-band data.

The *timeout* argument specifies how long the system call is to wait before returning. A positive value specifies the number of milliseconds to wait. Figure 7.22 shows the possible values for the *timeout* argument.

timeout value	Description
−1	wait indefinitely (until signal occurs)
0	return immediately, don't block
> 0	wait specified number of milliseconds

Figure 7.22 *timeout* values for `poll` system call.

If the system does not provide a timer with millisecond accuracy, the value is rounded up to the nearest supported value.

The return value from this system call is −1 if an error occurred, otherwise it is the number of descriptors that have a nonzero *revents* field. A return value of zero indicates that the system call timed out and no descriptors are ready.

7.12 Asynchronous I/O

Asynchronous I/O is another feature provided by the streams system, and not TLI. A process first notifies the system that it wants to receive the `SIGPOLL` signal for a given streams descriptor. The `ioctl` system call, with a *request* of `I_SETSIG` does this.

```
#include <stropts.h>

int ioctl(int fd, int request, int arg);
```

The *arg* is an integer value that specifies the conditions for which a `SIGPOLL` signal should be generated. This integer value is formed as the bitwise-OR of the following constants:

`S_INPUT`   A nonpriority message has arrived for a stream, and no other messages were on the stream's queue before this message arrived.

`S_HIPRI`   A priority message has arrived for a stream.

`S_OUTPUT`   The output queue for the stream is no longer full. This notifies us that we may now write data.

`S_MSG`   A streams signal message is at the front of the stream's read queue.

If the *arg* value is zero, the process will no longer receive SIGPOLL signals for this stream. If *arg* is set to S_HIPRI, we are signaled only when priority messages are present.

> This one signal, SIGPOLL, is similar to the 4.3BSD SIGIO and SIGURG signals. The steps required to register the process to receive these signals (ioctl) are similar in both environments. Under 4.3BSD the process that receives the signal has to execute a select to determine which descriptor is ready for I/O, and under System V the process has to execute a poll to accomplish the same result.

7.13 Out-of-Band Data

Support for out-of-band data (termed "expedited data" by TLI) is provided by the transport provider and the streams system. The TLI t_snd function allows the sender to specify the T_EXPEDITED flag. This flag value is also returned to the caller by the t_rcv function. The interpretation of expedited data, however, is left up to the transport provider.

Expedited data is usually handled by treating it as a priority message by the streams system. There are, however, problems with the implementation of this in System V Release 3, which should be corrected in System V Release 4.0 [Rago 1989]. The following points should be considered when using expedited data in System V Release 3.

- Only one priority message is allowed on a stream read queue at a time.† The reason for this is because these priority messages are not subject to the normal streams flow control. Any additional priority messages that arrive are silently discarded.

- You cannot use the read and write interface (the tirdwr module that we showed in Section 7.5 in our accept_call function). You must use the t_snd and t_rcv functions. If you use the tirdwr module and it receives expedited data from the other end, a fatal protocol error results.

  > 4.3BSD has a similar limitation—you must use one of the six send and recv system calls to handle out-of-band data.

- Since expedited data corresponds to priority messages, the POLLPRI event described in Section 7.11 with the poll system call corresponds to the receipt of expedited data.

- The getmsg and putmsg system calls use a flag of RS_HIPRI to indicate priority messages. This corresponds to the M_PCPROTO priority message (i.e., expedited data).

---

† Technically only one M_PCPROTO message, the type used by TLI. There are other types of priority messages.

7.14 **Summary**

This has been another long chapter containing many details. We have covered the differences and similarities between the AT&T Unix System V Transport Layer Interface and the socket interface provided by 4.3BSD. Our presentation was similar to the one we used in Chapter 6.

- Elementary TLI functions
- Client–server example using only the elementary TLI functions
- Advanced TLI functions
- Advanced TLI features and options

We also presented the streams concept, which is required to understand the details of using TLI.

The remaining examples in the text use the Berkeley socket interface. Most vendors that supply a transport provider for TLI also supply a socket library that emulates the 4.3BSD socket interface. We do, however, return to the System V streams concept in Chapter 15, when we describe pseudo-terminals.

Exercises

7.1 Write a program that prints all the values in the `t_info` structure, after calling the `t_open` function. Print all the values for each of the transport providers available on your system.

7.2 Can you use the stream pipes provided by System V to implement something similar to the Unix domain protocols supplied with 4.3BSD? If so, implement the Unix stream example from Section 6.6 (a connection-oriented server that can handle multiple clients using either a concurrent server or an iterative server). Can you also implement a datagram client–server?

7.3 Write a program that provides a higher precision timer, using the `poll` system call, similar to the example we showed in Section 6.13 that used the `select` system call.

7.4 Write a program that uses an unnamed stream pipe to connect two processes (a parent and child). Have one process copy standard input to the stream pipe and the other copy the stream pipe to standard output.

7.5 Modify the program in the previous exercise to use the asynchronous I/O feature described in Section 7.12. Since asynchronous I/O is only usable on streams devices, use it for both ends of the stream pipe.

8

Library Routines

8.1 Introduction

This chapter first discusses some network utility functions provided by 4.3BSD (and many other systems, too) for converting human readable names of network entities into the appropriate numeric representations. We then develop some network utility functions that we'll use in other examples in the book. These functions are designed to handle most cases when we want to open a network connection with a server. Finally we develop some functions that add reliability to a datagram service. These functions handle the typical needs of a datagram client: timeout and retransmission.

8.2 Berkeley Network Library Routines

In the examples we've shown so far, in Chapters 6 and 7, we used hard coded numbers to identify the host systems that we wanted to communicate with. This is not a good technique and we'll now describe some library functions that are provided to make the handling of names and addresses easier. Although these functions were first developed for 4BSD, some System V TCP/IP implementations provide them also. For example, the WIN/TCP package used in Chapter 7 provides these functions.

Host computers are normally known by human readable names. These are used when asking for a service from a network, such as ''I want to login to the system named apple'' or ''copy the file main.c from the system orange to the current system.'' As we've seen up to this point, the packets that are communicated between hosts use numeric addresses of some form to get to their destination, but humans deal much better with names instead of numbers.

Constructing Internet Addresses

The functions that we now define are available only for Internet services. This is partly because the Internet protocols are the ones most often used by a 4.3BSD system, and also because the other widely available protocol family (XNS) has its own set of services for locating network services (described later in this section). It is expected that additional functions or features will be provided with future BSD systems, as other protocols are added.

Let's consider the normal case, where we know the *service* we want (remote login, file transfer, etc.) and the name of the *host* we want to contact to provide that service. We first look up the host

```
#include <netdb.h>

struct hostent *gethostbyname(char *hostname);
```

The `gethostbyname` function returns a pointer to a `hostent` structure that is defined in the `<netdb.h>` header file.

```
struct hostent {
    char   *h_name;          /* official name of host */
    char   **h_aliases;      /* alias list */
    int    h_addrtype;       /* host address type */
    int    h_length;         /* length of address */
    char   **h_addr_list;    /* list of addresses from name server */
                             /* a NULL terminates the list */
};

#define h_addr   h_addr_list[0]   /* first address in list */
```

Currently the `h_addrtype` field always contains `AF_INET`, and similarly the `h_length` field always contains 4 (the length of an Internet address). For Internet addresses, the array of pointers `h_addr_list[0]`, `h_addr_list[1]`, and so on, are not pointers to characters, but are pointers to structures of type `in_addr`, which we defined in Section 6.4. As you can see, lots of generality has been built into the `hostent` structure, most of which is not currently used. The reason a given host might have more than one address is that a multihomed host has more than one Internet interface, each with a different Internet address.

The following program prints host entries, using the `gethostbyname` function:

```
/*
 * Print the "hostent" information for every host whose name is
 * specified on the command line.
 */

#include        <stdio.h>
#include        <sys/types.h>
#include        <netdb.h>              /* for struct hostent */
#include        <sys/socket.h>         /* for AF_INET */
#include        <netinet/in.h>         /* for struct in_addr */
```

```
#include        <arpa/inet.h>               /* for inet_ntoa() */

main(argc, argv)
int     argc;
char    **argv;
{
        register char           *ptr;
        char                    *host_err_str();        /* our lib function */
        register struct hostent *hostptr;

        while (--argc > 0) {
                ptr = *++argv;
                if ( (hostptr = gethostbyname(ptr)) == NULL) {
                        err_ret("gethostbyname error for host: %s %s",
                                        ptr, host_err_str());
                        continue;
                }
                printf("official host name: %s\n", hostptr->h_name);

                /* go through the list of aliases */
                while ( (ptr = *(hostptr->h_aliases)) != NULL) {
                        printf("        alias: %s\n", ptr);
                        hostptr->h_aliases++;
                }
                printf("        addr type = %d, addr length = %d\n",
                                hostptr->h_addrtype, hostptr->h_length);

                switch (hostptr->h_addrtype) {
                case AF_INET:
                        pr_inet(hostptr->h_addr_list, hostptr->h_length);
                        break;

                default:
                        err_ret("unknown address type");
                        break;
                }
        }
}

/*
 * Go through a list of Internet addresses,
 * printing each one in dotted-decimal notation.
 */

pr_inet(listptr, length)
char    **listptr;
int     length;
{
        struct in_addr  *ptr;

        while ( (ptr = (struct in_addr *) *listptr++) != NULL)
                printf("        Internet address: %s\n", inet_ntoa(*ptr));
}
```

We call the function `host_err_str` if an error is returned by the `gethostbyname` function. This error routine is shown in Appendix A. It looks at the variable `h_errno` that is set by the `gethostbyname` function, if an error occurs.

If the program above is named `hostent` and invoked as

```
hostent hsi hsivm
```

the resulting output is

```
official host name: hsi
        alias: hsi
        addr type = 2, addr length = 4
        Internet address: 192.43.235.2
official host name: hsivm
        alias: hsivm
        addr type = 2, addr length = 4
        Internet address: 192.43.235.31
```

In Section 14.3 we'll have the condition where a server (the 4.3BSD `rshd` server) knows the Internet address of the client host and wants to find its name. The function `gethostbyaddr` does this address-to-name mapping.

```
#include <netdb.h>

struct hostent *gethostbyaddr(char *addr, int len, int type);
```

The *addr* is a pointer to a `sockaddr_in` structure containing the Internet address and *len* is the size of this structure. The *type* argument must be specified as `AF_INET`. As with the `gethostbyname` function, there is more generality provided by this function than is currently used.

The next function, `getservbyname`, looks up a service.

```
#include <netdb.h>

struct servent *getservbyname(char *servname, char *protname);
```

This function returns a pointer to the following structure:

```
struct servent {
  char  *s_name;       /* official service name */
  char  **s_aliases;   /* alias list */
  int   s_port;        /* port number, network byte order */
  char  *s_proto;      /* protocol to use */
};
```

The information for this function is taken from the file `/etc/services`. A search is made of this file, looking for the requested *servname*. If a protocol is also specified (i.e., if the *protname* argument is not NULL), then the entry must also have a matching protocol. There are some Internet services that are provided using either TCP or UDP (the echo service, for example), and others that support only a single protocol (FTP, for example, requires TCP.) The field of main interest in the `servent` structure is the Internet port number. Note that this structure handles integer port numbers, even though Internet port numbers are 16-bit quantities.

Figure 8.1 shows the use of these two library functions to fill in an Internet address structure.

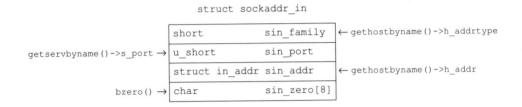

Figure 8.1   Filling in an Internet address structure.

We'll show some actual code to do this in the next section of this chapter.

Internet Name Servers

There are two ways for the `gethostbyname` function to obtain information about a specified host.

- The information about all accessible hosts can be stored in the file `/etc/hosts`. This technique requires that this file be updated on every host, whenever a host is added, deleted, or has its address changed. This technique is used only on those networks comprised of a few hosts.

- On larger networks such as the Internet, the `gethostbyname` and `gethostbyaddr` functions send queries to a name server. A name server is a program (a daemon) running on some system that client processes contact to obtain the addresses of other systems on the network. 4.3BSD provides the Berkeley Internet Name Domain (BIND) server system that can operate as a name server. This system consists of the actual server, `/etc/named`, and versions of the `gethostbyname` and `gethostbyaddr` functions that contact a name server.

Using the first technique corresponds to the name-to-number translation that you do when looking up a telephone number in a telephone book. The name server technique, on the other hand, is similar to calling directory assistance. For additional details on Internet name servers, see Chapter 18 of Comer [1988].

Constructing XNS Addresses

Most XNS applications use the Xerox Clearinghouse service to locate a named object and convert the name into an address. This is similar to an Internet name server. Oppen and Dalal [1983] along with Xerox [1984] give additional details on this system. Courier, the Xerox remote procedure call that we discuss in Section 18.4, is used for contacting the Clearinghouse server.

8.3   Network Utility Routines

The steps required by a client to start a dialogue with a server are standard. Our simple examples in Section 6.6 showed this. For a connection-oriented protocol we go through the sequence: `socket` and `connect`. For a connectionless protocol we call: `socket`, `bind`, and optionally `connect` to have the system record the server's address for future output on the socket. Additionally, we sometimes want to create a TCP socket that is bound to a reserved port on the local system. We would also like the TCP and UDP sockets to use the 4.3BSD Internet library functions described in Section 8.2 that allow names to be used for hosts and services. We can provide some utility functions that handle 90% of the services required by a typical client application, to avoid having to duplicate this code in each example. We provide four functions

```
tcp_open, udp_open, spp_open, idp_open
```

to handle TCP, UDP, SPP, and IDP client connections.

An additional feature that we provide in the TCP and UDP versions is to allow the host's name to be specified either as an Internet dotted-decimal address or as a name. We check for the dotted-decimal form first, to avoid calling the `gethostbyname` function unless required. This is because the `gethostbyname` function might have to contact a name server, and there is no reason to do this if the name is just a dotted-decimal address. Any application program that uses the Internet protocols (TCP/UDP/IP) and allows a host name to be specified, should allow either a dotted-decimal address or an actual name.

Our TCP function is the first one we've shown that uses the `gethostbyname` and `getservbyname` functions, which we described in the previous section.

```
/*
 * Open a TCP connection.
 */

#include        "netdefs.h"

#include        <netinet/in.h>
#include        <arpa/inet.h>

#ifndef INADDR_NONE
#define INADDR_NONE     0xffffffff     /* should be in <netinet/in.h> */
#endif
```

```
/*
 * The following globals are available to the caller, if desired.
 */

struct sockaddr_in      tcp_srv_addr;   /* server's Internet socket addr */
struct servent          tcp_serv_info;  /* from getservbyname() */
struct hostent          tcp_host_info;  /* from gethostbyname() */

int                     /* return socket descriptor if OK, else -1 on error */
tcp_open(host, service, port)
char    *host;          /* name or dotted-decimal addr of other system */
char    *service;       /* name of service being requested */
                        /* can be NULL, iff port > 0 */
int     port;           /* if == 0, nothing special - use port# of service */
                        /* if < 0, bind a local reserved port */
                        /* if > 0, it's the port# of server (host-byte-order) */
{
        int             fd, resvport;
        unsigned long   inaddr;
        char            *host_err_str();
        struct servent  *sp;
        struct hostent  *hp;

        /*
         * Initialize the server's Internet address structure.
         * We'll store the actual 4-byte Internet address and the
         * 2-byte port# below.
         */

        bzero((char *) &tcp_srv_addr, sizeof(tcp_srv_addr));
        tcp_srv_addr.sin_family = AF_INET;

        if (service != NULL) {
                if ( (sp = getservbyname(service, "tcp")) == NULL) {
                        err_ret("tcp_open: unknown service: %s/tcp", service);
                        return(-1);
                }
                tcp_serv_info = *sp;                    /* structure copy */
                if (port > 0)
                        tcp_srv_addr.sin_port = htons(port);
                                                        /* caller's value */
                else
                        tcp_srv_addr.sin_port = sp->s_port;
                                                        /* service's value */
        } else {
                if (port <= 0) {
                        err_ret("tcp_open: must specify either service or port");
                        return(-1);
                }
                tcp_srv_addr.sin_port = htons(port);
        }

        /*
         * First try to convert the host name as a dotted-decimal number.
```

```
                     * Only if that fails do we call gethostbyname().
                     */

                    if ( (inaddr = inet_addr(host)) != INADDR_NONE) {
                                                    /* it's dotted-decimal */
                            bcopy((char *) &inaddr, (char *) &tcp_srv_addr.sin_addr,
                                            sizeof(inaddr));
                            tcp_host_info.h_name = NULL;

                    } else {
                            if ( (hp = gethostbyname(host)) == NULL) {
                                    err_ret("tcp_open: host name error: %s %s",
                                                            host, host_err_str());
                                    return(-1);
                            }
                            tcp_host_info = *hp;    /* found it by name, structure copy */
                            bcopy(hp->h_addr, (char *) &tcp_srv_addr.sin_addr,
                                    hp->h_length);
                    }

                    if (port >= 0) {
                            if ( (fd = socket(AF_INET, SOCK_STREAM, 0)) < 0) {
                                    err_ret("tcp_open: can't create TCP socket");
                                    return(-1);
                            }

                    } else if (port < 0) {
                            resvport = IPPORT_RESERVED - 1;
                            if ( (fd = rresvport(&resvport)) < 0) {
                                    err_ret("tcp_open: can't get a reserved TCP port");
                                    return(-1);
                            }
                    }

                    /*
                     * Connect to the server.
                     */

                    if (connect(fd, (struct sockaddr *) &tcp_srv_addr,
                                                    sizeof(tcp_srv_addr)) < 0) {
                            err_ret("tcp_open: can't connect to server");
                            close(fd);
                            return(-1);
                    }

                    return(fd);       /* all OK */
            }
```

Our UDP function optionally calls the `connect` system call. Recall from Section 6.5 that for a datagram socket this merely establishes the address to be used in future output to the socket. It does not establish an actual connection with the server.

```
/*
 * Establish a UDP socket and optionally call connect() to set up
 * the server's address for future I/O.
 */

#include         "netdefs.h"

#include         <netinet/in.h>
#include         <arpa/inet.h>

#ifndef INADDR_NONE
#define INADDR_NONE      0xffffffff        /* should be in <netinet/in.h> */
#endif

/*
 * The following globals are available to the caller, if desired.
 */

struct sockaddr_in       udp_srv_addr;    /* server's Internet socket addr */
struct sockaddr_in       udp_cli_addr;    /* client's Internet socket addr */
struct servent           udp_serv_info;   /* from getservbyname() */
struct hostent           udp_host_info;   /* from gethostbyname() */

int                      /* return socket descriptor if OK, else -1 on error */
udp_open(host, service, port, dontconn)
char    *host;           /* name of other system to communicate with */
char    *service;        /* name of service being requested */
                         /* can be NULL, iff port > 0 */
int     port;            /* if == 0, nothing special - use port# of service */
                         /* if < 0, bind a local reserved port */
                         /* if > 0, it's the port# of server (host-byte-order) */
int     dontconn;        /* if == 0, call connect(), else don't */
{
        int             fd;
        unsigned long   inaddr;
        char            *host_err_str();
        struct servent  *sp;
        struct hostent  *hp;

        /*
         * Initialize the server's Internet address structure.
         * We'll store the actual 4-byte Internet address and the
         * 2-byte port# below.
         */

        bzero((char *) &udp_srv_addr, sizeof(udp_srv_addr));
        udp_srv_addr.sin_family = AF_INET;

        if (service != NULL) {
                if ( (sp = getservbyname(service, "udp")) == NULL) {
                        err_ret("udp_open: unknown service: %s/udp", service);
                        return(-1);
                }
```

```
                udp_serv_info = *sp;                              /* structure copy */
                if (port > 0)
                        udp_srv_addr.sin_port = htons(port);
                                                                  /* caller's value */
                else
                        udp_srv_addr.sin_port = sp->s_port;
                                                                  /* service's value */
        } else {
                if (port <= 0) {
                        err_ret("udp_open: must specify either service or port");
                        return(-1);
                }
                udp_srv_addr.sin_port = htons(port);
        }

        /*
         * First try to convert the host name as a dotted-decimal number.
         * Only if that fails do we call gethostbyname().
         */

        if ( (inaddr = inet_addr(host)) != INADDR_NONE) {
                                                        /* it's dotted-decimal */
                bcopy((char *) &inaddr, (char *) &udp_srv_addr.sin_addr,
                        sizeof(inaddr));
                udp_host_info.h_name = NULL;

        } else {
                if ( (hp = gethostbyname(host)) == NULL) {
                        err_ret("udp_open: host name error: %s %s",
                                                host, host_err_str());
                        return(-1);
                }
                udp_host_info = *hp;    /* found it by name, structure copy */
                bcopy(hp->h_addr, (char *) &udp_srv_addr.sin_addr,
                        hp->h_length);
        }

        if (port < 0)
                err_quit("udp_open: reserved ports not implemeneted yet");

        if ( (fd = socket(AF_INET, SOCK_DGRAM, 0)) < 0) {
                err_ret("udp_open: can't create UDP socket");
                return(-1);
        }

        /*
         * Bind any local address for us.
         */

        bzero((char *) &udp_cli_addr, sizeof(udp_cli_addr));
        udp_cli_addr.sin_family      = AF_INET;
        udp_cli_addr.sin_addr.s_addr = htonl(INADDR_ANY);
        udp_cli_addr.sin_port        = htons(0);
        if (bind(fd, (struct sockaddr *) &udp_cli_addr,
```

```
                                              sizeof(udp_cli_addr)) < 0) {
                    err_ret("udp_open: bind error");
                    close(fd);
                    return(-1);
            }

            /*
             * Call connect, if desired.  This is used by most caller's,
             * as the peer shouldn't change.  (TFTP is an exception.)
             * By calling connect, the caller can call send() and recv().
             */

            if (dontconn == 0) {
                    if (connect(fd, (struct sockaddr *) &udp_srv_addr,
                                                sizeof(udp_srv_addr)) < 0) {
                            err_ret("udp_open: connect error");
                            return(-1);
                    }
            }

            return(fd);
}
```

The following SPP example is similar to the TCP example.

```
/*
 * Open a SPP connection.
 */

#include        "netdefs.h"

#include        <netns/ns.h>

/*
 * The following globals are available to the caller, if desired.
 */

struct sockaddr_ns      spp_srv_addr;    /* server's XNS socket addr */

int                     /* return socket descriptor if OK, else -1 on error */
spp_open(host, service, port)
char    *host;          /* name of other system to communicate with */
                                /* must be acceptable to ns_addr(3N) */
                                /* <netid><separator><hostid><separator><port> */
char    *service;       /* name of service being requested */
                                /* not currently used */
int     port;           /* if < 0, bind a local reserved port (TODO) */
                        /* if > 0, it's the port# of server */
{
        int             fd;
        struct ns_addr  ns_addr();      /* BSD library routine */

        if ( (fd = socket(AF_NS, SOCK_STREAM, 0)) < 0) {
                err_ret("spp_open: can't create SPP stream socket");
```

```
                            return(-1);
                    }

                    /*
                     * Set up the server's address.
                     */

                    bzero((char *) &spp_srv_addr, sizeof(spp_srv_addr));
                    spp_srv_addr.sns_family = AF_NS;
                    spp_srv_addr.sns_addr   = ns_addr(host);
                                            /* stores net-ID, host-ID and port */
                    if (port > 0)
                            spp_srv_addr.sns_addr.x_port = htons(port);
                    else if (port < 0)
                            err_quit("spp_open: reserved ports not implemeneted yet");

                    /*
                     * And connect to the server.
                     */

                    if (connect(fd, (struct sockaddr *) &spp_srv_addr,
                                            sizeof(spp_srv_addr)) < 0) {
                            err_ret("spp_open: can't connect to server");
                            close(fd);
                            return(-1);
                    }

                    return(fd);        /* all OK */
}
```

Our IDP example also has an option to call `connect` for the datagram socket, as we discussed earlier for the UDP example.

```
/*
 * Establish an IDP socket and optionally call connect() to set up
 * the server's address for future I/O.
 */

#include        "netdefs.h"

#include        <netns/ns.h>

/*
 * The following globals are available to the caller, if desired.
 */

struct sockaddr_ns      idp_srv_addr;   /* server's XNS socket addr */
struct sockaddr_ns      idp_cli_addr;   /* client's XNS socket addr */

int                     /* return socket descriptor if OK, else -1 on error */
idp_open(host, service, port, dontconn)
char    *host;          /* name of other system to communicate with */
                        /* must be acceptable to ns_addr(3N) */
                        /* <netid><separator><hostid><separator><port> */
```

```
char    *service;       /* name of service being requested */
                        /* not currently used */
int     port;           /* if < 0, bind a local reserved port (TODO) */
                        /* if > 0, it's the port# of server */
int     dontconn;       /* if == 0, call connect(), else don't */
{
        int             fd;
        struct ns_addr  ns_addr();       /* BSD library routine */

        /*
         * Create an IDP socket.
         */

        if ( (fd = socket(AF_NS, SOCK_DGRAM, 0)) < 0) {
                err_ret("idp_open: can't create IDP datagram socket");
                return(-1);
        }

        /*
         * Bind any local address for us.
         */

        bzero((char *) &idp_cli_addr, sizeof(idp_cli_addr));
        idp_cli_addr.sns_family = AF_NS;
        if (bind(fd, (struct sockaddr *) &idp_cli_addr,
                                        sizeof(idp_cli_addr)) < 0) {
                err_ret("idp_open: bind error");
                close(fd);
                return(-1);
        }

        /*
         * Set up the server's address.
         */

        bzero((char *) &idp_srv_addr, sizeof(idp_srv_addr));
        idp_srv_addr.sns_family = AF_NS;
        idp_srv_addr.sns_addr   = ns_addr(host);
                                /* stores net-ID, host-ID and port */
        if (port > 0)
                idp_srv_addr.sns_addr.x_port = htons(port);
        else if (port < 0)
                err_quit("idp_open: reserved ports not implemeneted yet");

        /*
         * Call connect, if desired.  This is used by most caller's,
         * as the peer shouldn't change.
         * By calling connect, the caller can call send() and recv().
         */

        if (dontconn == 0) {
                if (connect(fd, (struct sockaddr *) &idp_srv_addr,
                                        sizeof(idp_srv_addr)) < 0) {
                        err_ret("idp_open: connect error");
```

```
                                return(-1);
                }
        }

        return(fd);
}
```

8.4   Providing a Reliable Message Service

In both the UDP and IDP echo examples from Section 6.6 we mentioned that the client and server did not provide a reliable service. We now add some reliability to the UDP example. By definition a datagram is unreliable. Therefore the term "reliable datagram" is an oxymoron. What we show here is a reliable message service on top of a datagram service.

We add two features to the client.

- If the server doesn't respond to a packet sent by the client, the client retransmits the packet. This is to handle datagrams that might get lost or discarded somewhere in the network. We put an upper limit on the retransmitting, and if it appears the server is not responding at all, the client terminates. Recall from Section 5.2 that one reason for UDP packets disappearing in the network can be an invalid checksum, detected by either the server's host or the client's host.

- The client adds a sequence number to each packet, so it can ignore duplicate packets and detect missing packets.

Recall from Section 5.3 that the Xerox Packet Exchange Protocol (PEX) performs timeout and retransmission but does not provide duplicate detection. An additional feature that could be added to our example is a checksum. This should be added if the underlying datagram service does not provide it (e.g., if IP were being used for the datagram service). Partridge [1987] describes an implementation of the Reliable Data Protocol (RDP) which uses IP as the network protocol.

The classic method for handling timeout and retransmission is to send a message and wait for N seconds. If no response is received, retransmit and wait another N seconds. After this has happened some number of times, we finally give up. This is a linear retransmit timer. One problem with this technique is that the amount of time required for a datagram to make a round-trip on an internet can vary from fractions of a second to many seconds. Factors affecting the round-trip time (RTT) are distance, network speed and congestion. The congestion can apply to the sending host, the receiving host, and all the intermediate gateways. What we need is a timeout and retransmission algorithm that takes into account the actual round-trip times that can be measured. Much work has been focused on this area, mostly relating to TCP—see Karn and Partridge [1987] and Jacobson [1988b] for the details.

The timeout and retransmission technique we show in the code below is called an adaptive timeout with an exponential back off. The term "adaptive" means that we measure the RTT of every datagram we send, and change our timeout values as the RTT changes. The technique we use is called Jacobson's algorithm. We not only measure the RTT values, but calculate both a smoothed RTT value (SRTT) and the mean deviation of the RTT values. The mean deviation is a good approximation of the standard deviation and is easier to compute.

The term "exponential back off" means that the first time we retransmit a datagram we multiply the timeout value by 2. If another timeout occurs for that datagram, we multiply the timeout by 4, and so on.

Karn's algorithm handles the following condition: a timeout occurs, the packet is retransmitted one or more times, and a response is finally received. When a response arrives for a packet that has been retransmitted

1. Don't use the round-trip time for this packet in updating the estimators. Since the packet has been sent more than once, we don't know which transmission this response refers to. This is called the retransmission ambiguity problem.

2. Since this response arrived before our timeout expired, reuse this timeout value for the next packet. Since the packet was retransmitted one or more times, the last timeout value that was used was multiplied by some power of 2 by the exponential back off. Only when we receive a response to the first transmission of a later packet, will we recalculate the retransmission timeout value based on the RTT measurements.

We'll define some RTT functions that use these algorithms. The following header file, `rtt.h`, is used by the RTT functions.

```
/*
 * Definitions for RTT timing.
 */

#include        "systype.h"
#include        <stdio.h>

#ifdef BSD
#include        <sys/time.h>
#include        <sys/resource.h>
#endif

#ifdef SYS5
#include        <sys/times.h>       /* requires <sys/types.h> */
#include        <sys/param.h>       /* need the definition of HZ */
#define         TICKS   HZ          /* see times(2); usually 60 or 100 */
#endif

/*
 * Structure to contain everything needed for RTT timing.
 * One of these required per socket being timed.
```

```
 * The caller allocates this structure, then passes its address to
 * all the rtt_XXX() functions.
 */

struct rtt_struct {
  float rtt_rtt;        /* most recent round-trip time (RTT), seconds */
  float rtt_srtt;       /* smoothed round-trip time (SRTT), seconds */
  float rtt_rttdev;     /* smoothed mean deviation, seconds */
  short rtt_nrexmt;     /* #times retransmitted: 0, 1, 2, ... */
  short rtt_currto;     /* current retransmit timeout (RTO), seconds */
  short rtt_nxtrto;     /* retransmit timeout for next packet, if nonzero */

#ifdef BSD
  struct timeval      time_start;   /* for elapsed time */
  struct timeval      time_stop;    /* for elapsed time */
#endif

#ifdef SYS5
  long                time_start;   /* for elapsed time */
  long                time_stop;    /* for elapsed time */
  struct tms          tms_start;    /* arg to times(2), but not used */
  struct tms          tms_stop;     /* arg to times(2), but not used */
#endif

};

#define RTT_RXTMIN      2       /* min retransmit timeout value, seconds */
#define RTT_RXTMAX    120       /* max retransmit timeout value, seconds */
#define RTT_MAXNREXMT   4       /* max #times to retransmit: must also
                                   change exp_backoff[] if this changes */

#ifdef  SYS5
long    times();                /* the system call */
#endif

extern int      rtt_d_flag;     /* can be set nonzero by caller for addl info */
```

We now show the RTT functions. These functions are intended to be used by an application that uses datagrams.

```
/*
 * Timer routines for round-trip timing of datagrams.
 *
 *      rtt_init()      Called to initialize everything for a given
 *                      "connection."
 *      rtt_newpack()   Called before each new packet is transmitted on
 *                      a "connection."  Initializes retransmit counter to 0.
 *      rtt_start()     Called before each packet either transmitted or
 *                      retransmitted.  Calculates the timeout value for
 *                      the packet and starts the timer to calculate the RTT.
 *      rtt_stop()      Called after a packet has been received.
 *      rtt_timeout()   Called after a timeout has occurred.  Tells you
 *                      if you should retransmit again, or give up.
 *
```

```
 * The difference between rtt_init() and rtt_newpack() is that the former
 * knows nothing about the "connection," while the latter makes use of
 * previous RTT information for a given "connection."
 */

#include         <sys/types.h>
#include         "rtt.h"

int     exp_backoff[ RTT_MAXNREXMT + 1 ] =
                { 1, 2, 4, 8, 16 };
        /* indexed by rtt_nrexmt: 0, 1, 2, ..., RTT_MAXNREXMT.
           [0] entry (==1) is not used;
           [1] entry (==2) is used the second time a packet is sent; ... */

int     rtt_d_flag = 0;         /* can be set nonzero by caller */

/*
 * Initialize an RTT structure.
 * This function is called before the first packet is transmitted.
 */

rtt_init(ptr)
register struct rtt_struct      *ptr;   /* ptr to caller's structure */
{
        ptr->rtt_rtt   = 0;
        ptr->rtt_srtt  = 0;
        ptr->rtt_rttdev = 1.5;
                /* first timeout at (srtt + (2 * rttdev)) = 3 seconds */
        ptr->rtt_nxtrto = 0;
}

/*
 * Initialize the retransmit counter before a packet is transmitted
 * the first time.
 */

rtt_newpack(ptr)
register struct rtt_struct      *ptr;   /* ptr to caller's structure */
{
        ptr->rtt_nrexmt = 0;
}

/*
 * Start our RTT timer.
 * This should be called right before the alarm() call before a packet
 * is received.  We calculate the integer alarm() value to use for the
 * timeout (RTO) and return it as the value of the function.
 */

int
rtt_start(ptr)
register struct rtt_struct      *ptr;   /* ptr to caller's structure */
{
        register int    rexmt;
```

```
            if (ptr->rtt_nrexmt > 0) {
                    /*
                     * This is a retransmission.  No need to obtain the
                     * starting time, as we won't use the RTT for anything.
                     * Just apply the exponential back off and return.
                     */

                    ptr->rtt_currto *= exp_backoff[ ptr->rtt_nrexmt ];
                    return(ptr->rtt_currto);
            }

#ifdef BSD
            if (gettimeofday(&ptr->time_start, (struct timezone *) 0) < 0)
                    err_sys("rtt_start: gettimeofday() error");
#endif

#ifdef SYS5
            if ( (ptr->time_start = times(&ptr->tms_start)) == -1)
                    err_sys("rtt_start: times() error");
#endif

            if (ptr->rtt_nxtrto > 0) {
                    /*
                     * This is the first transmission of a packet *and* the
                     * last packet had to be retransmitted.  Therefore, we'll
                     * use the final RTO for the previous packet as the
                     * starting RTO for this packet.  If that RTO is OK for
                     * this packet, then we'll start updating the RTT estimators.
                     */

                    ptr->rtt_currto = ptr->rtt_nxtrto;
                    ptr->rtt_nxtrto = 0;
                    return(ptr->rtt_currto);
            }

            /*
             * Calculate the timeout value based on current estimators:
             *      smoothed RTT plus twice the deviation.
             */

            rexmt = (int) (ptr->rtt_srtt + (2.0 * ptr->rtt_rttdev) + 0.5);
            if (rexmt < RTT_RXTMIN)
                    rexmt = RTT_RXTMIN;
            else if (rexmt > RTT_RXTMAX)
                    rexmt = RTT_RXTMAX;
            return( ptr->rtt_currto = rexmt );
}

/*
 * A response was received.
 * Stop the timer and update the appropriate values in the structure
 * based on this packet's RTT.  We calculate the RTT, then update the
 * smoothed RTT and the RTT variance.
 * This function should be called right after turning off the
```

```
 * timer with alarm(0), or right after a timeout occurs.
 */

rtt_stop(ptr)
register struct rtt_struct        *ptr;    /* ptr to caller's structure */
{
        double          start, stop, err;

        if (ptr->rtt_nrexmt > 0) {
                /*
                 * The response was for a packet that has been retransmitted.
                 * We don't know which transmission the response corresponds to.
                 * We didn't record the start time in rtt_start(), so there's
                 * no need to record the stop time here.  We also don't
                 * update our estimators.
                 * We do, however, save the RTO corresponding to this
                 * response, and it'll be used for the next packet.
                 */

                ptr->rtt_nxtrto = ptr->rtt_currto;
                return;
        }
        ptr->rtt_nxtrto = 0;                    /* for next call to rtt_start() */

#ifdef BSD
        if (gettimeofday(&ptr->time_stop, (struct timezone *) 0) < 0)
                err_sys("rtt_stop: gettimeofday() error");
        start = ((double) ptr->time_start.tv_sec) * 1000000.0
                            + ptr->time_start.tv_usec;
        stop = ((double) ptr->time_stop.tv_sec) * 1000000.0
                            + ptr->time_stop.tv_usec;
        ptr->rtt_rtt = (stop - start) / 1000000.0;      /* in seconds */
#endif

#ifdef SYS5
        if ( (ptr->time_stop = times(&ptr->tms_stop)) == -1)
                err_sys("t_stop: times() error");
        ptr->rtt_rtt = (double) (ptr->time_stop - ptr->time_start)
                            / (double) TICKS;       /* in seconds */
#endif

        /*
         * Update our estimators of RTT and mean deviation of RTT.
         * See Jacobson's SIGCOMM '88 paper, Appendix A, for the details.
         * This appendix also contains a fixed-point, integer implementation
         * (that is actually used in all the post-4.3 TCP code).
         * We'll use floating point here for simplicity.
         *
         * First
         *      err = (rtt - old_srtt) = difference between this measured value
         *                               and current estimator.
         * and
         *      new_srtt = old_srtt*7/8 + rtt/8.
         * Then
```

```
 *          new_srtt = old_srtt + err/8.
 *
 * Also
 *          new_rttdev = old_rttdev + (|err| - old_rttdev)/4.
 */

        err = ptr->rtt_rtt - ptr->rtt_srtt;
        ptr->rtt_srtt += err / 8;

        if (err < 0.0)
                err = -err;       /* |err| */

        ptr->rtt_rttdev += (err - ptr->rtt_rttdev) / 4;
}

/*
 * A timeout has occurred.
 * This function should be called right after the timeout alarm occurs.
 * Return -1 if it's time to give up, else return 0.
 */

int
rtt_timeout(ptr)
register struct rtt_struct       *ptr;   /* ptr to caller's structure */
{
        rtt_stop(ptr);

        if (++ptr->rtt_nrexmt > RTT_MAXNREXMT)
                return(-1);                /* time to give up for this packet */

        return(0);
}

/*
 * Print debugging information on stderr, if the "rtt_d_flag" is nonzero.
 */

rtt_debug(ptr)
register struct rtt_struct       *ptr;   /* ptr to caller's structure */
{
        if (rtt_d_flag == 0)
                return;

        fprintf(stderr, "rtt = %.5f, srtt = %.3f, rttdev = %.3f, currto = %d\n",
                    ptr->rtt_rtt, ptr->rtt_srtt, ptr->rtt_rttdev,
                    ptr->rtt_currto);
        fflush(stderr);
}
```

Now we can show the actual function, dgsendrecv, that sends a datagram and waits for a response, handling timeout and retransmission, using the RTT functions shown above.

```
/*
 * Send a datagram to a server, and read a response.
 * Establish a timer and resend as necessary.
 * This function is intended for those applications that send a datagram
 * and expect a response.
 * Returns actual size of received datagram, or -1 if error or no response.
 */

#include         <sys/types.h>
#include         <sys/socket.h>
#include         <signal.h>
extern int       errno;

#include         "rtt.h"          /* our header for RTT calculations */

static struct rtt_struct    rttinfo;     /* used by rtt_XXX() functions */
static int                  rttfirst = 1;
static int                  tout_flag;   /* used in this file only */

int
dgsendrecv(fd, outbuff, outbytes, inbuff, inbytes, destaddr, destlen)
int             fd;              /* datagram socket */
char            *outbuff;        /* pointer to buffer to send */
int             outbytes;        /* #bytes to send */
char            *inbuff;         /* pointer to buffer to receive into */
int             inbytes;         /* max #bytes to receive */
struct sockaddr *destaddr;       /* destination address */
                                 /* can be 0, if datagram socket is connect'ed */
int             destlen;         /* sizeof(destaddr) */
{
        int     n;
        int     to_alarm();                  /* our alarm() signal handler */

        if (rttfirst == 1) {
                rtt_init(&rttinfo);    /* initialize first time we're called */
                rttfirst = 0;
        }

        rtt_newpack(&rttinfo);               /* initialize for new packet */
rexmit:
        /*
         * Send the datagram.
         */

        if (sendto(fd, outbuff, outbytes, 0, destaddr, destlen) != outbytes) {
                err_ret("dgsendrecv: sendto error on socket");
                return(-1);
        }

        signal(SIGALRM, to_alarm);
        tout_flag = 0;                       /* for signal handler */
        alarm(rtt_start(&rttinfo));          /* calc timeout value & start timer */
```

```
                n = recvfrom(fd, inbuff, inbytes, 0,
                              (struct sockaddr *) 0, (int *) 0);
                if (n < 0) {
                        if (tout_flag) {
                                /*
                                 * The recvfrom() above timed out.
                                 * See if we've retransmitted enough, and
                                 * if so quit, otherwise try again.
                                 */

                                if (rtt_timeout(&rttinfo) < 0) {
#ifdef  DEBUG
                                        err_ret("dgsendrecv: no response from server");
#endif
                                        rttfirst = 1;   /* reinit if called again */
                                        return(-1);
                                                /* errno will be EINTR */
                                }

                                /*
                                 * We have to send the datagram again.
                                 */

                                errno = 0;                  /* clear the error flag */
#ifdef  DEBUG
                                err_ret("dgsendrecv: timeout, retransmitting");
                                rtt_d_flag = 1;
                                rtt_debug(&rttinfo);
#endif
                                goto rexmit;
                        } else {
                                err_ret("dgsendrecv: recvfrom error");
                                return(-1);
                        }
                }

        alarm(0);                   /* stop signal timer */
        rtt_stop(&rttinfo);         /* stop RTT timer, calc & store new values */

#ifdef  DEBUG
        rtt_debug(&rttinfo);
#endif

        return(n);                  /* return size of received datagram */
}

/*
 * Signal handler for timeouts (SIGALRM).
 * This function is called when the alarm() value that was set counts
 * down to zero.  This indicates that we haven't received a response
 * from the server to the last datagram we sent.
 * All we do is set a flag and return from the signal handler.
 * The occurrence of the signal interrupts the recvfrom() system call
 * (errno = EINTR) above, and we then check the tout_flag flag.
```

```
    */

to_alarm()
{
        tout_flag = 1;                /* set flag for function above */
}
```

This function can be used by any datagram client, not just those that use UDP. This is because we handle the destination address as an opaque structure, and require the caller to specify its length. Note also that we don't provide any way to return the address of the sender of the datagram that is received. While this feature could have been added, it would require two additional arguments to the function. Since this function is meant to be called by a client process, and not a server process, the client's socket address should be bound to any local address. The only datagrams received for this address should be those specifically sent to it by the server that the client is communicating with.

Note that the `rtt_debug` function optionally prints the timing information for the most recent datagram, based on the variable `rtt_d_flag`. This function is in turn called by the `dgsendrecv` function. We'll show some of this sample output from the `rtt_debug` function in Section 11.3.

Now we'll use the `dgsendrecv` function and redo the UDP client–server example from Section 6.6. Here is the header file, `rudp.h`, used by the client and the server.

```
/*
 * Definitions for more reliable UDP client/server programs.
 */

#include         <stdio.h>
#include         <sys/types.h>
#include         <sys/socket.h>
#include         <netinet/in.h>
#include         <sys/errno.h>
extern int       errno;

#define HOST            "hsi86"
#define MYECHO_SERVICE  "myecho"

#define MAXLINE         255

char          *pname;
```

We modify our client program so that it prepends a long integer sequence number to the front of every datagram that it sends to the server. The UDP server that we showed in Section 6.6 just echoed whatever it received, so the presence of this sequence number has no effect on this server. Our modified client program is

```
/*
 * Example of a more reliable echo client using UDP protocol.
 */

#include        "rudp.h"
```

```
main(argc, argv)
int     argc;
char    *argv[];
{
        int     sockfd;

        pname = argv[0];

        if ( (sockfd = udp_open(HOST, MYECHO_SERVICE, 0, 0)) < 0)
                err_sys("udp_open error");

        doit(stdin, sockfd);            /* do it all */

        exit(0);
}

/*
 * Read the contents of the FILE *fp, write each line to the
 * socket (to the server process), then read a line back from
 * the socket and print it on the standard output.
 */

doit(fp, sockfd)
register FILE           *fp;
register int            sockfd;
{
        int     n, sendlen;
        long    seqsend;
        char    sendline[MAXLINE], recvline[MAXLINE];

        seqsend = 0;            /* initialize sequence number to send */
        while (fgets(sendline + sizeof(long), MAXLINE, fp) != NULL) {
                seqsend++;              /* increment sequence number */
                bcopy((char *) &seqsend, sendline, sizeof(long));
                sendlen = strlen(sendline + sizeof(long)) + sizeof(long);
rexmit:
                if ( (n = dgsendrecv(sockfd, sendline, sendlen, recvline,
                                                                MAXLINE,
                                (struct sockaddr *) 0, 0)) < 0) {
                        if (errno == EINTR)
                                err_sys("client: no response from server");
                        else
                                err_dump("client: dgsendrecv error");
                }

                if (bcmp((char *) &seqsend, recvline, sizeof(long)) != 0) {
                        err_ret("incorrect sequence# received");
                        goto rexmit;    .
                }

                recvline[n] = 0;                /* null terminate */
                fputs(recvline + sizeof(long), stdout);
        }
```

```
        if (ferror(fp))
                err_dump("client: error reading file");
}
```

As mentioned above, we could use the UDP server from Section 6.6, but to test this client we'll change the server to discard packets on purpose, and to modify the sequence number on packets. We also provide an option for the server to add a delay into all its responses. This allows us to further test our round-trip timing calculations.

```
/*
 * Example of server using UDP protocol.
 * This server has a run-time option to discard packets and to
 * modify the sequence number, to allow testing of the more
 * reliable client side.
 *
 *        rudpserv [ -e <delay> ] [ -d <percent> ] [ -s <percent> ]
 */

#include        "rudp.h"
#include        <netdb.h>

int     discardrate = 0;        /* should be [0-100] */
int     delay = 0;              /* delay in responding, seconds */
int     seqmodrate  = 0;        /* should be [0-100] */

main(argc, argv)
int     argc;
char    *argv[];
{
        int                     sockfd;
        char                    *s;
        struct sockaddr_in      serv_addr;
        struct servent          *sp;

        pname = argv[0];
        while (--argc > 0 && (*++argv)[0] == '-')
                for (s = argv[0]+1; *s != '\0'; s++)
                        switch (*s) {

                        case 'd':       /* next arg is discard rate */
                                if (--argc <=0)
                                        err_quit("-d requires another argument");
                                discardrate = atoi(*++argv);
                                break;

                        case 'e':       /* next arg is delay in seconds */
                                if (--argc <=0)
                                        err_quit("-e requires another argument");
                                delay = atoi(*++argv);
                                break;

                        case 's':       /* next arg is sequence mod rate */
                                if (--argc <=0)
                                        err_quit("-s requires another argument");
```

```
                                    seqmodrate = atoi(*++argv);
                                    break;

                            default:
                                    err_quit("illegal option %c", *s);
                    }

        /*
         * Open a UDP socket (an Internet datagram socket).
         */

        if ( (sockfd = socket(AF_INET, SOCK_DGRAM, 0)) < 0)
                err_dump("server: can't open datagram socket");

        /*
         * Find out what port we should be listening on, then bind
         * our local address so that the client can send to us.
         */

        if ( (sp = getservbyname(MYECHO_SERVICE, "udp")) == NULL)
                err_quit("server: unknown service: %s/udp", MYECHO_SERVICE);

        bzero((char *) &serv_addr, sizeof(serv_addr));
        serv_addr.sin_family      = AF_INET;
        serv_addr.sin_addr.s_addr = htonl(INADDR_ANY);
        serv_addr.sin_port        = sp->s_port;

        if (bind(sockfd, (struct sockaddr *) &serv_addr, sizeof(serv_addr)) < 0)
                err_dump("server: can't bind local address");

        echo(sockfd);           /* do it all */
                /* NOTREACHED */
}

/*
 * Read the contents of the socket and write each line back to
 * the sender.
 */

echo(sockfd)
int     sockfd;
{
        int                     n, clilen;
        long                    percent, random(), time();
        char                    line[MAXLINE];
        struct sockaddr_in      cli_addr;

        if (discardrate || seqmodrate)  /* init random number sequence */
                srandom( (int) time((long *) 0) );

        for ( ; ; ) {
                /*
                 * Read a message from the socket and send it back
                 * to whomever sent it.
```

```
                        */

ignore:
                clilen = sizeof(cli_addr);
                n = recvfrom(sockfd, line, MAXLINE, 0,
                             (struct sockaddr *) &cli_addr, &clilen);
                if (n < 0)
                        err_dump("server: recvfrom error");

                /*
                 * First see if we should delay before doing anything.
                 */

                if (delay)
                        sleep(delay);

                /*
                 * See if we should discard this packet.
                 */

                if (discardrate) {
                        percent = (random() % 100) + 1;          /* [1, 100] */
                        if (percent <= discardrate)
                                goto ignore;
                }

                /*
                 * See if we should modify the sequence number of
                 * this packet.
                 */

                if (seqmodrate) {
                        percent = (random() % 100) + 1;          /* [1, 100] */
                        if (percent <= seqmodrate)
                                line[percent & 3]++;
                                /* change one of line[0], [1], [2] or [3] */
                }

                if (sendto(sockfd, line, n, 0, (struct sockaddr *)
                              &cli_addr, clilen) != n)
                        err_dump("server: sendto error");
        }
}
```

There are instances where a datagram service makes more sense than a connection-oriented protocol, and when using a datagram service, as shown above, it doesn't take much effort to make the client robust.

8.5   Summary

Names are typically used in networking to identify hosts and services. In this chapter we described the library functions provided by most Unix systems to convert Internet names into Internet addresses.

Since a large amount of the code required by a client to open a network connection with a server is the same, from one application to another, we then developed four functions that do these repetitive tasks. We provided one function for each of the following protocols: TCP, UDP, SPP, and IDP.

The final section of this chapter added reliability to a datagram service. To do this we first developed some general timing functions that can be used by any datagram application. We used these functions to develop the `dgsendrecv` function, which can be used by any datagram protocol. Finally we used this function in our client–server application from Section 6.6, along with a modified server program, to illustrate a more robust datagram application.

9

Security

9.1 Introduction

When computers were stand-alone entities, security was provided by physical means. Computer rooms were sealed and locked, and punched cards went in one window with line printer listings out another. The magnetic tapes used by programs usually never left the computer room. Even with the change from batch mode to interactive mode, the interactive terminals were usually connected directly to the computer and the terminals and computers were often in a single physical plant. The interactive users had a time-sharing system of some form between themselves, other users, and the hardware. The first change that occurred was the use of dial-in telephone lines for access to these time-shared systems. But this still allowed the normal password security mechanisms used by the time-sharing system to be used. Networking, however, changes all the rules.

First, consider the different types of environments where networking is used. In a *closed* environment, all the systems on the network are under a central administrative control, and the required security features are minimal. In a more *open* environment, some systems might be under a central control, however, other uncontrolled systems could also be connected to the network. Nevertheless, even with uncontrolled systems on the network, we still want to provide network services (line printer access, file storage, etc.) to users. The problem is how the provider of a service determines if a specific client's request for the service is to be honored.

In a university environment, for example, some hosts on the network might be under a central control, but there can be many workstations also connected to the network and some of these might be trusted and others might be untrusted. We'll use the term

420

workstation to mean either a personal computer running an unsecure operating system (such as MS-DOS) or some other type of system capable of running a time-sharing system (such as Unix) but not under central control.

There are three different approaches we can take towards security on a group of networked systems.

1. Do nothing and assume that the system requesting the service is secure. This is feasible in a closed environment where all the systems on the network are under a central control.

2. Require the host to prove its identity, and trust the host's identification of the user on that host. 4.3BSD, for example, uses this approach. The hosts are identified by their Internet address.

3. Every time a service is requested, require the user to enter a password. For example, every time we want to print a file on another system's line printer, we would have to enter a password.

Option 2 is used by 4.3BSD and we'll discuss it in the next section. The third option is used by the Kerberos system that was developed as part of Project Athena at M.I.T., and we'll discuss it in Section 9.3.

9.2   4.3BSD Routines

The network security features provided by 4.3BSD were designed to operate in an open environment where some hosts were designated as trusted. Hosts are identified by their Internet address and trusted hosts are assumed to identify correctly the user on that host requesting a particular service. An integral part of the 4.3BSD security scheme is the concept of reserved Internet ports that we described in Section 6.8. Recall that only a process with superuser privileges can bind a reserved port. But there is nothing to stop any user who knows the root password on a workstation from binding a reserved Internet port. Also, TCP/IP software under MS-DOS typically allows anyone to bind a reserved Internet port, since there isn't the concept of a superuser under MS-DOS.

Pitfalls exist even when some of the hosts are under a central control. For example, if a host that is under central control is taken down for maintenance, there is nothing to stop someone from changing their system to masquerade as the system that is down.

Nevertheless, despite these shortcomings, the network security measures provided by 4.3BSD are widely used. In later chapters we discuss in detail some typical network services. The specific servers that we'll discuss are

lpd   The line printer server that is invoked by a client to print a file on the server's system. We describe this server in Section 13.2.

rshd   The remote execution server. It is invoked by a client to execute a program on the server's system. This server is used by many of the

4.3BSD ''r'' commands: `rcp` and `rsh`, for example. We describe it in detail in Section 14.3.

`rexecd`   Another remote execution server, similar to `rshd`, but a different authentication protocol is used. It is described in Section 14.4.

`rlogind`   The remote login server used by the `rlogin` command. It is described in detail in Chapter 15.

All these servers, other than `rexecd`, base their authentication on the Internet address of the client—both the 32-bit Internet network ID and host ID, and the 16-bit TCP port number.

The `rshd` and `rlogind` servers both require two login names to accompany each request for service.

- The name of the user on the client's system making the request. We'll call this the *client-user-name*.

- The name of the user on the server's system. We'll call this the *server-user-name*.

These two servers also differentiate between a client that is seeking superuser permissions on the server's system (i.e., a server-user-name that maps into a user ID of zero) and other server-user-names.

Figure 9.1 summarizes the different techniques used by some of the 4.3BSD servers to allow or disallow access to a particular server. Each column should be read downwards to see the sequence of steps performed by each server to grant or refuse access to a given client's request for service. Empty boxes are not performed by that server.

`/etc/hosts.equiv` **and** `.rhosts` **Files**

Almost every server shown in Figure 9.1 uses either the `/etc/hosts.equiv` or `.rhosts` file as part of the authentication process. For requests that do not specify a server-user-name of root, the `rshd` and `rlogind` servers first check the file `/etc/hosts.equiv` and if a match is not found, then check the file `.rhosts` in the user's home directory. The home directory used is the one specified in the password file for the server-user-name on the server's system. These two servers also verify that this `.rhosts` file in the user's home directory is really owned by that user. These two servers only check the file `/.rhosts` in the root directory for service requests that are for superuser access on the server's system.

Action	rshd	rshd root	rexecd	rlogind	rlogind root	lpd
Check client's address for reserved TCP port; abort if not.	1	1		1	1	1
Check for password file entry on server for specified server-user-name. Abort if no entry.	2	2	1	2	2	
Allow access if password file entry for server-user-name does not specify a password.	3	3	2			
Encrypt password that was received across the network and compare with value in password file; abort if not equal.			3			
Check /etc/hosts.equiv file for client's system.	4			3		2
Check .rhosts file in home directory of server-user-name for client's system.	5			4		
Check /.rhosts file for client's system.		4			3	
Check /etc/hosts.lpd file for client's system.						3
Prompt user for a password if password file entry for server-user-name requires one, and if none of the above tests passed.				5	4	
Check if root logins allowed on this terminal; abort if not.					5	

Figure 9.1 Security checks performed by 4.3BSD servers.

These files are ASCII text files that list the names of client hosts that are allowed to make requests for services on the server's host. The format of each line of these files is either

> *client-host-name*

or

> *client-host-name   client-user-name*

Lines of the first form allow service requests from the specified host. In this case the server-user-name and the client-user-name must be the same. Lines of the second form also allow service requests from the specified host, if the client-user-name in the file equals the client-user-name passed to the server. Both files, `/etc/hosts.equiv` and `.rhosts` are scanned from beginning to end, looking for a successful match.

There are three different locations for this type of file, each for a different purpose.

1. The `/etc/hosts.equiv` file allows a system administrator to allow access by specific hosts. This allows us, for example, to use the commands such as `rcp` to copy files between these different systems, and login from one of these systems using `rlogin`.

2. The file `/.rhosts`, however, should only list those hosts that the administrator knows to be trustworthy. This is because anyone who appears as the superuser on these remote systems can obtain superuser privileges on the current host.

3. The purpose of the `.rhosts` file in your home directory is to allow you to specify additional hosts that might not appear in the `/etc/hosts.equiv` file, but from which you want to access the current host. If that remote host is untrustworthy, you should be aware that anyone appearing to be you on that system can access your account on the current host.

`ruserok` **Function**

The following function is called to validate a remote user. It is called by the `/etc/rshd` server (which we describe in Section 14.3) and also by the standard login program, `/bin/login`, when it is invoked by the remote login server, `/etc/rlogind` (which we discuss in Section 15.12). Additionally, the `_validuser` function that is part of the file is called directly by the line printer server, `lpd`, which is interested in validating only a host and not a particular user. We describe this printer server in Section 13.2.

```
/*
 * Copyright (c) 1983 Regents of the University of California.
 * All rights reserved.
 *
 * Redistribution and use in source and binary forms are permitted
 * provided that the above copyright notice and this paragraph are
 * duplicated in all such forms and that any documentation,
 * advertising materials, and other materials related to such
 * distribution and use acknowledge that the software was developed
 * by the University of California, Berkeley.  The name of the
 * University may not be used to endorse or promote products derived
 * from this software without specific prior written permission.
 * THIS SOFTWARE IS PROVIDED ``AS IS'' AND WITHOUT ANY EXPRESS OR
 * IMPLIED WARRANTIES, INCLUDING, WITHOUT LIMITATION, THE IMPLIED
 * WARRANTIES OF MERCHANTIBILITY AND FITNESS FOR A PARTICULAR PURPOSE.
 */
```

```
/*
 * From the file: "@(#)rcmd.c   5.20 (Berkeley) 1/24/89";
 */

/*
 * Validate a remote user.  This function is called on the server's system.
 *
 * Called by: /etc/rshd (the server for the rcmd() function);
 *            /bin/login (when invoked by /etc/rlogind for a remote login).
 */

#include         <sys/types.h>
#include         <sys/param.h>
#include         <sys/stat.h>
#include         <stdio.h>
#include         <pwd.h>
#include         <ctype.h>

int     _check_rhosts_file = 1; /* set to 0 by rlogind and rshd, if they're
                                   invoked with -l option */

int                                     /* return 0 if OK, else -1 */
ruserok(rhost, superuser, cliuname, servuname)
char    *rhost;          /* "hostname" or "hostname.domain" of client; obtained
                            by caller: gethostbyaddr( getpeername( ) ) */
int     superuser;       /* 1 if caller wants to be root on this (server's) sys */
char    *cliuname;       /* username on client's system */
char    *servuname;      /* username on this (server's) system */
{
        register int    first, hostlen;
        register char   *src, *dst;
        char            clihostname[MAXHOSTNAMELEN];
        register FILE   *hostfp;

        /*
         * First make a copy of the client's host name, remembering if
         * it contains a domain suffix.  Also convert everything to
         * lower case.
         */

        src = rhost;
        dst = clihostname;
        hostlen = -1;
        while (*src) {
                if (*src == '.') {
                        /*
                         * When we hit a period, check if it's the first period,
                         * and if so, save the length of the host name
                         * (i.e., everything up to the first period).
                         */

                        if (hostlen == -1)
                                hostlen = src - rhost;
                        *dst++ = *src++;
```

```
                } else {
                        *dst++ = isupper(*src) ? tolower(*src++) : *src++;
                }
        }
        *dst = '\0';

        /*
         * If the caller wants to be the superuser on this system, then all
         * we check is the file "/.rhosts".  Else we'll check the file
         * "/etc/hosts.equiv" the first time through the loop below.
         */

        hostfp = superuser ? (FILE *) 0 : fopen("/etc/hosts.equiv", "r");

        first = 1;
again:
        if (hostfp) {
                if (_validuser(hostfp, clihostname, servuname, cliuname,
                                                                hostlen) == 0) {
                        fclose(hostfp);            /* all OK, close file */
                        return(0);                 /* we're done */
                }
                fclose(hostfp);            /* not valid, close file */
        }
        if (first == 1 && (_check_rhosts_file || superuser)) {
                struct stat     statbuff;
                struct passwd   *pwd;
                char            buff[MAXPATHLEN];

                first = 0;
                if ( (pwd = getpwnam(servuname)) == NULL)
                        return(-1);     /* no password file entry */

                strcpy(buff, pwd->pw_dir); /* get home directory of servuname */
                strcat(buff, "/.rhosts");  /* will be "//.rhosts" if root */
                if ( (hostfp = fopen(buff, "r")) == NULL)
                        return(-1);     /* can't open user's .rhosts file */

                /*
                 * If the user is not root, then the owner of the .rhosts file
                 * has to be the user.  Also, the .rhosts file can't be
                 * writable by anyone other than the owner.
                 */

                if ((fstat(fileno(hostfp), &statbuff) < 0) ||
                    (statbuff.st_uid != 0 && statbuff.st_uid != pwd->pw_uid) ||
                    (statbuff.st_mode & 022)) {
                        fclose(hostfp);
                        return(-1);
                }
                goto again;     /* go and call _validuser() */
        }
        return(-1);                /* not a valid user */
}
```

```
/*
 * Validate a user.  This is called from the ruserok() function above, and
 * directly by the lpd server.  When the lpd server calls us, it sets both
 * "servuname" and "cliuname" to point to the same string, so that they'll
 * compare as equal.
 */

int                              /* return 0 if valid, else -1 */
_validuser(hostfp, clihostname, servuname, cliuname, hostlen)
FILE    *hostfp;        /* FILE pointer to "/etc/hosts.equiv", ".rhosts",
                           or "/etc/hosts.lpd" file */
char    *clihostname;   /* client's "hostname" or "hostname.domain" */
char    *servuname;     /* username on this (server's) system */
char    *cliuname;      /* username on client's system */
int     hostlen;        /* -1 if "hostname"; else its "hostname.domain" and this
                           is the #chars in hostname */
{
        register char   *ptr;
        char            *user;
        char            hostname[MAXHOSTNAMELEN];

        /*
         * Read and process each line of the file.
         */

        while (fgets(hostname, sizeof(hostname), hostfp)) {
                ptr = hostname;
                while (*ptr != '\n' && *ptr != ' ' &&
                    *ptr != '\t' && *ptr != '\0') {
                        *ptr = isupper(*ptr) ? tolower(*ptr) : *ptr;
                        ptr++;
                }
                if (*ptr == ' ' || *ptr == '\t') {
                        /*
                         * If the host name was terminated with either a blank
                         * or a tab, then there's a user name following.
                         * We set "user" to point to the first character of
                         * this user name.
                         */

                        *ptr++ = '\0';          /* null terminate host name */

                        while (*ptr == ' ' || *ptr == '\t')
                                ptr++;          /* skip over the white space */
                        user = ptr;

                        /*
                         * We have to skip to the end of the user name, so that
                         * we can assure it's terminated with a null byte.
                         */

                        while (*ptr != '\n' && *ptr != ' ' &&
                            *ptr != '\t' && *ptr != '\0')
                                ptr++;
```

```
                } else {
                        /*
                         * If there's not a user name in the line from the file,
                         * we have "user" point to the null byte that terminates
                         * the host name.  This means the user name is a C null
                         * string.  This fact is used in the strcmp() below.
                         */

                        user = ptr;
                }
                *ptr = '\0';     /* null terminate host name or user name */

                /*
                 * If the host fields match (_checkhost() function below), then:
                 * (a) if a user name appeared in the line from the file that
                 *     we processed above, then that user name has to equal the
                 *     user name on the server (servuname).
                 * (b) if no user name appeared in the line from the file, then
                 *     the user name on the server (servuname) has to equal the
                 *     user name on the client (cliuname).
                 */

                if (_checkhost(clihostname, hostname, hostlen) &&
                    (strcmp(cliuname, *user ? user : servuname) == 0) )
                        return(0);       /* OK */

                /* else read next line of file */
        }
        return(-1);                      /* end-of-file, no match found */
}

/*
 * Validate only the client's host name.
 * We compare the client's host name, either "hostname" or "hostname.domain"
 * to the host name entry from a line of the /etc/hosts.equiv or .rhosts file.
 * If there is not a domain qualifier in the client's host name, then things
 * are simple: the client's hostname has to exactly equal the hostname
 * field from the line of the file.
 *
 * However, domains complicate this routine.  See the comments below.
 */

static char     locdomname[MAXHOSTNAMELEN + 1];
static char     *locdomptr = NULL;
static int      locdomerror = 0;

static int                                  /* return 1 if OK, else 0 */
_checkhost(clihostname, hostfield, hostlen)
char    *clihostname;   /* client's "hostname" or "hostname.domain" */
char    *hostfield;     /* the hostname field from the file */
int     hostlen;        /* -1 if no ".domain", else length of "hostname" */
{
        register char   *ptr;
        char            *index();
```

```
/*
 * If there isn't a domain qualifier on the client's hostname,
 * then just compare the host names.  They have to be equal
 * to return 1 (OK).
 */

if (hostlen == -1)
        return(strcmp(clihostname, hostfield) == 0);    /* 1 if equal */

/*
 * There is a domain qualifier on the client's hostname.  If the
 * client's hostname (everything up to the first period) doesn't equal
 * the host name in the file, then return an error now.
 */

if (strncmp(clihostname, hostfield, hostlen) != 0)
        return(0);      /* not a valid host */

/*
 * If the client's "hostname.domain" exactly equals the entry from
 * the file, then return OK now.
 */

if (strcmp(clihostname, hostfield) == 0)
        return(1);      /* valid host */

/*
 * If the entry in the file is not "hostname." (a terminating period,
 * without a domain name), then return an error now.
 */

if (*(hostfield + hostlen) != '\0')
        return(0);      /* not a valid host */

/*
 * When we get here, the entry from the file is "hostname.",
 * meaning "use the local domain" as the domain.
 * If we've already tried to obtain the local domain and encountered
 * an error, return an error.
 */

if (locdomerror == 1)
        return(0);      /* couldn't get local domain name */

if (locdomptr == NULL) {
        /*
         * Try once to get the local domain name.
         */

        if (gethostname(locdomname, sizeof(locdomname)) == -1) {
                locdomerror = 1;        /* system call error */
                return(0);              /* return not valid */
        }
        locdomname[MAXHOSTNAMELEN] = '\0';
```

```
                              /* assure it's null terminated */

        /*
         * We got the "localhostname.localdomainmame" string from the
         * kernel.  Save the pointer to the "locdomainmame" part,
         * then assure it's lower case.
         */

        if ( (locdomptr = index(locdomname, '.')) == NULL) {
                locdomerror = 1;        /* humm, no period */
                return(0);              /* return not valid */
        }

        for (ptr = ++locdomptr; *ptr; ptr++)
                if (isupper(*ptr))
                        *ptr = tolower(*ptr);
    }

    /*
     * We know the host names are identical, and the entry in the file was
     * "hostname.".  So now we compare the client's domain with the local
     * domain, and if equal, all is OK.
     */

    return(strcmp(locdomptr, clihostname + hostlen + 1) == 0);
                              /* returns 1 if equal, 0 otherwise */
}
```

In the _checkhost function we call the gethostname system call. This system call
returns a pointer to the name of the current host. This name is usually set when the system is booted, using the hostname program under 4.3BSD. It may be either a simple
name such as orange, or a domain-qualified name such as orange.foo.edu. Refer
to Chapter 18 of Comer [1988] for additional information on the domain name system.

9.3   Kerberos

Project Athena was started at M.I.T. in 1983 and its goal was to create an educational
computing environment built around high-performance graphic workstations, high-speed
networking, and servers of various types. The operating system for the project is based
on 4.3BSD. A discussion of the project appears in seven papers published in the Conference Proceedings of the 1988 USENIX Winter Conference. The first of these papers,
Treese [1988], provides an overview.

The authentication system used by Athena is called Kerberos.[†] It is a trusted third-
party authentication service. It is worth an overview here since it is based on 4.3BSD
and it provides an interesting comparison to the techniques discussed in the previous

---

† In Greek mythology, Kerberos is the name of the 3-headed watch dog that guards the entrance to
Hades (the underground abode of the dead).

section of this chapter. This overview is based on the paper by Steiner, Neuman, and Schiller [1988].

Kerberos assumes that the workstations are not trustworthy and requires you, the client, to identify yourself every time a service is requested. For example, every time you want to send a file to a print server, you have to identify yourself to that server. Any system could implement a strict security mechanism such as this, by requiring you to enter a password of some form every time you request a network service. The techniques used by Kerberos, however, are unobtrusive. Kerberos follows these guidelines:

- You only have to identify yourself once, at the beginning of a workstation session. This involves entering your login name and password, and is automatically built in to the standard Unix `login` program.

- Passwords are never sent across the network in cleartext. They are always encrypted. Additionally, passwords are never stored on a workstation or server in cleartext.

- Every user has a password and every service has a password.

- The *only* entity that knows all passwords is the authentication server. This authentication server operates under considerable physical security.

Figure 9.2 shows all the pieces that are involved.

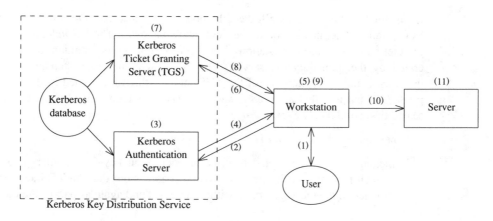

Figure 9.2 Kerberos authentication scheme.

The numbered steps, 1 to 11, in Figure 9.2 do the following:

1. You, the user, walk up to a workstation and login. You enter your login name in response to the normal Unix `login:` prompt.

2. As part of the login sequence, and *before* you're prompted for your password, a message is sent across the network to the Kerberos authentication server. This message

contains your login name along with the name of one particular Kerberos server: the
Kerberos ticket-granting server (TGS).

message = { *login-name, TGS-name* }

Since this message only contains two names, it need not be encrypted. Names are not
considered secret since everyone has to know other names to communicate. You
need to know other login names to send mail. You have to know the names of the
different network services, to use a particular service. We'll see as we progress
through the steps that follow that names are the *only* entities exchanged in cleartext
between the workstation and Kerberos. Everything else is encrypted.

3. The authentication server looks up your login name and the service name (TGS) in
    the Kerberos database, and obtains an encryption key for each. The encryption keys
    used by Kerberos are one-way encrypted passwords, similar to what is stored in the
    password field entry of the normal Unix password file.

4. The authentication server forms a response to send back to the login program on the
    workstation. This response contains a *ticket* that grants you access to the requested
    server (the TGS). The concept of a ticket and what makes up a ticket is central to the
    Kerberos system. Tickets are always sent across the network encrypted—they are
    never sent in cleartext. The ticket is a 4-tuple containing

    ticket = { *login-name, TGS-name, WS-net-address, TGS-session-key* }

    (At the end of this section we'll describe how a ticket also contains a time stamp and
    an expiration date, in addition to the fields shown above.) The *WS-net-address* is the
    Internet address of the workstation. The *TGS-session-key* is a random number gen-
    erated by the authentication server. The authentication server then encrypts this
    ticket using the encryption key of the TGS server (which it obtained in step 3). This
    produces what is called a *sealed ticket*. A message is then formed consisting of the
    sealed ticket and the *TGS-session-key*

    message = { *TGS-session-key, sealed-ticket* }

    This message is then encrypted using your encryption key—your encrypted pass-
    word, which is contained in the Kerberos database. Note that the TGS session key
    appears twice in the message: once within the ticket and again as part of the message
    itself.

5. The login program receives the encrypted message and only then prompts you for
    your password. This cleartext password that you enter is first processed through the
    standard Unix one-way encryption algorithm and the result, what we've called the
    user's encryption key, is used to decrypt the message (TGS session key and sealed
    ticket) that was received. Your cleartext password is then erased from memory. All
    that the workstation has now is a sealed ticket that has been encrypted using the TGS
    encryption key along with a TGS session key. This sealed ticket is incomprehensible
    to the workstation since it was encrypted using the TGS encryption key, that is
    known only to the TGS and Kerberos. The TGS session key is comprehensible to the

workstation, but it is just some random bit string that the authentication server created.

At this point the workstation software saves a copy of the sealed ticket and the TGS session key. Every workstation contains similar information: a sealed ticket for the ticket-granting service along with the corresponding random TGS session key. Even though all the sealed tickets are encrypted using the same encryption key (that of the ticket-granting server), since each ticket contains the name of the user the ticket was granted to, the workstation address, along with a different random TGS session key, each is different.

Now consider the scenario when you request some network service. You might want to read your mail from the mail server, print a file on a print server, or access a file from a file server. We'll call the requested server the *end-server*, to differentiate it from the Kerberos ticket-granting server and the Kerberos authentication server described above. *Every* service request of this form requires first obtaining a ticket for the particular service. To obtain the ticket, the workstation software has to contact the Kerberos ticket-granting server. The following steps, however, are transparent to you when you access the service. This was a goal of Kerberos.

6. The workstation builds a message to be sent to the ticket-granting service. This message is a 3-tuple, consisting of

    message = { *sealed-ticket, sealed-authenticator, end-server-name* }

    The *authenticator* is created by the workstation software, and is a 3-tuple consisting of

    authenticator = { *login-name, WS-net-address, current-time* }

    To seal the authenticator, the workstation encrypts it using the TGS session key that it obtained in step 5. This message is sent to the ticket-granting service. Note that the first two elements of the message are encrypted (sealed) and the last element is a name that need not be encrypted.

7. The ticket-granting service receives the message and first decrypts the sealed ticket using its TGS encryption key. Recall that this ticket was originally sealed by the Kerberos authentication server in step 4 using this same key. From the unencrypted ticket the TGS obtains the TGS session key. It uses this session key to decrypt the sealed-authenticator. There are multiple items for the TGS to check for validity: the login name in both the ticket and the authenticator, and the TGS server name in the ticket. It also compares the network address in the ticket, the authenticator, and in the received message, and all must be equal. Finally, it compares the current time in the authenticator to make certain the message is recent. This requires that all the workstations and servers maintain their clocks within some prescribed tolerance. (We describe some techniques for clock synchronization on an internet in Chapter 10.) The TGS now looks up the *end-server-name* from the message in the Kerberos database, and obtains the encryption key for the specified service.

8.   The TGS forms a new random session key and then creates a new ticket based on the requested end service name and the new session key.

ticket = { *login-name, end-server-name, WS-net-address, new-session-key* }

This ticket format contains the same fields as the one we showed in step 4 earlier. We have just labelled the session key with the qualifier "new" to differentiate it from the TGS session key that was created by the Kerberos authentication service. This ticket is sealed using the encryption key for the requested end server. The TGS forms a message and sends it to the workstation.

message = { *new-session-key, sealed-ticket* }

This message is then sealed using the TGS session key that the workstation knows, and sent to the workstation.

9.   The workstation receives this sealed message and decrypts it using the TGS session key that it knows. From this message it again receives a sealed ticket that it cannot decrypt. This sealed ticket is what it has to send to the end server. It also obtains the new session key that it uses in the next step.

10.   The workstation builds an authenticator

authenticator = { *login-name, WS-net-address, current-time* }

and seals it using the new session key. Finally, the workstation is able to send a message to the end-server. This message is of the same format as the message it sent to the TGS.

message = { *sealed-ticket, sealed-authenticator, end-server-name* }

This message isn't encrypted, since both the ticket and authenticator within the message are sealed, and the name of the end server isn't a secret.

11.   The end-server receives this message and first decrypts the sealed-ticket using its encryption key, which only it and Kerberos know. It then uses the new session key contained in the ticket to decrypt the authenticator and does the same validation process that we described in step 7.

Tickets and *authenticators* are the key points to understand in the implementation of Kerberos. Let's review some of the central points to this scheme and some of the details that we've ignored.

• In order for the workstation to use any end-server, a ticket is required. All tickets, other than the first ticket, are obtained from the TGS. The first ticket is special: it is a ticket for the TGS and is obtained from the Kerberos authentication server.

• The tickets held by a workstation are not comprehensible to the workstation. They are encrypted using the key of the server for whom the ticket is to be used for.

- Every ticket is associated with a session key that is assigned every time a ticket is allocated.

- Tickets are reusable. We didn't mention this above, but once a ticket has been allocated to a workstation for a particular service, that ticket can be reused. Every ticket has a lifetime, typically eight hours. After a ticket has expired, you have to identify yourself to Kerberos again, entering your login name and password. To accomplish this expiration of tickets, each ticket also contains the time the ticket was issued and the amount of time the ticket is valid for.

- Unlike the ticket, which can be reused, a new authenticator is required every time the client initiates a new connection with a server. The authenticator carries a time stamp within it, and the authenticator expires a few minutes after it is issued. This is why we mentioned that all the workstations and servers have to maintain synchronized clocks. The preciseness of this synchronization and the size of the network determines the maximum reasonable lifetime for an authenticator.

- A server should maintain a history of previous client requests for which the time stamp in the authenticator is still valid (i.e., a history of all requests within the past few minutes). This way a server can reject duplicate requests that could arise from a stolen ticket and authenticator.

- Since both the ticket and authenticator contain the network address of the client, another workstation can't use stolen copies of these without changing their system to impersonate the owner's network address. Furthermore, since an authenticator has a short lifetime and is only valid once, the impersonating system has to do all the following before the authenticator expires: steal the ticket and authenticator, assure that the original copies of the ticket and authenticator don't arrive at the specified end-server, and modify its network address to look like the original client.

- Once a server has validated a client's request for service, that client and server share a private encryption key (the session key that is part of the ticket for that client and server) that no one else besides Kerberos knows. If desired, the client and server can encrypt all their session data using this key, or they can choose not to encrypt the session data at all. Kerberos provides the private key, but it is the application's choice whether to use it or not for all the session data.

- During a workstation session, a list of

    { *server-name, sealed-ticket, session-key* }

3-tuples is constructed by the workstation on behalf of the user. The first entry will be for the ticket-granting server, and the others for each end-server contacted by the workstation on your behalf. Someone else cannot legitimately login to the workstation and use entries from this list (should they find this list in memory), since your name (the client to whom the tickets were issued) is contained in the sealed ticket. Also, when you log out from a workstation, this list of 3-tuples is destroyed.

- Once a server has validated a client, an option exists for the client to validate the server. This handles the problem of an intruder impersonating as a server. The client in this case requires that the server send back a message consisting of the time stamp from the client's authenticator, with one added to the time stamp value. This message is encrypted using the session key that was passed from the client to the server. If the server is bogus, it won't know the real server's encryption key, so it won't be able to obtain the session key from the sealed ticket or the time stamp from the sealed authenticator.

We described Kerberos as a trusted third-party authentication scheme. The adjective "third-party" is because Kerberos is a third party to the client and end-server. Trust is inherent throughout the system: You trust Kerberos, if it correctly provides your encryption key. The server trusts you, the client, if you pass the server a ticket that was sealed using the server's encryption key. As with most contemporary computer security schemes, an intruder that successfully obtains a legitimate user's login name and password can impersonate that user.

9.4   Summary

In this chapter we've covered two types of security that can be provided in a network environment. We'll encounter the techniques used by 4.3BSD in most of the remaining chapters of this text. We'll also refer to Figure 9.1 as we discuss each of the servers shown in this figure. These techniques aren't foolproof, but they are in widespread use.

Next, we provided an overview of the Kerberos system. Kerberos provides additional security, compared to 4.3BSD. It is the type of security system that will probably be used in post–4.3BSD systems.

10

Time and Date Routines

10.1 Introduction

A simple example is a client program to obtain the current time and date from a server on the network. In this chapter we describe the Internet daytime protocol and the Internet time protocol and show client implementations of both. We then briefly describe other forms of network clock synchronization.

10.2 Internet Time and Date Client

RFC 867 [Postel 1983d] and RFC 868 [Postel and Harrenstein 1983] define the *daytime protocol* and the *time protocol*, respectively. Both can be implemented using either TCP or UDP.

The *daytime protocol* returns a value that is intended for human consumption, and the protocol is as follows. The server listens on TCP port 13 for a connection. When a connection is made the server responds with the current time and date in ASCII. The server then closes the connection. There is no fixed format for the ASCII string returned by the server, although the RFC recommends that the result string be limited to printable ASCII characters, the space, the carriage return, and the line feed characters. The 4.3BSD server returns a string in the following format:

```
Sat Jun 11 19:17:19 1988\r\n
```

The UDP version is similar, with the server listening on UDP port 13. When the server receives a datagram, it responds with a datagram containing the ASCII string.

The *time protocol* returns a value that is intended for machine consumption. The value returned is a 32-bit binary number, in network byte order, representing the number of seconds since January 1, 1900 GMT. Both the UDP version and the TCP version for this protocol are similar to the protocol given for the daytime protocol above, with the time protocol using TCP port 37 and UDP port 37.

Here is a client program, `inettime`, that prints the time and date using all 4 variations of the two protocols.

- daytime protocol, using TCP
- daytime protocol, using UDP
- time protocol, using TCP
- time protocol, using UDP

Executing

```
inettime hsi
```

generates

```
daytime from host hsi using TCP/IP = Tue Feb 21 09:48:18 1989
time from host hsi using TCP/IP = 2813064498
daytime from host hsi using UDP/IP = Tue Feb 21 09:48:18 1989
time from host hsi using UDP/IP = 2813064498
```

The file `main.c` processes the command line arguments and calls the appropriate functions for every host name that is specified.

```
/*
 * This program is an example using the DARPA "Daytime Protocol"
 * (see RFC 867 for the details) and the DARPA "Time Protocol"
 * (see RFC 868 for the details).
 *
 * BSD systems provide a server for both of these services,
 * using either UDP/IP or TCP/IP for each service.
 * These services are provided by the "inetd" daemon under 4.3BSD.
 *
 *      inettime  [ -t ]  [ -u ]  hostname ...
 *
 * The -t option says use TCP, and the -u option says use UDP.
 * If neither option is specified, both TCP and UDP are used.
 */

#include        <stdio.h>

#define MAXHOSTNAMELEN  64

char    hostname[MAXHOSTNAMELEN];
char    *pname;

main(argc, argv)
int     argc;
char    **argv;
{
```

```
int     dotcp, doudp;
char    *s;

pname = argv[0];
dotcp = doudp = 0;

while (--argc > 0 && (*++argv)[0] == '-')
        for (s = argv[0]+1; *s != '\0'; s++)
                switch (*s) {

                case 't':
                        dotcp = 1;
                        break;

                case 'u':
                        doudp = 1;
                        break;

                default:
                        err_quit("unknown command line option: %c", *s);
                }

if (dotcp == 0 && doudp == 0)
        dotcp = doudp = 1;                      /* default */

while (argc-- > 0) {
        strcpy(hostname, *(argv++));

        if (dotcp) {
                tcp_daytime(hostname);
                tcp_time(hostname);
        }

        if (doudp) {
                udp_daytime(hostname);
                udp_time(hostname);
        }
}

exit(0);
}
```

The file `inettime.c` defines the four functions that contact the appropriate server using the appropriate protocol. These functions use the `tcp_open` and `udp_open` functions from Section 8.3 and the `dgsendrecv` function from Section 8.4.

```
#include     "systype.h"       /* for index() function */
#include     <sys/types.h>
#include     <sys/socket.h>
#include     <stdio.h>
#include     <sys/errno.h>
extern int   errno;

#define MAXLINE            512  /* max line length */
```

```
#define TVAL_SIZE           4    /* 4 bytes in the 32-bit binary timeval */

/*
 * Contact the time server using TCP/IP and print the result.
 */

tcp_time(host)
char    *host;
{
        int             fd, i;
        unsigned long   temptime, timeval;

        /*
         * Initiate the connection and receive the 32-bit time value
         * (in network byte order) from the server.
         */

        if ( (fd = tcp_open(host, "time", 0)) < 0) {
                err_ret("tcp_open error");
                return;
        }

        if ( (i = readn(fd, (char *) &temptime, TVAL_SIZE)) != TVAL_SIZE)
                err_dump("received %d bytes from server", i);

        timeval = ntohl(temptime);
        printf("time from host %s using TCP/IP = %lu\n", host, timeval);

        close(fd);
}

/*
 * Contact the daytime server using TCP/IP and print the result.
 */

tcp_daytime(host)
char    *host;
{
        int     fd;
        char    *ptr, buff[MAXLINE], *index();

        /*
         * Initiate the session and receive the netascii daytime value
         * from the server.
         */

        if ( (fd = tcp_open(host, "daytime", 0)) < 0) {
                err_ret("tcp_open error");
                return;
        }

        if(readline(fd, buff, MAXLINE) < 0)
                err_dump("readline error");
```

```
              if ( (ptr = index(buff, '\n')) != NULL)
                      *ptr = 0;
              printf("daytime from host %s using TCP/IP = %s\n", host, buff);

              close(fd);
}

/*
 * Contact the time server using UDP/IP and print the result.
 */

udp_time(host)
char    *host;
{
        int             fd, i;
        unsigned long   temptime, timeval;

        /*
         * Open the socket and send an empty datagram to the server.
         */

        if ( (fd = udp_open(host, "time", 0, 0)) < 0) {
                err_ret("udp_open error");
                return;
        }

        /*
         * Send a datagram, and read a response.
         */

        if ( (i = dgsendrecv(fd, (char *) &temptime, 1, (char *) &temptime,
                        TVAL_SIZE, (struct sockaddr *) 0, 0)) != TVAL_SIZE)
                if (errno == EINTR) {
                        err_ret("udp_time: no response from server");
                        close(fd);
                        return;
                } else
                        err_dump("received %d bytes from server", i);

        timeval = ntohl(temptime);
        printf("time from host %s using UDP/IP = %lu\n", host, timeval);

        close(fd);
}

/*
 * Contact the daytime server using UDP/IP and print the result.
 */

udp_daytime(host)
char    *host;
{
        int     fd, i;
        char    *ptr, buff[MAXLINE], *index();
```

```
    /*
     * Open the socket and send an empty datagram to the server.
     */

    if ( (fd = udp_open(host, "daytime", 0, 0)) < 0) {
            err_ret("udp_open error");
            return;
    }

    if ( (i = dgsendrecv(fd, buff, 1, buff, MAXLINE,
                            (struct sockaddr *) 0, 0)) < 0)
            if (errno == EINTR) {
                    err_ret("udp_daytime: no response from server");
                    close(fd);
                    return;
            } else
                    err_dump("read error");

    buff[i] = 0;                 /* assure its null terminated */
    if ( (ptr = index(buff, '\n')) != NULL)
            *ptr = 0;
    printf("daytime from host %s using UDP/IP = %s\n", host, buff);

    close(fd);
}
```

It is optional for a host that supports the Internet protocols to provide servers for the time and daytime protocols. 4.3BSD provides these servers in its Internet superserver, inetd, as we mentioned in Section 6.16.

What happens when we use our client program to contact a host that doesn't provide these servers? Since TCP is a connection-oriented protocol, a TCP client gets an error return from its connect system call, which is done by the tcp_open function. 4.3BSD returns a "connection refused" error (ECONNREFUSED). UDP, however, is a connectionless protocol. When we described the connect system call for connectionless clients in Section 6.5, we mentioned that a host should generate an ICMP port unreachable message if it receives a UDP datagram specifying a UDP port for which no process has issued a read for. Notice that our calls to udp_open have a final argument of zero, specifying that the datagram socket is to be connected. When a 4.3BSD host receives an ICMP port unreachable message for a connected UDP socket, it generates a "connection refused" error on the next system call that the process executes for that socket. In our case the next system call will be a recvfrom, which is executed by our dgsendrecv function. If the server's host does not generate the ICMP port unreachable message, our client retransmits until it finally gives up. If the server's host does generate the ICMP message, and if the client's UDP socket were not connected, then our client would still retransmit until it finally gave up, however an ICMP message is generated for every client transmission.

10.3   Network Time Synchronization

The time protocol and the daytime protocol from the previous section are simple and only provide accuracy to the second. The next step is to provide additional accuracy and the ability for a host to act as the server for multiple clients. Two application protocols that provide these features are NTP, the Internet Network Time Protocol, and the 4.3BSD `timed` protocol.

1. NTP, the Network Time Protocol, is defined in RFC 1119 [Mills 1989a] and RFC 1129 [Mills 1989b]. Its purpose is to connect several primary reference sources to widely available locations on the Internet, such as gateways. These gateways act as primary time servers and are each synchronized to some national time standard. Secondary time servers are then run on other gateways or hosts and these secondary time servers communicate with the primary servers using NTP. It is intented that only a few hosts on a LAN would be secondary time servers and these hosts then propagate the time to all the remaining hosts on the LAN. NTP uses UDP to communicate between the clients and servers. NTP contains sophisticated algorithms for synchronizing the clocks on an internet. These algorithms are described in RFC 1119.

2. The clock synchronization routines provided with 4.3BSD are intended for use in a LAN. It is intended to keep the clocks synchronized to within 20 milliseconds. The BSD implementation consists of a program, `timed`, that is run as a daemon. It is typically started by the `/etc/rc` initialization process. One host on the LAN runs as the master and the remaining hosts are designated slaves. The master computes the network time from the times of all the slaves, and the master sends each slave a correction that should be applied to the clock on that host. The slaves can detect if the master disappears and the protocol contains an election algorithm used by the slaves to elect a new master. This election algorithm requires the ability to broadcast, restricting the types of networks on which this protocol can be used.

10.4   Summary

This is a short chapter that describes a simple, yet essential, network application: providing the time and date. We first described the Internet time and daytime protocols, and provided a client program that contacts a server using these protocols. We then introduced the concept of network time synchronization, providing references to the Internet Network Time Protocol and the 4.3BSD time daemon.

Recall from our discussion of Kerberos in Section 9.3, that one requirement of Kerberos is that the workstations all maintain their clocks within some prescribed tolerance. The reason for this is because the Kerberos authenticators contain the current time.

Exercises

10.1   Compare the actual number of network messages exchanged between a client and server using the time protocol, for UDP versus TCP.

10.2   Compare the ICMP timestamp request and timestamp reply messages with the Internet time and daytime protocols. Which are more accurate?

10.3   Explain how Kerberos security can be compromised if the clocks on the network aren't synchronized.

11

Ping Routines

11.1 Introduction

In this chapter we examine the Internet ping program that is distributed with 4.3BSD. The word "ping" stands for Packet InterNet Groper. It is also used to describe the transmission of a sound wave to detect an underwater object. Indeed, the Internet ping program is often used to test the reachability of another site on the internet. We ping the other site by sending it echo requests that it must respond to, if the site is operational.

11.2 Internet Ping Client

The Internet ping program is one that sends an ICMP echo request message to a specified host and waits for a reply. Recall from Section 5.2 that the Internet Control Message Protocol is at the same layer as IP. In Figure 5.1, we show an arrow from the ICMP box to the IP box, since ICMP messages are encapsulated in IP datagrams. A nice feature in using ICMP for sending an echo request is that the operation of ICMP doesn't depend on the higher level protocols—TCP and UDP. Most TCP/IP implementations provide a ping program, and it has proved to be a useful tool.

In this section we'll examine the ping program that is distributed with 4.3BSD. It was originally written by Mike Muuss. This program shows one use of raw sockets in the Berkeley system.

First let's look at the format of an ICMP echo request message. We show a picture of an ICMP message in Figure 11.1, with the IP header preceding the ICMP header.

IP header	ICMP header	ICMP data

Figure 11.1   ICMP message.

The echo request and echo reply messages are only two of the 13 currently defined ICMP messages. Refer to Chapter 9 of Comer [1988] for additional details on the other ICMP messages, along with the official specification for ICMP, RFC 792 [Postel 1981b].

The following structure, from the file `<netinet/ip_icmp.h>` defines the format of an ICMP header.

```
/*
 * Structure of an icmp header.
 */
struct icmp {
    u_char  icmp_type;      /* type of message */
    u_char  icmp_code;      /* type sub code */
    u_short icmp_cksum;     /* ones complement cksum of struct */
    u_short icmp_id;        /* identifier */
    u_short icmp_seq;       /* sequence number */
    char    icmp_data[1];   /* start of optional data */
};
```

The actual structure in the header file is different from this, as it handles the various ICMP message formats using `unions`. The above, however, is the format of the ICMP header for an echo request and its echo reply. The `icmp_type` field specifies the type of the ICMP message. The two values we'll use are `ICMP_ECHO` and `ICMP_ECHOREPLY`. The `icmp_code` field is a subcode for some of the ICMP messages. Neither the echo request nor the echo reply use this field, which should be zero. The next two fields, `icmp_id` and `icmp_seq`, are used by the client, and are returned by the server. We use the identifier field to identify the sender of the ICMP echo requests: we set it to the Unix process ID of the ping program. By doing it this way, if the ping program is being run multiple times on a given host, each instance will generate messages with a unique ID field. We use the next field, `icmp_seq`, as a sequence number to identify each message that a client transmits. There is no guarantee that successive packets travel the same route, so the return packets can arrive in a different order from which they were transmitted. This sequence number field lets us identify each message.

We'll store the time that each message is transmitted in the optional data portion, and use this when the packet is returned to calculate the round-trip time. The time value is stored in the host's byte order, as are the identifier and sequence number fields. This doesn't present a problem, as it is only the sending process that interprets these fields when the message returns. The server doesn't interpret these at all.

The ping program contains two logical portions: one transmits an ICMP echo request message every second and the other receives any echo reply messages that are returned. The transmit portion is simple—it uses the Unix `alarm` system call to enable a `SIGALRM` signal every second. The receive portion is just an infinite loop that receives every ICMP message on a socket.

The semantics of a raw socket under 4.3BSD are as follows. We create a raw Internet socket and specify one particular Internet protocol, ICMP in this case. The kernel prepends an appropriate IP header to any data that we write to this socket. The protocol field in this IP header is the value that we specified when the socket was created. Whenever data is received by the kernel for this protocol, once the kernel has finished with the data, a copy is passed to all processes that have created raw sockets for this protocol. This data contains the IP header that was received. This means that our receive function has to look at each received ICMP message to verify that it is an ICMP echo reply *and* that it was sent by this process. Otherwise the packet can be ignored—it's either some other type of ICMP message or it's an ICMP echo reply that was probably sent by another copy of this program.

First we have the `main` function.

```
/*
 * Copyright (c) 1987 Regents of the University of California.
 * All rights reserved.
 *
 * Redistribution and use in source and binary forms are permitted
 * provided that the above copyright notice and this paragraph are
 * duplicated in all such forms and that any documentation,
 * advertising materials, and other materials related to such
 * distribution and use acknowledge that the software was developed
 * by the University of California, Berkeley.  The name of the
 * University may not be used to endorse or promote products derived
 * from this software without specific prior written permission.
 * THIS SOFTWARE IS PROVIDED ``AS IS'' AND WITHOUT ANY EXPRESS OR
 * IMPLIED WARRANTIES, INCLUDING, WITHOUT LIMITATION, THE IMPLIED
 * WARRANTIES OF MERCHANTIBILITY AND FITNESS FOR A PARTICULAR PURPOSE.
 */

#ifndef lint
char copyright[] =
"@(#) Copyright (c) 1987 Regents of the University of California.\n\
 All rights reserved.\n";
#endif /* not lint */

#ifndef lint
static char sccsid[] = "@(#)ping.c      4.10 (Berkeley) 10/10/88";
#endif /* not lint */

#include        "defs.h"

/*
 *
 *                      P I N G . C
 *
 * Using the InterNet Control Message Protocol (ICMP) "ECHO" facility,
 * measure round-trip-delays and packet loss across network paths.
 *
```

```
 * Author -
 *      Mike Muuss
 *      U. S. Army Ballistic Research Laboratory
 *      December, 1983
 * Modified at Uc Berkeley
 *
 * Status -
 *      Public Domain.  Distribution Unlimited.
 *
 * Bugs -
 *      More statistics could always be gathered.
 *      This program has to run SUID to ROOT to access the ICMP socket.
 */

char    usage[] = "Usage:  ping [ -drv ] host [ datasize ] [ npackets ]\n";
char    hnamebuf[MAXHOSTNAMELEN];
char    *pname;

main(argc, argv)
int     argc;
char    **argv;
{
        int                     sockoptions, on;
        char                    *destdotaddr;
        char                    *host_err_str();
        struct hostent          *host;
        struct protoent         *proto;

        on = 1;
        pname = argv[0];
        argc--;
        argv++;

        sockoptions = 0;
        while (argc > 0 && *argv[0] == '-') {
                while (*++argv[0]) switch (*argv[0]) {
                        case 'd':
                                sockoptions |= SO_DEBUG;
                                break;
                        case 'r':
                                sockoptions |= SO_DONTROUTE;
                                break;
                        case 'v':
                                verbose++;
                                break;
                }
                argc--, argv++;
        }
        if (argc < 1)
                err_quit(usage);

        /*
         * Assume the host is specified by numbers (Internet dotted-decimal)
         * and call inet_addr() to convert it.  If that doesn't work, then
```

```
        * assume its a name and call gethostbyname() to look it up.
        */

       bzero((char *) &dest, sizeof(dest));
       dest.sin_family = AF_INET;

       if ( (dest.sin_addr.s_addr = inet_addr(argv[0])) != INADDR_NONE) {
               strcpy(hnamebuf, argv[0]);
               hostname = hnamebuf;
               destdotaddr = NULL;
       } else {
               if ( (host = gethostbyname(argv[0])) == NULL) {
                       err_quit("host name error: %s %s",
                                               argv[0], host_err_str());
               }
               dest.sin_family = host->h_addrtype;
               bcopy(host->h_addr, (caddr_t) &dest.sin_addr, host->h_length);
               hostname = host->h_name;
               destdotaddr = inet_ntoa(dest.sin_addr.s_addr);
                              /* convert to dotted-decimal notation */
       }

       /*
        * If the user specifies a size, that is the size of the data area
        * following the ICMP header that is transmitted.  If the data area
        * is large enough for a "struct timeval", then enable timing.
        */

       if (argc >= 2)
               datalen = atoi(argv[1]);
       else
               datalen = DEF_DATALEN;

       packsize = datalen + SIZE_ICMP_HDR;
       if (packsize > MAXPACKET)
               err_quit("packet size too large");
       if (datalen >= SIZE_TIME_DATA)
               timing = 1;

       /*
        * The user can specify the maximum number of packets to receive.
        */

       if (argc > 2)
               npackets = atoi(argv[2]);

       /*
        * Fetch our Unix process ID.  We use that as the "ident" field
        * in the ICMP header, to identify this process' packets.
        * This allows multiple copies of ping to be running on a host
        * at the same time.  This identifier is needed to separate
        * the received ICMP packets (since all readers of an ICMP
        * socket get all the received packets).
        */
```

```
        ident = getpid() & 0xffff;

        /*
         * Create the socket.
         */

        if ( (proto = getprotobyname("icmp")) == NULL)
                err_quit("unknown protocol: icmp");
        if ( (sockfd = socket(AF_INET, SOCK_RAW, proto->p_proto)) < 0)
                err_sys("can't create raw socket");
        if (sockoptions & SO_DEBUG)
                if (setsockopt(sockfd, SOL_SOCKET, SO_DEBUG, &on,
                                                      sizeof(on)) < 0)
                        err_sys("setsockopt SO_DEBUG error");
        if (sockoptions & SO_DONTROUTE)
                if (setsockopt(sockfd, SOL_SOCKET, SO_DONTROUTE, &on,
                                                      sizeof(on)) < 0)
                        err_sys("setsockopt SO_DONTROUTE error");

        printf("PING %s", hostname);
        if (destdotaddr)
                printf(" (%s)", destdotaddr);
        printf(": %d data bytes\n", datalen);
        tmin = 99999999;

        setlinebuf(stdout);             /* one line at a time */

        signal(SIGINT, sig_finish);     /* to let user stop program */
        signal(SIGALRM, sig_alarm);     /* invoked every second */

        sig_alarm();    /* start the output going */

        recv_ping();    /* and start the receive */

        /* NOTREACHED */
}
```

The *protocol* argument for the socket system call is obtained by calling the getprotobyname function. This function searches the file /etc/protocols for the specified name, and returns a pointer to a structure that contains the corresponding protocol number.

The header file, defs.h, defines the global variables that are used by more than one file.

```
/*
 * Includes, defines and global variables used between functions.
 */

#include <stdio.h>
#include <errno.h>
extern int      errno;

#include <sys/time.h>
```

```
#include <sys/param.h>
#include <sys/socket.h>
#include <sys/file.h>

#include <netinet/in_systm.h>
#include <netinet/in.h>
#include <netinet/ip.h>
#include <netinet/ip_icmp.h>
#include <netdb.h>

#ifndef INADDR_NONE
#define INADDR_NONE       0xffffffff       /* should be in <netinet/in.h> */
#endif

#define MAXWAIT           10    /* max time to wait for response, sec. */
                                /* used only for final receive */

/*
 * Beware that the outgoing packet starts with the ICMP header and
 * does not include the IP header (the kernel prepends that for us).
 * But, the received packet includes the IP header.
 */

#define MAXPACKET         4096   /* max packet size */

#ifndef MAXHOSTNAMELEN
#define MAXHOSTNAMELEN    64     /* should be defined in <param.h> */
#endif

#define SIZE_ICMP_HDR     8      /* 8-byte ICMP header */
#define SIZE_TIME_DATA    8      /* then the BSD timeval struct (ICMP "data") */
#define DEF_DATALEN       56     /* default data area after ICMP header */

int           packsize;         /* size of ICMP packets to send */
                                /* this includes the 8-byte ICMP header */
int           datalen;          /* size of data after the ICMP header */
                                /* may be 0 */
                                /* if >= SIZE_TIME_DATA, timing is done */

int           verbose;          /* enables additional error messages */

u_char        sendpack[MAXPACKET];    /* the packet we send */
u_char        recvpack[MAXPACKET];    /* the received packet */

struct sockaddr_in    dest;    /* who to ping */
int                   sockfd;  /* socket file descriptor */

char          *hostname;
int           npackets;         /* max # of packets to send; 0 if no limit */
int           ident;            /* our process ID, to identify ICMP packets */
int           ntransmitted;     /* sequence # for outbound packets = #sent */
int           nreceived;        /* # of packets we got back */

int           timing;           /* true if time-stamp in each packet */
```

```
int              tmin;              /* min round-trip time */
int              tmax;              /* max round-trip time */
long             tsum;             /* sum of all round-trip times, for average */
                           /* above 3 times are in milliseconds */

char             *inet_ntoa();     /* BSD library routine */
int              sig_finish();     /* our function to finish up and exit */
int              sig_alarm();      /* our SIGALRM signal handler */
```

The `sig_alarm` function is called once by the `main` function to send the first message, then it is invoked every second as a signal handler. When invoked, it schedules another `SIGALRM` signal after one more second.

```
/*
 * This routine causes another PING to be transmitted, and then
 * schedules another SIGALRM for 1 second from now.
 *
 *      Our sense of time will slowly skew (i.e., packets will not be launched
 *      exactly at 1-second intervals).  This does not affect the quality
 *      of the delay and loss statistics.
 */

#include         "defs.h"

sig_alarm()
{
        int      waittime;

        send_ping();                /* first send another packet */

        if (npackets == 0 || ntransmitted < npackets)
                /*
                 * If we're not sending a fixed number of packets,
                 * or if we are sending a fixed number but we've still
                 * got more to send, schedule another signal for 1 second
                 * from now.
                 */

                alarm(1);

        else {
                /*
                 * We've sent the specified number of packets.
                 * But, we can't just terminate, as there is at least one
                 * packet still to be received (the one we sent at the
                 * beginning of this function).
                 * If we've received at least one packet already, then
                 * wait for 2 times the largest round-trip time we've seen
                 * so far.  Otherwise we haven't received anything yet from
                 * the host we're pinging, so just wait 10 seconds.
                 */

                if (nreceived) {
                        waittime = 2 * tmax / 1000;      /* tmax is millisec */
```

```
                              if (waittime == 0)
                                      waittime = 1;
                      } else
                              waittime = MAXWAIT;

                      signal(SIGALRM, sig_finish);   /* change the signal handler */
                      alarm(waittime);               /* schedule the signal */
              }
              return;
      }
```

The following function writes the ICMP message. It is called at the beginning of the
sig_alarm function above, to send a packet every second.

```
/*
 * Compose and transmit an ICMP ECHO REQUEST packet.  The IP header
 * will be prepended by the kernel.  The ID field is our UNIX process ID,
 * and the sequence number is an ascending integer.  The first 8 bytes
 * of the data portion are used to hold a BSD UNIX "timeval" struct in host
 * byte-order, to compute the round-trip time of each packet.
 */

#include        "defs.h"

send_ping()
{
        register int            i;
        register struct icmp    *icp;           /* ICMP header */
        register u_char         *uptr;          /* start of user data */

        /*
         * Fill in the ICMP header.
         */

        icp = (struct icmp *) sendpack; /* pointer to ICMP header */
        icp->icmp_type  = ICMP_ECHO;
        icp->icmp_code  = 0;
        icp->icmp_cksum = 0;            /* init to 0, then call in_cksum() below */
        icp->icmp_id    = ident;     /* our pid, to identify on return */
        icp->icmp_seq   = ntransmitted++;       /* sequence number */

        /*
         * Add the time stamp of when we sent it.
         * gettimeofday(2) is a BSD system call that returns the current
         * local time through its first argument.  The second argument is
         * for time zone information, which we're not interested in.
         */

        if (timing)
                gettimeofday((struct timeval *) &sendpack[SIZE_ICMP_HDR],
                        (struct timezone *) 0);

        /*
         * And fill in the remainder of the packet with the user data.
```

```
         * We just set each byte of udata[i] to i (although this is
         * not verified when the echoed packet is received back).
         */

        uptr = &sendpack[SIZE_ICMP_HDR + SIZE_TIME_DATA];
        for (i = SIZE_TIME_DATA; i < datalen; i++)
                *uptr++ = i;

        /*
         * Compute and store the ICMP checksum (now that we've filled
         * in the entire ICMP packet).  The checksum includes the ICMP
         * header, the time stamp, and our user data.
         */

        icp->icmp_cksum = in_cksum(icp, packsize);

        /*
         * Now send the datagram.
         */

        i = sendto(sockfd, sendpack, packsize, 0,
                      (struct sockaddr *) &dest, sizeof(dest));
        if (i < 0 || i != packsize)  {
                if (i < 0)
                        err_ret("sendto error");
                else
                        err_ret("wrote %s %d bytes, return=%d",
                                               hostname, packsize, i);

        }
}
```

When using a raw ICMP socket, it is the caller's responsibility to calculate and store the checksum in the ICMP header. This checksum includes the 8-byte ICMP header and any additional data following the header. In addition to this checksum, the kernel computes and stores another checksum in the IP header that it prepends. This IP checksum covers only the IP header.

```
/*
 * Checksum routine for Internet Protocol family headers (C Version).
 *
 * Refer to "Computing the Internet Checksum" by R. Braden, D. Borman and
 * C. Partridge, Computer Communication Review, Vol. 19, No. 2, April 1989,
 * pp. 86-101, for additional details on computing this checksum.
 */

#include        "defs.h"

int                                   /* return checksum in low-order 16 bits */
in_cksum(ptr, nbytes)
register u_short        *ptr;
register int            nbytes;
{
        register long           sum;            /* assumes long == 32 bits */
```

```
u_short                  oddbyte;
register u_short         answer;              /* assumes u_short == 16 bits */

/*
 * Our algorithm is simple, using a 32-bit accumulator (sum),
 * we add sequential 16-bit words to it, and at the end, fold back
 * all the carry bits from the top 16 bits into the lower 16 bits.
 */

sum = 0;
while (nbytes > 1)  {
        sum += *ptr++;
        nbytes -= 2;
}

                              /* mop up an odd byte, if necessary */
if (nbytes == 1) {
        oddbyte = 0;              /* make sure top half is zero */
        *((u_char *) &oddbyte) = *(u_char *)ptr;   /* one byte only */
        sum += oddbyte;
}

/*
 * Add back carry outs from top 16 bits to low 16 bits.
 */

sum  = (sum >> 16) + (sum & 0xffff);    /* add high-16 to low-16 */
sum += (sum >> 16);                     /* add carry */
answer = ~sum;              /* ones-complement, then truncate to 16 bits */
return(answer);
}
```

The following function is called at the end of the `main` function to receive every ICMP message from the socket.

```
/*
 * Infinite loop to receive every ICMP packet received on the socket.
 * For every packet that's received, we just call pr_pack() to look
 * at it and print it.
 */

#include        "defs.h"

recv_ping()
{
        register int        n;
        int                 fromlen;
        struct sockaddr_in  from;

        for ( ; ; ) {
                fromlen = sizeof(from);
                if ( (n = recvfrom(sockfd, recvpack, sizeof(recvpack), 0,
                             (struct sockaddr *) &from, &fromlen)) < 0) {
                        if (errno == EINTR)
```

```
                              continue;          /* normal */
                      err_ret("recvfrom error");
                      continue;
              }

          pr_pack(recvpack, n, &from);

          /*
           * If we're only supposed to receive a certain number of
           * packets, and we've reached the limit, stop.
           */

          if (npackets && (nreceived >= npackets))
                  sig_finish();    /* does not return */
      }
}
```

The comment "normal" when the `recvfrom` is interrupted is because the `alarm` system call that is being used by the sending portion of this program can cause the `recvfrom` to be interrupted. When this happens we just issue the `recvfrom` again.

The `pr_pack` function is called to examine every received message. As mentioned earlier, it has to check if the message is an echo reply that was sent by this process. Note that the received message includes the IP header at the front of the buffer. Also note that we use the actual length of the IP header, which is usually, but not always, 20 bytes, in stepping over the IP header to process the ICMP header that follows.

```
/*
 * Print out the packet, if it came from us.  This logic is necessary
 * because ALL readers of the ICMP socket get a copy of ALL ICMP packets
 * which arrive ('tis only fair).  This permits multiple copies of this
 * program to be run without having intermingled output (or statistics!).
 */

#include        "defs.h"

pr_pack(buf, cc, from)
char                    *buf;    /* ptr to start of IP header */
int                     cc;      /* total size of received packet */
struct sockaddr_in      *from;   /* address of sender */
{
        int                     i, iphdrlen, triptime;
        struct ip               *ip;             /* ptr to IP header */
        register struct icmp    *icp;            /* ptr to ICMP header */
        long                    *lp;
        struct timeval          tv;
        char                    *pr_type();

        from->sin_addr.s_addr = ntohl(from->sin_addr.s_addr);

        if (timing)
                gettimeofday(&tv, (struct timezone *) 0);

        /*
```

```
         * We have to look at the IP header, to get its length.
         * We also verify that what follows the IP header contains at
         * least an ICMP header (8 bytes minimum).
         */

        ip = (struct ip *) buf;
        iphdrlen = ip->ip_hl << 2;          /* convert # 16-bit words to #bytes */
        if (cc < iphdrlen + ICMP_MINLEN) {
                if (verbose)
                        printf("packet too short (%d bytes) from %s\n", cc,
                                    inet_ntoa(ntohl(from->sin_addr.s_addr)));
                return;
        }
        cc -= iphdrlen;

        icp = (struct icmp *)(buf + iphdrlen);
        if (icp->icmp_type != ICMP_ECHOREPLY) {
                /*
                 * The received ICMP packet is not an echo reply.
                 * If the verbose flag was set, we print the first 48 bytes
                 * of the received packet as 12 longs.
                 */

                if (verbose) {
                        lp = (long *) buf;       /* to print 12 longs */
                        printf("%d bytes from %s: ", cc,
                                    inet_ntoa(ntohl(from->sin_addr.s_addr)));
                        printf("icmp_type=%d (%s)\n",
                                    icp->icmp_type, pr_type(icp->icmp_type));
                        for (i = 0; i < 12; i++)
                            printf("x%2.2x: x%8.8x\n", i*sizeof(long), *lp++);
                        printf("icmp_code=%d\n", icp->icmp_code);
                }
                return;
        }

        /*
         * See if we sent the packet, and if not, just ignore it.
         */

        if (icp->icmp_id != ident)
                return;

        printf("%d bytes from %s: ", cc,
                                    inet_ntoa(ntohl(from->sin_addr.s_addr)));
        printf("icmp_seq=%d. ", icp->icmp_seq);
        if (timing) {
                /*
                 * Calculate the round-trip time, and update the min/avg/max.
                 */

                tvsub(&tv, (struct timeval *) &icp->icmp_data[0]);
                triptime = tv.tv_sec * 1000 + (tv.tv_usec / 1000);
                printf("time=%d. ms", triptime);         /* milliseconds */
```

```
                        tsum += triptime;
                        if (triptime < tmin)
                                tmin = triptime;
                        if (triptime > tmax)
                                tmax = triptime;
                }
        putchar('\n');

        nreceived++;      /* only count echo reply packets that we sent */
}

/*
 * Convert an ICMP "type" field to a printable string.
 * This is called for ICMP packets that are received that are not
 * ICMP_ECHOREPLY packets.
 */

char *
pr_type(t)
register int t;
{
        static char     *ttab[] = {
                "Echo Reply",
                "ICMP 1",
                "ICMP 2",
                "Dest Unreachable",
                "Source Quence",
                "Redirect",
                "ICMP 6",
                "ICMP 7",
                "Echo",
                "ICMP 9",
                "ICMP 10",
                "Time Exceeded",
                "Parameter Problem",
                "Timestamp",
                "Timestamp Reply",
                "Info Request",
                "Info Reply"
        };

        if (t < 0 || t > 16)
                return("OUT-OF-RANGE");

        return(ttab[t]);
}

/*
 * Subtract 2 BSD timeval structs:  out = out - in.
 */

tvsub(out, in)
register struct timeval *out;    /* return value through pointer */
register struct timeval *in;
```

```
{
        if ( (out->tv_usec -= in->tv_usec) < 0) {          /* subtract microsec */
                out->tv_sec--;
                out->tv_usec += 1000000;
        }
        out->tv_sec -= in->tv_sec;        /* subtract seconds */
}
```

Finally we have the function `sig_finish` that is called at the end. The program stops when either an interrupt key (`SIGINT`) is entered, or when the specified number of packets have been received.

```
/*
 * Print out statistics, and stop.
 * We're called both when a SIGINT signal is received, or if the
 * specified number of packets have been received.
 */

#include        "defs.h"

sig_finish()
{
        printf("\n----%s PING Statistics----\n", hostname );
        printf("%d packets transmitted, ", ntransmitted );
        printf("%d packets received, ", nreceived );
        if (ntransmitted)
                printf("%d%% packet loss",
                        (int) (((ntransmitted-nreceived)*100) / ntransmitted) );
        printf("\n");
        if (nreceived && timing)
                printf("round-trip (ms)  min/avg/max = %d/%d/%d\n",
                                tmin, tsum / nreceived, tmax );
        fflush(stdout);
        exit(0);
}
```

Here is some sample output from the program:

```
PING hsi (192.43.235.2): 56 data bytes
64 bytes from 192.43.235.2: icmp_seq=0. time=9. ms
64 bytes from 192.43.235.2: icmp_seq=1. time=8. ms
64 bytes from 192.43.235.2: icmp_seq=2. time=8. ms
64 bytes from 192.43.235.2: icmp_seq=3. time=8. ms
64 bytes from 192.43.235.2: icmp_seq=4. time=8. ms
64 bytes from 192.43.235.2: icmp_seq=5. time=8. ms
64 bytes from 192.43.235.2: icmp_seq=6. time=10. ms
64 bytes from 192.43.235.2: icmp_seq=7. time=8. ms
64 bytes from 192.43.235.2: icmp_seq=8. time=8. ms

----hsi PING Statistics----
9 packets transmitted, 9 packets received, 0% packet loss
round-trip (ms)  min/avg/max = 8/8/10
```

These times are typical for a LAN such as an Ethernet. In calculating these round-trip times we use the 4.3BSD `gettimeofday` system call in the `send_ping` and `pr_pack` functions. This system call returns the current time in microsecond units. Under System V, however, we must use the `times` system call. Unfortunately this system call returns a value that is only maintained in 60ths of a second or 100ths of a second, depending on the system. This would restrict the output to 100ths of a second, instead of the milliseconds shown above.

11.3   XNS Echo Client

The following program implements an XNS echo client, as specified by Section 6 of Xerox [1981b]. This client program is based on the datagram client programs that we showed in Section 6.6 for UDP and IDP. To fit the Xerox specification, however, we must now set the packet type field in the IDP header. This 2-byte field is what we called a *bridge field* in Section 5.3. To set this field we must use the SO_DEFAULT_HEADERS socket option. An additional change from the datagram client programs in Section 6.6 is that we now use the reliable datagram function, `dgsendrecv`, that we developed in Section 8.4, to send and receive the datagrams. We also use the `idp_open` function from Section 8.3.

We present this program in this chapter on ping routines since it is a low-level echo program. Its server implementation requires only IDP and none of the higher level protocols, such as SPP. Most Xerox NS implementations provide this service, similar to all TCP/IP implementations providing an ICMP echo function.

In 4.3BSD, the XNS routines in the kernel detect these echo-request datagrams that arrive. If a user process has not arranged to receive these datagrams, then the kernel routines send the echo-reply datagram themselves. This guarantees that a 4.3BSD system always responds to XNS echo requests, similar to a 4.3BSD system always responding to an ICMP echo request.

We could implement this client program just like the Internet ping program from the previous section: send an echo request every second and time the responses. It is left as an exercise for the reader to modify the Internet ping program to use the XNS protocol.

Figure 11.2 shows a picture of the XNS echo packets.

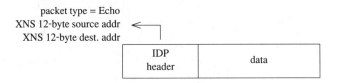

Figure 11.2   XNS echo packets.

The packet type field in the IDP header must be set to 2 (the 4.3BSD constant NSPROTO_ECHO). Then the first 16 bits in the data that follows the IDP header is

considered the "operation field." A value of 1 for the operation field is an echo request
and a value of 2 is an echo reply. The server takes the echo request packets, changes the
operation field to a 2 (echo reply), and returns the packet to the sender. Any data that follows the operation field is returned to the sender (echoed).

Here is the client program.

```
/*
 * This is an example of an XNS echo client.
 * It uses the protocol defined in the Xerox manual "Internet Transport
 * Protocols" (XNSS 028112, Dec. 1981), Chapter 6, pp. 37-38.
 * Notice that on 4.3BSD systems, the kernel handles these requests,
 * if a server isn't listening on the echo port.
 */

#include        <stdio.h>
#include        <sys/types.h>
#include        <sys/socket.h>
#include        <netns/ns.h>
#include        <netns/idp.h>

#define ECHO_SERV_ADDR   "123:02.07.01.00.6d.82:2"
                                /* <netid>:<hostid>:<port> */
                                /* the <port> of 2 is the well-known port
                                   (XNS "socket") for an XNS echo server */

#define ECHO_REQUEST    1       /* client sends a request as operation field */
#define ECHO_REPLY      2       /* server responds with this as op field */
#define OP_SIZE         sizeof(short)
                                /* size of the operation field at front of packet */

#define MAXLINE         255

extern int      rtt_d_flag;     /* defined in the rtt.h header file */
                                /* to print the RTT timing info */
char    *pname;

main(argc, argv)
int     argc;
char    *argv[];
{
        FILE                    *fp, *fopen();
        register int            i, sock;
        struct idp              idp_hdr;

        pname = argv[0];
        --argc; ++argv;

        rtt_d_flag = 1;         /* to print the RTT timing info */

        /*
         * Create an IDP socket, bind any local address and record the
         * server's address.
         */
```

```
        if ( (sock = idp_open(ECHO_SERV_ADDR, (char *) 0, 0)) < 0)
                err_sys("can't create IDP socket");

        /*
         * Set the socket option for default headers on output.
         * We set the packet type field of the IDP header to NSPROTO_ECHO.
         * Note that all the system uses from this structure is the packet
         * type field (idp_pt), and this will be the packet type on all
         * datagrams sent on this socket.
         * Note that the packet type field is a single byte, so there are
         * no byte-ordering problems.
         */

        idp_hdr.idp_pt = NSPROTO_ECHO;              /* packet type */
        if (setsockopt(sock, 0, SO_DEFAULT_HEADERS,
                        (char *) &idp_hdr, sizeof(idp_hdr)) < 0)
                err_sys("setsockopt error");

        /*
         * Main loop.
         * For every command line argument (or stdin) call doit();
         */

        i = 0;
        fp = stdin;
        do {
                if (argc > 0 && (fp = fopen(argv[i], "r")) == NULL) {
                        fprintf(stderr, "%s: can't open %s\n", pname, argv[i]);
                        continue;
                }

                doit(sock, fp);

        } while (++i < argc);

        close(sock);
        exit(0);
}

/*
 * Read the contents of the FILE *fp, write each line to the
 * socket (to the server process), then read a line back from
 * the socket and print it on the standard output.
 */

doit(sock, fp)
register int    sock;
register FILE   *fp;
{
        int     n, sendlen;
        char    *fgets();
        char    sendline[MAXLINE], recvline[MAXLINE];

        while (fgets(sendline + OP_SIZE, MAXLINE, fp) != NULL) {
```

```
                /*
                 * Set the first 2 bytes of the packet to ECHO_REQUEST.
                 */

                *( u_short * ) sendline = htons(ECHO_REQUEST);
                                                /* op = echo request */
                sendlen = strlen(sendline + OP_SIZE) + OP_SIZE;

                if ( (n = dgsendrecv(sock, sendline, sendlen, recvline, MAXLINE,
                            (struct sockaddr *) 0, 0)) < 0)
                        err_sys("drsendrecv error");

                /*
                 * There had better be at least 2 bytes in the datagram, and
                 * the first 2 bytes must be ECHO_REPLY.
                 */

                if (n < OP_SIZE)
                        err_dump("invalid length");
                if ( (*(u_short *) recvline) != htons(ECHO_REPLY))
                        err_dump("unexpected operation field");

                recvline[n] = 0;           /* null terminate */
                fputs(recvline + OP_SIZE, stdout);
        }

        if (ferror(fp))
                err_sys("error reading file");

        fclose(fp);     /* close the FILE, leave the socket open */
}
```

In this program we set the variable `rtt_d_flag` nonzero. This flag is used by the `rtt_debug` function from Section 8.4 to print additional information for each datagram. This function is in turn called by the `dgsendrecv` function which is called by our XNS echo client. Some sample output from this program, when echoing 60-byte lines, is

```
rtt = 0.00724, srtt = 0.001, rttdev = 1.127, currto = 3
rtt = 0.00678, srtt = 0.002, rttdev = 0.847, currto = 2
rtt = 0.00703, srtt = 0.002, rttdev = 0.636, currto = 2
rtt = 0.00746, srtt = 0.003, rttdev = 0.478, currto = 2
rtt = 0.00920, srtt = 0.004, rttdev = 0.360, currto = 2
rtt = 0.00686, srtt = 0.004, rttdev = 0.271, currto = 2
rtt = 0.00679, srtt = 0.004, rttdev = 0.204, currto = 2
rtt = 0.00653, srtt = 0.005, rttdev = 0.154, currto = 2
rtt = 0.00794, srtt = 0.005, rttdev = 0.116, currto = 2
rtt = 0.00706, srtt = 0.005, rttdev = 0.087, currto = 2
```

The server for this sample output is a different host on the same Ethernet as the client. Notice that the round-trip times are between 6 and 9 milliseconds, similar to the Internet ping times shown at the end of the previous section.

11.4 Summary

Whenever a network is installed or changes are made to an existing network, a ping program is the first test that should be run. If the low-level echo reply provided by a ping program doesn't work, then higher level protocols usually won't work either.

In the two ping programs presented in this chapter we've seen lower level socket options in use. The Internet ping program has to use a raw Internet socket and also has to specify the ICMP protocol. The XNS echo client has to set the packet-type field in the IDP header.

Exercises

11.1 The following anomaly has been observed on the Internet: multiple responses to a given ICMP ECHO_REQUEST packet have been received by the sender. Explain some possible causes.

11.2 Investigate the IP "record route" option. Add this feature as an option to the ping program. Consider adding the IP "timestamp" option also. Compare the IP timestamp option with the ICMP timestamp option.

12

Trivial File Transfer Protocol

12.1 Introduction

File transfer is an important part of any network. In this chapter we develop a client and server implementation of the Internet Trivial File Transfer Protocol (TFTP). This program is specified by RFC 783 [Sollins 1981]. Although its specification calls for it to be implemented using UDP, a cooperating client and server pair can be implemented using almost any desired protocol. A complete implementation of a TFTP client and server is shown at the end of this chapter.

TFTP is a simple method of transferring files between two systems. It was designed to be small and easy to implement. It is much smaller than the Internet File Transfer Protocol (FTP) and does not provide many of the features that FTP provides (directory listings, user authentication, etc.). The only service provided by TFTP is the ability to send and receive files between a client process and a server process. TFTP can be used to bootstrap a workstation on a LAN, since it is simple enough to implement in read-only memory. A protocol to do this is given in RFC 906 [Finlayson 1984b] and RFC 951 [Croft and Gilmore 1985].

12.2 Protocol

There are five types of packets used by TFTP, as shown in Figure 12.1. Every packet begins with a 2-byte opcode.

	opcode	string	EOS	string	EOS

read request (RRQ)

opcode	string	EOS	string	EOS
01	filename	0	mode	0
2 bytes	n bytes	1 byte	n bytes	1 byte

write request (WRQ)

opcode	string	EOS	string	EOS
02	filename	0	mode	0
2 bytes	n bytes	1 byte	n bytes	1 byte

data

opcode		
03	block#	data
2 bytes	2 bytes	n bytes, $0 \leq n \leq 512$

acknowledgment (ACK)

opcode	
04	block#
2 bytes	2 bytes

error

opcode		string	EOS
05	errcode	errstring	0
2 bytes	2 bytes	n bytes	1 byte

Figure 12.1   TFTP packet formats.

The RRQ and WRQ packets are sent by the client to the server to receive a file from the server (RRQ) or send a file to the server (WRQ). They specify the filename and its transfer mode. The *filename* and *mode* are both specified in ASCII. Both of these strings are variable length and terminated by a byte of zero, which is shown explicitly in Figure 12.1 as EOS (end of string). The *mode* must be the string netascii or the string octet. (We discuss these two file transfer modes in a Section 12.4.)

A data packet contains the actual *data* bytes along with a block number. The length of the data in a data packet is between 0 and 512 bytes. If the length of the data is between 0 and 511 bytes, that data packet is the final one, otherwise the length is 512 and there is more data to be sent. The block number is used by the other end to acknowledge which packet was the most recently received valid data packet.

The error packet is sent when an error occurs and it contains both an error code and an optional message string providing additional detail on the error condition. The *errstring* is specified in ASCII and is variable length, terminated with a byte of zero. The error codes are given in Figure 12.2. The *errstring* can be present with any *errcode* value, to provide additional information.

All the 2-byte fields in these packets, the *opcode*, *block#*, and *errcode*, are stored in network byte order.

errcode	Description
0	Not defined, see the *errstring*, if present
1	File not found
2	Access violation
3	Disk full or allocation exceeded
4	Illegal TFTP operation
5	Unknown port number
6	File already exists
7	No such user

Figure 12.2 TFTP error codes.

Let's show some examples of the packets that are exchanged between a client and server.

1. The client asks to receive a file from the server.

CLIENT (receiver)		**SERVER** (sender)
RRQ	→	
	←	data, block# 1
ACK, block# 1	→	
	←	data, block# 2
ACK, block# 2	→	
	←	data, block# 3
ACK, block# 3	→	
(etc.)		

With TFTP we use the term *receiver* to designate the end that is receiving the data packets, and the term *sender* for the end that is sending the data packets.

2. The client asks to send a file to the server.

CLIENT (sender)		**SERVER** (receiver)
WRQ	→	
	←	ACK, block# 0
Data, block# 1	→	
	←	ACK, block# 1
Data, block# 2	→	
	←	ACK, block# 2
Data, block# 3	→	
	←	ACK, block# 3
(etc.)		

The protocol handles lost packets by having the sender of the data packets use a timeout with retransmission. If a data packet is lost, the sender eventually times out when an acknowledgment is not received, and retransmits the packet. Note that either the client or the server can be the sender of data packets, depending whether the client has issued a read-request or a write-request. If an acknowledgment packet is lost, the sender of the data packet still times out and retransmits the data packet. In this case the receiver of the data packets notes from the block number in the data packet that it is a duplicate, so it ignores the duplicate data packet and retransmits the acknowledgment. This timeout with retransmission is similar to the enhanced reliability that we added to our datagram example in Section 8.4. For TFTP, the block number in every data packet and in every acknowledgment packet serves to detect missing or duplicate packets.

Most errors other than timeout cause termination of the process. When one side sends an error packet, the other side does not acknowledge it, nor does the side that sent the error packet retransmit it. The most common types of errors are "File not found" for an RRQ request, and "Access violation" for a WRQ request. Once a file transfer is in progress, it is possible to get the error "Disk full or allocation exceeded." Most other errors signify some fatal condition that aborts the transfer.

Note that once the initial RRQ or WRQ packet is sent by the client, the remainder of the protocol is symmetrical between the client and server. Both can send and receive data packets, acknowledgments, and error packets. We'll take advantage of this fact in our implementation to use as much of the source code as possible in both client and server.

There is a subtle problem in the original specification of the protocol. If both the sender and receiver use a timeout with retransmission, and both retransmit whatever they last sent, a condition termed the *sorcerer's apprentice syndrome* results—see RFC 1123 [Braden 1989b]. Figure 12.3 shows a time line of the packets between a client and server.

Assume that the ACK(n) sent by the receiver is delayed somehow in the network. We show this as the dashed arrow in Figure 12.3. What results is that every data packet and every acknowledgment from that point on is sent twice. The file is still transferred correctly, assuming the remainder of the transfer doesn't abort for some other reason.

The correction for this syndrome is for the sender never to retransmit a data packet if it receives a duplicate acknowledgment. If we implement this change, the new time line is shown in Figure 12.4.

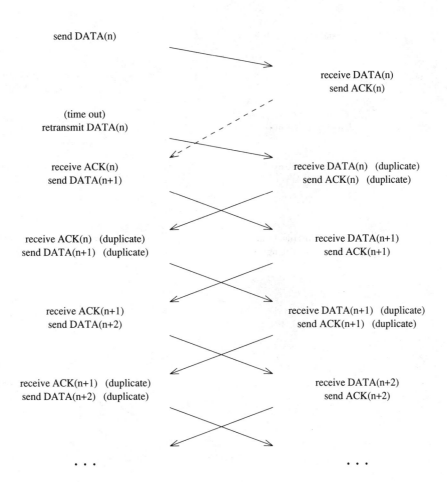

Figure 12.3 Sorcerer's apprentice syndrome.

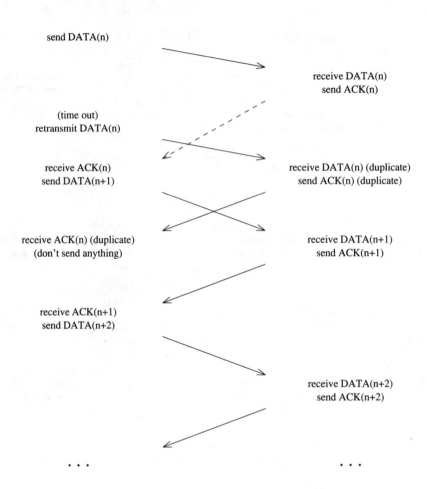

Figure 12.4 Correction for sorcerer's apprentice syndrome.

An effect of this correction is that the receiver of the data packets does not need a retransmission timer. This can simplify the implementation of TFTP if it is being used as a bootstrap program. When TFTP is used as a bootstrap program, it would only issue RRQs and would always be the receiver of data.

This syndrome is typical of a problem that often appears in networking software: some network condition occurs that causes poorly designed software to exacerbate the condition. In this example, the original condition could be congestion somewhere in the network that causes the ACK(n) packet to be delayed. Then the sorcerer's apprentice syndrome is started, and the congestion only gets worse, with all the duplicate packets consuming network resources.

12.3 Security

There is no user validation performed by TFTP. Each implementation must carefully consider the file access rights allowed by RRQ and WRQ operations.

Our strategy is for the server only to allow read access (RRQ requests) for files that have read access to all users (the equivalent of "other-read permission" under Unix). Our server also restricts write access (WRQ requests) to those directories that have write access to all users. Also note that the server is running as a detached process that specifically sets its home directory to '/' (the root directory). It therefore requires that all filenames requested by a client be fully qualified pathnames that begin with a slash.

The 4.3BSD version of the TFTP server is started by the `inetd` daemon, as we described in Section 6.16. Before the `inetd` superserver `execs` the TFTP server, it first sets the login name to `nobody`. This is an entry in the password file that typically has a numeric user ID of 32767, a value that no normal user has. This entry also specifies a numeric group ID that is not normally used (9999). This is done to assure that the server can't access any files that don't allow world access. If the TFTP server didn't specify this login name in the `inetd.conf` file, it would run with superuser privileges.

The intent of TFTP is to provide a simple file transfer program, but its use should be restricted to cooperating host systems.

12.4 Data Formats

There are two formats of data transfer supported by TFTP: netascii and octet. The *netascii* format is used for transferring text files between the client and server. The standard ASCII character set is used and the end of each text line is designated by a carriage return (octal 15) followed by a line feed (octal 12). If there is a carriage return in the text file, it is transferred as a carriage return followed by a null byte (octal 0). The presence of a carriage return followed by any other character is undefined. By defining a standard format for the text file that is being transferred, it is possible to transfer data between two different systems. It is the responsibility of the client and the server to convert the local file representation to and from netascii. For example, to transfer a text file between an IBM 370 and a VAX Unix system, the IBM implementation of TFTP has to convert a file from EBCDIC to ASCII and insert the carriage return, line feed pairs at the end of every line. The VAX Unix system has to look for the carriage return, line feed pairs and remove the carriage return, since Unix stores text files with only a line feed separating the lines. The receiving Unix system also has to look for a carriage return followed by a null, and remove the null.

The *octet* data format is used for transferring binary files. We defined the term octet in Chapter 4 as being an 8-bit quantity, which we call a byte. There are two primary uses of TFTP to transfer binary data between systems. First, two systems with the same architecture can obviously exchange a binary file without any problems. Second, if a system receives a binary file and then returns it to the system that sent it originally, the format of the file must not change. This scenario can be used to provide a file server. The clients send their files to the server in binary mode and retrieve them later in binary mode. The server would not be trying to interpret the contents of the binary file, it is merely storing it on its local filesystem. As long as it uses the same storage technique to store and fetch a binary file, the actual contents of the file won't change.

12.5 Connections

TFTP is unique in its handling of a ''pseudo'' connection between the client and server. TFTP is based on UDP, but UDP is a connectionless protocol. Few files are small enough to be transferred in a single packet, so there must be some way for the client and server to establish a connection between themselves. This allows the multiple packets that comprise a typical file to be handled between a single invocation of a client and server.

Since the server is listening for a UDP packet on a well-known port, the server is initially contacted by the client on that port. But multiple clients can contact the server on that well-known port during the time it takes the server to transfer a single file with some client. We need a concurrent server. But the child process that the server spawns can't continue using the well-known port number. The technique used by TFTP is as follows:

1. The client `binds` a local address that forms a unique socket 3-tuple (protocol, local-address, and local-process) on the client's system.

2. The client sends its first datagram (an RRQ or a WRQ request) to the server at the server's well-known port. This datagram contains the client's address from the previous step, so that the server knows where to send its response.

3. The server receives the datagram from the new client and spawns a child process to handle the request. This child process `binds` a local address on its system that forms a unique socket 3-tuple.

4. The child process sends its response to the RRQ or WRQ packet that the client sent. This datagram is sent to the client's address from step 1 above. The return address in the datagram is the new port that the child process obtained in step 3.

5. The client and server continue exchanging packets, with the client sending packets to the server's address from step 3.

This technique provides a connection between the client and server. It is not a true connection, in the sense of a TCP connection (which is handled by TCP itself) but it is a pseudo-connection that is handled by the two application processes. Since each process, the client and the child server, obtain unique socket 3-tuples on their systems, the association 5-tuple is unique, allowing them to exchange packets only with each other.

This protocol requires that the client look at the return address in the first received response from the server, and use that address as its destination address in all future exchanges with the server.

12.6   Client User Interface

In developing the client implementation of TFTP, a user interface is needed. We have copied the interface provided by the `tftp` program that is provided with the 4.3BSD system. The commands provided to an interactive user are described here.

connect *host* [*port*]
> Set the name of the host for future transfers. This command is optional, since the name of the other host system can be specified in both the `get` and `put` commands (see below). The *host* can be either a dotted-decimal number, or a name.
>
> An optional *port* number can also be specified, but its use depends on the underlying network protocol being used. In a typical UDP implementation, this *port* specifies the UDP port to use to contact the server, instead of the default UDP port of 69.

mode *transfer-mode*
> Set the mode for file transfer. The *transfer-mode* must be either `ascii` (for a net-ascii transfer) or `binary` (for an octet transfer). The default file transfer mode is ascii.

binary
> Set the mode for file transfer to binary (octet). This command is shorthand for `mode binary`.

ascii
> Set the mode for file transfer to ascii (netascii). This command is shorthand for `mode ascii`.

get *remotename localname*
> Get a file from the server. The *remotename* can be either the name of a file, in which case the name of the host is taken from the most previous `connect` command, or it can be of the form *host:filename* to specify both the name of the host and the name of the file. The *host* can be either a dotted-decimal number, or a name. The mode for the file transfer depends on the most previous `mode` command.

put *localname remotename*
> Send a file to the server. The *remotename* can be either the name of a file, in which case the name of the host is taken from the most previous `connect` command, or it can be of the form *host:filename* to specify both the name of the host and the name of the file. The *host* can be either a dotted-decimal number, or a name. The mode for the file transfer depends on the most previous `mode` command.

exit
> Terminate the program. Equivalent to the `quit` command.

quit
> Terminate the program. Equivalent to the `exit` command.

trace
> Toggle the packet tracing facility. By default the packet trace is disabled. It can be

enabled either by this command, or by the −t command line option when the tftp client program is started.

verbose

Toggle the verbose option. By default this option is disabled. It can be enabled either by this command, or by the −v command line option when the tftp client program is started.

status

Shows the current status of the program.

help

Print a 1-line summary of each command. Equivalent to the ? command.

?

Print a 1-line summary of each command. Equivalent to the help command.

We have not implemented the rexmt and timeout commands, which are provided by many client implementations. The reason for this is because the timeout and retransmit algorithm that we use (from Section 8.4) is adaptive and doesn't allow user modification of the initial parameters. Most client implementations still use a linear retransmit timer which can require user modification.

12.7 UDP Implementation

Here we provide the complete source code for a TFTP implementation. The TFTP program consists of both a client program and a server program. Since the client and server protocols are identical, once a file transfer is started, the same source code files and functions are used whenever possible. For the UDP version, the files are listed in Figure 12.5.

Filename	Client	Server	Notes
cmd.c	yes		only client processes user commands
cmdgetput.c	yes		only client processes user commands
cmdsubr.c	yes		only client processes user commands
file.c	yes	yes	client and server file I/O
fsm.c	yes	yes	finite state machine to drive system
initvars.c	yes	yes	initialize all global variables
maincli.c	yes		client main function
mainserv.c		yes	server main function
netudp.c	yes	yes	client and server network I/O—UDP
sendrecv.c	yes	yes	client and server TFTP functions

Figure 12.5   Files for UDP implementation of TFTP.

Throughout these files we use the two identifiers CLIENT and SERVER for code that is conditionally compiled.

First we have the file `defs.h` that contains the global definitions.

```
/*
 * Definitions for TFTP client and server.
 */

#include         <stdio.h>
#include         <sys/types.h>
#include         <setjmp.h>

#include         "systype.h"

#define MAXBUFF          2048    /* transmit and receive buffer length */
#define MAXDATA           512    /* max size of data per packet to send or rcv */
                                 /* 512 is specified by the RFC */
#define MAXFILENAME       128    /* max filename length */
#define MAXHOSTNAME       128    /* max host name length */
#define MAXLINE           512    /* max command line length */
#define MAXTOKEN          128    /* max token length */

#define TFTP_SERVICE     "tftp"  /* name of the service */
#define DAEMONLOG        "/tmp/tftpd.log"
                                 /* log file for daemon tracing */

/*
 * Externals.
 */

extern char      command[];      /* the command being processed */
extern int       connected;      /* true if we're connected to host */
extern char      hostname[];     /* name of host system */
extern int       inetdflag;      /* true if we were started by a daemon */
extern int       interactive;    /* true if we're running interactive */
extern jmp_buf   jmp_mainloop;   /* to return to main command loop */
extern int       lastsend;       /* #bytes of data in last data packet */
extern FILE      *localfp;       /* fp of local file to read or write */
extern int       modetype;       /* see MODE_xxx values */
extern int       nextblknum;     /* next block# to send/receive */
extern char      *pname;         /* the name by which we are invoked */
extern int       port;           /* port number - host byte order */
                                 /* 0 -> use default */
extern char      *prompt;        /* prompt string, for interactive use */
extern long      totnbytes;      /* for get/put statistics printing */
extern int       traceflag;      /* -t command line option, or "trace" cmd */
extern int       verboseflag;    /* -v command line option */

#define MODE_ASCII       0       /* values for modetype */
                                 /* ascii == netascii */
#define MODE_BINARY      1       /* binary == octet */

/*
 * One receive buffer and one transmit buffer.
 */

extern char      recvbuff[];
```

```
extern char      sendbuff[];
extern int       sendlen;            /* #bytes in sendbuff[] */

/*
 * Define the tftp opcodes.
 */

#define OP_RRQ        1              /* Read Request */
#define OP_WRQ        2              /* Write Request */
#define OP_DATA       3              /* Data */
#define OP_ACK        4              /* Acknowledgment */
#define OP_ERROR      5              /* Error, see error codes below also */

#define OP_MIN        1              /* minimum opcode value */
#define OP_MAX        5              /* maximum opcode value */

extern int       op_sent;            /* last opcode sent */
extern int       op_recv;            /* last opcode received */

/*
 * Define the tftp error codes.
 * These are transmitted in an error packet (OP_ERROR) with an
 * optional netascii Error Message describing the error.
 */

#define ERR_UNDEF     0              /* not defined, see error message */
#define ERR_NOFILE    1              /* File not found */
#define ERR_ACCESS    2              /* Access violation */
#define ERR_NOSPACE   3              /* Disk full or allocation exceeded */
#define ERR_BADOP     4              /* Illegal tftp operation */
#define ERR_BADID     5              /* Unknown TID (port#) */
#define ERR_FILE      6              /* File already exists */
#define ERR_NOUSER    7              /* No such user */

/*
 * Debug macros, based on the trace flag (-t command line argument,
 * or "trace" command).
 */

#define DEBUG1(fmt, arg1)       if (traceflag) { \
                                        fprintf(stderr, fmt, arg1); \
                                        fputc('\n', stderr); \
                                        fflush(stderr); \
                                } else ;

#define DEBUG2(fmt, arg1, arg2) if (traceflag) { \
                                        fprintf(stderr, fmt, arg1, arg2); \
                                        fputc('\n', stderr); \
                                        fflush(stderr); \
                                } else ;

/*
 * Define macros to load and store 2-byte integers, since these are
 * used in the TFTP headers for opcodes, block numbers and error
```

```
 * numbers.  These macros handle the conversion between host format
 * and network byte ordering.
 */

#define ldshort(addr)           ( ntohs (*( (u_short *)(addr) ) ) )
#define stshort(sval,addr)      ( *( (u_short *)(addr) ) = htons(sval) )

#ifdef  lint              /* hush up lint */
#undef  ldshort
#undef  stshort
short   ldshort();
#endif  /* lint */

/*
 * Datatypes of functions that don't return an int.
 */

char    *gettoken();
FILE    *file_open();
double  t_getrtime();   /* our library routine to return elapsed time */
char    *sys_err_str(); /* our library routine for system error messages */
```

Next we have the file `netudp.c`. This file defines five functions that are used by both the client and server.

net_init	initialize a network connection (server only)
net_open	open a network connection
net_close	close a network connection
net_send	send a packet
net_recv	receive a packet

By using these functions in the TFTP functions that follow, we can easily replace them with functions that use another protocol. (In the next section we provide a TCP implementation.) This way we can avoid having explicit socket calls, for example, in the generic TFTP functions.

```
/*
 * TFTP network handling for UDP/IP connection.
 */

#include         "netdefs.h"

#include         <netinet/in.h>
#include         <arpa/inet.h>
#include         <errno.h>
extern int       errno;

#ifndef CLIENT
#ifndef SERVER
either CLIENT or SERVER must be defined
#endif
#endif
```

```
int     sockfd = -1;                                    /* fd for socket of server */
char    openhost[MAXHOSTNAMELEN] = { 0 };               /* remember host's name */

extern int                      traceflag;      /* TFTP variable */

#ifdef  CLIENT

extern struct sockaddr_in       udp_srv_addr;   /* set by udp_open() */
extern struct servent           udp_serv_info;  /* set by udp_open() */
static int                      recv_first;


/*
 * Open the network connection.
 */

int
net_open(host, service, port)
char    *host;          /* name of other system to communicate with */
char    *service;       /* name of service being requested */
int     port;           /* if > 0, use as port#, else use value for service */
{
        struct sockaddr_in      addr;

        /*
         * Call udp_open() to create the socket.  We tell udp_open to
         * not connect the socket, since we'll receive the first response
         * from a port that's different from where we send our first
         * datagram to.
         */

        if ( (sockfd = udp_open(host, service, port, 1)) < 0 )
                return(-1);

        DEBUG2("net_open: host %s, port# %d",
                        inet_ntoa(udp_srv_addr.sin_addr),
                        ntohs(udp_srv_addr.sin_port));

        strcpy(openhost, host);         /* save the host's name */
        recv_first = 1;                 /* flag for net_recv() */

        return(0);
}

/*
 * Close the network connection.
 */

net_close()
{
        DEBUG2("net_close: host = %s, fd = %d", openhost, sockfd);

        close(sockfd);
```

```
                sockfd = -1;
}

/*
 * Send a record to the other end.
 * We use the sendto() system call, instead of send(), since the address
 * of the server changes after the first packet is sent.
 */

net_send(buff, len)
char    *buff;
int     len;
{
        register int    rc;

        DEBUG3("net_send: sent %d bytes to host %s, port# %d",
                        len, inet_ntoa(udp_srv_addr.sin_addr),
                        ntohs(udp_srv_addr.sin_port));

        rc = sendto(sockfd, buff, len, 0, (struct sockaddr *) &udp_srv_addr,
                                        sizeof(udp_srv_addr));
        if (rc < 0)
                err_dump("send error");
}

/*
 * Receive a record from the other end.
 */

int                             /* return #bytes in packet, or -1 on EINTR */
net_recv(buff, maxlen)
char    *buff;
int     maxlen;
{
        register int            nbytes;
        int                     fromlen;        /* value-result parameter */
        struct sockaddr_in      from_addr;      /* actual addr of sender */

        fromlen = sizeof(from_addr);
        nbytes = recvfrom(sockfd, buff, maxlen, 0,
                        (struct sockaddr *) &from_addr, &fromlen);
        /*
         * The recvfrom() system call can be interrupted by an alarm
         * interrupt, in case it times out.  We just return -1 if the
         * system call was interrupted, and the caller must determine
         * if this is OK or not.
         */

        if (nbytes < 0) {
                if (errno == EINTR)
                        return(-1);
                else
                        err_dump("recvfrom error");
        }
```

```
        DEBUG3("net_recv: got %d bytes from host %s, port# %d",
                    nbytes, inet_ntoa(from_addr.sin_addr),
                    ntohs(from_addr.sin_port));

    /*
     * The TFTP client using UDP/IP has a funny requirement.
     * The problem is that UDP is being used for a
     * "connection-oriented" protocol, which it wasn't really
     * designed for.  Rather than tying up a single well-known
     * port number, the server changes its port after receiving
     * the first packet from a client.
     *
     * The first packet a client sends to the server (an RRQ or a WRQ)
     * must be sent to its well-known port number (69 for TFTP).
     * The server is then to choose some other port number for all
     * subsequent transfers.  The recvfrom() call above will return
     * the server's current address.  If the port number that we
     * sent the last packet to (udp_srv_addr.sin_port) is still equal to
     * the initial well-known port number (udp_serv_info.s_port), then we
     * must set the server's port for our next transmission to be
     * the port number from the recvfrom().  See Section 4 of the RFC
     * where it talks about the TID (= port#).
     *
     * Furthermore, after we have determined the port number that
     * we'll be receiving from, we can verify each datagram to make
     * certain its from the right place.
     */

    if (recv_first) {
            /*
             * This is the first received message.
             * The server's port should have changed.
             */

            if (udp_srv_addr.sin_port == from_addr.sin_port)
                    err_dump("first receive from port %d",
                                    ntohs(from_addr.sin_port));

            udp_srv_addr.sin_port = from_addr.sin_port;
                            /* save the new port# of the server */
            recv_first = 0;

    } else if (udp_srv_addr.sin_port != from_addr.sin_port) {
            err_dump("received from port %d, expected from port %d",
                            ntohs(from_addr.sin_port),
                            ntohs(udp_srv_addr.sin_port));
    }

    return(nbytes);             /* return the actual length of the message */
}

#endif  /* CLIENT */

#ifdef  SERVER
```

```
#include         <sys/ioctl.h>

struct sockaddr_in       udp_srv_addr;     /* server's Internet socket addr */
struct sockaddr_in       udp_cli_addr;     /* client's Internet socket addr */
struct servent           udp_serv_info;    /* from getservbyname() */

static int       recv_nbytes = -1;
static int       recv_first = 0;

extern char      recvbuff[];                     /* this is declared in initvars.c */

/*
 * Initialize the network connection for the server, when it has *not*
 * been invoked by inetd.
 */

net_init(service, port)
char     *service;        /* the name of the service we provide */
int      port;            /* if nonzero, this is the port to listen on;
                             overrides the standard port for the service */
{
        struct servent  *sp;

        /*
         * We weren't started by a master daemon.
         * We have to create a socket ourselves and bind our well-known
         * address to it.
         */

        if ( (sp = getservbyname(service, "udp")) == NULL)
                err_dump("net_init: unknown service: %s/udp", service);

        if (port > 0)
                sp->s_port = htons(port);          /* caller's value */
        udp_serv_info = *sp;                       /* structure copy */

        if ( (sockfd = socket(AF_INET, SOCK_DGRAM, 0)) < 0)
                err_dump("net_init: can't create datagram socket");

        /*
         * Bind our local address so that any client can send to us.
         */

        bzero((char *) &udp_srv_addr, sizeof(udp_srv_addr));
        udp_srv_addr.sin_family      = AF_INET;
        udp_srv_addr.sin_addr.s_addr = htonl(INADDR_ANY);
        udp_srv_addr.sin_port = sp->s_port;

        if (bind(sockfd, (struct sockaddr *) &udp_srv_addr,
                                  sizeof(udp_srv_addr)) < 0)
                err_dump("net_init: can't bind local address");
}

/*
```

```
 * Initiate the server's end.
 * We are passed a flag that says whether or not we were started
 * by a "master daemon," such as the inetd program under 4.3BSD.
 * A master daemon will have already waited for a message to arrive
 * for us, and will have already set up the connection to the client.
 * If we weren't started by a master daemon, then we must wait for a
 * client's request to arrive.
 */

int
net_open(inetdflag)
int     inetdflag;         /* true if inetd started us */
{
        register int    childpid, nbytes;
        int             on;

        on = 1;

        if (inetdflag) {
#ifdef  BSD             /* assumes 4.3BSD inetd */
                /*
                 * When we're fired up by inetd under 4.3BSD, file
                 * descriptors 0, 1 and 2 are sockets to the client.
                 * We want to first receive the message that's waiting
                 * for us on the socket, and then close the socket.
                 * This will let inetd go back to waiting for another
                 * request on our "well-known port."
                 */

                sockfd = 0;     /* descriptor for net_recv() to recvfrom() */

                /*
                 * Set the socket to nonblocking, since inetd won't invoke
                 * us unless there's a datagram ready for us to read.
                 */

                if (ioctl(sockfd, FIONBIO, (char *) &on) < 0)
                        err_dump("ioctl FIONBIO error");

#endif  /* BSD inetd specifics */

        }

        /*
         * Now read the first message from the client.
         * In the inetd case, the message is already here and the call to
         * net_recv() returns immediately.  In the other case, net_recv()
         * blocks until a client request arrives.
         */

        recv_first = 1;         /* tell net_recv to save the address */
        recv_nbytes = -1;       /* tell net_recv to do the actual read */
        nbytes = net_recv(recvbuff, MAXBUFF);
```

```
/*
 * Fork a child process to handle the client's request.
 * In the inetd case, the parent exits, which allows inetd to
 * handle the next request that arrives to this well-known port
 * (inetd's wait mode for a datagram socket).
 * Otherwise the parent returns the child pid to the caller, which
 * is probably a concurrent server that'll call us again, to wait
 * for the next client request to this well-known port.
 */

if ( (childpid = fork()) < 0)
        err_dump("server can't fork");

else if (childpid > 0) {            /* parent */
        if (inetdflag)
                exit(0);                   /* inetd case; we're done */
        else
                return(childpid);          /* independent server */
}


/*
 * Child process continues here.
 * First close the socket that is bound to the well-known address:
 * the parent will handle any further requests that arrive there.
 * We've already read the message that arrived for us to handle.
 */

if (inetdflag) {
        close(0);
        close(1);
        close(2);
} else {
        close(sockfd);
}
errno = 0;                   /* in case it was set by a close() */

/*
 * Create a new socket.
 * Bind any local port# to the socket as our local address.
 * We don't connect(), since net_send() uses the sendto()
 * system call, specifying the destination address each time.
 */

if ( (sockfd = socket(AF_INET, SOCK_DGRAM, 0)) < 0)
        err_dump("net_open: can't create socket");

bzero((char *) &udp_srv_addr, sizeof(udp_srv_addr));
udp_srv_addr.sin_family      = AF_INET;
udp_srv_addr.sin_addr.s_addr = htonl(INADDR_ANY);
udp_srv_addr.sin_port        = htons(0);
if (bind(sockfd, (char *) &udp_srv_addr, sizeof(udp_srv_addr)) < 0)
        err_dump("net_open: bind error");

/*
```

```
             * Now we'll set a special flag for net_recv(), so that
             * the next time it's called, it'll know that the recvbuff[]
             * already has the received packet in it (from our call to
             * net_recv() above).
             */

            recv_nbytes = nbytes;

            return(0);
    }

    /*
     * Close a socket.
     */

    net_close()
    {
            DEBUG2("net_close: host = %s, fd = %d", openhost, sockfd);

            close(sockfd);

            sockfd = -1;
    }

    /*
     * Send a record to the other end.
     * The "struct sockaddr_in cli_addr" specifies the client's address.
     */

    net_send(buff, len)
    char    *buff;
    int     len;
    {
            register int    rc;

            DEBUG3("net_send: sent %d bytes to host %s, port# %d",
                        len, inet_ntoa(udp_cli_addr.sin_addr),
                        ntohs(udp_cli_addr.sin_port));

            rc = sendto(sockfd, buff, len, 0, (struct sockaddr *) &udp_cli_addr,
                            sizeof(udp_cli_addr));
            if (rc != len)
                    err_dump("sendto error");
    }

    /*
     * Receive a record from the other end.
     * We're called not only by the user, but also by net_open() above,
     * to read the first datagram after a "connection" is established.
     */

    int
    net_recv(buff, maxlen)
    char    *buff;
```

```
int     maxlen;
{
        register int            nbytes;
        int                     fromlen;        /* value-result parameter */
        extern int              tout_flag;      /* set by SIGALRM */
        struct sockaddr_in      from_addr;

        if (recv_nbytes >= 0) {
                /*
                 * First message has been handled specially by net_open().
                 * It's already been read into recvbuff[].
                 */

                nbytes = recv_nbytes;
                recv_nbytes = -1;
                return(nbytes);
        }

again:
        fromlen = sizeof(from_addr);
        nbytes = recvfrom(sockfd, buff, maxlen, 0,
                                (struct sockaddr *) &from_addr, &fromlen);
        /*
         * The server can have its recvfrom() interrupted by either an
         * alarm timeout or by a SIGCLD interrupt.  If it's a timeout,
         * "tout_flag" will be set and we have to return to the caller
         * to let them determine if another receive should be initiated.
         * For a SIGCLD signal, we can restart the recvfrom() ourself.
         */

        if (nbytes < 0) {
                if (errno == EINTR) {
                        if (tout_flag)
                                return(-1);

                        errno = 0;      /* assume SIGCLD */
                        goto again;
                }
                err_dump("recvfrom error");
        }

        DEBUG3("net_recv: got %d bytes from host %s, port# %d",
                        nbytes, inet_ntoa(from_addr.sin_addr),
                        ntohs(from_addr.sin_port));

        /*
         * If "recv_first" is set, then we must save the received
         * address that recvfrom() stored in "from_addr" in the
         * global "udp_cli_addr".
         */

        if (recv_first) {
                bcopy((char *) &from_addr, (char *) &udp_cli_addr,
                                        sizeof(from_addr));
```

```
                  recv_first = 0;
            }

            /*
             * Make sure the message is from the expected client.
             */

            if (udp_cli_addr.sin_port != 0 &&
                udp_cli_addr.sin_port != from_addr.sin_port)
                    err_dump("received from port %d, expected from port %d",
                          ntohs(from_addr.sin_port), ntohs(udp_cli_addr.sin_port));

            return(nbytes);          /* return the actual length of the message */
}

#endif  /* SERVER */
```

The file `maincli.c` contains the `main` function for the client. The `while` loop at the bottom of the `mainloop` function calls the `docmd` function to process every user command.

```
/*
 * tftp - Trivial File Transfer Program.  Client side.
 *
 * See RFC 783 for details.  Also see the "Requirements for Internet Hosts"
 * RFC for additional explanations and clarifications.
 */

#include        "defs.h"
#include        <signal.h>

main(argc, argv)
int    argc;
char   **argv;
{
        register int    i;
        register char   *s;
        register FILE   *fp;

        pname = argv[0];

        while (--argc > 0 && (*++argv)[0] == '-')
                for (s = argv[0]+1; *s != '\0'; s++)
                        switch (*s) {

                        case 'h':                    /* specify host name */
                                if (--argc <= 0)
                                    err_quit("-h requires another argument");
                                strcpy(hostname, *++argv);
                                break;

                        case 't':
                                traceflag = 1;
                                break;
```

```
                                case 'v':
                                        verboseflag = 1;
                                        break;

                                default:
                                        err_quit("unknown command line option: %c", *s);
                                }

        /*
         * For each filename argument, execute the tftp commands in
         * that file.  If no filename arguments were specified on the
         * command line, we process the standard input by default.
         */

        i = 0;
        fp = stdin;
        do {
                if (argc > 0 && (fp = fopen(argv[i], "r")) == NULL) {
                        err_sys("%s: can't open %s for reading", argv[i]);
                }

                mainloop(fp);                   /* process a given file */

        } while (++i < argc);

        exit(0);
}

mainloop(fp)
FILE    *fp;
{
        int             sig_intr();

        if (signal(SIGINT, SIG_IGN) != SIG_IGN)
                signal(SIGINT, sig_intr);

        /*
         * Main loop.  Read a command and execute it.
         * This loop is terminated by a "quit" command, or an
         * end-of-file on the command stream.
         */

        if (setjmp(jmp_mainloop) < 0) {
                err_ret("Timeout");
        }

        if (interactive)
                printf("%s", prompt);

        while (getline(fp)) {
                if (gettoken(command) != NULL)
                        docmd(command);

                if (interactive)
```

```
                      printf("%s", prompt);
         }
}

/*
 * INTR signal handler.  Just return to the main loop above.
 * In case we were waiting for a read to complete, turn off any possible
 * alarm clock interrupts.
 *
 * Note that with TFTP, if the client aborts a file transfer (such as with
 * the interrupt signal), the server is not notified.  The protocol counts
 * on the server eventually timing out and exiting.
 */

int
sig_intr()
{
        signal(SIGALRM, SIG_IGN);        /* first ignore the signal */
        alarm(0);                        /* then assure alarm is off */

        longjmp(jmp_mainloop, 1);
        /* NOTREACHED */
}
```

The following file cmd.h, is a header file that is used by the files cmdsubr.c and cmd.c.

```
/*
 * Header file for user command processing functions.
 */

#include        "defs.h"

extern char     temptoken[];    /* temporary token for anyone to use */

typedef struct Cmds {
  char  *cmd_name;                      /* actual command string */
  int   (*cmd_func)();                  /* pointer to function */
} Cmds;

extern Cmds     commands[];
extern int      ncmds;          /* number of elements in array */
```

The file cmdsubr.c contains the miscellaneous functions for command processing. The function docmd that is called from the main loop is in this file.

```
/*
 * Miscellaneous functions for user command processing.
 */

#include        "cmd.h"

        /* all of the following functions are in cmd.c */
int     cmd_ascii(), cmd_binary(), cmd_connect(), cmd_exit(),
```

```
            cmd_get(), cmd_help(), cmd_mode(), cmd_put(),
            cmd_status(), cmd_trace(), cmd_verbose();

Cmds    commands[] = {   /* keep in alphabetical order for binary search */
                "?",            cmd_help,
                "ascii",        cmd_ascii,
                "binary",       cmd_binary,
                "connect",      cmd_connect,
                "exit",         cmd_exit,
                "get",          cmd_get,
                "help",         cmd_help,
                "mode",         cmd_mode,
                "put",          cmd_put,
                "quit",         cmd_exit,
                "status",       cmd_status,
                "trace",        cmd_trace,
                "verbose",      cmd_verbose,
};
#define NCMDS   (sizeof(commands) / sizeof(Cmds))

int     ncmds = NCMDS;

static char     line[MAXLINE] = { 0 };
static char     *lineptr = NULL;

/*
 * Fetch the next command line.
 * For interactive use or batch use, the lines are read from a file.
 *
 * Return 1 if OK, else 0 on error or end-of-file.
 */

int
getline(fp)
FILE    *fp;
{
        if (fgets(line, MAXLINE, fp) == NULL)
                return(0);                      /* error or end-of-file */
        lineptr = line;

        return(1);
}

/*
 * Fetch the next token from the input stream.
 * We use the line that was set up in the most previous call to
 * getline().
 *
 * Return a pointer to the token (the argument), or NULL if no more exist.
 */

char *
gettoken(token)
char    token[];
```

```
{
        register int     c;
        register char    *tokenptr;

        while ((c = *lineptr++) == ' ' || c == '\t')
                ;                       /* skip leading white space */

        if (c == '\0' || c == '\n')
                return(NULL);    /* nothing there */

        tokenptr = token;
        *tokenptr++ = c;              /* first char of token */

        /*
         * Now collect everything up to the next space, tab, newline, or null.
         */

        while ((c = *lineptr++) != ' ' && c != '\t' && c != '\n' && c != '\0')
                *tokenptr++ = c;

        *tokenptr = 0;                /* null terminate token */
        return(token);
}

/*
 * Verify that there aren't any more tokens left on a command line.
 */

checkend()
{
        if (gettoken(temptoken) != NULL)
                err_cmd("trailing garbage");
}

/*
 * Execute a command.
 * Call the appropriate function.  If all goes well, that function will
 * return, otherwise that function may call an error handler, which will
 * call longjmp() and branch back to the main command processing loop.
 */

docmd(cmdptr)
char    *cmdptr;
{
        register int     i;

        if ( (i = binary(cmdptr, ncmds)) < 0)
                err_cmd(cmdptr);

        (*commands[i].cmd_func)();

        checkend();
}
```

```
/*
 * Perform a binary search of the command table
 * to see if a given token is a command.
 */

binary(word, n)
char    *word;
int     n;
{
        register int    low, high, mid, cond;

        low  = 0;
        high = n - 1;
        while (low <= high) {
                mid = (low + high) / 2;
                if ( (cond = strcmp(word, commands[mid].cmd_name)) < 0)
                        high = mid - 1;
                else if (cond > 0)
                        low = mid + 1;
                else
                        return(mid);    ' /* found it, return index in array */
        }
        return(-1);      /* not found */
}

/*
 * Take a "host:file" character string and separate the "host"
 * portion from the "file" portion.
 */

striphost(fname, hname)
char    *fname;          /* input:  "host:file" or just "file" */
char    *hname;          /* store "host" name here, if present */
{
        char            *index();
        register char   *ptr1, *ptr2;

        if ( (ptr1 = index(fname, ':')) == NULL)
                return;          /* there is not a "host:" present */

        /*
         * Copy the entire "host:file" into the hname array,
         * then replace the colon with a null byte.
         */

        strcpy(hname, fname);
        ptr2 = index(hname, ':');
        *ptr2 = 0;       /* null terminates the "host" string */

        /*
         * Now move the "file" string left in the fname array,
         * removing the "host:" portion.
         */
```

```
        strcpy(fname, ptr1 + 1);              /* ptr1 + 1 to skip over the ':' */
}

/*
 * User command error.
 * Print out the command line too, for information.
 */

err_cmd(str)
char    *str;             /* may be a 0-length string, i.e., "" */
{
        fprintf(stderr, "%s: '%s' command error", pname, command);
        if (strlen(str) > 0)
                fprintf(stderr, ": %s", str);
        fprintf(stderr, "\n");
        fflush(stderr);

        longjmp(jmp_mainloop, 1);           /* 1 -> not a timeout, we've already
                                               printed our error message */
}
```

The file `cmd.c` contains one function for every user command. These functions are called by the `docmd` function from the previous file.

```
/*
 * Command processing functions, one per command.
 * (Only the client side processes user commands.)
 * In alphabetical order.
 */

#include        "cmd.h"

/*
 * ascii
 *
 *      Equivalent to "mode ascii".
 */

cmd_ascii()
{
        modetype = MODE_ASCII;
}

/*
 * binary
 *
 *      Equivalent to "mode binary".
 */

cmd_binary()
{
        modetype = MODE_BINARY;
}
```

```
/*
 * connect <hostname> [ <port> ]
 *
 *      Set the hostname and optional port number for future transfers.
 *      The port is the well-known port number of the tftp server on
 *      the other system.  Normally this will default to the value
 *      specified in /etc/services (69).
 */

cmd_connect()
{
        register int    val;

        if (gettoken(hostname) == NULL)
                err_cmd("missing hostname");

        if (gettoken(temptoken) == NULL)
                return;
        val = atoi(temptoken);
        if (val < 0)
                err_cmd("invalid port number");
        port = val;
}

/*
 * exit
 */

cmd_exit()
{
        exit(0);
}

/*
 * get <remotefilename> <localfilename>
 *
 *      Note that the <remotefilename> may be of the form <host>:<filename>
 *      to specify the host also.
 */

cmd_get()
{
        char    remfname[MAXFILENAME], locfname[MAXFILENAME];
        char    *index();

        if (gettoken(remfname) == NULL)
                err_cmd("the remote filename must be specified");
        if (gettoken(locfname) == NULL)
                err_cmd("the local filename must be specified");

        if (index(locfname, ':') != NULL)
                err_cmd("can't have 'host:' in local filename");

        striphost(remfname, hostname);  /* check for "host:" and process */
```

```
            if (hostname[0] == 0)
                    err_cmd("no host has been specified");

            do_get(remfname, locfname);
}

/*
 * help
 */

cmd_help()
{
            register int    i;

            for (i = 0; i < ncmds; i++) {
                    printf("  %s\n", commands[i].cmd_name);
            }
}

/*
 * mode ascii
 * mode binary
 *
 *      Set the mode for file transfers.
 */

cmd_mode()
{
            if (gettoken(temptoken) == NULL) {
                    err_cmd("a mode type must be specified");
            } else {
                    if (strcmp(temptoken, "ascii") == 0)
                            modetype = MODE_ASCII;
                    else if (strcmp(temptoken, "binary") == 0)
                            modetype = MODE_BINARY;
                    else
                            err_cmd("mode must be 'ascii' or 'binary'");
            }
}

/*
 * put <localfilename> <remotefilename>
 *
 *      Note that the <remotefilename> may be of the form <host>:<filename>
 *      to specify the host also.
 */

cmd_put()
{
            char    remfname[MAXFILENAME], locfname[MAXFILENAME];

            if (gettoken(locfname) == NULL)
                    err_cmd("the local filename must be specified");
            if (gettoken(remfname) == NULL)
```

```
                        err_cmd("the remote filename must be specified");

        if (index(locfname, ':') != NULL)
                err_cmd("can't have 'host:' in local filename");

        striphost(remfname, hostname);   /* check for "host:" and process */
        if (hostname[0] == 0)
                err_cmd("no host has been specified");

        do_put(remfname, locfname);
}

/*
 * Show current status.
 */

cmd_status()
{
        if (connected)
                printf("Connected\n");
        else
                printf("Not connected\n");

        printf("mode = ");
        switch (modetype) {
        case MODE_ASCII:        printf("netascii");             break;
        case MODE_BINARY:       printf("octet (binary)");       break;
        default:
                err_dump("unknown modetype");
        }

        printf(", verbose = %s", verboseflag ? "on" : "off");
        printf(", trace = %s\n", traceflag ? "on" : "off");
}

/*
 * Toggle debug mode.
 */

cmd_trace()
{
        traceflag = !traceflag;
}

/*
 * Toggle verbose mode.
 */

cmd_verbose()
{
        verboseflag = !verboseflag;
}
```

The file `cmdgetput.c` has additional processing for the `get` and `put` commands.

```
/*
 * File get/put processing.
 *
 * This is the way the client side gets started - either the user
 * wants to get a file (generates a RRQ command to the server)
 * or the user wants to put a file (generates a WRQ command to the
 * server).  Once either the RRQ or the WRQ command is sent,
 * the finite state machine takes over the transmission.
 */

#include        "defs.h"

/*
 * Execute a get command - read a remote file and store on the local system.
 */

do_get(remfname, locfname)
char    *remfname;
char    *locfname;
{
        if ( (localfp = file_open(locfname, "w", 1)) == NULL) {
                err_ret("can't fopen %s for writing", locfname);
                return;
        }

        if (net_open(hostname, TFTP_SERVICE, port) < 0)
                return;

        totnbytes = 0;
        t_start();                      /* start timer for statistics */

        send_RQ(OP_RRQ, remfname, modetype);

        fsm_loop(OP_RRQ);

        t_stop();                       /* stop timer for statistics */

        net_close();

        file_close(localfp);

        printf("Received %ld bytes in %.1f seconds\n", totnbytes, t_getrtime());
                                /* print stastics */
}

/*
 * Execute a put command - send a local file to the remote system.
 */

do_put(remfname, locfname)
char    *remfname;
char    *locfname;
{
```

```
            if ( (localfp = file_open(locfname, "r", 0)) == NULL) {
                    err_ret("can't fopen %s for reading", locfname);
                    return;
            }

            if (net_open(hostname, TFTP_SERVICE, port) < 0)
                    return;

            totnbytes = 0;
            t_start();                      /* start timer for statistics */

            lastsend = MAXDATA;
            send_RQ(OP_WRQ, remfname, modetype);

            fsm_loop(OP_WRQ);

            t_stop();                       /* stop timer for statistics */

            net_close();

            file_close(localfp);

            printf("Sent %ld bytes in %.1f seconds\n", totnbytes, t_getrtime());
                                    /* print stastics */
    }
```

The functions `t_start`, `t_stop`, and `t_getrtime` that are used above are shown in Appendix A.

The file `file.c` handles all the Unix file I/O. This includes any required conversions between the TFTP formats, netascii and octet, and the Unix file format.

```
/*
 * Routines to open/close/read/write the local file.
 * For "binary" (octet) transmissions, we use the UNIX open/read/write
 * system calls (or their equivalent).
 * For "ascii" (netascii) transmissions, we use the UNIX standard i/o routines
 * fopen/getc/putc (or their equivalent).
 */

#include         "defs.h"

/*
 * The following are used by the functions in this file only.
 */

static int      lastcr   = 0;   /* 1 if last character was a carriage-return */
static int      nextchar = 0;

/*
 * Open the local file for reading or writing.
 * Return a FILE pointer, or NULL on error.
 */

FILE *
```

```
file_open(fname, mode, initblknum)
char    *fname;
char    *mode;              /* for fopen() - "r" or "w" */
int     initblknum;
{
        register FILE   *fp;

        if (strcmp(fname, "-") == 0)
                fp = stdout;
        else if ( (fp = fopen(fname, mode)) == NULL)
                return((FILE *) 0);

        nextblknum = initblknum;        /* for first data packet or first ACK */
        lastcr    = 0;                  /* for file_write() */
        nextchar  = -1;                 /* for file_read() */

        DEBUG2("file_open: opened %s, mode = %s", fname, mode);

        return(fp);
}

/*
 * Close the local file.
 * This causes the standard i/o system to flush its buffers for this file.
 */

file_close(fp)
FILE    *fp;
{
        if (lastcr)
                err_dump("final character was a CR");
        if (nextchar >= 0)
                err_dump("nextchar >= 0");

        if (fp == stdout)
                return;             /* don't close standard output */
        else if (fclose(fp) == EOF)
                err_dump("fclose error");
}

/*
 * Read data from the local file.
 * Here is where we handle any conversion between the file's mode
 * on the local system and the network mode.
 *
 * Return the number of bytes read (between 1 and maxnbytes, inclusive)
 * or 0 on EOF.
 */

int
file_read(fp, ptr, maxnbytes, mode)
FILE            *fp;
register char   *ptr;
register int    maxnbytes;
```

```
int             mode;
{
        register int    c, count;

        if (mode == MODE_BINARY) {
                count = read(fileno(fp), ptr, maxnbytes);
                if (count < 0)
                        err_dump("read error on local file");

                return(count);              /* will be 0 on EOF */

        } else if (mode == MODE_ASCII) {
                /*
                 * For files that are transferred in netascii, we must
                 * perform the reverse conversions that file_write() does.
                 * Note that we have to use the global "nextchar" to
                 * remember if the next character to output is a linefeed
                 * or a null, since the second byte of a 2-byte sequence
                 * may not fit in the current buffer, and may have to go
                 * as the first byte of the next buffer (i.e., we have to
                 * remember this fact from one call to the next).
                 */

                for (count = 0; count < maxnbytes; count++) {
                        if (nextchar >= 0) {
                                *ptr++ = nextchar;
                                nextchar = -1;
                                continue;
                        }

                        c = getc(fp);

                        if (c == EOF) { /* EOF return means eof or error */
                                if (ferror(fp))
                                    err_dump("read err from getc on local file");
                                return(count);

                        } else if (c == '\n') {
                                c = '\r';                       /* newline -> CR,LF */
                                nextchar = '\n';

                        } else if (c == '\r') {
                                nextchar = '\0';         /* CR -> CR,NULL */

                        } else
                                nextchar = -1;

                        *ptr++ = c;
                }

                return(count);
        } else
                err_dump("unknown MODE value");
```

```
        /* NOTREACHED */
}

/*
 * Write data to the local file.
 * Here is where we handle any conversion between the mode of the
 * file on the network and the local system's conventions.
 */

file_write(fp, ptr, nbytes, mode)
FILE            *fp;
register char   *ptr;
register int    nbytes;
int             mode;
{
        register int    c, i;

        if (mode == MODE_BINARY) {
                /*
                 * For binary mode files, no conversion is required.
                 */

                i = write(fileno(fp), ptr, nbytes);
                if (i != nbytes)
                        err_dump("write error to local file, i = %d", i);

        } else if (mode == MODE_ASCII) {
                /*
                 * For files that are transferred in netascii, we must
                 * perform the following conversions:
                 *
                 *      CR,LF               ->  newline = '\n'
                 *      CR,NULL             ->  CR      = '\r'
                 *      CR,anything_else    ->  undefined (we don't allow this)
                 *
                 * Note that we have to use the global "lastcr" to remember
                 * if the last character was a carriage-return or not,
                 * since if the last character of a buffer is a CR, we have
                 * to remember that when we're called for the next buffer.
                 */

                for (i = 0; i < nbytes; i++) {
                        c = *ptr++;
                        if (lastcr) {
                                if (c == '\n')
                                        c = '\n';
                                else if (c == '\0')
                                        c = '\r';
                                else
                                        err_dump("CR followed by 0x%02x", c);
                                lastcr = 0;

                        } else if (c == '\r') {
                                lastcr = 1;
```

```
                        continue;          /* get next character */
                }

                if (putc(c, fp) == EOF)
                        err_dump("write error from putc to local file");
        }
    } else
        err_dump("unknown MODE value");
}
```

The file `fsm.c` contains the finite state machine that drives the protocol processing. When a user enters either a `get` or `put` command, the functions `do_get` and `do_put` that we showed in the file `cmdgetput.c` send the first packet to the server. Then the function `fsm_loop` is called to do the rest of the protocol processing. The `fsm_loop` function is also called by the server's `main` function to do all its protocol processing.

The finite state machine in the following file can be represented as a table, similar to the state transition matrices that we discussed in Section 7.6 with TLI. The table for the client is shown in Figure 12.6.

Packet type	Packet type received				
sent	RRQ	WRQ	DATA	ACK	ERROR
RRQ			●		●
WRQ				●	●
DATA				●	
ACK			●		
ERROR					●

Figure 12.6 TFTP protocol—finite state machine for client.

Blank entries are not valid. The table for the server is shown in Figure 12.7.

Packet type	Packet type received				
sent	RRQ	WRQ	DATA	ACK	ERROR
(nothing)	●	●			
RRQ					
WRQ					
DATA				●	
ACK			●		
ERROR					

Figure 12.7 TFTP protocol—finite state machine for server.

For the server we have added another row to handle the initial state—the first packet that the server receives.

Note that all the timeout handling is done using the functions that we developed in Section 8.4. We use the identifier DATAGRAM to include the code required for a datagram protocol such as UDP. We'll see in the next section, when we present a TCP version, that this timeout handling isn't required when a reliable protocol is used.

```
/*
 * Finite state machine routines.
 */

#include        "defs.h"
#include        <signal.h>

#include        "rtt.h"          /* for RTT timing */

#ifdef  CLIENT
int     recv_ACK(), recv_DATA(), recv_RQERR();
#endif

#ifdef  SERVER
int     recv_RRQ(), recv_WRQ(), recv_ACK(), recv_DATA();
#endif

int     fsm_error(), fsm_invalid();

/*
 * Finite state machine table.
 * This is just a 2-d array indexed by the last opcode sent and
 * the opcode just received.  The result is the address of a
 * function to call to process the received opcode.
 */

int     (*fsm_ptr [ OP_MAX + 1 ] [ OP_MAX + 1 ] ) () = {

#ifdef  CLIENT
        fsm_invalid,    /* [sent = 0]          [recv = 0]          */
        fsm_invalid,    /* [sent = 0]          [recv = OP_RRQ]     */
        fsm_invalid,    /* [sent = 0]          [recv = OP_WRQ]     */
        fsm_invalid,    /* [sent = 0]          [recv = OP_DATA]    */
        fsm_invalid,    /* [sent = 0]          [recv = OP_ACK]     */
        fsm_invalid,    /* [sent = 0]          [recv = OP_ERROR]   */

        fsm_invalid,    /* [sent = OP_RRQ]     [recv = 0]          */
        fsm_invalid,    /* [sent = OP_RRQ]     [recv = OP_RRQ]     */
        fsm_invalid,    /* [sent = OP_RRQ]     [recv = OP_WRQ]     */
    recv_DATA,          /* [sent = OP_RRQ]     [recv = OP_DATA]    */
        fsm_invalid,    /* [sent = OP_RRQ]     [recv = OP_ACK]     */
    recv_RQERR,         /* [sent = OP_RRQ]     [recv = OP_ERROR]   */

        fsm_invalid,    /* [sent = OP_WRQ]     [recv = 0]          */
        fsm_invalid,    /* [sent = OP_WRQ]     [recv = OP_RRQ]     */
        fsm_invalid,    /* [sent = OP_WRQ]     [recv = OP_WRQ]     */
        fsm_invalid,    /* [sent = OP_WRQ]     [recv = OP_DATA]    */
    recv_ACK,           /* [sent = OP_WRQ]     [recv = OP_ACK]     */
    recv_RQERR,         /* [sent = OP_WRQ]     [recv = OP_ERROR]   */

        fsm_invalid,    /* [sent = OP_DATA]    [recv = 0]          */
        fsm_invalid,    /* [sent = OP_DATA]    [recv = OP_RRQ]     */
        fsm_invalid,    /* [sent = OP_DATA]    [recv = OP_WRQ]     */
```

```
            fsm_invalid,    /* [sent = OP_DATA]  [recv = OP_DATA]          */
        recv_ACK,           /* [sent = OP_DATA]  [recv = OP_ACK]           */
            fsm_error,      /* [sent = OP_DATA]  [recv = OP_ERROR]         */

            fsm_invalid,    /* [sent = OP_ACK]   [recv = 0]                */
            fsm_invalid,    /* [sent = OP_ACK]   [recv = OP_RRQ]           */
            fsm_invalid,    /* [sent = OP_ACK]   [recv = OP_WRQ]           */
        recv_DATA,          /* [sent = OP_ACK]   [recv = OP_DATA]          */
            fsm_invalid,    /* [sent = OP_ACK]   [recv = OP_ACK]           */
            fsm_error,      /* [sent = OP_ACK]   [recv = OP_ERROR]         */

            fsm_invalid,    /* [sent = OP_ERROR] [recv = 0]                */
            fsm_invalid,    /* [sent = OP_ERROR] [recv = OP_RRQ]           */
            fsm_invalid,    /* [sent = OP_ERROR] [recv = OP_WRQ]           */
            fsm_invalid,    /* [sent = OP_ERROR] [recv = OP_DATA]          */
            fsm_invalid,    /* [sent = OP_ERROR] [recv = OP_ACK]           */
            fsm_error       /* [sent = OP_ERROR] [recv = OP_ERROR]         */
#endif  /* CLIENT */

#ifdef  SERVER
            fsm_invalid,    /* [sent = 0]        [recv = 0]                */
        recv_RRQ,           /* [sent = 0]        [recv = OP_RRQ]           */
        recv_WRQ,           /* [sent = 0]        [recv = OP_WRQ]           */
            fsm_invalid,    /* [sent = 0]        [recv = OP_DATA]          */
            fsm_invalid,    /* [sent = 0]        [recv = OP_ACK]           */
            fsm_invalid,    /* [sent = 0]        [recv = OP_ERROR]         */

            fsm_invalid,    /* [sent = OP_RRQ]   [recv = 0]                */
            fsm_invalid,    /* [sent = OP_RRQ]   [recv = OP_RRQ]           */
            fsm_invalid,    /* [sent = OP_RRQ]   [recv = OP_WRQ]           */
            fsm_invalid,    /* [sent = OP_RRQ]   [recv = OP_DATA]          */
            fsm_invalid,    /* [sent = OP_RRQ]   [recv = OP_ACK]           */
            fsm_invalid,    /* [sent = OP_RRQ]   [recv = OP_ERROR]         */

            fsm_invalid,    /* [sent = OP_WRQ]   [recv = 0]                */
            fsm_invalid,    /* [sent = OP_WRQ]   [recv = OP_RRQ]           */
            fsm_invalid,    /* [sent = OP_WRQ]   [recv = OP_WRQ]           */
            fsm_invalid,    /* [sent = OP_WRQ]   [recv = OP_DATA]          */
            fsm_invalid,    /* [sent = OP_WRQ]   [recv = OP_ACK]           */
            fsm_invalid,    /* [sent = OP_WRQ]   [recv = OP_ERROR]         */

            fsm_invalid,    /* [sent = OP_DATA]  [recv = 0]                */
            fsm_invalid,    /* [sent = OP_DATA]  [recv = OP_RRQ]           */
            fsm_invalid,    /* [sent = OP_DATA]  [recv = OP_WRQ]           */
            fsm_invalid,    /* [sent = OP_DATA]  [recv = OP_DATA]          */
        recv_ACK,           /* [sent = OP_DATA]  [recv = OP_ACK]           */
            fsm_error,      /* [sent = OP_DATA]  [recv = OP_ERROR]         */

            fsm_invalid,    /* [sent = OP_ACK]   [recv = 0]                */
            fsm_invalid,    /* [sent = OP_ACK]   [recv = OP_RRQ]           */
            fsm_invalid,    /* [sent = OP_ACK]   [recv = OP_WRQ]           */
        recv_DATA,          /* [sent = OP_ACK]   [recv = OP_DATA]          */
            fsm_invalid,    /* [sent = OP_ACK]   [recv = OP_ACK]           */
            fsm_error,      /* [sent = OP_ACK]   [recv = OP_ERROR]         */
```

```
          fsm_invalid,      /* [sent = OP_ERROR] [recv = 0]          */
          fsm_invalid,      /* [sent = OP_ERROR] [recv = OP_RRQ]     */
          fsm_invalid,      /* [sent = OP_ERROR] [recv = OP_WRQ]     */
          fsm_invalid,      /* [sent = OP_ERROR] [recv = OP_DATA]    */
          fsm_invalid,      /* [sent = OP_ERROR] [recv = OP_ACK]     */
          fsm_error         /* [sent = OP_ERROR] [recv = OP_ERROR]   */
#endif  /* SERVER */
};

#ifdef  DATAGRAM
static struct rtt_struct   rttinfo;      /* used by the rtt_XXX() functions */
static int                 rttfirst = 1;

int     tout_flag;       /* set to 1 by SIGALRM handler */
#endif  /* DATAGRAM */

/*
 * Main loop of finite state machine.
 *
 * For the client, we're called after either an RRQ or a WRQ has been
 * sent to the other side.
 *
 * For the server, we're called after either an RRQ or a WRQ has been
 * received from the other side.  In this case, the argument will be a
 * 0 (since nothing has been sent) but the state table above handles
 * this.
 */

int             /* return 0 on normal termination, -1 on timeout */
fsm_loop(opcode)
int     opcode;          /* for client: RRQ or WRQ */
                         /* for server: 0 */
{
        register int    nbytes;

        op_sent = opcode;

#ifdef  DATAGRAM

        if (rttfirst) {
                rtt_init(&rttinfo);
                rttfirst = 0;
        }

        rtt_newpack(&rttinfo);           /* initialize for a new packet */

        for ( ; ; ) {
                int     func_timeout();           /* our signal handler */

                signal(SIGALRM, func_timeout);
                tout_flag = 0;
                alarm(rtt_start(&rttinfo));      /* calc timeout & start timer */

                if ( (nbytes = net_recv(recvbuff, MAXBUFF)) < 0) {
```

```
                               if (tout_flag) {
                                       /*
                                        * The receive timed out.  See if we've tried
                                        * enough, and if so, return to caller.
                                        */

                                       if (rtt_timeout(&rttinfo) < 0) {
#ifdef  CLIENT
                                               printf("Transfer timed out\n");
#endif
                                               return(-1);
                                       }

                                       if (traceflag)
                                               rtt_debug(&rttinfo);
                               } else
                                       err_dump("net_recv error");

                               /*
                                * Retransmit the last packet.
                                */

                               net_send(sendbuff, sendlen);
                               continue;
                       }

                       alarm(0);                       /* stop signal timer */
                       tout_flag = 0;
                       rtt_stop(&rttinfo);     /* stop RTT timer, calc new values */

                       if (traceflag)
                               rtt_debug(&rttinfo);

#else   /* else we have a connection-oriented protocol (makes life easier) */

               for ( ; ; ) {
                       if ( (nbytes = net_recv(recvbuff, MAXBUFF)) < 0)
                               err_dump("net_recv error");

#endif  /* DATAGRAM */

                       if (nbytes < 4)
                               err_dump("receive length = %d bytes", nbytes);

                       op_recv = ldshort(recvbuff);

                       if (op_recv < OP_MIN || op_recv > OP_MAX)
                               err_dump("invalid opcode received: %d", op_recv);

                       /*
                        * We call the appropriate function, passing the address
                        * of the receive buffer and its length.  These arguments
                        * ignore the received-opcode, which we've already processed.
                        *
```

```
                            * We assume the called function will send a response to the
                            * other side.  It is the called function's responsibility to
                            * set op_sent to the op-code that it sends to the other side.
                            */

                           if ((*fsm_ptr[op_sent][op_recv])(recvbuff + 2, nbytes - 2) < 0){
                                   /*
                                    * When the called function returns -1, this loop
                                    * is done.  Turn off the signal handler for
                                    * timeouts and return to the caller.
                                    */

                                   signal(SIGALRM, SIG_DFL);
                                   return(0);
                           }
                   }
       }


#ifdef  DATAGRAM

/*
 * Signal handler for timeouts.
 * Just set the flag that is looked at above when the net_recv()
 * returns an error (interrupted system call).
 */

int
func_timeout()
{
        tout_flag = 1;             /* set flag for function above */
}

#endif  /* DATAGRAM */

/*
 * Error packet received and we weren't expecting it.
 */

/*ARGSUSED*/
int
fsm_error(ptr, nbytes)
char    *ptr;
int     nbytes;
{
        err_dump("error received: op_sent = %d, op_recv = %d",
                                        op_sent, op_recv);

}

/*
 * Invalid state transition.  Something is wrong.
 */

/*ARGSUSED*/
int
```

```
fsm_invalid(ptr, nbytes)
char    *ptr;
int     nbytes;
{
        err_dump("protocol botch: op_sent = %d, op_recv = %d",
                                            op_sent, op_recv);
}
```

The file `sendrecv.c` contains all the functions that send and receive packets to the peer process. Some of these functions are for only the client or server, and some are used by both.

```
/*
 * Send and receive packets.
 */

#include         "defs.h"
#include         <sys/stat.h>
#include         <ctype.h>

#ifdef  CLIENT

/*
 * Send a Read-Request or a Write-Request to the other system.
 * These two packets are only sent by the client to the server.
 * This function is called when either the "get" command or the
 * "put" command is executed by the user.
 */

send_RQ(opcode, fname, mode)
int     opcode;             /* OP_RRQ or OP_WRQ */
char    *fname;
int     mode;
{
        register int    len;
        char            *modestr;

        DEBUG2("sending RRQ/WRQ for %s, mode = %d", fname, mode);

        stshort(opcode, sendbuff);

        strcpy(sendbuff+2, fname);
        len = 2 + strlen(fname) + 1;    /* +1 for null byte at end of fname */

        switch(mode) {
        case MODE_ASCII:            modestr = "netascii";   break;
        case MODE_BINARY:           modestr = "octet";      break;
        default:
                err_dump("unknown mode");
        }
        strcpy(sendbuff + len, modestr);
        len += strlen(modestr) + 1;     /* +1 for null byte at end of modestr */

        sendlen = len;
```

```
        net_send(sendbuff, sendlen);
        op_sent = opcode;
}

/*
 * Error packet received in response to an RRQ or a WRQ.
 * Usually means the file we're asking for on the other system
 * can't be accessed for some reason.  We need to print the
 * error message that's returned.
 * Called by finite state machine.
 */

int
recv_RQERR(ptr, nbytes)
char    *ptr;                /* points just past received opcode */
int     nbytes;             /* doesn't include received opcode */
{
        register int    ecode;

        ecode = ldshort(ptr);
        ptr += 2;
        nbytes -= 2;
        ptr[nbytes] = 0;            /* assure it's null terminated ... */

        DEBUG2("ERROR received, %d bytes, error code %d", nbytes, ecode);

        fflush(stdout);
        fprintf(stderr, "Error# %d: %s\n", ecode, ptr);
        fflush(stderr);

        return(-1);     /* terminate finite state loop */
}

#endif  /* CLIENT */

/*
 * Send an acknowledgment packet to the other system.
 * Called by the recv_DATA() function below and also called by
 * recv_WRQ().
 */

send_ACK(blocknum)
int     blocknum;
{
        DEBUG1("sending ACK for block# %d", blocknum);

        stshort(OP_ACK, sendbuff);
        stshort(blocknum, sendbuff + 2);

        sendlen = 4;
        net_send(sendbuff, sendlen);

#ifdef  SORCERER
        /*
```

```
               * If you want to see the Sorcerer's Apprentice syndrome,
               * #define SORCERER, then run this program as the client and
               * get a file from a server that doesn't have the bug fixed
               * (such as the 4.3BSD version).
               * Turn on the trace option, and you'll see the duplicate
               * data packets sent by the broken server, starting with
               * block# 2.  Yet when the transfer is complete, you'll find
               * the file was received correctly.
               */

              if (blocknum == 1)
                      net_send(sendbuff, sendlen);    /* send the first ACK twice */
#endif

              op_sent = OP_ACK;
}

/*
 * Send data to the other system.
 * The data must be stored in the "sendbuff" by the caller.
 * Called by the recv_ACK() function below.
 */

send_DATA(blocknum, nbytes)
int     blocknum;
int     nbytes;             /* #bytes of actual data to send */
{
        DEBUG2("sending %d bytes of DATA with block# %d", nbytes, blocknum);

        stshort(OP_DATA, sendbuff);
        stshort(blocknum, sendbuff + 2);

        sendlen = nbytes + 4;
        net_send(sendbuff, sendlen);
        op_sent = OP_DATA;
}

/*
 * Data packet received.  Send an acknowledgment.
 * Called by finite state machine.
 * Note that this function is called for both the client and the server.
 */

int
recv_DATA(ptr, nbytes)
register char   *ptr;              /* points just past received opcode */
register int    nbytes;           /* doesn't include received opcode */
{
        register int    recvblknum;

        recvblknum = ldshort(ptr);
        ptr += 2;
        nbytes -= 2;
```

```
        DEBUG2("DATA received, %d bytes, block# %d", nbytes, recvblknum);

    if (nbytes > MAXDATA)
            err_dump("data packet received with length = %d bytes", nbytes);

    if (recvblknum == nextblknum) {
            /*
             * The data packet is the expected one.
             * Increment our expected-block# for the next packet.
             */

            nextblknum++;
            totnbytes += nbytes;

            if (nbytes > 0) {
                    /*
                     * Note that the final data packet can have a
                     * data length of zero, so we only write the
                     * data to the local file if there is data.
                     */

                    file_write(localfp, ptr, nbytes, modetype);
            }
#ifdef SERVER
            /*
             * If the length of the data is between 0-511, this is
             * the last data block.  For the server, here's where
             * we have to close the file.  For the client, the
             * "get" command processing will close the file.
             */

            if (nbytes < MAXDATA)
                    file_close(localfp);
#endif

    } else if (recvblknum < (nextblknum - 1)) {
            /*
             * We've just received data block# N (or earlier, such as N-1,
             * N-2, etc.) from the other end, but we were expecting data
             * block# N+2.  But if we were expecting N+2 it means we've
             * already received N+1, so the other end went backwards from
             * N+1 to N (or earlier).  Something is wrong.
             */

            err_dump("recvblknum < nextblknum - 1");

    } else if (recvblknum > nextblknum) {
            /*
             * We've just received data block# N (or later, such as N+1,
             * N+2, etc.) from the other end, but we were expecting data
             * block# N-1.  But this implies that the other end has
             * received an ACK for block# N-1 from us.  Something is wrong.
             */
```

```
                        err_dump("recvblknum > nextblknum");
        }

        /*
         * The only case not handled above is "recvblknum == (nextblknum - 1)".
         * This means the other end never saw our ACK for the last data
         * packet and retransmitted it.  We just ignore the retransmission
         * and send another ACK.
         *
         * Acknowledge the data packet.
         */

        send_ACK(recvblknum);

        /*
         * If the length of the data is between 0-511, we've just
         * received the final data packet, else there is more to come.
         */

        return( (nbytes == MAXDATA) ? 0 : -1 );
}

/*
 * ACK packet received.  Send some more data.
 * Called by finite state machine.  Also called by recv_RRQ() to
 * start the transmission of a file to the client.
 * Note that this function is called for both the client and the server.
 */

int
recv_ACK(ptr, nbytes)
register char    *ptr;          /* points just past received opcode */
register int     nbytes;        /* doesn't include received opcode */
{
        register int     recvblknum;

        recvblknum = ldshort(ptr);
        if (nbytes != 2)
                err_dump("ACK packet received with length = %d bytes",
                                                nbytes + 2);

        DEBUG1("ACK received, block# %d", recvblknum);

        if (recvblknum == nextblknum) {
                /*
                 * The received acknowledgment is for the expected data
                 * packet that we sent.
                 * Fill the transmit buffer with the next block of data
                 * to send.
                 * If there's no more data to send, then we might be
                 * finished.  Note that we must send a final data packet
                 * containing 0-511 bytes of data.  If the length of the
                 * last packet that we sent was exactly 512 bytes, then we
                 * must send a 0-length data packet.
```

```
                    */

            if ( (nbytes = file_read(localfp, sendbuff + 4,
                                        MAXDATA, modetype)) == 0) {
                    if (lastsend < MAXDATA)
                            return(-1);       /* done */
                    /* else we'll send nbytes=0 of data */
            }

            lastsend = nbytes;
            nextblknum++;                 /* incr for this new packet of data */
            totnbytes += nbytes;
            send_DATA(nextblknum, nbytes);

            return(0);

    } else if (recvblknum < (nextblknum - 1)) {
            /*
             * We've just received the ACK for block# N (or earlier, such
             * as N-1, N-2, etc) from the other end, but we were expecting
             * the ACK for block# N+2.  But if we're expecting the ACK for
             * N+2 it means we've already received the ACK for N+1, so the
             * other end went backwards from N+1 to N (or earlier).
             * Something is wrong.
             */

            err_dump("recvblknum < nextblknum - 1");

    } else if (recvblknum > nextblknum) {
            /*
             * We've just received the ACK for block# N (or later, such
             * as N+1, N+2, etc) from the other end, but we were expecting
             * the ACK for block# N-1.  But this implies that the other
             * end has already received data block# N-1 from us.
             * Something is wrong.
             */

            err_dump("recvblknum > nextblknum");

    } else {
            /*
             * Here we have "recvblknum == (nextblknum - 1)".
             * This means we received a duplicate ACK.  This means either:
             * (1) the other side never received our last data packet;
             * (2) the other side's ACK got delayed somehow.
             *
             * If we were to retransmit the last data packet, we would start
             * the "Sorcerer's Apprentice Syndrome."  We'll just ignore this
             * duplicate ACK, returning to the FSM loop, which will initiate
             * another receive.
             */

            return(0);
    }
```

```
                /* NOTREACHED */
}

#ifdef  SERVER

/*
 * RRQ packet received.
 * Called by the finite state machine.
 * This (and receiving a WRQ) are the only ways the server gets started.
 */

int
recv_RRQ(ptr, nbytes)
char    *ptr;
int     nbytes;
{
        char    ackbuff[2];

        recv_xRQ(OP_RRQ, ptr, nbytes);  /* verify the RRQ packet */

        /*
         * Set things up so we can just call recv_ACK() and pretend we
         * received an ACK, so it'll send the first data block to the
         * client.
         */

        lastsend = MAXDATA;
        stshort(0, ackbuff);     /* pretend its an ACK of block# 0 */

        recv_ACK(ackbuff, 2);    /* this sends data block# 1 */

        return(0);       /* the finite state machine takes over from here */
}

/*
 * WRQ packet received.
 * Called by the finite state machine.
 * This (and receiving an RRQ) are the only ways the server gets started.
 */

int
recv_WRQ(ptr, nbytes)
char    *ptr;
int     nbytes;
{
        recv_xRQ(OP_WRQ, ptr, nbytes);  /* verify the WRQ packet */

        /*
         * Call send_ACK() to acknowledge block# 0, which will cause
         * the client to send data block# 1.
         */

        nextblknum = 1;
        send_ACK(0);
```

```
        return(0);        /* the finite stat machine takes over from here */
}

/*
 * Process an RRQ or WRQ that has been received.
 * Called by the 2 routines above.
 */

int
recv_xRQ(opcode, ptr, nbytes)
int             opcode;         /* OP_RRQ or OP_WRQ */
register char   *ptr;           /* points just past received opcode */
register int    nbytes;         /* doesn't include received opcode */
{
        register int    i;
        register char   *saveptr;
        char            filename[MAXFILENAME], dirname[MAXFILENAME],
                        mode[MAXFILENAME];
        struct stat     statbuff;

        /*
         * Assure the filename and mode are present and
         * null-terminated.
         */

        saveptr = ptr;          /* points to beginning of filename */
        for (i = 0; i < nbytes; i++)
                if (*ptr++ == '\0')
                        goto FileOK;
        err_dump("Invalid filename");

FileOK:
        strcpy(filename, saveptr);
        saveptr = ptr;          /* points to beginning of Mode */

        for ( ; i < nbytes; i++)
                if (*ptr++ == '\0')
                        goto ModeOK;
        err_dump("Invalid Mode");

ModeOK:
        strlccpy(mode, saveptr);        /* copy and convert to lower case */

        if (strcmp(mode, "netascii") == 0)
                modetype = MODE_ASCII;
        else if (strcmp(mode, "octet") == 0)
                modetype = MODE_BINARY;
        else
                send_ERROR(ERR_BADOP, "Mode isn't netascii or octet");

        /*
         * Validate the filename.
         * Note that as a daemon we might be running with root
         * privileges.  Since there are no user-access checks with
```

```
         * tftp (as compared to ftp, for example) we will only
         * allow access to files that are publicly accessible.
         *
         * Also, since we're running as a daemon, our home directory
         * is the root, so any filename must have it's full
         * pathname specified (i.e., it must begin with a slash).
         */

        if (filename[0] != '/')
                send_ERROR(ERR_ACCESS, "filename must begin with '/'");

        if (opcode == OP_RRQ) {
                /*
                 * Read request - verify that the file exists
                 * and that it has world read permission.
                 */

                if (stat(filename, &statbuff) < 0)
                        send_ERROR(ERR_ACCESS, sys_err_str());
                if ((statbuff.st_mode & (S_IREAD >> 6)) == 0)
                        send_ERROR(ERR_ACCESS,
                                    "File doesn't allow world read permission");

        } else if (opcode == OP_WRQ) {
                /*
                 * Write request - verify that the directory
                 * that the file is being written to has world
                 * write permission.  We've already verified above
                 * that the filename starts with a '/'.
                 */

                char    *rindex();

                strcpy(dirname, filename);
                *(rindex(dirname, '/') + 1) = '\0';
                if (stat(dirname, &statbuff) < 0)
                        send_ERROR(ERR_ACCESS, sys_err_str());
                if ((statbuff.st_mode & (S_IWRITE >> 6)) == 0)
                        send_ERROR(ERR_ACCESS,
                                    "Directory doesn't allow world write permission");

        } else
                err_dump("unknown opcode");

        localfp = file_open(filename, (opcode == OP_RRQ) ? "r" : "w", 0);
        if (localfp == NULL)
                send_ERROR(ERR_NOFILE, sys_err_str());   /* doesn't return */
}

/*
 * Send an error packet.
 * Note that an error packet isn't retransmitted or acknowledged by
 * the other end, so once we're done sending it, we can exit.
 */
```

```
send_ERROR(ecode, string)
int     ecode;          /* error code, ERR_xxx from defs.h */
char    *string;        /* some additional info */
                        /* can't be NULL, set to "" if empty */
{
        DEBUG2("sending ERROR, code = %d, string = %s", ecode, string);

        stshort(OP_ERROR, sendbuff);
        stshort(ecode, sendbuff + 2);

        strcpy(sendbuff + 4, string);

        sendlen = 4 + strlen(sendbuff + 4) + 1;          /* +1 for null at end */
        net_send(sendbuff, sendlen);

        net_close();

        exit(0);
}


/*
 * Copy a string and convert it to lower case in the process.
 */

strlccpy(dest, src)
register char   *dest, *src;
{
        register char   c;

        while ( (c = *src++) != '\0') {
                if (isupper(c))
                        c = tolower(c);
                *dest++ = c;
        }
        *dest = 0;
}

#endif  /* SERVER */
```

The file `mainserv.c` contains the `main` function for the server. The server is complicated by allowing it to be started either by the 4.3BSD `inetd` superserver, or independently. When started by the `inetd` daemon, the `wait` mode is specified, as we described in Section 6.16. Once the TFTP server has read the datagram from the client on its well-known port, we want the TFTP server to `fork` with the parent `exit`ing. This allows the `inetd` daemon to start another read on the server's well-known port to process the next request from some other client. The sequence of steps is shown in Figure 12.8.

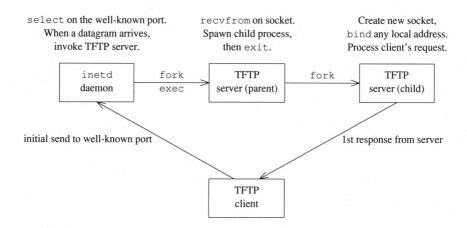

Figure 12.8   TFTP server, when invoked by 4.3BSD inetd.

When the server is started independently of the inetd superserver, the TFTP server must provide the concurrency. The TFTP parent must start another recvfrom after a child process is spawned. Here we have the processes shown in Figure 12.9.

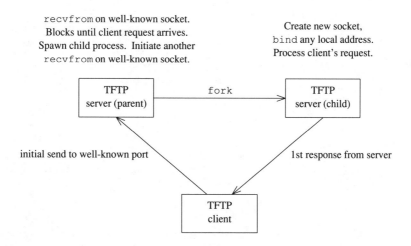

Figure 12.9   TFTP server, when run as daemon.

Here is the `main` function for the TFTP server.

```
/*
 * tftp - Trivial File Transfer Program.  Server side.
 *
 *      -i                says we were *not* started by inted.
 *      -p port#          specifies a different port# to listen on.
 *      -t                turns on the traceflag - writes to a file.
 */

#include         "defs.h"

main(argc, argv)
int    argc;
char   **argv;
{
        int             childpid;
        register char   *s;

        err_init("rich's tftpd");

        while (--argc > 0 && (*++argv)[0] == '-')
                for (s = argv[0]+1; *s != '\0'; s++)
                        switch (*s) {
                        case 'i':
                                inetdflag = 0;  /* turns OFF the flag */
                                                /* (it defaults to 1) */
                                break;

                        case 'p':                  /* specify server's port# */
                                if (--argc <= 0)
                                    err_quit("-p requires another argument");
                                port = atoi(*++argv);
                                break;

                        case 't':
                                traceflag = 1;
                                break;

                        default:
                                err_quit("unknown command line option: %c", *s);
                        }

        if (inetdflag == 0) {
                /*
                 * Start us up as a daemon process (in the background).
                 * Also initialize the network connection - create the socket
                 * and bind our well-known address to it.
                 */

                daemon_start(1);

                net_init(TFTP_SERVICE, port);
        }
```

```
        /*
         * If the traceflag is set, open a log file to write to.
         * This is used by the DEBUG macros.  Note that all the
         * err_XXX() functions still get handled by syslog(3).
         */

        if (traceflag) {
                if (freopen(DAEMONLOG, "a", stderr) == NULL)
                        err_sys("can't open %s for writing", DAEMONLOG);
                DEBUG2("pid = %d, inetdflag = %d", getpid(), inetdflag);
        }

        /*
         * Concurrent server loop.
         * The child created by net_open() handles the client's request.
         * The parent waits for another request.  In the inetd case,
         * the parent from net_open() never returns.
         */

        for ( ; ; ) {
                if ( (childpid = net_open(inetdflag)) == 0) {
                        fsm_loop(0);    /* child processes client's request */
                        net_close();    /* then we're done */
                        exit(0);
                }

                /* parent waits for another client's request */
        }
        /* NOTREACHED */
}
```

The file `initvars.c` declares all the global variables and initializes them.

```
/*
 * Initialize the external variables.
 * Some link editors (on systems other than UNIX) require this.
 */

#include        "defs.h"

char    command[MAXTOKEN]        = { 0 };
int     connected                = 0;
char    hostname[MAXHOSTNAME]    = { 0 };
int     inetdflag                = 1;
int     interactive              = 1;
jmp_buf jmp_mainloop             = { 0 };
int     lastsend                 = 0;
FILE    *localfp                 = NULL;
int     modetype                 = MODE_ASCII;
int     nextblknum               = 0;
int     op_sent                  = 0;
int     op_recv                  = 0;
int     port                     = 0;
char    *prompt                  = "tftp: ";
```

```
char      recvbuff[MAXBUFF]        = { 0 };
char      sendbuff[MAXBUFF]        = { 0 };
int       sendlen                  = 0;
char      temptoken[MAXTOKEN]      = { 0 };
long      totnbytes                = 0;
int       traceflag                = 0;
int       verboseflag              = 0;
```

12.8 TCP Implementation

We now present a version of our TFTP client and server that uses TCP. By coding all the
protocol-specific functions in a single file, `netudp.c`, we can replace it with another set
of similar functions that use some other protocol.

In many ways, the UDP implementation is a worst-case example. The underlying
transport protocol, UDP, is unreliable, so we had to handle timeout and retransmission
ourselves. We also had to maintain a pseudo-connection between the client and server,
since multiple datagrams had to be exchanged for the transfer of a single file, using the
connectionless UDP.

The following file, `nettcp.c`, replaces the file `netudp.c` that we presented in the
previous section. The only other change we make is not to define the DATAGRAM
identifier when we compile the file `fsm.c`, since the timeout and retransmission code is
not needed with TCP. The `nettcp.c` file is about one-half the size of the corresponding UDP file. Using a reliable, connection-oriented protocol simplifies things for the
application.

```
/*
 * TFTP network handling for TCP/IP connection.
 */

#include        "netdefs.h"

#include        <netinet/in.h>
#include        <arpa/inet.h>
#include        <signal.h>
#include        <errno.h>
extern int      errno;

#ifndef CLIENT
#ifndef SERVER
either CLIENT or SERVER must be defined
#endif
#endif

int     sockfd = -1;                            /* fd for socket of server */
char    openhost[MAXHOSTNAMELEN] = { 0 };       /* remember host's name */

extern int                      traceflag;      /* TFTP variable */

extern struct sockaddr_in       tcp_srv_addr;   /* set by tcp_open() */
```

```
extern struct servent           tcp_serv_info;  /* set by tcp_open() */

#ifdef  CLIENT

/*
 * Open the network connection.  Client version.
 */

int
net_open(host, service, port)
char    *host;          /* name of other system to communicate with */
char    *service;       /* name of service being requested */
int     port;           /* if > 0, use as port#, else use value for service */
{
        if ( (sockfd = tcp_open(host, service, port)) < 0)
                return(-1);

        DEBUG2("net_open: host %s, port# %d",
                        inet_ntoa(tcp_srv_addr.sin_addr),
                        ntohs(tcp_srv_addr.sin_port));

        strcpy(openhost, host);            /* save the host's name */

        return(0);
}

#endif  /* CLIENT */

/*
 * Close the network connection.  Used by client and server.
 */

net_close()
{
        DEBUG2("net_close: host = %s, fd = %d", openhost, sockfd);

        close(sockfd);

        sockfd = -1;
}

/*
 * Send a record to the other end.  Used by client and server.
 * With a stream socket we have to preface each record with its length,
 * since TFTP doesn't have a record length as part of each record.
 * We encode the length as a 2-byte integer in network byte order.
 */

net_send(buff, len)
char    *buff;
int     len;
{
        register int    rc;
        short           templen;
```

```
        DEBUG1("net_send: sent %d bytes", len);

        templen = htons(len);
        rc = writen(sockfd, (char *) &templen, sizeof(short));
        if (rc != sizeof(short))
                err_dump("writen error of length prefix");

        rc = writen(sockfd, buff, len);
        if (rc != len)
                err_dump("writen error");
}


/*
 * Receive a record from the other end.  Used by client and server.
 */

int                             /* return #bytes in packet, or -1 on EINTR */
net_recv(buff, maxlen)
char    *buff;
int     maxlen;
{
        register int    nbytes;
        short           templen;        /* value-result parameter */

again1:
        if ( (nbytes = readn(sockfd, (char *) &templen, sizeof(short))) < 0) {
                if (errno == EINTR) {
                        errno = 0;                  /* assume SIGCLD */
                        goto again1;
                }
                err_dump("readn error for length prefix");
        }
        if (nbytes != sizeof(short))
                err_dump("error in readn of length prefix");

        templen = ntohs(templen);               /* #bytes that follow */
        if (templen > maxlen)
                err_dump("record length too large");

again2:
        if ( (nbytes = readn(sockfd, buff, templen)) < 0) {
                if (errno == EINTR) {
                        errno = 0;                  /* assume SIGCLD */
                        goto again2;
                }
                err_dump("readn error");
        }
        if (nbytes != templen)
                err_dump("error in readn");

        DEBUG1("net_recv: got %d bytes", nbytes);

        return(nbytes);          /* return the actual length of the message */
}
```

```
#ifdef  SERVER

struct sockaddr_in                  tcp_cli_addr;   /* set by accept() */

/*
 * Initialize the network connection for the server, when it has *not*
 * been invoked by inetd.
 */

net_init(service, port)
char    *service;       /* the name of the service we provide */
int     port;           /* if nonzero, this is the port to listen on;
                           overrides the standard port for the service */
{
        struct servent  *sp;

        /*
         * We weren't started by a master daemon.
         * We have to create a socket ourselves and bind our well-known
         * address to it.
         */

        bzero((char *) &tcp_srv_addr, sizeof(tcp_srv_addr));
        tcp_srv_addr.sin_family     = AF_INET;
        tcp_srv_addr.sin_addr.s_addr = htonl(INADDR_ANY);

        if (service != NULL) {
                if ( (sp = getservbyname(service, "tcp")) == NULL)
                        err_dump("net_init: unknown service: %s/tcp", service);
                tcp_serv_info = *sp;                    /* structure copy */

                if (port > 0)
                        tcp_srv_addr.sin_port = htons(port);
                                                        /* caller's value */
                else
                        tcp_srv_addr.sin_port = sp->s_port;
                                                        /* service's value */
        } else {
                if (port <= 0) {
                        err_ret("tcp_open: must specify either service or port");
                        return(-1);
                }
                tcp_srv_addr.sin_port = htons(port);
        }

        /*
         * Create the socket and Bind our local address so that any
         * client can send to us.
         */

        if ( (sockfd = socket(AF_INET, SOCK_STREAM, 0)) < 0)
                err_dump("net_init: can't create stream socket");

        if (bind(sockfd, (struct sockaddr *) &tcp_srv_addr,
```

```
                                        sizeof(tcp_srv_addr)) < 0)
                err_dump("net_init: can't bind local address");

        /*
         * And set the listen parameter, telling the system that we're
         * ready  to accept incoming connection requests.
         */

        listen(sockfd, 5);
}

/*
 * Initiate the server's end.
 * We are passed a flag that says whether or not we were started
 * by a "master daemon," such as the inetd program under 4.3BSD.
 * A master daemon will have already waited for a message to arrive
 * for us, and will have already set up the connection to the client.
 * If we weren't started by a master daemon, then we must wait for a
 * client's request to arrive.
 */

int
net_open(inetdflag)
int     inetdflag;         /* true if inetd started us */
{
        register int    newsockfd, childpid, nbytes;
        int             clilen, on;

        on = 1;

        if (inetdflag) {
#ifdef  BSD             /* assumes 4.3BSD inetd */
                /*
                 * When we're fired up by inetd under 4.3BSD, file
                 * descriptors 0, 1 and 2 are sockets to the client.
                 */

                sockfd = 0;     /* descriptor for net_recv() to read from */

                return(0);      /* done */

#endif  /* BSD inetd specifics */
        }

        /*
         * For the concurrent server that's not initiated by inetd,
         * we have to wait for a connection request to arrive,
         * then fork a child to handle the client's request.
         * Beware that the accept() can be interrupted, such as by
         * a previously spawned child process that has terminated
         * (for which we caught the SIGCLD signal).
         */

again:
```

```
        clilen = sizeof(tcp_cli_addr);
        newsockfd = accept(sockfd, (struct sockaddr *) &tcp_cli_addr, &clilen);
        if (newsockfd < 0) {
                if (errno == EINTR) {
                        errno = 0;
                        goto again;       /* probably a SIGCLD that was caught */
                }
                err_dump("accept error");
        }

        /*
         * Fork a child process to handle the client's request.
         * The parent returns the child pid to the caller, which is
         * probably a concurrent server that'll call us again, to wait
         * for the next client request to this well-known port.
         */

        if ( (childpid = fork()) < 0)
                err_dump("server can't fork");

        else if (childpid > 0) {                    /* parent */
                close(newsockfd);        /* close new connection */
                return(childpid);        /* and return */
        }

        /*
         * Child process continues here.
         * First close the original socket so that the parent
         * can accept any further requests that arrive there.
         * Then set "sockfd" in our process to be the descriptor that
         * we are going to process.
         */

        close(sockfd);
        sockfd = newsockfd;

        return(0);                       /* return to process the connection */
}

#endif  /* SERVER */
```

Note that if we used a connection-oriented protocol that was record-oriented, such as the XNS SPP, we would not have to prepend the 2-byte record-length to each record.

12.9 Summary

TFTP is a simple application, yet we have taken over 2000 lines of C code to provide both a client and server. Some of this C code, however, is for comments and additional features (command line processing) that wouldn't be required in a simple application such as a bootstrap implementation in read-only memory.

This application has shown many of the details that have to be handled when the transport layer (UDP) doesn't provide an error-free connection—block numbers, timeout, and retransmission. We've also seen how the naive approach of having both the sender and receiver timeout and retransmit can lead to subtle problems such as the sorcerer's apprentice syndrome.

Readers interested in the additional features provided by FTP should consult RFC 959 [Postel and Reynolds 1985] and Stallings et al. [1988].

Exercises

12.1 To send a file to the other end, the client or server executes a loop consisting of the following three operations: read the data from a file, write the data to the other end, wait for an acknowledgment. What would it take to have the transfer of a file use multiple buffers? Add multiple buffering and compare the speeds with the 4.3BSD version (which uses double buffering).

12.2 Assume that a host is receiving a file with TFTP (using UDP) and it receives the final data packet. If the acknowledgment for this final data packet is lost, what happens? Propose and implement a solution. What would happen in this case if a connection-oriented protocol, such as TCP, were used instead?

12.3 How much code in the TFTP client and server could be removed if only reliable protocols were used (TCP or SPP, for example)?

13

Line Printer Spoolers

13.1 Introduction

Using a network to print a file on a system that does not have an attached printer, is commonplace today. In addition to the use of a network, line printer spooling systems provide a good example of the interaction between processes, since more than one process is typically involved.

In this chapter we look at the 4.3BSD line printer spooling system and the System V line printer spooler. This section is not intended to be an in-depth look at these spoolers. Line printer spooling systems tend to be complicated by the fact that they provide many options (number of copies, titles, banner pages, and so on) and many ancillary functions (see what jobs are in the queue, remove a job from the queue, stop a printer, etc.). Our interest is in their overall design, their process control arrangement and their use of IPC and networking. We also develop a client program that sends files to a 4.3BSD `lpd` server for printing.

13.2 4.3BSD Print Spooler

First we consider a 4.3BSD system without any network connections. You execute the `lpr` command to print one or more files on any local printer. For example

```
lpr -Plp main.c subr.c
```

prints the two files `main.c` and `subr.c` on the printer whose symbolic name is `lp`. The mapping of symbolic printer names into physical device names, along with a complete specification of the printer's capabilities, is specified by the system administrator in the file `/etc/printcap`. We won't go into all the features and options provided by the `/etc/printcap` file in this text. Refer to Chapter 11 of Nemeth, Snyder, and Seebas [1989] for all the details. Also, there are many options available with the `lpr` command that we won't go into in this text—specifying the number of copies to print, the number of lines per page, and so on.

The actions of the `lpr` command shown above are as follows:

1. The two files `main.c` and `subr.c` are read by the `lpr` program and copied to the spooling directory. The name of the spooling directory for a given printer is specified in the `/etc/printcap` entry for each printer. Assume that for the printer `lp` the spooling directory is `/usr/spool/lpd`. Also assume that the symbolic name of the host is `orange`. The `lpr` command creates three files in the spooling directory

   ```
   dfA123orange
   dfB123orange
   cfA123orange
   ```

   The first is a copy of the file `main.c`, the second a copy of the file `subr.c`, and the third file is a "control file" that specifies the printing parameters for the program that prints the file. We show these spool files in Figure 13.1.

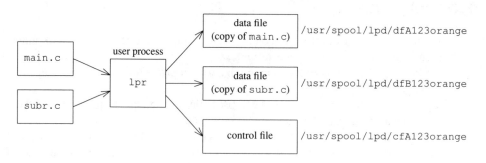

Figure 13.1   Spool files created by 4.3BSD `lpr` command.

An example of what the control file, `cfA123orange`, looks like for the example given above is

```
Horange
Pstevens
Jmain.c
Corange
Lstevens
fdfA123orange
UdfA123orange
Nmain.c
fdfB123orange
```

```
UdfB123orange
Nsubr.c
```

Each line in the control file starts with a letter that specifies a parameter for the printer daemon that eventually prints the file. The characters and their meaning are

f	filename of text file to print
C	class name for banner page
H	name of host system on which the `lpr` was executed
J	job name for banner page
N	name of file (used by `lpq`)
P	person (login name of user)
U	name of file to unlink after printing is complete

Note that in this example, the first five lines in the control file specify parameters for the entire job, and following these lines are three lines for every file to be printed.

2. Once the data files and the control file are written to the spooling directory, the `lpr` process sends an IPC message to the line printer daemon, `lpd`, notifying it that there is a job to print. The message contains the name of the printer (`lp`), so the daemon knows which directory to look at for the control files and data files. We show this in Figure 13.2.

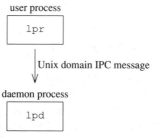

Figure 13.2 IPC from `lpr` process to `lpd` daemon.

This IPC message is sent using a Unix domain stream socket, since the daemon process is running on the same system as the `lpr` process.

3. The daemon process, which has been waiting for an IPC message on a Unix domain socket, does a `fork` of itself. This provides another copy of itself that handles the request, while the original `lpd` process waits for another IPC message notifying it that there are jobs to print. This is an example of a concurrent server, as described in Section 1.6.

4. The `lpr` process is now complete. It has copied the files to be printed to the spooling directory, created a control file for the spooling program, and notified the master print daemon that there is work to do. The `forked` copy of the printer daemon now looks at the files in the spool directory and sends them to the actual printer. This is shown in Figure 13.3.

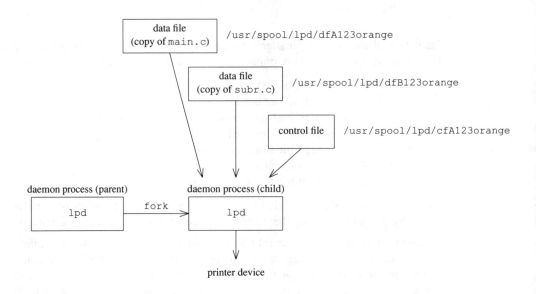

Figure 13.3   Processing of spool files by lpd daemon.

There are some fine points that were ignored in the description above. First, what if two different users send files to the same printer at almost the same time? This is where the 3-digit sequence number in the df filenames and cf filename is used. Each user's data files and control files have a different sequence number. The assignment of the sequence number is done by each client's lpr process. A file is maintained in each printer's spooling directory with the 4-character name ".seq". The pathname in the above example would be /usr/spool/lpd/.seq. This file itself has a length of four bytes—it contains the next 3-digit sequence number to be used, and a newline. The lpr process opens this file and then calls flock to obtain an "exclusive lock" on the file. The system doesn't return from the flock call until the process has an exclusive lock on the file. Otherwise the process is blocked until it can get the lock. When the lpr process obtains the exclusive lock, it reads the sequence number, and uses the value for its data files and control files. It immediately increments this number (cycling back to 000 if its value was 999), writes it back to the file, and closes the file. The close system call releases the exclusive lock that the process has on the file, in case another lpr process is waiting to get a lock on the same sequence number file. The actual code fragment to implement this is

```
sprintf(buf, "%s/.seq", SPOOLDIR);
if ( (fd = open(buf, O_RDWR | O_CREAT, 0661)) < 0)
        err_sys("cannot create %s", buf);

if (flock(fd, LOCK_EX))
```

```
        err_sys("cannot lock %s", buf);

seq = 0;
if ( (len = read(fd, buf, sizeof(buf))) > 0) {
        for (cp = buf; len--; ) {          /* convert ASCII to binary */
                if (*cp < '0' || *cp > '9')
                        break;
                seq = seq * 10 + (*cp++ - '0');
        }
}
        /* seq = sequence number to use */

seq = (seq + 1) % 1000;         /* increment seq# modulo 1000 */
if (lseek(fd, 0L, 0) < 0)
        err_sys("lseek error");
sprintf(buf, "%03d\n", seq); /* convert binary to ASCII */
if (write(fd, buf, strlen(buf)) != strlen(buf))
        err_sys("write error");
close(fd);                      /* unlocks the file too */
```

The names of the data files and control files do not conflict for jobs that are destined for different printers, since each printer has its own spooling directory. For example, assume two different users executed the lpr program at the same time, one printer on the printer named lp and the other on the printer named laser1. If the sequence numbers for the two printers just happened to be identical (345, for example), then the files are

```
/usr/spool/lpd/.seq
/usr/spool/lpd/dfA345orange
/usr/spool/lpd/cfA345orange
```

and

```
/usr/spool/laser1d/.seq
/usr/spool/laser1d/dfA345orange
/usr/spool/laser1d/cfA345orange
```

Note that the pathnames of all the files are unique. Note also that since the sequence number files are unique, neither process has to wait for the other to obtain a lock on its sequence number file.

The second point that was ignored above is what happens if there is already a printer daemon process that is busy printing a file on the requested printer. In each printer's spooling directory a file named lock is maintained. Whenever an lpd child process is active for a given printer, that process holds an exclusive lock on its lock file. When a copy of the lpd daemon is forked by the master lpd daemon, the first thing it does is try to obtain an exclusive lock on its lock file. If this fails, and if the reason for the failure is that another process already holds an exclusive lock on the file, then this new copy of the lpd daemon gracefully exits, since a copy of the daemon for this particular printer already exists. The actual code segment that implements this is

```
if ( (lfd = open(MASTERLOCK, O_WRONLY | O_CREAT, 0644)) < 0) {
        syslog(LOG_ERR, "%s: %m", MASTERLOCK);
        exit(1);
}
if (flock(lfd, LOCK_EX | LOCK_NB) < 0) {
        if (errno == EWOULDBLOCK)
                exit(0); /* active daemon present, normal exit */
        syslog(LOG_ERR, "%s: %m", MASTERLOCK);
        exit(1);
}
```

When a daemon is active for a given printer, it prints all files that appear in the spool directory for that printer. Even though the active copy of the daemon was invoked to print one specific print job, when it is done it looks in its spooling directory to see if any other jobs have been placed there for printing.

While the lpd child process has the exclusive lock on its lock file, it maintains the file as an ASCII text file containing two lines. The first line is the process ID of the lpd child process itself, and the second line is the name of the control file for the job currently being printed by the process. By keeping these two pieces of information in a file, it is easy for the lpq program (described later) to determine if a daemon is active for a given printer, and if so, which job is currently being printed. The way to determine if a process exists, given its process ID, is to use the kill system call and send it a signal 0, as we described in Section 2.4.

Output Filters

The description above is valid if there are no output filters being used for the print job. But the 4.3BSD spooling system supports several different output filters. These handle different types of data files and do resource accounting. The invocation of these filters by the printer daemon provides some interesting uses of process control.

A particular filter is specified with the lpr command. For example, to print the file plot.out that was produced by the Unix plot command on the printer named raster, we execute

```
lpr -Praster -g plot.out
```

The -g option causes lpr to change the first character of the control file from an f to a g. When the printer daemon reads the control file, this character tells it which output filter to use.

Figure 13.4 shows the lpr options that cause the different filters to be invoked. The interaction of these different filters is not at all obvious from an inspection of Figure 13.4.

`lpr` option	`printcap` keyword	Control file character	Description
	`of`		per-job filter—see description below
	`if`	f	default text filter for per-file accounting
`-l`	`if`	l	same as above with ''literal'' mode
`-p`		p	use `/bin/pr` command
`-c`	`cf`	c	`cifplot` filter
`-d`	`df`	d	TEX filter
`-g`	`gf`	g	`plot` filter
`-n`	`nf`	n	`ditroff` filter
`-f`	`rf`	r	FORTRAN-style output filter
`-t`	`tf`	t	`troff` filter
`-v`	`vf`	v	raster filter

Figure 13.4   `lpr` options and filters.

- First, group the filters into four categories, as shown in Figure 13.4.
  - the `of` filter
  - the `if` filter
  - the `/bin/pr` filter
  - the other seven data filters (the last seven entries in the table)

- The `-l` option to `lpr` specifies that the file is to be printed in *literal* mode—control characters are to be printed as is and the usual page breaks (form feeds by default) are not printed. All this option does is pass a special command line option to the `if` filter, so we can consider it equivalent to the `if` filter, for our purposes.

- The `if` filter is used by default. It is invoked for every file that is printed. It usually does the printer accounting function, appending a line to an accounting file specifying the login name and the number of pages printed, for every file.

- We can consider the other seven data filters equivalent to the `if` filter. These seven filters handle special data formats, while the `if` filter is for text files.

- If an `if` filter or one of the seven special data filters isn't specified for a file, the `of` filter is used instead. But the `of` filter is invoked only a single time for a print job, which might be comprised of multiple files.

- If the `if` filter or one of the seven special data filters is being used, the `of` filter is bypassed, even if it is specified for the printer.

- The $-p$ option, to use the Unix /bin/pr program before the file is printed, can be used with the other filters, or by itself.

We can now consider six cases that handle all the different combinations of output filters. These cases are shown in Figure 13.5.

if or other special data filter	of filter	/bin/pr	Case below
no	no	no	(1)
no	yes	no	(2)
yes	(ignored)	no	(3)
no	no	yes	(4)
no	yes	yes	(5)
yes	(ignored)	yes	(6)

Figure 13.5 Cases to consider for combinations of filters.

1. This case was shown in the example earlier in this section. The lpd daemon spawns a child process that prints all the data files on the printer device. No filters are involved.

2. When only an of filter is specified, the lpd child process first creates a pipe and then forks to create another process. This new child process uses the dup system call to assign the output end of the pipe to its standard input and to assign the printer device to its standard output. It then execs the filter program. The lpd child reads each data file and writes it to the pipe for the filter process to print. We show this in Figure 13.6.

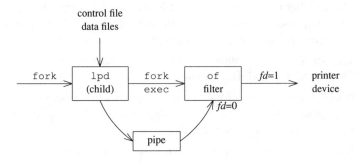

Figure 13.6 Processes and IPC for only an of filter.

3. When either an if filter or one of the seven special data filters is specified, the output filter is invoked for every file to print. Also, even if an of filter was specified, it is

not used. Before invoking the filter, the `lpd` child uses the `dup` system call to attach the input data file to its standard input, and the printer device to its standard output. This is shown in Figure 13.7.

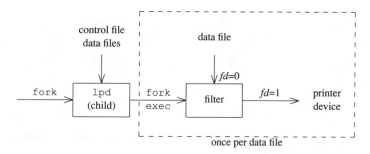

Figure 13.7 Processes and IPC for `if` or other data filter.

4. If the `/bin/pr` program is used as a filter, without an `if` or an `of` filter, we have the same case as the previous, with the `/bin/pr` program being used as the output filter. Figure 13.8 shows this case.

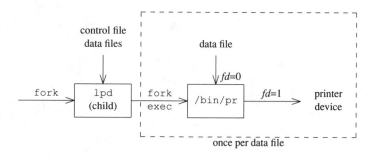

Figure 13.8 Processes and IPC for `/bin/pr` without other filters.

Since the `/bin/pr` program reads from its standard input and writes to its standard output, it can be used just like the printer specific filters.

5. When we have two filters between the `lpd` child process and printer device (the `/bin/pr` filter and the `of` filter), the two filters must be connected with some form of IPC. The technique used is a pipe. The first step is for the `lpd` child to create a pipe using the `pipe` system call, `fork` a copy of itself, and then `exec` the `of` filter. These are exactly the same steps used in case 2. This is shown in Figure 13.9. This first step is done only once by the `lpd` child.

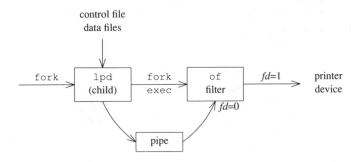

Figure 13.9   First step when two filters are being used.

Then, for every data file to be printed, the /bin/pr filter is invoked. This is done by forking and execing the /bin/pr filter, having it use the previously created pipe for its standard output, and the data file as its standard input. We show this in Figure 13.10.

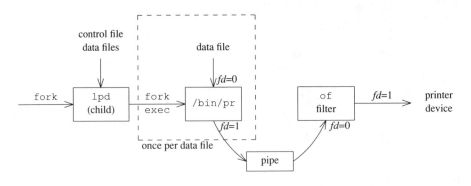

Figure 13.10   Final arrangement when two filters are used.

6. The final case also involves two filters between the lpd child and the printer device, but unlike the previous case, now both of these filters are invoked for every data file. Again, a pipeline is used as the form of IPC between the two filters. For each data file, the first step is to create a pipe and then fork and exec the /bin/pr program, connecting the pipe *from* /bin/pr back to the lpd child process. Figure 13.11 shows this arrangement. Note that the data file to be printed is attached to the standard input of the /bin/pr filter.

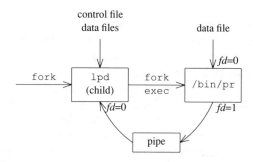

Figure 13.11 First step when two filters are invoked for every data file.

Next the `lpd` child process spawns the filter program, setting up the file descriptors before the `exec` so that the standard input for the filter is the pipe and the standard output is the printer device. This final arrangement is shown in Figure 13.12.

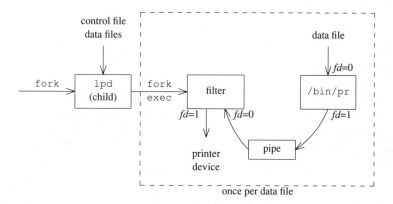

Figure 13.12 Final arrangement when two filters are invoked for every file.

For simplicity, we do not show that the `lpd` process opens the printer's log file on its standard error before `exec`ing any of the filters. By doing this, any of the filters can write error messages to their standard error.

Remote Printing

We now consider a request to print a file on a printer that resides on a remote host. The system administrator can set a flag for a printer in the /etc/printcap file that designates the printer as a remote printer and specifies the name of the remote host to send files to for printing. It is transparent to the users of the lpr command that the actual printer is connected to a different computer system. If we assume that the name of the local system (the system on which the lpr command is executed) is named orange and that the remote system (the one on which the files are printed) is named apple, we can pick up the example from above at the point where the master lpd daemon has forked a copy of itself to handle the request. This lpd child process recognizes that the request is for a remote printer from the printer's entry in the /etc/printcap file. Instead of sending it to the printer device, it opens a TCP connection to the printer service on the remote host, which is the lpd daemon on a 4.3BSD system. This gives us the processes shown in Figure 13.13. (The service name printer is converted to its TCP port number using the getservbyname function, described in Section 8.2.)

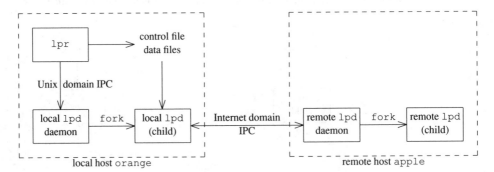

Figure 13.13 Processes and IPC for remote printing.

The master lpd daemon on the remote host is waiting for one of two events to occur

- a local connection on a Unix domain socket from a local lpr command, as described previously,

- a remote connection on an Internet domain socket from a remote lpd daemon, which we now describe.

The lpd process uses the select system call to wait for either connection to occur. When a remote connection is received, the remote lpd daemon first verifies that the sending host has permission to send it print jobs, and then forks a copy of itself. As before, it is the child process that does the actual work, allowing the parent to go back to its wait for a socket connection. This is another example of a concurrent server as shown in Figure 13.14.

Figure 13.14 Actual communication is between the two child processes for remote printing.

The first communication across the socket occurs when the local process writes the following 4 bytes to the socket

    \0021p\n

This line consists of a byte containing the binary value 2 (shown above as \002), followed by the ASCII name of the printer (1p in this example), followed by a newline. This is the standard format for IPC messages to or from the daemon: a binary byte that specifies the message type, followed by the variable-length ASCII message, followed by a newline. Acknowledgments usually consist of a single byte, with a byte of binary zero meaning all is OK, and other values indicating various error conditions. The first byte of this message, 2, specifies that the local host wants to send the remote daemon one or more files to print. This line is read by the remote process and it writes an acknowledgment message to the socket consisting of a single byte of zero. The local process now sends the data files to be printed, followed by the control file, to the remote process. The actual data flow is

1. The local writes a message of the form

        \003*size filename*\n

    to the remote process. The message type, 3, specifies that a data file is being sent. The first file transferred in our example is main.c. By specifying its *size* in bytes, the remote system can check that it has enough room for the file. Knowing the size before the file transfer also allows the receiving process to know when it has received the entire file. The *filename* in our example is dfA123orange. Note that the first line that was transferred across the socket between the two daemons specified the name of the destination printer (1p), so the receiving daemon can write the data file to the appropriate spool directory on the remote system. There is no need that the spool directory on the remote system be the same as on the local system. The /etc/printcap file on the remote system contains all the parameters for the remote spooling system.

    Note also that there cannot be filename conflicts in the remote spool directory with print files arriving from multiple hosts, each with their own sequence numbers. (Recall that the sequence number is assigned by the local host.) This is because the filename in the remote spool directory contains the host name.

2. If there is room on the remote system, the remote process responds with an acknowledgment consisting of a single byte of zero. If the file won't fit, the response is a single byte of two.

3. If there is room on the remote host, the local host now sends the actual data file. The entire file is transferred across the socket, followed by a byte of zero. Since the receiving host knows the size of the file, it knows when the entire file has been received. Note also that since the size of the file is known by the receiver before the file is transferred, there are no restrictions on what characters can be in the file. Either text files or binary files can be handled.

4. If the remote host receives the entire file and the final byte of zero, it responds with an acknowledgment of a byte of zero, otherwise it responds with a single byte of one.

Note that the network protocol being used by the two processes, TCP, is a reliable protocol with error handling built into it. The simple application protocol that we described above is between the two application processes (the two daemons). There are no checksums or block numbers specifically sent by the daemons in their messages—this is handled by TCP.

The four steps listed above are then repeated for the next data file, dfB123orange, which is a copy of the file subr.c, and then repeated again for the control file, cfA123orange. When the control file is transferred, the first byte of the message in step 1 is 2, instead of 3, indicating that the file is a control file and not a data file. Once the files are successfully transferred to the remote system, they can be deleted from the local system. The local process goes through the control file and for every U line, unlinks the corresponding file. The control file is then deleted.

Before closing the socket connection to the remote host, the local process first checks if any other print jobs have arrived that are to be sent to the remote host. If so, they are transferred. When there are no more jobs to transfer to the remote host, the local process terminates, which closes the socket. The remote process, which has executed a read on the socket, waiting for some more files to be transferred, gets an end-of-file return from the read. It then goes through its spool directory and prints the files that have been queued (i.e., the jobs that it received from the local host, along with any other jobs that are queued for the lp printer).

Two copies of the file are made when the file is printed on a remote printer. The first is made by the lpr process on the local host, and the other copy is made by the remote lpd daemon when it receives the file. Doing it this way makes it transparent to the local lpr process that the file is going to a remote host—the only process that needs to worry about sending the file to the remote host is the lpd process. Also, another benefit of the additional copy is that it is transparent to the local lpr process if the remote host is not available. The file is still spooled on the local system and can be transferred to the remote system by the lpd daemon as soon as the remote host is available. If we wanted to avoid the extra copy that is made, the lpr process would have to handle the transmission to the remote host and it would not be able to do the transfer if the remote host were down.

Security Issues for Remote Printing

We gave an overview of the network security used by 4.3BSD in Section 9.2. Figure 9.1 listed the steps taken by the `lpd` server. The steps are

1. First, any request from a remote host to access a printer must arrive with a reserved TCP port number. (Reserved Internet ports were discussed in Section 6.8.)

2. Next, the remote host must appear in either the file `/etc/hosts.equiv` or the file `/etc/hosts.lpd`. If a host is not considered an equivalent host for the `rshd` and `rlogind` servers (which we describe in Chapters 14 and 15), you can still give it access to your line printers by entering the host name in your `/etc/hosts.lpd` file. This file is used only by the printer daemon, to allow printer access to nonequivalent hosts.

3. Finally, the administrator has the option of specifying an option in the `/etc/printcap` file for any printer that restricts remote usage of the printer to users with accounts on the server's system. This option is handled by the `lpd` daemon. Recall from the comments in the `_validuser` function that we showed in Section 9.2, that the line printer server calls this function to validate a login name.

Ancillary Daemon Functions

We described in detail one IPC message that the master `lpd` daemon handles

   `\002`*printer*`\n`

This line was read by the daemon on its Internet domain socket and asked the daemon to receive one or more files from a remote system for queueing on the local system. The five message lines of this form that the daemon handles are as follows:

- check the queue for jobs and print any that are there,
- receive a job from a remote system,
- list the queue, short form,
- list the queue, long form,
- remove some jobs from the queue.

Step 2 from the first example of this chapter, when the `lpr` process sent a Unix domain message to the daemon after placing a job in the queue for a printer, sends the first of these messages to the daemon. The third and fourth messages are used by the `lpq` program to print the status of the queue for a given printer. The final message is used by the lprm program to remove a job from a print queue. The three programs, lpr, lpq, and lprm are the ones available for general users.

An additional program, /etc/lpc is available for the system administrator for additional control over the spooling system. The commands provided by this program are

abort   Kills an existing daemon (if one exists) and disables printing for one or more printers. The method used to disable printing is to turn on the owner-execute bit of the lock file in the spooling directory for a given printer.

start   Enables printing and starts a daemon for one or more printers. This command turns off the owner-execute bit of the lock file in the spooling directory.

clean   Remove any control files, data files, and temporary files that do not form a complete print job.

enable   Enables lpr to queue jobs for one or more printers. Queueing is enabled for a given printer if the group-execute bit of the lock file in the printer's spool directory is off.

disable   Disables queueing of print jobs by lpr by turning on the group-execute bit of the lock file in a printer's spool directory.

restart   Attempts to start a new lpd child process for a given printer.

stop   Stops an lpd child process after the current job completes, then disables printing on the printer.

up   Enables queueing and enables printing for a given printer.

down   Turns queueing off and disables printing for a given printer.

topq   Moves one or more print jobs to the top of the queue for a given printer. Since the processing of a printer's queue is done in a first-in, first-out order, based on the modification time of a job's control file, this command changes the modification time of the specified job's control files. Additionally, the world-execute bit of the printer's lock file is turned on to tell the lpd child process that the output queue for this printer must be rebuilt when it is finished with the current job.

`status`   Displays the status of a given printer—queueing status, printing status, number of jobs to print, and whether an `lpd` child process is active for the printer.

The features that a system administrator needs control over—enabling and disabling the queue for a printer, and starting and stopping a printer—are controlled by the owner-execute bit and the group-execute bit of the printer's `lock` file. Recall that the `lpd` child process for a given printer holds an exclusive lock on its `lock` file while it is active. Having the file locked by the `lpd` child process does not prevent the `lpc` process from modifying these execute bits in the file's access control word. Hence, a printer's `lock` file is used for six different purposes.

- The file is exclusively locked by an active `lpd` child process, to prevent multiple daemons from being invoked.
- If the owner-execute bit is on, printing is disabled.
- If the group-execute bit is on, queueing is disabled.
- If the world-execute bit is on, the `lpd` child process is to rebuild the queue after it is finished with the current job.
- The first line of the file is the ASCII process ID of the `lpd` child process, and is used by `lpc` to `kill` this process when turning a printer off.
- The second line is the name of the control file of the job being printed, and is used by the `lpq` process.

13.3   4.3BSD `lpr` **Client**

We now show a program that can act as a client to have one or more text files printed on a remote system. The remote system must provide a server that is compatible with the description of the 4.3BSD `lpd` server given in the previous section. It is intended that this program would be run on systems other than a 4.3BSD system. Our program does not spool the files to be printed on the local system, but instead it connects directly to the printer daemon on the 4.3BSD system. This means that if the daemon is not available (i.e., the system is down), this program returns an error message.

The following header file provides the global definitions and declarations.

```
/*
 * Definitions for line printer client program.
 */

#include         <stdio.h>
#include         <sys/types.h>
```

```
#define MAXFILENAME        128   /* max filename length */
#define MAXHOSTNAMELEN      64   /* max host name length */
#define MAXLINE            512   /* max ascii line length */

#define LPR_SERVICE     "printer"      /* name of the network service */
#define SEQNO_FILE      "/tmp/seqno"   /* name of the sequence# file */

/*
 * Externals.
 */

extern char     hostname[];      /* name of host providing the service */
extern char     printername[];   /* name of printer to use on hostname */
extern int      debugflag;       /* -d command line options */

/*
 * Debug macro, based on the debug flag (-d command line argument) with
 * two values to print.
 */

#define DEBUG2(fmt, arg1, arg2) if (debugflag) { \
                                    fprintf(stderr, fmt, arg1, arg2); \
                                    fputc('\n', stderr); \
                                } else ;
```

The function `main.c` processes the command line arguments and calls the function `send_file` for every file to be printed.

```
/*
 * Print one or more files on a remote line printer.
 *
 *      lpr  [ -h host ] [ -p printer ] [ -P printer ] [ -t ] [ file ... ]
 *
 * If no file arguments are specified, the standard input is read.
 * If any file argument is "-" it also implies the standard input.
 */

#include        "defs.h"

char    *pname;

main(argc, argv)
int     argc;
char    *argv[];
{
        FILE            *fp, *fopen();
        char            *s, *filename;
        int             i;

        pname = argv[0];
        while (--argc > 0 && (*++argv)[0] == '-')
                for (s = argv[0]+1; *s != '\0'; s++)
                        switch (*s) {
```

```
                        case 'P':                    /* specify printer name */
                        case 'p':                    /* specify printer name */
                                if (--argc <= 0)
                                    err_quit("-%c requires another argument", *s);
                                strcpy(printername, *++argv);
                                break;

                        case 'd':                    /* debug */
                                debugflag = 1;
                                break;

                        case 'h':                    /* specify host name */
                                if (--argc <= 0)
                                    err_quit("-h requires another argument");
                                strcpy(hostname, *++argv);
                                break;

                        default:
                                fprintf(stderr, "%s: illegal option %c\n",
                                                pname, *s);
                                break;
                        }

        i = 0;
        send_start();
        do {
                if (argc > 0) {
                        filename = argv[i];
                        if (strcmp(filename, "-") == 0) {
                                fp = stdin;
                                filename = "-stdin";
                        } else if ( (fp = fopen(argv[i], "r")) == NULL) {
                                fprintf(stderr, "%s: can't open %s\n",
                                                        pname, argv[i]);
                                continue;
                        }
                } else {
                        fp = stdin;
                        filename = "-stdin";
                }

                send_file(filename, fp);

                fclose(fp);

        } while (++i < argc);
        send_done();

        exit(0);
}
```

The file `printbsd.c` does all the work. It calls the function `tcp_open` that we showed in Section 8.3, to connect to the server.

```
/*
 * Send files to a Berkeley (BSD) line printer daemon.
 * This is done using a TCP connection, following the protocol
 * inherent (and undocumented) in the BSD printer daemon (/usr/lib/lpd).
 *
 * This program differs from the normal BSD lpr(1) command in the
 * following ways.  The BSD lpr command writes the files to be
 * printed into the spooling directory, and then notifies the
 * line printer daemon (lpd) that the files are there (using a
 * UNIX domain socket message).  The lpd program then sees that
 * the files get printed at some time.  If the files are to be
 * printed on another host's line printer, then the printer daemon
 * will contact the daemon on the other host (using an Internet
 * TCP socket) and will transfer the file to the other daemon,
 * who will then see to it that the file gets printed.
 * This program, however, acts like a UNIX printer daemon (lpd)
 * as we assume the files are to be printed on another system.
 * We go ahead and contact the UNIX lpd program on the remote host
 * (using an Internet TCP socket) and send the files to that
 * daemon for printing.
 *
 * There are three functions in this file that main() calls:
 *      send_start() - called once, before the first file
 *      send_file()  - called for every file that can be opened by main
 *      send_done()  - called at the end
 */

#include        "defs.h"
#include        "systype.h"

#include        <pwd.h>
#include        <sys/stat.h>

/*
 * Variables specific to this file.
 */

static FILE     *cfp;                       /* file pointer for control file */
static long     cfilesize;                  /* size of cfile, in bytes */
static char     myhostname[MAXHOSTNAMELEN]; /* name of host running lpr */
static char     username[MAXHOSTNAMELEN];   /* name of user running lpr */
static char     cfname[MAXFILENAME];        /* name of "cf" file */
static char     dfname[MAXFILENAME];        /* name of "df" file */
static char     buf[MAXLINE];               /* temp buffer */
static int      sockfd;                     /* network connection */
static int      seqnum;                     /* seq#, set to same value for now */

long    get_size();

/*
 * Start things up.
```

```
   */

send_start()
{
        register int    uid;
        struct passwd   *pw, *getpwuid();

        DEBUG2("send_start: host = %s, printer = %s", hostname, printername);

                                          /* we need a reserved port */
        if ( (sockfd = tcp_open(hostname, LPR_SERVICE, -1)) < 0)
                err_quit("can't connect to service: %s on host: %s",
                                          LPR_SERVICE, hostname);

        /*
         * If we got the reserved port, then we're either running as
         * root, or the program is set-user-ID root.  In the latter case,
         * the only reason we need to be set-user-ID root is to bind the
         * reserved port, so we can now go back to being the "real"
         * user who executed this program.  We really need to do
         * this anyway, to assure we can't read files as root
         * that the user doesn't have normal access to.
         */

        setuid(getuid());

        /*
         * Get the name of the local host.
         */

        if (gethostname(myhostname, MAXHOSTNAMELEN) < 0)
                err_dump("gethostname error");

        /*
         * Get the name of the user executing this program.
         */

        uid = getuid();
        if ( (pw = getpwuid(uid)) == NULL)
                err_quit("getpwuid failed, uid = %d; who are you", uid);
        strcpy(username, pw->pw_name);

        /*
         * We must insert a 3-digit sequence number into the filenames
         * that we're creating to send to the server.  This is to
         * distinguish between successive files that are sent to the
         * same server for the same printer.
         */

        seqnum = get_seqno();

        sprintf(cfname, "cfA%03d%s", seqnum, myhostname);
        sprintf(dfname, "dfA%03d%s", seqnum, myhostname);
        DEBUG2("cfname = %s, dfname = %s", cfname, dfname);
```

```c
/*
 * Create the control file and open it for writing.
 */

if ( (cfp = fopen(cfname, "w")) == NULL)
        err_dump("can't open control file: %s for writing", cfname);
cfilesize = 0L;

/*
 * Initialize the control file by inserting the following lines:
 *
 *      H<hostname>         (host on which the lpr was executed)
 *      P<username>         (person executing the lpr)
 *      J<jobname>          (for the banner page)
 *      C<classname>        (for the banner page)
 *      L<username>         (literal value for banner page)
 *
 * Then, for each file to be printed, send_file() will add
 * the following three lines:
 *
 *      f<df_filename>  (name of text file to print)
 *      U<df_filename>  (to unlink the file after printing)
 *      N<filename>     (real name of the file, used by lpq)
 *
 * The <df_filename> is of the form "df[A-Z]nnn<host>" where
 * "nnn" is the 3-digit sequence number from this host,
 * and "<host>" is the name of the host on which the lpr
 * was executed.
 */

add_H();
add_P();
add_C();
add_L();

/*
 * Send a line to the print server telling it we want
 * to send it some files to print, and specifying the
 * printer to be used.
 */

sprintf(buf, "%c%s\n", '\002', printername);
if (writen(sockfd, buf, strlen(buf)) != strlen(buf))
        err_dump("writen error");

if (readn(sockfd, buf, 1) != 1)
        err_dump("readn error");
if (buf[0] != '\0') {
        if (readline(sockfd, &buf[1], MAXLINE-1) > 0)
            err_quit("error, server returned: %s", buf);
        else
            err_dump("didn't get ACK from server, got 0x%02x", buf[0]);
}
}
```

```
/*
 * Send a single file.
 * This function is called by main once for every file to be printed.
 * Main has already opened the file for reading, but it still passes
 * us the actual filename from the command line, so that we can
 * use the filename for identifying the file to the server.
 */

send_file(filename, fp)
char      *filename;         /* filename from command line, or "-stdin" */
FILE      *fp;               /* file pointer on which file is open for reading */
{
        static int       filecount = 0;
        register char    *ptr;
        char             *rindex();

        /*
         * We don't currently handle standard input.  To do so requires
         * that we copy stdin to a temporary file, so that we can get
         * its size in bytes.  We have to know the file's size before
         * we send it to the server.
         */

        if (strcmp(filename, "-stdin") == 0) {
                err_ret("can't currently print standard input");
                return;
        }

        filecount++;

        /*
         * First strip any leading directory names off the filename.
         * This is to get the base filename for the job banner.
         */

        if ( (ptr = rindex(filename, '/')) != NULL) {
                filename = ptr + 1;
        }

        /*
         * If this is the first file, set the Job Class on the banner
         * page to the filename.
         */

        if (filecount == 1)
                add_J(filename);
        else
                dfname[2]++;      /* A, B, C, ... */

        /*
         * Add the 'f', 'U' and 'N' lines to the control file.
         */

        add_f(dfname);
```

```
                add_U(dfname);
                add_N(filename);

                DEBUG2("send_file: %s, dfname = %s", filename, dfname);

                xmit_file(filename, fp, dfname, '\003');
                                        /* transmit file across network */
}

/*
 * All done with the user's files.
 * Now we must transmit the control file that we've been building
 * to the other side.
 */

send_done()
{
        fclose(cfp);

        if ( (cfp = fopen(cfname, "r")) == NULL)
                err_dump("can't reopen cfile for reading");

        xmit_file("-cfile", cfp, cfname, '\002');

        fclose(cfp);

        /*
         * We're done with the control file, so delete it.
         * (Don't unlink if debugflag is 1, assuming we're debugging.)
         */

        if (debugflag == 0 && unlink(cfname) < 0)
                err_dump("can't unlink control file: %s", cfname);

        close(sockfd);
}

/*
 * Transmit one file to the server.
 * This routine is used to send both the actual text files (data files)
 * that the user wants printed, and to send the control file (cfile)
 * that we build up as we send the data files.
 * The only difference between transmitting these two types of files
 * is the first byte of the transmission (002 for the cfile and 003
 * for the dfiles).
 */

xmit_file(filename, fp, fname, xmittype)
char    *filename;      /* name from command line, or "-stdin" or "-cfile" */
FILE    *fp;
char    *fname;         /* the cfname or dfname */
char    xmittype;       /* '\002' or '\003' */
{
        register long   size;
```

```
        /*
         * We have to get the exact size of the file in bytes
         * to send to the server, so that it knows how much
         * data to read from the net.
         */

        size = get_size(filename, fp);
        DEBUG2("xmit_file: %s, size = %ld", filename, size);

        /*
         * Send a line to the print server giving the type of
         * file, the exact size of the file in bytes,
         * and the name of the file (its dfname, not its actual
         * name).
         */

        sprintf(buf, "%c%ld %s\n", xmittype, size, fname);
        if (writen(sockfd, buf, strlen(buf)) != strlen(buf))
                err_dump("writen error");
        if (readn(sockfd, buf, 1) != 1)
                err_dump("readn error");
        if (buf[0] != '\0')
                err_dump("didn't get an ACK from server, got 0x%02x", buf[0]);

        /*
         * Now send the actual file itself.
         */

        copyfile(fp);

        /*
         * Write a byte of zero to the server, and wait for
         * a byte of zero to be returned from the server,
         * telling us all is OK (I'm OK, you're OK).
         */

        if (writen(sockfd, "", 1) != 1)
                err_dump("writen error");
        if (readn(sockfd, buf, 1) != 1)
                err_dump("readn error");
        if (buf[0] != '\0')
                err_dump("didn't get an ACK from server, got 0x%02x", buf[0]);
}

/*
 * Copy a file to the network.
 * We read the file using standard i/o, one line at a time,
 * and write the data to the network one line at a time.
 */

copyfile(fp)
FILE    *fp;
{
        register int    len;
```

```
        char            line[MAXLINE];

        while (fgets(line, MAXLINE, fp) != NULL) {
                len = strlen(line);
                if (writen(sockfd, line, len) != len)
                        err_dump("writen error");
        }

        if (ferror(fp))
                err_dump("read error from fgets");
}

/*
 * Determine the exact size of a file.
 * Under UNIX this is easy - we just call the fstat() system call.
 * Under other operating systems it is harder, since they may not use
 * exactly one character to represent a newline.
 */

long
get_size(filename, fp)
char    *filename;
FILE    *fp;
{
        struct stat     statbuff;

        if (fstat(fileno(fp), &statbuff) < 0)
                err_dump("can't fstat");

        return(statbuff.st_size);
}

add_H()
{
        fprintf(cfp, "H%s\n", myhostname);
        cfilesize += strlen(myhostname) + 2;
}

add_P()
{
        fprintf(cfp, "P%s\n", username);
        cfilesize += strlen(username) + 2;
}

/*
 * We add the Job Class when the first file is processed.
 */

add_J(filename)
char    *filename;
{
        fprintf(cfp, "J%s\n", filename);
        cfilesize += strlen(filename) + 2;
}
```

```
add_C()
{
        fprintf(cfp, "C%s\n", myhostname);
        cfilesize += strlen(myhostname) + 2;
                                        /* just use this host's name */
}

add_L()
{
        fprintf(cfp, "L%s\n", username);
        cfilesize += strlen(username) + 2;
}

add_f(dfname)
char    *dfname;
{
        fprintf(cfp, "f%s\n", dfname);
        cfilesize += strlen(dfname) + 2;
}

add_U(dfname)
char    *dfname;
{
        fprintf(cfp, "U%s\n", dfname);
        cfilesize += strlen(dfname) + 2;
}

add_N(filename)
char    *filename;
{
        fprintf(cfp, "N%s\n", filename);
        cfilesize += strlen(filename) + 2;
}
```

The following function obtains the current sequence number and increments it for
the next user. We use the functions `my_lock` and `my_unlock` that we developed in
Section 3.2, to guarantee exclusive access to the sequence number file while we increment the value.

```
/*
 * Get the sequence number to use, and update it.
 */

#include        "defs.h"

int
get_seqno()
{
        int     seqno;
        FILE    *fp;

        if ( (fp = fopen(SEQNO_FILE, "r+")) == NULL)
                err_sys("can't open %s", SEQNO_FILE);
```

```
        my_lock(fileno(fp));                      /* exclusive lock on file */

        if (fscanf(fp, "%d", &seqno) != 1)
                err_quit("fscanf error for sequence number");

        rewind(fp);
        fprintf(fp, "%03d\n", (seqno+1) % 1000 );        /* next seq# to use */
        fflush(fp);

        my_unlock(fileno(fp));                    /* unlock file */

        fclose(fp);                               /* and close it, we're done */

        return(seqno);
}
```

Finally, the file `initvars.c` allocates space for and initializes the external variables.

```
/*
 * Initialize the external variables.
 * Some link editors (on systems other than UNIX) require this.
 */

#include        "defs.h"

char    hostname[MAXHOSTNAMELEN]        = "hsi";        /* default host */
char    printername[MAXHOSTNAMELEN]     = "lp";         /* default printer */
int     debugflag                       = 0;
```

13.4 System V Print Spooler

Under System V the `lp` command is executed by users to print one or more files on a line printer. If we execute

```
        lp -plaser1 main.c subr.c
```

the two files are queued for printing on the printer whose name, or class name, is `laser1`. Recall under 4.3BSD a printer is specified with the `-P` option to the `lpr` command, and the name following the `-P` is looked up in the `/etc/printcap` file. System V takes the naming one step further and allows names to be associated both with printers and with classes of printers. For example, we can create a class of printers with the name `laser` that might include 3 different printers. We then specify either a specific printer, perhaps `laser1`, `laser2`, or `laser3`, or the class name, in which case the system prints the job on the first available printer in the class.

When the `lp` command above is executed, the following steps take place:

1. Links are made to the two files to be printed, `main.c` and `subr.c`. If a link cannot be made (if the files are on a different filesystem from the `/usr/spool/lp`

directory), then the full pathname of the two files is remembered by `lp`. Additionally, an option can be specified to have `lp` make a copy of the files and print the copy. If a copy is not made, then any modifications made to the files before they are printed will appear in the printed output.

Assuming links can be made to the user's files, three files are created by `lp` in the directory `/usr/spool/lp/request/laser1`. These files are shown in Figure 13.15.

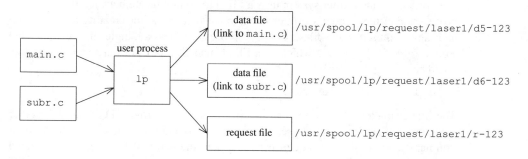

Figure 13.15   Spool files created by System V `lp` command.

Note that the System V line printer spooler requires that all directories and files start at the `/usr/spool/lp` directory, while the 4.3BSD only requires the file `/etc/printcap` to be in a known location, with all the spool directories pointed to by the `printcap` file.

The "request file" specifies the parameters for the print job. An example of what the request file looks like is

```
T
C 1
O
F d5-123
F d6-123
```

Each line in the request file starts with a letter that specifies a parameter for the printer daemon.

C	number of copies, `-n` option
F	name of file to print
O	printer-specific options, `-o` option
T	optional title, `-t` option

As with the 4.3BSD spooler, a sequence number is chosen for each print job by the `lp` command. Unlike the 4.3BSD system, the System V spooler uses a single sequence number file for all print jobs. The 4.3BSD system uses a separate sequence number file for each printer. A locking mechanism makes certain that multiple invocations of lp don't interfere with each other in obtaining the next sequence number. In the example above we assume the sequence number is 123. The names of the data files (the names of the links to the data files) are of the form d*n–seqno* where *n* is an integer that is incremented for every job that gets printed (the numbers 5 and 6 in our example) and *seqno* is the sequence number.

2. An entry is appended to the file /usr/spool/lp/outputq. This is a binary file whose function is described later in this section.

3. The System V line printer system uses a FIFO to communicate between the user's lp processes and the system's printer daemon lpsched. After creating a request file and any required data files, the lp process writes a single line to the file /usr/spool/lp/FIFO which is a FIFO (named pipe). In our example the line could be

```
r laser1 123 stevens\n
```

The first character, r, specifies that this is a print request (the FIFO is used for other messages between other processes and the daemon) and it is followed by the destination name (laser1), the sequence number and the name of the user who executed the lp command. The second and third parameters allow the daemon to go to the file /usr/spool/lp/request/laser1/r-123 to find the request file for this job. We specifically show the newline character at the end, as these are used as the message delimiters for the data in the FIFO. The communication between the user process and the daemon is shown in Figure 13.16.

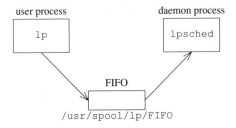

Figure 13.16 IPC through FIFO between lp and lpsched daemon.

After writing to the FIFO the lp process is finished. Note that multiple lp processes that might be executing at the same time have their writes to the FIFO handled correctly by the kernel. Recall from Section 3.5 that writes to a pipe or FIFO are guaranteed to be atomic, when the size of the write is less than the capacity of the FIFO, as it is here.

We now follow the actions of the system printer daemon, lpsched, when it receives a request to print a job. As with the 4.3BSD daemon, it does a fork to have a child process handle each job, but the actions of the System V daemon are more complicated.

1. If the requested printer is not busy, and it is enabled for printing, the daemon `forks` a copy of itself, and the "master" daemon (the parent) goes back to waiting for a request to be written to the FIFO. The parent remembers that the printer is now busy and it also remembers the process ID of the child process, so that it can `wait` for it later.

2. The child process (we'll call it the first child) opens and reads the request file. It builds a command line that is used for executing the interface program for the specified printer. In our example the command line is

```
interface/laser1 laser1-123 stevens "" 1 ""
    /usr/spool/lp/request/laser1/d5-123 /usr/spool/lp/request/laser1/d6-123
```

(The line above has been displayed as two lines to fit on the page.) The interface program expects its arguments to be as shown in Figure 13.17.

Argument	Description
0	Name of interface program. The interface program can obtain the name of the printer from the last portion of this argument, using the Unix `basename` command, for example.
1	Request name.
2	Login name.
3	Title. Shown above as an empty string.
4	Number of copies to print.
5	Options. Shown above as an empty string. This is where the `-o` options on the `lp` command are passed to the actual interface program.
6	First file to print.
7	Second file to print.
...	

Figure 13.17 Command line arguments to printer interface program.

(The first column in Figure 13.17, 0, 1, etc., is the index of the argument. In a C program the arguments would be `argv[0]`, `argv[1]`, and so on.) The first child opens the actual printer device and attaches it to both standard output and standard error. The standard input is attached to the empty device `/dev/null`, in case the interface program attempts to read from standard input. If the device file's permission bits allow reading, then both standard output and standard error are opened for reading and writing. Otherwise, they are opened for writing only. The attempt to open the device for reading is for those devices that present status information that the interface program might want to read. (The 4.3BSD print spooler has a similar feature that is specified as a per-printer option in the `/etc/printcap` entry for each printer.)

The first child does another `fork` and it is the second child that does the `exec` of the interface program, using a command line as shown above.

3. The second child does the `exec` and the first child `waits` for the interface program
    to complete. It is the interface program that reads the files to be printed and prints
    them. Most interface programs are shell scripts, and you can look at them by perus-
    ing through the files in `/usr/spool/lp/interface`. Note that there is no
    assumption by anyone whether the interface program is a shell script, a C program, or
    any other type of program—if a program can be `exec`ed and passed an argument
    list, it can be an interface program.

    When the second child has finished and calls `exit`, the first child has its `wait`
    return. The first child then deletes the request file and any data files that it created in
    the spool directory (the files `laser1/d5-123` and `laser1/d6-123` from the
    example). It then sends an IPC message back to the master daemon (the parent) noti-
    fying it that the specified printer has finished and is ready for more output.

The picture we have from these steps is shown in Figure 13.18.

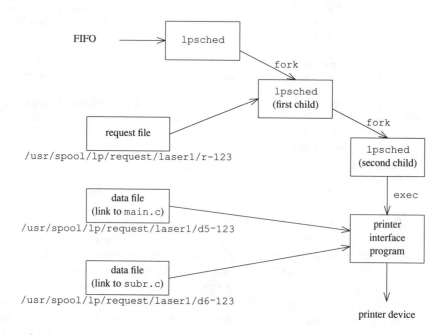

Figure 13.18   Processes and files used by System V print spooler.

    One point to note is that there is no requirement that the interface program print any-
thing. What is provided by the System V line printer spooler is a general purpose
scheduler that could be used for purposes other than printing files on a line printer. Since
it is easy to implement your own interface programs, you can have them do whatever you
wish. Be aware that there are some basic limitations in the scheduling algorithms

currently used by the spooler—for example, you cannot assign priorities to different requests, and you cannot have the spooler process the jobs in any order other than first-in, first-out.

When the master printer daemon is started, usually from the file `/etc/rc` during system initialization, it creates a file named `/usr/spool/lp/SCHEDLOCK` and locks this file. This is to prevent any additional copies of this daemon from starting, as long as the original daemon is still in existence. This same technique was used by the 4.3BSD daemon and it is a standard technique that programs can use to assure that only a single copy is running.

Ancillary Daemon Functions

The master `lpsched` daemon handles FIFO messages other than the "request to print a file" message that we have described. This is the method used by the other programs in the print spooler package to communicate with the daemon. The following programs make up the remainder of the print spooler package. It is worth going over the interactions of these programs with the daemon, as both an example of IPC usage, and to see how complicated a real spooling system is. Some of these programs can be executed by any user, while others are restricted to the system administrator.

accept   Allows the `lp` command to accept requests for a specific printer or class of printers. It modifies the file `/usr/spool/lp/qstatus`.

reject   The opposite of `accept`. It disallows requests for a specific printer or class of printers.

cancel   Stops the printing of the job that is currently being printed on a specified printer, or cancels a specific job, whether it is still in the queue or currently printing. If the job cancelled was currently printing, the printer then resumes with the next job in the queue, if any. To terminate a job that is currently printing, the process ID of the first child process is obtained from the `/usr/spool/lp/pstatus` file, and the `SIGTERM` signal is sent to that process. When the first child process receives this signal it sends the same signal to the process group of the second child process (the interface program). The `cancel` program also writes a `CANCEL` message to the FIFO for the daemon to `wait` for the terminated processes, and then restart the printer.

disable   Disables a specific printer and terminates any job currently printing on the printer. The job stays in the output queue, so it is reprinted in its entirety either on another printer in the same class, or on the same printer when it is `enabled` at a later time. A `DISABLE` message is written to the FIFO so that the daemon can try to find an available printer for any jobs that are queued for the destination that was just disabled.

enable   Enables a specific printer. An ENABLE request is written to the FIFO, notifying the daemon that the printer is available. The daemon then looks to see if any jobs are queued for that printer and starts the first job. Also modifies the file /usr/spool/lp/qstatus.

lp   The user program described earlier in this section that queues one or more files for printing. Creates the necessary data files and a request file, then writes a REQUEST message to the FIFO.

lpadmin   The program that manipulates all the files describing what printers are available, which printers belong to which classes, what the system default printer is, and the like. This command can only be run when the daemon is *not* running, so the first action of lpadmin is to write a NOOP request to the FIFO. If the write to the FIFO succeeds, the daemon is active and lpadmin aborts.

lpmove   Moves requests that were queued by lp between destinations. As with the lpadmin program described above, this program can only be executed when the daemon is not active.

lpsched   The master daemon for the print spooler system. Started at system initialization. Executes in an infinite loop reading requests from the FIFO and processing the requests. The daemon is terminated by the lpshut command, described below.

lpshut   Shuts down the spooling system. Writes a QUIT message to the FIFO. When the daemon processes this request it sends the SIGTERM signal to its process group, terminating any child processes it has spawned.

lpstat   User program to print the status of the print spooler system. This program determines if the daemon is active by writing a special request to the FIFO that the daemon just ignores. If the write to the FIFO succeeds, the FIFO is open for reading by the daemon and the daemon is active. If for some reason the daemon has died, the write to the FIFO fails, telling the lpstat program that the daemon is not active.

The print spooler programs also maintain three binary files that are used and maintained by the various programs.

```
/usr/spool/lp/outputq
/usr/spool/lp/pstatus
/usr/spool/lp/qstatus
```

- The `outputq` file contains one entry for every print job that is queued by the `lp` program. `lp` appends a binary record to the end of this file specifying the destination (printer or class), login name, sequence number, total number of bytes to be printed, and some flag bits. By maintaining this information in a disk file, should the system be stopped and restarted before the requested file has been printed, it is reprinted when the print spooler daemon is started again. When the daemon starts up, it goes through every record in this file, saving only those records that have not been printed. Note that the only way to delete entries from the middle of a file is to read the original file, write the desired records to a temporary file, then delete the original file, and rename the temporary file to the name of the original file.

- The `pstatus` file contains one binary record for every printer. The `lpadmin` program recreates this file when printers are added or deleted. Also, the programs `enable` and `disable` update the entries in this file as printers are enabled and disabled.

- The `qstatus` file contains one binary record for every destination (either a printer or a class of printers). The `lpadmin` program recreates this file when destinations are added or deleted, and the `accept` and `reject` programs update the entries in this file.

Since more than one program can try to access any of these three files at the same time, these files must be locked by the process that reads or writes the file. Indeed, each time a process needs to find a record in one of the files, it obtains an exclusive lock on the entire file, finds the desired entry, reads or updates the entry, then closes the file and releases the lock.

13.5 Summary

Line printer spoolers provide a nice example of process control. Multiple users are competing for a single resource (a printer). Some form of concurrency control is required so that each job is handled correctly. The 4.3BSD spooling system handles this at the user level by requiring the `lpr` command to obtain an exclusive lock on a sequence number file. At the `lpd` daemon level this is handled by having the daemon obtain an exclusive lock on its `lock` file, to assure that only a single daemon is active for any printer.

At the user level the System V print spooler also requires the user process, `lp`, to obtain a sequence number using a file locking mechanism. Requests from the user process to the master daemon, `lpsched`, are passed through a FIFO, using the fact that writes to a FIFO are guaranteed to be atomic (when less than the maximum size of a pipe or FIFO). The System V spooler programs also use three additional files to maintain various information about the print jobs, and these files are locked as required.

To handle the printing of files on a remote system, we examined the 4.3BSD spooler. We saw how the `lpd` process on a system is really waiting for either a print request from an `lpr` process on the same system, or for a print request from an `lpd` process on a remote system. We also examined the application protocol used by the two `lpd` processes to print a job on a remote system. Finally, we developed a simple `lpr` client that can be used to send files to a 4.3BSD `lpd` process on a remote system for printing.

Exercises

13.1   What is required for the System V `lp` program to print a file on a printer attached to a 4.3BSD system? Assume the two systems are connected with a TCP/IP link. Implement this.

13.2   What is required for the System V `lp` program to print a file on a printer attached to another System V system, assuming the two are connected with a TCP/IP link? Implement this.

13.3   What is required for the 4.3BSD `lpr` program to print a file on a printer on a System V system? Implement this.

14

Remote Command Execution

14.1 Introduction

Remote command execution is when a process on a host causes a program to be executed on another host. Usually the invoking process wants to pass data to the remote program, and capture its output also. 4.3BSD provides the `rsh` program that you can execute to invoke a program on another system. In this chapter we examine the building block for the `rsh` program: a function that a process can call to invoke a program on another system, with the input and output of the remote command connected to the invoking process.

Our task is to provide a function that can cause a program on a remote system to be executed. In the normal Unix tradition, we want to be able to write data that becomes the standard input of the remote process and be able to read what the remote process writes to its standard output. Additionally, we would like to be able to read what the remote process writes to its standard error, and be able to read this on a different channel from its standard output. If we don't separate these two output streams from the remote process, it'll be impossible to know which output corresponds to standard output or standard error. Finally, we would like a way to be able to send a signal to the remote process, as another way of controlling its execution. All these requirements lead to the picture shown in Figure 14.1.

We'll call the user process on the local host the *local process* and the user process on the remote host the *remote process*. What we've labelled as the *control process* has to run on the remote host, as it has to execute the `kill` system call on that host to send signals to the remote process.

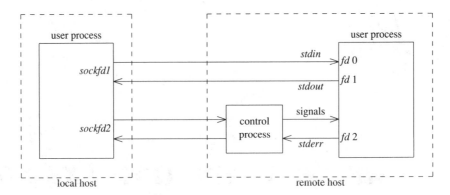

Figure 14.1 Remote command execution.

We'll discuss two functions that provide this type of process execution on a remote system: `rcmd` and `rexec`. The difference between the two has to do with the method used to verify that the caller of the function (the local process) has adequate permission to execute a particular process on the remote system. Also, the two functions invoke different servers on the remote system to set up the communication between the local process and the remote process. A summary of these two functions is given in Figure 14.2.

Function on local host	Server on remote host	Authentication
`rcmd()`	`rshd`	Caller must have superuser privileges so that a reserved port can be bound on the local host. No login name or password required.
`rexec()`	`rexecd`	Caller passes a login name and a cleartext password across the network to the server, for verification on remote host.

Figure 14.2 `rcmd` and `rexec` functions.

By *cleartext password* we mean the actual string of characters comprising the password that you enter when you login to the system. This is what gets encrypted into the "encrypted password" that is stored in the password file. Before describing the client and server code, let's consider the security issues.

14.2 Security Issues

We described the security features provided by 4.3BSD in Section 9.2, and showed the steps performed by the `rshd` and `rexecd` servers in Figure 9.1. Let's review the steps performed by the `rhsd` server, in the sequence in which they're performed.

1. The server checks the client's TCP port to verify that it is a reserved port. This port corresponds to the connection shown as *sockfdl* in Figure 14.1. If not, the connection is terminated.

2. The server reads the following three strings from the client: the client-user-name, the server-user-name, and the command string to be executed on the remote host.

3. The server-user-name is looked up in the password file by the server. If no entry is found, the connection is terminated.

4. If the password file entry doesn't contain a password, proceed to step 5. Otherwise,

    a. if the server-user-name is not root, the files `/etc/hosts.equiv` and `.rhosts` are used to verify the client. The latter file is looked for in the home directory on the server's system corresponding to the server-user-name. If the verification is successful, proceed to step 5.

    b. if the server-user-name is root, the file `/.rhosts` is used to verify the client. If the verification is successful, proceed to step 5.

5. If the server-user-name is not root, and if logins are currently disabled, the connection is terminated. On a 4.3BSD system, logins can be disabled for all users other than the superuser by creating a file named `/etc/nologin`.

All these steps can be seen when we present the source code for the rshd server in the next section.

14.3   rcmd **Function and** rshd **Server**

The rcmd client function and its corresponding rshd server, are central to the 4.3BSD networking system. Many of the 4.3BSD ''r'' commands call the rcmd function. The rcmd function is called by the programs shown in Figure 14.3.

Note the unfortunate choice of names. The rshd server is the server for the rcmd function, not just the rsh command. A better name for the rshd server would have been rcmdd. Also, System V implementations of the 4.3BSD ''r'' commands often rename the rsh program to be remsh, since the name rsh is already used by System V to mean a restricted shell. Also note that both the rcp and rdist programs function as either client or server. They both do this by using undocumented command line arguments to tell the other copy of itself to act as a server instead of a client.

Client Program	Remote Server	Command executed on remote system	Function
rcp	/etc/rshd	rsh, rcp	Remote file copy. Copies files and directories between systems.
rdist	/etc/rshd	rdist	Remote distribution. Allows the client system to update files automatically on a remote system.
rdump	/etc/rshd	/etc/rmt	Remote dump. Dumps filesystems on the client's system onto a tape drive on the remote system.
rlogin	/etc/rlogind	(special)	Remote login. Allows a user on the client system to login to the remote system.
rsh	/etc/rshd	user's command	Remote command execution. Allows a user on the client system to execute a command on the remote system.

Figure 14.3 4.3BSD programs that call the rcmd function.

The prototype for the rcmd function is

```
int rcmd(char **ahost, int remport, char *cliuname, char *servuname,
         char *cmd, int *sockfd2);
```

The first argument, *ahost* is a pointer to the address of the name of the remote host. The name of the host is looked up using the gethostbyname function, which we described in Section 8.2. Note that this is the address of a character pointer, not a character pointer. This is so that the official name of the host can be returned to the caller.

The rcmd function obtains a reserved TCP port, which implies that the calling process must have superuser privileges. The *remport* argument specifies the TCP port on the remote system that rcmd connects to. Normally the remote process is the rshd server, but the capability exists to connect to any process on the remote host. Beware, however, that the process that rcmd connects to must understand the application protocol used by rcmd and rshd, or nothing meaningful will result. The rlogin client uses this argument to have rcmd connect with the rlogind server. The rlogind server understands the application protocol used by rcmd and uses this to authenticate the user.

A typical code sequence that precedes the calling of the rcmd function is

```
#include  <netdb.h>

struct servent  *sp;

if ( (sp = getservbyname("shell", "tcp")) == NULL) {
        fprintf(stderr, "shell/tcp: unknown service\n");
        exit(1);
}

/* use "sp->s_port" as the "remport" in the call to rcmd() */
```

The *remport* argument must be in the network byte order, which is handled for us by the getservbyname library function.

The *cliuname* and *servuname* arguments specify the client-user-name and server-user-name, respectively. These login names are used to authenticate the user by the server on the remote system, as described in Section 9.2.

The *cmd* string contains the command string to be executed on the remote host. The rshd server executes this command string as

    shell -c *cmd*

where *shell* is the shell field from the password file entry for *servuname* on the remote system. Typically this field specifies one of the three common Unix shells: the Bourne shell, the C shell, or the KornShell. Since this command string is executed by a shell, it can contain special shell metacharacters, for interpretation by the shell on the remote host.

The final argument, *sockfd2*, is a pointer to an integer. If this pointer is not NULL, the rcmd function opens a second socket between the calling process and what we showed as the control process in Figure 14.1. The actual socket descriptor created by rcmd is returned to the caller through this pointer. If this pointer is NULL, the standard error of the remote process is duplicated onto the standard output (*sockfd1* in Figure 14.1) and there is no way to send signals to the remote process. This second socket is also bound to a reserved TCP port by the rcmd function. We'll call this second socket descriptor the secondary port.

The value returned by the rcmd function is the socket descriptor *sockfd1*. But if an error occurs, −1 is returned instead.

The application protocol used by the rcmd function is as follows:

Client—`rcmd()` function	Server—typically `rshd`
Create a socket with a reserved port. `connect` to server.	
	`accept` connection and get client's address (`getpeername`). If client did not bind a reserved port, terminate.
If a secondary port is requested by caller, create another socket with a reserved port. Write ASCII string specifying secondary port number. An empty string containing just the terminating null byte is written if a secondary port isn't needed.	
	Read secondary port number. If nonzero and not in the range of reserved ports, terminate. If nonzero, create a socket with a reserved port and `connect` to the client's secondary port.
If a secondary port is needed, `accept` connection from server, get server's address and if the server didn't bind a reserved port for its end of the secondary connection, return −1 to caller.	
Write three ASCII strings to server: *cliuname*, *servuname*, and *cmd*.	
	Read the three ASCII strings: client-user-name, server-user-name, and command string.
	Validate user. If OK, write a single byte of binary zero to client. If not OK, write a byte of binary one followed by an ASCII error message, followed by a newline, then terminate.
Read validation status from server. If an error occurred, read the error message and output it to standard error, then return −1 to caller. If OK, return socket descriptor to caller.	
	Server establishes process structure: establishes control process if a secondary port is needed and invokes shell to execute command for client.

We can now look at the `rcmd` function itself.

```
/*
 * Copyright (c) 1983 Regents of the University of California.
 * All rights reserved.
 *
 * Redistribution and use in source and binary forms are permitted
 * provided that the above copyright notice and this paragraph are
 * duplicated in all such forms and that any documentation,
 * advertising materials, and other materials related to such
 * distribution and use acknowledge that the software was developed
 * by the University of California, Berkeley.  The name of the
 * University may not be used to endorse or promote products derived
 * from this software without specific prior written permission.
 * THIS SOFTWARE IS PROVIDED ''AS IS'' AND WITHOUT ANY EXPRESS OR
 * IMPLIED WARRANTIES, INCLUDING, WITHOUT LIMITATION, THE IMPLIED
```

```
 * WARRANTIES OF MERCHANTIBILITY AND FITNESS FOR A PARTICULAR PURPOSE.
 */

#if defined(LIBC_SCCS) && !defined(lint)
static char sccsid[] = "@(#)rcmd.c      5.20 (Berkeley) 1/24/89";
#endif /* LIBC_SCCS and not lint */

#include       <sys/types.h>
#include       <sys/socket.h>
#include       <sys/file.h>
#include       <sys/signal.h>
#include       <netinet/in.h>
#include       <arpa/inet.h>

#include       <stdio.h>
#include       <netdb.h>
#include       <errno.h>
extern int     errno;

int                                     /* return socket descriptor - sockfd1 */
rcmd(ahost, rport, cliuname, servuname, cmd, fd2ptr)
char    **ahost;        /* pointer to address of host name */
u_short rport;          /* port on server to connect to - network byte order */
char    *cliuname;      /* username on client system (i.e., caller's username */
char    *servuname;     /* username to use on server system */
char    *cmd;           /* command string to execute on server */
int     *fd2ptr;        /* ptr to secondary socket descriptor (if not NULL) */
{
        int                     sockfd1, timo, lport;
        long                    oldmask;
        char                    c;
        struct sockaddr_in      serv_addr, serv2_addr;
        struct hostent          *hp;
        fd_set                  readfds;

        if ( (hp = gethostbyname(*ahost)) == NULL) {
                herror(*ahost);
                return(-1);
        }
        *ahost = hp->h_name;    /* return hostname we're using to caller */

        oldmask = sigblock(sigmask(SIGURG));

        lport = IPPORT_RESERVED - 1;
        timo  = 1;
        for ( ; ; ) {
                if ( (sockfd1 = rresvport(&lport)) < 0) {
                        if (errno == EAGAIN)
                                fprintf(stderr, "socket: All ports in use\n");
                        else
                                perror("rcmd: socket");
                        sigsetmask(oldmask);
                        return(-1);
                }
```

```
        fcntl(sockfd1, F_SETOWN, getpid());
                                /* set pid for socket signals */

        /*
         * Fill in the socket address of the server, and connect to
         * the server.
         */

        bzero((char *) &serv_addr, sizeof(serv_addr));
        serv_addr.sin_family = hp->h_addrtype;
        bcopy(hp->h_addr_list[0], (caddr_t)&serv_addr.sin_addr,
                                        hp->h_length);
        serv_addr.sin_port = rport;
        if (connect(sockfd1, (struct sockaddr *) &serv_addr,
                                sizeof(serv_addr)) >= 0)
                break;          /* OK, continue onward */

        close(sockfd1);
        if (errno == EADDRINUSE) {
                /*
                 * We were able to bind the local address, but couldn't
                 * connect to the server.  Decrement the starting
                 * port number for rresvport() and try again.
                 */

                lport--;
                continue;
        }

        if (errno == ECONNREFUSED && timo <= 16) {
                /*
                 * The connection was refused.  The server's system
                 * is probably overloaded.  Sleep for a while, then
                 * try again.  We try this 5 times (total of 31 sec).
                 */

                sleep(timo);
                timo *= 2;      /* increase timer: 1, 2, 4, 8, 16 sec */
                continue;
        }

        if (hp->h_addr_list[1] != NULL) {
                /*
                 * If there's another address for the host, try it.
                 */

                int     oerrno;

                oerrno = errno; /* save errno over call to fprintf */
                fprintf(stderr, "connect to address %s: ",
                                        inet_ntoa(serv_addr.sin_addr));
                errno = oerrno;
                perror((char *) 0);
```

```
                        hp->h_addr_list++;     /* incr. pointer for next time */
                        bcopy(hp->h_addr_list[0], (caddr_t) &serv_addr.sin_addr,
                                            hp->h_length);
                        fprintf(stderr, "Trying %s...\n",
                                            inet_ntoa(serv_addr.sin_addr));
                        continue;
                }

                perror(hp->h_name);        /* none of the above, quit */
                sigsetmask(oldmask);
                return(-1);
        }

        if (fd2ptr == (int *) 0) {
                /*
                 * Caller doesn't want a secondary channel.  Write a byte
                 * of 0 to the socket, to let the server know this.
                 */

                write(sockfd1, "", 1);
                lport = 0;

        } else {
                /*
                 * Create the secondary socket and connect it to the
                 * server also.  We have to bind the secondary socket to
                 * a reserved TCP port also.
                 */

                char    num[8];
                int     socktemp, sockfd2, len;

                lport--;        /* decrement for starting port# */
                if ( (socktemp = rresvport(&lport)) < 0)
                        goto bad;

                listen(socktemp, 1);

                /*
                 * Write an ASCII string with the port number to the server,
                 * so it knows which port to connect to.
                 */

                sprintf(num, "%d", lport);
                if (write(sockfd1, num, strlen(num)+1) != strlen(num)+1) {
                        perror("write: setting up stderr");
                        close(socktemp);
                        goto bad;
                }

                FD_ZERO(&readfds);
                FD_SET(sockfd1, &readfds);
                FD_SET(socktemp, &readfds);
                errno = 0;
```

```
                    if ((select(32, &readfds, (fd_set *) 0, (fd_set *) 0,
                                              (struct timeval *) 0) < 1) ||
                        !FD_ISSET(socktemp, &readfds)) {
                            if (errno != 0)
                                    perror("select: setting up stderr");
                            else
                                fprintf(stderr,
                                    "select: protocol failure in circuit setup.\n");
                            close(socktemp);
                            goto bad;
                    }

                    /*
                     * The server does the connect() to us on the secondary socket.
                     */

                    len = sizeof(serv2_addr);
                    sockfd2 = accept(socktemp, &serv2_addr, &len);
                    close(socktemp);          /* done with this descriptor */
                    if (sockfd2 < 0) {
                            perror("accept");
                            lport = 0;
                            goto bad;
                    }
                    *fd2ptr = sockfd2;        /* to return to caller */

                    /*
                     * The server has to bind its end of this connection to a
                     * reserved port also, or we don't accept it.
                     */

                    serv2_addr.sin_port = ntohs((u_short) serv2_addr.sin_port);
                    if ((serv2_addr.sin_family != AF_INET) ||
                        (serv2_addr.sin_port >= IPPORT_RESERVED) ||
                        (serv2_addr.sin_port <  IPPORT_RESERVED/2)) {
                            fprintf(stderr,
                                "socket: protocol failure in circuit setup.\n");
                            goto bad2;
                    }
            }

    write(sockfd1, cliuname, strlen(cliuname)+1);
    write(sockfd1, servuname, strlen(servuname)+1);
    write(sockfd1, cmd, strlen(cmd)+1);

    if (read(sockfd1, &c, 1) != 1) {          /* read one byte from server */
            perror(*ahost);
            goto bad2;
    }

    if (c != 0) {
            /*
             * We didn't get back the byte of zero.  There was an error
             * detected by the server.  Read everything else on the
```

```
                            * socket up through a newline, which is an error message from
                            * the server, and copy to stderr.
                            */

                           while (read(sockfd1, &c, 1) == 1) {
                                   write(2, &c, 1);
                                   if (c == '\n')
                                           break;
                           }
                           goto bad2;
                   }

           sigsetmask(oldmask);
           return(sockfd1);            /* all OK, return socket descriptor */

   bad2:
           if (lport)
                   close(*fd2ptr);
           /* then fall through */
   bad:
           close(sockfd1);
           sigsetmask(oldmask);
           return(-1);
   }
```

This is the first time we've encountered the function herror that is called at the beginning of the rcmd function. It is called if the gethostbyname library function returns
an error. The herror function is similar to the standard Unix function perror.
herror prints an error message based on the external variable h_errno. This external
is set by the gethostbyname and gethostbyaddr functions when an error is
encountered. The herror function was not in the original 4.3BSD release—it appeared
with the Tahoe release.

    The interesting process control is in the server process: rshd. Let's show the pro-
gram, then examine some of its details.

```
/*
 * Copyright (c) 1983, 1988 The Regents of the University of California.
 * All rights reserved.
 *
 * Redistribution and use in source and binary forms are permitted
 * provided that the above copyright notice and this paragraph are
 * duplicated in all such forms and that any documentation,
 * advertising materials, and other materials related to such
 * distribution and use acknowledge that the software was developed
 * by the University of California, Berkeley.  The name of the
 * University may not be used to endorse or promote products derived
 * from this software without specific prior written permission.
 * THIS SOFTWARE IS PROVIDED ``AS IS'' AND WITHOUT ANY EXPRESS OR
 * IMPLIED WARRANTIES, INCLUDING, WITHOUT LIMITATION, THE IMPLIED
 * WARRANTIES OF MERCHANTIBILITY AND FITNESS FOR A PARTICULAR PURPOSE.
 */

#ifndef lint
```

```
char copyright[] =
"@(#) Copyright (c) 1983, 1988 The Regents of the University of California.\n\
 All rights reserved.\n";
#endif /* not lint */

#ifndef lint
static char sccsid[] = "@(#)rshd.c      5.17.1.2 (Berkeley) 2/7/89";
#endif /* not lint */

/*
 * Remote shell server.  We're invoked by the rcmd(3) function.
 */

#include        <sys/param.h>
#include        <sys/ioctl.h>
#include        <sys/socket.h>
#include        <sys/file.h>
#include        <sys/time.h>
#include        <netinet/in.h>
#include        <arpa/inet.h>
#include        <stdio.h>
#include        <varargs.h>
#include        <pwd.h>
#include        <signal.h>
#include        <netdb.h>
#include        <syslog.h>
#include        <errno.h>
extern int      errno;

char    *index();
char    *rindex();
char    *strncat();

int     keepalive = 1;          /* flag for SO_KEEPALIVE socket option */
int     one = 1;                /* used for setsockopt() and ioctl() */

char    env_user[20]  = "USER=";        /* the environment strings we set */
char    env_home[64]  = "HOME=";
char    env_shell[64] = "SHELL=";
char    *env_ptrs[] =
        {env_home, env_shell, "PATH=/usr/ucb:/bin:/usr/bin:", env_user, 0};
char    **environ;

/*ARGSUSED*/
main(argc, argv)
int     argc;
char    **argv;
{
        int                     ch, addrlen;
        struct sockaddr_in      cli_addr;
        struct linger           linger;
        extern int              opterr, optind;         /* in getopt() */
        extern int              _check_rhosts_file;     /* in validuser() */
```

```
             openlog("rsh", LOG_PID | LOG_ODELAY, LOG_DAEMON);

             opterr = 0;
             while ( (ch = getopt(argc, argv, "ln")) != EOF)
                     switch((char) ch) {
                     case 'l':
                             _check_rhosts_file = 0; /* don't check .rhosts file */
                             break;

                     case 'n':
                             keepalive = 0;              /* don't enable SO_KEEPALIVE */
                             break;

                     case '?':
                     default:
                             syslog(LOG_ERR, "usage: rshd [-l]");
                             break;
                     }

         argc -= optind;
         argv += optind;

         /*
          * We assume we're invoked by inetd, so the socket that the connection
          * is on, is open on descriptors 0, 1 and 2.
          *
          * First get the Internet address of the client process.
          * This is required for all the authentication we perform.
          */

         addrlen = sizeof(cli_addr);
         if (getpeername(0, (struct sockaddr *) &cli_addr, &addrlen) < 0) {
                 fprintf(stderr, "%s: ", argv[0]);
                 perror("getpeername");
                 _exit(1);
         }

         /*
          * Set the socket options: SO_KEEPALIVE and SO_LINGER.
          */

         if (keepalive &&
             setsockopt(0, SOL_SOCKET, SO_KEEPALIVE, (char *) &one,
                                                         sizeof(one)) < 0)
                 syslog(LOG_WARNING, "setsockopt(SO_KEEPALIVE): %m");

         linger.l_onoff = 1;
         linger.l_linger = 60;
         if (setsockopt(0, SOL_SOCKET, SO_LINGER, (char *) &linger,
                         sizeof(linger)) < 0)
                 syslog(LOG_WARNING, "setsockopt(SO_LINGER): %m");

         doit(&cli_addr);
                 /* doit() never returns */
```

```
}

doit(cli_addrp)
struct sockaddr_in        *cli_addrp;      /* client's Internet address */
{
        int                       sockfd2, pipefd[2], childpid,
                                  maxfdp1, cc, oursecport;
        fd_set                    ready, readfrom;
        short                     clisecport;
        char                      *cp, *hostname;
        char                      servuname[16], cliuname[16], cmdbuf[NCARGS+1];
        char                      remotehost[2 * MAXHOSTNAMELEN + 1];
        char                      buf[BUFSIZ], c, sigval;
        struct passwd             *pwd;
        struct hostent            *hp;

        signal(SIGINT, SIG_DFL);
        signal(SIGQUIT, SIG_DFL);
        signal(SIGTERM, SIG_DFL);

#ifdef DEBUG
        {
                int t = open("/dev/tty", 2);
                if (t >= 0) {
                        ioctl(t, TIOCNOTTY, (char *) 0);
                        close(t);
                }
        }
#endif

        /*
         * Verify that the client's address is an Internet address.
         */

        if (cli_addrp->sin_family != AF_INET) {
                syslog(LOG_ERR, "malformed from address\n");
                exit(1);
        }

#ifdef IP_OPTIONS
    {
        u_char          optbuf[BUFSIZ/3], *optptr;
        char            lbuf[BUFSIZ], *lptr;
        int             optsize, ipproto;
        struct protoent *ip;

        if ( (ip = getprotobyname("ip")) != NULL)
                ipproto = ip->p_proto;
        else
                ipproto = IPPROTO_IP;

        optsize = sizeof(optbuf);
        if (getsockopt(0, ipproto, IP_OPTIONS, (char *) optbuf, &optsize) == 0
            && optsize != 0) {
```

```
                         /*
                          * The client has set IP options.  This isn't allowed.
                          * Use syslog() to record the fact.
                          */

                         lptr = lbuf;
                         optptr = optbuf;
                         for ( ; optsize > 0; optptr++, optsize--, lptr += 3)
                                 sprintf(lptr, " %2.2x", *optptr);
                                         /* print each option byte as 3 ASCII chars */
                         syslog(LOG_NOTICE,
                             "Connection received using IP options (ignored): %s", lbuf);

                         /*
                          * Turn off the options.  If this doesn't work, we quit.
                          */

                         if (setsockopt(0, ipproto, IP_OPTIONS,
                                             (char *) NULL, &optsize) != 0) {
                                 syslog(LOG_ERR, "setsockopt IP_OPTIONS NULL: %m");
                                 exit(1);
                         }
                 }
         }
#endif

         /*
          * Verify that the client's address was bound to a reserved port.
          */

     cli_addrp->sin_port = ntohs((u_short) cli_addrp->sin_port);
                             /* need host byte ordered port# to compare */
     if (cli_addrp->sin_port >= IPPORT_RESERVED   ||
         cli_addrp->sin_port <  IPPORT_RESERVED/2) {
             syslog(LOG_NOTICE, "Connection from %s on illegal port",
                                     inet_ntoa(cli_addrp->sin_addr));
             exit(1);
     }

     /*
      * Read the ASCII string specifying the secondary port# from
      * the socket.  We set a timer of 60 seconds to do this read,
      * else we assume something is wrong.  If the client doesn't want
      * the secondary port, they just send the terminating null byte.
      */

     alarm(60);
     clisecport = 0;
     for ( ; ; ) {
             if ( (cc = read(0, &c, 1)) != 1) {
                     if (cc < 0)
                             syslog(LOG_NOTICE, "read: %m");
                     shutdown(0, 2);
                     exit(1);
```

```
                }
                if (c == 0)                 /* null byte terminates the string */
                        break;
                clisecport = (clisecport * 10) + (c - '0');
        }
        alarm(0);

        if (clisecport != 0) {
                /*
                 * If the secondary port# is nonzero, then we have to
                 * connect to that port (which the client has already
                 * created and is listening on).  The secondary port#
                 * that the client tells us to connect to has to also be
                 * a reserved port#.  Also, our end of this secondary
                 * connection has to also have a reserved TCP port bound
                 * to it, plus.
                 */

                if (clisecport >= IPPORT_RESERVED) {
                        syslog(LOG_ERR, "2nd port not reserved\n");
                        exit(1);
                }

                oursecport = IPPORT_RESERVED - 1; /* starting port# to try */
                if ( (sockfd2 = rresvport(&oursecport)) < 0) {
                        syslog(LOG_ERR, "can't get stderr port: %m");
                        exit(1);
                }

                /*
                 * Use the cli_addr structure that we already have.
                 * The 32-bit Internet address is obviously that of the
                 * client's, just change the port# to the one specified
                 * by the client as the secondary port.
                 */

                cli_addrp->sin_port = htons((u_short) clisecport);
                if (connect(sockfd2, (struct sockaddr *) cli_addrp,
                                sizeof(*cli_addrp)) < 0) {
                        syslog(LOG_INFO, "connect second port: %m");
                        exit(1);
                }
        }

        /*
         * Get the "name" of the client from its Internet address.
         * This is used for the authentication below.
         */

        hp = gethostbyaddr((char *) &cli_addrp->sin_addr,
                        sizeof(struct in_addr), cli_addrp->sin_family);
        if (hp) {
                /*
                 * If the name returned by gethostbyaddr() is in our domain,
```

```
                        * attempt to verify that we haven't been fooled by someone
                        * in a remote net.  Look up the name and check that this
                        * address corresponds to the name.
                        */

                if (local_domain(hp->h_name)) {
                        strncpy(remotehost, hp->h_name, sizeof(remotehost) - 1);
                        remotehost[sizeof(remotehost) - 1] = 0;
                        if ( (hp = gethostbyname(remotehost)) == NULL) {
                                syslog(LOG_INFO,
                                    "Couldn't look up address for %s",
                                                          remotehost);
                                my_error("Couldn't look up addr for your host");
                                exit(1);
                        }
                        for ( ; ; hp->h_addr_list++) {
                                if (bcmp(hp->h_addr_list[0],
                                        (caddr_t) &cli_addrp->sin_addr,
                                        sizeof(cli_addrp->sin_addr)) == 0)
                                      break;  /* equal, OK */

                                if (hp->h_addr_list[0] == NULL) {
                                        syslog(LOG_NOTICE,
                                          "Host addr %s not listed for host %s",
                                              inet_ntoa(cli_addrp->sin_addr),
                                              hp->h_name);
                                        my_error("Host address mismatch");
                                        exit(1);
                                }
                        }
                }
                hostname = hp->h_name;
        } else
                hostname = inet_ntoa(cli_addrp->sin_addr);

        /*
         * Read three strings from the client.
         */

        getstr(cliuname, sizeof(cliuname), "cliuname");
        getstr(servuname, sizeof(servuname), "servuname");
        getstr(cmdbuf, sizeof(cmdbuf), "command");

        /*
         * Look up servuname in the password file.  The servuname has
         * to be a valid account on this system.
         */

        setpwent();
        if ( (pwd = getpwnam(servuname)) == (struct passwd *) NULL) {
                my_error("Login incorrect.\n");
                exit(1);
        }
        endpwent();
```

```
        /*
         * We'll execute the client's command in the home directory
         * of servuname.
         */

        if (chdir(pwd->pw_dir) < 0) {
                chdir("/");
#ifdef notdef
                my_error("No remote directory.\n");
                exit(1);
#endif
        }

        if (pwd->pw_passwd != NULL  &&  *pwd->pw_passwd != '\0'  &&
            ruserok(hostname, pwd->pw_uid == 0, cliuname, servuname) < 0) {
                my_error("Permission denied.\n");
                exit(1);
        }

        /*
         * If the servuname isn't root, then check if logins are disabled.
         */

        if (pwd->pw_uid != 0  &&  access("/etc/nologin", F_OK) == 0) {
                my_error("Logins currently disabled.\n");
                exit(1);
        }

        /*
         * Now write the null byte back to the client telling it
         * that everything is OK.
         * Note that this means that any error messages that we generate
         * from now on (such as the perror() if the execl() fails), won't
         * be seen by the rcmd() function, but will be seen by the
         * application that called rcmd() when it reads from the socket.
         */

        if (write(2, "", 1) != 1)
                exit(1);

        if (clisecport) {
                /*
                 * We need a secondary channel.  Here's where we create
                 * the control process that'll handle this secondary
                 * channel.
                 * First create a pipe to use for communication between
                 * the parent and child, then fork.
                 */

                if (pipe(pipefd) < 0) {
                        my_error("Can't make pipe.\n");
                        exit(1);
                }
```

```
if ( (childpid = fork()) == -1) {
        my_error("Try again.\n");
        exit(1);
}

if (pipefd[0] > sockfd2)            /* set max fd + 1 for select */
        maxfdp1 = pipefd[0];
else
        maxfdp1 = sockfd2;
maxfdp1++;

if (childpid != 0) {
        /*
         * Parent process == control process.
         * We: (1) read from the pipe and write to sockfd2;
         *     (2) read from sockfd2 and send corresponding
         *          signal.
         */

        close(0);         /* child handles the original socket */
        close(1);         /* (0, 1, and 2 were from inetd) */
        close(2);
        close(pipefd[1]);         /* close write end of pipe */

        FD_ZERO(&readfrom);
        FD_SET(sockfd2, &readfrom);
        FD_SET(pipefd[0], &readfrom);

        ioctl(pipefd[0], FIONBIO, (char *) &one);
                        /* should set sockfd2 nbio! */
        do {
                ready = readfrom;
                if (select(maxfdp1, &ready, (fd_set *) 0,
                        (fd_set *) 0, (struct timeval *) 0) < 0)
                                /* wait until something to read */
                        break;

                if (FD_ISSET(sockfd2, &ready)) {
                        if (read(sockfd2, &sigval, 1) <= 0)
                                FD_CLR(sockfd2, &readfrom);
                        else
                                killpg(childpid, sigval);
                }

                if (FD_ISSET(pipefd[0], &ready)) {
                        errno = 0;
                        cc = read(pipefd[0], buf, sizeof(buf));
                        if (cc <= 0) {
                                shutdown(sockfd2, 2);
                                FD_CLR(pipefd[0], &readfrom);
                        } else
                                write(sockfd2, buf, cc);
                }
        } while (FD_ISSET(sockfd2, &readfrom) ||
```

```
                                    FD_ISSET(pipefd[0], &readfrom));
                /*
                 * The pipe will generate an EOF when the shell
                 * terminates.  The socket will terminate when the
                 * client process terminates.
                 */

                exit(0);
        }

        /*
         * Child process.  Become a process group leader, so that
         * the control process above can send signals to all the
         * processes we may be the parent of.  The process group ID
         * (the getpid() value below) equals the childpid value from
         * the fork above.
         */

        setpgrp(0, getpid());
        close(sockfd2);         /* control process handles this fd */
        close(pipefd[0]);       /* close read end of pipe */
        dup2(pipefd[1], 2);     /* stderr of shell has to go through
                                   pipe to control process */
        close(pipefd[1]);
}

if (*pwd->pw_shell == '\0')
        pwd->pw_shell = "/bin/sh";

/*
 * Set the gid, then uid to become the user specified by "servuname".
 */

setgid((gid_t) pwd->pw_gid);
initgroups(pwd->pw_name, pwd->pw_gid);  /* BSD groups */
setuid((uid_t) pwd->pw_uid);

/*
 * Set up an initial environment for the shell that we exec().
 */

environ = env_ptrs;
strncat(env_home,  pwd->pw_dir,   sizeof(env_home)-6);
strncat(env_shell, pwd->pw_shell, sizeof(env_shell)-7);
strncat(env_user,  pwd->pw_name,  sizeof(env_user)-6);

if ( (cp = rindex(pwd->pw_shell, '/')) != NULL)
        cp++;                           /* step past first slash */
else
        cp = pwd->pw_shell;     /* no slash in shell string */

execl(pwd->pw_shell, cp, "-c", cmdbuf, (char *) 0);

perror(pwd->pw_shell);          /* error from execl() */
```

```
            exit(1);
    }

    /*
     * Read a string from the socket.  Make sure it fits, else fatal error.
     */

    getstr(buf, cnt, errmesg)
    char    *buf;
    int     cnt;              /* sizeof() the char array */
    char    *errmesg;        /* in case error message required */
    {
            char    c;

            do {
                    if (read(0, &c, 1) != 1)
                            exit(1);         /* error or EOF */
                    *buf++ = c;
                    if (--cnt == 0) {
                            my_error("%s too long.\n", errmesg);
                            exit(1);
                    }
            } while (c != 0);        /* null byte terminates the string */
    }

    /*
     * Send an error message back to the rcmd() client.
     * The first byte we send must be binary 1, followed by the ASCII
     * error message, followed by a newline.
     */

    my_error(va_alist)
    va_dcl
    {
            va_list         args;
            char            *fmt, buff[BUFSIZ];

            va_start(args);
            fmt = va_arg(args, char *);
            buff[0] = 1;
            vsprintf(buff + 1, fmt, args);
            va_end(args);

            write(2, buff, strlen(buff));    /* fd 2 = socket, from inetd */
    }

    /*
     * Check whether the specified host is in our local domain, as determined
     * by the part of the name following the first period, in its name and in ours.
     * If either name is unqualified (contains no period), assume that the host
     * is local, as it will be interpreted as such.
     */

    int                              /* return 1 if local domain, else return 0 */
```

```
local_domain(host)
char    *host;
{
        register char    *ptr1, *ptr2;
        char             localhost[MAXHOSTNAMELEN];

        if ( (ptr1 = index(host, '.')) == NULL)
                return(1);                      /* no period in remote host name */

        gethostname(localhost, sizeof(localhost));
        if ( (ptr2 = index(localhost, '.')) == NULL)
                return(1);                      /* no period in local host name */

        /*
         * Both host names contain a period.  Now compare both names,
         * starting with the first period in each name (i.e., the names
         * of their respective domains).  If equal, then the remote domain
         * equals the local domain, return 1.
         */

        if (strcasecmp(ptr1, ptr2) == 0)        /* case insensitive compare */
                return(1);

        return(0);
}
```

Note that the change to the home directory of the specified server-user-name has an error return that is commented out, if the `chdir` fails. For some unknown reason this error is commented out in the 4.3BSD release, the 4.3BSD Tahoe release, and the BSD networking release. Instead the remote user is started in the root directory.

Note also that the loop that becomes the control process uses the `killpg` system call, which we haven't described yet. This system call sends a signal to a specified process group. Our use of it here is equivalent to the call

```
kill(-childpid, sigval);
```

as we described in Section 2.4. The reason the `killpg` system call is used here is because 4.2BSD didn't support the option to the `kill` system call that sends a signal to a process group. This feature was added to 4.3BSD for System V compatibility.

When a secondary channel isn't requested by the client, the final picture is simple, as shown in Figure 14.4.

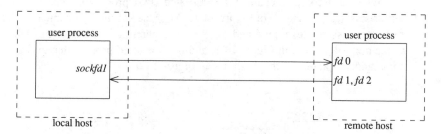

Figure 14.4 rshd connection without a secondary channel.

Let's examine the actual sequence of steps. When rcmd connects to the rshd server, on a 4.3BSD system the inetd superserver is listening on that port for the connection request. inetd invokes the rshd server through a fork followed by an exec. Then the rshd process execs the shell program, which in turn forks and execs the user's command. This is a minimum of two forks and three execs on the remote system, as shown in Figure 14.5.

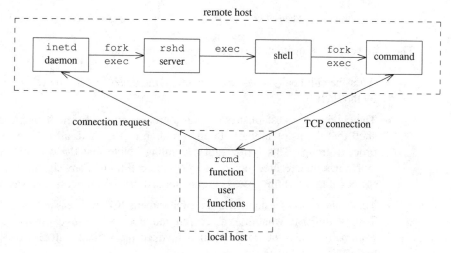

Figure 14.5 Sequence of steps to establish an rshd connection.

When a secondary channel is requested, two processes must be running on the server's system, as shown in Figure 14.1. After the secondary channel is established, the rshd process creates a pipe and forks. The parent process becomes what we showed as the control process in Figure 14.1, and it is the child process that executes the client's command. A picture of this is shown in Figure 14.6.

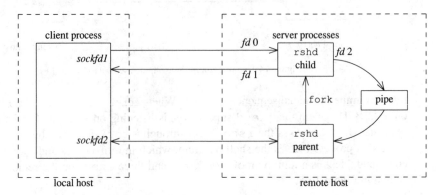

Figure 14.6   rshd connection with a secondary channel.

There are several points to note from the rshd source code.

- After the child calls the execl function, the upper box in Figure 14.6 is replaced by the shell.

- The child process establishes itself as a process group leader. This means that the shell that it execs along with any children of the shell, all belong to the same process group. This is ior signal handling. Note that the control process, the rshd parent, executes the killpg system call to send any signals received from the client to the entire process group, not just the shell process that was started.

- The child process establishes an environment list for the shell that it invokes. This is similar to what the login program does before invoking the user's shell. Minimally, when the user's shell is invoked the variables HOME, USER, PATH, and SHELL should be set.

- There is no way for the client process on the local system to obtain the exit status from the shell on the remote system.

14.4 `rexec` **Function and** `rexecd` **Server**

The `rexec` function is similar to the `rcmd` function, with one major difference. The process that calls `rexec` does not need superuser privileges, since a reserved port is not required. The authentication scheme used between `rexec` and its server, `rexecd`, is for the cleartext password of the user to be passed from the client to the server. The server takes the cleartext password and encrypts it. The server then compares its encrypted version with the encrypted version in the password file on the server's system.

The problem is that a cleartext copy of the user's password travels across the network, allowing anyone connected to the network (either legitimately, as on a broadcast network such as an Ethernet, or illegally if the listener has tapped the network medium) to see the password. Also, to pass the cleartext password to the `rexec` function, the caller might have their password in the source file, which is another potential security hole.

The calling sequence for `rexec` is similar to the calling sequence for `rcmd`.

```
int rexec(char **ahost, int remport, char *servuname, char *password,
          char *cmd, int *sockfd2);
```

The *ahost*, *remport*, *servuname*, *cmd*, and *sockfd2* arguments are identical to those described in Section 14.3 for the `rcmd` function. The cleartext *password* and the *servuname* are used to validate the caller on the server's system.

We won't show the source code for the `rexec` function and its `rexecd` server, as they are similar to the ones shown in the previous section for `rcmd` and `rshd`. The process control is identical. The only differences have to do with user authentication on the remote host.

14.5 Summary

The `rcmd` function is central to the 4.3BSD system, as shown by the list of programs that use it in Figure 14.3. One fundamental problem, however, is that a reserved port is required to use this function. The `rexec` function isn't of practical use, since it requires a cleartext password as an argument. A better authentication system, such as the Kerberos system that we described in Section 9.3, is required.

The initial statement of the problem that we were trying to solve, given in Section 14.1, along with the picture of the processes shown in Figure 14.1, is the starting point for any application that is to be divided among multiple processes. We must first be able to show which process is doing what, and how the I/O streams are connected, before trying to understand or write the actual source code.

Exercises

14.1   Propose changes to the `rshd` server so that it can return the `exit` status to the client process. What changes have to be made to the client?

14.2   It would appear that a nonprivileged process must use the `rexec` function to execute a program on another system. But, an alternative technique is as follows. Create a pair of pipes and `fork`. Have the child set up its ends of the pipes to be standard input and standard output and then `exec` the `rsh` program (`remsh` under System V). Since `rsh` is a set-user-ID program it can call `rcmd` to invoke your program on the remote host. Diagram the processes involved in this and develop a function to do this. Would you rather use a pair of regular pipes for the IPC between the client and `rsh`, or a stream pipe? What happens to the standard error from `rsh`?

14.3   The protocol used by `rcmd` sends a binary byte from the client process to the control process to send a signal to the remote command. Are the binary signal numbers the same between different versions of Unix? What happens if a System V client sends `SIGUSR1` to a 4.3BSD server?

14.4   Why can't the `rexec` function pass the encrypted password string to the `rexecd` server, instead of the cleartext password?

14.5   Why does the `rshd` server call the `access` system call to check the file `/etc/nologin`, instead of just `opening` the file to see if it exists?

15

Remote Login

15.1 Introduction

The ability to login from one computer to another is an important networking application. 4.3BSD provides two remote login applications: `rlogin`, which assumes the server is another Unix system, and `telnet`, which we mentioned in Section 5.2.5. TELNET is a standard Internet application that most TCP/IP implementations support, regardless of the host operating system. Most Unix implementations of TCP/IP (4.3BSD and others) support the `rlogin` protocol.

Any discussion of remote login from one computer system to another involves the details of terminal handling. The discussion also requires knowledge of *pseudo-terminals*. Instead of just presenting the details of pseudo-terminals and terminal I/O, we'll first develop a simple example: a program that can make a copy of all the input and output during a login session. We'll enhance this example in four steps as we proceed, showing where its shortcomings are, and fixing them. We'll develop this example under both 4.3BSD and System V Release 3.2. Pseudo-terminals have always been a mystical and undocumented feature of Unix. But to understand the use of a network to login to another computer, knowledge of pseudo-terminals is required.

After this example, we provide an overview of the 4.3BSD remote login facility. We then discuss some additional terminal features—dynamic window sizes and flow control, and their implications for a remote login application. This leads to a detailed presentation of the source code for the 4.3BSD `rlogin` client and its `rlogind` server.

589

15.2 Terminal Line Disciplines

Terminal drivers are complicated by the *line disciplines* associated with them. Also, a terminal is assumed to be a full-duplex device, so that the input path and output path are separate. The line discipline is within the kernel, somewhere between the actual device driver and the user's process. Figure 15.1 shows this for a normal interactive shell.

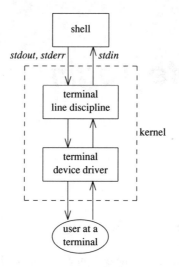

Figure 15.1 Normal interactive shell showing terminal line discipline.

Notice how similar this picture looks to the pictures of stream modules from Chapter 7. Indeed, with a stream implementation, the terminal line discipline is just a module that is pushed onto a stream on top of the actual terminal device driver. With systems that don't support streams, the link between the terminal line discipline and the terminal device driver is much tighter.

There are several functions that can be done by a line discipline module.

- Echo the characters that are entered.

- Assemble the characters entered into lines, so that a process reading from the terminal receives complete lines.

- Edit the lines that are input. Unix allows you to erase the preceding character and also to kill the entire line being input and start over with a new line.

- Generate signals when certain terminal keys are entered. The SIGINT and SIGQUIT signals can be generated this way, for example.

- Process flow control characters. For example, when you press the Control-S key, the output to the terminal is stopped. To restart the output, the Control-Q key is entered.

- Allow you to enter an end-of-file character.

- Do character conversions. For example, every time a process writes a newline character, the line discipline can convert it to a carriage return and a line feed. Also, tab characters that are output can be converted to spaces if the terminal doesn't handle tab characters.

There are numerous versions of line discipline modules. For example, 4.3BSD supplies five modules.

- The "old discipline" that is similar to the Version 7 Unix terminal handler. This discipline handles the features listed above (echoing, line building, signal generation, etc.) but does not provide the features needed for job control.

- The "new discipline" is a superset of the old discipline. It provides the features needed for job control along with enhanced editing capabilities (erase-previous-word and escape-next-character, for example).

- The Berknet line discipline. Berknet is an obsolete networking system that was originally used to connect PDP-11 Unix systems together using 9600 baud serial lines.

- The Serial Line Internet Protocol (SLIP) can be used to transfer IP datagrams across serial lines.

- The tablet line discipline is used for specific graphics tablet devices.

Part of the complication of terminal handling arises from the many different devices that can be connected to an asynchronous serial line on a computer. Not only are interactive terminals connected this way, but printers, modems, plotters, and the like are also attached to terminal lines. Even when a terminal line is being used for interactive input, different programs want to access the terminal differently. Some process lines, some are full-screen editors, and some want the echo facility disabled (when entering a password, for example).

We'll discuss the way a process changes the mode of a terminal device in Section 15.5.

15.3 A Simple Example

Our first task is to develop a program that can be invoked to keep a log of everything that is input or output on your terminal. This could be used, for example, to generate documentation for a particular program, by providing the exact sequence of what is output in response to a specific input. 4.3BSD provides a program named `script` that does this function. A picture of what we want is shown in Figure 15.2.

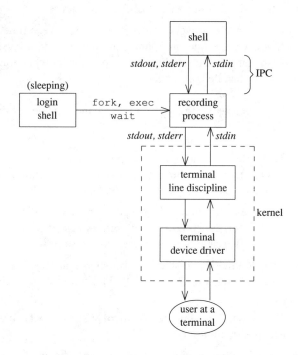

Figure 15.2 Recording process overview.

When you start the recording process from your login shell, the login shell `forks` and `execs` the new process, then the login shell goes to sleep, waiting for the recording process to complete. The recording process establishes an IPC channel of some form, then `forks` and `execs` another shell process, and this is the new shell that you interact with. The IPC channel that is set up by the recording process has to become the standard input, standard output, and standard error of the newly created shell process, in order for the shell to work normally. We'll put our recording process between the terminal and the shell you're interacting with, so we can look at all the data that is being input to and output from the shell and record it somewhere. The output includes what is generated by any program that the shell runs, since by default the shell duplicates its standard output and standard error before starting any program (see Section 2.5).

Two points should be noted. First, the login shell still has its standard input, standard output, and standard error connected to the terminal line discipline—although the arrows are not shown in the diagram, the shell has not closed these three descriptors. But since the login shell is asleep, waiting for its child process (the recording process) to terminate, there won't be any I/O by the login shell on any of these three file descriptors. Second, although we have talked about the recording process as being able to save a copy of all the input and output in a file, we won't show any code to do this, to avoid complicating our programs with this feature. The goal of the examples in this section is to understand the involvement of Unix terminals in remote logins.

In our first version of this program we'll use a stream pipe to do what we label as "IPC" in Figure 15.2. This provides a full-duplex channel between the newly invoked shell and the recording process. We could use a standard Unix unidirectional pipe, but that takes more work, as we showed in Section 3.4. First we have the `main` function for the recording process.

```
/*
 * Recording process, first try: use stream pipes.
 */

main(argc, argv, envp)
int     argc;
char    **argv;
char    **envp;
{
        int     fd[2], childpid;

        if (!isatty(0) || !isatty(1))
                err_quit("stdin and stdout must be a terminal");

        if (s_pipe(fd) < 0)
                err_sys("can't create stream pipe");

        if ( (childpid = fork()) < 0)
                err_sys("can't fork");
        else if (childpid == 0) {           /* child process */
                close(fd[0]);
                exec_shell(fd[1], argv, envp);
                        /* NOTREACHED */
        }

        close(fd[1]);                       /* parent process */
        pass_all(fd[0], childpid);
        exit(0);
}
```

This `main` function calls the `s_pipe` function that we developed in Sections 6.9 and 7.9 to create an unnamed stream pipe. The child process of the `main` function calls the function `exec_shell` to `exec` the new shell process.

```
/*
 * Exec a shell process, dup'ing the specified "fd" as its
 * standard input, standard output and standard error.
 */

#include        <stdio.h>
#include        "systype.h"

exec_shell(fd, argv, envp)
int     fd;                /* communication channel */
char    **argv;
char    **envp;
{
        char    *shell;
```

```
        char    *getenv(), *rindex();

        close(0); close(1); close(2);
        if (dup(fd) != 0 || dup(fd) != 1 || dup(fd) != 2)
                err_sys("dup error");
        close(fd);

        /*
         * We must set up the pathname of the shell to be exec'ed,
         * and its argv[0].
         */

        if ( (shell = getenv("SHELL")) == NULL) /* look at environment */
                shell = "/bin/sh";        /* default */
        if ( (argv[0] = rindex(shell, '/')) != NULL)
                argv[0]++;                       /* step past rightmost slash */
        else
                argv[0] = shell;          /* no slashes in pathname */

        execve(shell, argv, envp);
        err_sys("execve error");
                /* NOTREACHED */
}
```

Before calling `execve`, the child duplicates the communication channel descriptor so that it becomes the standard input, standard output, and standard error of the shell. This establishes the links that we show in Figure 15.2 between the shell box and the recording process.

Another picture of what we have, showing the stream pipe as being in the kernel, is shown in Figure 15.3.

Finally we have the recording process itself. This function copies data in two independent directions. With 4.3BSD we can do this in a single process, using the `select` system call, since data can arrive from either direction (the shell process or the terminal line discipline) at any time.

```
/*
 * This function copies standard input to "fd" and also copies
 * everything from "fd" to standard output.
 * In addition, all this data that is copied could also
 * be recorded in a log file, if desired.
 * This is the 4.3BSD version that uses the select(2) system call.
 */

#include         <sys/types.h>
#include         <sys/time.h>

#define BUFFSIZE        512

pass_all(fd, childpid)
int     fd;
int     childpid;
{
        int             maxfdp1, nfound, nread;
```

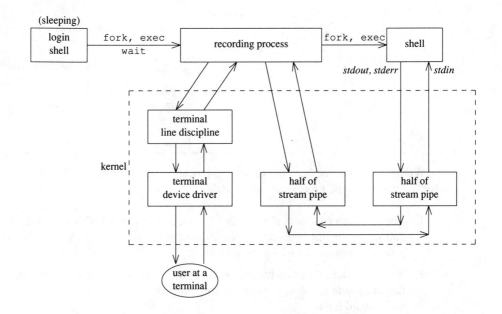

Figure 15.3 Recording process with stream pipes.

```
char            buff[BUFFSIZE];
fd_set          readmask;

FD_ZERO(&readmask);

for ( ; ; ) {
        FD_SET(0, &readmask);
        FD_SET(fd, &readmask);
        maxfdp1 = fd + 1;               /* check descriptors [0..fd] */

        nfound = select(maxfdp1, &readmask, (fd_set *) 0, (fd_set *) 0,
                                (struct timeval *) 0);
        if (nfound < 0)
                err_sys("select error");

        if (FD_ISSET(0, &readmask)) {   /* data to read on stdin */
                nread = read(0, buff, BUFFSIZE);
                if (nread < 0)
                        err_sys("read error from stdin");
                else if (nread == 0)
                        break;          /* stdin EOF -> done */

                if (writen(fd, buff, nread) != nread)
                        err_sys("writen error to stream pipe");
        }
```

```
            if (FD_ISSET(fd, &readmask)) {
                                /* data to read on stream pipe */
                nread = read(fd, buff, BUFFSIZE);
                if (nread <= 0)
                        break;              /* error or EOF, terminate */

                if (write(1, buff, nread) != nread)
                        err_sys("write error to stdout");
            }
        }
}
```

We have to examine how the recording process is terminated. There are two ways, when we use the single process as shown above.

1. The shell can terminate if you enter the `exit` command.† This closes the shell's half of the stream pipe, which causes the read from the other half of the stream pipe to return an end-of-file indication.

2. You can enter an end-of-file character on the terminal, which is interpreted by its line discipline and sent to the recording process by a return of zero from a `read` on standard input.

The `pass_all` function handles both these cases. In the second case, when the recording process terminates, its half of the stream pipe is closed, which sends an end-of-file indication to the shell (or whatever process the shell is running on your behalf), causing the shell to terminate.

Under System V we can't code the recording process as a single process, using the `poll` system call, since `poll` only works with streams devices. While a stream pipe is implemented using streams, the standard terminal handler supplied with System V Release 3.2 is *not* a streams device. Therefore, we'll have the `pass_all` function issue a `fork` system call to make another copy of itself. The child process copies its standard input to the stream pipe, and the parent process copies the stream pipe to its standard output. Note that we could have implemented our 4.3BSD version this same way, but we chose to use the `select` system call instead. A picture of the two process that we're using to pass all the data from the terminal to the new shell is shown in Figure 15.4.

Handling the termination of all the processes now involves more details than the single process version that used `select`. The problem is that *either* the parent or the child can receive the end-of-file indication, and whichever one receives this, has to notify the other. As you can guess, a signal is the easiest way for these processes to notify the other.

---

† All three shells, the Bourne shell, C shell, and KornShell, recognize this command. But the 4.3BSD version of the Bourne shell doesn't terminate an interactive shell with this command. It requires an end of file on its standard input to terminate. Nevertheless, we'll assume the invoked shell can terminate by itself in response to a user command.

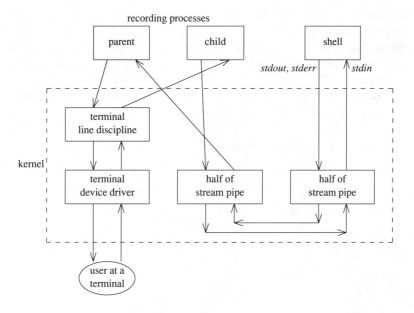

Figure 15.4 Recording process as two processes.

Both methods of termination that we described can still happen. In the first case, the shell exits, closing its half of the stream pipe. This eventually makes its way to the parent process, where the `read` on the stream pipe returns an end-of-file (0). The child process will be in a `read` from the standard input when this happens, and this read won't complete until you enter more input from the terminal. But we want the process to terminate now, so the parent has to notify the child that it's time to exit. To do this, the parent sends the child a `SIGTERM` signal. The default action of this signal is to terminate the receiving process, which is fine for this case.

In the second case, you enter an end-of-file character on the terminal. This causes the child's `read` to return with a value of zero, but the child has to notify the parent. We'll use the same technique, sending the `SIGTERM` signal from the child to the parent, *however* the parent has to catch this signal and return to its caller. (We'll discuss the reason for the parent having to return to its caller as we develop this example later in this chapter.) This means we need a signal handler in the parent to catch this signal, which isn't hard to do, but we run into a portability problem in having this function run under both 4.3BSD and System V. When the parent catches this signal, it'll be executing a `read` system call from the communication channel. Under System V this system call (termed a "slow" system call) then returns an error (a −1 return value) with `errno` set to `EINTR` (interrupted system call). But 4.3BSD, by default, automatically restarts an interrupted system call, which would cause the parent process to return to its `read`. Therefore, we must use the BSD-specific function, `siginterrupt`, to specify that for the `SIGTERM` signal, we do not want a slow system call restarted. There are other ways around this problem, but they involve doing more work in the signal handler itself. In general, the *only* operation a signal handler should do is set a flag for the interrupted routine to look at when the signal handler returns. Doing things like executing other system calls and nonlocal branches (`setjmp` and `longjmp`) are dangerous (i.e., nonportable) in a signal handler.

Having to worry about the differences between 4.3BSD and System V makes the routine messier, but it does work fine under both systems.

```
/*
 * This function copies standard input to "fd" and also copies
 * everything from "fd" to standard output.
 * In addition, all this data that is copied could also
 * be recorded in a log file, if desired.
 *
 * This version fork's into two processes - one to copy stdin to fd,
 * and one to copy fd to stdout.  This is required if you can't use
 * select(2) or poll(2) on any of the three descriptors.
 */

#include        <sys/types.h>
#include        <signal.h>

#define BUFFSIZE        512

static int      sigcaught;          /* set by signal handler */

pass_all(fd, childpid)
int     fd;
int     childpid;
{
        int             newpid, nread;
        int             sig_term();
        char            buff[BUFFSIZE];

        if ( (newpid = fork()) < 0) {
                err_sys("parent1: can't fork");

        } else if (newpid == 0) {          /* child: stdin -> fd */
                for ( ; ; ) {
                        nread = read(0, buff, BUFFSIZE);
                        if (nread < 0)
                                err_sys("read error from stdin");
                        else if (nread == 0)
                                break;          /* stdin EOF -> done */

                        if (writen(fd, buff, nread) != nread)
                                err_sys("writen error to stream pipe");
                }
                kill(getppid(), SIGTERM);       /* kill parent */
                exit(0);
        }
        /* parent: fd -> stdout */
```

```
#ifdef  SIGTTIN
        siginterrupt(SIGTERM, 1);          /* interrupt the system call */
#endif

        sigcaught = 0;
        signal(SIGTERM, sig_term);

        for ( ; ; ) {
                if ( (nread = read(fd, buff, BUFFSIZE)) <= 0)
                        break;             /* error, EOF or signal; terminate */

                if (write(1, buff, nread) != nread)
                        err_sys("write error to stdout");
        }

        /*
         * If we get here either there was an EOF on the stream pipe,
         * implying that the shell terminated, or the child process above
         * terminated and we received its SIGTERM.
         * If the shell terminated, we have to let the child process
         * that we fork'ed above know this, so that it can break out
         * of its read from the standard input.
         * If we received the signal, the child is already gone, so we're done.
         */

        if (sigcaught == 0)
                kill(newpid, SIGTERM);

        return;         /* parent returns to caller */
}
/*
 * If we get here, the child that was copying stdin to the IPC
 * channel got an EOF or error.  It has notified us with a SIGTERM
 * signal.  We set a flag for the parent process above.
 */

sig_term()
{
        sigcaught = 1;              /* set flag */
}
```

If you compile and link edit these C program files, and invoke the resulting program from your shell prompt, the first thing you'll notice is that the new shell doesn't generate a prompt character. But the shell still works and if you enter simple Unix commands, such as date or who, you get the expected output. Also, when you enter your end-of-file character, the recording process terminates as it should. The original login shell is woken up and resumes. The entire process also terminates correctly if you enter the exit command to the shell.

There are, however, some problems. When any of the shells start up, they check their standard input and standard output to see if both belong to a terminal device, using the standard Unix function isatty. Since both of these descriptors for the shell refer to the stream pipe that is created between the shell and the recording process, the isatty function returns false for both descriptors. This is why you don't get the prompt. You can get around this by invoking the recording process with a −i argument, which is passed by the child process to the shell. This argument tells the shell to consider itself interactive, even if its standard input or its standard output is not a terminal.

If you then invoke the recording process with the −i flag, you get a prompt and the simple Unix commands you tried above still work fine. But if your SHELL environment variable specifies the C shell, you get the message "Warning: no access to tty; thus no job control in this shell." Also, if you try to invoke a program that requires a terminal, such as the vi editor, the editor generates an error message saying that it requires an addressable cursor. Finally, if you execute the Unix command tty, which prints the pathname of the terminal device being used, both 4.3BSD and System V print the message "not a tty."

The problem is that the communication channel between the recording process and the shell that it invokes does not look like a terminal device to the system. If there is some way to put a block containing the "terminal line discipline" between the recording process and the shell, these problems disappear. Indeed, this is what pseudo-terminals are designed to do. Doing this, the shell thinks that it is talking to a terminal, so the −i flag isn't needed, and the vi editor works, since it can execute the terminal ioctls that it needs for full-screen control.

15.4 Pseudo-Terminals

A pseudo-terminal is a pair of devices. One half is called the master and the other half is called the slave. A process opens a pair of pseudo-terminal devices and gets two file descriptors. The slave portion of a pseudo-terminal presents an interface to the user process that looks like a terminal device. We can picture this as shown in Figure 15.5.

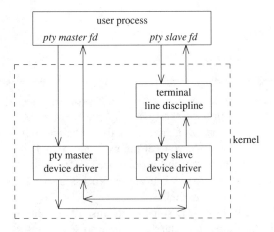

Figure 15.5 Pseudo-terminal.

We use the term "pty" as an abbreviation for pseudo-terminal. Note how this looks like the streams loop-around device that we covered in Section 7.9. Anything written to the master pty is looped around and appears as input from the slave pty. Similarly, anything written to the slave pty appears as input from the master pty.

The following functions are for 4.3BSD. The function `pty_master` opens the master-half of a pseudo-terminal, and the function `pty_slave` opens the slave-half. (We have separated the opening of both halves for reasons that will become clear as we proceed with the recording process example.)

```
/*
 * Pseudo-terminal routines for 4.3BSD.
 */

#include         <sys/types.h>
#include         <sys/stat.h>
#include         <sys/file.h>

/*
 * The name of the pty master device is stored here by pty_master().
 * The next call to pty_slave() uses this name for the slave.
 */

static char     pty_name[12];    /* "/dev/[pt]tyXY" = 10 chars + null byte */

int                     /* returns the file descriptor, or -1 on error */
pty_master()
{
        int             i, master_fd;
        char            *ptr;
        struct stat     statbuff;
        static char     ptychar[] = "pqrs";                    /* X */
        static char     hexdigit[] = "0123456789abcdef";       /* Y */

        /*
         * Open the master half - "/dev/pty[pqrs][0-9a-f]".
         * There is no easy way to obtain an available minor device
         * (similar to a streams clone open) - we have to try them
         * all until we find an unused one.
         */

        for (ptr = ptychar; *ptr != 0; ptr++) {
                strcpy(pty_name, "/dev/ptyXY");
                pty_name[8] = *ptr;       /* X */
                pty_name[9] = '0';        /* Y */

                /*
                 * If this name, "/dev/ptyX0" doesn't even exist,
                 * then we can quit now.  It means the system doesn't
                 * have /dev entries for this group of 16 ptys.
                 */

                if (stat(pty_name, &statbuff) < 0)
                        break;
```

```
                    for (i = 0; i < 16; i++) {
                            pty_name[9] = hexdigit[i];       /* 0-15 -> 0-9a-f */
                            if ( (master_fd = open(pty_name, O_RDWR)) >= 0)
                                    return(master_fd);       /* got it, done */
                    }
            }
            return(-1);       /* couldn't open master, assume all pty's are in use */
}


/*
 * Open the slave half of a pseudo-terminal.
 * Note that the master half of a pty is a single-open device,
 * so there isn't a race condition between opening the master
 * above and opening the slave below.  The only way the slave
 * open will fail is if someone has opened the slave without
 * first opening the master.
 */

int                     /* returns the file descriptor, or -1 on error */
pty_slave(master_fd)
int     master_fd;              /* from pty_master() */
{
        int     slave_fd;

        pty_name[5] = 't';       /* change "/dev/ptyXY" to "/dev/ttyXY" */
        if ( (slave_fd = open(pty_name, O_RDWR)) < 0) {
                close(master_fd);
                return(-1);
        }

        return(slave_fd);
}
```

System V Release 3.2 provides support for pseudo-terminals, but for some reason it is not documented. There are three functions in the library /usr/lib/libpt.a that help create a pair of pseudo-terminals. There is also an executable program, /usr/lib/pt_chmod, that is invoked by the grantpt function to change the permissions and ownership of the slave device to the caller. This program is a set-user-ID root program, as it requires superuser privilege to change the ownership of the slave device.

Here are the two pseudo-terminal functions, pty_master and pty_slave, for System V Release 3.2.

```
/*
 * Pseudo-terminal routines for Unix System V Release 3.2.
 */

#include         <stdio.h>
#include         <fcntl.h>
#include         <stropts.h>

#define PTY_MASTER       "/dev/ptmx"       /* System V Release 3.2 */
```

```
int                     /* returns the file descriptor, or -1 on error */
pty_master()
{
        int     master_fd;

        /*
         * Open the master half - "/dev/ptms".  This is a streams clone
         * device, so it'll allocate the first available pty master.
         */

        if ( (master_fd = open(PTY_MASTER, O_RDWR)) < 0)
                return(-1);

        return(master_fd);
}

/*
 * Open the slave half of a pseudo-terminal.
 */

int                     /* returns the file descriptor, or -1 on error */
pty_slave(master_fd)
int     master_fd;                      /* from pty_master() */
{
        int     slave_fd;
        char    *slavename;
        int     grantpt();      /* undocumented function - libpt.a */
        int     unlockpt();     /* undocumented function - libpt.a */
        char    *ptsname();     /* undocumented function - libpt.a */

        if (grantpt(master_fd) < 0) {   /* change permissions of slave */
                close(master_fd);
                return(-1);
        }

        if (unlockpt(master_fd) < 0) {  /* unlock slave */
                close(master_fd);
                return(-1);
        }

        slavename = ptsname(master_fd); /* determine the slave's name */
        if (slavename == NULL) {
                close(master_fd);
                return(-1);
        }

        slave_fd = open(slavename, O_RDWR);     /* open the slave */
        if (slave_fd < 0) {
                close(master_fd);
                return(-1);
        }

        /*
         * Now push two modules onto the slave's stream: "ptem" is the
```

```
 * pseudo-terminal hardware emulation module, and "ldterm" is
 * the standard terminal line discipline.
 */

if (ioctl(slave_fd, I_PUSH, "ptem") < 0) {
        close(master_fd);
        return(-1);
}
if (ioctl(slave_fd, I_PUSH, "ldterm") < 0) {
        close(master_fd);
        return(-1);
}

        return(slave_fd);
}
```

Once the two stream modules `ptem` and `ldterm` are pushed onto the slave's
stream, we have the picture shown in Figure 15.6.

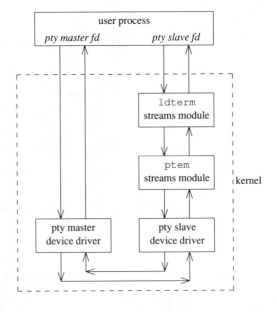

Figure 15.6   System V pseudo-terminal with streams modules.

Note that these two stream modules are pushed onto the slave's stream, not the master's
stream, as it is the slave device that we want to look like a terminal. In all the remaining
pictures of pseudo-terminals, we'll combine the `ldterm` module and the `ptem` module
into a single box called "terminal line discipline."

The typical use of a pseudo-terminal is for a process to open a pty master, then
`fork` a copy of itself. The child process then opens the pty slave and `exec`s another
process, passing the slave pty to the new process as its standard input, standard output,

and standard error. This new process thinks that it is connected to a terminal device. Using pseudo-terminals in our recording process example, Figure 15.7 shows what we want for the final picture.

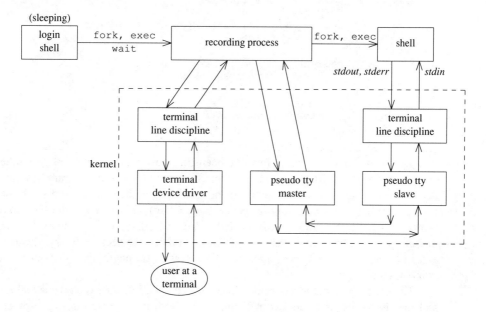

Figure 15.7   Recording process with pseudo-terminals.

Realize that in all the System V examples that we'll show, the box labelled "recording process" is really two processes, as we discussed in Section 15.3.

We are now ready to return to the recording program example that we started in Section 15.3. We must change the `main` function to open the pseudo-terminal devices.

```
/*
 * Recording process, second try: now use pseudo-terminals.
 */

main(argc, argv, envp)
int     argc;
char    **argv;
char    **envp;
{
        int     master_fd, slave_fd, childpid;

        if (!isatty(0) || !isatty(1))
                err_quit("stdin and stdout must be a terminal");

        master_fd = pty_master();
        if (master_fd < 0)
                err_sys("can't open master pty");
```

```
        if ( (childpid = fork()) < 0)
                err_sys("can't fork");
        else if (childpid == 0) {          /* child process */
                slave_fd = pty_slave(master_fd);
                if (slave_fd < 0)
                        err_sys("can't open pty slave");
                close(master_fd);

                exec_shell(slave_fd, argv, envp);
                        /* NOTREACHED */
        }

        pass_all(master_fd, childpid);
        exit(0);
}
```

As mentioned above, the `main` function opens the master half, then `fork`s, and the child opens the slave half. If you make no other changes at all to this program, it now works better. Assuming the `SHELL` environment variable specifies the Bourne shell, the shell prompt appears (without having to specify the `-i` flag) and executing the `tty` command prints `/dev/ttyp0` under 4.3BSD and `/dev/pts000` under System V. But even though the `vi` editor now starts up, it doesn't operate correctly. Every character you enter is echoed on the screen, and the editor doesn't do anything with your input until you enter a newline.

The problem is that there are two line discipline modules between the actual terminal and the shell process as shown in Figure 15.7. Both modules are trying to process the special characters. In general we only want a single line discipline module interpreting the characters being entered on a terminal. We want the line discipline module associated with the actual terminal just to pass everything through, and we want the line discipline associated with the slave's pseudo-terminal to do the normal terminal processing. When the `vi` editor determines that its standard input is a terminal device (as it is now) and it tries to turn off echoing on this descriptor, it is referring to the line discipline module associated with the slave pseudo-terminal. We need to initialize the mode of this pseudo-terminal to be identical to the mode of your terminal, and we need to put your terminal line discipline module in a raw mode that just passes every character through to the recording process.

15.5 Terminal Modes

We now consider the control a process has over what is done by a terminal line discipline module. (Here we are considering only standard terminal line discipline modules, such as the old line discipline and the new line discipline supported by 4.3BSD. We are not considering special line disciplines, such as Berknet or SLIP.) This section is not a complete coverage of terminal handling under Unix. This topic is complicated and detailed. Rochkind [1985], for example, devotes an entire chapter to this topic. Interested readers are referred to this book (which describes the System V terminal handler) and both the

4.3BSD *tty*(4) manual pages and the System V *termio*(7) manual pages, for all the gory details.

4.3BSD considers a terminal device in one of three modes.

- *Cooked mode* provides all the processing steps listed in Section 15.2. The input is collected into lines and all special character processing is done (erase processing, signal generation, etc.). This is the normal mode for interactive use.

- *Raw mode* lets the process receive every character as it is input, with no interpretation done by the system. Raw mode is used, for example, by full screen editors such as vi, and also by programs that use a serial line for something other than interactive use. An example of the latter is UUCP. A classic problem with raw mode is if a process enables this mode but terminates without changing the mode back to cooked mode. You are typically left with a "raw" terminal—echoing is probably disabled and you might have to enter the line feed key, instead of the normal return key to end a line, for example.

- *Cbreak mode* is somewhere between cooked mode and raw mode.† The cbreak mode provides character at a time input to the process reading from the terminal, instead of collecting the input into lines. The signal-generating keys are still processed, however, the editing features are disabled.

We need a function that puts a terminal into a raw mode. We don't want the characters echoed, and we want *all* characters passed through with no interpretation done by the system. We'll use this function with our recording process example so that the terminal line discipline module that is above the terminal device driver passes all input through to the recording process. The 4.3BSD version of this function is

```
/*
 * Put a terminal device into RAW mode with ECHO off.
 * Before doing so we first save the terminal's current mode,
 * assuming the caller will call the tty_reset() function
 * (also in this file) when it's done with raw mode.
 */

#include        <sys/types.h>
#include        <sys/ioctl.h>

static struct sgttyb    tty_mode;       /* save tty mode here */

int
tty_raw(fd)
int     fd;                     /* of terminal device */
{
        struct sgttyb   temp_mode;
```

† The Version 7 *tty*(4) manual page referred to the cbreak mode as "a sort of half-cooked (rare?) mode."

```
            if (ioctl(fd, TIOCGETP, (char *) &temp_mode) < 0)
                    return(-1);
            tty_mode = temp_mode;           /* save for restoring later */

            temp_mode.sg_flags |= RAW;      /* turn RAW mode on */
            temp_mode.sg_flags &= ~ECHO;    /* turn ECHO off */
            if (ioctl(fd, TIOCSETP, (char *) &temp_mode) < 0)
                    return(-1);

            return(0);
    }

    /*
     * Restore a terminal's mode to whatever it was on the most
     * recent call to the tty_raw() function above.
     */

    int
    tty_reset(fd)
    int     fd;             /* of terminal device */
    {
            if (ioctl(fd, TIOCSETP, (char *) &tty_mode) < 0)
                    return(-1);

            return(0);
    }
```

Additionally, we need to initialize the slave pseudo-terminal to some known state. When the slave is opened, there is no guarantee what state the terminal line discipline is in. To set its state, we want to take a copy of the line discipline mode for the terminal on the standard input and initialize the pseudo-terminal slave with this mode. Under 4.3BSD, copying the mode of a terminal involves copying four structures and two integers. We'll use the two functions `tty_getmode` and `tty_setmode` defined in the following file:

```
/*
 * Copy the existing mode of a terminal to another terminal.
 * Typically this is used to initialize a slave pseudo-terminal
 * to the state of the terminal associated with standard input.
 *
 * We provide two functions to do this in 2 separate steps.
 */

#include         <sys/types.h>
#include         <sys/ioctl.h>

         /* See the tty(4) man page for all the details */
static struct sgttyb    tty_sgttyb;     /* basic modes (V6 & V7) */
static struct tchars    tty_tchars;     /* basic control chars (V7) */
static struct ltchars   tty_ltchars;    /* control chars for new discipline */
static struct winsize   tty_winsize;    /* terminal and window sizes */
static int              tty_localmode;  /* local mode word */
static int              tty_ldisc;      /* line discipline word */
```

```
/*
 * Get a copy of the tty modes for a given file descriptor.
 * The copy is then used later by tty_setmode() below.
 */

int
tty_getmode(oldfd)
int     oldfd;          /* typically an actual terminal device */
{
        if (ioctl(oldfd, TIOCGETP,  (char *) &tty_sgttyb) < 0)     return(-1);
        if (ioctl(oldfd, TIOCGETC,  (char *) &tty_tchars) < 0)     return(-1);
        if (ioctl(oldfd, TIOCGLTC,  (char *) &tty_ltchars) < 0)    return(-1);
        if (ioctl(oldfd, TIOCLGET,  (char *) &tty_localmode) < 0)  return(-1);
        if (ioctl(oldfd, TIOCGETD,  (char *) &tty_ldisc) < 0)      return(-1);
        if (ioctl(oldfd, TIOCGWINSZ, (char *) &tty_winsize) < 0)   return(-1);

        return(0);
}


/*
 * Set the tty modes for a given file descriptor.
 * We set the modes from the values saved by tty_getmode() above.
 */

int
tty_setmode(newfd)
int     newfd;          /* typically a pseudo-terminal slave device */
{
        if (ioctl(newfd, TIOCSETP,  (char *) &tty_sgttyb) < 0)     return(-1);
        if (ioctl(newfd, TIOCSETC,  (char *) &tty_tchars) < 0)     return(-1);
        if (ioctl(newfd, TIOCSLTC,  (char *) &tty_ltchars) < 0)    return(-1);
        if (ioctl(newfd, TIOCLSET,  (char *) &tty_localmode) < 0)  return(-1);
        if (ioctl(newfd, TIOCSETD,  (char *) &tty_ldisc) < 0)      return(-1);
        if (ioctl(newfd, TIOCSWINSZ, (char *) &tty_winsize) < 0)   return(-1);

        return(0);
}
```

System V does not provide three specific modes similar to the three provided by 4.3BSD. Instead, each of the features that make up what we called cooked mode can be enabled or disabled independently: signal generation, building lines, editing the lines, and echo. The following System V function puts a terminal into raw mode.

```
/*
 * Put a terminal device into RAW mode with ECHO off.
 * Before doing so we first save the terminal's current mode,
 * assuming the caller will call the tty_reset() function
 * (also in this file) when it's done with raw mode.
 */

#include        <termio.h>

static struct termio    tty_mode;      /* save tty mode here */
```

```
int
tty_raw(fd)
int     fd;                 /* of terminal device */
{
        struct termio   temp_mode;

        if (ioctl(fd, TCGETA, (char *) &temp_mode) < 0)
                return(-1);
        tty_mode = temp_mode;           /* save for restoring later */

        temp_mode.c_iflag  = 0;         /* turn off all input control */
        temp_mode.c_oflag &= ~OPOST;    /* disable output post-processing */
        temp_mode.c_lflag &= ~(ISIG | ICANON | ECHO | XCASE);
                                        /* disable signal generation */
                                        /* disable canonical input */
                                        /* disable echo */
                                        /* disable upper/lower output */
        temp_mode.c_cflag &= ~(CSIZE | PARENB);
                                        /* clear char size, disable parity */
        temp_mode.c_cflag |= CS8;       /* 8-bit chars */

        temp_mode.c_cc[VMIN]  = 1;      /* min #chars to satisfy read */
        temp_mode.c_cc[VTIME] = 1;      /* 10'ths of seconds between chars */

        if (ioctl(fd, TCSETA, (char *) &temp_mode) < 0)
                return(-1);

        return(0);
}

/*
 * Restore a terminal's mode to whatever it was on the most
 * recent call to the tty_raw() function above.
 */

int
tty_reset(fd)
int     fd;                 /* of terminal device */
{
        if (ioctl(fd, TCSETA, (char *) &tty_mode) < 0)
                return(-1);

        return(0);
}
```

To copy the mode of a terminal under System V we need only copy a single `termio` structure.

```
/*
 * Copy the existing mode of a terminal to another terminal.
 * Typically this is used to initialize a slave pseudo-terminal
 * to the state of the terminal associated with standard input.
 *
 * We provide two functions to do this in 2 separate steps.
```

```
        */

#include        <termio.h>

        /* See the termio(7) man page for all the details */
static struct termio    tty_termio;     /* System V's structure */

/*
 * Get a copy of the tty modes for a given file descriptor.
 * The copy is then used later by tty_setmode() below.
 */

int
tty_getmode(oldfd)
int     oldfd;          /* typically an actual terminal device */
{
        if (ioctl(oldfd, TCGETA, (char *) &tty_termio) < 0)
                return(-1);

        return(0);
}

/*
 * Set the tty modes for a given file descriptor.
 * We set the modes from the values saved by tty_getmode() above.
 */

int
tty_setmode(newfd)
int     newfd;                  /* typically a pseudo-terminal slave device */
{
        if (ioctl(newfd, TCSETA, (char *) &tty_termio) < 0)
                return(-1);

        return(0);
}
```

Now we can change the `main` function of the recording process example to use the functions we defined in this section.

```
/*
 * Recording process, third try: use pseudo-terminals,
 * copying the mode of the pty slave from the tty on stdin.
 * We also set the mode of the tty on stdin to raw.
 */

main(argc, argv, envp)
int     argc;
char    **argv;
char    **envp;
{
        int     master_fd, slave_fd, childpid;

        if (!isatty(0) || !isatty(1))
```

```
                    err_quit("stdin and stdout must be a terminal");

        if ( (master_fd = pty_master()) < 0)
                err_sys("can't open master pty");
        if (tty_getmode(0) < 0)
                err_sys("can't get tty mode of standard input");

        if ( (childpid = fork()) < 0)
                err_sys("can't fork");
        else if (childpid == 0) {         /* child process */
                if ( (slave_fd = pty_slave(master_fd)) < 0)
                        err_sys("can't open pty slave");
                close(master_fd);
                if (tty_setmode(slave_fd) < 0)
                        err_sys("can't set tty mode of pty slave");

                exec_shell(slave_fd, argv, envp);
                        /* NOTREACHED */
        }

        if (tty_raw(0) < 0)                          /* set stdin tty to raw mode */
                err_sys("tty_raw error");

        pass_all(master_fd, childpid);

        if (tty_reset(0) < 0)                        /* reset stdin mode */
                err_sys("tty_reset error");
        exit(0);
}
```

Note that we get the mode of the terminal on the standard input *before* we change it to raw mode. We want to set the mode of the slave pseudo-terminal in the child process, which is why we divided the get and set mode routine into two functions. Note also that the copy of the terminal mode saved by `tty_getmode` is available to the child process, since the child's data area after a `fork` is a copy of the parent's data area. Finally, note that it is the `main` function that resets the mode of the standard input. This is why the `pass_all` function has to return to its caller. It cannot just let itself be terminated by a signal from its child process, as we described earlier, it must return so that the terminal mode can be restored to a sane state.

When you execute this latest version of our recording process, if your shell is the Bourne shell, the `vi` editor works fine, now that the terminal modes have been set up correctly. But if you execute `ps -x` on a 4.3BSD system the new shell process that you invoke shows your actual terminal as the associated terminal, not the pseudo-terminal that the shell is talking to. The shell should be associated with the pseudo-terminal, not your actual terminal. Also, if you try to use the C shell, it comes back immediately with the message "(Stopped) tty input" and you are unable to run the C shell.

The problem now is that the new shell process that is invoked has your original terminal as its controlling terminal. What we have to do is make the pseudo-terminal become the control terminal for this shell process.

15.6 Control Terminals (Again)

Recall our discussion of control terminals in Section 2.6. Our interest there was making certain that a daemon process does not have a control terminal and that it doesn't reacquire one. Our goal now is to *acquire* a control terminal for a process. Specifically, we want the shell associated with the pseudo-terminal slave to acquire that slave as its control terminal. At the same time, we want that shell process to disassociate from your terminal.

Under 4.3BSD we want to have the child process from the fork disassociate from its control terminal *before* it opens the pseudo-terminal slave device. This way, when the slave is opened, it becomes the control terminal. Since we only want the new shell process that this child process execs to disassociate from its control terminal—we don't want the recording process that is reading from your actual terminal to do this—we must do this in the child process and not in the parent. This is precisely why we divided the opening of a pseudo-terminal pair into two pieces. We don't want to open the slave device until we're in the child process. The final 4.3BSD version of our main function becomes

```
/*
 * Recording process, fourth try: use pseudo-terminals,
 * copying the mode of the pty slave from the tty on stdin.
 * We also set the mode of the tty on stdin to raw.
 * Additionally, we now disassociate the child from its controlling
 * terminal, so that the pty slave can become its control terminal.
 */

#include        <sys/types.h>
#include        <sys/ioctl.h>
#include        <fcntl.h>

main(argc, argv, envp)
int     argc;
char    **argv;
char    **envp;
{
        int     master_fd, slave_fd, childpid, fd;

        if (!isatty(0) || !isatty(1))
                err_quit("stdin and stdout must be a terminal");

        master_fd = pty_master();
        if (master_fd < 0)
                err_sys("can't open master pty");
        if (tty_getmode(0) < 0)
                err_sys("can't get tty mode of standard input");

        if ( (childpid = fork()) < 0)
                err_sys("can't fork");
        else if (childpid == 0) {       /* child process */
                /*
                 * First disassociate from control terminal.
```

```
                              */

                      if ( (fd = open("/dev/tty", O_RDWR)) >= 0) {
                              if (ioctl(fd, TIOCNOTTY, (char *) 0) < 0)
                                      err_sys("ioctl TIOCNOTTY error");
                              close(fd);
                      }

                      /*
                       * Now open slave pty device.
                       */

                      if ( (slave_fd = pty_slave(master_fd)) < 0)
                              err_sys("can't open pty slave");
                      close(master_fd);
                      if (tty_setmode(slave_fd) < 0)
                              err_sys("can't set tty mode of pty slave");

                      exec_shell(slave_fd, argv, envp);
                              /* NOTREACHED */
              }

              if (tty_raw(0) < 0)                       /* set stdin tty to raw mode */
                      err_sys("tty_raw error");

              pass_all(master_fd, childpid);

              if (tty_reset(0) < 0)                     /* reset stdin mode */
                      err_sys("tty_reset error");
              exit(0);
      }
```

Under System V we need to do the following steps in the child process, to disassociate it from its control terminal and make the pseudo-terminal slave its control terminal. We covered these points in Section 2.6.

1. Call `setpgrp` which makes the child process a process group leader and disassociates it from its control terminal (since it won't be a process group leader when it calls `setpgrp`).

2. Open the pseudo-terminal slave, which then becomes its control terminal.

Our final version for System V is

```
/*
 * Recording process, fourth try: use pseudo-terminals,
 * copying the mode of the pty slave from the tty on stdin.
 * We also set the mode of the tty on stdin to raw.
 * Additionally, we now disassociate the child from its controlling
 * terminal, so that the pty slave can become its control terminal.
 */

#include        <sys/types.h>
```

```
#include        <signal.h>

main(argc, argv, envp)
int     argc;
char    **argv;
char    **envp;
{
        int     master_fd, slave_fd, childpid;

        if (!isatty(0) || !isatty(1))
                err_quit("stdin and stdout must be a terminal");

        if ( (master_fd = pty_master()) < 0)
                err_sys("can't open master pty");
        if (tty_getmode(0) < 0)
                err_sys("can't get tty mode of standard input");

        if ( (childpid = fork()) < 0)
                err_sys("can't fork");
        else if (childpid == 0) {       /* child process */
                /*
                 * Disassociate from our control terminal so we can acquire
                 * the pseudo-terminal slave as our control tty.
                 * This call also makes us a process group leader, which is
                 * necessary to acquire a control tty.
                 */

                setpgrp();

                /*
                 * Now open slave pty device.
                 */

                if ( (slave_fd = pty_slave(master_fd)) < 0)
                        err_sys("can't open pty slave");
                close(master_fd);
                if (tty_setmode(slave_fd) < 0)
                        err_sys("can't set tty mode of pty slave");

                exec_shell(slave_fd, argv, envp);
                        /* NOTREACHED */
        }

        if (tty_raw(0) < 0)                             /* set stdin tty to raw mode */
                err_sys("tty_raw error");

        pass_all(master_fd, childpid);

        if (tty_reset(0) < 0)                           /* reset stdin mode */
                err_sys("tty_reset error");
        exit(0);
}
```

This final version works as desired, both with a Bourne shell and with a job-control shell. We have developed a working version for both 4.3BSD and System V. The `ps` command can be used to verify that this shell, along with any programs invoked by the shell, have the pseudo-terminal slave as their control terminal.

Let's recapitulate the steps that we've taken in the previous sections to develop our recording process example.

1. We used a stream pipe.

2. We used a pseudo-terminal.

3. We used a pseudo-terminal, and set the terminal modes such that the terminal was in a raw mode and the pseudo-terminal slave had its mode controlled by its shell and the programs it invoked (such as the `vi` editor).

4. We used a pseudo-terminal, and set the terminal modes as in step 3. Additionally, we set things up so that the newly invoked shell had the pseudo-terminal slave as its control terminal.

This final step is the version of the program that operates as desired.

15.7   `rlogin` Overview

Now that we've introduced the concepts of pseudo-terminals, terminal modes, control terminals, and the interactions of all these, we can begin to discuss an actual remote login process. Let's first show a picture of all the processes involved in the 4.3BSD remote login client and server. This is shown in Figure 15.8. We'll refer to the system that you initially login to as either the *local system* or *client system*. The system that you remotely login to is the *remote system* or *server system*.

The terminal line discipline on the local system is placed into the raw mode with echoing disabled by the `rlogin` client process, so that all keystrokes are passed to the remote system. As we saw earlier in this chapter, the raw mode is required to run programs such as the `vi` editor on the remote system. In the normal Unix fashion, characters that are entered on the local system are echoed by the remote system. If the remote system is in a cooked mode, then the echoing is done by the terminal line discipline on the remote system. If the remote system is in a raw mode (such as when the `vi` editor is being run on the remote system), then the echoing is done by that remote process itself (e.g., `vi`). Regardless of which box on the remote system is doing the echoing, every character that is echoed on your terminal has to go from the client system, through the network to the remote system, and then back, before being echoed on your terminal.

Notice that the `rlogin` client process `forks` so that two processes are running on the local system, each process handling the flow of data in a single direction. Conversely, on the remote system a single server process handles both directions of data flow. As you might guess, the 4.3BSD `select` system call is used by the `rlogind` server to multiplex its two input streams. Also, as we saw in our earlier examples in this

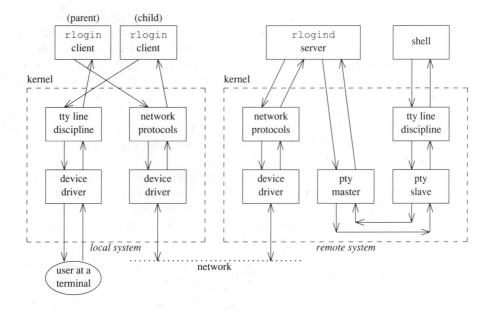

Figure 15.8 4.3BSD `rlogin` processes.

chapter, there has to be some form of information flow between the parent and child client processes on the local system.

The reason the client runs as two processes, instead of as a single process (that could use `select` to multiplex its two input streams), is to make it possible to stop the parent process without stopping the child process. By doing this, we can stop the parent, allowing you to enter other commands on the client system, while still allowing any output from the remote system to appear on your terminal. We'll see when we look at the source code for the client program, how it provides two job-control characters—one to stop both the parent and the child, and one to stop only the parent.

The 4.3BSD manual page for the pseudo-terminal driver, *pty*(4), describes the remote login facility as "remote-echoed, locally flow-controlled, with proper back-flushing of output." Now that we see the overall structure of a remote login session, to understand this description we present some additional terminal characteristics, before looking at the actual source code.

15.8 Windowing Environments

The typical method used by Unix to specify a terminal's features is to have a data file of terminal characteristics. 4.3BSD and early versions of System V use the *termcap* file for this, while more recent versions of System V use the *terminfo* file. Contained in either of these files for each terminal type is the size of the terminal's screen. Typical values are

24 lines by 80 columns. A problem with these terminal capability files is that they assume that the size of the terminal window doesn't change. Current technology, however, provides a variety of ways for you to change the size of a terminal's window dynamically during a login session. Software that uses the full capabilities of the screen, such as a full screen editor, has to be made aware of any changes in a window's size, so they can redraw the screen.

The ability to have a terminal device support multiple windows of varying sizes and to allow you to change the sizes of a window during a login session is not restricted to bit-mapped displays. 4.3BSD, for example, provides the `window` program that provides these capabilities on standard ASCII terminals.

To support a windowed environment, the current size of a window has to be stored in a central location during a login session. Also, there has to be some way to allow processes to read the current size, set the current size and be made aware whenever the size changes. 4.3BSD provides `ioctl`s to get and store the window size.

```
#include   <ioctl.h>

int ioctl(int fd, TIOCGWINSZ, struct winsize *winptr);   /* get */

int ioctl(int fd, TIOCSWINSZ, struct winsize *winptr);   /* set */

struct winsize {
  unsigned short   ws_row;      /* rows, in characters */
  unsigned short   ws_col;      /* columns, in characters */
  unsigned short   ws_xpixel;   /* horizontal size, pixels */
  unsigned short   ws_ypixel;   /* vertical size, pixels */
};
```

The kernel maintains a `winsize` structure for each terminal and pseudo-terminal, but does not use it for anything. All the kernel does is provide a central location for active processes to keep track of a window's size.

The kernel also generates the `SIGWINCH` signal whenever the size of a window changes. This signal is sent to the terminal process group associated with the terminal. Recall our discussion of terminal process groups and the signals associated with this group, in Section 2.6.

As an example, the 4.3BSD `vi` editor catches the `SIGWINCH` signal. This editor needs to know the size of the terminal's window so that it can wrap long lines from one line to the next, and to know where the bottom line of the screen is (its command and output line). Whenever the size of the window changes, it catches the signal and redraws the screen.

When a windowing environment is being used, such as the 4.3BSD `window` command that we mentioned above, pseudo-terminals are typically used to provide one login shell for each active window. As an example, consider the AT&T 630 MTG (MultiTasking Graphics) terminal. This bit-mapped terminal is a descendant of the Blit terminal developed at AT&T Bell Laboratories [Pike 1984]. Under 4.3BSD, if we have created two windows, we have the arrangement shown in Figure 15.9.

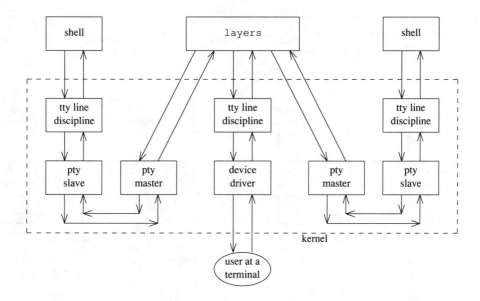

Figure 15.9 Multiple windows on a windowing terminal.

The `layers` process is the host process that handles the multiplexed terminal. It communicates over a single RS-232 line with the terminal. It also communicates with the processes running in each window (layer) using a pseudo-terminal. When you resize a window, the operation is done by the firmware in the terminal (a small operating system that executes in the terminal). This firmware sends a special sequence of bytes across the RS-232 line to the `layers` process. The `layers` process figures out which window was resized from the sequence of bytes it receives and executes the `TIOCSWINSZ` `ioctl` to set the new window size. This system call is applied to the master pseudo-terminal associated with the window that was resized. The kernel then sends the `SIGWINCH` signal to the corresponding slave side of the pseudo-terminal.

Not shown in Figure 15.9 is the login shell that was used to invoke the `layers` process. This login shell is `waiting` for the `layers` process to terminate.

Now, let's consider what effect resizing a window has on a remote login session. The problem is that resizing a window on the client's system has to be propagated to the server's system. Consider the `layers` system shown in Figure 15.9 and assume we have an `rlogin` client running in one window. This gives us the processes shown in Figure 15.10. The five steps that have to be taken by the remote login client and server are shown in Figure 15.10.

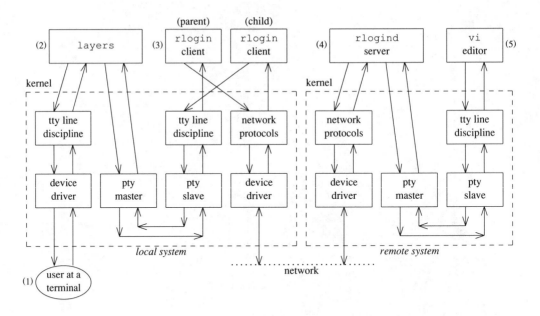

Figure 15.10 Remote login from a windowing terminal.

1. You resize the window which causes a special sequence of bytes to be sent to the
    `layers` process.

2. The `layers` process recognizes the sequence of characters as a window resize
    command and issues an `ioctl` of `TIOCSWINSZ` for the pseudo-terminal master
    device. This causes the `SIGWINCH` signal to be sent to the process group of the
    pseudo-terminal slave device, the `rlogin` parent process.

3. The `rlogin` parent process catches the `SIGWINCH` signal. It then issues an
    `ioctl` of `TIOCGWINSZ` to fetch the new window size. The new size of the
    window is then sent across the network connection to the `rlogind` server pro-
    cess. The method used by the 4.3BSD `rlogin` client–server to exchange this
    data is an in-band signaling method, which we describe later in more detail.

4. The `rlogind` server receives the new window size from the client and issues an
    `ioctl` of `TIOCSWINSZ` on its pseudo-terminal master device. The
    `SIGWINCH` signal is then sent by the kernel to the process group of the pseudo-
    terminal slave device, the `vi` editor in this example.

5. The `vi` editor catches the `SIGWINCH` signal and redraws the screen.

What we have done is change the window size on both host systems—the local host and
the remote host.

15.9 Flow Control

Most terminal line disciplines that are intended for interactive use, buffer characters in both directions. This allows a process to `write` data in chunks. Typically these chunks are either complete lines or buffers of some size. The driver accepts as much data as it can and then outputs it to the terminal as fast as possible. By doing it this way, the process that is producing the terminal output can continue executing while the line discipline and the terminal device driver output to the terminal device as fast as it can accept data. Terminal output is usually limited by the connection speed—9600 baud, for example. If the output is being displayed on the terminal device too fast for you to read or comprehend, you can stop the output by pressing a special character, termed the *stop* character. When you are ready to have more output displayed, enter the *start* character, and the terminal line discipline resumes the output. The stop character is typically Control-S and the start character is typically Control-Q.† In addition to this output buffering, terminal input is also buffered independently by the line discipline. By doing it this way, you can enter characters before a process is ready to `read` them. We can picture this as two somewhat independent queues within the terminal line discipline, as shown in Figure 15.11. There is an input queue and an output queue for every terminal and pseudo-terminal.

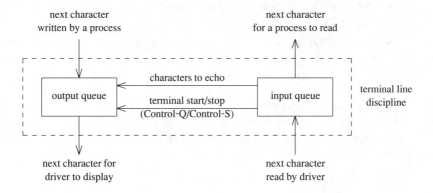

Figure 15.11 Input queue and output queue in terminal line discipline.

As shown by the two horizontal lines, there is typically a link within the line discipline

---

† Be aware of the different uses of the term ''stop'' in the 4.3BSD terminal driver and signal routines. Here we use the terms stop and start to refer to flow control. When referring to job control, the normal terms are suspend and continue. But, the suspend character and the delayed suspend character in the terminal driver (typically Control-Z and Control-Y, respectively) generate the ''stop process'' signal, SIGTSTP. A process can also be stopped with the SIGSTOP signal. The SIGCONT signal resumes a stopped process.

from the input queue to the output queue. If the line discipline is echoing the input characters, this is done by moving a copy of the character that is input to the output queue. Also, if flow control is being done, when the stop character is input this has to stop the output side of the discipline. Similarly, when the start character is entered, the output side has to be notified.

The interaction that we have to be concerned with is if the *interrupt* key or the *quit* key is entered. Normally, entering either of these keys flushes both the input queue and the output queue, in addition to terminating the process that is currently running. When a terminal discipline is in the raw mode, these two keys are no longer special and entering them won't flush the queues.

During a remote login session, the line discipline on the remote system processes the interrupt key. But consider all the characters that can be buffered between the local system on which you enter the interrupt key and the remote system that processes the interrupt key.

- The remote terminal line discipline can have characters in its output queue, waiting to be read by the `rlogind` server through the pseudo-terminal devices.

- The network buffers on the remote system can contain data waiting to be sent to the local system.

- The network buffers on the local system can also contain characters, waiting to be read by the `rlogin` client process.

- The terminal line discipline on the local system can contain characters ready to display on the terminal, since the terminal is usually slower than either the network or the remote process that is generating the output.

Still, when you enter the interrupt key on the local system, as soon as that key is processed by the remote line discipline, you would like all the pending output flushed as soon as possible. Otherwise, you have to sit and watch lines of unwanted output pass by for seconds after entering the interrupt key.

15.10 Pseudo-Terminal Packet Mode

Flow control is best handled by the client system. If it is handled by the remote system, then when you enter the stop character, that character has to be transmitted across the network to the remote system, where the remote line discipline module will stop the output. But in the time required to do this, all the data that was already going from the remote system to the local system will have been displayed on your screen. The problem with doing flow control on the client system is that whenever the remote system is in a raw mode, the stop and start characters cannot be interpreted as flow control. When the remote system is in a raw mode, the client has to transmit what it thinks are the start and stop characters to the remote system for it to interpret. But if the remote system is not in a raw mode, we can allow the local system to handle flow control. We need some way for the remote system's line discipline to notify the `rlogind` server when the start and stop characters are enabled or disabled.

There is another condition that we would like the client process to know as soon as possible. The terminal `ioctl` of `TIOCFLUSH` allows a process to flush everything that the line discipline has queued for input or output to the terminal device. If the process running on the remote system issues this terminal `ioctl`, in addition to having the line discipline module on the remote system flush its output buffer, we would also like to flush everything that is buffered across the network for output on your terminal. This is another condition that the remote system's line discipline module knows about, which we would like the `rlogind` server to also know.

To handle these cases, the 4.3BSD pseudo-terminal device driver supports an optional *packet mode*. This mode is enabled by issuing an `ioctl` of `TIOCPKT` to the pseudo-terminal master device, with a nonzero argument. What this mode provides is a notification from the terminal line discipline module that is above the pseudo-terminal slave device, to the pseudo-terminal master device, of certain events that happen in the slave's line discipline module. When this mode is enabled, every `read` of the pty master (by the `rlogind` server, in our example) returns either

- a single byte of zero, followed by the actual data from the pty slave. The first byte of zero is a flag byte indicating that the remainder of the buffer is normal data.

- a single nonzero byte. The length returned by the `read` should be one. This byte is a control byte that indicates a condition that happened on the slave pty. The include file `<ioctl.h>` contains the following definitions for this byte:

TIOCPKT_FLUSHREAD
: Indicates that the terminal's input queue was flushed (i.e., all the characters on the read queue were discarded).†

TIOCPKT_FLUSHWRITE
: Indicates that the terminal's output queue was flushed. Both the read queue and the write queue are flushed, for example, when you enter either the interrupt key or the quit key. This way, if you abort a running process with either of these keys, any output that the process has already written or any input that you have entered, is discarded.

TIOCPKT_STOP
: Indicates that the terminal output has been stopped.

TIOCPKT_START
: Indicates that the terminal output has been restarted.

---

† Be aware that the term "flush" when used with the terminal drivers means "to discard." Do not confuse it with the standard I/O function `fflush` which forces the writing of a buffer to a file or device.

`TIOCPKT_DOSTOP`

Indicates that something has changed so that the terminal stop character is Control-S, and the start character is Control-Q, and the terminal is not in raw mode.

`TIOCPKT_NOSTOP`

Indicates that something has changed so that the terminal stop character is not Control-S, or the start character is not Control-Q, or the terminal is in raw mode.

Whenever one of the above control bytes is available to be read from the master pty device, the file descriptor for the master pty indicates that an exceptional condition is present, if the `select` system call is issued. This way, the process that is reading from the master pty can differentiate between normal data and control information, before issuing the `read`.

The `rlogind` server is only interested in three of these control indicators.

`TIOCPKT_FLUSHWRITE`
`TIOCPKT_NOSTOP`
`TIOCPKT_DOSTOP`

When the server reads any of these three bytes from its master pty, it sends an out-of-band message to the `rlogin` client. Since the child `rlogin` process is reading from the network, it arranges to receive the out-of-band notifications (the `SIGURG` signal) and its actions are as follows:

`TIOCPKT_FLUSHWRITE`

Since the server's terminal output queue was flushed, the client should try to flush all the pending output that it can. It first issues an `ioctl` of `TIOCFLUSH` for its standard output (your terminal) to discard any output data that is buffered in the line discipline. It then reads everything from the network, up to the out-of-band byte, and throws the data away. This way, any data that is buffered in the network, is also discarded. This is a good example of when we want the notification of out-of-band data to arrive as soon as possible. As soon as the receiver reads the out-of-band byte, it is going to throw away all the in-band data that the out-of-band data was sent ahead of. We'll see exactly how the client handles the out-of-band data when we examine the source code.

`TIOCPKT_NOSTOP`

In this case, the slave pty is no longer using Control-Q and Control-S for its start and stop characters, or the slave pty is in the raw mode. In either case, the `rlogin` client can no longer do flow control and the client must pass all characters through to the server process. This is what happens, for example, when you start the `vi` editor on the remote system.

TIOCPKT_DOSTOP

>   Here the slave pty is not in raw mode and its start and stop characters are Control-Q and Control-S. This allows the rlogin client to handle flow control on the local system. To do this, the client puts the line discipline module for your terminal in cbreak mode (instead of raw mode) to have the client do the flow control processing. An example of this notification is if you terminate the vi editor, for example.

The notification provided by the packet mode of the pseudo-terminal is hard-wired for having Control-Q and Control-S as the start and stop characters. 4.3BSD allows you to set the start and stop characters to anything you like, yet the packet mode bases its notification on these two specific values. The reason for this is that few people change their start and stop characters from their defaults of Control-Q and Control-S. By assuming these values, the client and server processes don't have to exchange the actual values of these characters. This handles most cases. But as long as your start and stop characters on the remote system are not Control-Q and Control-S, the client will never do flow control.

Now we can reexamine the description that we mentioned earlier: the remote login facility is ''remote-echoed, locally flow-controlled, with proper back-flushing of output.''

- The remote-echo is because the client has the server do all the echoing.
- We described above how the flow control for the terminal output is done on the client's system, as long as the start and stop characters on the remote system are Control-Q and Control-S and if the remote line discipline is not in the raw mode.
- We also described how the client ''back flushes'' any pending terminal output, when it receives the flush notification from the server.

In addition to these three points, we can add that the remote login facility also propagates changes in the client's window size to the server.

15.11 rlogin **Client**

Before examining the source code for the rlogin client and server, let's first summarize the control information that is exchanged between the client and server. In Figure 15.8 we show the communication paths between the various processes and the kernel. In Figure 15.12 we show the control information that is exchanged.

Note in Figure 15.12 that the window-size changes are sent in-band from the client to the server, while the pseudo-terminal control information is sent as out-of-band data in the other direction.

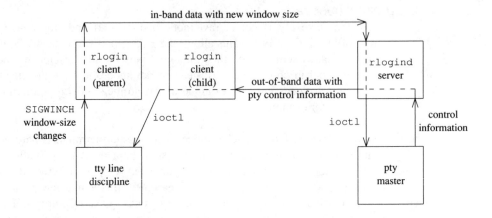

Figure 15.12   Control information between rlogin client and server.

We are now ready to examine the actual source code for the 4.3BSD rlogin client and server. We'll first examine the client.

```
/*
 * Copyright (c) 1983 The Regents of the University of California.
 * All rights reserved.
 *
 * Redistribution and use in source and binary forms are permitted
 * provided that the above copyright notice and this paragraph are
 * duplicated in all such forms and that any documentation,
 * advertising materials, and other materials related to such
 * distribution and use acknowledge that the software was developed
 * by the University of California, Berkeley.  The name of the
 * University may not be used to endorse or promote products derived
 * from this software without specific prior written permission.
 * THIS SOFTWARE IS PROVIDED ``AS IS'' AND WITHOUT ANY EXPRESS OR
 * IMPLIED WARRANTIES, INCLUDING, WITHOUT LIMITATION, THE IMPLIED
 * WARRANTIES OF MERCHANTIBILITY AND FITNESS FOR A PARTICULAR PURPOSE.
 */

#ifndef lint
char copyright[] =
"@(#) Copyright (c) 1983 The Regents of the University of California.\n\
 All rights reserved.\n";
#endif /* not lint */

#ifndef lint
static char sccsid[] = "@(#)rlogin.c    5.12 (Berkeley) 9/19/88";
#endif /* not lint */

/*
 * rlogin - remote login client.
 */
```

```
#include <sys/param.h>
#include <sys/file.h>
#include <sys/socket.h>
#include <sys/time.h>
#include <sys/resource.h>
#include <sys/wait.h>

#include <netinet/in.h>

#include <stdio.h>
#include <sgtty.h>
#include <pwd.h>
#include <signal.h>
#include <setjmp.h>
#include <netdb.h>
#include <errno.h>
extern int       errno;

/*
 * The server sends us a TIOCPKT_WINDOW notification when it starts up.
 * The value for this (0x80) can't overlap the kernel defined TIOCKPT_xxx
 * values.
 */

#ifndef TIOCPKT_WINDOW
#define TIOCPKT_WINDOW 0x80
#endif

#ifndef SIGUSR1
#define SIGUSR1 30      /* concession to sun */
#endif

char            *index(), *rindex(), *malloc(), *getenv(), *strcat(), *strcpy();
struct passwd   *getpwuid();
char            *name;
int             sockfd;                 /* socket to server */

char            escchar = '~';          /* can be changed with -e flag */
int             eight;                  /* can be changed with -8 flag */
int             litout;                 /* can be changed with -L flag */

char            *speeds[] = {
        "0", "50", "75", "110", "134", "150", "200", "300",
        "600", "1200", "1800", "2400", "4800", "9600", "19200", "38400"
};
char            term[256] = "network";
int             dosigwinch = 0;         /* set to 1 if the server supports
                                           our window-size-change protocol */

#ifndef sigmask
#define sigmask(m)      (1 << ((m)-1))
#endif

#ifdef sun
```

```
struct winsize {
        unsigned short  ws_row;
        unsigned short  ws_col;
        unsigned short  ws_xpixel;
        unsigned short  ws_ypixel;
};
#endif

struct winsize  currwinsize;                /* current size of window */

int     sigpipe_parent();                   /* our signal handlers */
int     sigwinch_parent();
int     sigcld_parent();
int     sigurg_parent();
int     sigusr1_parent();
int     sigurg_child();

/*
 * The following routine provides compatibility (such as it is)
 * between 4.2BSD Suns and others.  Suns have only a 'ttysize',
 * so we convert it to a winsize.
 */

#ifdef sun

int
get_window_size(fd, wp)
int             fd;
struct winsize  *wp;
{
        struct ttysize  ts;
        int             error;

        if ( (error = ioctl(0, TIOCGSIZE, &ts)) != 0)
                return(error);
        wp->ws_row    = ts.ts_lines;
        wp->ws_col    = ts.ts_cols;
        wp->ws_xpixel = 0;
        wp->ws_ypixel = 0;
        return(0);
}
#else
#define get_window_size(fd, wp)         ioctl(fd, TIOCGWINSZ, wp)
#endif  /* sun */

main(argc, argv)
int     argc;
char    **argv;
{
        char            *host, *cp;
        struct sgttyb   ttyb;
        struct passwd   *pwd;
        struct servent  *sp;
        int             uid, options = 0, oldsigmask;
```

```
        int             on = 1;

        if ( (host = rindex(argv[0], '/')) != NULL)
                host++;
        else
                host = argv[0];
        argv++, --argc;
        if (strcmp(host, "rlogin") == 0)
                host = *argv++, --argc;
another:
        if (argc > 0 && strcmp(*argv, "-d") == 0) {
                /*
                 * Turn on the debug option for the socket.
                 */

                argv++, argc--;
                options |= SO_DEBUG;
                goto another;
        }

        if (argc > 0 && strcmp(*argv, "-l") == 0) {
                /*
                 * Specify the server-user-name, instead of using the
                 * name of the person invoking us.
                 */

                argv++, argc--;
                if (argc == 0)
                        goto usage;
                name = *argv++; argc--;
                goto another;
        }

        if (argc > 0 && strncmp(*argv, "-e", 2) == 0) {
                /*
                 * Specify an escape character, instead of the default tilde.
                 */

                escchar = argv[0][2];
                argv++, argc--;
                goto another;
        }

        if (argc > 0 && strcmp(*argv, "-8") == 0) {
                /*
                 * 8-bit input.  Specifying this forces us to use RAW mode
                 * input from the user's terminal.  Also, in this mode we
                 * won't perform any local flow control.
                 */

                eight = 1;
                argv++, argc--;
                goto another;
        }
```

```
if (argc > 0 && strcmp(*argv, "-L") == 0) {
        /*
         * 8-bit output.  Causes us to set the LLITOUT flag,
         * which tells the line discpline: no output translations.
         */

        litout = 1;
        argv++, argc--;
        goto another;
}

if (host == NULL)
        goto usage;
if (argc > 0)
        goto usage;         /* too many command line arguments */

/*
 * Get the name of the user invoking us: the client-user-name.
 */

if ( (pwd = getpwuid(getuid())) == NULL) {
        fputs("Who are you?\n", stderr);
        exit(1);
}

/*
 * Get the name of the server we connect to.
 */

if ( (sp = getservbyname("login", "tcp")) == NULL) {
        fputs("rlogin: login/tcp: unknown service\n", stderr);
        exit(2);
}

/*
 * Get the name of the terminal from the environment.
 * Also get the terminal's speed.  Both the name and
 * the speed are passed to the server as the "cmd"
 * argument of the rcmd() function.  This is something
 * like "vt100/9600".
 */

if ( (cp = getenv("TERM")) != NULL)
        strcpy(term, cp);
if (ioctl(0, TIOCGETP, &ttyb) == 0) {
        strcat(term, "/");
        strcat(term, speeds[ttyb.sg_ospeed]);
}

get_window_size(0, &currwinsize);
signal(SIGPIPE, sigpipe_parent);

/*
 * Block the SIGURG and SIGUSR1 signals.  These will be handled
```

```
                * by the parent and the child after the fork.
                */

               oldsigmask = sigblock(sigmask(SIGURG) | sigmask(SIGUSR1));

               /*
                * Use rcmd() to connect to the server.  Note that even though
                * we're using rcmd, we specify the port number of the rlogin
                * server, not the rshd server.  We also pass the terminal-type/speed
                * as the "command" argument, but the server knows what it is.
                */

               sockfd = rcmd(&host, sp->s_port, pwd->pw_name,
                                      name ? name : pwd->pw_name, term, (int *) 0);
               if (sockfd < 0)
                       exit(1);

               if ((options & SO_DEBUG) &&
                   setsockopt(sockfd, SOL_SOCKET, SO_DEBUG, &on, sizeof(on)) < 0)
                       perror("rlogin: setsockopt (SO_DEBUG)");

               /*
                * Now change to the real user ID.  We have to be set-user-ID root
                * to get the privileged port that rcmd() uses,
                * however we now want to run as the real user who invoked us.
                */

               uid = getuid();
               if (setuid(uid) < 0) {
                       perror("rlogin: setuid");
                       exit(1);
               }

               doit(oldsigmask);
               /*NOTREACHED*/
       usage:
               fputs("usage: rlogin host [ -ex ] [ -l username ] [ -8 ] [ -L ]\n",
                       stderr);
               exit(1);
       }

       int     childpid;

       /*
        * tty flags.  Refer to tty(4) for all the details.
        */

       int             defflags;       /* the sg_flags word from the sgttyb struct */
       int             tabflag;        /* the two tab bits from the sg_flags word */
       int             deflflags;
       char            deferase;       /* client's erase character */
       char            defkill;        /* client's kill character */
       struct tchars   deftc;
       struct ltchars  defltc;
```

```
/*
 * If you set one of the special terminal characters to -1, that effectively
 * disables the line discipline from processing that special character.
 * We initialize the following two structures to do this.  However, the
 * code below replaces the -1 entries for "stop-output" and "start-output"
 * with the actual values of these two characters (such as ^Q/^S).
 * This way, we can use CBREAK mode but only have the line discipline do
 * flow control.  All other special characters are ignored by our end and
 * passed to the server's line discipline.
 */

struct tchars   notc = { -1, -1, -1, -1, -1, -1 };
                                /* disables all the tchars: interrupt, quit,
                                   stop-output, start-output, EOF */
struct ltchars  noltc = { -1, -1, -1, -1, -1, -1 };
                                /* disables all ltchars: suspend,
                                   delayed-suspend, reprint-line, flush,
                                   word-erase, literal-next */

doit(oldsigmask)
int     oldsigmask;             /* mask of blocked signals */
{
        int             exit();
        struct sgttyb   sb;

        ioctl(0, TIOCGETP, (char *) &sb);       /* get the basic modes */
        defflags = sb.sg_flags;
        tabflag  = defflags & TBDELAY;          /* save the 2 tab bits */
        defflags &= ECHO | CRMOD;
        deferase = sb.sg_erase;
        defkill  = sb.sg_kill;

        ioctl(0, TIOCLGET, (char *) &deflflags);

        ioctl(0, TIOCGETC, (char *) &deftc);
        notc.t_startc = deftc.t_startc;         /* replace -1 with start char */
        notc.t_stopc  = deftc.t_stopc;          /* replace -1 with stop char */

        ioctl(0, TIOCGLTC, (char *) &defltc);

        signal(SIGINT, SIG_IGN);
        setsignal(SIGHUP, exit);        /* HUP or QUIT go straight to exit() */
        setsignal(SIGQUIT, exit);

        if ( (childpid = fork()) < 0) {
                perror("rlogin: fork");
                done(1);
        }
        if (childpid == 0) {                    /* child process == reader */
                tty_mode(1);
                if (reader(oldsigmask) == 0) {
                        /*
                         * If the reader() returns 0, the socket to the
                         * server returned an EOF, meaning the client
```

```
                         * logged out of the remote system.
                         * This is the normal termination.
                         */

                        prf("Connection closed.");
                        exit(0);
                }

                /*
                 * If the reader() returns nonzero, the socket to the
                 * server returned an error.  Something went wrong.
                 */

                sleep(1);
                prf("\007Connection closed.");   /* 007 = ASCII bell */
                exit(3);
        }

        /*
         * Parent process == writer.
         *
         * We may still own the socket, and may have a pending SIGURG
         * (or might receive one soon) that we really want to send to
         * the reader.  Set a trap that copies such signals to
         * the child.  Once the two signal handlers are installed,
         * reset the signal mask to what it was before the fork.
         */

        signal(SIGURG, sigurg_parent);
        signal(SIGUSR1, sigusr1_parent);
        sigsetmask(oldsigmask);          /* reenables SIGURG and SIGUSR1 */

        signal(SIGCHLD, sigcld_parent);

        writer();

        /*
         * If the writer returns, it means the user entered "~." on the
         * terminal.  In this case we terminate and the server will
         * eventually get an EOF on its end of the network connection.
         * This should cause the server to log you out on the remote system.
         */

        prf("Closed connection.");
        done(0);
}

/*
 * Enable a signal handler, unless the signal is already being ignored.
 * This function is called before the fork(), for SIGHUP and SIGQUIT.
 */

setsignal(sig, action)
int     sig;
```

```
int     (*action)();
{
        register int    omask;

        omask = sigblock(sigmask(sig));            /* block the signal */

        if (signal(sig, action) == SIG_IGN)
                signal(sig, SIG_IGN);

        sigsetmask(omask);                         /* reset the signal mask */
}

/*
 * This function is called by the parent:
 *      (1) at the end (user terminates the client end);
 *      (2) SIGCLD signal - the sigcld_parent() function;
 *      (3) SIGPIPE signal - the connection has dropped.
 *
 * We send the child a SIGKILL signal, which it can't ignore, then
 * wait for it to terminate.
 */

done(status)
int     status;         /* exit() status */
{
        int     w;

        tty_mode(0);    /* restore the user's terminal mode */

        if (childpid > 0) {
                signal(SIGCHLD, SIG_DFL);          /* disable signal catcher */

                if (kill(childpid, SIGKILL) >= 0)
                        while ((w = wait((union wait *) 0)) > 0 &&
                               w != childpid)
                                ;
        }
        exit(status);
}

/*
 * Copy SIGURGs to the child process.
 * The parent shouldn't get any SIGURGs, but if it does, just pass
 * them to the child, as it's the child that handles the out-of-band
 * data from the server.
 */

sigurg_parent()
{
        kill(childpid, SIGURG);
}

/*
 * The child sends the parent a SIGUSR1 signal when the child receives
```

```
 * the TIOCPKT_WINDOW indicator from the server.  This tells the
 * client to enable the in-band window-changing protocol.
 */

sigusr1_parent()
{
        if (dosigwinch == 0) {              /* first time */
                /*
                 * First time.  Send the initial window sizes to the
                 * server and enable the SIGWINCH signal, so that we pick
                 * up any changes from this point on.
                 */

                sendwindow();
                signal(SIGWINCH, sigwinch_parent);
                dosigwinch = 1;
        }
}

/*
 * SIGCLD signal haldner in parent.
 */

sigcld_parent()
{
        union wait      status;
        register int    pid;

again:
        /*
         * WNOHANG -> don't block.
         * WUNTRACED -> tell us about stopped, untraced children.
         */

        pid = wait3(&status, WNOHANG | WUNTRACED, (struct rusage *) 0);
        if (pid == 0)
                return;              /* no processes wish to report status */

        /*
         * If the child (reader) dies, just quit.
         */

        if (pid < 0 || (pid == childpid && WIFSTOPPED(status) == 0))
                done( (int) (status.w_termsig | status.w_retcode) );
        goto again;
}

/*
 * SIGPIPE signal handler.  We're called if the connection drops.
 * This signal happens in the parent, since the signal is sent to the process
 * that writes to the socket (pipe) that has no reader.
 */

sigpipe_parent()
```

```
{
        signal(SIGPIPE, SIG_IGN);
        prf("\007Connection closed.");
        done(1);
}

/*****************************************************************************
 *
 * writer main loop: copy standard input (user's terminal) to network.
 *
 * The standard input is in raw mode, however, we look for three special
 * sequences of characters:
 *
 *        ~.         terminate;
 *        ~^D        terminate;
 *        ~^Z        suspend rlogin process;
 *        ~^Y        suspend rlogin process, but leave reader alone.
 *
 * This handling of escape sequences isn't perfect, however.  For example,
 * use rlogin, then run the vi editor on the remote system.  Enter return,
 * then tilde (vi's convert-case-of-character command), then dot (vi's redo
 * last command).  Voila, you're logged out.
 */

writer()
{
        char           c;
        register       n;
        register       bol = 1;                 /* beginning of line */
        register       local = 0;

        for ( ; ; ) {
                /*
                 * Since we have to look at every character entered by the
                 * user, we read the standard input one-character-at-a-time.
                 * For human input, this isn't too bad.
                 */

                n = read(0, &c, 1);
                if (n <= 0) {
                        if (n < 0 && errno == EINTR)
                                continue;
                        break;
                }

                /*
                 * If we're at the beginning of the line and recognize
                 * the escape character, then we echo the next character
                 * locally.  If the command character is doubled, for example
                 * if you enter ~~. at the beginning of a line, nothing
                 * is echoed locally and ~. is sent to the server.
                 */

                if (bol) {
```

```
                bol = 0;
                if (c == escchar) {
                        local = 1;          /* local echo next char */
                        continue;           /* next iteration of for-loop */
                }

        } else if (local) {
                /*
                 * The previous character (the first character of
                 * a line) was the escape character.  Look at the
                 * second character of the line and determine if
                 * something special should happen.
                 */

                local = 0;

                if (c == '.' || c == deftc.t_eofc) {
                        /*
                         * A tilde-period or tilde-EOF terminates
                         * the parent.  Echo the period or EOF
                         * then stop.
                         */

                        echo(c);
                        break;              /* breaks out of for-loop */
                }

                if (c == defltc.t_suspc || c == defltc.t_dsuspc) {
                        /*
                         * A tilde-^Z or tilde-^Y stops the parent
                         * process.
                         */

                        bol = 1;
                        echo(c);

                        stop(c); /* returns only when we're continued */

                        continue;          /* next iteration of for-loop */
                }

                /*
                 * If the input was tilde-someothercharacter,
                 * then we have to write both the tilde and the
                 * other character to the network.
                 */

                if (c != escchar)
                        if (write(sockfd, &escchar, 1) != 1) {
                                prf("line gone");
                                break;
                        }
        }
```

```
                        if (write(sockfd, &c, 1) != 1) {
                                prf("line gone");
                                break;
                        }

                        /*
                         * Set a flag if by looking at the current character
                         * we think the next character is going to be the first
                         * character of a line.  This ain't perfect.
                         */

                        bol = (c == defkill) ||          /* kill char, such as ^U */
                              (c == deftc.t_eofc) ||     /* EOF char, such as ^D */
                              (c == deftc.t_intrc) ||    /* interrupt, such as ^C */
                              (c == defltc.t_suspc) ||   /* suspend job, such as ^Z */
                              (c == '\r') ||             /* carriage-return */
                              (c == '\n');               /* newline */
                }
        }

/*
 * Echo a character on the standard output (the user's terminal).
 * This is called only by the writer() function above to handle the
 * escape characters that we echo.
 */

echo(c)
register char   c;
{
        char            buf[8];
        register char   *p = buf;

        *p++ = escchar;         /* print the escape character first */

        c &= 0177;
        if (c < 040) {
                /*
                 * Echo ASCII control characters as a caret, followed
                 * by the upper case character.
                 */

                *p++ = '^';
                *p++ = c + '@';

        } else if (c == 0177) {         /* ASCII DEL character */
                *p++ = '^';
                *p++ = '?';

        } else
                *p++ = c;

        *p++ = '\r';    /* need a return-linefeed, since it's in raw mode */
        *p++ = '\n';
```

```
            write(1, buf, p - buf);
}

/*
 * Stop the parent process (job control).
 * If the character entered by the user is the "stop process" (^Z) character,
 * then we send the SIGTSTP signal to both ourself and the reader (all the
 * processes in the sending processes process group).  When this happens,
 * anything sent by the server to us will be buffered by the network
 * until the reader starts up again and reads it.
 * However, if the character is the "delayed stop process" (^Y) character,
 * then we stop only ourself and not the reader.  This way, the reader
 * continues outputting any data that it receives from the server.
 */

stop(cmdc)
char    cmdc;
{
        tty_mode(0);               /* first reset the terminal mode to normal */

        signal(SIGCHLD, SIG_IGN);  /* ignore SIGCLD in case child stops too */

        kill( (cmdc == defltc.t_suspc) ? 0 : getpid() , SIGTSTP);

                /* resumes here when we're continued by user */
        signal(SIGCHLD, sigcld_parent);
        tty_mode(1);               /* reset terminal back to raw mode */

        sigwinch_parent();         /* see if the window size has changed */
}

/*
 * SIGWINCH signal handler.
 * We're also called above, after we've been resumed after being stopped.
 * We only send a window size message to the server if the size has changed.
 * Note that we use the flag "dosigwinch" to indicate if the server supports
 * our window-size-change protocol.  If the server doesn't tell us that
 * it supports it (see sigusr1_parent() above), we'll never send it.
 */

sigwinch_parent()
{
        struct winsize  ws;

        if (dosigwinch && (get_window_size(0, &ws) == 0) &&
            (bcmp((char *) &ws, (char *) &currwinsize,
                                    sizeof(struct winsize)) != 0)) {
                currwinsize = ws;        /* store new size for next time */
                sendwindow();            /* and tell the server */
        }
}

/*
 * Send the window size to the server via the magic escape.
```

```
 * Note that we send the 4 unsigned shorts in the structure in network byte
 * order, as it's possible to be running the client and server on systems
 * with different byte orders (a VAX and a Sun, for example).
 */

sendwindow()
{
        char                    obuf[4 + sizeof(struct winsize)];
        register struct winsize *wp;

        wp = (struct winsize *)(obuf + 4);

        obuf[0] = 0377;                 /* these 4 bytes are the magic sequence */
        obuf[1] = 0377;
        obuf[2] = 's';
        obuf[3] = 's';

        wp->ws_row    = htons(currwinsize.ws_row);
        wp->ws_col    = htons(currwinsize.ws_col);
        wp->ws_xpixel = htons(currwinsize.ws_xpixel);
        wp->ws_ypixel = htons(currwinsize.ws_ypixel);

        write(sockfd, obuf, sizeof(obuf));
}

/*****************************************************************************
 *
 * reader main loop: copy network to standard output (user's terminal).
 */

char    rcvbuf[8 * 1024];       /* read into here from network */
int     rcvcnt;                 /* amount of data in rvcbuf[] */
int     rcvstate;               /* READING or WRITING: so sigurg_child()
                                   knows whether a read or write system
                                   call was interrupted */
int     parentpid;              /* parent pid, from the fork */
jmp_buf rcvtop;                 /* setjmp/longjmp buffer */

#define READING 1               /* values for rcvstate */
#define WRITING 2

reader(oldsigmask)
int     oldsigmask;     /* signal mask from parent */
{
#if !defined(BSD) || BSD < 43
        int     pid = -getpid();
#else
        int     pid = getpid();
#endif
        int     n, remaining;
        char    *bufp = rcvbuf;

        signal(SIGTTOU, SIG_IGN);
        signal(SIGURG, sigurg_child);   /* out-of-band data from server */
```

```
        fcntl(sockfd, F_SETOWN, pid);      /* to receive SIGURG signals */

        parentpid = getppid();             /* for SIGUSR1 signal at beginning */

        setjmp(rcvtop);                    /* see the longjmps in sigurg_child() */

        sigsetmask(oldsigmask);            /* reset signal mask */
                                           /* reenables SIGURG and SIGUSR1 */

        for ( ; ; ) {
                /*
                 * Reader main loop - read as much as we can from
                 * the network and write it to standard output.
                 */

                while ( (remaining = rcvcnt - (bufp - rcvbuf)) > 0) {
                        /*
                         * While there's data in the buffer to write,
                         * write it to the standard output.
                         */

                        rcvstate = WRITING;
                        if ( (n = write(1, bufp, remaining)) < 0) {
                                if (errno != EINTR)
                                        return(-1);
                                continue;
                        }
                        bufp += n;       /* incr pointer past what we wrote */
                }

                /*
                 * There's nothing in our buffer to write, so read from
                 * the network.
                 */

                bufp = rcvbuf;            /* ptr to start of buffer */
                rcvcnt = 0;              /* #bytes in buffer */
                rcvstate = READING;

                rcvcnt = read(sockfd, rcvbuf, sizeof(rcvbuf));
                if (rcvcnt == 0)
                        return(0);       /* user logged out from remote system */
                if (rcvcnt < 0) {
                        if (errno == EINTR)
                                continue;
                        perror("read");
                        return(-1);
                }
        }
}

/*
 * This is the SIGURG signal handler in the child.  Here we process
 * the out-of-band signals that arrive from the server.
 */
```

```
        */

sigurg_child()
{
        int             flushflag, atoobmark, n, rcvd;
        char            waste[BUFSIZ], ctlbyte;
        struct sgttyb   sb;

        rcvd = 0;
        while (recv(sockfd, &ctlbyte, 1, MSG_OOB) < 0) {
                switch (errno) {

                case EWOULDBLOCK:
                        /*
                         * The Urgent data is not here yet.
                         * It may not be possible to send it yet if we are
                         * blocked for output and our input buffer is full.
                         *
                         * First try to read as much as the receive buffer
                         * has room for.  Note that neither of the reads
                         * below will go past the OOB mark.
                         */

                        if (rcvcnt < sizeof(rcvbuf)) {
                                n = read(sockfd, rcvbuf + rcvcnt,
                                                sizeof(rcvbuf) - rcvcnt);
                                if (n <= 0)
                                        return;

                                rcvd += n;       /* remember how much we read */

                        } else {
                                /*
                                 * The receive buffer is currently full.
                                 * We have no choice but to read into
                                 * our wastebasket.
                                 */

                                n = read(sockfd, waste, sizeof(waste));
                                if (n <= 0)
                                        return;
                        }
                        continue;        /* try to read to OOB byte again */

                default:
                        return;
                }
        }

        /*
         * Note that in the TIOCPKT mode, any number of the control
         * bits may be on in the control byte, so we have to test
         * for all the ones we're interested in.
         */
```

```
if (ctlbyte & TIOCPKT_WINDOW) {
        /*
         * We get this control byte from the server after it has
         * started.  It means that the server is started and
         * it needs to know the current window size.  We send
         * the SIGUSR1 signal to the parent, as it is the
         * parent who must send the window size to the server.
         */

        kill(parentpid, SIGUSR1);
}

if (!eight && (ctlbyte & TIOCPKT_NOSTOP)) {
        /*
         * Either the server is not using ^S/^Q or the server is
         * in raw mode.  We must set the user's terminal to
         * raw mode.  This disables flow control on the client system.
         */

        ioctl(0, TIOCGETP, (char *) &sb);
        sb.sg_flags &= ~CBREAK;                 /* CBREAK off */
        sb.sg_flags |= RAW;                     /* RAW on */
        ioctl(0, TIOCSETN, (char *) &sb);       /* doesn't delay */

        notc.t_stopc  = -1;                     /* no stop char */
        notc.t_startc = -1;                     /* no start char */
        ioctl(0, TIOCSETC, (char *) &notc);
}

if (!eight && (ctlbyte & TIOCPKT_DOSTOP)) {
        /*
         * The server is using ^S/^Q and it's not in raw mode,
         * so we can do flow control on the client system.
         */

        ioctl(0, TIOCGETP, (char *) &sb);
        sb.sg_flags &= ~RAW;                    /* RAW off */
        sb.sg_flags |= CBREAK;                  /* CBREAK on */
        ioctl(0, TIOCSETN, (char *) &sb);

        notc.t_stopc  = deftc.t_stopc;          /* enable stop */
        notc.t_startc = deftc.t_startc;         /* enable start */
        ioctl(0, TIOCSETC, (char *) &notc);
}

if (ctlbyte & TIOCPKT_FLUSHWRITE) {
        /*
         * The terminal output queue on the server was flushed.
         * First we flush our terminal output queue (the output
         * queue for the user's terminal).
         */

        flushflag = FWRITE;     /* flush output only, not input */
        ioctl(1, TIOCFLUSH, (char *) &flushflag);
```

```
                        /*
                         * Now we continue reading from the socket, throwing
                         * away all the data until we reach the out-of-band mark.
                         */

                        for ( ; ; ) {
                                if (ioctl(sockfd, SIOCATMARK, &atoobmark) < 0) {
                                        perror("ioctl SIOCATMARK error");
                                        break;
                                }
                                if (atoobmark)
                                        break;  /* we're at the oob mark */

                                if ( (n = read(sockfd, waste, sizeof(waste))) <= 0)
                                        break;
                        }

                        /*
                         * We don't want any pending data that we've already read
                         * into the receive buffer to be output, so clear the receive
                         * buffer (i.e., just set rcvcnt = 0).
                         * Also, if we were hanging on a write to standard output
                         * when interrupted, we don't want it to restart, so we
                         * longjmp back to the top of the loop.
                         * If we were reading, we want to restart it anyway.
                         */

                        rcvcnt = 0;
                        longjmp(rcvtop, 1);     /* back to the setjmp */
                                                /* the arg of 1 isn't used */
                }

                /*
                 * If we read data into the receive buffer above (so that we
                 * could read the OOB byte) and if we we're interrupted during
                 * a read, then longjmp to the top of the loop to write the
                 * data that was received.
                 * Don't abort a pending write, however, or we won't know how
                 * much was written.
                 */

                if (rcvd > 0 && rcvstate == READING)
                        longjmp(rcvtop, 1);

        return;         /* from the signal handler; probably causes an EINTR */
}

/*
 * Set the terminal mode.  This function affects the user's terminal.
 * We're called by both the parent and child.
 */

tty_mode(mode)
int     mode;                   /* 0 -> reset to normal; 1 -> set for rlogin */
```

```
{
        struct tchars    *tcptr;
        struct ltchars   *ltcptr;
        struct sgttyb    sb;            /* basic modes */
        int              lflags;        /* local mode word */

        ioctl(0, TIOCGETP, (char *) &sb);
        ioctl(0, TIOCLGET, (char *) &lflags);

        switch (mode) {

        case 0:
                /*
                 * This is called by the parent when it's done to reset
                 * the terminal state to how it found it.
                 * The parent also calls this to reset the terminal state
                 * before stopping itself with job control.
                 */

                sb.sg_flags &= ~(CBREAK | RAW | TBDELAY);
                sb.sg_flags |= defflags | tabflag;

                tcptr = &deftc;        /* restore all special chars */
                ltcptr = &defltc;
                sb.sg_kill = defkill;
                sb.sg_erase = deferase;
                lflags = deflflags;
                break;

        case 1:
                /*
                 * This is called by the child when it starts, to set the
                 * terminal to a raw mode.  Actually, we default to CBREAK
                 * unless the -8 flag was specified (8-bit input) in which
                 * case we have to use RAW mode.
                 * The parent also calls this when resumed, after being
                 * stopped by job control.
                 */

                sb.sg_flags |= (eight ? RAW : CBREAK);
                sb.sg_flags &= ~defflags;
                        /* preserve tab delays, but turn off XTABS */
                if ((sb.sg_flags & TBDELAY) == XTABS)
                        sb.sg_flags &= ~TBDELAY;

                tcptr = &notc;         /* disable all special chars */
                ltcptr = &noltc;
                sb.sg_kill = -1;
                sb.sg_erase = -1;
                if (litout)
                        lflags |= LLITOUT;    /* no output translations */
                break;

        default:
```

```
                        return;
                }

                ioctl(0, TIOCSLTC, (char *) ltcptr);
                ioctl(0, TIOCSETC, (char *) tcptr);
                ioctl(0, TIOCSETN, (char *) &sb);
                ioctl(0, TIOCLSET, (char *) &lflags);
        }

/*
 * Fatal error.
 */

prf(str)
char    *str;
{
        fputs(str, stderr);
        fputs("\r\n", stderr);  /* return & newline, in case raw mode */
}
```

15.12 `rlogind` Server

The remote login server, `rlogind`, is invoked by the Internet superserver, `inetd`, when a connection request arrives from a client on the TCP port used for remote login requests. The first part of the processing is done by the `rlogind` process itself, and it then invokes the standard Unix `login` program to complete the login. If you pass the authentication tests, which we presented in Figure 9.1, then the `login` process invokes your login shell. The steps we've described are shown in Figure 15.13.

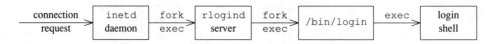

Figure 15.13 Steps required when invoking `rlogind` server.

Here is the source code for the server process.

```
/*
 * Copyright (c) 1983, 1988 The Regents of the University of California.
 * All rights reserved.
 *
 * Redistribution and use in source and binary forms are permitted
 * provided that the above copyright notice and this paragraph are
 * duplicated in all such forms and that any documentation,
 * advertising materials, and other materials related to such
 * distribution and use acknowledge that the software was developed
 * by the University of California, Berkeley.  The name of the
 * University may not be used to endorse or promote products derived
 * from this software without specific prior written permission.
```

```
 * THIS SOFTWARE IS PROVIDED ''AS IS'' AND WITHOUT ANY EXPRESS OR
 * IMPLIED WARRANTIES, INCLUDING, WITHOUT LIMITATION, THE IMPLIED
 * WARRANTIES OF MERCHANTIBILITY AND FITNESS FOR A PARTICULAR PURPOSE.
 */

#ifndef lint
char copyright[] =
"@(#) Copyright (c) 1983, 1988 The Regents of the University of California.\n\
 All rights reserved.\n";
#endif /* not lint */

#ifndef lint
static char sccsid[] = "@(#)rlogind.c   5.22.1.6 (Berkeley) 2/7/89";
#endif /* not lint */

/*
 * remote login server:  the following data is sent across the network
 * connection by the rcmd() function that the rlogin client uses:
 *       \0  (there is no auxiliary port used by the client and server)
 *       client-user-name\0
 *       server-user-name\0
 *       terminal-type/speed\0
 *       data
 *
 * Define OLD_LOGIN for compatibility with the 4.2BSD and 4.3BSD /bin/login.
 * If this isn't defined, a newer protocol is used whereby rlogind does
 * the user verification.  This only works if your /bin/login supports the
 * -f and -h flags.  This newer version of login is on the Berkeley
 * Networking Release 1.0 tape.
 */

#ifndef OLD_LOGIN
#define NEW_LOGIN          /* make the #ifdefs easier to understand */
#endif

#include <stdio.h>
#include <sys/param.h>
#include <sys/stat.h>
#include <sys/socket.h>
#include <sys/wait.h>
#include <sys/file.h>

#include <netinet/in.h>

#include <pwd.h>
#include <signal.h>
#include <sgtty.h>
#include <stdio.h>
#include <netdb.h>
#include <syslog.h>
#include <strings.h>
#include <errno.h>
extern int      errno;
```

```
/*
 * We send a TIOCPKT_WINDOW notification to the client when we start up.
 * This tells the client that we support the window-size-change protocol.
 * The value for this (0x80) can't overlap the kernel defined TIOCKPT_xxx
 * values.
 */

#ifndef TIOCPKT_WINDOW
#define TIOCPKT_WINDOW 0x80
#endif

char            *env[2];                /* the environment we build */
static char     term[64] = "TERM=";
#define ENVSIZE (sizeof("TERM=")-1)     /* skip null for concatenation */

#define NMAX 30
char            cliuname[NMAX+1];       /* user name on client's host */
char            servuname[NMAX+1];      /* user name on server's host */

int             keepalive = 1;          /* set to 0 with -n flag */

#define SUPERUSER(pwd)  ((pwd)->pw_uid == 0)

int             reapchild();
struct passwd   *getpwnam(), *pwd;
char            *malloc();
int             one = 1;                /* for setsockopt() */

main(argc, argv)
int     argc;
char    **argv;
{
        extern int              opterr, optind;
        int                     ch, addrlen;
        struct sockaddr_in      cli_addr;

        openlog("rlogind", LOG_PID | LOG_CONS, LOG_AUTH);

        opterr = 0;
        while ( (ch = getopt(argc, argv, "ln")) != EOF)
                switch (ch) {
                case 'l':
#ifdef  NEW_LOGIN
                        {
                            extern int      _check_rhosts_file;

                            _check_rhosts_file = 0; /* don't check .rhosts file */
                        }
#endif
                        break;

                case 'n':
                        keepalive = 0;          /* don't enable SO_KEEPALIVE */
                        break;
```

```
                case '?':
                default:
                        syslog(LOG_ERR, "usage: rlogind [-l] [-n]");
                        break;
                }

        argc -= optind;
        argv += optind;

        /*
         * We assume we're invoked by inetd, so the socket that the connection
         * is on, is open on descriptors 0, 1 and 2.
         *
         * First get the Internet address of the client process.
         * This is required for all the authentication we perform.
         */

        addrlen = sizeof(cli_addr);
        if (getpeername(0, &cli_addr, &addrlen) < 0) {
                syslog(LOG_ERR, "Couldn't get peer name of remote host: %m");
                fatalperror("Can't get peer name of host");
        }

        if (keepalive &&
            setsockopt(0, SOL_SOCKET, SO_KEEPALIVE, (char *) &one,
                                                        sizeof(one)) < 0)
                syslog(LOG_WARNING, "setsockopt (SO_KEEPALIVE): %m");

        doit(&cli_addr);
}

int             child;
int             cleanup();
char            *line;
extern char     *inet_ntoa();

struct winsize  win = { 0, 0, 0, 0 };

doit(cli_addrp)
struct sockaddr_in      *cli_addrp;     /* client's Internet address */
{
        int                     i, masterfd, slavefd, childpid;
#ifdef  NEW_LOGIN
        int                     authenticated = 0, hostok = 0;
        char                    remotehost[2 * MAXHOSTNAMELEN + 1];
#endif
        register struct hostent *hp;
        struct hostent          hostent;
        char                    c;

        /*
         * Read the null byte from the client.  This byte is really
         * written by the rcmd() function as the secondary port number.
         * However, the rlogin client calls rcmd() specifying a secondary
```

```
 * port of 0, so all that rcmd() sends is the null byte.
 * We set a timer of 60 seconds to do this read, else we assume
 * something is wrong.
 */

alarm(60);
read(0, &c, 1);
if (c != 0)
        exit(1);
alarm(0);

/*
 * Try to look up the client's name, given its internet
 * address, since we use the name for the authentication.
 */

cli_addrp->sin_port = ntohs((u_short)cli_addrp->sin_port);
hp = gethostbyaddr(&cli_addrp->sin_addr, sizeof(struct in_addr),
                                          cli_addrp->sin_family);
if (hp == NULL) {
        /*
         * Couldn't find the client's name.
         * Use its dotted-decimal address as its name.
         */

        hp = &hostent;
        hp->h_name = inet_ntoa(cli_addrp->sin_addr);
#ifdef  NEW_LOGIN
        hostok++;
#endif
}
#ifdef  NEW_LOGIN
    else if (local_domain(hp->h_name)) {
        /*
         * If the name returned by gethostbyaddr() is in our domain,
         * attempt to verify that we haven't been fooled by someone
         * in a remote net.  Look up the name and check that this
         * address corresponds to the name.
         */

        strncpy(remotehost, hp->h_name, sizeof(remotehost) - 1);
        remotehost[sizeof(remotehost) - 1] = 0;
        if ( (hp = gethostbyname(remotehost)) != NULL) {
                for ( ; hp->h_addr_list[0]; hp->h_addr_list++) {
                        if (bcmp(hp->h_addr_list[0],
                                (caddr_t)&cli_addrp->sin_addr,
                                sizeof(cli_addrp->sin_addr)) == 0) {
                        hostok++;        /* equal, OK */
                        break;
                }
        }
    }
} else
        hostok++;
```

```
#endif

        /*
         * Verify that the client's address is an internet address and
         * that it was bound to a reserved port.
         */

        if (cli_addrp->sin_family != AF_INET ||
            cli_addrp->sin_port >= IPPORT_RESERVED ||
            cli_addrp->sin_port <  IPPORT_RESERVED/2) {
                syslog(LOG_NOTICE, "Connection from %s on illegal port",
                                        inet_ntoa(cli_addrp->sin_addr));
                fatal(0, "Permission denied");
        }

#ifdef IP_OPTIONS
    {
        u_char          optbuf[BUFSIZ/3], *optptr;
        char            lbuf[BUFSIZ], *lptr;
        int             optsize, ipproto;
        struct protoent *ip;

        if ( (ip = getprotobyname("ip")) != NULL)
                ipproto = ip->p_proto;
        else
                ipproto = IPPROTO_IP;

        optsize = sizeof(optbuf);
        if (getsockopt(0, ipproto, IP_OPTIONS, (char *)optbuf, &optsize) == 0 &&
            optsize != 0) {
                /*
                 * The client has set IP options.  This isn't allowed.
                 * Use syslog() to record the fact.
                 */

                lptr = lbuf;
                optptr = optbuf;
                for ( ; optsize > 0; optptr++, optsize--, lptr += 3)
                        sprintf(lptr, " %2.2x", *optptr);
                                /* print each option byte as 3 ASCII chars */
                syslog(LOG_NOTICE,
                    "Connection received using IP options (ignored): %s", lbuf);

                /*
                 * Turn off the options.  If this doesn't work, we quit.
                 */

                if (setsockopt(0, ipproto, IP_OPTIONS,
                                        (char *) NULL, &optsize) != 0) {
                        syslog(LOG_ERR, "setsockopt IP_OPTIONS NULL: %m");
                        exit(1);
                }
        }
    }
```

```
#endif  /* IP_OPTIONS */

        /*
         * Write a null byte back to the client telling it that
         * everything is OK.  Note that this is different from the
         * sequence performed by rshd.  The rshd server first reads
         * the 3 strings on the socket before writing back the null
         * byte if all is OK.  We can get away with this, since we're
         * using a full-duplex socket.
         */

        write(0, "", 1);

#ifdef NEW_LOGIN
        if (do_rlogin(hp->h_name) == 0) {
                if (hostok)
                        authenticated++;
                else
                        write(0, "rlogind: Host address mismatch.\r\n",
                            sizeof("rlogind: Host address mismatch.\r\n") - 1);
        }
#endif

        /*
         * Allocate and open a master pseudo-terminal.
         */

        for (c = 'p'; c <= 's'; c++) {
                struct stat     statbuff;

                line = "/dev/ptyXY";
                line[8] = c;                    /* X = [pqrs] */
                line[9] = '0';                  /* Y = 0 */

                if (stat(line, &statbuff) < 0)
                        break;

                for (i = 0; i < 16; i++) {
                        line[9] = "0123456789abcdef"[i];
                        if ( (masterfd = open(line, O_RDWR)) > 0)
                                goto gotpty;    /* got the master ptr */
                }
        }
        fatal(0, "Out of ptys");
        /*NOTREACHED*/

gotpty:
        ioctl(masterfd, TIOCSWINSZ, &win);      /* set window sizes all to 0 */

        /*
         * Now open the slave pseudo-terminal corresponding to the
         * master that we opened above.
         */
```

```
        line[5] = 't';              /* change "/dev/ptyXY" to "/dev/ttyXY" */
        if ( (slavefd = open(line, O_RDWR)) < 0)
                fatalperror(0, line);
        if (fchmod(slavefd, 0))
                fatalperror(0, line);

        /*
         * The 4.3BSD vhangup() system call does a virtual hangup on the
         * current control terminal.  It goes through the kernel's tables
         * and for every reference it finds to the current control terminal,
         * it revokes that reference (i.e., unconnects any former processes
         * that may have had this terminal as their control terminal).
         * vhangup() also sends a SIGHUP to the process group of the control
         * terminal, so we ignore this signal.
         */

        signal(SIGHUP, SIG_IGN);
        vhangup();
        signal(SIGHUP, SIG_DFL);

        /*
         * Now reopen the slave pseudo-terminal again and set it's mode.
         * This gives us a "clean" control terminal.
         * line[] contains the string "/dev/ttyXY" which will be used
         * by the cleanup() function when we're done.
         */

        if ( (slavefd = open(line, O_RDWR)) < 0)
                fatalperror(0, line);

        setup_term(slavefd);

#ifdef DEBUG
        {
                int     tt;

                if ( (tt = open("/dev/tty", O_RDWR)) > 0) {
                        ioctl(tt, TIOCNOTTY, 0);
                        close(tt);
                }
        }
#endif

        if ( (childpid = fork()) < 0)
                fatalperror(0, "");

        if (childpid == 0) {
                /*
                 * Child process.  Becomes the login shell for the user.
                 */

                close(0);               /* close socket */
                close(masterfd);        /* close pty master */
                dup2(slavefd, 0);       /* pty slave is 0,1,2 of login shell */
```

```
                    dup2(slavefd, 1);
                    dup2(slavefd, 2);
                    close(slavefd);

#ifdef OLD_LOGIN
                    /*
                     * Invoke /bin/login with the -r argument, which tells
                     * it was invoked by rlogind.  This causes login to read the
                     * the socket for the client-user-name, the server-user-name
                     * and the terminal-type/speed.  login then calls the
                     * ruserok() function and possibly prompts the client for
                     * their password.
                     */

                    execl("/bin/login", "login", "-r", hp->h_name, (char *) 0);

#else /* NEW_LOGIN */
                    /*
                     * The -p flag tells login not to destroy the environment.
                     * The -h flag passes the name of the client's system to
                     * login, so it can be placed in the utmp and wtmp entries.
                     * The -f flag says the user has already been authenticated.
                     */

                    if (authenticated)
                            execl("/bin/login", "login", "-p", "-h", hp->h_name,
                                    "-f", servuname, (char *) 0);
                    else
                            execl("/bin/login", "login", "-p", "-h", hp->h_name,
                                    servuname, (char *) 0);
#endif /* OLD_LOGIN */

                    fatalperror(2, "/bin/login");    /* exec error */
                    /*NOTREACHED*/
            }

            /*
             * Parent process.
             */

            close(slavefd);                    /* close slave pty, child uses it */

            ioctl(0, FIONBIO, &one);         /* nonblocking I/O for socket */
            ioctl(masterfd, FIONBIO, &one);  /* nonblocking I/O for master pty */
            ioctl(masterfd, TIOCPKT, &one);  /* BSD pty packet mode */

            signal(SIGTSTP, SIG_IGN);
            signal(SIGCHLD, cleanup);

            setpgrp(0, 0);                     /* set our process group to 0 */

            protocol(0, masterfd);             /* this does it all */

            signal(SIGCHLD, SIG_IGN);
```

```
                cleanup();
}

/*
 * Define the pty packet-mode control bytes that we're interested in.
 * We ignore any other of the control bytes.
 */

#define pkcontrol(c)     ((c)&(TIOCPKT_FLUSHWRITE|TIOCPKT_NOSTOP|TIOCPKT_DOSTOP))

/*
 * The following byte always gets sent along with the pty packet-mode
 * control byte to the client.  It's initialized to TIOCPKT_WINDOW
 * but this bit gets turned off after the client has sent the first
 * window size.  Thereafter this byte is 0.
 */

char    oobdata[] = {TIOCPKT_WINDOW};

/*
 * Handle an in-band control request from the client.
 * These are signaled by two consecutive magic[] bytes appearing in
 * the data from the client.  The next two bytes in the data stream
 * tell us what type of control message this is.
 * For now, all we handle is a window-size-change.
 *
 * We return the number of bytes that we processed in the buffer, so that
 * the caller can skip over them.
 */

char    magic[2] = { 0377, 0377 };       /* in-band magic cookie */

int
control(pty, cp, n)
int     pty;            /* fd of pty master */
char    *cp;            /* pointer to first two bytes of control sequence */
int     n;
{
        struct winsize  w;

        if (n < 4+sizeof(w) || cp[2] != 's' || cp[3] != 's')
                return (0);

        /*
         * Once we receive one of these in-band control requests from
         * the client we know that it received the TIOCPKT_WINDOW
         * message that we sent it on startup.  We only send this
         * control byte at the beginning, to tell the client that we
         * support window-size-changes.  Now we can turn off the
         * TIOCPKT_WINDOW bit in our control byte.
         */

        oobdata[0] &= ~TIOCPKT_WINDOW;
```

```
        bcopy(cp+4, (char *) &w, sizeof(w));     /* copy into structure */
        w.ws_row    = ntohs(w.ws_row);  /* and change to host byte order */
        w.ws_col    = ntohs(w.ws_col);
        w.ws_xpixel = ntohs(w.ws_xpixel);
        w.ws_ypixel = ntohs(w.ws_ypixel);
        ioctl(pty, TIOCSWINSZ, &w);                /* set the new window size */

        return (4 + sizeof(w));
}

/*
 * rlogin server "protocol" machine.
 *
 * The only condition for which we return to the caller is if we get an
 * error or EOF on the network connection.
 */

protocol(socketfd, masterfd)
int     socketfd;         /* network connection to client */
int     masterfd;         /* master pseudo-terminal */
{
        char            mptyibuf[1024], sockibuf[1024], *mptybptr, *sockbptr;
        register int    mptycc, sockcc;
        int             cc, maxfdp1;
        int             mptymask, sockmask;
        char            cntlbyte;

        mptycc = 0;               /* count of #bytes in buffer */
        sockcc = 0;

        /*
         * We must ignore SIGTTOU, otherwise we'll stop when we try
         * and set the slave pty's window size (our controlling tty
         * is the master pty).
         */

        signal(SIGTTOU, SIG_IGN);

        /*
         * Send the TIOCPKT_WINDOW control byte to the client
         * (as an OOB data byte) telling it that we'll accept
         * window-size changes.
         */

        send(socketfd, oobdata, 1, MSG_OOB);

        /*
         * Set things up for the calls to select().
         * We cheat and store the file descriptor masks in an int,
         * knowing that they can't exceed 32 (or something else is wrong).
         */

        if (socketfd > masterfd)          /* determine max descriptor */
                maxfdp1 = socketfd + 1;
```

```
        else
                maxfdp1 = masterfd + 1;

        sockmask = 1 << socketfd;        /* select mask for this descriptor */
        mptymask = 1 << masterfd;

        /*
         * This loop multiplexes the 2 I/O "streams":
         *      network input -> sockibuf[]
         *                              sockibuf[] -> master pty (input from client)
         *
         *      master pty input -> mptyibuf[]
         *                              mptyibuf[] -> network (output for client)
         */

        for ( ; ; ) {
                int     ibits, obits, ebits;

                ibits = 0;
                obits = 0;
                if (sockcc)
                        obits |= mptymask;
                else
                        ibits |= sockmask;
                if (mptycc >= 0) {
                        if (mptycc)
                                obits |= sockmask;
                        else
                                ibits |= mptymask;
                }
                ebits = mptymask;
                if (select(maxfdp1, (fd_set *) &ibits,
                                obits ? (fd_set *) &obits : (fd_set *) NULL,
                                (fd_set *) &ebits, (struct timeval *) 0) < 0) {
                        if (errno == EINTR)
                                continue;
                        fatalperror(socketfd, "select");
                }

                if (ibits == 0 && obits == 0 && ebits == 0) {
                        /* shouldn't happen... */
                        sleep(5);
                        continue;
                }

                if ((ebits & mptymask) != 0) {
                        /*
                         * There is an exceptional condition on the master
                         * pty.  In the pty packet mode, this means there
                         * is a single TIOCPKT_xxx control byte available.
                         * Send that control byte to the client as OOB data.
                         */

                        cc = read(masterfd, &cntlbyte, 1);
```

```
                    if (cc == 1 && pkcontrol(cntlbyte)) {
                            cntlbyte |= oobdata[0];
                            send(socketfd, &cntlbyte, 1, MSG_OOB);

                            if (cntlbyte & TIOCPKT_FLUSHWRITE) {   .
                                    /*
                                     * If the pty slave flushed its output
                                     * queue, then we want to throw away
                                     * anything we have in our buffer to
                                     * send to the client.
                                     */

                                    mptycc = 0;
                                    ibits &= ~mptymask;
                            }
                    }
                    /* else could be a packet-mode control byte that
                       we're not interested in */
            }

        if ((ibits & sockmask) != 0) {
                /*
                 * There is input ready on the socket from the client.
                 */

                sockcc = read(socketfd, sockibuf, sizeof(sockibuf));
                if (sockcc < 0 && errno == EWOULDBLOCK)
                        sockcc = 0;
                else {
                        register char   *ptr;
                        int             left, n;

                        if (sockcc <= 0)
                                break;
                        sockbptr = sockibuf;

            top:
                        for (ptr = sockibuf; ptr < sockibuf+sockcc-1;
                                                        ptr++) {
                                if (ptr[0] == magic[0] &&
                                    ptr[1] == magic[1]) {
                                        /*
                                         * We have an in-band control
                                         * message.  Process it.  After
                                         * we've processed it we have to
                                         * move all the remaining data
                                         * in the buffer left, and check
                                         * for any more in-band control
                                         * messages.  Ugh.
                                         */

                                        left = sockcc - (ptr-sockibuf);
                                        n = control(masterfd, ptr, left);
                                        if (n) {
```

```
                                        left -= n;
                                        if (left > 0)
                                            bcopy(ptr+n, ptr, left);
                                        sockcc -= n;
                                        goto top; /* n^2 */
                                    }
                                }
                            }
                            obits |= mptymask;        /* try write */
                    }
            }

    if ((obits & mptymask) != 0  &&  sockcc > 0) {
            /*
             * The master pty is ready to accept data and there
             * is data from the socket to write to the mpty.
             * An error from the write is not fatal, since we
             * set the master pty to nonblocking and it may
             * not really be ready for writing (see "try write"
             * comment above).
             */

            cc = write(masterfd, sockbptr, sockcc);
            if (cc > 0) {
                    sockcc -= cc;   /* write succeeded */
                    sockbptr += cc; /* update counter and pointer */
            }
    }

    if ((ibits & mptymask) != 0) {
            /*
             * There is input from the master pty.  Read it into
             * the beginning of out "mptyibuf" buffer.
             */

            mptycc = read(masterfd, mptyibuf, sizeof(mptyibuf));
            mptybptr = mptyibuf;
            if (mptycc < 0 && errno == EWOULDBLOCK)
                    mptycc = 0;
            else if (mptycc <= 0)
                    break;  /* returns from function; done */
            else if (mptyibuf[0] == 0) {
                    /*
                     * If the first byte that we read is a 0, then
                     * there is real data in the buffer for us,
                     * not one of the packet-mode control bytes.
                     */

                    mptybptr++;     /* skip over the byte of 0 */
                    mptycc--;
                    obits |= sockmask;   /* try a write to socket */
            } else {
                    /*
                     * It's possible for the master pty to generate
```

```
                                         * a control byte for us, between the select
                                         * above and the read that we just did.
                                         */

                                        if (pkcontrol(mptyibuf[0])) {
                                            mptyibuf[0] |= oobdata[0];
                                            send(socketfd, &mptyibuf[0], 1, MSG_OOB);
                                        }
                                        /* else it has to be one of the packet-mode
                                           control bytes that we're not interested in */

                                        mptycc = 0;       /* there can't be any data after
                                                             the control byte */

                                }
                        }

                        if ((obits & sockmask) != 0  &&  mptycc > 0) {
                                /*
                                 * The socket is ready for more output and we have
                                 * data from the master pty to send to the client.
                                 */

                                cc = write(socketfd, mptybptr, mptycc);
                                if (cc < 0 && errno == EWOULDBLOCK) {
                                        /* also shouldn't happen */
                                        sleep(5);
                                        continue;
                                }
                                if (cc > 0) {
                                        mptycc -= cc;    /* update counter and pointer */
                                        mptybptr += cc;
                                }
                        }
                }
        }
}

/*
 * This function is called if a SIGCLD signal occurs.  This means that our
 * child, the login shell that we invoked through /bin/login, terminated.
 * This function is also called at the end of the parent, which only happens
 * if it gets an error or EOF on the network connection to the client.
 */

cleanup()
{
        char    *p;

        /*
         * Remove the /etc/utmp entry by calling the logout() function.
         * Then add the terminating entry to the /usr/adm/wtmp file.
         */

        p = line + 5;              /* p = pointer to "ttyXY" */
        if (logout(p))
```

```
                    logwtmp(p, "", "");

           chmod(line, 0666);       /* change mode of slave to rw-rw-rw */
           chown(line, 0, 0);       /* change owner=root, group-owner=wheel */

           *p = 'p';                /* change "ttyXY" to "ptyXY" */
           chmod(line, 0666);       /* change mode of master to rw-rw-rw */
           chown(line, 0, 0);       /* change owner=root, group-owner=wheel */

           shutdown(0, 2);          /* close both directions of socket */

           exit(1);
}

/*
 * Send an error message back to the rlogin client.
 * The first byte must be a binary 1, followed by the ASCII
 * error message, followed by a return/newline.
 */

fatal(fd, msg)
int     fd;
char    *msg;
{
           char buf[BUFSIZ];

           buf[0] = 1;
           sprintf(buf + 1, "rlogind: %s.\r\n", msg);
           write(fd, buf, strlen(buf));
           exit(1);
}

/*
 * Fatal error, as above, but include the errno value in the message.
 */

fatalperror(fd, msg)
int     fd;
char    *msg;
{
           char            buf[BUFSIZ];
           extern int      sys_nerr;
           extern char     *sys_errlist[];

           if ((unsigned) errno < sys_nerr)
                   sprintf(buf, "%s: %s", msg, sys_errlist[errno]);
           else
                   sprintf(buf, "%s: Error %d", msg, errno);

           fatal(fd, buf);
                   /* NOTREACHED */
}

#ifdef  OLD_LOGIN
```

```
/*
 * Set up the slave pseudo-terminal.
 * This is because the slave becomes standard input, standard output,
 * and standard error of /bin/login.
 * The mode of the slave's pty will be reset again by /bin/login.
 */

setup_term(fd)
int     fd;
{
        struct sgttyb   sgttyb;

        ioctl(fd, TIOCGETP, &sgttyb);
        sgttyb.sg_flags = RAW | ANYP;
                        /* raw mode */
                        /* accept any parity, send none */
        ioctl(fd, TIOCSETP, &sgttyb);
}

#endif  /* OLD_LOGIN */

#ifdef  NEW_LOGIN

/*
 * The new rlogind does the user authentication here.  In 4.2BSD & 4.3BSD
 * this was done by the login program when invoked with the -r flag.
 */

int                     /* return 0 if user validated OK, else -1 on error */
do_rlogin(host)
char    *host;
{
        /*
         * Read the 3 strings that the rcmd() function wrote to the
         * socket: the client-user-name, server-user-name and
         * terminal-type/speed.
         */

        getstr(cliuname, sizeof(cliuname), "remuser too long");
        getstr(servuname, sizeof(servuname), "locuser too long");
        getstr(term+ENVSIZE, sizeof(term)-ENVSIZE, "Terminal type too long");

        /*
         * The real-user-ID has to be root since we're invoked by the
         * inetd daemon.
         */

        if (getuid())
                return(-1);

        /*
         * The server-user-name has to correspond to an account on
         * this system.
         */
```

```
            if ( (pwd = getpwnam(servuname)) == NULL)
                    return(-1);

        /*
         * Call the ruserok() function to authenticate the client.
         * This function returns 0 if OK, else -1 on error.
         */

            return( ruserok(host, SUPERUSER(pwd), cliuname, servuname) );
}

/*
 * Read a string from the socket.  Make sure it fits, else fatal error.
 */

getstr(buf, cnt, errmsg)
char    *buf;           /* the string that's read goes into here */
int     cnt;            /* sizeof() the char array */
char    *errmsg;        /* in case error message required */
{
        char    c;

        do {
                if (read(0, &c, 1) != 1)
                        exit(1);                /* error or EOF */
                if (--cnt < 0)
                        fatal(1, errmsg);       /* no return */
                *buf++ = c;
        } while (c != 0);                       /* null byte terminates the string */
}

extern  char **environ;

char    *speeds[] = {   /* the order *IS* important - see tty(4) */
        "0", "50", "75", "110", "134", "150", "200", "300", "600",
        "1200", "1800", "2400", "4800", "9600", "19200", "38400",
};
#define NSPEEDS (sizeof(speeds) / sizeof(speeds[0]))

/*
 * Set up the slave pseudo-terminal device.
 * We take the terminal name that was sent over by the rlogin client,
 * along with the speed.  We set the speed of the slave pty accordingly
 * (since programs such as vi do things differently based on the user's
 * terminal speed) and propagate the terminal type into the initial
 * environment.
 */

setup_term(fd)
int     fd;
{
        register char   *cp, **cpp;
        struct sgttyb   sgttyb;
        char            *speed;
```

```
        ioctl(fd, TIOCGETP, &sgttyb);    /* fetch modes for slave pty */

    if ( (cp = index(term, '/')) != NULL) {
            /*
             * The rlogin client sends a string such as "vt100/9600"
             * which was stored in the term[] array by do_rlogin().
             */

            *cp++ = '\0';    /* null terminate the terminal name */
            speed = cp;      /* and get pointer to ASCII speed */

            /*
             * Assure the ASCII speed is null terminated, in case
             * it's followed by another slash.  This allows the client
             * to append additional things to the string, separated
             * by slashes, even though we don't currently look at them.
             */

            if ( (cp = index(speed, '/')) != NULL)
                    *cp++ = '\0';

            /*
             * Compare the ASCII speed with the array above, and set
             * the slave pty speed accordingly.
             */

            for (cpp = speeds; cpp < &speeds[NSPEEDS]; cpp++) {
                    if (strcmp(*cpp, speed) == 0) {
                            sgttyb.sg_ispeed = sgttyb.sg_ospeed = cpp - speeds;
                            break;
                    }
            }
    }
    sgttyb.sg_flags = ECHO|CRMOD|ANYP|XTABS;
                    /* echo on */
                    /* map CR into LF; output LF as CR-LF */
                    /* accept any parity, send none */
                    /* replace tabs by spaces on output */

    ioctl(fd, TIOCSETP, &sgttyb);

    /*
     * Initialize the environment that we'll ask /bin/login to
     * maintain.  /bin/login will then append its variables
     * (HOME, SHELL, USER, PATH, ...) to this.
     */

    env[0] = term;          /* the "TERM=..." string */
    env[1] = (char *) 0;    /* one element is all we initialize it with */
    environ = env;          /* stuff it away for our execl of /bin/login */
}

/*
 * Check whether the specified host is in our local domain, as determined
```

```
 * by the part of the name following the first period, in its name and in ours.
 * If either name is unqualified (contains no period), assume that the host
 * is local, as it will be interpreted as such.
 */

int                               /* return 1 if local domain, else return 0 */
local_domain(host)
char    *host;
{
        register char    *ptr1, *ptr2;
        char             localhost[MAXHOSTNAMELEN];

        if ( (ptr1 = index(host, '.')) == NULL)
                return(1);                 /* no period in remote host name */

        gethostname(localhost, sizeof(localhost));
        if ( (ptr2 = index(localhost, '.')) == NULL)
                return(1);                 /* no period in local host name */

        /*
         * Both host names contain a period.  Now compare both names,
         * starting with the first period in each name (i.e., the names
         * of their respective domains).  If equal, then the remote domain
         * equals the local domain, return 1.
         */

        if (strcasecmp(ptr1, ptr2) == 0)          /* case insensitive compare */
                return(1);

        return(0);
}
#endif /* NEW_LOGIN */
```

The `cleanup` function calls the functions `logout` and `logwtmp`. The first function deletes the user's entry from the `/etc/utmp` file. This file has one entry for each terminal currently logged in. The `logwtmp` function appends an entry to the file `/usr/adm/wtmp`. This file has an entry appended to it each time a user logs in or out. These two files are normally maintained by the `/bin/login` and `/etc/init` programs. Indeed, the `login` program does its part (see Figure 15.13), but since the parent of the login shell is not the `init` process (see Figure 2.9), the terminating entries in these two files must be handled by the `rlogind` server.

15.13 Summary

Remote login is the most complicated networking example that we've described so far. Part of the complication comes from the required details of terminal handling, which isn't simple under any operating system. Also, users expect a remote login session to be as similar as possible to a local login. This requires that we handle the back flushing of output and changes in the client's window size.

Our approach to describing the 4.3BSD `rlogin` client and server was to describe all the facilities that are required in a stepwise mode. We first developed a recording process, to understand terminal line disciplines and pseudo-terminals. We then described windowing environments and the effects of a dynamic window size on a user process. Flow control and the pseudo-terminal packet mode were then examined, since these are used by the 4.3BSD remote login programs. The chapter ended with the actual source code to the 4.3BSD `rlogin` client and server.

Given the number of user processes and kernel modules involved in a remote login, as shown in Figure 15.8, you might wonder how much CPU time is required to do everything. In an actual measurement of a remote login session, the CPU times required by the different processes are shown in Figure 15.14.

Process	CPU time (seconds)
`rlogin` client, parent (VAX 785)	40.0
`rlogin` client, child (VAX 785)	34.0
`rlogind` server (VAX 8650)	34.1

Figure 15.14   CPU times required for a five-hour remote login.

These CPU times were for a five-hour remote login session, during which most of the time was spent editing with the `vi` editor. Even on a system like the VAX 785 (whose CPU performance is similar to the smaller microprocessors and workstations today) just over 1 minute was required to support the `rlogin` client.

Exercises

15.1   What happens with the 4.3BSD `rlogind` when there are already 64 remote logins and the next client request arrives? What is necessary to correct this?

15.2   In Section 15.3 we showed how a single process can use the `select` system call to multiplex two independent flows of data. But the 4.3BSD `rlogin` client uses two processes to do this, instead of using `select`. Why?

15.3   Why does the cbreak terminal mode handle interrupt-generating characters but not line editing?

15.4   If the remote login server prompts the client for a password, how is the password transferred across the network from the client to the server?

15.5   Why is the pseudo-terminal control information sent from the server to the client as out-of-band data, but the window size changes are sent in the other direction as in-band data?

15.6   Follow the three strings that the `rcmd` function writes to its socket: the client-user-name, server-user-name, and terminal type. If `OLD_LOGIN` is defined, which process reads these three strings and processes them? Be sure you understand all the processes involved in transferring these three strings. If NEW_LOGIN is defined, which process reads these three strings and processes them?

15.7 Describe the steps that are probably performed by the three System V pseudo-terminal functions: grantpt, unlockpt, and ptsname.

15.8 Compare the rlogin client and server to the TELNET facility.

15.9 Assume that you are logged in to host 1 and use the rlogin client to login to the same host, host 1. Modify Figure 15.8 to show the flow of data between your terminal and the new login shell.

15.10 The 4.3BSD program tip and the System V program cu provide a feature similar to a remote login. These two programs are typically used with dial-up telephone lines and modems. Modify Figure 15.8 to show what is involved when this type of remote login is used. (Hint: modems are typically connected to Unix systems similar to terminals.) Indicate the state of each terminal line discipline box (cooked mode or raw mode).

16

Remote Tape Drive Access

16.1 Introduction

A practical use of a LAN is for systems without tape drives to back up their disks across the network to a system that has a tape drive. Indeed, there are many workstations attached to LANs such as an Ethernet, that do not have a tape drive. In this chapter we examine the 4.3BSD rmt protocol. It is a simple protocol, much simpler than the true sharing of files across a network, and solves a current problem. This protocol is used by the rdump and rrestore commands in 4.3BSD.

16.2 Unix Tape Drive Handling

Unix presents a simple interface between a user process and a tape drive. A write system call writes a block of the specified size to the tape drive. The read system call reads an entire block from a tape drive, returning the actual number of bytes read. This is an example where the number of bytes returned by the read might not equal the request amount of data. It is the user's responsibility to assure that the buffer size for the read is large enough to handle the largest block size on the tape, or else an error occurs. When a tape drive is closed, if the last operation was a write, two end-of-file marks are written to the tape. When an end-of-file mark is encountered on the tape, the next read returns a value of 0. If there is more data on the tape, the program can continue reading, and the next read returns the first block of the next file on the tape. This is a rare instance where it makes sense to continue reading after receiving an end-of-file indication from a read system call.

668

Tape drives under 4.3BSD are known by names such as `/dev/rmt8`, which is the pathname that is passed to the `open` system call, to open a tape drive. If the name is specified as `/dev/nrmt8`, for example, the ''n'' prefix specifies that the tape is not to be rewound when closed.

4.3BSD also provides an `ioctl` for tape devices that allows additional operations to be performed on a tape: write end-of-file marks, space over a specified number of records or files, take the tape drive off-line, and the like.

16.3 `rmt` **Protocol**

4.3BSD provides a remote tape server known as the `rmt` daemon. It is usually found in the file `/etc/rmt`. This program is started by the remote shell server, `rshd`, that we described in Section 14.3. It can also be started by the `rexecd` server, which we also mentioned in Section 14.4. The only difference between these two servers is the authentication used by the server to allow the client to run the `rmt` server on the host. We show these processes in Figure 16.1.

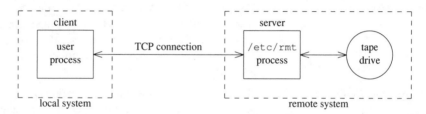

Figure 16.1 Processes for remote tape drive access.

Realize that the client process has called either `rcmd` or `rexec` to cause the `rmt` process to execute on the remote host. This provides an Internet stream socket to the client process.

There is an application protocol that the client must adhere to when communicating with the server over the TCP connection. This protocol is partly documented in the *rmt*(8) manual page in the 4.3BSD System Manager's Manual, but there are errors in that description. The protocol is simple and consists mainly of short ASCII strings, terminated by the newline character. The client sends the first command. The responses from the server are either

A*retval*\n

or

E*errornum*\n*errorstring*\n

The first response is an ASCII 'A', followed by an ASCII representation of a number, followed by a newline. This response indicates successful completion of the command. The second response is generated by the server whenever an error occurs and consists of an ASCII 'E', followed by an ASCII representation of an error number (the Unix `errno` value), followed by a newline, followed by an ASCII error message string, followed by a newline.

The client requests all start with an ASCII character also. The actual format of these requests is

O*pathname*\n*mode*\n
: Open the specified *pathname*. The *mode* is a decimal value specifying the mode for the `open` system call, which we discussed in Section 2.3. Typical values for *mode* are 0 for reading, 1 for writing, and 2 for reading and writing. On a successful open, the response is

    ```
    A0\n
    ```

C*pathname*\n
: Close the currently open device. The required *pathname* argument is ignored. On a successful close, the response is

    ```
    A0\n
    ```

L*offset*\n*whence*\n
: Does an `lseek` on the currently open device, if the device supports random access. The *offset* and *whence* are as described in Section 2.3 for the `lseek` system call. On a successful operation, the *retval* returned is the long integer value returned by `lseek`.

W*count*\n*data*
: Write *count* bytes to the currently open device. The bytes of *data* to be written are sent by the client immediately following the newline of this command. On a successful `write`, the *retval* is the return value from the `write` system call. This should equal the specified *count*.

R*count*\n
: Read up to *count* bytes of data from the currently open device. If the `read` is successful, the response is

    A*count*\n*data*

    where *count* is the actual number of bytes read. The actual *data* immediately follows the newline of the response.

I*operation*\n*count*\n
: Does an `ioctl` operation on the tape drive. The allowable values for the *operation* are found in the `<sys/mtio.h>` header file. These values are shown in Figure 16.2. There are some other values, but they are hardware dependent. The return value from this operation, *retval*, is not defined by the 4.3BSD manual.

S\n
: Returns the status of the currently open device. This request should be avoided, as the value returned is a binary structure containing hardware-dependent information.

operation	Description
0	write *count* end-of-file marks
1	forward space over *count* end-of-file marks
2	space backwards over *count* end-of-file marks
3	forward space over *count* records
4	space backwards over *count* records
5	rewind (*count* ignored)
6	rewind (*count* ignored) and place drive off-line

Figure 16.2 ioctl operations for /etc/rmt.

In normal operation the only commands needed are: open, close, read, and write. Other than the I and S commands, there is nothing in this protocol that assumes the remote device is a tape drive. There is a footnote in the *rmt*(8) manual page stating, "People tempted to use this for a remote file access protocol are discouraged."

16.4   rmt **Server**

We can now show the rmt program that runs on the server.

```
/*
 * Copyright (c) 1983 Regents of the University of California.
 * All rights reserved.
 *
 * Redistribution and use in source and binary forms are permitted
 * provided that the above copyright notice and this paragraph are
 * duplicated in all such forms and that any documentation,
 * advertising materials, and other materials related to such
 * distribution and use acknowledge that the software was developed
 * by the University of California, Berkeley.  The name of the
 * University may not be used to endorse or promote products derived
 * from this software without specific prior written permission.
 * THIS SOFTWARE IS PROVIDED ''AS IS'' AND WITHOUT ANY EXPRESS OR
 * IMPLIED WARRANTIES, INCLUDING, WITHOUT LIMITATION, THE IMPLIED
 * WARRANTIES OF MERCHANTIBILITY AND FITNESS FOR A PARTICULAR PURPOSE.
 */

#ifndef lint
char copyright[] =
"@(#) Copyright (c) 1983 Regents of the University of California.\n\
 All rights reserved.\n";
#endif /* not lint */

#ifndef lint
static char sccsid[] = "@(#)rmt.c       5.4 (Berkeley) 6/29/88";
#endif /* not lint */

/*
 * rmt daemon.
 */
```

```
#include      <stdio.h>
#include      <sgtty.h>
#include      <sys/types.h>
#include      <sys/socket.h>
#include      <sys/mtio.h>
#include      <errno.h>
extern int    errno;

int    tapefd = -1;            /* file descriptor for tape device */

char   *record = NULL;         /* pointer to our malloc'ed buffer */

#define MAXSTRING      64
char    device[MAXSTRING];     /* device/filename to open */
char    count[MAXSTRING];      /* count for read(2) and write(2) and others */
char    offset[MAXSTRING];     /* offset for lseek(2) */
char    whence[MAXSTRING];     /* whence for lseek(2) */
char    mode[MAXSTRING];       /* mode for open(2) */
char    op[MAXSTRING];         /* operation for mt ioctl */

char    respstr[BUFSIZ];       /* response string we send back to client */

long    lseek();
long    atol();
char    *malloc();
char    *checkbuf();           /* our function, at end of file */

FILE    *debug;
#define DEBUG(f)         if (debug) fprintf(debug, f)
#define DEBUG1(f,a)      if (debug) fprintf(debug, f, a)
#define DEBUG2(f,a1,a2)  if (debug) fprintf(debug, f, a1, a2)

main(argc, argv)
int    argc;
char   **argv;
{
        int         n, i, cc, respval;
        long        lrespval;
        char        c;
        struct mtop     mtop;
        struct mtget    mtget;

        argc--, argv++;
        if (argc > 0) {
                /*
                 * If a command line argument is specified, take that as the
                 * name of a file to write debugging information into.
                 */

                if ( (debug = fopen(*argv, "w")) == NULL)
                        exit(1);
                setbuf(debug, NULL);    /* completely unbuffered */
        }
```

```
            /*
             * We communicate with the client on descriptors 0 and 1.
             * Since we're invoked by rshd, both are set to the stream socket
             * that inetd accepts from the client.
             * We read from fd 0 and write to fd 1, so that for testing we can
             * just invoke this program interactively and it'll work with
             * stdin and stdout.
             */
top:
            errno   = 0;                    /* Unix errno, clear before every operation */

            if (read(0, &c, 1) != 1)
                    exit(0);        /* EOF (normal way to end) or error */

            switch (c) {

            case 'O':                                               /* open */
                    if (tapefd >= 0)
                            close(tapefd);  /* implies a close of currently-open
                                                    device */
                    get_string(device);
                    get_string(mode);
                    DEBUG2("rmtd: O %s %s\n", device, mode);

                    if ( (tapefd = open(device, atoi(mode))) < 0)
                            resp_ioerr(errno);
                    else
                            resp_val((long) 0);
                    break;

            case 'C':                                               /* close */
                    DEBUG("rmtd: C\n");
                    get_string(device);                     /* required, but ignored */

                    if (close(tapefd) < 0)
                            resp_ioerr(errno);
                    else
                            resp_val((long) 0);

                    tapefd = -1;    /* will force any i/o operations to generate
                                            an error, until another device is opened */
                    break;

            case 'L':                                               /* lseek */
                    get_string(offset);
                    get_string(whence);
                    DEBUG2("rmtd: L %s %s\n", offset, whence);

                    if ( (lrespval = lseek(tapefd, atol(offset), atoi(whence))) < 0)
                            resp_ioerr(errno);
                    else
                            resp_val(lrespval);     /* lseek return value */
                    break;
```

```
        case 'W':                                              /* write */
                get_string(count);
                DEBUG1("rmtd: W %s\n", count);

                n = atoi(count);
                record = checkbuf(record, n, SO_RCVBUF);

                /*
                 * We have to loop, to read a record of the specified size
                 * from the socket.
                 */

                for (i = 0; i < n; i += cc) {
                        if ( (cc = read(0, &record[i], n - i)) <= 0) {
                                DEBUG("rmtd: premature eof\n");
                                exit(2);
                        }
                }

                /*
                 * Write a single tape record.  Note that we don't respond to
                 * the client until the write(2) system call returns.
                 */

                if ( (respval = write(tapefd, record, n)) < 0)
                        resp_ioerr(errno);
                else
                        resp_val((long) respval);        /* #bytes written */
                break;

        case 'R':                                              /* read */
                get_string(count);
                DEBUG1("rmtd: R %s\n", count);

                n = atoi(count);
                record = checkbuf(record, n, SO_SNDBUF);

                if ( (respval = read(tapefd, record, n)) < 0)
                        resp_ioerr(errno);
                else {
                        resp_val((long) respval);        /* #bytes */
                        resp_buff(record, respval);      /* the actual data */
                }
                break;

        case 'I':                                              /* MT ioctl */
                get_string(op);
                get_string(count);
                DEBUG2("rmtd: I %s %s\n", op, count);

                mtop.mt_op    = atoi(op);
                mtop.mt_count = atoi(count);
                if (ioctl(tapefd, MTIOCTOP, (char *) &mtop) < 0)
                        resp_ioerr(errno);
```

```
                        else
                                resp_val((long) mtop.mt_count);
                        break;

                case 'S':                                          /* MT status */
                        DEBUG("rmtd: S\n");

                        if (ioctl(tapefd, MTIOCGET, (char *) &mtget) < 0)
                                resp_ioerr(errno);
                        else {
                                resp_val((long) sizeof(mtget));
                                resp_buff((char *) &mtget, sizeof(mtget));
                        }
                        break;

                default:
                        DEBUG1("rmtd: garbage command %c\n", c);
                        exit(3);
                }
                goto top;
}

/*
 * Send a normal response to the client.
 */

resp_val(lval)
long    lval;              /* has to be a long, for lseek() return value */
{
        register int    n;

        DEBUG1("rmtd: A %ld\n", lval);

        sprintf(respstr, "A%ld\n", lval);
        n = strlen(respstr);
        if (write(1, respstr, n) != n) {
                DEBUG("rmtd: resp_val: write error\n");
                exit(5);
        }
}

/*
 * Send a response buffer to the client.
 */

resp_buff(buff, nbytes)
char    *buff;
int     nbytes;
{
        if (write(1, buff, nbytes) != nbytes) {
                DEBUG("rmtd: resp_buff: write error\n");
                exit(6);
        }
}
```

```
/*
 * Send an error response to the client.
 * Notice that we send the error string associated with "errno" to the
 * client, not just the errno value, since if it is a different flavor
 * of Unix (or not even Unix at all) the errno values may not be
 * meaningful.
 */

resp_ioerr(errnum)
int     errnum;         /* the Unix errno */
{
        char            msgstr[100];
        extern int      sys_nerr;
        extern char     *sys_errlist[];

        if (errnum > 0 && errnum < sys_nerr)
                sprintf(msgstr, "%s", sys_errlist[errnum]);
        else
                sprintf(msgstr, "errno = %d", errnum);

        DEBUG2("rmtd: E %d (%s)\n", errnum, msgstr);
        sprintf(respstr, "E%d\n%s\n", errnum, msgstr);
        resp_buff(respstr, strlen(respstr));
}


/*
 * Get a string from the command line (the socket).
 */

get_string(bp)
char    *bp;            /* string gets stored here by us */
{
        register int    i;
        register char   *cp;

        cp = bp;
        for (i = 0; i < (MAXSTRING - 1); i++) {
                /*
                 * Read one byte at a time, looking for the newline.
                 * Note that this differs from the rmt(8C) man page.
                 * Commands with multiple arguments (such as 'O') require
                 * a newline between the arguments.  Also, we do not skip
                 * over any leading white space, so the command character
                 * must be immediately followed by the first argument.
                 */

                if (read(0, cp+i, 1) != 1)
                        exit(0);

                if (cp[i] == '\n')
                        break;
        }
        cp[i] = '\0';
}
```

```
/*
 * The following function is called before every record is written or read
 * to or from the tape.  Since we have to read or write every tape record
 * with a single read(2) or write(2) system call, we have to assure
 * we have a buffer that is big enough.
 * What we do is keep track of the largest record we've seen so far, and
 * whenever a larger record is required, we free(3) the old buffer and
 * malloc(3) a new one.
 *
 * Additionally, when we malloc a buffer, we set the socket's buffer size
 * to the new size (or as close to it as possible).
 */

static int       maxrecsize = -1;          /* largest record we've seen so far */

char *                     /* return pointer to buffer to use */
checkbuf(ptr, size, option)
char    *ptr;              /* pointer to current buffer */
int     size;             /* size of current buffer */
int     option;           /* for setsockopt: SO_SNDBUF or SO_RCVBUF */
{

        if (size <= maxrecsize)
                return(ptr);              /* current buffer is big enough */

        if (ptr != NULL)
                free(ptr);                /* first free the existing buffer */
                                          /* then malloc a new buffer */
        if ( (ptr = malloc(size)) == NULL) {
                DEBUG("rmtd: cannot allocate buffer space\n");
                exit(4);
        }

        maxrecsize = size;                /* remember new buffer size */

        while ((size > 1024) &&
                (setsockopt(0, SOL_SOCKET, option, (char *) &size,
                                sizeof(size)) < 0))
                size -= 1024;

        return(ptr);              /* return pointer to the new buffer */
}
```

This server is intended to be invoked by either the rshd server or the rexecd server. The 4.3BSD rdump program, for example, calls the rcmd function to invoke the rmt server. The actual connection between the client process and the rmt process is as shown in Figure 14.1.

Since this program is written to read commands from standard input and write results to standard output, we can invoke it interactively for testing. Assuming the program is compiled and link edited into the file a.out we can show the following interaction. User input is shown *like this* and computer output is shown like this. Explanations are shown in *italics*.

```
% cat temp.foo                          Here is the file we'll demonstrate with
now is the time
for all good computers
to come to the aid
of their programmer
% ls -l temp.foo                        Let's get its exact size in bytes
-rw-rw-r--  1 stevens        78 Mar  7 11:57 temp.foo
% a.out                                 Start the program interactively
Otemp.foo
0                                       Open the file temp.foo for reading
A0                                      Normal response from program
R50                                     Read 50 bytes
A50                                     Normal return—50 bytes follow
now is the time
for all good computers
to come to R60                          Read 60 bytes
A28                                     Normal response—only 28 bytes follow
the aid
of their programmer
L50
0                                       Position to byte 50 from the start of the file
A50                                     Normal response, positioned to byte 50
R60                                     Read 60 bytes
A28                                     Normal response—only 28 bytes follow
the aid
of their programmer
C                                       Close file
A0                                      Normal response
%
```

This simple example shows that it is worth considering the use of ASCII commands in the application protocol. This can simplify debugging.

The comment in the source code for the W command notes that a response is not returned to the client until the write system call returns. It is possible to modify the rmt server so that it sends its response to the client *before* invoking the write system call to write the data block to the tape drive. This means that the server then has to remember the result of its write system call for the *next* response that it sends back to the client, as there still has to be a way to signal the client when a write error occurs.† This also means that the client has to execute some command, such as the C command to close the device, after it has written the last data block, so that it can obtain the results of the final write system call. By changing the server in this fashion, it lets the server overlap the writing of a tape block with the reading of the next block from the network.

---

† The typical user of the rmt server is the rdump program, and it is possible to get write errors when writing to a magnetic tape.

16.5 Summary

In this chapter we've shown a simple example—writing to a tape drive on a remote system. This application built on the remote command execution functions from Chapter 14.

We also mentioned how the performance of this application can be improved by allowing the local process and the remote process to overlap execution. This is a form of overlapping the reading and writing using multiple buffers, as we mentioned in Section 3.11. In Section 3.11 we were using two processes on a single system, communicating through shared memory. Here we would use two processes, one on each system, communicating across a network.

In the next chapter we'll examine some typical performance figures for disks, tapes, and networks.

Exercises

16.1   Modify the `rmt` server so that it sends a response to the client before doing the `write` to the tape drive. How would you handle errors from the `write` system call?

16.2   An alternative technique for increasing the throughput of the `rmt` server is for the client to send its next `W` command before reading the server's response to the previous command. How does this work? Which technique is preferable—this one or the technique from the previous exercise?

16.3   What happens with the call to `setsockopt` in the function `checkbuf` when file descriptor zero is a terminal, as in the example from the text?

16.4   Assume that a client on host 1 uses the `rmt` server to access the file `/usr/foo` on host 2. At the same time a client on host 3 also uses the `rmt` server on host 2 to access the same file, `/usr/foo`. If both clients perform the three steps described in Section 3.2 to use and update a sequence number in the file `/usr/foo`, describe the possible outcomes. What is needed to handle this scenario? Is this still a problem if the `rmt` server is used with a tape drive?

17

Performance

17.1 Introduction

We've talked about various methods of communicating between different processes. In Chapter 3 we described numerous IPC techniques for communicating between processes on a single host, and in Chapters 6 and 7 we covered the techniques used to communicate between different processes using a network.

How fast are the various IPC techniques? Also, how fast is a typical network, and how does a network compare to devices such as disk drives and tape drives? Since a network is often used to transfer files, the speed of the network compared to a local disk drive is of interest. But there are few generic answers to these hard questions. Still some appreciation of performance makes it easier to understand if performance improvements are possible for a given client–server. For example, when considering the `rmt` server from the previous chapter, we're dealing with a disk drive, a network and a tape drive. An understanding of performance becomes important since any of the three can be the limiting factor in throughput. In this chapter we'll look at some typical performance values for the various IPC techniques, tape drives, disk drives, and networks.

17.2 IPC Performance

Let's first look at the performance of the various forms of IPC that we presented in Chapter 3. The intent is to get some benchmark figures so that we can make reasonable decisions when selecting IPC for an application.

Our performance test consists of a process sending and receiving 20,000 "messages." The program using a pipe consists of

```
#define COUNT            20000
#define BUFFSIZE         128

char            buff[BUFFSIZE];

main()
{
        register int    i;
        int             pipefd[2];

        if (pipe(pipefd) < 0)
                err_sys("pipe error");

        for (i = 0; i < COUNT; i++) {
                if (write(pipefd[1], buff, BUFFSIZE) < 0)
                        err_sys("write error");

                if (read(pipefd[0], buff, BUFFSIZE) != BUFFSIZE)
                        err_sys("read error");
        }

        close(pipefd[0]);
        close(pipefd[1]);

        exit(0);
}
```

For any form of IPC, the overhead is usually attributable to the time required to execute the system calls (`read`, `write`, `msgsnd`, etc.) and the time required to move the data between the processes. Figure 3.24 shows that this typically requires the kernel to copy the data between the user process and the kernel. The program shown above exercises these features, even though only one process is used.

The version using a message queue is

```
#include         <sys/types.h>
#include         <sys/ipc.h>
#include         <sys/msg.h>

#define KEY      ((key_t) 54321)

#define COUNT            20000
#define BUFFSIZE          128
#define PERMS            0666

main()
{
        register int    i, msqid;
        struct {
          long  m_type;
          char  m_text[BUFFSIZE];
```

```
        } msgbuff;

        if ( (msqid = msgget(KEY, PERMS | IPC_CREAT)) < 0)
                err_sys("msgget error");
        msgbuff.m_type = 1L;

        for (i = 0; i < COUNT; i++) {
                if (msgsnd(msqid, &msgbuff, BUFFSIZE, 0) < 0)
                        err_sys("msgsnd error");

                if (msgrcv(msqid, &msgbuff, BUFFSIZE, 0L, 0) != BUFFSIZE)
                        err_sys("msgrcv error");
        }

        if (msgctl(msqid, IPC_RMID, (struct msqid_ds *) 0) < 0)
                err_sys("IPC_RMID error");

        exit(0);
}
```

The programs using FIFOs and semaphores are similar. Two versions of the semaphore version were written—one that does not use the SEM_UNDO feature, and one that uses this feature. The reason for these two versions of the semaphore test is to see what effect the undo feature has on performance. There is no processing of the data that is being transmitted—we are only interested in seeing how fast messages can be sent using each of the techniques, and how they compare to each other. The programs were run using four values for BUFFSIZE: 32, 128, 512, and 2048 bytes. We naturally expect larger messages to require more time, but want to see just what effect the message size has on performance. Since the two semaphore tests only do an increment of a semaphore's value, followed by a decrement of its value, the time required for this does not depend on the BUFFSIZE value. This semaphore test assumes that a shared memory segment is being used for the actual message, so the time required for the system to process a message in the shared memory segment depends on the synchronization overhead—the semaphore time.

These five programs were run on three different computer systems.

- A Compaq 386 (a 20 MHz Intel 80386 processor), running AT&T Unix System V/386 Release 3.2.

- A DEC MicroVAX II, running Ultrix (a 4.3BSD derivative).

- An AT&T Unix PC (a 10 MHz Motorola 68010 processor), running AT&T System V Unix.

First, let us look at the results on a single computer system. Figure 17.1 shows the performance of the five types of IPC on the Compaq 386/20. The values for "Messages per second" were obtained by dividing 20,000 by the number of seconds of clock time used by the program. Each program was run three times and the three results averaged.

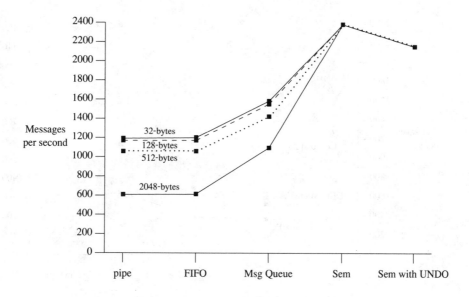

Figure 17.1 IPC performance on the Compaq 386/20.

The results make sense—the values for a pipe and a FIFO should be similar, as the two techniques are similar and use the same system calls to send and receive data. Both use the standard Unix block buffers for holding the data while in the kernel. Also, we're not surprised that message queues are faster than pipes and FIFOs, since the latter two techniques use the general `read` and `write` system calls, while message queues have their own system calls, which can be implemented efficiently. Since the semaphore calls don't transfer a message between the user process and the kernel, we expect them to be the fastest, as they are. We can also see the effect of the undo feature on the performance of the semaphore system calls.

We also note the similarity between the results for 32-byte messages and for 128-byte messages. Even though the size of the message changes by a factor of four, the results are within a few percent of each other. This is because the fundamental limitation for these small messages is the overhead involved in executing the system calls (`read`, `write`, `msgsnd`, or `msgrcv`), and the setup time involved in moving any amount of data between the user process and the kernel. This implies that there is a fixed cost for any form of IPC, along with a variable cost that depends on the actual amount of data being transferred. Further evidence of this is that the throughput for 512-byte messages is not four times greater than the throughput for 2048-byte messages.

We can now compare the performance of the three different computer systems. Figure 17.2 shows the number of messages per second for each of the three systems, for a 512-byte message.

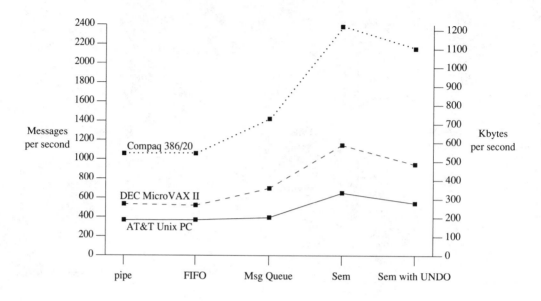

Figure 17.2 IPC performance for 512-byte messages.

We see here that the shape of the graphs is similar for all three systems, but the relative values change for each system. It appears from this small sample that the slower the system, the flatter the curve for that system. Conversely, the faster the system, the greater the improvement in message queues and semaphores.

In Figure 17.2 we have labelled the right side in Kbytes per second, for comparison with the remaining figures in this chapter.

17.3 Tape Performance

The throughput of a start–stop tape drive is given by the following equation:†

$$throughput = \frac{speed \times blocksize}{(2 \times gapsize) + \dfrac{blocksize}{density}}$$

If the *speed* is given in inches/second (ips), the *blocksize* in bytes, the *gapsize* in inches, and the *density* in bytes/inch (bpi), the *throughput* value is in units of bytes/sec. Typical values for the *density* are 1600 bpi and 6250 bpi. For 1600 bpi, the gap size is usually 0.7 inches. For 6250 bpi, the gap size is usually 0.4 inches. The reason for multiplying the gap size by two is that between one tape block and the next (the interrecord gap whose size is specified by the *gapsize*), the tape drive is first slowing down and then speeding

---

† This equation is attributed to Don Speck of Caltech.

up. By doubling the gap size, we assume that the tape is moving at one-half the *speed* during the gap.

Figure 17.3 shows the maximum transfer rates, in bytes per second, for reading or writing 32768-byte blocks. Three tape speeds are shown, and two different tape densities.

Density	45 ips	75 ips	125 ips
1600 bpi	67,000	112,000	187,000
6250 bpi	244,000	406,000	678,000

Figure 17.3 Tape drive performance, bytes/sec, writing 32768-byte blocks.

These values can be verified by writing a small program that executes the `write` system call many times, writing the data blocks to a tape drive. On an idle system, your results should be within a few percent of the values in Figure 17.3.

Let's show the results from Figure 17.3, along with the corresponding values for a *blocksize* of 10240 bytes, in a graphical format (Figure 17.4), for comparisons later in the chapter with disk performance and network performance.

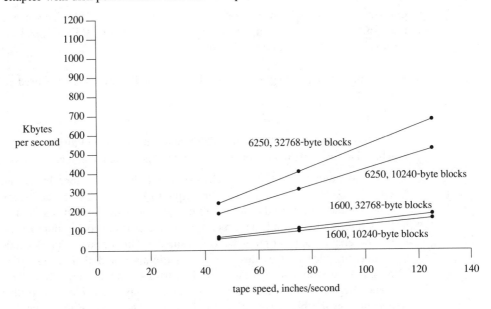

Figure 17.4 Tape drive performance.

Be aware that in units of Kbytes/sec, the "K" means 1000, not 1024. Similarly the "M" in Mbytes/sec refers to 1,000,000 not 1024×1024. About the only measurements in which the K and M refer to the powers of 2 are memory capacities—512 Kbytes, 16 Mbytes—for example.

17.4 Disk Performance

Figure 17.5 shows some typical transfer rates for five different disk drives.

- A Control Data 9720–850 disk drive connected to a VAX 8650 on a Massbus.
- A Fujitsu Eagle (M2351) disk drive connected to a VAX 785 on a Massbus.
- A DEC RA81 disk drive connected to a VAX 8650 on a Unibus.
- A Compaq 386/20 ESDI disk drive.
- An IBM PC AT disk drive.

	IBM PC AT	Compaq 386/20	DEC RA81	Fujitsu Eagle	CDC 9720–850
max. reading speed	149,000	318,000	720,000	917,000	981,000
max. dump speed	40,000	295,000	300,000	555,000	704,000

Figure 17.5 Disk performance, bytes/sec.

The operating system used for the three VAX examples was 4.3BSD. The operating system used for the PC AT and Compaq examples was SCO Xenix, Release 2.2.3.

Two values are shown for each disk drive.

- The maximum reading speed in Kbytes/second. This was measured using the command:

      dd if=*raw-disk-device* of=/dev/null bs=32768 count=1000

  This command does 1000 reads, 32768 bytes at a time, and throws away the data. This gives us some indication about how fast the system can read the disk drive.

- The maximum dump speed in Kbytes/second. This was done by executing the Unix dump program and writing the output to /dev/null. Since the amount of time that the program takes to write the first tape is the longest (the first tape contains information for all the directories on the partition being dumped), only the second and subsequent tapes were measured.† This timing value depends on the number of files in the filesystem being dumped and their sizes. The dump program's performance is best when the partition contains large files. The performance degrades when the partition contains many small files. Also, this metric depends on the block size of the filesystem. The three VAX examples used a

---

† The dump program calculates the actual amount of data written, as it writes to its output device. Since the output is typically going to a tape device, we specify the size of the tape reel and the density of the tape. The dump program does not wait until it passes the physical end-of-tape marker, but usually stops writing to a tape before this point is reached. This way, we are able to talk about how long it takes to write a tape, even though the output is being sent to the sink device, /dev/null.

block size of 8192 bytes with a fragment size of 1024 bytes. This is the largest block size supported by 4.3BSD. Our interest in this number is to see how much slower the dump program is, compared to a raw-read of the filesystem.

Figure 17.6 shows a graphical representation of these numbers, using the same scale on the y-axis as we used in Figure 17.4.

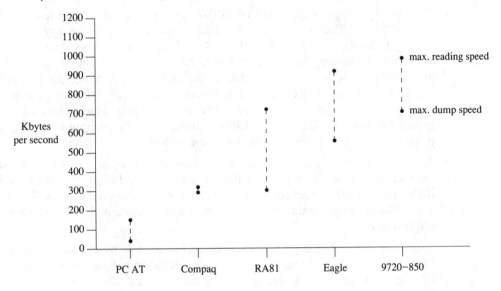

Figure 17.6 Disk performance.

17.5 Network Performance

Network performance has been improving over time. This is because of improvements in both the code that implements the network protocols and in the underlying operating system. Let's look at some of the published results on network performance.

- Let's start with the maximum throughput we could ever see on an Ethernet using TCP/IP. On a 10 megabit/sec Ethernet, after accounting for the minimum interpacket gap, the 22-byte Ethernet headers, the 20-byte IP header, the 20-byte TCP header and the 4-byte Ethernet trailer, the maximum theoretical throughput for user data is 1,185,840 bytes/sec. This assumes the maximum Ethernet packet size, which contains 1464 bytes of user data after all the headers and trailers are accounted for. It also assumes only a single host is transmitting on the Ethernet and that the host is capable of transmitting packets with the minimum allowable interpacket gap. We show this value as the dotted line at the top of Figure 17.7.

- Chesson [1987] describes the effect of a layered protocol implementation on performance. You start with the media clock rate, 10 megabits/sec for an Ethernet, and decrease it for each layer. The first loss is caused by the Ethernet interface hardware and software, then the IP layer, then the TCP layer, then the application layer. Chesson claims around 350,000 bytes/sec being available for the TCP layer, but this is not based on actual measurements. This is only 30% of the maximum.

- The paper by Boggs, Mogul, and Kent [1988] shows performance measurements on an actual Ethernet. Their throughput values are for the Ethernet only—they did not use any higher level protocols such as IP or TCP. Their measurements show that with a single host transmitting 1024-byte packets as fast as it can, they are able to obtain just over 1000 packets/sec throughput. The maximum theoretical throughput for this size packet is 1192 packets/sec, which corresponds to 1,203,920 bytes/sec of user data. Their loss of 15% from the maximum is because of the time required by their system to start the transmission of another Ethernet frame when the interrupt-complete signal is received from the previous frame (100 microseconds).

- An early paper that provides actual performance measurements of TCP/IP is Walsh and Gurwitz [1984]. They describe the integration of the TCP/IP code developed by BBN into 4.2BSD. Their performance measurements, between a VAX 750 and a VAX 780 on an Ethernet, shows TCP throughput between 80,000 bytes/sec and 100,000 bytes/sec.

- Another of the earlier papers on network performance is by Cabrera et al. [1988]. This paper provides performance measurements of user processes under 4.2BSD in an Ethernet environment. For unloaded hosts and unloaded ethers, they show a maximum TCP throughput of about 90,000 bytes/sec and a maximum UDP throughput of about 185,000 bytes/sec. This value of 90,000 bytes/sec for TCP corresponds to the values from the Walsh and Gurwitz paper, but both are less than 10% of the theoretical value. When the host systems were kept busy through an artificial workload, the throughput was reduced to around 30,000 bytes/sec.

- The NETBLT protocol, specified in RFC 998 [Clark, Lambert, and Zhang 1987a], is designed for high throughput transmission of bulk data. NETBLT is a transport protocol that runs on top of IP, similar to TCP and UDP. An analysis of the protocol is given in Clark, Lambert, and Zhang [1987b]. The values given in this paper show a throughput of 182,000 bytes/sec on a heavily used Ethernet and a throughput of 218,000 bytes/sec on a 10 megabit/sec Proteon ring.

- The most recent work on network throughput is by Jacobson [1988a; 1988c]. His efforts have gone into speeding up the kernel and the protocol processing (IP and TCP) for SunOS, a derivative of 4BSD. In [1988a] he claims a TCP throughput between two out-of-the-box Sun Microsystems 3/60s as being 380,000 bytes/sec. Note that this is significantly higher than the 4.2BSD values described above, but still only 33% of the theoretical maximum. With his modifications to the kernel and the TCP/IP code he then obtains 890,000 bytes/sec using TCP between two Sun 3/60s. In

[1988c] he shows example output of an FTP application (this is one layer above TCP) with a throughput of 816,000 bytes/sec.

• Another set of interesting values, for comparison purposes, is from the networking systems used on many personal computers. These systems frequently use a dedicated personal computer as the network server. This server often runs a special network operating system that is optimized for network throughput. An example is the NetWare operating system available from Novell, Inc. The values given in Novell [1986] for an Ethernet LAN show a maximum throughput of 144,000 bytes/sec when the server is an IBM PC AT (an Intel 80286 processor, running at 6 MHz with one wait state), and a throughput of 175,000 bytes/sec with Novell's own server (an Intel 80286 running at 8 MHz with no wait states). While the protocol being used on the Ethernet is not TCP, it is similar to the Xerox IDP protocol.

We show all these figures graphically in Figure 17.7.

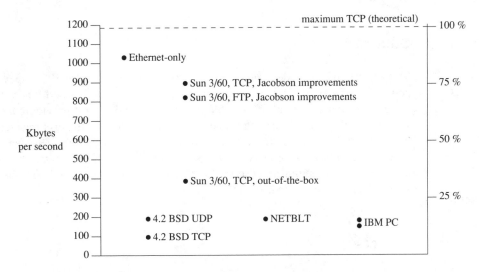

Figure 17.7 Network performance on a 10 Mbit/sec Ethernet.

What do we learn from all these numbers? First, network performance differs greatly from one implementation to the next. Also, as shown by Jacobson's results, it is possible to obtain network throughput within 75% of the theoretical maximum, for an Ethernet using current hardware. Chesson [1987] provides insight about some potential problems when the raw network speed increases the next order of magnitude, from the 10 megabit/sec Ethernet to the 100 megabit/sec FDDI.

Another set of interesting numbers is from Borman [1989]. Using two Cray computers and HYPERchannel interfaces he obtained TCP transfer rates of 1500 Kbytes/sec. This value is just above the top of the graph in Figure 17.7. But, his measurements between two Cray computers connected with an HSX high-speed channel show a TCP transfer rate of 23,750 Kbytes/sec. This value is 20 times the maximum theoretical value shown in Figure 17.7.

Clark et al. [1989] perform a detailed analysis of TCP and IP. Their analysis was to determine the amount of overhead imposed by the transport protocol—TCP, which requires IP. To do this they took the existing BSD implementation of TCP, optimized the source code and determined the number of machine instructions required to send and receive packets. They then determined that for a 10 MIPS processor and a packet size of 4000 bytes the throughput could be 530 Mbits/sec. Since the next generation of LANs will operate around 100 Mbits/sec, they claim it is not necessary to redesign the transport protocols to handle these higher speeds, it is just necessary to implement them properly. Additionally, their analysis of an existing system, the BSD TCP on a Sun 3/60, shows that the normal overhead imposed by the operating system and the overhead involved in moving the data between the user process and TCP, exceeds the overhead imposed by the transport protocol.

17.6 Summary

This chapter has provided some typical performance figures for IPC, tapes, disks, and networks. The reason for examining these figures is to understand where the limiting factor is in an application. If your file transfer application isn't providing the speed that you expect, you should first determine if the limiting factor is the disk transfer or the network. If you're going to use a tape drive for backing up remote filesystems, it doesn't make sense to buy a tape drive whose performance exceeds your network. Also, before using the rdump command described in Chapter 16, you should measure the disk dump speed, the tape drive speed, and the TCP speed.

Exercises

17.1 Perform the IPC performance tests from Section 17.2 on the computer system that you use. Compare your results to Figure 17.2.

17.2 Derive the maximum theoretical Ethernet throughput for TCP that is shown in Figure 17.7. In addition to the sizes of the headers and trailers given at the beginning of Section 17.5 you need the fact that the minimum interpacket gap of 9.6 microseconds corresponds to 12 byte-times.

17.3 What happens when dumping an Eagle disk to a 6250 bpi 75 ips tape drive, if the TCP throughput is 100 Kbytes/sec?

17.4   Write a pair of programs to be used to measure TCP performance. The sender should just execute `write` system calls in a loop, until a specified number of megabytes of data have been sent. The program should accept a option that enables the `SO_DEBUG` socket option. It should also require the following command line arguments: name or dotted-decimal address of receiver, TCP port number that receiver is listening on, number of megabytes of data to send, number of bytes per `write` system call, and size of socket buffer (`SO_SNDBUF` socket option). The receive program should accept a TCP connection and execute a `read` loop. It should also accept an optional debug command line option and should require the following command line arguments: port number to listen on, number of bytes per `read` system call, and size of socket buffer (`SO_RCVBUF` socket option). Use the programs to measure the TCP throughput between some of the systems you have access to.

18

Remote Procedure Calls

18.1 Introduction

The procedure call (sometimes referred to as a function call or a subroutine call) is a well-known method for transferring control from one part of a process to another, with a return of control to the caller. Many computer architectures implement this with an instruction of the form "jump-to-subroutine." Associated with the procedure call is the passing of arguments from the caller (the client) to the callee (the server). Similarly, there are often one or more return values from the called procedure. In most current systems the caller and callee are within a single process on a given host system. They are linked together using a link editor when the program file is generated. We'll refer to these types of procedure calls as *local procedure calls*.

In a *remote procedure call* (RPC) a process on the local system invokes a procedure on a remote system. The reason we even call this a "procedure call" is because the intent is to make it appear to the programmer that a normal procedure call is taking place. We use the term *request* to refer to the client calling the remote procedure, and the term *response* to describe the remote procedure returning its results to the client.

We'll see as we proceed, that remote procedure calls are different from local procedure calls. Figure 18.1 shows the steps that normally take place in a remote procedure call. The numbered steps in Figure 18.1 are executed in order.

1. The client calls a local procedure, called the *client stub*. It appears to the client that the client stub is the actual server procedure that it wants to call. The purpose of the stub is to package up the arguments to the remote procedure, possibly put them into some standard format (more about this in the next section) and then build one or

692

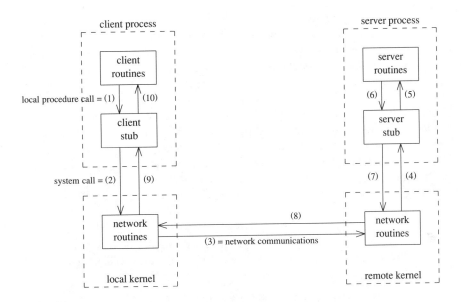

Figure 18.1 Remote Procedure Call (RPC) model.

more network messages. The packaging of the client's arguments into a network message is termed *marshaling*.

2. These network messages are sent to the remote system by the client stub. This requires a system call into the local kernel.

3. The network messages are transferred to the remote system. Either a connection-oriented or a connectionless protocol is used. We'll see examples of both later in this chapter.

4. A *server stub* procedure is waiting on the remote system for the client's request. It unmarshals the arguments from the network messages and possibly converts them.

5. The server stub executes a local procedure call to invoke the actual server function, passing it the arguments that it received in the network messages from the client stub.

6. When the server procedure is finished, it returns to the server stub, returning whatever its return values are.

7. The server stub converts the return values, if necessary, and marshals them into one or more network messages to send back to the client stub.

8. The messages get transferred back across the network to the client stub.

9. The client stub reads the network messages from the local kernel.

10. After possibly converting the return values, the client stub finally returns to the client function. This appears to be a normal procedure return to the client.

What the concept of remote procedure calls provides is the hiding of all the network code into the stub procedures. This prevents the application programs, the client and server, from having to worry about details such as sockets, network byte order, and the like. One goal of RPC is to make the writing of distributed applications easier.

RPC falls somewhere between the transport layer and the application layer, in the OSI model. Typically it is considered part of layer 6, the presentation layer. Since one intent of RPC is to hide the application layer from some of the networking details, RPC usually includes a specification for exchanging the arguments and results between the client and server in some standard format. This enhances portability between different systems and prevents the application programs from having to worry about details such as byte ordering.

In this chapter we examine three different implementations of RPC.

1. Sun Microsystems' Open Network Computing (ONC). Two parts of ONC are RPC, the Remote Procedure Call specification, and XDR, the eXternal Data Representation standard. Sun RPC typically uses either UDP or TCP as the transport protocol.

2. Xerox Courier. This is an early implementation of RPC. It includes an RPC model, built on XNS SPP as the transport protocol, and a data representation standard also.

3. Apollo's Network Computing Architecture (NCA). NCA/RPC specifies a remote procedure call protocol and NDR, Network Data Representation, defines a data representation standard.

18.2 Transparency Issues

As you might guess, taking something as simple as a procedure call and transforming it into system calls, data conversions, and network communications, leads to a greater chance of something going wrong. The goal is to make the use of RPC transparent to the application, compared to calling a local procedure, but the following issues need to be considered:

- parameter passing,
- binding,
- transport protocol,
- exception handling,
- call semantics,
- data representation,
- performance,
- security.

We'll describe each of these now in more detail, then when we get to some concrete examples later in the chapter, we'll see how the different RPC implementations handle each of these issues.

Parameter Passing

The passing of parameters between the client and the server can be nontransparent. Parameters that are passed by value are simple—the client stub copies the value from the client and packages it into a network message. The problem arises if parameters can be passed by reference. This is done, for example, in C when we pass the address of a variable, instead of passing its value. Here it makes no sense for the client stub to pass the address to the server, since the server has no way of referencing memory locations on the client's system.

A typical solution is for the RPC protocol only to allow the client to pass arguments by value. For each remote procedure, we specifically define what the input arguments are and what the return values are.

Binding

Binding refers to the client contacting the appropriate remote system to have a particular remote procedure executed. There are two components to binding:

- finding a remote host for a desired server,
- finding the correct server process on a given host.

To locate a host that provides a given type of server, one technique is to provide a centralized database. Birrell and Nelson [1984] describe one particular example of this. The servers on any host in the internet register their willingness to accept remote procedure calls, by having the server send a special message to a central authority when the server is booted. The clients then contact this central authority whenever they need to locate a particular service.

Another technique is to require the client to know which host they want to contact, and provide a superserver on that host that knows the network address of any servers that are available on that host.

Transport Protocol

Some RPC implementations use only a single transport layer protocol while others allow a choice to be made. Most RPC implementations claim to be transport-independent, but typically they support only one or two different protocols.

We can show the protocols typically used by the RPC systems that we'll cover in this chapter.

Sun RPC: UDP, TCP
Xerox Courier: SPP
Apollo RPC: UDP, DDS†

Sun RPC is designed to work with either a connection-oriented or a connectionless protocol, while Courier is designed only for a connection-oriented protocol and Apollo is
designed for a connectionless protocol.

When a connectionless protocol is used, the client stub typically has to worry about
lost packets and the like. A connection-oriented protocol handles these issues for us, but
the overhead is higher when a connection-oriented protocol is used.

Exception Handling

With a local procedure there are a limited number of things that can go wrong, and we're
usually aware of the problem when it happens—an invalid memory reference, divide by
zero, and so on. The Unix shells, for example, print a message when an error of this
form occurs, and the program that is aborted sometimes generates a core image file. As
we've mentioned, with a remote procedure the possibility of something going wrong
increases. Not only can the actual server procedure itself generate an error, but either the
client stub or the server stub can encounter network problems. The detection of a server
crash usually requires a timeout by the client stub.

Another exception condition is a request by the client to stop the server. We covered
this in Section 14.3 with the `rcmd` function, which has the option of providing a secondary channel to the remote server process so that the client can send signals to the server.
This is how a client can stop a long-running server, for example.

If the client process terminates after invoking a remote procedure but before obtaining its result, the server is termed an orphan. There are instances where the server needs
to know that its client has disappeared.

Call Semantics

When we call a local procedure, there is never any question as to how many times the
procedure executed. If it returns to the caller we know that it executed exactly once.
With a remote procedure, however, if we don't get a response after a certain interval, we
don't know how many times the remote procedure was executed. If the server crashed,
for instance, before being called by the server stub, it didn't execute at all. If it crashed
after the server returned to the server stub, it executed once. Furthermore, if the client
times out and retransmits a request, this only confuses things more. Now it is possible
for the original request to have been delayed somewhere in the network yet eventually
executed, along with the retransmitted request also being executed.

---

† DDS is a proprietary networking protocol implemented by Apollo.

When an operation such as a procedure call can be executed any number of times, with no harm done, it is said to be *idempotent*. Some examples of remote procedures that are idempotent are: a procedure to return the time-of-day, a procedure to calculate the square root, a procedure to read the first 512 bytes from a disk file, and a procedure to return the current balance of a bank account. Some examples of procedures that are *nonidempotent* are: a procedure to append 512 bytes to the end of a file, and a procedure to subtract an amount from a bank account.

There are three different forms of RPC semantics.

1. *Exactly once* means that the remote procedure was executed one time, period. This type of operation is hard to achieve, owing to the possibility of server crashes.

2. *At most once* means that the remote procedure was either not executed at all or it was executed one time at most. If a normal return is made to the caller, we know the remote procedure was executed one time. But if an error return is made, we're not certain if the remote procedure was executed once or not at all.

3. *At least once* means that the remote procedure was executed at least one time, but perhaps more. This is typical for idempotent procedures—the client keeps transmitting its request until it receives a valid response. But if the client has to send its request more than once to receive a valid response, there is a possibility that the remote procedure was executed more than once.

Data Representation

With a local procedure, both the client and the server are executing on the same system, so there aren't any data incompatibility problems. The binary format of all data types is the same. But when RPC is used, what happens when the client passes a floating point number to the server? If the client and server are on systems with different architectures, there has to be a data conversion somewhere.

All the implementations that we consider in this chapter handle this issue by defining one or more standard formats for the data types supported by that RPC implementation. Notice that we have to worry about all data items, not just binary values. It is feasible for the client to be on a system that uses ASCII and the server to use EBCDIC.

Before examining the techniques used by the RPC implementations, it is worth going back over some of the earlier examples from this text to see how we've handled the problem so far.

- The TCP/IP protocol suite uses the big-endian byte order for all the 16-bit and 32-bit fields in the various protocol headers. This includes fields such as the 32-bit network and host ID, and the 16-bit UDP port number.

- The XNS protocol suite also uses the big-endian byte order for all its 16-bit and 32-bit fields.

- The Trivial File Transfer Protocol uses the big-endian byte order for its 16-bit fields (block number and error code) and uses ASCII for character data (the filename, mode, and error string).

- The 4.3BSD line printer spooler restricts its binary values to single-byte fields, so byte ordering isn't an issue. It also uses ASCII for fields such as the printer name, filename, file size and login name.

- The remote login client and server use the big-endian byte order for the 16-bit window-size fields in their protocol that handles changes in the window size.

- The 4.3BSD `rmt` server uses ASCII strings in all its commands other than the "return status" command. As we noted in Section 16.3, this particular command isn't even portable between different Unix systems and should be avoided totally. This server has no restrictions on the data that it reads and writes to the tape device.

We now compare the three RPC implementations that we mentioned earlier.

1. Sun RPC. The data representation standard used by Sun RPC is called XDR. It imposes a big-endian byte ordering and the minimum size of any field is 32 bits. This means, for example, that when a VAX client passes a 16-bit integer to a server that is also running on a VAX, the 16-bit value is first converted to a 32-bit big-endian integer by the client, then converted back to a little-endian 16-bit integer by the server. (Recall from Chapter 4 that the VAX is a little-endian architecture.)

2. Xerox Courier. This RPC protocol also imposes a standard that both the client and server must use. It is a big-endian byte ordering and the minimum size of any field is 16 bits. Character data is encoded in the 16-bit Xerox NS character set. This uses 8-bit ASCII for normal characters, with escapes to other specialized character sets, such as Greek. This is used, for example, when sending mathematical text to certain printers.

3. Apollo RPC. Instead of imposing a single network standard, Apollo's NDR supports multiple formats. It allows the sender to use its own internal format, if it is one of the supported formats. The receiver then has to convert this to its format, if different from the sender's format. This is called the "receiver makes it right" approach. This technique has the advantage that when two systems with the same architecture are communicating, they don't have to convert the data at all (assuming they both belong to one of the supported architectures).

Figure 18.2 compares the data types and formats supported by these three RPC implementations. In the columns for each RPC implementation we show a • if it supports the corresponding data type. If the entry is blank, the data type isn't supported by that implementation.

Data type	Sun RPC	Xerox Courier	Apollo NDR
8-bit logical			•
16-bit logical		•	
32-bit logical	•		
8-bit signed integer			•
8-bit unsigned integer			•
16-bit signed integer		•	•
16-bit unsigned integer		•	•
32-bit signed integer	•	•	•
32-bit unsigned integer	•	•	•
64-bit signed integer	•		•
64-bit unsigned integer	•		•
byte order	`big-endian`	`big-endian`	`big-endian or little-endian`
signed integer format	`2's-complement`	`2's-complement`	`2's-complement`
32-bit floating point	•		•
64-bit floating point	•		•
floating-point format		`IEEE`	`IEEE, VAX IBM or Cray`
character type	`ASCII`	`16-bit NS`	`ASCII or EBCDIC`
enumeration	•	•	•
structure (record)	•	•	•
fixed-length single-dimensional array	•	•	•
variable-length single-dimensional array	•	•	•
fixed-length multidimensional array			•
variable-length multidimensional array			•
discriminated union	•		•
fixed-length opaque data	•	•	•
variable-length opaque data	•	•	•

Figure 18.2 Data types supported by RPC packages.

All three of these implementations use what is called *implicit typing*. That is, only the value of a variable is transmitted across the network, not the type of the variable. In contrast to this, the ISO technique for data representation, termed ASN.1 (Abstract Syntax Notation 1), uses *explicit typing*. ASN.1 transmits the type of every data field in a message (typically encoded in an 8-bit byte) along with the value of each field. As an example, when Courier sends a 32-bit integer value as either a procedure argument or a procedure result, only the 32-bit value is transmitted across the network. ASN.1 would transfer an 8-bit byte, specifying that the next value is an integer, followed by another byte specifying the length of the integer field (in bytes), followed by either one, two, three, four, or five bytes containing the actual value of the integer.

Performance

Taking something as simple as a local procedure call and turning it into network communications between two processes, has to affect the performance. Usually the performance loss in using RPC, versus a local procedure call, is a factor of 10 or more. But the use of RPC should be viewed as simplifying network programming, and not just replacing local procedure calls with remote procedure calls. There is usually an underlying reason why you want to distribute your application between the local system and a remote system. It is sometimes hard to realize this when reading about RPC, because the textbook examples are often contrived for display purposes. Most examples could be executed easier on a single system and don't provide any justification for using RPC. Realize that these examples are purposely made simple, to avoid confusing the presentation of RPC with details about the actual application.

Birrell and Nelson [1984] present some performance numbers for RPC on an Ethernet LAN. The system that is described in their paper does not correspond to any of the systems described in this chapter, nevertheless their performance numbers are still relevant to RPC in general. Their results were obtained for various numbers of arguments and results. For a procedure that is called with two 16-bit arguments and returns two 16-bit results, the difference between a local call and a remote call was a factor of 100 (two orders of magnitude). For a procedure with an argument of 40 16-bit words and a result of 40 16-bit words, the remote call increased the time by a factor of 33.

Another performance consideration is the technique used to invoke the server every time a client request arrives. The simplest technique is to handle each client call of a remote procedure in the concurrent-server method we've used throughout the text: a new process (containing the server stub and the server functions) is `forked` for each client call. But if a client knows that it needs to call a certain remote procedure multiple times, it would be more efficient to leave the server process running as long as the client is running.

Security

With RPC we have all the potential security problems that we had with the execution of commands on a remote system in Chapter 14. Allowing a remote program to call a procedure on your system is similar to someone executing a command on your system. We'll examine the different techniques used by Sun RPC and Courier.

18.3 Sun RPC

We start our description of an actual RPC implementation with the Sun RPC system. The 4.3BSD implementation of this system is available in source code from Sun Microsystems for a minimal charge. It is also available electronically from many of the Usenet archive sites. The version described here is called ''RPCSRC 3.9.'' The actual RPC protocol is termed Version 2. RFC 1057 [Sun 1988] provides a specification of the

Version 2 protocol used by Sun RPC. This includes the format of the packets exchanged between the client and the server, along with a description of the authentication options available with Sun RPC. RFC 1014 [Sun 1987] provides a description of XDR.

Sun RPC consists of the following parts:

- `rpcgen`, a compiler that takes the definition of a remote procedure interface, and generates the client stubs and the server stubs.

- XDR (eXternal Data Representation), a standard way of encoding data in a portable fashion between different systems.

- A run-time library to handle all the details.

We'll use a simple example to shows what is involved in writing both the client and server using RPC. We'll define two functions that the client calls using RPC: `bin_date_1` returns the current time as the number of seconds since 00:00:00 GMT, January 1, 1970. This function has no arguments and returns a long integer. The other function, `str_date_1`, takes a long integer value from the previous function and converts it into an ASCII string that is fit for human consumption. Figure 18.3 shows the steps involved in creating both the client and server programs.

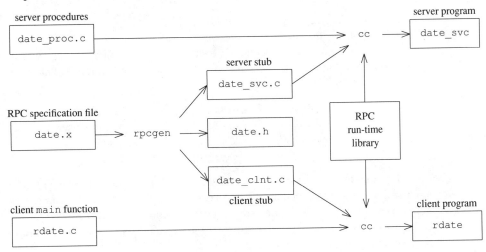

Figure 18.3 Files involved in generating a Sun RPC program.

Minimally we have to provide the three files shown on the left side of Figure 18.3: the server procedures that are called remotely from the client, the RPC specification file, and the client `main` function.

The `rpcgen` compiler takes the `date.x` file and generates two C files, the client stub and the server stub, along with a header file that is included by both stub files. The client stub is compiled with our client `main` function to generate the executable client program.

```
cc -o rdate rdate.c date_clnt.c -lrpclib
```

Similarly, we generate the server program by compiling the server stub (which contains the `main` function for the server) along with our server functions.

```
cc -o date_svc date_proc.c date_svc.c -lrpclib
```

Let's first look at the specification file that is the input for the `rpcgen` compiler.

```
/*
 * date.x - Specification of remote date and time service.
 */

/*
 * Define 2 procedures:
 *      bin_date_1() returns the binary time and date (no arguments).
 *      str_date_1() takes a binary time and returns a human-readable string.
 */

program DATE_PROG {
    version DATE_VERS {
        long    BIN_DATE(void) = 1;      /* procedure number = 1 */
        string  STR_DATE(long) = 2;      /* procedure number = 2 */
    } = 1;                               /* version number = 1 */
} = 0x31234567;                          /* program number = 0x31234567 */
```

We declare both of the procedures and specify the argument and return value for each. We also assign a procedure number to each function (1 and 2), along with a program number (0x31234567) and a version number (1). The program numbers are 32-bit integers that are assigned as follows:

$$
\begin{array}{ll}
\texttt{0x00000000 - 0x1fffffff} & \text{defined by Sun} \\
\texttt{0x20000000 - 0x3fffffff} & \text{defined by user} \\
\texttt{0x40000000 - 0x5fffffff} & \text{transient} \\
\texttt{0x60000000 - 0xffffffff} & \text{reserved}
\end{array}
$$

Procedure numbers start at 0. Every remote program and version must define procedure number 0 as the "null procedure." It doesn't require any arguments and it returns nothing. It is automatically generated by the `rpcgen` compiler. Its use is to allow a client to call it, to verify that the particular program and version exist. It is also useful to the client for calculating the round-trip time.

The `rpcgen` compiler generates the actual remote procedure names by converting the names `BIN_DATE` and `STR_DATE` to `bin_date_1` and `str_date_1`. To do this it converts to lower case and appends an underscore and the version number.

We define the `BIN_DATE` procedure as taking no arguments (`void`) and returning a long integer result. Similarly, `STR_DATE` takes a long integer argument and returns a string result. Sun RPC allows only a single argument and a single result. If more arguments are desired, we must use a structure as the argument. Similarly, to return more than one value, a structure is used as the return value.

Let's look at the header file, date.h, that is generated by the rpcgen compiler.

```
#define DATE_PROG       ((u_long)0x31234567)
#define DATE_VERS       ((u_long)1)
#define BIN_DATE        ((u_long)1)
extern long    *bin_date_1();
#define STR_DATE        ((u_long)2)
extern char    **str_date_1();
```

It defines our function bin_date_1 as returning a pointer to a long integer. It also defines the return value from our str_date_1 function as being a pointer to a character pointer. Indeed, Sun RPC specifies that the remote procedure return the address of its return value. Also, the remote procedure is passed the address of its argument when it is called by the server stub. We'll see this handling of arguments and return values in both our client program and in the remote procedures.

Here is the client program that we'll invoke to call the remote procedures.

```
/*
 * rdate.c - client program for remote date service.
 */

#include        <stdio.h>
#include        <rpc/rpc.h>     /* standard RPC include file */
#include        "date.h"        /* this file is generated by rpcgen */

main(argc, argv)
int     argc;
char    *argv[];
{
        CLIENT          *cl;            /* RPC handle */
        char            *server;
        long            *lresult;       /* return value from bin_date_1() */
        char            **sresult;      /* return value from str_date_1() */

        if (argc != 2) {
                fprintf(stderr, "usage: %s hostname\n", argv[0]);
                exit(1);
        }
        server = argv[1];

        /*
         * Create the client "handle."
         */

        if ( (cl = clnt_create(server, DATE_PROG, DATE_VERS, "udp")) == NULL) {
                /*
                 * Couldn't establish connection with server.
                 */

                clnt_pcreateerror(server);
                exit(2);
        }

        /*
```

```
     * First call the remote procedure "bin_date".
     */

    if ( (lresult = bin_date_1(NULL, cl)) == NULL) {
            clnt_perror(cl, server);
            exit(3);
    }
    printf("time on host %s = %ld\n", server, *lresult);

    /*
     * Now call the remote procedure "str_date".
     */

    if ( (sresult = str_date_1(lresult, cl)) == NULL) {
            clnt_perror(cl, server);
            exit(4);
    }
    printf("time on host %s = %s", server, *sresult);

    clnt_destroy(cl);                     /* done with the handle */
    exit(0);
}
```

We call `clnt_create` to create an RPC handle to the specified program and version on a host. We also specify UDP as the protocol. We could have specified the final argument as `"tcp"` to use TCP as the transport protocol. (We'll cover the RPC differences between the two protocols later in this section.) Once we have the handle, we're able to call any of the procedures defined for that particular program and version.

When we call `bin_date_1`, the first argument of the call is the argument we defined in the `date.x` specification file—a `void` argument that we specify as a `NULL` pointer. The second argument is the client handle. The return value is a pointer to a long integer, as we saw in the `date.h` file that was generated by the `rpcgen` compiler. If a `NULL` pointer is returned from the remote procedure call, an error occurred. When we call the `str_date_1` function, the first argument is a pointer to a long integer.

Finally we have the server functions that define the remote procedures.

```
/*
 * dateproc.c - remote procedures; called by server stub.
 */

#include         <rpc/rpc.h>        /* standard RPC include file */
#include         "date.h"           /* this file is generated by rpcgen */

/*
 * Return the binary date and time.
 */

long *
bin_date_1()
{
        static long     timeval;        /* must be static */
        long            time();         /* Unix function */
```

```
        timeval = time((long *) 0);

        return(&timeval);
}

/*
 * Convert a binary time and return a human readable string.
 */
char **
str_date_1(bintime)
long    *bintime;
{
        static char     *ptr;           /* must be static */
        char            *ctime();       /* Unix function */

        ptr = ctime(bintime);           /* convert to local time */

        return(&ptr);                /* return the address of pointer */
}
```

The reason for commenting that the return values must be static variables is because both functions return the address of these variables. If the variables weren't static or external, but were automatic variables instead, their values would be undefined after the return statement passes control back to the server stub that calls our remote procedure.

Let's look at the steps that are involved when we use RPC. First we start our server as a background process

```
date_svc &
```

Then we invoke it from another system (or the same system) using our client program

```
rdate hsi86
```

This generates the following output:

```
time on host hsi86 = 609264219
time on host hsi86 = Sat Apr 22 12:03:39 1989
```

Pictorially we have the processes shown in Figure 18.4. The steps shown in Figure 18.4 are executed in the following order:

1. When we start the server program on the remote system it creates a UDP socket and binds any local port to the socket. It then calls a function in the RPC library, svc_register, to register its program number and version. This function contacts the port mapper process to register itself. The port mapper keeps track of the program number, version number, and port number. (The port mapper is usually started as a daemon when the system is started.) Our server then waits for a client request. Note that all the actions in this step are done by the server stub, the main function that is generated by the rpcgen compiler.

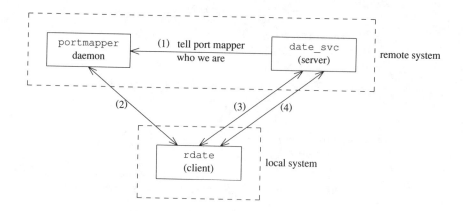

Figure 18.4 Steps involved in RPC calls.

2. We start our client program and it calls the `clnt_create` function. This call
    specifies the name of the remote system, the program number, version number,
    and the protocol. This function contacts the port mapper on the remote system to
    find out the UDP port for the server.

3. Our client program calls the `bin_date_1` function. This function is defined in
    the client stub that was generated by the `rpcgen` compiler. This function in the
    client stub sends a datagram to the server, using the UDP port number from the
    previous step. It then waits for a response, retransmitting the request a fixed
    number of times if a response isn't received. The datagram is received on the
    remote system by the server stub associated with our server program. This stub
    determines which procedure is being called and calls our `bin_date_1` func-
    tion. When our function returns to the server stub, the stub takes the return
    value, converts it into the XDR standard format, and packages it into a datagram
    for transmission back to the client. When the response if received, the client stub
    takes the value from the datagram, converts it as required, and returns it to our
    client program.

4. Our client calls the `str_date_1` function, which goes through a similar
    sequence of operations as described in the previous step. One difference is that
    the client stub has to pass an argument to the remote procedure.

The port mapper process on the remote system only needs to be contacted if a new client
handle is created. This occurs if a different program or version is called.
    Let's look at how Sun RPC handles the transparency issues that we mentioned in
Section 18.2.

Parameter Passing

A single argument and a single result are allowed. Multiple arguments or multiple return values must be packaged into a structure.

Binding

The port mapper daemon on the desired remote system is contacted to locate a specific program and version. The caller has to specify the name of the remote system and the transport protocol.

The port mapper also provides support for broadcast requests to a specified remote program. The client program sends a broadcast request for a particular program, version and procedure to the port mapper's well-known port. If the specified procedure is registered with the port mapper, the port mapper passes the request to the procedure. When the procedure is finished, it returns its response to the port mapper, who sends it back to the client. This response contains the port number of the actual procedure, so that later requests from the client can be made directly to the remote program. If the requested procedure isn't registered with the port mapper, no response is sent to the client.

Transport Protocol

Sun RPC currently supports either UDP or TCP. There are some differences in the call semantics for each one that we discuss below.

When a stream-oriented protocol such as TCP is used, there has to be some way to delimit the records in the byte stream. We encountered this same problem in Section 12.8 when we implemented the TFTP program using TCP. Sun RPC uses a record marking protocol that is defined in RFC 1057 [Sun 1988]. It uses a 32-bit integer at the beginning of every record to specify the number of bytes in the record.

When using UDP, the total size of the arguments must not generate a UDP packet that exceeds 8192 bytes in length. Similarly, the total size of the return values must also be less than 8192 bytes. This limitation is just an implementation parameter. Recall from Section 5.2 that this is not a fundamental UDP limitation. There is no such limit when using TCP.

Exception Handling

When UDP is used as the transport protocol, it automatically times out and retransmits an RPC request, if necessary. It terminates and returns an error to the caller after a fixed number of unsuccessful tries. If TCP is used, an error is also returned to the caller if the connection is terminated by the server. There is no way for the client to send an interrupt to the server.

Call Semantics

One part of the Sun RPC protocol is that every client request carries a unique transaction ID, a 32-bit integer termed the *xid*. The server is not allowed to examine this value in any way other than to test for equality. Both the TCP and UDP client functions initialize this ID to a random value when the client handle is created. This value is then changed every time a new RPC request is made. Both the TCP and UDP server functions return the ID value that was sent by the client. Additionally, both the TCP and UDP client functions test for a matching transaction ID before returning with an RPC result. This assures the client that the response is from the request that it made.

The UDP server functions have an option that causes the UDP server to remember the client requests that it receives. To do this it maintains a cache of its responses, indexed by the transaction ID, program number, version number, procedure number, and the client's UDP address. Each time a request is received, the UDP server looks in the cache to see if the request is a duplicate, and if so, the remote procedure is not called again. Instead, the response that was saved in the cache is returned to the caller again. This assumes that the previous response must have been lost or damaged. This technique attempts to provide the at-most-once semantics for UDP.

Data Representation

We showed the data types supported by XDR in Figure 18.2. The `rpcgen` compiler automatically generates the code required to reference the correct XDR run-time functions that convert the data between the host format and the standard format.

Security

Sun RPC has provisions for supporting three forms of authentication:

- null authentication,
- Unix authentication,
- DES authentication.

The default is null authentication. Unix authentication causes the following fields to be transmitted with every RPC request: a time stamp, the name of the local host, the client's effective user ID, the client's effective group ID, and a list of all the other group IDs that the client belongs to. (Recall from Section 2.2 that 4.3BSD allows a user to belong to more than one group.) The server is then able to examine these fields to determine if it wants to grant the client's request or not.

DES authentication is available with a later version of the Sun RPC package, RPCSRC 4.0. An overview of the DES authentication is provided in RFC 1057 [Sun 1988].

18.4 Xerox Courier

We continue our examples of actual RPC implementations with the Xerox Courier system. Courier is both a protocol and a specification language. It is used mainly under Unix to communicate with other Xerox systems—Xerox print servers or Xerox file servers, for example. The official description of Courier is given in Xerox [1981a]. Our examples are based on the Courier implementation under 4.3BSD. The source code for this implementation is provided on the BSD Networking Release, which we mentioned in the Preface. This source code also contains the documentation required to install and use the system.

Courier also defines an additional protocol called Bulk Data Transfer (BDT). If the application is going to transfer lots of data between the client and server, as either an argument or a result, bulk data transfer should be used. The Unix implementation of Courier supports bulk data transfer, but we won't cover it in this text.

Now we'll use Courier to show the client and server programs from the previous section. As with Sun RPC, to use Courier we must write three pieces of code:

- the RPC specification, written in the Courier language,
- the client program, written in C,
- the server functions, written in C.

We use the Courier compiler, `xnscourier` to translate the specification file into five files, as shown in Figure 18.5. The Courier compiler requires that the specification file be named with a `.cr` suffix. The function `Date1_support.c` defines various support functions that are used by both the client and server.

Let's show the Courier specification file first.

```
Date : PROGRAM 876 VERSION 1 =

BEGIN
        -- Define the two remote procedures.

        BinDate : PROCEDURE []
                RETURNS [bindate : LONG INTEGER]
                = 0;

        StrDate : PROCEDURE [bindate: LONG INTEGER]
                RETURNS [strdate : STRING]
                = 1;
END.
```

The Courier keywords must be in upper case. Our choice of a program number, 876, is arbitrary—Appendix B of Xerox [1981b] describes how to obtain a block of program numbers from Xerox. The prefix `Date1` that is prepended to all the filenames generated by the Courier compiler is taken from the name of the program and its version.

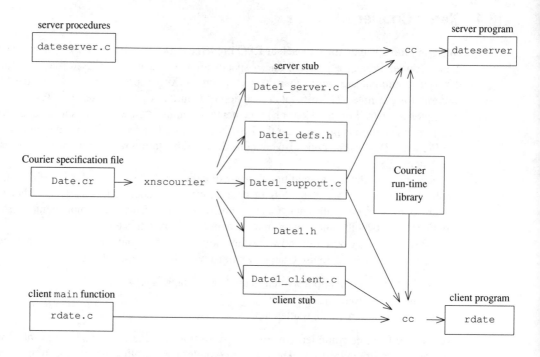

Figure 18.5 Files involved in generating a Courier program.

Let's look at one header file that is generated by the Courier compiler, `Date1.h`:

```
/*
 * Definitions for Date VERSION 1 NUMBER 876.
 */

#ifndef __Date1
#define __Date1
#include         <xnscourier/courier.h>
#include         <xnscourier/courierconnection.h>

typedef struct {
        LongInteger bindate;
} BinDateResults;

extern BinDateResults    BinDate();

typedef struct {
        String strdate;
} StrDateResults;

extern StrDateResults    StrDate();

#endif __Date
```

We see that Courier defines the result of each function as a structure. This is because a remote procedure can return any number of values. Since the C language doesn't support multiple return values from a function, all remote procedures in Courier return a structure that contains one element for each return value. Courier also allows any number of arguments to be passed to a remote procedure.

Here is the client program.

```
/*
 * rdate.c - client program for remote date service.
 */

#include         <stdio.h>
#include         "Date1_defs.h"           /* this file generated by xnscourier */

#include         <sys/types.h>
#include         <netns/ns.h>             /* definition of struct ns_addr */

main(argc, argv)
int     argc;
char    *argv[];
{
        CourierConnection       *conn;          /* RPC handle */
        char                    *server;
        struct ns_addr          ns_addr(),      /* BSD library routine */
                                servaddr;
        BinDateResults          binresult;      /* result from BinDate() */
        StrDateResults          strresult;      /* result from StrDate() */

        if (argc != 2) {
                fprintf(stderr, "usage: %s hostaddr\n", argv[0]);
                exit(1);
        }
        server = argv[1];
        servaddr = ns_addr(argv[1]);    /* convert to an ns_addr structure */

        /*
         * Create the client "handle."
         */

        if ( (conn = CourierOpen(&servaddr)) == NULL) {
                fprintf(stderr, "Can't open connection to %s\n", server);
                exit(2);
        }

        /*
         * First call the remote procedure BinDate().
         */

        binresult = BinDate(conn, NULL);
        printf("time on host %s = %ld\n", server, binresult.bindate);

        /*
         * Now call the remote procedure StrDate().
         */
```

```
    */

    strresult = StrDate(conn, NULL, binresult.bindate);
    printf("time on host %s = %s", server, strresult.strdate);

    CourierClose(conn);              /* close the connection cleanly */
    exit(0);
}
```

The file `Date1_defs.h`, which we include in the client program, was generated by the Courier compiler. It includes the header file `Date1.h` which we showed earlier.

The client opens a Courier connection with the `CourierOpen` function, calls the two remote procedures, then closes the connection. Note that the call to `CourierOpen` specifies only the name of the remote system—there is nothing regarding which remote procedures the client is going to call. We'll see later in this section exactly what happens when this function is called.

The first two arguments to both of the remote procedures are the same—the RPC handle (`conn`) and a `NULL` pointer. This second argument is used only when bulk data is being transferred, so we set it to `NULL` for our example. The actual long integer argument to the `StrDate` function is passed as the third argument when it is called.

Each Courier remote procedure returns a structure whose type is the procedure name appended with `Results`. The C `typedefs` for `BinDateResults` and `StrDateResults` are in the `Date1.h` file that we showed.

A Courier remote procedure can return one of three ways:

- normal return,
- rejection by the remote system to execute the procedure,
- an abort generated by the remote procedure.

Our client example shows only the normal return. The reject and abort can be handled by the program, if desired. If the client program doesn't handle these potential errors, the client program is terminated if they occur.

Now let's look at the server procedures. As with the Sun RPC example, we only have to code the server procedures. The run-time library provides a `main` function that is invoked when an RPC request arrives for one of our procedures.

```
/*
 * dateserver.c - remote procedures; called by server stub.
 */

#include       "Date1_defs.h"  /* this file is generated by xnscourier */

/*
 * Return the binary date and time.
 */

BinDateResults
BinDate(conn, bdtptr)
CourierConnection       *conn;           /* ignored */
char                    *bdtptr;         /* ignored */
```

```
{
        BinDateResults   result;
        long             time();                      /* Unix function */

        result.bindate = time((long *) 0);

        return(result);
}

/*
 * Convert a binary time and return a human readable string.
 */

StrDateResults
StrDate(conn, bdtptr, bintime)
CourierConnection        *conn;           /* ignored */
char                     *bdtptr;         /* ignored */
long                     bintime;
{
        StrDateResults   result;
        char             *ctime();                    /* Unix function */

        result.strdate = ctime(&bintime);             /* convert to local time */

        return(result);
}
```

Our server procedures return a structure. There is no need for this structure to be statically allocated, as with our Sun RPC example, since the procedures return the entire structure, not its address.

Now let's look at the steps involved in executing a remote procedure using Courier. Any Unix system that supports Courier RPC has to be running a Courier daemon that listens on a well-known SPP port (port 5) for client connection requests. This program is called xnscourierd in the implementation we're describing. Once we've compiled and linked our server program, we have to tell the Courier daemon that our server is available to be invoked. To do this we have to add an entry to the file /etc/Courierservices specifying the program number, version number, and pathname of the executable file for the server program. This file is similar in concept to the inetd.conf file that we described in Section 6.16. Typically the xnscourierd daemon is started when the system is started. Figure 18.6 shows the steps that are then involved when we execute our client program.

1. The client calls CourierOpen to open a connection to the specified host. This causes an SPP connection to be established to port 5 on the remote host, on which the xnscourierd process is listening for client requests.

2. This daemon forks a child process to handle the connection. The child process reads the first few bytes from the connection to verify that the client is a Courier client. The child then waits for the client to issue its first RPC request, which

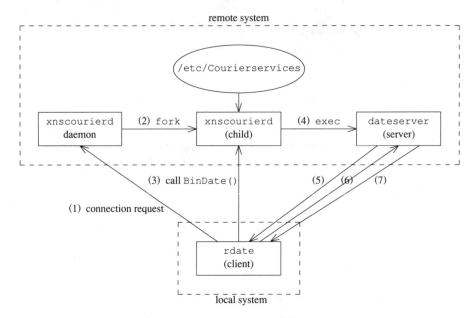

remote system

Figure 18.6 Steps involved in calling Courier procedures.

specifies the program, version, and procedure to be called. Details of this initial protocol between the client and server are given in Xerox [1981a].

3. When the client calls the `BinDate` function, the client stub writes the desired program number, version number and procedure number to the connection.

4. The child reads this information from the connection and then reads the `/etc/Courierservices` file to determine which server program to execute. The child then does an `exec` of the appropriate server program. Note that the child has already read the procedure number from the connection. It has to pass this value to our server program when it is invoked, as it is the server stub in our server program that has to determine which of the two remote procedures is being called. This procedure number is passed to the server program as a command line argument as part of the `exec`.

5. Our `dateserver` program is started and the server stub, the `main` function, processes its command line arguments to determine which remote procedure is being called. It then calls our `BinDate` function. When our function returns, the server stub converts the results into the Courier standard format and sends them back to the client.

6. Our client then calls the `StrDate` function. The client stub sends the corresponding program, version, and procedure numbers across the connection where they are read by the server stub. The server stub in our `dateserver` process recognizes that the program and version haven't changed, so it calls our

`StrDate` function. Before calling our function, the server stub reads the arguments from the connection and converts them from the Courier format to the format required by the function.

If the server stub receives a request for a different program or a different version, it has to `exec` the appropriate program to handle the new request. As long as the program and version don't change, a single process on the remote system handles the client requests.

7. When our function returns to the server stub, the stub converts the return value and sends it back to the client.

After all this, the client calls `CourierClose` to close the SPP connection, which causes the server process to terminate normally.

Now we'll look at how Courier handles the transparency issues from Section 18.2.

Parameter Passing

Any number of arguments are allowed and each is passed individually to the remote procedure. Any number of return values are also allowed, and they are packaged into a single structure that is the return value.

Binding

Most Xerox applications use the Clearinghouse to locate a particular network service. This is a database of objects that can be queried by an application. Details of the Clearinghouse protocol are given in Xerox [1984] and Oppen and Dalal [1983]. The 4.3BSD implementation of Courier, which we have been describing in this section, provides limited support for the Clearinghouse.

Transport Protocol

Courier uses only the XNS Sequenced Packet Protocol (SPP) for the network connection between the client and server. Since this is a connection-oriented protocol, there is no inherent limit on the amount of data that can be exchanged between the client and server. Courier uses both the end-of-message flag and the datastream type field which are in the SPP header. These are bridge fields that we described in Section 5.3.

Exception Handling

Since a connection-oriented transport protocol is used for Courier, a server failure is detected by a dropped connection. Additionally, the implementation we've been using supports the return of exceptional conditions to the caller, although we didn't show this in our example.

Call Semantics

Courier relies on SPP to provide a reliable connection between the client and server. A normal return to the client implies that the remote procedure was executed exactly once. An error return implies that the remote procedure was executed at most once. This provides the at-most-once call semantics to the caller.

Courier includes a 16-bit transaction ID with every request and reply. But this value is always zero and Xerox [1981a] specifies that it is currently unused, but included for future expansion.

Data Representation

Figure 18.2 shows the data types supported by Courier. The `xnscourier` compiler automatically generates the C code required to convert the arguments and results between the host format and the standard format.

Security

Most Xerox applications use the Xerox Authentication protocol for validating user access to network resources. Two types of authentication are provided:

- simple authentication,
- strong authentication.

This protocol is described in Xerox [1986] with an overview given in Xerox [1985]. Strong authentication is similar in principle to the Kerberos system we described in Section 9.3. The 4.3BSD implementation of Courier that we have been describing provides limited support for simple authentication but no support for strong authentication.

18.5 Apollo RPC

Network Computing Architecture (NCA) is Apollo's architecture for remote computing. Dineen et al. [1987] provide an overview and Zahn et al. [1990] provide additional details. Although the architecture is publicly specified, Apollo's implementation, termed NCS for Network Computing System, is a proprietary product. Details on NCS are given in Kong et al. [1990]. NCS is comprised of the following pieces:

- NIDL, the Network Interface Definition Language. A compiler is provided to translate this language into the client and server stubs.

- NDR, the Network Data Representation. This defines the standard formats used for passing the supported data types.

- A run-time library.

In this section we'll just go through the transparency issues that we went over for Sun RPC and Courier. We won't redo our previous remote-date example.

Parameter Passing

NCA/RPC allows any number of arguments and any number of return values. When writing the RPC function prototype in NIDL, we specify whether each parameter is input (passed from client to server), output (returned from server to client) or both input and output.

Binding

Apollo provides a forwarding agent that is similar to the port mapper that we described with Sun's RPC implementation. Recall however, from Figure 18.4, that the Sun RPC client first has to exchange a message with the port mapper to determine the server's address, and then the client contacts the server. The Apollo approach has the client send its first request to the forwarding agent, who then forwards the request to the server. The server sends its response directly to the client. It is assumed the client looks at the return address in this first response packet to determine the actual address of the server, and uses this address for all subsequent requests.

This forwarding agent is part of a larger binding agent, called the Location Broker. If a client knows the type of service it is looking for, but doesn't know the name of a host that supplies that service, the location broker can provide the host name along with the address of the appropriate server on that host. The location broker is contacted by having the client send a broadcast message on its local network, stating what type of service the client is looking for. All the appropriate servers will respond, and the client typically uses the first response.

Transport Protocol

Apollo RPC is designed to run over a connectionless transport protocol. Either UDP or DDS (a proprietary networking protocol of Apollo) is typically used. The logic required to provide the *at-most-once* call semantics, when using a connectionless protocol, is discussed below.

The Apollo implementation does fragmentation and reassembly of its network messages if they are too large to fit into a network packet. Recall from Section 5.2 that UDP has an upper limit of almost 64 Kbytes while Xerox IDP has a much smaller limit of 546 bytes.

The location broker returns complete socket addresses (as we described in Section 6.4), not just port numbers within some protocol. (Recall that the Sun port mapper requires the client to specify the transport protocol, typically UDP or TCP, and it returns a port number appropriate to that protocol.) Furthermore, the client handle that identifies a particular server contains the entire socket address of the server. This means that the client can be written in a protocol-independent fashion, since the complete socket address is part of the handle for each call. The client need not know what transport protocol is being used until it binds its handle to a specific server. Even when the handle is bound to a server, the handle is considered an opaque structure to the client, so the client does not need to know the protocol.

Exception Handling

NCA/RPC provides the reporting of server exceptions back to the client. NCA/RPC also allows the client to send signals to a server that is executing on its behalf.

Call Semantics

By default, the Apollo implementation provides the *at-most-once* call semantics. To do this the server keeps track of the previous request for each client with which it has communicated. If the server detects a retransmission of a prior request, it resends the saved response, instead of reexecuting the remote procedure. While this is similar to the Sun RPC implementation, the Apollo implementation goes further. First, the server retransmits the response packet until it receives an acknowledgment from the client indicating that the client has received the response. The acknowledgment from the client can be implicit, by having the client send a new request, or the client can send an explicit acknowledgment. The server is allowed to remove entries from its cache of saved responses, after not hearing from a client for a while. Hence, there is a possibility that a duplicate request can arrive from a client after the server has flushed its cache entry for that client. To handle this case, the server sends a message back to the client asking for the client's current sequence number. This additional packet exchange typically happens when a new client program is started. But after the client has issued its first RPC request, the server should keep the client's last packet in its cache, avoiding the additional packet exchange.

One additional feature is provided—the ability for the client to ask the server for the server's current status. This way, a client that doesn't receive a response can time out and send a query to the server, instead of assuming the request was lost and just retransmitting its previous request. The server can respond to this status request with either a packet indicating that it is currently working on the request, or with a packet stating that the server never received the request.

Apollo allows the programmer to specify that a remote procedure is idempotent. In this case the server does not save previous responses. If it receives a duplicate request from the client, it just calls the procedure again. Also, the client is not expected to acknowledge the receipt of responses from the server.

Data Representation

Figure 18.2 shows the data types supported by NDR. As mentioned in Section 18.2, the Apollo implementation has the receiver do any required data conversion.

18.6 Summary

Our coverage of RPC has been a brief overview, to give a feeling of the steps involved in writing a simple, remote application. The three implementations that we described are similar, despite many minor technical differences. The steps involved in generating an RPC application are also similar for all three.

Exercises

18.1   Given the timeout handling described in Section 18.3 for Sun RPC using UDP, what happens if a procedure call takes longer to execute than the default? Even if some form of adaptive timeout were used, what would happen if some procedure calls were performed quickly and others required much more time?

18.2   Propose a solution to the problems described in the previous exercise. (Hint: examine the Apollo NCA techniques.)

18.3   Compare the advantages and disadvantages between explicit typing (ASN.1) and implicit typing (Courier, Sun RPC, Apollo NCA).

Appendix A

Miscellaneous Source Code

A.1   System Type Header File

The following header file, named `systype.h`, is used by the some of the programs in the text to determine at *compile-time* the type of system. This allows certain differences to be handled by the conditional compilation feature of any C program. It is best if this header file can automatically determine its compile-time environment from the pre-defined names provided by most C compilers, but there might be systems that require this file to be edited by hand when compiling on a different system.

```
/*
 * Figure out the type of system that we're running on.
 *
 * Try to determine the environment automatically from the C compiler's
 * predefined symbols.
 * The following can be determined automatically:
 * BSD VAX, Pyramid, Xenix, AT&T 3b1, AT&T 80386, Celerity and MS-DOS.
 * If this doesn't work on some new system, ifdef this out, and set it
 * by hand.
 */

#ifdef  unix            /* true for most UNIX systems, BSD and Sys5 */
                        /* but not for Xenix !! */
#define UNIX    1       /* OS type */

#ifdef  vax             /* true for BSD on a VAX */
/* also true for VAX Sys5, but we don't have to worry about that (for now) */
#define VAX     1       /* hardware */
#define BSD     1       /* OS type */
```

720

```
#else
#ifdef  pyr

#define PYRAMID 1        /* hardware */
#define BSD      1       /* OS type */
#else
#ifdef  mc68k            /* assume AT&T UNIX pc, aka 7300 or 3b1 */
                         /* what about other 68000 unix systems ?? */
#define UNIXPC   1       /* hardware */
#define SYS5     1       /* OS type */
#else
#ifdef  i386             /* AT&T System V Release 3.2 on the Intel 80386 */

#define IBMPC    1       /* hardware */
#define SYS5     1       /* OS type */
#else
#ifdef  accel

#define CELERITY 1       /* hardware */
#define BSD      1       /* OS type */
#else
what type of unix system is this
#endif  /* accel */
#endif  /* i386 */
#endif  /* mc68k */
#endif  /* pyr */
#endif  /* vax */

#endif  /* unix */

#ifdef  M_XENIX          /* true for SCO Xenix */
#define UNIX    1        /* OS type */
#define XENIX   1        /* OS type */
#define SYS5    1        /* OS type */
#define IBMPC   1        /* hardware */
#endif  /* M_XENIX */

#ifdef  MSDOS            /* true for Microsoft C and Lattice, assume former */
#define IBMPC       1       /* hardware */
#define MICROSOFT   1       /* C compiler type */
#endif  /* MSDOS */

/*
 * Define replacement names for the BSD names that we use.
 */

#ifdef  SYS5
#define rindex          strrchr
#define index           strchr

#define u_char          unchar
#define u_short         ushort
#define u_int           uint
#define u_long          ulong
```

```
#endif

#ifdef  MICROSOFT
#define rindex           strrchr
#define index            strchr

#define u_char           unchar
#define u_short          ushort
#define u_int            uint
#define u_long           ulong
#endif
```

A.2   System Type Shell Script

The following shell script is used in `Makefiles` to determine the type of Unix system
that the program is being made on. This file is required to handle the different library
files, loader arguments, and the like that different Unix systems use.

```
 # (leading space required for Xenix /bin/sh)

#
# Determine the type of *ix operating system that we're
# running on, and echo an appropriate value.
# This script is intended to be used in Makefiles.
# (This is a kludge.  Gotta be a better way.)
#

if (test -f /vmunix)
then
        echo "bsd"
elif (test -f /xenix)
then
        echo "xenix"
elif (test -c /dev/spx)
then
        echo "sys5"
elif (test -f /etc/lddrv)
then
        echo "unixpc"
fi
```

A.3   Standard Error Routines

The following functions are used in most of the examples throughout the text to handle
error conditions. Note that they can be used in either client or server programs. In the
former case the error messages are generated on the `stderr` stream, while the latter
case uses the 4.3BSD `syslog` facility.

These functions define three levels of errors.

1. Nonfatal, return to caller: `err_ret`.
2. Fatal, terminate process: `err_quit`.
3. Fatal, terminate process and dump core: `err_dump`.

The second two cases allow us to write our error handling with a single line of C code

```
if (error condition)
        err_dump (printf format with any number of arguments) ;
```

instead of

```
if (error condition) {
        char buff[200];
        sprintf(buff, printf format with any number of arguments) ;
        perror(buff);
        abort();
}
```

Our error functions use the variable-length argument list facility, which is provided my most C libraries today. See Section 7.3 of Kernighan and Ritchie [1988] for additional details, along with the 4.3BSD *varargs*(3) manual page or the System V *varargs*(5) manual page.

```c
/*
 * Error handling routines.
 *
 * The functions in this file are independent of any application
 * variables, and may be used with any C program.
 * Either of the names CLIENT or SERVER may be defined when compiling
 * this function.  If neither are defined, we assume CLIENT.
 */

#include        <stdio.h>
#include        <varargs.h>

#include        "systype.h"

#ifdef  CLIENT
#ifdef  SERVER
cant define both CLIENT and SERVER
#endif
#endif

#ifndef CLIENT
#ifndef SERVER
#define CLIENT  1               /* default to client */
#endif
#endif

#ifndef NULL
```

```
#define NULL    ((void *) 0)
#endif

char    *pname = NULL;

#ifdef  CLIENT                      /* these all output to stderr */

/*
 * Fatal error.  Print a message and terminate.
 * Don't dump core and don't print the system's errno value.
 *
 *       err_quit(str, arg1, arg2, ...)
 *
 * The string "str" must specify the conversion specification for any args.
 */

/*VARARGS1*/
err_quit(va_alist)
va_dcl
{
        va_list         args;
        char            *fmt;

        va_start(args);
        if (pname != NULL)
                fprintf(stderr, "%s: ", pname);
        fmt = va_arg(args, char *);
        vfprintf(stderr, fmt, args);
        fputc('\n', stderr);
        va_end(args);

        exit(1);
}

/*
 * Fatal error related to a system call.  Print a message and terminate.
 * Don't dump core, but do print the system's errno value and its
 * associated message.
 *
 *       err_sys(str, arg1, arg2, ...)
 *
 * The string "str" must specify the conversion specification for any args.
 */

/*VARARGS1*/
err_sys(va_alist)
va_dcl
{
        va_list         args;
        char            *fmt;

        va_start(args);
        if (pname != NULL)
                fprintf(stderr, "%s: ", pname);
```

```
        fmt = va_arg(args, char *);
        vfprintf(stderr, fmt, args);
        va_end(args);

        my_perror();

        exit(1);
}

/*
 * Recoverable error.  Print a message, and return to caller.
 *
 *      err_ret(str, arg1, arg2, ...)
 *
 * The string "str" must specify the conversion specification for any args.
 */

/*VARARGS1*/
err_ret(va_alist)
va_dcl
{
        va_list         args;
        char            *fmt;

        va_start(args);
        if (pname != NULL)
                fprintf(stderr, "%s: ", pname);
        fmt = va_arg(args, char *);
        vfprintf(stderr, fmt, args);
        va_end(args);

        my_perror();

        fflush(stdout);
        fflush(stderr);

        return;
}

/*
 * Fatal error.  Print a message, dump core (for debugging) and terminate.
 *
 *      err_dump(str, arg1, arg2, ...)
 *
 * The string "str" must specify the conversion specification for any args.
 */

/*VARARGS1*/
err_dump(va_alist)
va_dcl
{
        va_list         args;
        char            *fmt;
```

```
        va_start(args);
        if (pname != NULL)
                fprintf(stderr, "%s: ", pname);
        fmt = va_arg(args, char *);
        vfprintf(stderr, fmt, args);
        va_end(args);

        my_perror();

        fflush(stdout);            /* abort doesn't flush stdio buffers */
        fflush(stderr);

        abort();                   /* dump core and terminate */
        exit(1);                   /* shouldn't get here */
}

/*
 * Print the UNIX errno value.
 */

my_perror()
{
        char    *sys_err_str();

        fprintf(stderr, " %s\n", sys_err_str());
}

#endif  /* CLIENT */

#ifdef  SERVER

#ifdef  BSD
/*
 * Under BSD, these server routines use the syslog(3) facility.
 * They don't append a newline, for example.
 */

#include       <syslog.h>

#else   /* not BSD */
/*
 * There really ought to be a better way to handle server logging
 * under System V.
 */

#define syslog(a,b)     fprintf(stderr, "%s\n", (b))
#define openlog(a,b,c)  fprintf(stderr, "%s\n", (a))

#endif  /* BSD */

char    emesgstr[255] = {0};     /* used by all server routines */

/*
 * Identify ourself, for syslog() messages.
```

```
 *
 * LOG_PID is an option that says prepend each message with our pid.
 * LOG_CONS is an option that says write to console if unable to send
 * the message to syslogd.
 * LOG_DAEMON is our facility.
 */

err_init(ident)
char    *ident;
{
        openlog(ident, (LOG_PID | LOG_CONS), LOG_DAEMON);
}

/*
 * Fatal error.  Print a message and terminate.
 * Don't print the system's errno value.
 *
 *      err_quit(str, arg1, arg2, ...)
 *
 * The string "str" must specify the conversion specification for any args.
 */

/*VARARGS1*/
err_quit(va_alist)
va_dcl
{
        va_list         args;
        char            *fmt;

        va_start(args);
        fmt = va_arg(args, char *);
        vsprintf(emesgstr, fmt, args);
        va_end(args);

        syslog(LOG_ERR, emesgstr);

        exit(1);
}

/*
 * Fatal error related to a system call.  Print a message and terminate.
 * Don't dump core, but do print the system's errno value and its
 * associated message.
 *
 *      err_sys(str, arg1, arg2, ...)
 *
 * The string "str" must specify the conversion specification for any args.
 */

/*VARARGS1*/
err_sys(va_alist)
va_dcl
{
        va_list         args;
```

```
        char            *fmt;

        va_start(args);
        fmt = va_arg(args, char *);
        vsprintf(emesgstr, fmt, args);
        va_end(args);

        my_perror();
        syslog(LOG_ERR, emesgstr);

        exit(1);
}

/*
 * Recoverable error.  Print a message, and return to caller.
 *
 *      err_ret(str, arg1, arg2, ...)
 *
 * The string "str" must specify the conversion specification for any args.
 */

/*VARARGS1*/
err_ret(va_alist)
va_dcl
{
        va_list         args;
        char            *fmt;

        va_start(args);
        fmt = va_arg(args, char *);
        vsprintf(emesgstr, fmt, args);
        va_end(args);

        my_perror();
        syslog(LOG_ERR, emesgstr);

        return;
}

/*
 * Fatal error.  Print a message, dump core (for debugging) and terminate.
 *
 *      err_dump(str, arg1, arg2, ...)
 *
 * The string "str" must specify the conversion specification for any args.
 */

/*VARARGS1*/
err_dump(va_alist)
va_dcl
{
        va_list         args;
        char            *fmt;
```

```
            va_start(args);
            fmt = va_arg(args, char *);
            vsprintf(emesgstr, fmt, args);
            va_end(args);

            my_perror();
            syslog(LOG_ERR, emesgstr);

            abort();                    /* dump core and terminate */
            exit(1);                    /* shouldn't get here */
}

/*
 * Print the UNIX errno value.
 * We just append it to the end of the emesgstr[] array.
 */

my_perror()
{
            register int    len;
            char            *sys_err_str();

            len = strlen(emesgstr);
            sprintf(emesgstr + len, " %s", sys_err_str());
}

#endif  /* SERVER */

                        /* remainder is for both CLIENT and SERVER */
extern int      errno;          /* Unix error number */
extern int      sys_nerr;       /* # of error message strings in sys table */
extern char     *sys_errlist[]; /* the system error message table */

#ifdef SYS5
int     t_errno;        /* in case caller is using TLI, these are "tentative
                            definitions"; else they're "definitions" */
int     t_nerr;
char    *t_errlist[1];
#endif


/*
 * Return a string containing some additional operating-system
 * dependent information.
 * Note that different versions of UNIX assign different meanings
 * to the same value of "errno" (compare errno's starting with 35
 * between System V and BSD, for example).  This means that if an error
 * condition is being sent to another UNIX system, we must interpret
 * the errno value on the system that generated the error, and not
 * just send the decimal value of errno to the other system.
 */

char *
sys_err_str()
```

```
{
        static char     msgstr[200];

        if (errno != 0) {
                if (errno > 0 && errno < sys_nerr)
                        sprintf(msgstr, "(%s)", sys_errlist[errno]);
                else
                        sprintf(msgstr, "(errno = %d)", errno);
        } else {
                msgstr[0] = '\0';
        }

#ifdef  SYS5
        if (t_errno != 0) {
                char    tmsgstr[100];

                if (t_errno > 0 && t_errno < sys_nerr)
                        sprintf(tmsgstr, " (%s)", t_errlist[t_errno]);
                else
                        sprintf(tmsgstr, ", (t_errno = %d)", t_errno);

                strcat(msgstr, tmsgstr);            /* catenate strings */
        }
#endif

        return(msgstr);
}
```

The server routines under 4.3BSD use the `openlog` and `syslog` functions to record error messages in the system log. Refer to the *syslog*(3) manual page for the details on these functions.

The following function is used when an error is detected by the `gethostbyname` or `gethostbyaddr` functions. It prints the additional error information available in the `h_errno` variable. We call this error routine from our `tcp_open` and `udp_open` functions, described in Section 8.3. We also call it from our Internet ping program in Chapter 11.

```
/*
 * Return a string containing some additional information after a
 * host name or address lookup error - gethostbyname() or gethostbyaddr().
 */

int     h_errno;                     /* host error number */
int     h_nerr;                      /* # of error message strings */
char    *h_errlist[];                /* the error message table */

char *
host_err_str()
{
        static char     msgstr[200];

        if (h_errno != 0) {
                if (h_errno > 0 && h_errno < h_nerr)
```

```
                    sprintf(msgstr, "(%s)", h_errlist[h_errno]);
              else
                    sprintf(msgstr, "(h_errno = %d)", h_errno);
       } else {
              msgstr[0] = '\0';
       }

       return(msgstr);
}
```

A.4   Timer Routines

The following functions are used by the TFTP client program in Chapter 12.

```
/*
 * Timer routines.
 *
 * These routines are structured so that there are only the following
 * entry points:
 *
 *      void    t_start()       start timer
 *      void    t_stop()        stop timer
 *      double  t_getrtime()    return real (elapsed) time (seconds)
 *      double  t_getutime()    return user time (seconds)
 *      double  t_getstime()    return system time (seconds)
 *
 * Purposely, there are no structures passed back and forth between
 * the caller and these routines, and there are no include files
 * required by the caller.
 */

#include         <stdio.h>
#include         "systype.h"

#ifdef BSD
#include         <sys/time.h>
#include         <sys/resource.h>
#endif

#ifdef SYS5
#include         <sys/types.h>
#include         <sys/times.h>
#include         <sys/param.h>    /* need the definition of HZ */
#define          TICKS   HZ        /* see times(2); usually 60 or 100 */
#endif

#ifdef BSD
static  struct timeval          time_start, time_stop; /* for real time */
static  struct rusage           ru_start, ru_stop;      /* for user & sys time */
#endif

#ifdef SYS5
```

```
static  long                      time_start, time_stop;
static  struct tms                tms_start, tms_stop;
long                              times();
#endif

static  double                    start, stop, seconds;

/*
 * Start the timer.
 * We don't return anything to the caller, we just store some
 * information for the stop timer routine to access.
 */

void
t_start()
{

#ifdef BSD
        if (gettimeofday(&time_start, (struct timezone *) 0) < 0)
                err_sys("t_start: gettimeofday() error");
        if (getrusage(RUSAGE_SELF, &ru_start) < 0)
                err_sys("t_start: getrusage() error");
#endif

#ifdef SYS5
        if ( (time_start = times(&tms_start)) == -1)
                err_sys("t_start: times() error");
#endif

}

/*
 * Stop the timer and save the appropriate information.
 */

void
t_stop()
{

#ifdef BSD
        if (getrusage(RUSAGE_SELF, &ru_stop) < 0)
                err_sys("t_stop: getrusage() error");
        if (gettimeofday(&time_stop, (struct timezone *) 0) < 0)
                err_sys("t_stop: gettimeofday() error");
#endif

#ifdef SYS5
        if ( (time_stop = times(&tms_stop)) == -1)
                err_sys("t_stop: times() error");
#endif

}

/*
```

```
 * Return the user time in seconds.
 */

double
t_getutime()
{

#ifdef BSD
        start = ((double) ru_start.ru_utime.tv_sec) * 1000000.0
                             + ru_start.ru_utime.tv_usec;
        stop = ((double) ru_stop.ru_utime.tv_sec) * 1000000.0
                             + ru_stop.ru_utime.tv_usec;
        seconds = (stop - start) / 1000000.0;
#endif

#ifdef SYS5
        seconds = (double) (tms_stop.tms_utime - tms_start.tms_utime) /
                                    (double) TICKS;
#endif

        return(seconds);
}

/*
 * Return the system time in seconds.
 */

double
t_getstime()
{

#ifdef BSD
        start = ((double) ru_start.ru_stime.tv_sec) * 1000000.0
                             + ru_start.ru_stime.tv_usec;
        stop = ((double) ru_stop.ru_stime.tv_sec) * 1000000.0
                             + ru_stop.ru_stime.tv_usec;
        seconds = (stop - start) / 1000000.0;
#endif

#ifdef SYS5
        seconds = (double) (tms_stop.tms_stime - tms_start.tms_stime) /
                                    (double) TICKS;
#endif

        return(seconds);
}

/*
 * Return the real (elapsed) time in seconds.
 */

double
t_getrtime()
{
```

```
#ifdef BSD
        start = ((double) time_start.tv_sec) * 1000000.0
                            + time_start.tv_usec;
        stop = ((double) time_stop.tv_sec) * 1000000.0
                            + time_stop.tv_usec;
        seconds = (stop - start) / 1000000.0;
#endif

#ifdef SYS5
        seconds = (double) (time_stop - time_start) / (double) TICKS;
#endif

        return(seconds);
}
```

Bibliography

The specifications for the TCP/IP Internet protocols are provided in the RFCs. The term *RFC* stands for *request for comment*. Comer [1988] provides a detailed list of all RFCs, arranged by topic. A nice feature of the RFCs is that they are maintained on-line and can be retrieved by electronic mail or through FTP. Refer to Appendix 3 of Comer [1988] for details. Since the size of the RFCs range from 1 page to over 200 pages, the size of each one is given in the bibliography that follows.

The "BSD Networking Software" that was mentioned in the text is available from

> CSRG, Computer Science Division
> University of California
> Berkeley, CA 94720
> (415) 642-7780
>
> bsd-dist@ucbvax.berkeley.edu (Internet)
> uunet!ucbvax!bsd-dist (UUCP)

Unlike the complete 4BSD source code distributions, the BSD Networking Software does not contain source code that is derived from AT&T source code. While this Berkeley source code is available to anyone, it is not in the public domain. The code is copyrighted by The Regents of the University of California, but may be redistributed in source or binary form, as long as the original copyright notice is retained and appropriate credit is given to the Electrical Engineering and Computer Science Department of the University of California at Berkeley. This software is also available from other sources, such as the UUNET archives.

The 4.3BSD manuals can be ordered through

> USENIX Association
> P.O. Box 2299
> Berkeley, CA 94710
> (415) 528-8649
>
> office@usenix.org (Internet)
> uunet!usenix!office (UUCP)

One must first join the Usenix Association for a nominal charge.

AT&T Unix System V manuals are available from

> AT&T Customer Information Center
> Marketing Department
> P.O. Box 19901
> Indianapolis, IN 46219
> (800) 432−6600 (U.S.)
> (800) 255−1242 (Canada)
> (317) 352−8556

The System V Release 3.2 and System V/386 Release 3.2 manuals are also published by Prentice Hall.

The referenced Xerox documents can be ordered from

> Xerox Corporation
> Xerox Systems Institute
> 475 Oakmead Parkway
> Sunnyvale, CA 94086
> (408) 737−4652

IEEE Standards can be ordered from

> Publication Sales
> IEEE Service Center
> P.O. Box 1331
> 445 Hoes Lane
> Piscataway, NJ 08854−1331
> (201) 981−0060

This bibliography does not contain references to each of the ISO standards that was mentioned in Section 5.6. Refer to Chapin [1989] for a detailed list of the ISO standards. Adopted ISO standards have the prefix "ISO." The "DIS" prefix stands for "Draft International Standard" and indicates the standard is in the final stage of approval. The prefix "DP" stands for "Draft Proposal" indicating that it is in the initial stage of approval. ISO standards are available from

> Omnicon, Inc.
> 115 Park Street, SE
> Vienna, VA 22180−4607
> (800) 666−4266
> (703) 281−1135

The ISODE package that was described in Section 5.6 is available from a variety of sources for a modest handling fee. The starting point is to obtain the current announcement letter, which details the different ways to obtain it. The announcement letter is published in Appendix A of Rose [1990]. The announcement letter can also be obtained from

> NYSERNet, Inc.
> Western Development Office
> Attn: Marshall T. Rose
> 420 Whisman Court
> Mountain View, CA 94043−2112
> (415) 961−3380

All referenced IBM documents must be ordered through your local IBM sales office.

Alphabetical Bibliography

AT&T 1989a, *UNIX System V Release 3.2—Network Programmer's Guide,* Prentice Hall, Englewood Cliffs, N.J., 1989.

> Contains TLI examples and descriptions. This manual should be used with the Section 3N manual pages for the TLI functions in the *Programmer's Reference Manual.*

AT&T 1989b, *UNIX System V Release 3.2—Programmer's Reference Manual,* Prentice Hall, Englewood Cliffs, N.J., 1989.

> Contains the Unix manual pages for the System V Release 3 system calls (Section 2) and functions (Section 3). Specifically, it contains the manual pages for all TLI functions in Section 3N.

AT&T 1989c, *UNIX System V Release 3.2—STREAMS Primer,* Prentice Hall, Englewood Cliffs, N.J., 1989.

> An overview of the streams facility. This manual should be used with the *STREAMS Programmer's Guide.*

AT&T 1989d, *UNIX System V Release 3.2—STREAMS Programmer's Guide,* Prentice Hall, Englewood Cliffs, N.J., 1989.

> Contains detailed information on the streams facility. Intended for developers writing their own streams modules.

Bach, M. J. 1986, *The Design of the UNIX Operating System,* Prentice Hall, Englewood Cliffs, N.J., 1986.

> A book on the details of the design and implementation of the Unix operating system. Although actual Unix source code is not provided in this text (since it is proprietary to AT&T) many of the algorithms and data structures used by the Unix kernel are presented and discussed.

Baratz, A. E., Gray, J. P., Green, P. E. Jr., Jaffe, J. M., and Pozefsky, D. P. 1985, "SNA Networks of Small Systems," *IEEE Journal on Selected Areas in Communications*, vol. SAC-3, no. 3, pp. 416–425, May 1985.

> The original reference for SNA/LEN (Advanced Peer-to-Peer Networking). Describes the design and implementation of the APPN prototype. Details such as the dynamic routing used by APPN are discussed.

Berkeley 1986a, *UNIX User's Reference Manual (URM), 4.3 Berkeley Software Distribution,* Computer Systems Research Group, Computer Science Division, Univ. of California, Berkeley, Calif., Apr. 1986.

> Contains Sections 1 (commands), 6 (games), and 7 (macro packages and language conventions) of the 4.3BSD manuals.

Berkeley 1986b, *UNIX Programmer's Reference Manual (PRM), 4.3 Berkeley Software Distribution,* Computer Systems Research Group, Computer Science Division, Univ. of California, Berkeley, Calif., Apr. 1986.

> Contains Sections 2 (system calls), 3 (subroutines), 4 (special files), and 5 (file formats and conventions) of the 4.3BSD manuals.

Berkeley 1986c, *UNIX System Manager's Manual (SMM), 4.3 Berkeley Software Distribution,* Computer Systems Research Group, Computer Science Division, Univ. of California, Berkeley, Calif., Apr. 1986.

> Contains Section 8 (maintenance commands) and other system-related documents of the 4.3BSD manuals.

Birrell, A. D. and Nelson, B. J. 1984, "Implementing Remote Procedure Calls," *ACM Transactions on Computer Systems*, vol. 2, no. 1, pp. 39–59, Feb. 1984.

> This is an early paper on RPC. It describes an actual RPC facility, the design decisions made during its implementation, and some performance measurements.

Boggs, D. R., Shoch, J. F., Taft, E. A., and Metcalfe, R. M. 1980, "Pup: An Internetwork Architecture," *IEEE Transactions on Communications*, vol. COM-28, no. 4, pp. 612–624, Apr. 1980.

> A description of the predecessor to XNS, Pup (PARC Universal Packet). This paper gives some of the rationale and insight for the design decisions made in the implementation of XNS.

Boggs, D. R., Mogul, J. C., and Kent, C. A. 1988, "Measured Capacity of an Ethernet: Myths and Reality," *Computer Communication Review*, vol. 18, no. 4, pp. 222–234, Proceedings of the ACM SIGCOMM '88 Workshop, Aug. 1988.

> Describes a set of measurements made on an actual Ethernet to compare the actual performance to various theoretical models. The tests were performed for various packet sizes, different numbers of transmitting hosts, and different lengths of coaxial cable.

Borman, D. A. 1989, "Implementing TCP/IP on a Cray Computer," *Computer Communication Review*, vol. 19, no. 2, pp. 11–15, Apr. 1989.

> This paper describes the improvements and optimizations made to the TCP/IP implementation that runs under the UNICOS operating system.

Braden, R. and Postel, J. 1987, "Requirements for Internet Gateways," RFC 1009, 55 pages, June 1987.

> This RFC supplements the primary RFCs relating to gateway support for the Internet protocols. The next two references apply to Internet hosts.

Braden, R. ed. 1989a, "Requirements for Internet Hosts—Communication Layers," RFC 1122, 116 pages, Oct. 1989.

> This RFC is one of a pair that amends, corrects, and supplements the primary RFCs relating to host support for the Internet protocols. This RFC covers the link layer, IP layer, and transport layer.

Braden, R. ed. 1989b, "Requirements for Internet Hosts—Application and Support," RFC 1123, 98 pages, Oct. 1989.

> This RFC is one of a pair that amends, corrects, and supplements the primary RFCs relating to host support for the Internet protocols. This RFC covers the application protocol layers.

Cabrera, L., Hunter, E., Karels, M. J., and Mosher, D. A. 1988, "User-Process Communication Performance in Networks of Computers," *IEEE Transactions on Software Engineering*, vol. 14, no. 1, pp. 38−53, Jan. 1988.

> This paper studies the networking performance of the 4.2BSD Unix system from a user-process perspective. Measurements are provided for the UDP/IP and TCP/IP protocols.

Chapin, A. L. 1989, "Status of OSI Standards," *Computer Communication Review*, vol. 19, no. 3, pp. 99−118, July 1989.

> Provides a detailed list of the ISO (and related) standards. This article is a regular feature of *Computer Communication Review*.

Chesson, G. 1987, "Protocol Engine Design," *Proceedings of the 1987 Summer USENIX Conference*, Phoenix, Ariz., pp. 209−215, 1987.

> This paper describes some of the problems that can be encountered when the speed of a LAN increases the next order of magnitude with FDDI (100 Mbits/sec). A proposal is made to implement the transport layer in VLSI.

Clark, D. D., Lambert, M. L., and Zhang, L. 1987a, "NETBLT: A Bulk Data Transfer Protocol," RFC 998, 21 pages, Mar. 1987.

> NETBLT is a transport protocol that uses IP. It was designed for the high throughput of large quantities of data. This RFC describes the NETBLT protocol.

Clark, D. D., Lambert, M. L., and Zhang, L. 1987b, "NETBLT: A High Throughput Transport Protocol," *Computer Communication Review*, vol. 17, no. 5, pp. 353−359, Proceedings of the ACM SIGCOMM '87 Workshop, Aug. 1987.

> This paper describes the design of the NETBLT protocol and provides some performance measurements.

Clark, D. D., Jacobson, V., Romkey, J. L., and Salwen, H. 1989, "An Analysis of TCP Processing Overhead," *IEEE Communications Magazine*, vol. 27, no. 6, pp. 23−29, June 1989.

> This paper provides a detailed analysis of the overhead imposed by the TCP layer. The conclusion is that TCP is not the source of overhead that is typically observed and that it could support high speeds, if properly implemented.

Comer, D. E. 1987, *Operating System Design—Volume II: Internetworking with Xinu*, Prentice Hall, Englewood Cliffs, N.J., 1987.

> This text provides a sample implementation of UDP and IP in the Xinu operating system.

Comer, D. E. 1988, *Internetworking with TCP/IP: Principles, Protocols, and Architecture*, Prentice Hall, Englewood Cliffs, N.J., 1988.

> A detailed reference for the TCP/IP protocol suite. This text should be consulted before reading the detailed RFCs. Contains details on gateways, naming and routing.

Crocker, D. H. 1982, "Standard for the Format of ARPA Internet Text Messages," RFC 822, 47 pages, Aug. 1982.

> This RFC specifies the syntax for electronic mail in the Internet. The format of all the headers, for example, is specified here.

Croft, W. and Gilmore, J. 1985, "Bootstrap Protocol (BOOTP)," RFC 951, 12 pages, Sept. 1985.

> BOOTP is a bootstrap protocol based on UDP that allows a diskless client to discover its Internet address, the Internet address of a server, and the name of a file to be loaded into memory.

Dineen, T. H., Leach, P. J., Mishkin, N. W., Pato, J. N., and Wyant, G. L. 1987, "The Network Computing Architecture and System: An Environment for Developing Distributed Applications," *Proceedings of the 1987 Summer USENIX Conference*, Phoenix, Ariz., pp. 385–398, 1987.

> An overview of Apollo's NCA and its implementation.

Dixon, R. C. and Pitt, D. A. 1988, "Addressing, Bridging, and Source Routing," *IEEE Network*, vol. 2, no. 1, pp. 25–32, Jan. 1988.

> A description of the source routing used by the IBM token ring network. Additionally, this issue of the *IEEE Network* contains 16 papers on bridges, routers, and gateways.

Dunsmuir, M. R. M. 1989, "OS/2 to UNIX LAN," pp. 237–284 in *UNIX Networking*, eds. S. G. Kochan and P. H. Wood, Howard W. Sams and Company, Indianapolis, Ind., 1989.

> Contains information on the Microsoft Lan Manager/X product, which allows a Unix system to be a server for a personal computer running MS-DOS or OS/2.

Finlayson, R. 1984, "Bootstrap Loading using TFTP," RFC 906, 4 pages, June 1984.

> This RFC proposes to use TFTP to bootstrap a diskless workstation.

Finlayson, R., Mann, T., Mogul, J., and Theimer, M. 1984, "A Reverse Address Resolution Protocol," RFC 903, 4 pages, June 1984.

> The standard for RARP. It allows a workstation to determine its Internet address, given only its hardware address.

Fritz, T. E., Hefner, J. E., and Raleigh, T. M. 1984, "A Network of Computers Running the UNIX System," *AT&T Bell Laboratories Technical Journal*, vol. 63, no. 8, pp. 1877–1896, Oct. 1984.

> Discusses an early network developed at AT&T that connected various Unix systems using a high-speed LAN (HYPERchannel).

Henshall, J. and Shaw, S. 1988, *OSI Explained: End-to-End Computer Communication Standards,* John Wiley & Sons, New York, 1988.

> This book covers the upper four layers of the OSI model with entire chapters on FTAM and X.400/MOTIS.

IBM 1980, "Systems Network Architecture, Format and Protocol Reference Manual: Architecture Logic," SC30–3112–2, IBM Corp., Nov. 1980.

> The technical reference for SNA. This 1300-page manual provides a formal definition of SNA protocols. A form of pseudo-PL/1 code is provided to show the implementation of many SNA features. This manual does not cover the newer features of SNA, such as LU 6.2, PU 2.1 and APPN, but is more applicable to the traditional mainframe-oriented SNA networks.

IBM 1983, "An Introduction to Advanced Program-to-Program Communication (APPC)," GG24−1584−0, IBM Corp., July 1983.

> A detailed introduction to LU 6.2 and PU 2.1.

IBM 1984, "Systems Network Architecture, Format and Protocol Reference Manual: Architecture Logic for LU Type 6.2," SC30−3269−2, IBM Corp., Dec. 1984.

> The technical reference for LU 6.2. This 620-page manual provides a formal definition of the LU 6.2 protocols. Pseudocode is provided to show the implementation of many LU 6.2 features.

IBM 1985, "Systems Network Architecture, Technical Overview," GC30−3073−1, IBM Corp., May 1985.

> A technical overview of SNA, describing the organization of SNA networks. Covers items such as routing, flow control and SNA protocols.

IBM 1986a, "Systems Network Architecture, Concepts and Products," GC30−3072−3, IBM Corp., Oct. 1986.

> An overview of SNA and the SNA products available from IBM.

IBM 1986b, "Systems Network Architecture, Format and Protocol Reference Manual: Architecture Logic for Type 2.1 Nodes," SC30−3422−0, IBM Corp., Nov. 1986.

> The technical reference for PU 2.1. This manual provides the formal definition of PU Type 2.1 nodes.

IBM 1987, "NETBIOS Application Development Guide," S68X–2270−00, IBM Corp., Apr. 1987.

> A reference for the NetBIOS implementation used with the IBM PC Network. Contains descriptions of each NetBIOS command, along with a pseudocode implementation of each command. Additionally, the format of each type of frame used by NetBIOS on the IBM PC Network is described.

IBM 1988, "Systems Application Architecture, Common Programming Interface, Communications Reference," SC26−4399−0, IBM Corp., May 1988.

> A reference for IBM's programming interface to LU 6.2, as it relates to IBM's Systems Application Architecture (SAA). It describes LU 6.2 conversations in general and provides a description of every function available to the application program, the arguments to the function, its return values, and a general description of the function.

IEEE 1988, "Portable Operating System Interface for Computer Environments (POSIX)," 1003.1−1988, IEEE, Sept. 1988.

> The first 162 pages of this standard define the standard C language interface based on the Unix operating system. The remaining 120 pages are appendices that cover related standards and the rationale and background of the standard.

Jacobson, V. 1988a, "Some Interim Notes on the BSD Network Speedup," Message-ID <8807200426.AA01221@helios.ee.lbl.gov>, Usenet, comp.protocols.tcp-ip Newsgroup, July 1988.

> This Usenet posting details some enhancements made to the 4.3BSD TCP/IP software to increase its performance.

Jacobson, V. 1988b, "Congestion Avoidance and Control," *Computer Communication Review*, vol. 18, no. 4, pp. 314–329, Proceedings of the ACM SIGCOMM '88 Workshop, Aug. 1988.

> This paper describes modifications made to the 4.3BSD TCP/IP software that provide: slow start, improved round-trip timing, and congestion avoidance.

Jacobson, V. 1988c, "Performance," Message-ID <8811231121.AA19744@helios.ee.lbl.gov>, Usenet, comp.protocols.tcp-ip Newsgroup, Nov. 1988.

> This Usenet posting shows an actual FTP transfer between two Sun 3/60s on an Ethernet that achieves 816,000 bytes/sec throughput.

Karn, P. and Partridge, C. 1987, "Improving Round-Trip Estimates in Reliable Transport Protocols," *Computer Communication Review*, vol. 17, no. 5, pp. 2–7, Proceedings of the ACM SIGCOMM '87 Workshop, Aug. 1987.

> This paper contains details on selecting the responses on which to base an estimate of the round-trip time.

Kent, C. A. and Mogul, J. C. 1987, "Fragmentation Considered Harmful," *Computer Communication Review*, vol. 17, no. 5, pp. 390–401, Proceedings of the ACM SIGCOMM '87 Workshop, Aug. 1987.

> This paper argues that a network protocol such as IP should not allow fragmentation. A variety of methods are proposed to reduce the likelihood of fragmentation.

Kernighan, B. W. and Ritchie, D. M. 1978, *The C Programming Language,* Prentice Hall, Englewood Cliffs, N.J., 1978.

> A reference for the pre-ANSI standard version of the C programming language.

Kernighan, B. W. and Pike, R. 1984, *The UNIX Programming Environment,* Prentice Hall, Englewood Cliffs, N.J., 1984.

> A general reference for additional details on Unix programming.

Kernighan, B. W. and Ritchie, D. M. 1988, *The C Programming Language, Second Edition,* Prentice Hall, Englewood Cliffs, N.J., 1988.

> A reference for the ANSI standard version of the C programming language. Appendix B contains a description of the libraries defined by the ANSI standard.

Knightson, K. G., Knowles, T., and Larmouth, J. 1988, *Standards for Open Systems Interconnection,* McGraw-Hill, New York, 1988.

> A complete book on the OSI model and ISO-related standards.

Kong, M., Dineen, T. H., Leach, P. J., Martin, E. A., Mishkin, N. W., Pato, J. N., and Wyant, G. L. 1990, *Network Computing System Reference Manual,* Prentice Hall, Englewood Cliffs, N.J., 1990.

> The reference manual for Apollo's NCS.

Krol, E. 1989, "The Hitchhikers Guide to the Internet," RFC 1118, 24 pages, Sept. 1989.

> This RFC contains information for new members of the Internet and details on obtaining on-line information.

Leffler, S. J., Fabry, R. S., Joy, W. N., Lapsley, P., Miller, S., and Torek, C. 1986a, "An Advanced 4.3BSD Interprocess Communication Tutorial," UNIX Programmer's Supplementary Documents, Volume 1 (PS1), 4.3 Berkeley Software Distribution, Computer Systems Research Group, Computer Science Division, Univ. of California, Berkeley, Calif., Apr. 1986.

> This article, which is part of the 4.3BSD distribution, describes the networking features of 4.3BSD.

Leffler, S. J., Joy, W. N., Fabry, R. S., and Karels, M. J. 1986b, "Networking Implementation Notes, 4.3BSD Edition," UNIX System Manager's Manual (SMM), 4.3 Berkeley Software Distribution, Computer Systems Research Group, Computer Science Division, Univ. of California, Berkeley, Calif., June 1986.

> This article is also part of the 4.3BSD distribution, and describes the actual implementation of the 4.3BSD networking system. This article is intended for implementors of communication protocols and networking services.

Leffler, S. J., McKusick, M. K., Karels, M. J., and Quarterman, J. S. 1989, *The Design and Implementation of the 4.3BSD UNIX Operating System,* Addison-Wesley, Reading, Mass., 1989.

> An entire book on the 4.3BSD Unix system.

Lennert, D. C. 1986, "A System V Compatible Implementation of 4.2BSD Job Control," *Proceedings of the 1986 Summer USENIX Conference,* Atlanta, Ga., pp. 459−474, 1986.

> Provides a summary of process groups, control terminals, and job control.

Lennert, D. C. 1987, "How to Write a UNIX Daemon," *;login:,* vol. 12, no. 4, pp. 17−23, July/Aug. 1987.

> The paper that inspired Section 2.6 of this text. This paper was later reprinted in the December 1988 issue of *UNIX World.*

Mills, D. L. 1989a, "Network Time Protocol (Version 2) Specification and Implementation," RFC 1119, 61 pages, Sept. 1989.

> Describes NTP and information relevant to its implementation.

Mills, D. L. 1989b, "Internet Time Synchronization: the Network Time Protocol," RFC 1129, 27 pages, Oct. 1989.

> This RFC describes the architectures, algorithms, and protocols which have evolved over several years to become the Network Time Protocol. It is required reading for anyone interested in network clock synchronization.

Mogul, J. and Postel, J. 1985, "Internet Standard Subnetting Procedure," RFC 950, 18 pages, Aug. 1985.

> The reference for TCP/IP subnetting.

Narten, T. 1989, "Internet Routing," *Computer Communication Review,* vol. 19, no. 4, pp. 271−282, Proceedings of the ACM SIGCOMM '89 Workshop, Sept. 1989.

> This paper reviews the routing techniques that have been used on the TCP/IP Internet between the late 1970s through 1988: EGP, GGP, RIP, and HELLO.

Nemeth, E., Snyder, G., and Seebass, S. 1989, *UNIX System Administration Handbook,* Prentice Hall, Englewood Cliffs, N.J., 1989.

> A book with many details on administering a Unix system.

Novell 1986 1986, *LAN Evaluation Report,* Novell, Inc., Provo, Utah, 1986.

> This report provides a comparison of various IBM PC LANs.

Olander, D. J., McGrath, G. J., and Israel, R. K. 1986, "A Framework for Networking in System V," *Proceedings of the 1986 Summer USENIX Conference*, Atlanta, Ga., pp. 38−45, 1986.

> This paper describes the original implementation of streams and TLI for System V.

Oppen, D. C. and Dalal, Y. K. 1983, "The Clearinghouse: A Decentralized Agent for Locating Named Objects in a Distributed Environment," *ACM Transactions on Office Information Systems*, vol. 1, no. 3, pp. 230−253, July 1983.

> Clearinghouse is the XNS server for translating names into addresses.

O'Toole, J., Torek, C., and Weiser, M. 1985, "Implementing XNS Protocols for 4.2BSD," *Proceedings of the 1985 Winter USENIX Conference*, Dallas, Tex., pp. 90−97, 1985.

> A description of the first implementation of the XNS protocols in 4.2BSD, and the changes that were required to the BSD networking support. Also contains a formal specification of SPP.

Partridge, C. 1986, "Mail Routing and the Domain System," RFC 974, 7 pages, Jan. 1986.

> This RFC describes how mailers route mail messages when the addresses are specified by Internet domain names.

Partridge, C. 1987, "Implementing the Reliable Data Protocol (RDP)," *Proceedings of the 1987 Summer USENIX Conference*, Phoenix, Ariz., pp. 367−379, 1987.

> Describes an implementation of RDP for 4.2BSD and 4.3BSD.

Pike, R. 1984, "The Blit: a Multiplexed Graphics Terminal," *AT&T Bell Laboratories Technical Journal*, vol. 63, no. 8, pp. 1607−1631, Oct. 1984.

> Describes the predecessor to the AT&T 630 MTG terminal. Also describes the Unix processes used to multiplex one or more login sessions on a windowed terminal.

Plummer, D. C. 1982, "An Ethernet Address Resolution Protocol," RFC 826, 10 pages, Nov. 1982.

> The reference for ARP—mapping 32-bit Internet addresses into 48-bit Ethernet addresses.

Postel, J. 1980, "User Datagram Protocol," RFC 768, 3 pages, Aug. 1980.

Postel, J. ed. 1981a, "Internet Protocol," RFC 791, 45 pages, Sept. 1981.

Postel, J. 1981b, "Internet Control Message Protocol," RFC 792, 21 pages, Sept. 1981.

Postel, J. ed. 1981c, "Transmission Control Protocol," RFC 793, 85 pages, Sept. 1981.

> The standard reference for TCP. There are also many RFCs that came after this one, clarifying points about TCP. Consult Comer [1988] for additional details and RFC references.

Postel, J. 1982, "Simple Mail Transfer Protocol," RFC 821, 68 pages, Aug. 1982.

Postel, J. 1983a, "Echo Protocol," RFC 862, 1 page, May 1983.

Postel, J. 1983b, "Discard Protocol," RFC 863, 1 page, May 1983.

Postel, J. 1983c, "Character Generator Protocol," RFC 864, 3 pages, May 1983.

Postel, J. 1983d, "Daytime Protocol," RFC 867, 2 pages, May 1983.

Postel, J. and Harrenstien, K. 1983, "Time Protocol," RFC 868, 2 pages, May 1983.

Postel, J. and Reynolds, J. 1983, "Telnet Protocol Specification," RFC 854, 15 pages, May 1983.

Postel, J. and Reynolds, J. 1985, "File Transfer Protocol (FTP)," RFC 959, 69 pages, Oct. 1985.

Presotto, D. L. and Ritchie, D. M. 1985, "Interprocess Communication in the Eighth Edition UNIX System," *Proceedings of the 1985 Summer USENIX Conference*, Portland, Oreg., 1985.

> This paper describes the IPC facilities provided by the Eighth Edition of Unix, developed at the Information Sciences Research Division of AT&T Bell Laboratories. The features are built on the stream input-output system and include full-duplex pipes and the ability to pass file descriptors between processes.

Rago, S. 1989, "Out-of-Band Communications in STREAMS," *Proceedings of the 1989 Summer USENIX Conference*, Baltimore, Md., pp. 29−37, 1989.

> Describes enhancements made to the streams mechanism for System V Release 4.0 to provide generalized support for out-of-band messages.

Redman, B. E. 1989, "UUCP UNIX-to-UNIX Copy," pp. 5−48 in *UNIX Networking*, eds. S. G. Kochan and P. H. Wood, Howard W. Sams and Company, Indianapolis, Ind., 1989.

> This chapter contains additional details on Honey DanBer UUCP. It also contains a detailed history of the UUCP programs.

Ritchie, D. M. 1984a, "The Evolution of the UNIX Time-sharing System," *AT&T Bell Laboratories Technical Journal*, vol. 63, no. 8, pp. 1577−1593, Oct. 1984.

> This paper is a history of the early development of Unix.

Ritchie, D. M. 1984b, "A Stream Input-Output System," *AT&T Bell Laboratories Technical Journal*, vol. 63, no. 8, pp. 1897−1910, Oct. 1984.

> This is the original paper on streams.

Rochkind, M. J. 1985, *Advanced UNIX Programming*, Prentice Hall, Englewood Cliffs, N.J., 1985.

> A general text on Unix programming, for an experienced C programmer.

Rose, M. T. 1990, *The Open Book: A Practical Perspective on OSI*, Prentice Hall, Englewood Cliffs, N.J., 1990.

> A comprehensive book on the OSI protocols.

Schwaderer, W. D. 1988, *C Programmer's Guide to NetBIOS*, Howard W. Sams and Company, Indianapolis, Ind., 1988.

> This book describes NetBIOS on an IBM PC using the C programming language.

Sollins, K. R. 1981, "The TFTP Protocol (Revision 2)," RFC 783, 19 pages, June 1981.

> The official specification for the Trivial File Transfer Protocol.

Stallings, W. 1987a, *Handbook of Computer-Communications Standards, Volume 1: The Open Systems Interconnection (OSI) Model and OSI-Related Standards,* Macmillan, New York, 1987.

> An overview of the ISO-related standards.

Stallings, W. 1987b, *Handbook of Computer-Communications Standards, Volume 2: Local Network Standards,* Macmillan, New York, 1987.

> An overview of LAN standards, including the IEEE 802 standards (LLC, CSMA/CD, token bus and token ring) and FDDI.

Stallings, W., Mockapetris, P., McLeod, S., and Michel, T. 1988, *Handbook of Computer-Communications Standards, Volume 3: Department of Defense (DOD) Protocol Standards,* Macmillan, New York, 1988.

> An overview of the TCP/IP protocol suite. Contains chapters on IP, TCP, FTP, SMTP, and TELNET.

Steiner, J. G., Neuman, C., and Schiller, J. I. 1988, "Kerberos: An Authentication Service for Open Network Systems," *Proceedings of the 1988 Winter USENIX Conference,* Dallas, Tex., pp. 191–202, 1988.

> A description of the Kerberos system used by M.I.T.'s Project Athena.

Sun Microsystems 1987, "XDR: External Data Representation Standard," RFC 1014, 20 pages, June 1987.

Sun Microsystems 1988, "RPC: Remote Procedure Call, Protocol Specification, Version 2," RFC 1057, 25 pages, June 1988.

Tanenbaum, A. S. 1989, *Computer Networks, Second Edition,* Prentice Hall, Englewood Cliffs, N.J., 1989.

> A general text on computer networks. Many of the items that have been glossed over in the current text are discussed in more detail in Tanenbaum's text.

Treese, G. W. 1988, "Berkeley UNIX on 1000 Workstations: Athena Changes to 4.3BSD," *Proceedings of the 1988 Winter USENIX Conference,* Dallas, Tex., pp. 175–182, 1988.

> An overview of M.I.T.'s Project Athena.

Walsh, R. and Gurwitz, R. 1984, "Converting the BBN TCP/IP to 4.2BSD," *Proceedings of the 1984 Summer USENIX Conference,* Salt Lake City, Utah, pp. 52–61, 1984.

Williams, T. 1989, "Session Management in System V Release 4," *Proceedings of the 1989 Winter USENIX Conference,* San Diego, Calif., pp. 365–375, 1989.

> Describes the session architecture to be implemented in System V Release 4.0. This includes process groups, job control and control terminals. Also describes the security concerns of existing approaches.

Xerox 1981a, "Courier: The Remote Procedure Call Protocol," XNSS 038112, Xerox Corp., Dec. 1981.

> The formal reference for Version 3 of the Courier protocol.

Xerox 1981b, "Internet Transport Protocols," XNSS 028112, Xerox Corp., Dec. 1981.

> The official reference for the XNS protocols. It describes the formats of the headers and contains prose descriptions of the protocols.

Xerox 1984, "Clearinghouse Protocol," XNSS 078404, Xerox Corp., Apr. 1984.

> Clearinghouse is the XNS server for translating names into addresses.

Xerox 1985, "Xerox Network Systems Architecture, General Information Manual," XNSG 068504, Xerox Corp., Apr. 1985.

> An overview of XNS, its protocols and some of its typical applications.

X/Open 1989, *X/Open Portability Guide*, Prentice Hall, Englewood Cliffs, N.J., 1989.

> This is a set of 7 volumes covering the following areas: commands and utilities (Vol. 1), system interfaces and headers (Vol. 2), supplementary definitions (Vol. 3), programming languages (Vol. 4), data management (Vol. 5), window management (Vol. 6), networking services (Vol. 7).

Zahn, L., Dineen, T. H., Leach, P. J., Martin, E. A., Mishkin, N. W., Pato, J. N., and Wyant, G. L. 1990, *Network Computing Architecture*, Prentice Hall, Englewood Cliffs, N.J., 1990.

> The reference manual for Apollo's NCA.

Index

Networking is a field that is pockmarked with acronyms. The primary entry for the acronym in this index is found under the acronym name. This is because you are more likely to look up the acronym ICMP, for example, than the compound term "Internet Control Message Protocol." A second reference is also found under the compound term, with a note to *see* the acronym.

To aid the reader in locating examples of the concepts presented in Chapters 2 through 7, references to significant system calls, functions, and magic constants are also found in this index. For example, the `getsockopt` system calls in the `rshd` and `rlogin` servers are found in the index.

MSG_DONTROUTE constant, 275, 319
msgget system call, 121–122, 124–125,
    127–128, 131, 134–135, 682
msghdr structure, 301, 311–312
MSG_NOERROR constant, 129–130
MSG_OOB constant, 275, 319, 332–333, 642, 656,
    658, 660
MSG_PEEK constant, 275
MSG_R constant, 128
msgrcv system call, 121, 128–130, 132–133,
    682–683
msgsnd system call, 121, 124, 128–129, 132,
    681–683
MSG_W constant, 128
msqid_ds structure, 126
MTA (message transfer agent), 251
MTU (maximum transmission unit), 186, 207, 209,
    212, 317
multicast, 192, 202, 239
multihomed, 173, 181, 202, 285, 393
multiple buffers, 161–168, 170, 526
multiple sessions, SNA, 230
multiplexing, 181, 207, 248
multiplexing and demultiplexing, 181–183
multiplexing, I/O, 328–331, 341, 388–389, 616
multiplexing messages, 133–136
multiplexor, streams, 376
Muuss, M., 445
mycat program, 308
my_lock function, 89–90, 94–95, 97, 99,
    142–144, 553
my_open function, 309, 386
my_unlock function, 89–90, 94–95, 98–100,
    143–144, 553

name servers, Internet, 396
name service, NetBIOS, 241–242
name space, IPC, 119–121
named pipe, *see* FIFO
named server, 396
Narten, T., 194, 743
National Science Foundation, *see* NSF
National Science Foundation network, *see*
    NSFNET
NCA (Network Computing Architecture, Apollo
    RPC), 694, 716, 740, 747
NCS (Network Computing System, Apollo RPC),
    716, 742
NDR (Network Data Representation, Apollo RPC),
    694, 698, 716

Nelson, B. J., 695, 700, 738
Nemeth, E., 201, 252, 528, 744
NetBIOS (Network Basic Input/Output System,
    IBM), 238–245, 741, 745
NetBIOS association, 245
NetBIOS datagram service, 243–244
NetBIOS general commands, 244
NetBIOS group name, 241
NetBIOS local name number, 241
NetBIOS local session number, 242
NetBIOS name service, 241–242
NetBIOS protocols, 238–245
NetBIOS session service, 242–243
NetBIOS unique name, 241
NetBIOS well-known address, 242
NETBLT (Network Block Transfer, Internet), 688,
    739
netbuf structure, 345, 348–350, 378
<netdb.h> header file, 393
<net/if_arp.h> header file, 325
<netinet/in.h> header file, 264, 269, 303
<netinet/ip_icmp.h> header file, 446
<netns/ns.h> header file, 264, 269
network address, 191
Network Basic Input/Output System, IBM, *see*
    NetBIOS
Network Block Transfer, Internet, *see* NETBLT
network byte order, 178–179, 438, 466, 567, 640,
    694
network, computer, 171
Network Computing Architecture, Apollo RPC, *see*
    NCA
Network Computing System, Apollo RPC, *see*
    NCS
Network Data Representation, Apollo RPC, *see*
    NDR
Network File System, Sun Microsystems, *see* NFS
Network Information Center, Internet, *see* NIC
Network Interface Definition Language, Apollo
    RPC, *see* NIDL
network layer, Internet, 201–204
network layer, OSI, 247
network layer, XNS, 216–218
network library routines, Berkeley, 392–397
network performance, 687–690
Network Time Protocol, Internet, *see* NTP
network time synchronization, 443, 743
network utility routines, 397–405
network-qualified LU name, SNA, 228
networks, subarea SNA, 227

Neuman, C., 431, 746
newgrp program, 26
_NFILE constant, 74
NFS (Network File System, Sun Microsystems), 341
NIC (Network Information Center, Internet), 201–202
NIDL (Network Interface Definition Language, Apollo RPC), 716
nobody login name, 471
NOFILE constant, 74
nonblocking, 93
nonblocking I/O, 42, 93, 321–322, 328, 370, 373
nonblocking lock, 93
nonidempotent, 697
Novell, Inc., 689, 744
Nowitz, D. A., 252
ns_addr function, 277
ns_addr structure, 265, 278
NSF (National Science Foundation), 2, 198
NSFNET (National Science Foundation network), 198
ns_pipe function, 305–306, 384–385
NSPROTO_ECHO constant, 460, 462
NSPROTO_ERROR constant, 268
NSPROTO_PE constant, 314
NSPROTO_RAW constant, 268, 314
NSPROTO_SPP constant, 268, 314
ntohl function, 276
ntohs function, 276
NTP (Network Time Protocol, Internet), 443, 743

O_APPEND constant, 39–40, 42, 85
O_CREAT constant, 39, 99
octets, bytes and, 178
O_EXCL constant, 39, 99
Olander, D. J., 9, 378, 744
Omnicon Inc., 736
ONC (Open Network Computing, Sun RPC), 694
O_NDELAY constant, 39, 42, 110–111, 113, 370
open, active, 195
open environment, 420
Open Network Computing, Sun RPC, see ONC
open, passive, 195
open system call, 28, 32, 38–40, 54, 71, 85, 96–97, 99, 110, 112–113, 258, 263, 306, 309–310, 346, 376–377, 380, 382, 386, 530, 588, 669–670
Open Systems Interconnect model, ISO, see OSI
openlog function, 730

operation, atomic, 53, 99, 111, 138, 141–142, 251, 300, 556, 561
Oppen, D. C., 397, 715, 744
option set, SNA, 237
options, socket, 312–325
orderly release, 356
ordinary file, 30
O_RDONLY constant, 39
O_RDWR constant, 39
organization of book, x–x', 6–8
OSI (Open Systems Interconnect model, ISO), 245–252
OSI application layer, 250–252
OSI data-link layer, 247
OSI electronic mail, 251
OSI file transfer, 252
OSI model, 3–4, 173–177, 342, 694
OSI model, simplified, 4–5
OSI network layer, 247
OSI presentation layer, 250
OSI protocols, 245–252, 739, 742, 745–746
OSI session layer, 249
OSI transport layer, 247–249, 342
OSI virtual terminal, 251–252
O_SYNC constant, 42
O'Toole, J., 216, 339, 744
O_TRUNC constant, 39
out-of-band data, 190, 319, 324, 332–333, 390–391, 625–626, 666
out-of-band data, buffering and, 189–190
out-of-band data, Internet buffering and, 212
out-of-band data, SNA buffering and, 236
out-of-band data, SPP, 332–333
out-of-band data, TCP, 333
out-of-band data, XNS buffering and, 223
output filters, printer, 532–537
O_WRONLY constant, 39

pacing, 188
packet, 181, 183
Packet Exchange Protocol, XNS, see PEX
packet, IDP, 217–218, 223–224, 317, 460
packet, IP, 201, 212
packet mode, pseudo-terminal, 622–625
packet switching, 183–184
packet type bridge field, 223, 460
packet-stream, SPP, 218, 341
parallel sessions, SNA, 230
parameter passing, Apollo RPC, 717
parameter passing, Courier RPC, 715